T0324890

## Fundamentals of Digital Imaging

Designing complex and practical imaging systems requires a strong foundation in the accurate capture, display and analysis of digital images. This introduction to digital imaging covers the core techniques of image capture and the display of monochrome and color images. The basic tools required to describe sampling and image display on real devices are presented within a powerful mathematical framework. Starting with an overview of digital imaging, mathematical representation, and the elementary display of images, the topics progressively move to quantization, spatial sampling, photometry and colorimetry, and color sampling, and conclude with the estimation of image model parameters and image restoration. The characterization of input and output devices is also covered in detail. The reader will learn the processes used to generate accurate images, and appreciate the mathematical basis required to test and evaluate new devices.

With numerous illustrations, real-world examples, and end-of-chapter homework problems, this text is suitable for advanced undergraduate and graduate students taking courses in digital imaging in electrical engineering and computer science departments. This will also be an invaluable resource for practitioners in the industry.

Further resources for this title, including instructor-only solutions, MATLAB scripts and reference data for problems, are available online at www.cambridge.org/9780521868532.

**H. J. Trussell** is Professor and Director of Graduate Programs in the Electrical and Computer Engineering Department at North Carolina State University. He is an IEEE Fellow and has written over 200 technical papers.

**M. J. Vrhel** is the color scientist at Artifex Software, Inc. in Sammamish WA. A senior member of the IEEE, he is the author of numerous papers and patents in the areas of image and signal processing.

# Fundamentals of Digital Imaging

H. J. TRUSSELL
*North Carolina State University*

and

M. J. VRHEL
*Artifex Software, Inc.*

 CAMBRIDGE
UNIVERSITY PRESS

Shaftesbury Road, Cambridge CB2 8EA, United Kingdom

One Liberty Plaza, 20th Floor, New York, NY 10006, USA

477 Williamstown Road, Port Melbourne, VIC 3207, Australia

314–321, 3rd Floor, Plot 3, Splendor Forum, Jasola District Centre, New Delhi – 110025, India

103 Penang Road, #05–06/07, Visioncrest Commercial, Singapore 238467

Cambridge University Press is part of Cambridge University Press & Assessment,
a department of the University of Cambridge.

We share the University's mission to contribute to society through the pursuit of
education, learning and research at the highest international levels of excellence.

www.cambridge.org
Information on this title: www.cambridge.org/9780521868532

© Cambridge University Press & Assessment 2008

First published 2008

*A catalogue record for this publication is available from the British Library*

ISBN    978-0-521-86853-2    Hardback

# Contents

*The colour plates are situated between pages 206 and 207*

# Preface

## Purpose of this book

This book is written as an introduction for people who are new to the area of digital imaging. Readers may be planning to go into the imaging business, to use imaging for purposes peripheral to their main interest or to conduct research in any of the many areas of image processing and analysis. For each of these readers, this text covers the basics that will be used at some point in almost every task.

The common factors in all of image processing are the capture and display of images. While many people are engaged in the high-level processing that goes on between these two points, the starting and ending points are critical. The imaging worker needs to know exactly what the image data represents before meaningful analysis or interpretation can be done. The results of most image processing results in an output image that must be displayed and interpreted by an observer. To display such an image accurately, the worker must know the characteristics of the image and the display device. This book introduces the reader to the methods used for analyzing and characterizing image input and output devices. It presents the techniques necessary for interpreting images to determine the best ways to capture and display them.

Since accuracy of both capture and display is a major motivation for this text, it is necessary to emphasize a mathematical approach. The characterizations of devices and the interpretation of images will rely heavily on analysis in both the spatial and frequency domains. In addition, basic statistical and probability concepts will be used frequently. The prerequisites for courses based on this text include a junior-level course in signals and systems that covered convolution and Fourier transforms, and a basic probability or statistics course that covered basic probability distributions, means, variance and covariance concepts. These are required in Electrical and Computer Engineering departments, from which the authors come. The basic concepts from these courses are briefly reviewed in the text chapters or appendices. If more than a jog of the memory is needed, it is recommended that the reader consult any of the many undergraduate texts written specifically for these courses.

## Who should use this book

This text should be useful to anyone who deals with digital images. Anyone who has the task of digitizing an image with the intent of accurately displaying that image later will find topics in this text that will help improve the quality of the final product. Note that we emphasize the concept of *accuracy*. The topics in this text are not needed by the casual snapshot photographer, who wishes to email pictures to a friend or relative, who in turn will glance at them and soon forget where they are stored on the computer. The more serious photographer can use this text to discover the basis for many of the processing techniques used in commercial image manipulation packages, such as Adobe's Photoshop™, Corel's Paint Shop™ or Microsoft's Digital Image Suite™.

For those workers in the imaging industry, this text provides the foundation needed to build more complex and useful systems. The designers of digital imaging devices will find the mathematical basis that is required for the testing and evaluation of new devices. Since it is far cheaper to test ideas in software simulation than to build hardware, this text will be very useful in laying the foundation for basic simulation of blurring, noise processes and reproduction. The analysis tools used for evaluating performance, such as Fourier analysis and statistical analysis, are covered to a depth that is appropriate for the beginner in this area.

Many workers in the imaging industry are concerned with creating algorithms to modify images. The designers of the image manipulation packages are examples of this group. This group of people should be familiar with the concepts introduced in this text.

Researchers in image processing are concerned with higher-level topics such as restoration of degradations of recorded images, encoding of images or extraction of information from images. These higher level tasks form the cutting edge of image processing research. In most of these tasks, knowledge of the process that created the original image on which the researcher is working is required in order to produce the best final result. In addition, many of these tasks are judged by the appearance of the images that are produced by the processing that is done. The basic concepts in this text must be understood if the researcher is to obtain and display the best results.

## Approaches to this book

The text can be used for senior undergraduate level, introductory graduate and advanced graduate level courses. At the undergraduate level, the basic material of Chapters 2–6 is covered in detail but without heavy emphasis on the mathematical derivations. The step from one to two dimensions is large for most undergraduates. The first basic undergraduate course should include Sections 7.1 and 7.2, since these are required for fundamental characterization of images. The subspace material in Chapter 7 may be omitted from the undergraduate course. Likewise, since color is now ubiquitous, Chapter 8 is fundamental for understanding basic imaging. In a single-semester undergraduate course, it would be necessary to select only parts of Chapters 10–12. The device that is both common and representative of input devices is the scanner, Section 10.1. The analogous output device is the flat-panel display, Section 11.2. Basic characterization of these devices, as discussed in Chapter 12, should be included in the basic course.

At the introductory graduate level, the material of Chapters 2–6 can be covered quickly since the students either have had the basic course or are much more advanced mathematically. This gives time to cover the material of Chapters 10–12 in depth, after a review of Chapters 7 and 8. Projects at the graduate level may include the use of the instrumentation of Section 8.7.

An advanced graduate course would include the mathematical modeling details of Chapters 10–12, along with the derivation of the statistics used for the characterization of Chapter 7. The mathematics of Chapters 13 and 14 would be covered with applications to correction or compensation of physical imaging problems associated with input and output devices.

# Acknowledgments

The authors would like to thank Scott Daly and Dean Messing of Sharp Labs for discussions on soft-copy displays. David Rouse was extremely helpful in catching many errors and offering valuable suggestions throughout the text. He is the only guinea pig who suffered through the entire text before publication. Any problems with the grammar, punctuation or English should not be blamed on our resident English majors, Stephanie and Lynne, who tried to correct our misteaks. We simply failed to consult them frequently enough.

# 1     Introduction

Digital imaging is now so commonplace that we tend to forget how complicated and exacting the process of recording and displaying a digital image is. Of course, the process is not very complicated for the average consumer, who takes pictures with a digital camera or video recorder, then views them on a computer monitor or television. It is very convenient now to obtain prints of the digital pictures at local stores or make your own with a desktop printer. Digital imaging technology can be compared to automotive technology. Most drivers do not understand the details of designing and manufacturing an automobile. They do appreciate the qualities of a good design. They understand the compromises that must be made among cost, reliability, performance, efficiency and aesthetics. This book is written for the designers of imaging systems to help them understand concepts that are needed to design and implement imaging systems that are tailored for the varying requirements of diverse technical and consumer worlds. Let us begin with a bird's eye view of the digital imaging process.

## 1.1     Digital imaging: overview

A digital image can be generated in many ways. The most common methods use a digital camera, video recorder or image scanner. However, digital images are also generated by image processing algorithms, by analysis of data that yields two-dimensional discrete functions and by computer graphics and animation. In most cases, the images are to be viewed and analyzed by human beings. For these applications, it is important to capture or create the image data appropriately and display the image so that it is most pleasing or best interpreted. Exceptions to human viewing are found in computer vision and automated pattern recognition applications. Even in these cases, the relevant information must be captured accurately by the imaging system. Many detection and recognition tasks are modeled on analogies to the human visual system, so recording images as the human viewer sees the scene can be important.

The most common operations in digital imaging may be illustrated by examining the capture and display of an image with a common digital camera. The camera focuses an optical image onto a sensor. The basics of the optical system of the camera are the same regardless of whether the sensor is film or a solid-state sensing array. The optics, which include lenses and apertures, must be matched to the sensitivity and resolution of the sensor. The technology has reached a point where the best digital imaging chips are comparable to high-quality consumer film. In the cases of both film and digital sensors, the characteristics of the sensors must be taken into account. In a color system, the responses of each of the color bands should be known and any interaction between them should be determined. Once the image data are recorded, the processing of film and digital images diverges. It is common to scan film, in which case the processing proceeds as in the case of a digital image.

An advantage of the digital system is that operations are performed by digital processors that have more latitude and versatility than the analog chemical-optical systems for film. Computational speed and capability have increased to the point where all the necessary processing can be done within the normal time between successive shots of the camera. At low resolution, digital cameras are capable of recording short video sequences.

The recorded data are processed to compensate for nonlinearities of the sensor and to remove any bias and nonuniform gain across the sensor array. Any defects in the sensor array can be corrected at this point by processing. Compensation for some optical defects, such as flare caused by bright light sources, is also possible. The image is then prepared for storage or output. Storage may include encoding the data to reduce the memory required. Information about the camera settings may be appended to the image data to aid the accurate interpretation and reproduction of the image. When the image is prepared for viewing on an output device, this information is combined with information about the characteristics of the output device to produce the optimal image for the user's purposes.

This text will present the material that will allow the reader to understand, analyze and evaluate each of these steps. The goal is to give the reader the analytical tools and guidance necessary to design, improve and create new digital imaging systems.

## 1.2     Digital imaging: short history

Electronic imaging has a longer history than most readers in this digital age would imagine. As early as 1851, the British inventor Frederick Bakewell demonstrated a device that could transmit line drawings over telegraph wires at the World's Fair in London. This device, basically the first facsimile machine, used special insulating inks at the transmitter and special paper at the receiver. It used a scanning mechanism much like a drum scanner. The drawing was wrapped around a cylinder and a stylus, attached to a lead-screw, controlled the current that was sent to a receiving unit with a synchronized scanning cylinder where the current darkened the special electro-sensitive paper.

As photography developed, methods of transforming tonal images to electronic form were considered. Just after the turn of the century, two early versions of facsimile devices were developed that used scanning but different methods for sensing tonal images. Arthur Korn, in Germany, used a selenium cell to scan a photograph directly. Edouard Belin, in France, created a relief etching from a photograph, which was scanned with a stylus. The variable resistance produced a variable current that transmitted the image. Belin's method was used to transmit the first trans-Atlantic image in 1921. Korn's methods did the same in 1923. The images could be reproduced at the receiver by modulating a light source on photographic paper or by modulating the current with electro-sensitive paper.

The first digital image was produced by the Bartlane method in 1920. This was named for the British co-inventors, Harry G. Bartholomew and Maynard D. McFarlane. This method used a series of negatives on zinc plates that were exposed for varying lengths of time, which produced varying densities. The first system used five plates, corresponding to five quantization levels. The plates were scanned simultaneously on a cylinder. A hole was punched in a paper tape to indicate that the corresponding plate was clear. The method was later increased to 15 levels. On playback, the holes could be used to modulate a light beam with the same number of intensity levels.

The first electronic television was demonstrated by Philo T. Farnsworth in 1927. This had an electronic scanning tube as well as a CRT that could be controlled to display an image. Of interest is the fact that in 1908, A. A. C. Swinton proposed, in a paper published in *Nature*, an electronic tube for recording images and sending them to a receiver. Commercial television did not appear until after World War II.

Electronic image scanners were also used in the printing industry to make color separations in the 1930s, but these were analog devices, using the electronic signals to expose film simultaneously with the scan. Thus, there was no electronic storage of the image data. The first digital image, in the sense that we know it, was produced in 1957 by Russell Kirsch at the National Bureau of Standards. His device was basically a drum scanner with a photomultiplier tube that produced digital data that could be stored in a computer.

The first designs for digital cameras were based on these scanning ideas; thus, they took a significantly long time to take a picture and were not suitable for consumer purposes. The military was very instrumental in the development of the technology and supported research that led to the first digital spy satellite, the KH-11 in 1976. Previous satellites recorded the images on film and ejected a canister that was caught in mid-air by an airplane. The limited bandwidth of the system was a great motivator for image coding and compression research in the 1970s.

The development of the charge-coupled device (CCD) in an array format made the digital camera possible. The first imaging systems to use these devices were astronomical telescopes, as early as 1973. The first black and white digital cameras were used in the 1980s but were confined to experimental and research uses. The technology made the consumer video recorder possible in the 1980s, but the low resolution of these arrays restricted their use in consumer cameras. Color could be produced by using three filters and three arrays in an arrangement similar to the common television camera, which used an electronic tube. Finally, color was added directly to the CCD array in the form of a mosaic of filters laid on top of the CCD elements. Each element recorded one band of a three-band image. A full resolution color image was obtained by spatial interpolation of the three signals. This method remains the basis of color still cameras today.

## 1.3    Applications

As mentioned, there are many ways to generate digital images. The emphasis of this text is on accurate input and output. Let us consider the applications that require this attention to precision. The digital still camera is the most obvious application. Since the object is to reproduce a recorded scene, accuracy on both the input and output are required. In addition to consumer photography, there are many applications where accuracy in digital imaging is important. In the medical world, color images are used to record and diagnose diseases and conditions in areas that include dermatology, ophthalmology, surgery and endoscopy. Commercial printing has a fundamental requirement for accurate color reproduction. Poor color in catalogs can lead to customer dissatisfaction and costly returns. The accuracy of commercial printing has historically been more art than science, but with innovations in technology, this application area will move to a more analytical plane. Electrophotography and copying of documents is another important application area. This combines the same basic elements of digital cameras, except the input is usually a scanner and the output device is totally under the control of the manufacturer. More exotic applications include imaging systems used on satellites and space probes. We will see that multispectral systems that record many more than the usual three color bands can be analyzed using the methods presented in this text.

There are many applications where the reproduction of the image is not the end product. In most computer vision applications, a machine interprets the recorded image. To obtain the best performance from the algorithms, the input image data should be as accurate as possible. Since many algorithms are based on human visual properties for discrimination of objects, attention to accurate input is important. Satellite imagery can be interpreted by human beings or automated, and serves as another example. The bands recorded by satellites are usually not compatible with reproduction of true color. Digital astronomy must record spatial data accurately for proper interpretation. Infrared imaging, which is common in both ground-based and satellite systems, can be accurately recorded for analysis purposes, but cannot be displayed accurately for humans, since it is beyond the range of our sensitivities.

It should be noted that several imaging modalities are not covered by this text. X-ray images from medical or industrial applications are beyond the scope of this text. The transformation from X-ray energy distributions to quantitative data is not sufficiently well modeled to determine its accuracy. X-ray computed tomography (CT) and magnetic resonance imaging (MRI) are important medical modalities, but the relationships of the physical quantities that produce the images are highly complex and still the subject of research.

## 1.4    Methodology

Since our goal is to present the basic methods for accurate image capture and display, it is necessary to use a mathematical approach. We have to define what we mean by accuracy and quantify errors in a meaningful way. There will be many cases where the user must make decisions about the underlying assumptions that make a mathematical algorithm optimal. We will indicate these choices and note that if the system fails to satisfy the assumed conditions, then the results may be quite useful but suboptimal.

The error measures that will be chosen are often used for mathematical convenience. For example, mean square error is often used for this reason. The use of such measures is appropriate since the methods based on them produce useful, if suboptimal, results. The analysis that is used for these methods is also important since it builds a foundation for extensions and improvements that are more accurate in the visual sense.

Errors can be measured in more than one way and in more than one space. It is not just the difference in values of the input pixel and the output pixel that is of interest. We are often interested in the difference in color values of pixels. The color values may be represented in a variety of color spaces. The transformations between the measured values and the various color spaces are important. In addition, it is not just the difference in color values of pixels that is important, but the effect of the surrounding area and the response of the human visual system. To study these effects, we need the mathematical concepts of spatial convolution and transformation to the frequency domain. Just as the eye may be more sensitive to some color ranges than others, it is more sensitive to some spatial frequency ranges than others.

The algorithms used to process images often require the setting of various parameters. The proper values for these parameters are determined by the characteristics of the images. The characteristics that are important are almost always mathematical or statistical. This text will explore the relationships between these quantitative characteristics and the qualitative visual characteristics of the images. The background that is needed to make these connections will be reviewed in the text and the appendices. We will use many examples to help the reader gain insight into these relationships.

## 1.5 Prerequisite knowledge

Since we are taking a mathematical approach, it is appropriate to review the mathematical and statistical concepts that are required to get the most from this text. The details of the required mathematics are reviewed in Chapter 2. The reader's background should be equivalent to an undergraduate degree in engineering or computer science. A course in linear systems is assumed. We will review the concepts of system functions, transformations and convolution from this topic. The major extension is from one dimension to two dimensions. Included in linear systems courses is an introduction to the frequency domain. The reader should have a working knowledge of the Fourier transform in both its continuous and discrete forms. Of course, knowledge of Fourier transforms requires the basic manipulation of complex numbers, along with the use of Euler's identity that relates the complex exponential to the trigonometric functions

$$e^{j\theta} = \cos(\theta) + j\sin(\theta), \tag{1.1}$$

where we will use the engineering symbol j for the imaginary number $\sqrt{-1}$. The frequency domain is important for both computational efficiency and for interpretation.

Thus, the material in Chapter 5 is the basis for much of the analysis and many methods introduced later.

The use of vectors and matrices to represent images and operations allows the use of the very powerful tools of linear algebra. The level of knowledge that is required is that covered in most undergraduate engineering programs. The reader is expected to be familiar with basic matrix-vector operations, such as addition and multiplication. The concepts of diagonalization, eigenvectors and eigenvalues should be familiar. A review of these concepts and their use in representing operations with digital images is given in Chapter 2 and Appendix B.

As mentioned previously, the optimal processing of an image depends on its characterization. The characterization is most often done statistically. The mean and variance, which is related to the signal power when computing signal-to-noise ratios, are the most common statistics. The reader should be familiar with second-order statistics, such as covariance, autocovariance and cross-covariance. These concepts are based on elementary probability, which includes knowledge of random variables, probability density functions, expected values and expected values of functions of random variables. These concepts are reviewed, along with basic probability concepts, in Appendix C. This background should be part of any undergraduate engineering degree.

## 1.6      Overview of the book

Because of our emphasis on the analytical methods for obtaining accurate images, we begin with a review of the basic mathematics that will be used in the rest of the book. The review in Chapter 2 uses some concepts for which the reader may need further review. For this reason, we have included additional review material on generalized functions (Dirac delta functions), matrix algebra, and probability and stochastic signals in Appendices A, B and C, respectively.

The major emphasis of the text is on accuracy in imagery. Thus, before we start using examples of images to demonstrate various concepts, we need to discuss the fundamentals of image display. Chapter 3 discusses the important points that will be used throughout the text. The rules of this chapter are used for monochrome images, which will be used to demonstrate most of the basic concepts of image capture and reproduction. The discussion of accurate reproduction of monochrome and color must await a presentation of basic photometry and colorimetry in Chapter 8.

A digital image is defined by a finite number of values for a finite number of pixels. We first consider the quantization process and its effects in Chapter 4. We use some of our statistical and probability background to derive optimal quantizers and measure the goodness of other methods. The effects of spatial sampling would naturally follow. However, the analysis of spatial sampling requires a good understanding of the two-dimensional frequency domain. We review one-dimensional Fourier transforms and extend that knowledge to two dimensions in Chapter 5. Having obtained the necessary background, we present spatial sampling in Chapter 6.

In the first six chapters, we have covered most of the basic properties of monochrome images. In Chapter 7, we put these properties in context and use them to describe image characteristics. The frequency domain is used to describe the bandwidth of an image. That concept can be extended to describe an image in terms of its relation to various subspaces. The statistical concepts can be used to characterize images by their stochastic properties, such as the signal-to-noise ratio. The statistical approach also lets us characterize an image by a stochastic model that represents the class of images to which our particular image belongs.

To capture and reproduce color images accurately, it is necessary to understand the definition and measurement of monochrome and colored objects. The imaging scientist needs to understand the relationship between the quantized pixel values and the physical quantities that they represent. While this text cannot present a complete background, Chapter 8 covers the fundamentals that are needed for practical applications. This foundation can be enhanced by further study of more complete and specialized texts. In Chapter 9, we present a topic that is missing from many color science texts. The relationship of color sampling to the concepts of sampling in the spatial domain is important in the design of digital color imaging systems and in the simulation of any color imaging system by digital computers.

Chapter 10 describes image input devices. The characterization of the images is necessary to design a device that will capture that data accurately. Likewise, in Chapter 11, we describe the various devices and methods used for image reproduction. In Chapter 12, we discuss the various methods used to characterize the input and output devices. These characterizations, together with the characterization of the images, are used to complete the cycle of accurate image capture and reproduction.

We have mentioned that characterization of images is often determined by various statistics or model parameters. These formed the basis for the image characterization of Chapter 7. In that chapter, examples are used to illustrate the effects of the parameters. However, when determining the optimal processing for a particular image, it is necessary to estimate the appropriate value of the parameters for that image. In Chapter 13, we discuss methods to estimate the important parameters that are needed for processing algorithms.

Finally, in all imaging systems, the actual components have limited accuracy. Optical systems can never produce an unblurred image. Digital systems are always subject to quantization noise, but in practical systems this is rarely the limiting noise component. A final step in producing accurate images may be the restoration of degradations caused by imperfections in a less than ideal system. The degradations of interest include noise, blurring, nonideal scanning filters, illuminant and color distortions. The basics of restoration are presented in Chapter 14. Restoration differs from enhancement in that restoration seeks to restore accurately what was degraded, whereas enhancement seeks to improve an image subjectively. While enhancement is a valid step in processing images, it requires a much different background and assumptions than does restoration. This text does not provide the background for the subjective improvement of images, and thus, we will stay within the bounds of what is quantitatively optimal.

With this motivation for the order of the topics in the text, let us begin our journey.

# 2     Mathematical representation

For any type of structured analysis on imaging systems, we must first have some model for the system. Most often it is a mathematical model that is most useful. Even if the model is simplified to the point that it ignores many real world physical effects, it is still very useful to give first order approximations to the behavior of the system.

In this chapter, we will review the tools needed to construct the mathematical models that are most often used in image analysis. It is assumed that the reader is already familiar with the basics of one-dimensional signals and systems. Thus, while a quick review is given for the various basic concepts, it is the relation between one and two dimensions and the two-dimensional operations that will be discussed in more depth here.

As mentioned, the mathematical models are often better or worse approximations to the real systems that are realized with optics, electronics and chemicals. As we review the concepts that are needed, we will point out where the most common problems are found and how close some of the assumptions are to reality.

## 2.1     Images as functions

Since images are the main topic of this book, it makes sense to discuss their representation first. Images are, by definition, defined in two spatial dimensions. Many, if not most, images represent the projection of some three-dimensional object or scene onto a two-dimensional plane. The geometrical relationship between the object and the image is left for other texts on image analysis. We will be concerned with other aspects of the physical object or scene on the recorded data. Images may be monochrome or color; they may be continuous or discrete; they may be still or moving; but always there are exactly two spatial dimensions. The value of the representation of the image may reflect the physical quantity that is measured by some imaging device, or it may reflect only the relative brightness imagined by a user.

Let us consider the common case where $f(x, y)$ is a function of two spatial variables whose value represents some physical quantity that can be measured by some instrument. Examples include:

- light intensity,
- optical or electromagnetic reflectivity,
- optical density,

- material density or attenuation,
- distance.

The cases of light intensity and reflectivity are the most common and will receive the most attention. The other cases can be modeled using the same mathematical tools. The details of the optical cases are covered in Chapter 8 on photometry and colorimetry.

For the optical cases, we are often interested in the color characteristics of the image. The model can easily be extended to include this aspect. The function $f(x, y, \lambda)$ includes the effect of wavelength or frequency of the measured radiation. Visible light has wavelengths, $\lambda$, from about 400 nm (blue) to 700 nm (red). The usual color images are represented by three bands that represent integrated power in roughly the red, green and blue regions of the spectrum. The exact representation will be discussed later. Hyperspectral images may use 100–400 bands in the visible to the near and middle infrared (IR) for satellite image applications. To reduce the problem back to the case of only two dimensions, the wavelength dimension can be eliminated by integrating the intensity over some range of wavelengths. This will produce a single-band image,

$$f_i(x, y) = \int_{\lambda_{\min}}^{\lambda_{\max}} f(x, y, \lambda) s_i(\lambda) \, d\lambda, \tag{2.1}$$

where $s_i(\lambda)$ is the sensitivity of the $i$th sensor, which defines the $i$th band. We often denote the $N$-band image by the vector

$$\mathbf{f}(x, y) = [f_1(x, y), f_2(x, y), \dots f_N(x, y)]^T. \tag{2.2}$$

It is often the case that each of the bands is treated as a monochrome image. We will make the case that this is inappropriate many times. The exact details of handling color bands are discussed in Chapter 8.

Light can have attributes other than intensity and wavelength. Light can be characterized as *coherent, partially coherent* and *noncoherent*. Coherent light is defined by a single wavelength at a single phase, $s(t) = e^{j(\omega t + \phi)}$. Because coherent light includes a phase parameter, it is usually represented by a complex function. Physically, coherent light is produced by a laser. Noncoherent light consists of a stochastic mixture of phases and is measured only by its power. Thus, it can be represented by a real number. Noncoherent light can be monochromatic, i.e., single wavelength, as can coherent light. The major difference is that the mixture of phases in noncoherent light prevents the narrow collimated beams possible with lasers. Almost all examples of imaging systems discussed in this course will be based on noncoherent light.

In addition, light can be polarized, that is, it has directional properties. This is most commonly observed when using polarized sunglasses. The effect has been used to display three-dimensional images in movies and on computer monitors. It is used in liquid crystal displays (see Section 11.2). Both coherent and noncoherent light can be polarized. Almost all examples of imaging systems are based on unpolarized light.

There are many applications of imaging that use radiation other than the visible band. For reference, the electromagnetic spectrum and its characteristics are given in Table 2.1.

**Table 2.1.** Regions of the electromagnetic spectrum

| Name | Wavelength Range | Frequency | Character |
| --- | --- | --- | --- |
| Cosmic and gamma rays | $10^{-7}$–$10^{-2}$ nm | 300000–$0.3 \times 10^{20}$ Hz | Emissive |
| X-rays | $10^{-2}$–$10^{-1}$ nm | 300–$30 \times 10^{17}$ Hz | Heavy industrial |
| X-rays | $10^{-1}$–1 nm | 30–$3 \times 10^{17}$ Hz | Medical, industrial |
| Ultraviolet | 1–380 nm | 3000–$7.5 \times 10^{14}$ Hz | Optical |
| Visible | 400–700 nm | 7.5–$4.2 \times 10^{14}$ Hz | Optical |
| Infrared (near) | 720–1300 nm | 4.2–$2.3 \times 10^{14}$ Hz | Optical |
| Infrared (middle) | 1.3–3 µm | 2.3–$1 \times 10^{14}$ Hz | Optical |
| Infrared (far) | 7–15 µm | 4.3–$2 \times 10^{13}$ Hz | Emissive |
| Super high (SHF) | 1–10 mm | 3–30 GHz | Satellite communications |
| Ultra high (UHF) | 10–100 mm | 3–0.3 GHz | UHF television, radar |
| Very high (VHF) | 0.1–1 m | 300–30 MHz | FM radio, VHF television |
| High (HF) | 1–10 m | 30–3 MHz | Amateur radio, telephone |
| Medium (MF) | 10–100 m | 3000–300 kHz | AM broadcast |
| Low (LF) | 0.1–1 km | 300–30 kHz | Marine communications |
| Very low (VLF) | 1–10 km | 30–3 kHz | Long range navigation |

There are various problems for each of the various ranges that are peculiar to that band. For example, X-rays cannot be focused by ordinary means. The mathematics that is described in this text can be used for almost all bands, but should be modified according to the physical properties of each band.

The temporal aspect of the imaging can be taken into account by adding another argument to the function of spatial coordinates to represent time, $f(x, y, t)$. As with wavelength, the time variable can be discretized to produce a two-dimensional function, or series of functions,

$$f_i(x, y) = \int_{t_i}^{t_{i+1}} f(x, y, t) a_i(t) \, dt, \tag{2.3}$$

where $a_i(t)$ is the aperture function during the $i$th time interval. Note that the image has to be integrated over some finite time interval in order to capture a finite amount of energy. The aperture function might represent the response of a CCD cell between read cycles of the array or the time integration function of an analog-to-digital converter. This will be discussed further in Chapter 6 on sampling. Examples of this actually include virtually all real still images. They all represent the image at a particular instant of time. Sequences of images are found in television, motion pictures and medical imaging.

The time and wavelength effects can be combined to produce

$$f(x, y) = \int_{t_1}^{t_2} \int_{\lambda_1}^{\lambda_2} f(x, y, \lambda, t) s(\lambda) a(t) \, d\lambda \, dt. \tag{2.4}$$

This is actually what occurs in most imaging applications. It is often convenient to ignore this step and work with the two-dimensional result as if it is the starting point for processing. This will be the approach of many sections of this text.

### 2.1.1    Continuous vs. discrete variables

For all digital images, the spatial variables are discretized and the image is represented by $f(m, n)$, where the function is defined only at integer values, $(m, n)$. The mathematics of handling the discrete functions is much the same as handling continuous functions. We will note any differences as they come up in the discussions. The sampling of a continuous signal to obtain a discrete signal is very important and will be discussed in detail in Chapter 6. All of the fundamental operations on images have both continuous and discrete counterparts. These will be presented in parallel for each operation.

The discrete function can be represented naturally as a matrix or vector. For all practical cases, the extent of the image of interest is finite. If a function has zero value outside of a finite region, we say the function has *finite support*. It is easy to represent functions of infinite support in the continuous domain, but representing matrices and vectors of infinite support is more difficult. For this reason, we will assume that all of our images have finite support. There are no practical problems associated with this assumption, since the region of support may be taken as large as necessary to contain the portions that affect the part that is recorded. The truncation of parts of the image, caused by boundaries of the recording area, can be represented by the mathematics that will be presented here.

### 2.1.2    Deterministic vs. stochastic

Images may be viewed as deterministic processes represented by a functional form or defined pixel-by-pixel. A deterministic function is one whose exact value can be determined at any time or place. For example,

$$f(x, y) = 5e^{-x^2/10} \cos(2\pi y/5)$$

is deterministic. The value at any position, $(x, y)$, e.g., $(-3.5, 4.7)$, is known exactly. There are many properties that are easily determined for such functions: maximum and minimum values, maximum frequencies in each direction, etc. It is convenient to think of images as being composed of such functions, even though the functions may be unknown. While the functions may be unknown, the properties of the functions can be known, or assumed to be known.

Alternatively, the image may be assumed to represent one sample of an ensemble of images that is characterized by its statistical properties. In fact, virtually all sampled images are stochastic in nature since they are obtained by some sort of measurement process. Every measurement is subject to noise of some kind. Of course, digital images are represented by quantized values and thus, at the minimum, are subject to uncertainty caused by the quantization process.

Generally, a stochastic characterization is advantageous, since it allows the use of more practical knowledge. It is rare that we claim to know the functional form of the deterministic function that represents an image. On the other hand, it is common to assume that the average (mean) is known, as are limits on signal power (variance) and characteristics about smoothness (covariance). Furthermore, stochastic processing usually avoids problems caused by ill-conditioned systems. When dealing with inverse problems, such as minimum mean square error estimators, accounting for the noise in measurements is beneficial.

The knowledge of probability and statistics that is required for this text is very basic. It is assumed that the reader has been exposed to the relevant concepts somewhere prior to encountering this text. The concepts used for analysis include mean, variance, covariance and the effects of linear systems on these quantities. The property of stationarity will also be important for several applications. These concepts are reviewed in Appendix C. Chapter 7 contains examples of images that have various statistical characteristics. This will enable the reader to get a feel for what these concepts mean for images.

### 2.1.3    Philosophical aspects of the problem

Before one begins processing an image, there are several aspects of the problem that need to be determined in order to know what operations will be valid and what assumptions can be made. Many of these are more philosophical in nature than physical, that is, the user is considering more than the physical attributes of the imaging systems. He or she must consider what knowledge can be assumed and how certain that knowledge is. Consider the following aspects of processing an image.

- Processing one image or many: if the image is unique, it is almost impossible to define meaningful limitations on its characteristics. Saying the image is $512 \times 512$ tells one little about the image. On the other hand, it may be possible to characterize the image as a member of some ensemble or class of images. Saying the image is a member of a class of images that represent optical reflectance, indicates that the values of the image are limited to be between zero and one. The methods used for this particular image would be the same as that for any image in this class. If the knowledge about the image is not easily expressed in the statistical forms of mean and correlations, deterministic processing can produce better results.
- A priori knowledge about an image: after it is determined that the image belongs to a class of images of interest, the characteristics of that class need to be defined. The covariance structure of the ensemble is often assumed or perhaps estimated by various methods. The estimation method assumes certain knowledge about the ensemble. For example, a common estimation is usually obtained from prototype images or from subsections of the image under investigation. Selecting the prototypes requires significant knowledge about the image ensemble. Structural properties, such as region of support, region boundaries and value bounds, are often known but are difficult to characterize statistically.
- Tractable mathematics: assumptions are often made based on the difficulty of computing and manipulating the mathematical solution. If linear processing is to be

done, then nonlinear constraints, such as those on the region of support and bounds on the image values, cannot be implemented. The assumption that the image is a member of a stationary ensemble permits tractable solutions that use first-order and second-order statistics. Linear approximations are often used to simplify computation of physically nonlinear phenomena.

### 2.1.4     Two dimensions vs. one dimension

Processing two-dimensional functions is clearly more costly than processing one-dimensional functions with the same characteristics. In most cases, there is also a conceptual leap. However, it should be emphasized that, in many cases, this leap is not too great. Many two-dimensional concepts are relatively straightforward extensions of their one-dimensional counterparts. Let us compare some of the similarities of $f(x, y)$ vs. $f(t)$. We will use the time domain argument, $t$, for the one-dimensional signals and the spatial arguments, $x$ and $y$, for the two-dimensional signals.

#### Similarities of 1-D and 2-D functions
(1)  Continuity: a function is continuous in the variable $x$ if the limit

$$\lim_{h \to 0} f(x + h, y) = f(x, y)$$

exists. Of course, there are many directions to consider for the two-dimensional case. For most functions that represent images, continuity in both coordinate directions is sufficient to assume total continuity.
(2)  Derivatives and Taylor expansions are extensions of one-dimension. Here there are directional derivatives, but, again, it is usually sufficient to consider the partial derivatives along the coordinate axes. Since it can be useful in approximations, the two-dimensional Taylor expansion is given here. The expansion about the origin is given by

$$f(x, y) = f(0, 0) + \frac{\partial f(0, 0)}{\partial x} x + \frac{\partial f(0, 0)}{\partial y} y + \frac{\partial^2 f(0, 0)}{\partial x^2} x^2$$
$$+ \frac{\partial^2 f(0, 0)}{\partial y^2} y^2 + \frac{\partial^2 f(0, 0)}{\partial xy} xy + \cdots,$$

where the notation $\partial f(0, 0)/\partial x$ is used to represent the value of the partial derivative of $f(x, y)$ with respect to $x$ and evaluated at $(x, y) = (0, 0)$.
(3)  Two-dimensional Fourier transforms are straightforward extensions of 1-D transforms. This is covered in Chapter 5. While the mathematics is relatively straightforward for rectangular coordinate systems, the interpretation is more complicated. In addition, there are more possible variations on the properties, for example, region of support and periodicity.
(4)  Linear systems theory is the same. This will be discussed in the next section.
(5)  Two-dimensional sampling theory is a straightforward extension of 1-D sampling. This is discussed in Chapter 6.

(6) Separable 2-D signals are treated as two 1-D signals. A two-dimensional function, $f(x, y)$ is *separable* if it can be written as the product of two one-dimensional functions, $f(x, y) = f_x(x)f_y(y)$. Many operations on separable functions are simply two successive operations on one-dimensional functions, e.g., first in the $x$ direction and then in the $y$ direction. Two-dimensional Fourier transforms are computed this way.

There are some differences between 1-D and 2-D functions that occur, beyond just dealing with a more complicated function. Some concepts do not transfer and others are not useful in practical cases.

### Differences of 1-D and 2-D functions

(1) Two-dimensional signals are usually not causal; causality is not intuitive. In the case of images, it is not clear that one pixel or position is ahead or behind another. The question of which pixels come first in spatial coordinates is unanswerable in general. For the case of raster scanning of television images, it is somewhat artificial to say the pixel to the left and above comes before the pixel located at a certain position.
(2) Two-dimensional polynomials cannot always be factored; this limits use of rational polynomial models.[1]
(3) More variation in 2-D sampling; hexagonal lattices are common in nature, random sampling makes interpolation much more difficult. Multiple lattices such as those encountered in halftone printing make for much more complicated analysis.
(4) Periodic functions may have a wide variety of 2-D periods. The hexagonal lattice mentioned above is relatively simple. While there are extremely complicated periodic patterns, such as are seen in textile patterns, they are rarely useful in image processing.
(5) Two-dimensional regions of support are more variable, defining boundaries of objects are often irregular instead of rectangular or elliptical.
(6) Two-dimensional systems can be mixed infinite and finite impulse response, causal and noncausal. These properties are of primary interest to filter designers. Fortunately, these problems do not bother most image processors.
(7) Algebraic representation using stacked notation for 2-D signals is more difficult to manipulate and understand. To use the power of matrix algebra, two-dimensional images are rearranged to form one-dimensional vectors called stacked notation. This notation is discussed in Section 2.7.

## 2.2    Systems and operators

It is simple enough to give the notation for an image in continuous or discrete space, as shown in the preceding sections. The task of interest is the processing of images. This means that we change an image in some way. This change is represented by an operator

---

[1] It is possible to approximate to any arbitrary precision a nonfactorable polynomial by a factorable one. However, finding the approximation is not trivial.

or a system that takes an image as input and produces another image as output. There are many different systems and operators that are used in image processing. For example, a digital camera is a system that takes an image represented by physical quantities of energy at various wavelengths and transforms it into discrete values at discrete locations. An operator might be any of many mathematical operations that are used in analysis, such as differentiation, clipping of negative values and transformation to the frequency domain. Let us consider the general notation.

A simple example of a system might take a single band image and transform it into another single band image. Let $T[\cdot]$ denote the system. The transformation of the input image $f(x, y)$ to the output image $g(x, y)$ is given by

$$T[f(x, y)] = g(x, y).$$

We can denote this also by using vector notation, $T[\mathbf{f}] = \mathbf{g}$, where the vectors may be multidimensional to represent spatial, temporal and wavelength attributes. There are several common transformations that we will encounter in image processing. We will review three of the most common; amplitude scaling, spatial translation (shifting) and spatial scaling, to illustrate the concepts.

### 2.2.1    Amplitude scaling

A common transformation is a linear stretching of the range of the image for better display. The transformation defined by

$$T[f(x, y)] = 2f(x, y) + 20$$

doubles the range of the image and adds 20 units to the resulting mean, i.e., if the mean of $f(x, y)$ is 10, then the mean of $T[f(x, y)]$ is 40. We will show examples of this operation in Chapter 3.

A look-up table transforms one digital image into another by using a mapping defined by a table or array. A digital image has only a finite number of values, commonly between

**Table 2.2.** Look-up table example, $L[f(x, y)]$

| $f(x, y)$ | $g(x, y)$ |
|-----------|-----------|
| 0 | 0 |
| 1 | 0 |
| 2 | 2 |
| 3 | 4 |
| 4 | 6 |
| 5 | 7 |
| 6 | 7 |
| 7 | 7 |

0 and 255. A look-up table defines how each of these values is to be mapped by the system. To illustrate the concept, let us suppose we have an image with only eight values, 0 to 7. A mapping, $L[\cdot]$, can be defined by the Table 2.2 as

$$T[f(x,y)] = g(x,y) = L[f(x,y)].$$

In a more complicated example, but one of great importance, a multidimensional image or set of images, can be transformed to a new multidimensional image. The dimensionality of the input and output images need not be the same. The operator $T[\cdot]$ may transform a set of $M$ images, $\{f_i(x,y,t,\lambda)\}_{i=1}^{M}$ into a set of $N$ images, $\{g_j(x,y,t,\lambda)\}_{j=1}^{N}$.

---

**Example 2.1.**   Let a 31-band (hyperspectral) image be represented by

$$f_i(x,y) = f(x,y,t_0,\lambda_i), \ \lambda_i = 400 + 10i, \ 0 \le i \le 30,$$

and define $T[\cdot]$ by

$$g_j(x,y) = \sum_{i=0}^{30} \alpha_{ij} f_i(x,y),$$

where $\alpha_{ij}$ is the sensitivity of the $j$th sensor at wavelength $\lambda_i$ for $j = 1,2,3$. Using vector notation, we can write

$$\mathbf{T[f]} = \mathbf{g}.$$

This system transforms a 31-band, two-dimensional image into a three-band, two-dimensional image. This is common when simulating the capturing of a color image in red, green and blue bands. The input vector has 33 dimensions (2 spatial and 31 wavelength); the output vector has 5 dimensions.

---

### 2.2.2  Spatial translation

A time delay of $t_0$ of a one-dimensional signal, $s(t)$, is given by $T[s(t)] = s(t - t_0)$. This generalizes easily to two dimensions when we shift an image spatially. To move the image, $s(x,y)$, to the right by $x_0$ units and up by $y_0$ units, we write the shifted image as $T[s(x,y)] = s(x - x_0, y - y_0)$. Note that $x_0$ and $y_0$ can be either positive or negative.

### 2.2.3  Spatial scaling

The time scaling of a one-dimensional signal, $s(t)$, by $\alpha$ is given by $T[s(t)] = s(\alpha t)$. This generalizes in two dimensions when we enlarge or shrink the size of an image. In those cases, it is usually the case that the scale factors are the same in each direction.

For example, to enlarge an image by a factor of two, we would use the transformation $T[s(x, y)] = s(x/2, y/2)$. In general, the scale factors in each direction can be different and we write the scaled image as $T[s(x, y)] = s(\alpha x, \beta y)$. Note that $\alpha$ and $\beta$ can be either positive or negative. A negative scale factor would result in a reflection about the corresponding axis.

## 2.3    Linear systems (operators)

The notation for systems and operators is general and can represent virtually any transformation of images. In many cases, we can restrict our interest to special classes of system that have properties that make analysis and computation much easier. The linear system is the first and most important special class of interest. A system is *linear* if the superposition principle holds, that is, if the result of adding images together and putting the result through the system is the same as putting the two images through the system and adding the two results. For two input images, $f_1$ and $f_2$, this can be written

$$T[f_1 + f_2] = T[f_1] + T[f_2].$$

In addition, the linear scaling property must hold, that is, the result of transforming a scaled version of the input image is the same as scaling the output of the unscaled input image. This is written

$$T[\alpha f_1] = \alpha T[f_1].$$

These two conditions can be combined into one equation:

$$T[\alpha_1 f_1 + \alpha_2 f_2] = \alpha_1 T[f_1] + \alpha_2 T[f_2]. \tag{2.5}$$

We can include spatial arguments (or time or wavelength) if desired and write the conditions as

$$T[\alpha_1 f_1(x, y) + \alpha_2 f_2(x, y)] = \alpha_1 T[f_1(x, y)] + \alpha_2 T[f_2(x, y)],$$

or using the output functions, $g_i(x, y)$,

$$T[\alpha_1 f_1(x, y) + \alpha_2 f_2(x, y)] = \alpha_1 g_1(x, y) + \alpha_2 g_2(x, y).$$

---

**Example 2.2.**    The transformations described in the previous section, amplitude scaling with no offset, spatial translation and spatial scaling, are all linear operations. To see this, let us consider amplitude scaling. Let $r(x, y) = T[s(x, y)] = 2s(x, y)$. Then, for any $\alpha$ and $\beta$, and any images $s_1(x, y)$ and $s_2(x, y)$, the output of the weighted sum is given by

$$s_o(x, y) = T[\alpha s_1(x, y) + \beta s_2(x, y)]$$
$$= 2(\alpha s_1(x, y) + \beta s_2(x, y)) = 2\alpha s_1(x, y) + 2\beta s_2(x, y).$$

This is the same as the sum after scaling output of the two signals by $\alpha$ and $\beta$, that is,

$$s_o(x, y) = \alpha T[s_1(x, y)] + \beta T[s_2(x, y)]$$
$$= \alpha(2s_1(x, y)) + \beta(2s_2(x, y))$$
$$= 2\alpha s_1(x, y) + 2\beta s_2(x, y).$$

Note that if we include an offset value in the transformation, e.g., $r(x, y) = T[s(x, y)] = 2s(x, y) + 1$, the transformation is no longer linear.

---

**Example 2.3.**  Most optical systems are linear, that is, adding another light emitting object at the input will increase the response at the output in a linear manner. This includes the case of objects that produce overlapping images. Consider the case shown in Figs. 2.1a–c. The image of a point source with intensity $p_1$ at position $x_1$ is shown in Fig. 2.1a. Likewise, the image of a point source with intensity $p_2$ at position $x_2$ is shown in Fig. 2.1b. The image of the combined sources, shown in Fig. 2.1c, is the sum of the two output images of the individual sources. This is easy to see since the intensity at any point is given by the number of photons per unit time, and the sum of photons is conserved in the output image.

---

**Example 2.4.**  Even within the operating limits of a particular film, an optical film camera is a nonlinear device. The film has a logarithmic response to light power. The system might be defined as

$$T[f(x, y)] = \gamma \log_{10}[f(x, y)].$$

It is easily seen that the relationship of Eq. (2.5) does not hold.

---

**Example 2.5.**  The transformation defined by the look-up table in Table 2.2 is nonlinear. While we might have to make some odd adjustments for integer arithmetic defined on an eight-valued image, it should be clear that this look-up table would represent a nonlinear system. Indeed, modeling nonlinear functions is one of the most important uses of look-up tables. We will use these tables often when characterizing input and output devices, as discussed in later chapters.

---

**Example 2.6.**  A linear system can be defined using more than a single position in an image. An important transformation is one that produces the weighted sum of several

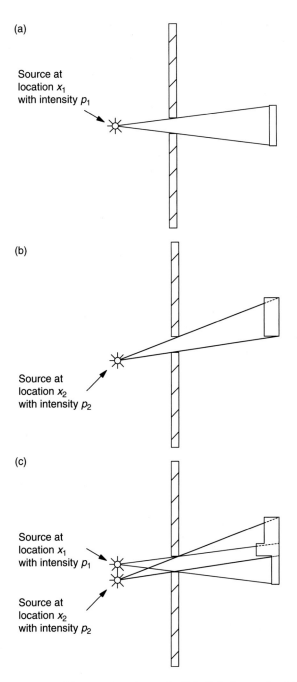

(a)

Source at
location $x_1$
with intensity $p_1$

(b)

Source at
location $x_2$
with intensity $p_2$

(c)

Source at
location $x_1$
with intensity $p_1$

Source at
location $x_2$
with intensity $p_2$

**Figure 2.1.** Linear optics: the result of the light from point (a) and the light from point (b) add linearly to produce the result in (c). Note that the difference in the extent (not intensity) between (a) and (b) indicates a shift-variant system.

positions in an input image. One such transformation might be

$$T[f(x, y)] = \frac{\frac{1}{4}f(x - dx, y) - \frac{1}{2}f(x, y) + \frac{1}{4}f(x + dx, y)}{(dx)^2}. \tag{2.6}$$

This operator would be used to approximate a second derivative in the $x$-direction, where the value of $dx$ would be some small distance.

---

**Example 2.7.** The most important use of linear systems in imaging is the modeling of optical systems by the superposition integral. This is a generalized version of the transformation of Eq. (2.5), where the discrete weights are replaced by a weighting function, $h(\xi, \eta, x, y)$, and the sum is replaced by an integral. The output image $g(x, y)$ is obtained from the input image $f(x, y)$ by

$$g(x, y) = \int_{-\infty}^{\infty} \int_{-\infty}^{\infty} h(\xi, \eta, x, y) f(\xi, \eta) \, d\xi \, d\eta. \tag{2.7}$$

Note that the weighting function, $h(\xi, \eta, x, y)$, has arguments that specify both the position of the input image and the output image. We will discuss this form in depth in Section 2.5.

---

In describing linear systems, we have used continuous notation. The definitions and examples can easily be changed to discrete images by replacing the continuous arguments $(x, y)$ by the discrete arguments $(m, n)$ in all cases except Example 2.7. For this case, the integral must be replaced by a summation. This gives

$$g(m, n) = \sum_{i=-\infty}^{\infty} \sum_{j=-\infty}^{\infty} h(i, j, m, n) f(i, j).$$

## 2.4        Sampling representation

The process of sampling transforms a continuous signal into a discrete one. We will treat this process in depth in Chapter 6. At this point, it is necessary to introduce the Dirac delta function and the mathematical representation for sampling. The delta function will be used in the following section to describe convolution.

Mathematically, ideal sampling is usually represented with the use of a *generalized function*, the Dirac delta function, $\delta(t)$ [201]. A more detailed description is included in Appendix A. The function is defined as zero for $t \neq 0$ and having an *area* of unity. The most useful property of the delta function is that of sifting, e.g., extracting single values

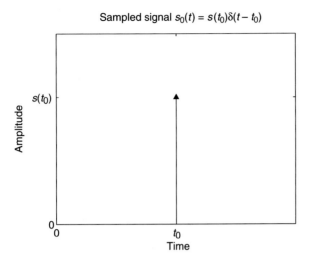

Figure 2.2. Sampled signal at $t = t_0$.

of a continuous function. This is defined by the integral

$$s(t_0) = \int_{-\infty}^{\infty} s(t)\delta(t - t_0)\,\mathrm{d}t$$
$$= \int_{-\infty}^{\infty} s(t_0)\delta(t - t_0)\,\mathrm{d}t = s(t_0)\int_{-\infty}^{\infty} \delta(t - t_0)\,\mathrm{d}t, \qquad (2.8)$$

where we use the property that the last integral is the area under the $\delta(t)$, which is unity. This shows the production of a single sample. We would represent the sampled signal as a signal that is zero everywhere except at the sampling time, $s_0(t) = s(t_0)\delta(t - t_0)$. The sampled signal can be represented graphically by using the arrow, as shown in Fig. 2.2.

The entire sampled sequence can be represented using the *comb* function, defined as

$$\mathrm{comb}(t) = \sum_{n=-\infty}^{\infty} \delta(t - n), \qquad (2.9)$$

where the sampling interval is unity. The sampled signal is obtained by multiplication,

$$s_\mathrm{d}(t) = s(t)\mathrm{comb}(t) = s(t)\sum_{n=-\infty}^{\infty} \delta(t - n) = \sum_{n=-\infty}^{\infty} s(t)\delta(t - n), \qquad (2.10)$$

where the subscript d denotes the discrete domain. The sampling is represented graphically in Fig. 2.3. It is common to use the notation of $\{s(n)\}$ or $s(n)$ to represent a collection of samples in discrete space. The arguments $n$ and $t$ will serve to distinguish the discrete or continuous spaces, respectively.

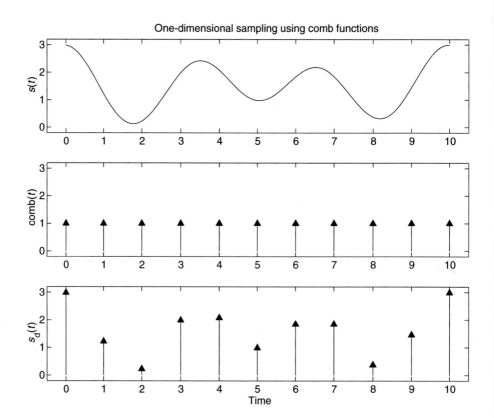

**Figure 2.3.** One-dimensional sampling.

## 2.5      Shift-invariant (space-invariant) linear systems

In addition to linearity, a second important restriction of systems is that of *shift-invariance*. Ideal optical systems have the property that if the input image is shifted in space, the output image is shifted by an equivalent amount. We saw in Fig. 2.1 that shifting the input image (a point) from $x_1$ to $x_2$ resulted in an image that differed from that obtained from just shifting the image that resulted from the point at $x_1$. To obtain a close approximation to a shift-invariant system, we could increase the distance from the point to the aperture and limit the range of the image in the $x$-direction.

### 2.5.1      One-dimensional continuous convolution

To formalize the definition of shift-invariance, let us first review the one-dimensional case. We assume that the reader has seen one-dimensional convolution, but we include a review of the necessary Dirac delta function in Appendix A. The one-dimensional form of a linear system that can be described by an impulse response can be written in the general form

$$g(t) = \int_{-\infty}^{\infty} h(\xi, t) f(\xi) \, d\xi, \tag{2.11}$$

where $h(\xi, t)$ is the system response at time $t$ to an impulse at time $\xi$. If the system is shift-invariant, the integral becomes a *convolution*

$$g(t) = \int_{-\infty}^{\infty} h(t - \xi) f(\xi) \, d\xi, \tag{2.12}$$

where $h(\xi)$ is the system response at time $\xi$ to an impulse at time zero. The response at time $\xi$ to an impulse at time $t$ is obtained by a simple shift, $h(\xi, t) = h(t - \xi)$. The case when the input signal is an impulse $f(t) = \delta(t)$ produces the identity

$$h(t) = \int_{-\infty}^{\infty} h(t - \xi) f(\xi) \, d\xi. \tag{2.13}$$

From the above, we can see that a linear shift-invariant system is completely defined by its impulse response.

Convolution is a commutative operation, that is, it does not matter whether you convolve $f(t)$ with $h(t)$, or $h(t)$ with $f(t)$. From a mathematical view, the signal and the impulse response are interchangeable,

$$g(t) = \int_{-\infty}^{\infty} f(\xi) h(t - \xi) \, d\xi = \int_{-\infty}^{\infty} h(\xi) f(t - \xi) \, d\xi. \tag{2.14}$$

The visualization of the operation is shown in Fig. 2.4 as time-reversal and shifting. The input signal and the impulse response are shown at the top. The first step is to create the time-reversed function, $h(-\xi)$. The time-reversed signal is then shifted to the appropriate time ($t_0 = 1.5$ in Fig. 2.4), $t$, giving $h(t - \xi)$; the resulting function is multiplied by the input signal, $f(t)$, to produce the product $f(\xi) h(t - \xi)$, and finally, the product is integrated to obtain the value of $g(t)$. The last graph in Fig. 2.4 shows the single value at $t = t_0$ with an asterisk on the curve of $g(t)$, which represents the total convolution. One-dimensional convolution can be visualized using sequences of graphs like Fig. 2.4 or animations. Such an animation is found on the website that supports this book (www.cambridge.org/9780521868532).

For shorthand notation, we will use $g(t) = h(t) * f(t)$ to represent convolution. As mentioned, convolution is commutative: $f(t) * h(t) = h(t) * f(t)$. We will use $*$ to denote both continuous and discrete convolution.

## 2.5.2 Two-dimensional continuous convolution

Convolution in two dimensions can be described by using a two-dimensional Dirac delta function (impulse). The two-dimensional impulse function can be defined analogously

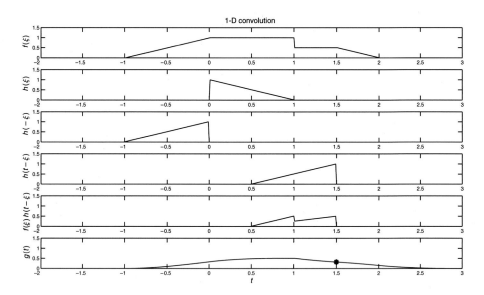

**Figure 2.4.** Graphical 1-D convolution: the shift for the graph is $t_0 = 1.5$.

to the one-dimensional function. See Appendix A for details. We see that $h(\xi, \eta, x, y)$ is the output of the system at $(x, y)$ to an impulse at the input position $(\xi, \eta)$. Letting $T[\cdot]$ represent the system, we have

$$h(\xi, \eta, x, y) = T[\delta(x - \xi, y - \eta)].$$

As in the 1-D case, the function, $h(\xi, \eta, x, y)$, is called the impulse response of the linear system. Since our mental image of the 2-D impulse, $\delta(x, y)$, is a point of light (infinitely bright and infinitely small) and $h(\xi, \eta, x, y)$ shows how that point is spread over the 2-D plane, the function is often called the *point spread function* or *PSF*. It is important to note that, in general, the response of a system may vary from point-to-point in the input image. An example of this is shown in the one-dimensional case of Fig. 2.1. The image of the point at $x_1$ has a larger extent than the image of the point at $x_2$. Note that it is the extent that is of interest here and not the magnitude.

For shift-invariant systems, the point spread function can be expressed in terms of the output of an impulse at $(0, 0)$,

$$h(x, y) = T[\delta(x, y)].$$

Then, the output of the shifted input is shifted by the same amount:

$$h(x - \xi, y - \eta) = T[\delta(x - \xi, y - \eta)].$$

In this case, the impulse response is represented by a function of two variables instead of four, i.e., $h(\xi, \eta, x, y) = h(x-\xi, y-\eta)$. Substitution into Eq. (2.7) leads to the convolution integral,

$$g(x, y) = \int_{-\infty}^{\infty} \int_{-\infty}^{\infty} f(\xi, \eta) h(x - \xi, y - \eta) \, d\xi \, d\eta. \tag{2.15}$$

The graphical representation of 2-D convolution is more difficult. The principles of time reversal and shifting are the same. Of course, time reversal corresponds to spatial reversal, and shifting must be done over a two-dimensional plane. Let us begin with a 2-D function (image), shown in Fig. 2.5a and 2.5b as isometric and grayscale displays, respectively. The advantages and disadvantages of these display methods are discussed in Chapter 3.

Many of the common point spread functions encountered in image processing are symmetric, e.g., circular and rectangular apertures in cameras and scanners. For our convolution example, we will use an asymmetric function, which will make it easier to follow the spatial reversal and shifting. The overlapping of the functions in the 1-D convolution example is easy to do by placing the graphs over one another. The same technique with 2-D functions requires more imagination.

Let us assume for ease of visualization that both the 2-D signal (input object) and the point spread function have finite support. The original image is shown using isometric plotting in Fig. 2.5a and in grayscale in Fig. 2.5b. The PSF is shown in Figs. 2.6a and 2.6b. As in 1-D convolution, the first step is the spatial reversal of the PSF (impulse response in 1-D) to obtain $h(-\xi, -\eta)$. The 2-D spatial reversal is shown in Figs. 2.7a and 2.7b. The result of the convolution is shown in Figs. 2.8a and 2.8b.

It is difficult to show the shift and overlap in the 2-D examples and include the value of the function. Let us try to make the point using only the region of support (RoS) of the functions, Fig. 2.9. For this example, assume the PSF and the object are nonnegative over their regions of support. For this example, the (0,0) location is denoted by the cross. We show the PSF, $h(x, y)$, in the upper left and the spatially reversed function, $h(-x, -y)$, below it. The value of $g(x, y)$ is computed by 1) sliding $h(-\xi, -\eta)$ so that (0,0) is located at (x,y), i.e., $h(x - \xi, y - \eta)$; then 2) integrating the product of the functions over the common region of support, which is represented by the shaded area in the figures. Figure 2.9a shows a position of $(x, y)$ that has partial overlap of the regions of support for the object and PSF. Figure 2.9b shows a position of $(x, y)$ that has total overlap of the RoS. Figure 2.9c shows a position of $(x, y)$ that has no overlap of the RoS. The region of support for the output, $g(x, y)$, is obtained from the position of the shifted, reversed PSF as its RoS just touches the RoS of the input, $f(x, y)$. This is denoted in Fig. 2.9d by the dashed line.

## 2.5.3     Discrete convolution

Discrete convolution is primarily used for approximating continuous convolution using computers. To refresh the reader's memory, we will first give the one-dimensional

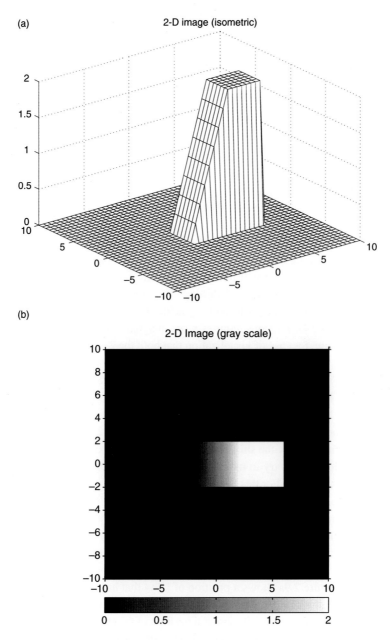

**Figure 2.5.** (a) Isometric display of 2-D function $f(x, y)$ for convolution example: (b) grayscale display of 2-D function $f(x, y)$ for convolution example.

(a)

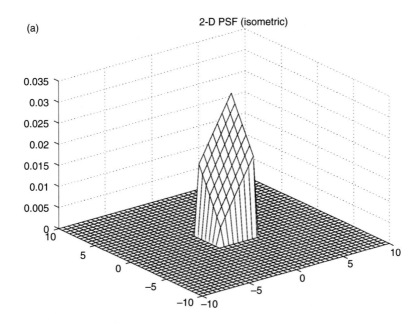

(b)

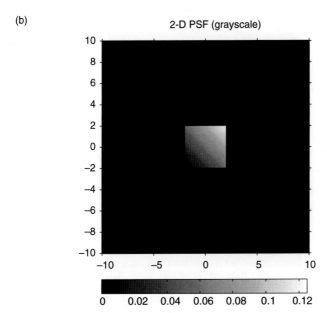

**Figure 2.6.** (a) Isometric display of point spread function $h(x, y)$ for convolution example: (b) grayscale display of point spread function $h(x, y)$ for convolution example.

(a)

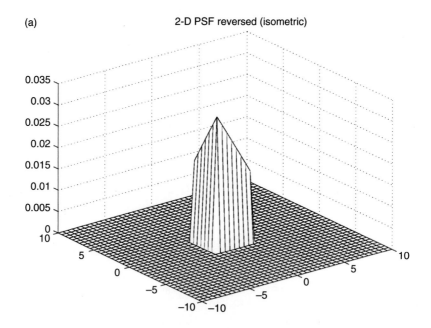

(b)

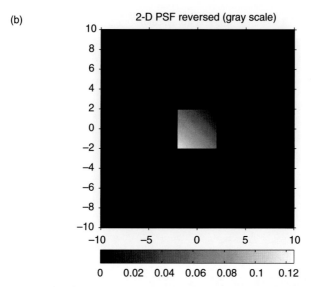

**Figure 2.7.** (a) Isometric display of spatially reversed point spread function, $h(-x, -y)$: (b) grayscale display of spatially reversed point spread function, $h(-x, -y)$.

(a)

2-D convolution of H*X (isometric)

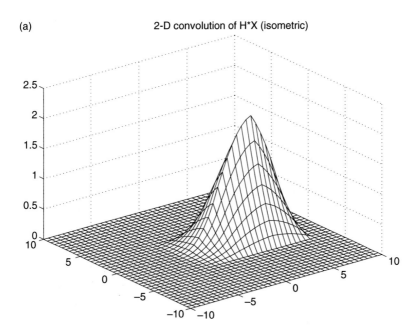

(b)

2-D Convolution of H*X (gray scale)

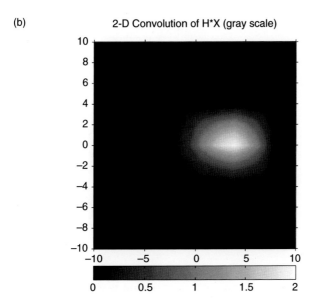

**Figure 2.8.** (a) Isometric display of 2-D convolution of $h(x, y)$ and $f(x, y)$: (b) grayscale display of 2-D convolution of $h(x, y)$ and $f(x, y)$.

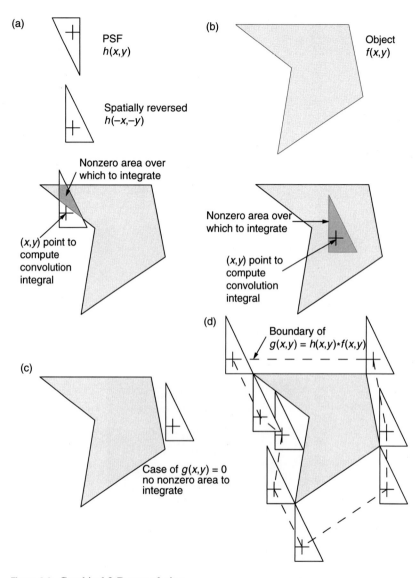

**Figure 2.9.** Graphical 2-D convolution.

formulation. The equation for discrete convolution is a straightforward extension of the continuous case,

$$g(n) = \sum_{k=-\infty}^{\infty} f(k)h(n-k). \qquad (2.16)$$

The methodology for visualizing the operation is the same as continuous convolution: time reversal of the impulse response, followed by shifting. As in the 1-D case, two-dimensional discrete convolution is an extension of the continuous case. The defining equation of the convolution of $f(k, l)$ and $h(k, l)$ is given by

$$g(m, n) = \sum_{k=-\infty}^{\infty} \sum_{l=-\infty}^{\infty} f(k, l) h(m - k, n - l). \tag{2.17}$$

Consider the example given below, where $(m, n) = (0, 0)$ is in the center of each array,

$$f(m, n) = \begin{bmatrix} 0 & 0 & 0 & 0 & 0 & 0 & 0 \\ 0 & 1 & 1 & 0 & 0 & 0 & 0 \\ 0 & 1 & 2 & 1 & 2 & 0 & 0 \\ 0 & 0 & 1 & 2 & 3 & 1 & 0 \\ 0 & 0 & 1 & 1 & 2 & 1 & 0 \\ 0 & 1 & 1 & 0 & 0 & 0 & 0 \\ 0 & 0 & 0 & 0 & 0 & 0 & 0 \end{bmatrix},$$

$$h(m, n) = \begin{bmatrix} 0 & 0 & 0 & 0 & 0 \\ 0 & 1 & 3 & 0 & 0 \\ 0 & 2 & 1 & 4 & 0 \\ 0 & 0 & 0 & 1 & 0 \\ 0 & 0 & 0 & 0 & 0 \end{bmatrix}.$$

The spatial reversal yields

$$h(-m, -n) = \begin{bmatrix} 0 & 0 & 0 & 0 & 0 \\ 0 & 1 & 0 & 0 & 0 \\ 0 & 4 & 1 & 2 & 0 \\ 0 & 0 & 3 & 1 & 0 \\ 0 & 0 & 0 & 0 & 0 \end{bmatrix}.$$

The output is given by

$$g(m, n) = \begin{bmatrix} 0 & 0 & 0 & 0 & 0 & 0 & 0 & 0 & 0 & 0 & 0 \\ 0 & 0 & 0 & 0 & 0 & 0 & 0 & 0 & 0 & 0 & 0 \\ 0 & 0 & 1 & 4 & 3 & 0 & 0 & 0 & 0 & 0 & 0 \\ 0 & 0 & 3 & 8 & 12 & 9 & 6 & 0 & 0 & 0 & 0 \\ 0 & 0 & 2 & 6 & 14 & 23 & 16 & 11 & 0 & 0 & 0 \\ 0 & 0 & 0 & 3 & 10 & 19 & 21 & 18 & 4 & 0 & 0 \\ 0 & 0 & 1 & 6 & 6 & 10 & 10 & 12 & 5 & 0 & 0 \\ 0 & 0 & 2 & 3 & 5 & 5 & 1 & 2 & 1 & 0 & 0 \\ 0 & 0 & 0 & 0 & 1 & 1 & 0 & 0 & 0 & 0 & 0 \\ 0 & 0 & 0 & 0 & 0 & 0 & 0 & 0 & 0 & 0 & 0 \\ 0 & 0 & 0 & 0 & 0 & 0 & 0 & 0 & 0 & 0 & 0 \end{bmatrix}.$$

The example was created using the MATLAB routine conv2. Note that it is up to the user to keep track of the indices. If we assume the (0,0) location is in the center of the PSF and the image, then the same is true of the output. Likewise, if the upper left corner is (0,0) for both the input image and the PSF, then the same is true of the output. To represent noncentered matrices with arbitrary (0,0) locations within the stored matrix, we need two sets of indices: one to represent the storage location (range 1:$N$) and one to represent the actual spatial location. Since convolution is a shift-invariant process, the easy approach is to shift the matrices to a standard location, perform the convolution and shift the result accordingly.

## 2.6          Differential operators

The characterization of an image by local smoothness requires the use of a derivative operator. With the addition of another dimension to the one-dimensional case, the number of possibilities is increased significantly. The simple derivatives of the continuous image become directional, given by the partial derivatives

$$d_x f = \frac{\partial f(x,y)}{\partial x}, \quad d_y f = \frac{\partial f(x,y)}{\partial y}.$$

The $\nabla$ (del) operator is a vector quantity defined by

$$\nabla f = \left[ \frac{\partial f(x,y)}{\partial x}, \frac{\partial f(x,y)}{\partial y} \right].$$

Note that this is not the same as the directional derivative.

To further complicate matters, there are several ways to define second-order derivatives. The second partial derivatives can be taken individually to produce a directional value or can be combined to produce a scalar quantity.

The Laplacian is defined by

$$\nabla^2 f = \frac{\partial^2 f(x,y)}{\partial x^2} + \frac{\partial^2 f(x,y)}{\partial y^2}.$$

Of course, digital image processing is concerned with discrete images. For the discrete case, it is common to simply use differences as approximations to the derivatives. Thus, we have

$$d_x f(m,n) = f(m,n) - f(m-1,n),$$
$$d_y f(m,n) = f(m,n) - f(m,n-1).$$

The discrete $\nabla$ operator is a vector quantity defined by

$$\nabla f(m,n) = [d_x f(m,n), d_y f(m,n)].$$

The discrete Laplacian is defined by

$$\nabla^2 f(m,n) = [d_x f(m,n)]^2 + [d_y f(m,n)]^2.$$

## 2.7  Matrix representation of images

The power of matrix algebra is simply too great to avoid using it in digital image processing. Of course, the use of matrices is restricted to discrete images, but since this is the only type processed by computers, it is not a real limitation. Fortunately, for most users only the elementary matrix operations are needed. The fact that image blurring in the presence of noise can be represented by a matrix equation, $\mathbf{g} = \mathbf{Hf} + \boldsymbol{\epsilon}$, makes the solution to the restoration problem extremely easy to write. At this point, let us not define all the terms of the restoration model, but consider only the simplicity of the notation. The matrix representation can yield extremely elegant and understandable solutions.

The digital image is represented by a function of discrete variables, $f(m, n)$. It has been noted that in practice the image must be confined to a region of finite support. This region will be designated

$$A = \{(m, n) \mid 0 \leq m \leq M - 1 \quad \text{and} \quad 0 \leq n \leq N - 1\}.$$

This leads to a natural representation of the digital image as a matrix. Unfortunately, this natural representation is not the most convenient for mathematical manipulations. To introduce the most tractable notation for images, let us first review the matrix representation of 1-D signals.

The digital signal with finite support is naturally represented by a vector

$$\mathbf{f} = [f(0), f(1), \ldots, f(M - 1)]^{T}. \tag{2.18}$$

Note that the vectors are represented as column vectors.

The defining operation for shift-invariant linear systems is convolution. Consider the 1-D analog system,

$$g_{a}(t) = \int_{-\infty}^{\infty} h_{a}(u) f_{a}(t - u)\, du, \tag{2.19}$$

where we use the subscript a to emphasize the analog nature of the signal. The discrete approximation to continuous convolution is given by

$$g(n) = \sum_{k=-\infty}^{\infty} h(n - k) f(k) = \sum_{k=-\infty}^{\infty} h(k) f(n - k), \tag{2.20}$$

where the indices $n$ and $k$ represent sampling of the analog signals, e.g., $f(n) = f_{a}(n\Delta T)$. Since convolution is commutative, both forms of the summation are given. Since it is assumed that the signals under investigation have finite support, the summation is over a finite number of terms. From elementary linear systems, it is known that if $f(n)$ has $M$ nonzero samples and $h(n)$ has $L$ nonzero samples, then $g(n)$ can have at most $N = M + L - 1$ nonzero samples. Let us assume the indices of the nonzero samples begin at $n = 0$; then the convolution is now written

$$g(n) = \sum_{k=0}^{L-1} h(n - k) f(k), \quad 0 \leq n \leq (M + L - 2) = N - 1. \tag{2.21}$$

Let us first write this in matrix notation, then consider under what conditions we can represent the analog system by the discrete approximation. Using the definition of the signal as a vector of Eq. (2.18), the summation of Eq. (2.21) can be written

$$\mathbf{g} = \mathbf{H}\mathbf{f}, \tag{2.22}$$

where the vectors $\mathbf{f}$ and $\mathbf{g}$ are of length $M$ and $N$, respectively and the $N \times M$ matrix $\mathbf{H}$ is defined by

$$\mathbf{H} = \begin{bmatrix}
h_0 & 0 & 0 & \cdots & 0 & 0 & 0 \\
h_1 & h_0 & 0 & \cdots & 0 & 0 & 0 \\
h_2 & h_1 & h_0 & \cdots & 0 & 0 & 0 \\
\vdots & \vdots & \vdots & \vdots & \vdots & \vdots & \vdots \\
h_{L-1} & h_{L-2} & h_{L-3} & \cdots & 0 & 0 & 0 \\
0 & h_{L-1} & h_{L-2} & \cdots & 0 & 0 & 0 \\
\vdots & \vdots & \vdots & \vdots & \vdots & \vdots & \vdots \\
0 & 0 & 0 & \cdots & h_0 & 0 & 0 \\
0 & 0 & 0 & \cdots & h_1 & h_0 & 0 \\
0 & 0 & 0 & \cdots & h_2 & h_1 & h_0 \\
0 & 0 & 0 & \cdots & h_3 & h_2 & h_1 \\
\vdots & \vdots & \vdots & \vdots & \vdots & \vdots & \vdots \\
0 & 0 & 0 & \cdots & 0 & h_{L-1} & h_{L-2} \\
0 & 0 & 0 & \cdots & 0 & 0 & h_{L-1}
\end{bmatrix}.$$

It is often desirable to work with square matrices. In this case, the input vector can be padded with zeros to make it the same size as $\mathbf{g}$ and the matrix $\mathbf{H}$ modified to produce an $N \times N$ Toeplitz[2] form

$$\mathbf{H}_t = \begin{bmatrix}
h_0 & 0 & 0 & \cdots & 0 & 0 & 0 & \cdots & 0 & 0 & 0 \\
h_1 & h_0 & 0 & \cdots & 0 & 0 & 0 & \cdots & 0 & 0 & 0 \\
h_2 & h_1 & h_0 & \cdots & 0 & 0 & 0 & \cdots & 0 & 0 & 0 \\
\vdots & \vdots & \vdots & \vdots & \vdots & \vdots & \vdots & \vdots & \vdots & \vdots & \vdots \\
h_{L-1} & h_{L-2} & h_{L-3} & \cdots & h_0 & 0 & 0 & \cdots & 0 & 0 & 0 \\
0 & h_{L-1} & h_{L-2} & \cdots & h_1 & h_0 & 0 & \cdots & 0 & 0 & 0 \\
\vdots & \vdots & \vdots & \vdots & \vdots & \vdots & \vdots & \vdots & \vdots & \vdots & \vdots \\
0 & 0 & 0 & \cdots & h_k & h_{k-1} & h_{k-2} & \cdots & 0 & 0 & 0 \\
0 & 0 & 0 & \cdots & h_{k+1} & h_k & h_{k-1} & \cdots & 0 & 0 & 0 \\
0 & 0 & 0 & \cdots & h_{k+2} & h_{k+1} & h_k & \cdots & 0 & 0 & 0 \\
\vdots & \vdots & \vdots & \vdots & \vdots & \vdots & \vdots & \vdots & \vdots & \vdots & \vdots \\
0 & 0 & 0 & \cdots & 0 & h_{L-1} & h_{L-2} & \cdots & h_1 & h_0 & 0 \\
0 & 0 & 0 & \cdots & 0 & 0 & h_{L-1} & \cdots & h_2 & h_1 & h_0
\end{bmatrix}. \tag{2.23}$$

---

[2] Recall that a Toeplitz form is a matrix with diagonal elements equal, mathematically $h(i,j) = h(i+k, j+k)$ for all $i$ and $j$ and for any $k$.

The output can now be written

$$\mathbf{g} = \mathbf{H_t f_0},$$

where $\mathbf{f_0} = [f(0), f(1), \ldots f(M-1), 0, \ldots 0]^T$ is the padded input.

It is often useful, because of the efficiency of the fast Fourier transform (FFT), to approximate the Toeplitz form by a circulant form

$$\mathbf{H_c} = \begin{bmatrix}
h_0 & 0 & 0 & \cdots & 0 & h_{L-1} & h_{L-2} & \cdots & h_3 & h_2 & h_1 \\
h_1 & h_0 & 0 & \cdots & 0 & 0 & 0 & \cdots & h_4 & h_3 & h_2 \\
h_2 & h_1 & h_0 & \cdots & 0 & 0 & 0 & \cdots & h_5 & h_4 & h_3 \\
\vdots & \vdots & \vdots & \vdots & \vdots & \vdots & \vdots & \vdots & \vdots & \vdots & \vdots \\
h_{L-1} & h_{L-2} & h_{L-3} & \cdots & 0 & 0 & 0 & \cdots & 0 & 0 & 0 \\
0 & h_{L-1} & h_{L-2} & \cdots & 0 & 0 & 0 & \cdots & 0 & 0 & 0 \\
\vdots & \vdots & \vdots & \vdots & \vdots & \vdots & \vdots & \vdots & \vdots & \vdots & \vdots \\
0 & 0 & 0 & \cdots & h_k & h_{k-1} & h_{k-2} & \cdots & 0 & 0 & 0 \\
0 & 0 & 0 & \cdots & h_{k+1} & h_k & h_{k-1} & \cdots & 0 & 0 & 0 \\
0 & 0 & 0 & \cdots & h_{k+2} & h_{k+1} & h_k & \cdots & 0 & 0 & 0 \\
\vdots & \vdots & \vdots & \vdots & \vdots & \vdots & \vdots & \vdots & \vdots & \vdots & \vdots \\
0 & 0 & 0 & \cdots & 0 & h_{L-1} & h_{L-2} & \cdots & h_1 & h_0 & 0 \\
0 & 0 & 0 & \cdots & 0 & 0 & h_{L-1} & \cdots & h_2 & h_1 & h_0
\end{bmatrix},$$

$$(2.24)$$

where each row of the circulant is a circular shift of one unit of the previous or succeeding row. The use of the circulant form will be discussed in Chapter 5.

The approximation of a Toeplitz matrix by a circulant improves as the dimension of the matrix increases. Consider the matrix norm

$$||\mathbf{H}||^2 = \frac{1}{N^2} \sum_{k=1}^{N} \sum_{l=1}^{N} h_{kl}^2,$$

then $||\mathbf{H_t} - \mathbf{H_c}|| \to 0$ as $N \to \infty$, since the matrices differ by the same elements in the corner but the dimension increases.

This works well with impulse response matrices (point spread functions) of short duration and autocorrelation matrices with small correlation distances.

---

**Example 2.8.** Consider the convolution $\mathbf{g} = \mathbf{h} * \mathbf{f}$ with

$$\mathbf{h} = [1, 2, 3, 4] \quad \text{and} \quad \mathbf{f} = [2, -3, 0, 1, -2, 1],$$

where the first elements are assumed to start with index $i = 0$. We can compute $\mathbf{g}$ by Eq. (2.20) to obtain

$$\mathbf{g} = [2, 1, 0, 0, -12, 0, 0, -5, 4].$$

The matrix version of the equation using a square Toeplitz form is given by

$$\mathbf{g} = \begin{bmatrix} 2 \\ 1 \\ 0 \\ 0 \\ -12 \\ 0 \\ 0 \\ -5 \\ 4 \end{bmatrix} = \begin{bmatrix} 1 & 0 & 0 & 0 & 0 & 0 & 0 & 0 & 0 \\ 2 & 1 & 0 & 0 & 0 & 0 & 0 & 0 & 0 \\ 3 & 2 & 1 & 0 & 0 & 0 & 0 & 0 & 0 \\ 4 & 3 & 2 & 1 & 0 & 0 & 0 & 0 & 0 \\ 0 & 4 & 3 & 2 & 1 & 0 & 0 & 0 & 0 \\ 0 & 0 & 4 & 3 & 2 & 1 & 0 & 0 & 0 \\ 0 & 0 & 0 & 4 & 3 & 2 & 1 & 0 & 0 \\ 0 & 0 & 0 & 0 & 4 & 3 & 2 & 1 & 0 \\ 0 & 0 & 0 & 0 & 0 & 4 & 3 & 2 & 1 \end{bmatrix} \begin{bmatrix} 2 \\ -3 \\ 0 \\ 1 \\ -2 \\ 1 \\ 0 \\ 0 \\ 0 \end{bmatrix}.$$

The circulant matrix form gives the same result because of the zero padding of the input signal,

$$\mathbf{g} = \begin{bmatrix} 2 \\ 1 \\ 0 \\ 0 \\ -12 \\ 0 \\ 0 \\ -5 \\ 4 \end{bmatrix} = \begin{bmatrix} 1 & 0 & 0 & 0 & 0 & 0 & 4 & 3 & 2 \\ 2 & 1 & 0 & 0 & 0 & 0 & 0 & 4 & 3 \\ 3 & 2 & 1 & 0 & 0 & 0 & 0 & 0 & 4 \\ 4 & 3 & 2 & 1 & 0 & 0 & 0 & 0 & 0 \\ 0 & 4 & 3 & 2 & 1 & 0 & 0 & 0 & 0 \\ 0 & 0 & 4 & 3 & 2 & 1 & 0 & 0 & 0 \\ 0 & 0 & 0 & 4 & 3 & 2 & 1 & 0 & 0 \\ 0 & 0 & 0 & 0 & 4 & 3 & 2 & 1 & 0 \\ 0 & 0 & 0 & 0 & 0 & 4 & 3 & 2 & 1 \end{bmatrix} \begin{bmatrix} 2 \\ -3 \\ 0 \\ 1 \\ -2 \\ 1 \\ 0 \\ 0 \\ 0 \end{bmatrix}.$$

Now, let us consider the two-dimensional convolution problem. To make use of matrix algebra, we need to write the image in the form of a vector. We will do this using stacked notation. Without loss of generality, let us assume that an image is defined on a square $M \times N$ grid. A single band, two-dimensional image is denoted by the $M \times N$ matrix $\mathbf{F}_{M \times N}$, and is defined by

$$\mathbf{F} = [\mathbf{f}_1, \mathbf{f}_2, ..., \mathbf{f}_N] = \begin{bmatrix} f_{0,0} & f_{0,1} & f_{0,2} & \cdots & f_{0,N-1} \\ f_{1,0} & f_{1,1} & f_{1,2} & \cdots & f_{1,N-1} \\ f_{2,0} & f_{2,1} & f_{2,2} & \cdots & f_{2,N-1} \\ \vdots & \vdots & \vdots & \vdots & \vdots \\ f_{M-1,0} & f_{M-1,1} & f_{M-1,2} & \cdots & f_{M-1,N-1} \end{bmatrix}, \quad (2.25)$$

where the $\mathbf{f}_k$ are column vectors of length $M$. The $MN \times 1$ stacked vector, $\mathbf{f}_{MN \times 1}$, representing the image is given by

$$\mathbf{f} = [\mathbf{f}_1^T, \mathbf{f}_2^T, ..., \mathbf{f}_M^T]^T = \begin{bmatrix} f_{0,0} \\ f_{1,0} \\ \vdots \\ f_{M-1,0} \\ f_{0,1} \\ f_{1,1} \\ \vdots \\ f_{M-1,1} \\ f_{0,2} \\ \vdots \\ f_{M-1,N-1} \end{bmatrix}. \tag{2.26}$$

Two-dimensional convolution for a single band $M \times M$ image with a $K \times K$ point spread function (PSF) is defined by

$$g(m,n) = \sum_{k=0}^{K-1} \sum_{l=0}^{K-1} h(k,l) f(m-k, n-l), \tag{2.27}$$

and is written using the stacked notation as

$$\mathbf{g}_{(M+K-1)^2 \times 1} = \mathbf{H}_{(M+K-1)^2 \times M^2} \; \mathbf{f}_{M^2 \times 1},$$

or

$$\mathbf{g}_{(M+K-1)^2 \times 1} = \begin{bmatrix} g_{0,0} \\ g_{1,0} \\ \vdots \\ g_{M+K-2,0} \\ g_{0,1} \\ g_{1,1} \\ \vdots \\ g_{M+K-2,1} \\ g_{0,2} \\ \vdots \\ g_{M+K-2,M+K-2} \end{bmatrix} = \mathbf{H}_{(M+K-1)^2 \times M^2} \begin{bmatrix} f_{0,0} \\ f_{1,0} \\ \vdots \\ f_{M-1,0} \\ f_{0,1} \\ x_{1,1} \\ \vdots \\ f_{M-1,1} \\ f_{0,2} \\ \vdots \\ f_{M-1,M-1} \end{bmatrix}, \tag{2.28}$$

where the 2-D point spread function array $\mathbf{H}_{(M+K-1)^2 \times M^2}$ is defined by

$$
\begin{bmatrix}
h_{0,0} & 0 & 0 & \cdots & 0 & 0 & 0 & 0 & \cdots & 0 & \cdots & 0 & 0 & 0 & \cdots & 0 \\
h_{1,0} & h_{0,0} & 0 & \cdots & 0 & 0 & 0 & 0 & \cdots & 0 & \cdots & 0 & 0 & 0 & \cdots & 0 \\
h_{2,0} & h_{1,0} & h_{0,0} & \cdots & 0 & 0 & 0 & 0 & \cdots & 0 & \cdots & 0 & 0 & 0 & \cdots & 0 \\
\vdots & \vdots & \vdots & \vdots & \vdots & \vdots & \vdots & \vdots & \vdots & \vdots & \cdots & \vdots & \vdots & \vdots & \vdots & \vdots \\
0 & 0 & 0 & \cdots & h_{K-1,0} & 0 & 0 & 0 & \cdots & 0 & \cdots & 0 & 0 & 0 & \cdots & 0 \\
h_{0,1} & 0 & 0 & \cdots & 0 & h_{0,0} & 0 & 0 & \cdots & 0 & \cdots & 0 & 0 & 0 & \cdots & 0 \\
h_{1,1} & h_{0,1} & 0 & \cdots & 0 & h_{1,0} & h_{0,0} & 0 & \cdots & 0 & \cdots & 0 & 0 & 0 & \cdots & 0 \\
h_{2,1} & h_{1,1} & h_{0,1} & \cdots & 0 & h_{2,0} & h_{1,0} & h_{0,0} & \cdots & 0 & \cdots & 0 & 0 & 0 & \cdots & 0 \\
\vdots & \vdots & \vdots & \vdots & \vdots & \vdots & \vdots & \vdots & \vdots & \vdots & \cdots & \vdots & \vdots & \vdots & \vdots & \vdots \\
0 & 0 & 0 & \cdots & h_{K-1,1} & 0 & 0 & 0 & \cdots & h_{K-1,0} & \cdots & 0 & 0 & 0 & \cdots & 0 \\
\vdots & \vdots & \vdots & \vdots & \vdots & \vdots & \vdots & \vdots & \vdots & \vdots & \vdots & \vdots & \vdots & \vdots & \vdots & \vdots \\
0 & 0 & 0 & \cdots & 0 & 0 & 0 & 0 & \cdots & 0 & \cdots & h_{0,K-1} & 0 & 0 & \cdots & 0 \\
0 & 0 & 0 & \cdots & 0 & 0 & 0 & 0 & \cdots & 0 & \cdots & h_{1,K-1} & h_{0,K-1} & 0 & \cdots & 0 \\
0 & 0 & 0 & \cdots & 0 & 0 & 0 & 0 & \cdots & 0 & \cdots & h_{2,K-1} & h_{1,K-1} & h_{0,K-1} & \cdots & 0 \\
\vdots & \vdots & \vdots & \vdots & \vdots & \vdots & \vdots & \vdots & \vdots & \vdots & \vdots & \vdots & \vdots & \vdots & \vdots & \vdots \\
0 & 0 & 0 & \cdots & 0 & 0 & 0 & 0 & \cdots & 0 & \cdots & 0 & 0 & 0 & \cdots & h_{K-1,K-1}
\end{bmatrix}
$$

$$(2.29)$$

Since each $(M + K - 1) \times M$ block of the large matrix is Toeplitz, the form is called *block Toeplitz*.

As in the one-dimensional case, let us pad the input image so that we produce a square point spread function matrix, $\mathbf{H}$, that is $N \times N$, where $N = (M + K - 1)$. If the convolution of Eq. (2.27) is approximated by a 2-D circulant operation, the matrix will be *block circulant* of the form

$$
\begin{bmatrix}
h_{0,0} & 0 & 0 & \cdots & h_{K-1,0} & 0 & 0 & 0 & \cdots & 0 & \cdots & h_{0,1} & 0 & 0 & \cdots & h_{K-1,1} \\
h_{1,0} & h_{0,0} & 0 & \cdots & h_{K-2,0} & 0 & 0 & 0 & \cdots & 0 & \cdots & h_{1,1} & h_{0,1} & 0 & \cdots & h_{K-2,1} \\
h_{2,0} & h_{1,0} & h_{0,0} & \cdots & h_{K-3,0} & 0 & 0 & 0 & \cdots & 0 & \cdots & h_{2,1} & h_{1,1} & h_{0,1} & \cdots & h_{K-3,1} \\
\vdots & \vdots & \vdots & \vdots & \vdots & \vdots & \vdots & \vdots & \vdots & \vdots & \cdots & \vdots & \vdots & \vdots & \vdots & \vdots \\
0 & 0 & 0 & \cdots & h_{0,0} & 0 & 0 & 0 & \cdots & 0 & \cdots & 0 & 0 & 0 & \cdots & h_{0,1} \\
h_{0,1} & 0 & 0 & \cdots & h_{K-1,1} & h_{0,0} & 0 & 0 & \cdots & h_{K-1,0} & \cdots & h_{0,2} & 0 & 0 & \cdots & h_{K-1,2} \\
h_{1,1} & h_{0,1} & 0 & \cdots & h_{K-2,1} & h_{1,0} & h_{0,0} & 0 & \cdots & h_{K-2,0} & \cdots & h_{1,2} & h_{0,2} & 0 & \cdots & h_{K-2,2} \\
h_{2,1} & h_{1,1} & h_{0,1} & \cdots & h_{K-3,1} & h_{2,0} & h_{1,0} & h_{0,0} & \cdots & h_{K-3,0} & \cdots & h_{2,2} & h_{1,2} & h_{0,2} & \cdots & h_{K-3,2} \\
\vdots & \vdots & \vdots & \vdots & \vdots & \vdots & \vdots & \vdots & \vdots & \vdots & \cdots & \vdots & \vdots & \vdots & \vdots & \vdots \\
0 & 0 & 0 & \cdots & h_{0,1} & 0 & 0 & 0 & \cdots & h_{0,0} & \cdots & 0 & 0 & 0 & \cdots & h_{0,2} \\
\vdots & \vdots & \vdots & \vdots & \vdots & \vdots & \vdots & \vdots & \vdots & \vdots & \vdots & \vdots & \vdots & \vdots & \vdots & \vdots \\
0 & 0 & 0 & \cdots & 0 & 0 & 0 & 0 & \cdots & 0 & \cdots & h_{0,K-1} & 0 & 0 & \cdots & h_{1,K-1} \\
0 & 0 & 0 & \cdots & 0 & 0 & 0 & 0 & \cdots & 0 & \cdots & h_{1,K-1} & h_{0,K-1} & 0 & \cdots & h_{2,K-1} \\
0 & 0 & 0 & \cdots & 0 & 0 & 0 & 0 & \cdots & 0 & \cdots & h_{2,K-1} & h_{1,K-1} & h_{0,K-1} & \cdots & h_{3,K-1} \\
\vdots & \vdots & \vdots & \vdots & \vdots & \vdots & \vdots & \vdots & \vdots & \vdots & \vdots & \vdots & \vdots & \vdots & \vdots & \vdots \\
0 & 0 & 0 & \cdots & 0 & 0 & 0 & 0 & \cdots & 0 & \cdots & 0 & 0 & 0 & \cdots & h_{0,K-1}
\end{bmatrix}
$$

$$(2.30)$$

**Example 2.9.** Using the nonzero portion of the two-dimensional convolution example given previously in Section 2.5.3, the block Toeplitz square matrix version of the convolution matrix $\mathbf{H}_t$ is written

$$
\begin{bmatrix}
1 & 0 & 0 & 0 & 0 & 0 & 0 & 0 & 0 & 0 & 0 & 0 & 0 & 0 & 0 & \cdots & 0 & 0 & 0 & 0 & 0 & 0 & 0 & 0 & 0 & 0 & 0 & 0 & 0 & 0 & 0 \\
2 & 1 & 0 & 0 & 0 & 0 & 0 & 0 & 0 & 0 & 0 & 0 & 0 & 0 & 0 & \cdots & 0 & 0 & 0 & 0 & 0 & 0 & 0 & 0 & 0 & 0 & 0 & 0 & 0 & 0 & 0 \\
0 & 2 & 1 & 0 & 0 & 0 & 0 & 0 & 0 & 0 & 0 & 0 & 0 & 0 & 0 & \cdots & 0 & 0 & 0 & 0 & 0 & 0 & 0 & 0 & 0 & 0 & 0 & 0 & 0 & 0 & 0 \\
0 & 0 & 2 & 1 & 0 & 0 & 0 & 0 & 0 & 0 & 0 & 0 & 0 & 0 & 0 & \cdots & 0 & 0 & 0 & 0 & 0 & 0 & 0 & 0 & 0 & 0 & 0 & 0 & 0 & 0 & 0 \\
0 & 0 & 0 & 2 & 1 & 0 & 0 & 0 & 0 & 0 & 0 & 0 & 0 & 0 & 0 & \cdots & 0 & 0 & 0 & 0 & 0 & 0 & 0 & 0 & 0 & 0 & 0 & 0 & 0 & 0 & 0 \\
0 & 0 & 0 & 0 & 2 & 1 & 0 & 0 & 0 & 0 & 0 & 0 & 0 & 0 & 0 & \cdots & 0 & 0 & 0 & 0 & 0 & 0 & 0 & 0 & 0 & 0 & 0 & 0 & 0 & 0 & 0 \\
0 & 0 & 0 & 0 & 0 & 2 & 1 & 0 & 0 & 0 & 0 & 0 & 0 & 0 & 0 & \cdots & 0 & 0 & 0 & 0 & 0 & 0 & 0 & 0 & 0 & 0 & 0 & 0 & 0 & 0 & 0 \\
3 & 0 & 0 & 0 & 0 & 0 & 0 & 1 & 0 & 0 & 0 & 0 & 0 & 0 & 0 & \cdots & 0 & 0 & 0 & 0 & 0 & 0 & 0 & 0 & 0 & 0 & 0 & 0 & 0 & 0 & 0 \\
1 & 3 & 0 & 0 & 0 & 0 & 0 & 2 & 1 & 0 & 0 & 0 & 0 & 0 & 0 & \cdots & 0 & 0 & 0 & 0 & 0 & 0 & 0 & 0 & 0 & 0 & 0 & 0 & 0 & 0 & 0 \\
0 & 1 & 3 & 0 & 0 & 0 & 0 & 0 & 2 & 1 & 0 & 0 & 0 & 0 & 0 & \cdots & 0 & 0 & 0 & 0 & 0 & 0 & 0 & 0 & 0 & 0 & 0 & 0 & 0 & 0 & 0 \\
0 & 0 & 1 & 3 & 0 & 0 & 0 & 0 & 0 & 2 & 1 & 0 & 0 & 0 & 0 & \cdots & 0 & 0 & 0 & 0 & 0 & 0 & 0 & 0 & 0 & 0 & 0 & 0 & 0 & 0 & 0 \\
0 & 0 & 0 & 1 & 3 & 0 & 0 & 0 & 0 & 0 & 2 & 1 & 0 & 0 & 0 & \cdots & 0 & 0 & 0 & 0 & 0 & 0 & 0 & 0 & 0 & 0 & 0 & 0 & 0 & 0 & 0 \\
0 & 0 & 0 & 0 & 1 & 3 & 0 & 0 & 0 & 0 & 0 & 2 & 1 & 0 & 0 & \cdots & 0 & 0 & 0 & 0 & 0 & 0 & 0 & 0 & 0 & 0 & 0 & 0 & 0 & 0 & 0 \\
0 & 0 & 0 & 0 & 0 & 1 & 3 & 0 & 0 & 0 & 0 & 0 & 2 & 1 & & \cdots & 0 & 0 & 0 & 0 & 0 & 0 & 0 & 0 & 0 & 0 & 0 & 0 & 0 & 0 & 0 \\
0 & 0 & 0 & 0 & 0 & 0 & 0 & 3 & 0 & 0 & 0 & 0 & 0 & 0 & 0 & \cdots & 0 & 0 & 0 & 0 & 0 & 0 & 0 & 0 & 0 & 0 & 0 & 0 & 0 & 0 & 0 \\
4 & 0 & 0 & 0 & 0 & 0 & 0 & 1 & 3 & 0 & 0 & 0 & 0 & 0 & & \cdots & 0 & 0 & 0 & 0 & 0 & 0 & 0 & 0 & 0 & 0 & 0 & 0 & 0 & 0 & 0 \\
1 & 4 & 0 & 0 & 0 & 0 & 0 & 0 & 1 & 3 & 0 & 0 & 0 & 0 & & \cdots & 0 & 0 & 0 & 0 & 0 & 0 & 0 & 0 & 0 & 0 & 0 & 0 & 0 & 0 & 0 \\
0 & 1 & 4 & 0 & 0 & 0 & 0 & 0 & 0 & 1 & 3 & 0 & 0 & 0 & & \cdots & 0 & 0 & 0 & 0 & 0 & 0 & 0 & 0 & 0 & 0 & 0 & 0 & 0 & 0 & 0 \\
0 & 0 & 1 & 4 & 0 & 0 & 0 & 0 & 0 & 0 & 1 & 3 & 0 & 0 & & \cdots & 0 & 0 & 0 & 0 & 0 & 0 & 0 & 0 & 0 & 0 & 0 & 0 & 0 & 0 & 0 \\
0 & 0 & 0 & 1 & 4 & 0 & 0 & 0 & 0 & 0 & 0 & 1 & 3 & 0 & & \cdots & 0 & 0 & 0 & 0 & 0 & 0 & 0 & 0 & 0 & 0 & 0 & 0 & 0 & 0 & 0 \\
0 & 0 & 0 & 0 & 1 & 4 & 0 & 0 & 0 & 0 & 0 & 0 & 1 & 3 & & \cdots & 0 & 0 & 0 & 0 & 0 & 0 & 0 & 0 & 0 & 0 & 0 & 0 & 0 & 0 & 0 \\
\vdots & \vdots & \vdots & \vdots & \vdots & \vdots & \vdots & \vdots & \vdots & \vdots & \vdots & \vdots & \vdots & \vdots & \vdots & & \vdots & \vdots & \vdots & \vdots & \vdots & \vdots & \vdots & \vdots & \vdots & \vdots & \vdots & \vdots & \vdots & \vdots & \vdots \\
0 & 0 & 0 & 0 & 0 & 0 & 0 & 0 & 0 & 0 & 0 & 0 & 0 & 0 & 0 & \cdots & 1 & 0 & 0 & 0 & 0 & 0 & 0 & 0 & 0 & 0 & 0 & 0 & 0 & 0 & 0 \\
0 & 0 & 0 & 0 & 0 & 0 & 0 & 0 & 0 & 0 & 0 & 0 & 0 & 0 & 0 & \cdots & 2 & 1 & 0 & 0 & 0 & 0 & 0 & 0 & 0 & 0 & 0 & 0 & 0 & 0 & 0 \\
0 & 0 & 0 & 0 & 0 & 0 & 0 & 0 & 0 & 0 & 0 & 0 & 0 & 0 & 0 & \cdots & 0 & 2 & 1 & 0 & 0 & 0 & 0 & 0 & 0 & 0 & 0 & 0 & 0 & 0 & 0 \\
0 & 0 & 0 & 0 & 0 & 0 & 0 & 0 & 0 & 0 & 0 & 0 & 0 & 0 & 0 & \cdots & 0 & 0 & 2 & 1 & 0 & 0 & 0 & 0 & 0 & 0 & 0 & 0 & 0 & 0 & 0 \\
0 & 0 & 0 & 0 & 0 & 0 & 0 & 0 & 0 & 0 & 0 & 0 & 0 & 0 & 0 & \cdots & 0 & 0 & 0 & 2 & 1 & 0 & 0 & 0 & 0 & 0 & 0 & 0 & 0 & 0 & 0 \\
0 & 0 & 0 & 0 & 0 & 0 & 0 & 0 & 0 & 0 & 0 & 0 & 0 & 0 & 0 & \cdots & 0 & 0 & 0 & 0 & 2 & 1 & 0 & 0 & 0 & 0 & 0 & 0 & 0 & 0 & 0 \\
0 & 0 & 0 & 0 & 0 & 0 & 0 & 0 & 0 & 0 & 0 & 0 & 0 & 0 & 0 & \cdots & 0 & 0 & 0 & 0 & 0 & 2 & 1 & 0 & 0 & 0 & 0 & 0 & 0 & 0 & 0 \\
0 & 0 & 0 & 0 & 0 & 0 & 0 & 0 & 0 & 0 & 0 & 0 & 0 & 0 & 0 & \cdots & 3 & 0 & 0 & 0 & 0 & 0 & 0 & 1 & 0 & 0 & 0 & 0 & 0 & 0 & 0 \\
0 & 0 & 0 & 0 & 0 & 0 & 0 & 0 & 0 & 0 & 0 & 0 & 0 & 0 & 0 & \cdots & 1 & 3 & 0 & 0 & 0 & 0 & 0 & 2 & 1 & 0 & 0 & 0 & 0 & 0 & 0 \\
0 & 0 & 0 & 0 & 0 & 0 & 0 & 0 & 0 & 0 & 0 & 0 & 0 & 0 & 0 & \cdots & 0 & 1 & 3 & 0 & 0 & 0 & 0 & 0 & 2 & 1 & 0 & 0 & 0 & 0 & 0 \\
0 & 0 & 0 & 0 & 0 & 0 & 0 & 0 & 0 & 0 & 0 & 0 & 0 & 0 & 0 & \cdots & 0 & 0 & 1 & 3 & 0 & 0 & 0 & 0 & 0 & 2 & 1 & 0 & 0 & 0 & 0 \\
0 & 0 & 0 & 0 & 0 & 0 & 0 & 0 & 0 & 0 & 0 & 0 & 0 & 0 & 0 & \cdots & 0 & 0 & 0 & 1 & 3 & 0 & 0 & 0 & 0 & 0 & 2 & 1 & 0 & 0 & 0 \\
0 & 0 & 0 & 0 & 0 & 0 & 0 & 0 & 0 & 0 & 0 & 0 & 0 & 0 & 0 & \cdots & 0 & 0 & 0 & 0 & 1 & 3 & 0 & 0 & 0 & 0 & 0 & 2 & 1 & 0 & 0 \\
0 & 0 & 0 & 0 & 0 & 0 & 0 & 0 & 0 & 0 & 0 & 0 & 0 & 0 & 0 & \cdots & 0 & 0 & 0 & 0 & 0 & 1 & 3 & 0 & 0 & 0 & 0 & 0 & 2 & 1 & 0 \\
0 & 0 & 0 & 0 & 0 & 0 & 0 & 0 & 0 & 0 & 0 & 0 & 0 & 0 & 0 & \cdots & 0 & 0 & 0 & 0 & 0 & 1 & 3 & 0 & 0 & 0 & 0 & 0 & 2 & 1 \\
\end{bmatrix}
$$

(2.31)

The block circulant square matrix version of the convolution matrix $\mathbf{H_c}$ is written

$$
\begin{bmatrix}
1 & 0 & 0 & 0 & 0 & 0 & 2 & 0 & 0 & 0 & 0 & 0 & 0 & 0 & \cdots & 0 & 0 & 0 & 0 & 0 & 1 & 4 & 3 & 0 & 0 & 0 & 0 & 0 & 1 \\
2 & 1 & 0 & 0 & 0 & 0 & 0 & 0 & 0 & 0 & 0 & 0 & 0 & 0 & \cdots & 4 & 0 & 0 & 0 & 0 & 0 & 1 & 1 & 3 & 0 & 0 & 0 & 0 & 0 \\
0 & 2 & 1 & 0 & 0 & 0 & 0 & 0 & 0 & 0 & 0 & 0 & 0 & 0 & \cdots & 1 & 4 & 0 & 0 & 0 & 0 & 0 & 0 & 1 & 3 & 0 & 0 & 0 & 0 \\
0 & 0 & 2 & 1 & 0 & 0 & 0 & 0 & 0 & 0 & 0 & 0 & 0 & 0 & \cdots & 0 & 1 & 4 & 0 & 0 & 0 & 0 & 0 & 0 & 1 & 3 & 0 & 0 & 0 \\
0 & 0 & 0 & 2 & 1 & 0 & 0 & 0 & 0 & 0 & 0 & 0 & 0 & 0 & \cdots & 0 & 0 & 1 & 4 & 0 & 0 & 0 & 0 & 0 & 0 & 1 & 3 & 0 & 0 \\
0 & 0 & 0 & 0 & 2 & 1 & 0 & 0 & 0 & 0 & 0 & 0 & 0 & 0 & \cdots & 0 & 0 & 0 & 1 & 4 & 0 & 0 & 0 & 0 & 0 & 0 & 1 & 3 & 0 \\
0 & 0 & 0 & 0 & 0 & 2 & 1 & 0 & 0 & 0 & 0 & 0 & 0 & 0 & \cdots & 0 & 0 & 0 & 0 & 1 & 4 & 0 & 0 & 0 & 0 & 0 & 0 & 1 & 3 \\
3 & 0 & 0 & 0 & 0 & 0 & 1 & 1 & 0 & 0 & 0 & 0 & 0 & 2 & \cdots & 0 & 0 & 0 & 0 & 0 & 0 & 0 & 0 & 0 & 0 & 0 & 0 & 1 & 4 \\
1 & 3 & 0 & 0 & 0 & 0 & 0 & 2 & 1 & 0 & 0 & 0 & 0 & 0 & \cdots & 0 & 0 & 0 & 0 & 0 & 0 & 0 & 4 & 0 & 0 & 0 & 0 & 0 & 1 \\
0 & 0 & 1 & 3 & 0 & 0 & 0 & 0 & 0 & 2 & 1 & 0 & 0 & 0 & \cdots & 0 & 0 & 0 & 0 & 0 & 0 & 0 & 0 & 1 & 4 & 0 & 0 & 0 & 0 \\
0 & 0 & 0 & 1 & 3 & 0 & 0 & 0 & 0 & 0 & 2 & 1 & 0 & 0 & \cdots & 0 & 0 & 0 & 0 & 0 & 0 & 0 & 0 & 0 & 1 & 4 & 0 & 0 & 0 \\
0 & 0 & 0 & 0 & 1 & 3 & 0 & 0 & 0 & 0 & 0 & 2 & 1 & 0 & \cdots & 0 & 0 & 0 & 0 & 0 & 0 & 0 & 0 & 0 & 0 & 1 & 4 & 0 & 0 \\
0 & 0 & 0 & 0 & 0 & 1 & 3 & 0 & 0 & 0 & 0 & 0 & 2 & 1 & \cdots & 0 & 0 & 0 & 0 & 0 & 0 & 0 & 0 & 0 & 0 & 0 & 1 & 4 & 0 \\
0 & 0 & 0 & 0 & 0 & 1 & 4 & 3 & 0 & 0 & 0 & 0 & 0 & 1 & \cdots & 0 & 0 & 0 & 0 & 0 & 0 & 0 & 0 & 0 & 0 & 0 & 0 & 0 & 0 \\
4 & 0 & 0 & 0 & 0 & 0 & 1 & 1 & 3 & 0 & 0 & 0 & 0 & 0 & \cdots & 0 & 0 & 0 & 0 & 0 & 0 & 0 & 0 & 0 & 0 & 0 & 0 & 0 & 0 \\
1 & 4 & 0 & 0 & 0 & 0 & 0 & 0 & 1 & 3 & 0 & 0 & 0 & 0 & \cdots & 0 & 0 & 0 & 0 & 0 & 0 & 0 & 0 & 0 & 0 & 0 & 0 & 0 & 0 \\
0 & 1 & 4 & 0 & 0 & 0 & 0 & 0 & 0 & 1 & 3 & 0 & 0 & 0 & \cdots & 0 & 0 & 0 & 0 & 0 & 0 & 0 & 0 & 0 & 0 & 0 & 0 & 0 & 0 \\
0 & 0 & 1 & 4 & 0 & 0 & 0 & 0 & 0 & 0 & 1 & 3 & 0 & 0 & \cdots & 0 & 0 & 0 & 0 & 0 & 0 & 0 & 0 & 0 & 0 & 0 & 0 & 0 & 0 \\
0 & 0 & 0 & 1 & 4 & 0 & 0 & 0 & 0 & 0 & 0 & 1 & 3 & 0 & \cdots & 0 & 0 & 0 & 0 & 0 & 0 & 0 & 0 & 0 & 0 & 0 & 0 & 0 & 0 \\
0 & 0 & 0 & 0 & 1 & 4 & 0 & 0 & 0 & 0 & 0 & 0 & 1 & 3 & \cdots & 0 & 0 & 0 & 0 & 0 & 0 & 0 & 0 & 0 & 0 & 0 & 0 & 0 & 0 \\
\vdots &  &  &  &  &  &  &  &  &  &  &  &  &  &  &  &  &  &  &  &  &  &  &  &  &  &  &  & \vdots \\
0 & 0 & 0 & 0 & 0 & 0 & 0 & 0 & 0 & 0 & 0 & 0 & 0 & 0 & \cdots & 1 & 0 & 0 & 0 & 0 & 0 & 2 & 0 & 0 & 0 & 0 & 0 & 0 & 0 \\
0 & 0 & 0 & 0 & 0 & 0 & 0 & 0 & 0 & 0 & 0 & 0 & 0 & 0 & \cdots & 2 & 1 & 0 & 0 & 0 & 0 & 0 & 0 & 0 & 0 & 0 & 0 & 0 & 0 \\
0 & 0 & 0 & 0 & 0 & 0 & 0 & 0 & 0 & 0 & 0 & 0 & 0 & 0 & \cdots & 0 & 2 & 1 & 0 & 0 & 0 & 0 & 0 & 0 & 0 & 0 & 0 & 0 & 0 \\
0 & 0 & 0 & 0 & 0 & 0 & 0 & 0 & 0 & 0 & 0 & 0 & 0 & 0 & \cdots & 0 & 0 & 2 & 1 & 0 & 0 & 0 & 0 & 0 & 0 & 0 & 0 & 0 & 0 \\
0 & 0 & 0 & 0 & 0 & 0 & 0 & 0 & 0 & 0 & 0 & 0 & 0 & 0 & \cdots & 0 & 0 & 0 & 2 & 1 & 0 & 0 & 0 & 0 & 0 & 0 & 0 & 0 & 0 \\
0 & 0 & 0 & 0 & 0 & 0 & 0 & 0 & 0 & 0 & 0 & 0 & 0 & 0 & \cdots & 0 & 0 & 0 & 0 & 2 & 1 & 0 & 0 & 0 & 0 & 0 & 0 & 0 & 0 \\
0 & 0 & 0 & 0 & 0 & 0 & 0 & 0 & 0 & 0 & 0 & 0 & 0 & 0 & \cdots & 0 & 0 & 0 & 0 & 0 & 2 & 1 & 0 & 0 & 0 & 0 & 0 & 0 & 0 \\
0 & 0 & 0 & 0 & 0 & 0 & 0 & 0 & 0 & 0 & 0 & 0 & 0 & 0 & \cdots & 3 & 0 & 0 & 0 & 0 & 0 & 1 & 1 & 0 & 0 & 0 & 0 & 0 & 2 \\
0 & 0 & 0 & 0 & 0 & 0 & 0 & 0 & 0 & 0 & 0 & 0 & 0 & 0 & \cdots & 1 & 3 & 0 & 0 & 0 & 0 & 0 & 2 & 1 & 0 & 0 & 0 & 0 & 0 \\
0 & 0 & 0 & 0 & 0 & 0 & 0 & 0 & 0 & 0 & 0 & 0 & 0 & 0 & \cdots & 0 & 1 & 3 & 0 & 0 & 0 & 0 & 0 & 2 & 1 & 0 & 0 & 0 & 0 \\
0 & 0 & 0 & 0 & 0 & 0 & 0 & 0 & 0 & 0 & 0 & 0 & 0 & 0 & \cdots & 0 & 0 & 1 & 3 & 0 & 0 & 0 & 0 & 0 & 2 & 1 & 0 & 0 & 0 \\
0 & 0 & 0 & 0 & 0 & 0 & 0 & 0 & 0 & 0 & 0 & 0 & 0 & 0 & \cdots & 0 & 0 & 0 & 1 & 3 & 0 & 0 & 0 & 0 & 0 & 2 & 1 & 0 & 0 \\
0 & 0 & 0 & 0 & 0 & 0 & 0 & 0 & 0 & 0 & 0 & 0 & 0 & 0 & \cdots & 0 & 0 & 0 & 0 & 1 & 3 & 0 & 0 & 0 & 0 & 0 & 2 & 1 & 0 \\
0 & 0 & 0 & 0 & 0 & 0 & 0 & 0 & 0 & 0 & 0 & 0 & 0 & 0 & \cdots & 0 & 0 & 0 & 0 & 0 & 1 & 3 & 0 & 0 & 0 & 0 & 0 & 2 & 1
\end{bmatrix}
$$

$$(2.32)$$

The convolution equations in matrix form are the same as for the one-dimensional case:

$$\mathbf{g} = \mathbf{H_t f_0},$$

$$\mathbf{g} = \mathbf{H_c f_0},$$

where $\mathbf{f}_0$ and $\mathbf{g}$ are given in stacked notation

$$\mathbf{f}_0 = \begin{array}{l} [1, 1, 0, 0, 1, 0, 0, 1, 2, 1, 1, 1, 0, 0, 0, 1, 2, 1, 0, 0, 0, 0, 2, 3, 2, 0, 0, 0, 0, 0, 1, 1, 0, 0, 0, \\ 0, 0, 0, 0, 0, 0, 0, 0, 0, 0, 0, 0, 0, 0]^\mathrm{T}, \end{array}$$

where we have padded the $5 \times 5$ image $\mathbf{f}$ with zeros on the right and bottom, and

$$\mathbf{g} = \begin{array}{l} [1, 3, 2, 0, 1, 2, 0, 4, 8, 6, 3, 6, 3, 0, 3, 12, 14, 10, 6, 5, 1, 0, 9, 23, 19, 10, 5, 1.0, 6, 16, \\ 21, 10, 1, 0, 0, 0, 11, 18, 12, 2, 0, 0, 0, 0, 4, 5, 1, 0]^\mathrm{T}. \end{array}$$

Since matrix-vector algebra plays such an important part in the presentation and explanation of image processing, Appendix B summarizes the properties of matrices and matrix-vector operations that are important for image processing.

## 2.8 Problems

**2.1** Consider the image in Fig. 2.6. Assume that this is the image of an object that is isolated in free space.

(a) If the object is self-luminous, what are the approximate coordinates of the point that emits the most light?
(b) If the image is taken with a range camera of a reflective object, what are the approximate coordinates of the closest point?
(c) If the image represents material density and is obtained using a common X-ray system, what are the approximate coordinates of the densest point?

**2.2** Consider the image of Fig. 7.3(a). Repeat the exercise of Problem 2.1.

**2.3** Consider the image of Fig. 3.5. What aspects of the image could reasonably be considered deterministic? What aspects of the image could reasonably be considered stochastic?

**2.4** Systems and operators: Which of the operators below are linear? Which are shift-invariant? The function $f(x, y)$ can be considered arbitrary.

(a) $T[f(x, y)] = \int_{-\infty}^{x} f(\eta, y) \, d\eta$.
(b) $T[f(x, y)] = \int_{0}^{x} f(\eta, y) \, d\eta$.
(c) $T[f(x, y)] = f(x, y)(x + y)$.
(d) $T[f(x, y)] = af(x, y) + c$, where $a$ and $c$ are constants and $c \neq 0$.
(e) $T[f(x, y)] = f(x - x_0, y - y_0)$, where $x_0$ and $y_0$ are constant.
(f) $T[f(x, y)] = f(x_0, y_0)$, where $x_0$ and $y_0$ are constant.
(g) $T[f(x, y)] = \frac{\partial f(x,y)}{\partial y}$, where we assume $f(x, y)$ is differentiable.
(h) $T[f(x, y)] = f(x, y)g(x, y)$ where $g(x, y)$ is arbitrary.

**2.5** Let $T[f(x, y)]$ represent a transformation of pixel values associated with a computer monitor. Assume that the input values for $f(x, y)$ are measured in volts. Write a functional form for the transformation $T[f(x, y)]$, if the function represents the standard controls on a monitor:

(a) $T_b[f(x, y)]$ represents brightness control.
(b) $T_c[f(x, y)]$ represents contrast control.
(c) Which of your functions are linear? You may wish to experiment with your monitor to verify that your functions behave in a qualitatively correct way.

**2.6** Show that sampling is a linear operation but not shift-invariant.

**2.7** Compute the 1-D convolution, $g(x) = f(x) * h(x)$, for the following combinations of $f(x)$ and $h(x)$, where

$$\text{rect}(x) = \begin{cases} 1 & \text{for } -\frac{1}{2} < x \le \frac{1}{2} \\ 0 & \text{else,} \end{cases}$$

$$\text{tri}(x) = \begin{cases} 1 + x & \text{for } -1 \le x \le 0 \\ 1 - x & \text{for } 0 \le x \le 1 \\ 0 & \text{else.} \end{cases}$$

(a) $f(x) = \text{rect}(x - 1)$ and $h(x) = \text{rect}(x + 1)$.
(b) $f(x) = \cos(2\pi x)$ and $h(x) = \text{rect}(x)$.
(c) $f(x) = \text{tri}(x)$ and $h(x) = \text{rect}(x)$.
(d) $f(x) = \text{tri}(x)$ and $h(x) = \delta(x - 2)$.
(e) $f(x) = 2\text{rect}(x - 1) + \text{rect}(x)$ and $h(x) = \delta(x + 1)$.
(f) $f(x) = 2\text{rect}(x - 1) + \text{rect}(x)$ and $h(x) = 3\delta(x + \frac{1}{2}) + \delta(x - \frac{1}{2})$.

**2.8** Compute the 2-D convolution, $g(x, y) = f(x, y) * h(x, y)$, (give the functional form of the result, not a numerical approximation from MATLAB) for the following combinations of $f(x, y)$ and $h(x, y)$, where

$$\text{sq}(x, y) = \begin{cases} 1 & \text{for } -\frac{1}{2} < x \le \frac{1}{2} \text{ and } -\frac{1}{2} < y \le \frac{1}{2} \\ 0 & \text{else.} \end{cases}$$

(a) $f(x, y) = \text{sq}(x, y)$ and $h(x, y) = \delta(x - 2, y + 1)$.
(b) $f(x, y) = \text{sq}(x, y)$ and $h(x, y) = \delta(x - \frac{1}{2}, y) + 2\delta(x, y + \frac{1}{2})$.
(c) $f(x, y) = \text{sq}(x, y)$ and $h(x, y) = \text{sq}(x, y)$.
(d) $f(x, y) = \cos[2\pi(x + y)]$ and $h(x, y) = \text{sq}(x, y)$.
(e) $f(x, y) = \text{sq}(x/4, y/8)$ and $h(x, y) = \delta(x - 1, y) + 2\delta(x, y + 1)$.
(f) $f(x, y) = \text{sq}(x/4, y - 2) + 2\text{sq}(x - 1, y/8)$ and $h(x, y) = \delta(x - 1, y - 1) + 2\delta(x, y + 1)$.

**2.9** Compute and sketch the regions of support for the convolution of various combinations of nonnegative functions defined by

$f_1(x, y)$ is nonzero for the region defined by the triangle with vertices $\{(-1,0),(0,2),(1,0)\}$,

$f_2(x, y)$ is nonzero for the region defined by the triangle with vertices $\{(-1,0),(0,1),(3,0)\}$,

$f_3(x, y)$ is nonzero for the region defined by the rectangle with vertices
$\{(-1/2, -1), (-1/2, 1)(1/2, 1)(1/2, -1)\}$,
$f_4(x, y)$ is nonzero for the region defined by the quadrilateral with vertices
$\{(-2, -1), (-1, 1)(1, 1)(2, -1)\}$.

(a) $g_1(x, y) = f_1(x, y) * f_1(x, y)$.
(b) $g_2(x, y) = f_1(x, y) * f_2(x, y)$.
(c) $g_3(x, y) = f_1(x, y) * f_3(x, y)$.
(d) $g_4(x, y) = f_1(x, y) * f_4(x, y)$.
(e) $g_5(x, y) = f_2(x, y) * f_3(x, y)$.
(f) $g_6(x, y) = f_3(x, y) * f_3(x, y)$.
(g) $g_7(x, y) = f_4(x, y) * f_3(x, y)$.

**2.10** Compute the 2-D discrete convolution for the input matrix, $f(x, y)$, of Table 2.3 and the three point spread functions defined below. It is recommended that you use MATLAB to compute the values. Note the coordinates of the functions. Be sure to label the coordinates of the output functions. Be sure to look at your answers to see that they are reasonable and the relationship of the outputs of the three point spread functions.

| PSF $h_1(x, y)$ | | | | PSF $h_2(x, y)$ | | | | PSF $h_3(x, y)$ | | | |
|---|---|---|---|---|---|---|---|---|---|---|---|
| | | $x$ | | | | $x$ | | | | $x$ | |
| $y$ | $-1$ | $0$ | $1$ | $y$ | $-1$ | $0$ | $1$ | $y$ | $-1$ | $0$ | $1$ |
| $-1$ | 1 | 1 | 1 | $-1$ | 1 | 0 | 0 | $-1$ | 1 | 0 | 0 |
| $0$ | 0 | 0 | 0 | $0$ | 1 | 0 | 0 | $0$ | 0 | 1 | 0 |
| $1$ | 0 | 0 | 0 | $1$ | 1 | 0 | 0 | $1$ | 0 | 0 | 1 |

**Table 2.3.** Input matrix for Problem 2.10

| | | | | | | input matrix $f(x, y)$ | | | | | | |
|---|---|---|---|---|---|---|---|---|---|---|---|---|
| | | | | | | $x$ | | | | | | |
| $y$ | $-5$ | $-4$ | $-3$ | $-2$ | $-1$ | $0$ | $1$ | $2$ | $3$ | $4$ | $5$ | $6$ |
| $-5$ | 3 | 3 | 1 | 1 | 0 | 0 | 2 | 2 | 2 | 2 | 2 | 2 |
| $-4$ | 3 | 3 | 1 | 1 | 0 | 0 | 2 | 2 | 2 | 2 | 2 | 2 |
| $-3$ | 1 | 1 | 1 | 1 | 0 | 0 | 2 | 2 | 2 | 2 | 2 | 2 |
| $-2$ | 1 | 1 | 1 | 1 | 0 | 0 | 2 | 2 | 2 | 2 | 2 | 2 |
| $-1$ | 1 | 2 | 1 | 1 | 0 | 0 | 2 | 2 | 2 | 2 | 2 | 2 |
| $0$ | 1 | 0 | 2 | 1 | 0 | 0 | 2 | 2 | 2 | 2 | 2 | 2 |
| $1$ | 1 | 1 | 0 | 3 | 0 | 0 | 0 | 1 | 1 | 1 | 0 | 0 |
| $2$ | 0 | 1 | 1 | 0 | 3 | 0 | 0 | 0 | 1 | 1 | 1 | 0 |
| $3$ | 0 | 0 | 1 | 1 | 0 | 2 | 0 | 0 | 0 | 1 | 1 | 1 |
| $4$ | 0 | 0 | 0 | 1 | 1 | 0 | 2 | 0 | 0 | 0 | 1 | 1 |
| $5$ | 0 | 0 | 0 | 0 | 1 | 1 | 0 | 1 | 0 | 0 | 0 | 1 |
| $6$ | 0 | 0 | 0 | 0 | 0 | 1 | 1 | 0 | 0 | 0 | 0 | 0 |

**2.11** Write the 2-D convolution of the point spread function given below and the image in Table 2.4 in matrix form using stacked notation. It is suggested that you use ruled paper or a computer spreadsheet to keep the matrix entries aligned. Use the stacked notation where **H** has square Toeplitz form and is non circulant.

| PSF $h(x, y)$ | | | |
|---|---|---|---|
| | | $x$ | |
| $y$ | 0 | 1 | 2 |
| 0 | 1 | 0 | 3 |
| 1 | 0 | 4 | 2 |
| 2 | −2 | 0 | −1 |

**Table 2.4.** Input matrix for Problem 2.11

| input matrix $f(x, y)$ | | | | |
|---|---|---|---|---|
| | | | $x$ | |
| $y$ | −1 | 0 | 1 | 2 |
| −1 | 1 | 2 | 1 | 1 |
| 0 | 1 | 0 | 2 | 1 |
| 1 | 3 | 0 | 1 | 0 |
| 2 | 1 | 3 | 0 | 0 |

**2.12** Repeat the previous problem using circulant extension and representing circulant convolution.

# 3  Elementary display of images

One difference between one-dimensional and two-dimensional functions is the way in which they are displayed. One-dimensional functions are easily displayed on a graph where the scaling is obvious. One dimension, usually the horizontal, is used to represent the abscissa or independent axis; the second dimension of the display is used to represent the ordinate or dependent axis. The function, $y = f(x)$, is usually represented as ordered pairs, $[x, f(x)]$. The value of points along the axes are usually displayed adjacent to the axes as in Fig. 3.1. The observer need only examine the numbers that label the axes to determine the scale of the graph and get a mental picture of the function.

With two-dimensional scalar-valued functions, the display becomes more complicated, since there are more degrees of freedom in the function than are available on the two-dimensional display, i.e., two independent coordinate values and one dependent value. The two-dimensional function, $z = f(x, y)$, is represented by an ordered triple, $[x, y, f(x, y)]$. There are many ways of displaying such functions. The reader has probably seen several. There are advantages and disadvantages to all of them. The point here is not

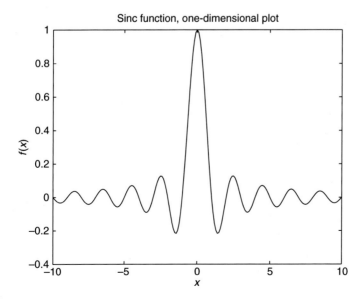

**Figure 3.1.** One-dimensional plot.

to summarize all the possibilities but to relate the characteristics of those representations to the display of images. The main emphasis will be on the scaling of the displays and the representation of the value of the function. The accurate display of vector-valued, two-dimensional functions, e.g., color images, will be discussed after covering the necessary material on sampling (Chapter 6) and colorimetry (Chapter 8).

The three most common two-dimensional representations are the isometric plot, the contour plot and the grayscale plot. All are supported by MATLAB [183]. The user should choose the correct display for the information to be conveyed. Let us consider each of the three display modalities. As a simple example, consider the two-dimensional functional form

$$f(m, n) = \text{sinc}\left(\frac{m^2}{a^2} + \frac{n^2}{b^2}\right),$$

where, for the following plots, $a = 1$ and $b = 2$. This form is chosen to show both positive and negative values, something that occurs even when processing nonnegative signals such as images.

## 3.1　　　Isometric plots

Isometric or surface plots give the appearance of three-dimensional drawings. The surface can be represented as a wire mesh or as a shaded solid, as in Figs. 3.2a and b, respectively. In both cases, portions of the function will be obscured by other portions. For example, one cannot see through the main lobe, so some part of the surface is hidden. This form works well with functions where the unseen part can be predicted, as with symmetric or very smooth functions. Typical examples include point spread functions and filters in the space or frequency domains. An advantage of the surface plot is that it gives some indication of the values of the function since a scale is readily displayed on the axes. However, it is difficult to read values accurately, or even approximately, from the graph. It is rarely effective for the display of images.

## 3.2　　　Contour plots

Contour plots are analogous to the contour or topographic maps used to describe geographical locations. The sinc function is shown using this method in Fig. 3.3. All points that have a specific value are connected to form a continuous line. For a continuous function, the lines must form closed loops. This type of plot is useful in locating the relative position of maxima or minima in images or two-dimensional functions. It is used primarily in spectrum analysis and pattern recognition applications. It is difficult to read values from the contour plot and takes some effort to determine whether the functional trend is up or down. The relative gradient of the function can be qualitatively observed by the closeness of the contour lines. The steep gradient near the origin can be seen in

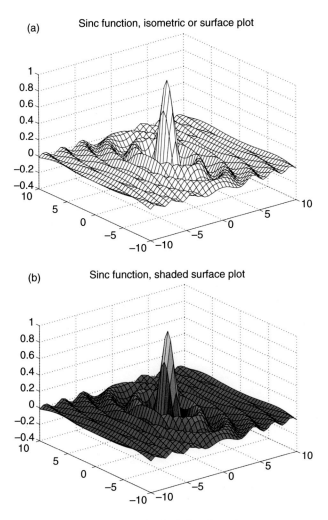

**Figure 3.2.** (a) Surface plot, (b) shaded surface plot.

Fig. 3.3a. The filled contour plot, shown in Fig. 3.3b and available in MATLAB, helps in this last task. Again, it is not possible to obtain very accurate values from the graph.

## 3.3  Grayscale graphs

Most monochrome images are displayed using the grayscale plot, where the value of a pixel is represented by its relative lightness. For images, it is easy to find monotonic mappings from pixel values to gray levels of the display that preserve the qualitative features of the image; namely that light pixels are light and dark pixels are dark. The exact or more precise mappings that will preserve the appearance of the image will be covered after the discussion of characterization of display devices (Chapter 12). The intent of

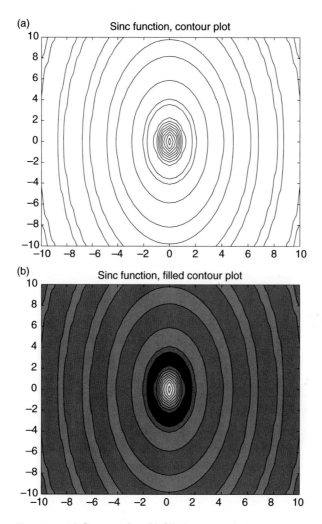

**Figure 3.3.** (a) Contour plot, (b) filled contour plot.

this section is to outline the major characteristics of the mappings, which will lead to producing images that can be accurately interpreted.

Since, in most cases, high values are displayed as light and low values are displayed as dark, it is easy to determine functional trends or relative shading. It is almost impossible to determine exact values. For images, which are nonnegative functions, the display is natural; for functions that have negative values, this type of display can be quite artificial.

In order to use this type of display with images or functions, the representation must be scaled to fit in the range of displayable gray levels. This is most often done using a min/max scaling, where the values are linearly mapped such that the minimum value appears as black and the maximum value appears as white. This method was used for the sinc function shown in Fig. 3.4. A scale of gray-level values can be added to aid the observer in estimating actual pixel values. The grayscale will be discussed in more

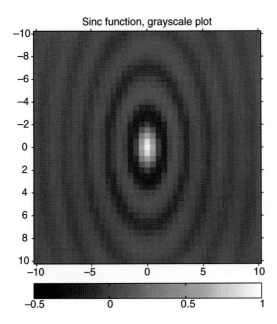

**Figure 3.4.** Grayscale plot.

detail later. For the display of functions, the min/max scaling can be effective to indicate trends in the behavior. Scaling for images is another matter.

Let's consider a monochrome image that has been digitized by some device, e.g., a scanner or camera. The values of the image function represent some physical quantity, as mentioned in Chapter 2. Without knowing the physical process of digitization, it is impossible to determine the best or most accurate way to display the image. The proper display of images requires calibration of both the input and output devices. However, before the accurate display of images can be discussed in detail, it will be necessary to build a foundation. During this building, it will be helpful to consider both 2-D functions and images. In order to proceed, it is reasonable to give some general rules about the display of monochrome images.

1. For the comparison of a sequences of images (comparative display), it is *imperative* that all images be displayed using the same scaling.
2. Display a step-wedge, a strip of sequential gray levels from minimum to maximum values, with the image to show how the image gray levels are mapped to brightness or density.
3. Use a graytone mapping that allows a wide range of gray levels to be distinguished visually.

### 3.3.1    Comparative display

It is hard to emphasize the comparative display rule sufficiently and hard to count all the misleading results that have occurred when it has been ignored. The most common violation of this rule occurs when comparing an original and processed image. The user scales both images independently using min/max scaling. The min/max scaling is done by finding the minimum and maximum of the image to be displayed and mapping those values linearly to the minimum and maximum values of the display device. In many cases, the scaling can produce significant enhancement of low contrast images, which can be mistaken for improvements produced by an algorithm under investigation.

For example, consider an algorithm designed to reduce noise. The noisy image is modeled by

$$\mathbf{g} = \mathbf{f} + \mathbf{n},$$

where we are using the stacked notation of Section 2.7. Since the noise is both positive and negative, the noisy image, $\mathbf{g}$, has a larger range than the clean image, $\mathbf{f}$. To obtain an accurate impression of the effect of the noise, both $\mathbf{g}$ and $\mathbf{f}$ should be displayed using the same scaling. In considering the effects of processing, it is noted that almost any noise reduction method will reduce the range of the processed image, thus, the smoothed (processed) image undergoes additional contrast enhancement if min/max scaling is used. The result is greater apparent dynamic range and a better looking image.

Examples of the effects of this rule are shown in Figs. 3.5–3.9. The original image is shown in Fig. 3.5. The image in Fig. 3.5 has been scaled to the range between 30 and 220, denoted henceforth as $[30, 220]$. This allows the manipulations presented later to produce values within the usual range $[0, 255]$. The image can be enhanced by using min/max scaling as shown in Fig. 3.6. This maps the range $[30, 220]$ to $[0, 255]$, which improves contrast, as noted in Section 7.1.1. If the only reason for the display was to discuss features of the image, this might be a suitable display. However, if the reasons for display include a comparison with processed images, then this display can produce misleading images. Noise is added to the original and shown in Fig. 3.7. The noise has been created to produce an image with a maximum range of $[0, 255]$. Thus, this image will not change appearance with min/max scaling and represents a valid comparison with the original, Fig. 3.5. A comparison of Figs. 3.6 and 3.7 would give a misleading impression of the effect of the noise. Note the easily observable differences in the average values of very dark and very light regions of the images. To continue the example, the noisy image is smoothed (using a 5 × 5 median filter – [134]). The smoothed image is shown in Fig. 3.8 with its min/max version in Fig. 3.9. The obvious differences between the two images emphasizes the need for controlled display for accurate comparisons.

There are several ways to implement the comparative display rule. The most appropriate way will depend on the application. The scaling may be made using the min/max of the collection of all images to be compared. In some cases, it is appropriate to truncate values at the limits of the display, rather than force the entire range into the range of the display. This is particularly true of images containing a few outliers. If the noise that was added to the image in Fig. 3.5 had been Gaussian, the resulting image would have had values out of the range [0,255]. Since the number of the values affected would be small, it would be appropriate to truncate the noisy image for display since the visual effect would have been almost unnoticeable. It may also be advantageous to

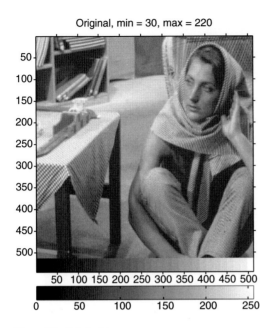

**Figure 3.5.** Original image.

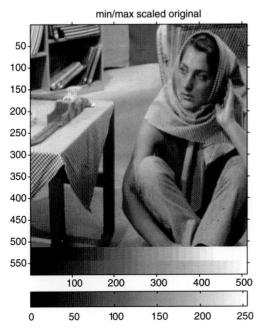

**Figure 3.6.** Minimum/maximum scaled original.

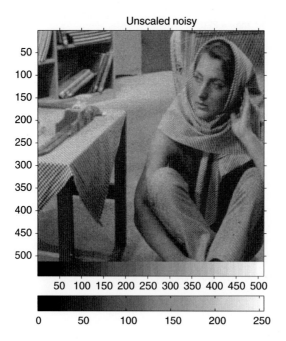

**Figure 3.7.** Noisy original.

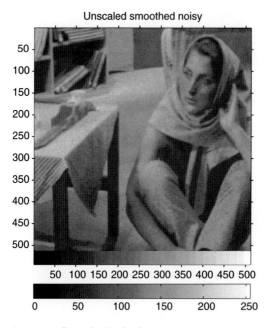

**Figure 3.8.** Smoothed noisy image.

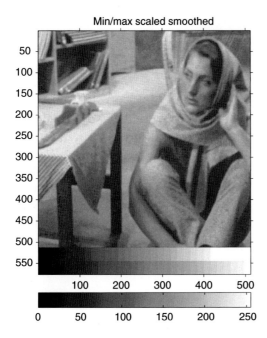

**Figure 3.9.** Minimum/maximum scaled smoothed image.

reduce the display of the image to a particular region of interest, which will usually reduce the range to be reproduced.

### 3.3.2 Grayscale inclusion

The inclusion of a grayscale allows some idea of the quantitative values associated with the pixels. This is routinely done on images that are used for analysis, such as digital photographs from space probes. The comparison of grayscales of processed and unprocessed images gives an indication of the effect of any scalings that have been made for the display. A grayscale has been included in the original image of Fig. 3.5. This scale shows values in 32 equally spaced intervals. Note that the grayscale that is used to show the mapping of the image values to the display should not be included in any computation of the minimum and maximum of the image for display purposes. In this image, the grayscale range is [15, 255], which includes values below and above the range of the image. The MATLAB software that was used to generate the examples shown here includes the capability to generate a grayscale, called a colormap. This scale should represent exactly the same information that is contained in the grayscale that is included in the image. It has the additional feature of denoting the numerical values of the relative gray levels. Since not all readers have access to MATLAB software, the authors have used the alternative method of inserting the grayscale in the image.

In addition to indicating where the range of the image fits within the range of the display, the inclusion of a grayscale can demonstrate the effect of any mappings used to display the image. Consider the min/max scaling used to display Fig. 3.6. The figure shows the grayscale of the display mapping, i.e., the gray levels [15, 255] on the bottom. This scale agrees with the MATLAB scale. The result of min/max scaling is shown by the top scale. From a comparison of the two scales, it is easy to see how the range of the original has been increased. Note that there are several gray values at the extremes of the scaled version (top) that are indistinguishable after the scaling. This will not matter in this case, since there are no values in this range in the original image. In cases where the user is making a judgment of what range of the image to display, this effect may be significant.

A typical case where a choice of omitting values of the image occurs when displaying an image with larger grayscale resolution than the display. For example, a 12-bit image (4096 gray levels) cannot be accurately displayed on an 8-bit device. The user has several choices for display mappings that include: (1) reducing the range of the image by linear scaling and (2) displaying a limited range of the image at full resolution. The choice will depend on the application and the intent of the investigator. In any case, the basic principle of comparative display should be followed.

### 3.3.3      Display of processed and nonpictorial images

The output of many image analysis tasks is a two-dimensional array that is related to an input image, but is itself not an image in the sense that it does not represent a pictorial scene. Examples of such output are created by many applications, including edge detection, segmentation and tomographic algorithms. In these cases, there is no original image that can be used to guide the display. There are a few good rules to follow in the display of these images. The first rule is the rule of comparative display. This rule applies when comparing nonpictorial images. If two edge detection methods are being compared, then care should be taken to present the results of each in its most effective manner. In this case, the intent of the process under investigation needs to be considered.

Let us consider an example to illustrate the concepts. The original image in Fig. 3.5 is filtered using a Laplacian kernel [134]. This is an edge enhancement filter and produces an image that will have approximately zero mean. For this result, the minimum and maximum are $-324$ and 285, respectively. There is no ideal way to display this image, since it does not represent an image that one could actually see in the real world. The obvious method of displaying the image is to use min/max scaling. This image is shown in Fig. 3.10. It represents strong positive edges as white and strong negative edges as black. Areas with low contrast (little variation) are a mid-gray. For this image, the strong edges in the clothing are the dominant features. Note that the scale map shows the actual pixel values corresponding to the gray level that is displayed. If the interest in the image were in the more subtle edge information of other objects, a rescaling is appropriate. To allow enhancement of the lower contrast edges, a new scaling has been created that linearly maps the range $[-100, 100]$ in the filtered image to $[0, 255]$ on the display. Pixel values above 100 are mapped to 100 and values below $-100$ are mapped to $-100$. This rescaling is shown in Fig. 3.11. Some information is lost, while other information is made more visible.

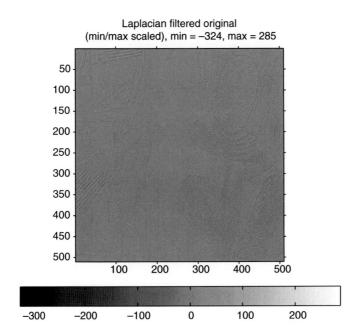

**Figure 3.10.** Laplacian filtered – actual min/max scaling.

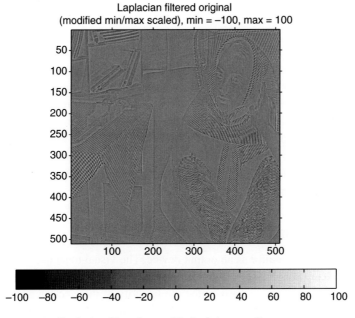

**Figure 3.11.** Laplacian filtered – modified min/max scaling.

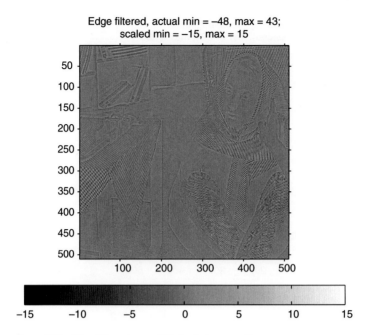

**Figure 3.12.** Edge filtered – modified min/max scaling.

The scale map indicates the gray-level assignment that aids the observer in evaluating the relative strength of the edges. However, it does not indicate the effect of the truncation. The user should be aware of this and annotate the displayed images to reflect the fact that truncation has occurred. Other than telling the observer that the image is displayed in an enhanced form, there is little that can be done to display all the information in the image. There is no standard that can be applied to comparing several edge enhancement methods that have different ranges. It is the investigator's responsibility to display the processed images in their best light. Consider the result of a second edge enhancement filter, shown in Fig. 3.12. The range is significantly different from the Laplacian filtered image of Fig. 3.10. The scaling has been adjusted to enhance the lower contrast edges and, thus, should be compared with Fig. 3.11. It is an open question whether the adjustment is comparable. For this example, the reduction in range is about one-third for both images and the results appear about the same. Clearly, a change in the scaling could make one or the other more appealing to an observer.

### 3.3.4     Nonlinear mappings and monitor adjustments

Consider the CRT monitor as an output device. The visual tonal qualities of the output depend on many factors, including the brightness and contrast setting of the monitor, the specific phosphors used in the monitor, the linearity of the electron guns or solid-state elements and the ambient lighting. It is recommended that adjustments be made so that a user is able to distinguish all levels of a step-wedge of about 32 levels. The gray strips used on the examples of the previous section can be used to check the monitor settings.

It should be noted here that monitors do change with time. They will certainly vary during the warm-up period. The length of warm-up depends on ambient conditions and the type of monitor. Even after warm-up, monitors can vary within the time frame of a few hours. Using gray strips on the images allows the user to monitor the display device continually. Most displays have problems with gray levels at the ends of the range being indistinguishable. This can be overcome by proper adjustment of the contrast and gain controls and an appropriate mapping from image values to display values. For hard-copy devices, the medium should be taken into account. For example, changes in paper type or manufacturer can result in significant tonal variations.

In software such as MATLAB, the user can control the mapping between the continuous values of the image and the values sent to the display device. This will achieve the same goal as changing the image. However, care must be taken when doing this. It is possible to be confused when viewing the gray strip, since it now undergoes the same transformation as the image.

There are cases where the investigator is interested in particular tonal regions of the image. For these cases, it may be advantageous to emphasize these regions in the display. A nonlinear mapping of the gray levels allows this. A second case, where nonlinear mappings are useful, is when linearizing a device that has a nonlinear response. This application will be discussed in later chapters on characterization and profiling (Chapters 10–12). An example of the effect of a nonlinear mapping is shown in Fig. 3.13. The mapping in this case is

$$y = 255 \left[ (x/255)^{0.75} \right].$$

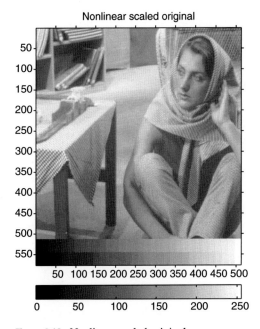

Figure 3.13. Nonlinear scaled original.

This mapping has the effect of maintaining the range of $[0, 255]$ while spreading out the darker (lower) values and compressing the lighter (higher) values. The tonal detail in the dark regions, e.g., the wood grain of the table leg, are more readily apparent. However, there is a loss of detail in the light regions, e.g., the rug. Note the effect of the mapping on the grayscale that has been processed. Again, the value of such mappings is subjective.

## 3.4        Problems

Since this chapter is concerned with display of images, the exercises must necessarily require the display of functions and images. It is assumed that most readers will use MATLAB for these. However, other software can be used if it is more convenient.

Several of the problems in this chapter ask you to perform certain operations on an image. We suggest that you find an image on the internet that is of particular interest to you. This will make life a bit more interesting as you manipulate the image in the problems in this and subsequent chapters. Some suggestions for the characteristics of the image that you select include:

- The image should be no smaller than $256 \times 256$ pixels. Larger images will take more time to process, so we recommend staying below $1024 \times 1024$. You can crop a larger image to suit your needs.
- The image should be in either TIFF or JPEG format.
- Check the image by enlarging it greatly to determine if there are any coding artifacts. Coding artifacts are usually noticed as ringing around high contrast edges, such as text, or regular low contrast blocks that occur because JPEG encodes $8 \times 8$ blocks of pixels. Artifacts are most apparent in JPEG images that have been saved using the highest compression settings of the camera or encoder.
- The image should be RGB color. We'll do most monochrome manipulation using the green band. We will use color later. The color image will be referred to as *image-one* later; the monochrome version as *gray-one*.
- The image should contain areas that are low contrast and smooth, like the carpet in Fig. 3.5, and high contrast with fine detail, like the striped clothing of the same figure.
- It will be helpful if the image contains some objects that have an approximately periodic pattern. The clothing of Fig. 3.5 is an example. Buildings with periodic windowing or brick walls are common.
- The image should have at least eight bits per color band. We will assume that your images will be scaled within the range $[0, 255]$. If yours is not, you can scale it using a simple linear transformation.
- The image should have a smooth histogram, but this is getting ahead of ourselves. We will discuss this in Chapter 7.
- Find the minimum and maximum values of each band of your image. Avoid images that have a maximum value of 255. This indicates possible saturation and will be discussed in Chapter 7.

Finally, if you cannot find a novel image among your own photographs or on the internet, there are several available at the text's website: www.cambridge.org/9780521868532.

To display images in MATLAB, use the imshow function. An example of using these functions is found in www.cambridge.org/9780521868532. Note how to set the colormap to various grayscales. Do **not** use PCOLOR for setting the colormap or displaying the image as it uses interpolation over which you have little control.

**3.1** Consider a generalization of the sinc function that we used for the example in the text,

$$f(m, n) = \text{sinc}(am^2 + bmn + cn^2),$$

where for this problem, $a = 1$, $b = 1$ and $c = \frac{1}{16}$. Plot the function in various ways over the range $-10 \le m \le 10$ and $-10 \le n \le 10$.

(a) Plot the function using the isometric plot. You may use shading or not.
(b) Plot the function using the contour plot. You may use filling or not.
(c) Plot the function using a grayscale plot. Show the effect of two distinctly different colormaps.

**3.2** Read your image into MATLAB using imread and extract the green band (band 2). Save this image as a monochrome TIFF image. We will refer to this image as *gray-one*. Find the minimum and maximum of *gray-one*. Using these min and max values, display the image using imshow(gray-one,[min,max]). Remember to display the grayscale using *colorbar('horiz')*.

**3.3** Using the *gray-one* image of Problem 3.2, display the image using various upper and lower limits, e.g., imshow(gray-one,[lower_lim,upper_lim]). Determine an optimal set of limits for creating a visually pleasing display. You are the judge of what is pleasing.

**3.4** Construct a colormap, named *cmap*, for the MATLAB display using the functions below. Remember that the colormap function must be a $256 \times 3$ array and have values between 0 and 1. For your monochrome image, all three columns will be identical. Display your *gray-one* using these colormaps, e.g., imshow(gray-one,cmap). Describe the qualitative visual effects of the mappings for $n = 1, ..., 256$.

(a) $\text{cmap1}(n) = (n - 1)/255$.
(b) $\text{cmap2}(n) = \text{cmap1}(n)^k$, for $k = 2$. Consider what would happen if $k$ is allowed to be an arbitrary positive integer.
(c) $\text{cmap3}(n) = \text{cmap1}(n)^{1/k}$, for $k = 2$. Consider what would happen if $k$ is allowed to be an arbitrary positive integer.

**3.5** For the images in Problem 3.4, construct transformations $T[\cdot]$ that operate directly on the image data and will create the same image when displayed using imshow(gray-one,[0,255]).

**3.6** Create images by using the transformations of Problem 3.5 and display them both using the minimum and maximum of each image and using a standard $[0, 255]$ range in imshow. Note the differences in appearance that occur when the standard range is used. Note that this exercise gives examples of the problems that may occur when the display rules of Section 3.3.1 are violated.

**3.7** Using your image *gray-one*, create edge images using the transformations below and compare the results. Reduce the image size by one pixel in each direction to avoid edge effects caused by using a zero row or column to start.

(a) $T[f(m,n)] = f(m,n) - f(m,n-1)$, a horizonal edge filter.
(b) $T[f(m,n)] = f(m,n) - f(m-1,n)$, a vertical edge filter.
(c) Use the rule of comparative display to compare the two images, (a) and (b).

# 4 Quantization

When an analog signal is transformed to a digital one, it is necessary to limit the representation to a fixed number of bits. This chapter discusses the best way to distribute those bits across the range of possible values. The quantization problem is no different in two dimensions than in one dimension. The first task of quantization is the definition of the term "best." This task requires not only the definition of an error metric, e.g., mean square error, but also the definition of the space in which the error is measured. The choice of the appropriate space is determined by the physical properties of the image that is being digitized, as well as the intent of the user of the digital data.

Most mathematically based quantization schemes use the mean square error as the error metric because of the ease of analytical manipulation. Since the eye is not a mean square error detector, quantizing for minimum mean square error (MMSE) is not usually visually optimal. However, such quantization rarely results in unacceptable images if an appropriate space is chosen for the quantization. Subjective quantization schemes are common and are often implemented using a look-up table (LUT).

We will first briefly consider the selection of an appropriate space for the image data. After a space is chosen, mathematically optimum quantization can be obtained by use of the MMSE criterion. We will show how to use this for both monochrome and color images.

## 4.1 Appropriate quantization spaces

In Chapters 2 and 3, we have discussed images as functions and how to display gray-level images. The exact quantity that is represented by the image values has not been discussed, and, indeed, will not be discussed in detail until Chapter 8. Nevertheless, we must anticipate this discussion to indicate the options that are available to the user.

The two main spaces of interest are linear and logarithmic. Colorimetric spaces will be defined in Chapter 8; however, the principles given by using the linear and logarithmic spaces can be applied to the colorimetric spaces also. The linear space is derived from the reflectance property of print material or the transmission property of films or transparencies. The *transmission* of an optically transmissive material is defined as the ratio of the intensity of the light that passes through the material to the intensity

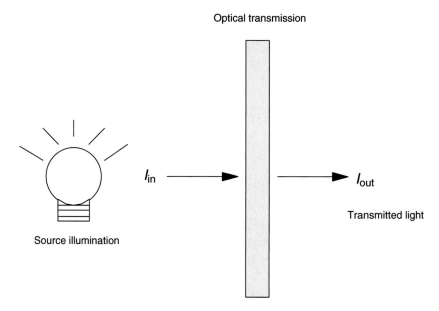

**Figure 4.1.** Geometry for transmission through a material.

of the source, as shown in Fig. 4.1. The equation is given by

$$T = \frac{I_{out}}{I_{in}}. \tag{4.1}$$

The transmission can be thought of as either the fraction of photons that pass through the material or the probability that a photon will pass through the material. The *reflectance* of a surface is defined in an analogous manner, where $I_{out}$ represents the reflected light intensity, rather than the transmitted light intensity. Either of these representations would be considered linear.

Optical density is defined by

$$d = -\log_{10}(T) \tag{4.2}$$

and is related to the physical density of the material. The density representation is obviously logarithmic. In Chapter 8, we will see that the sensitivity of the eye can be approximated by either a cube root function or logarithm. Furthermore, the transformation from light intensity to density on photographic film is a nearly logarithmic function over its useful range. The printing industry has long used density as the measurement of choice. For these reasons, the logarithmic space is often chosen as the one in which to quantize the image.

Digital cameras and many scanners use CCD or photodiode detectors that are nearly linear in their response to light intensity. It is easy and economical to quantize these measurements directly, rather than insert a nonlinear amplifier in the A/D conversion process. Furthermore, computer generated images are most easily created using a linear scale from dark to light. It is left to the display device and color management software to make a transformation that is visually pleasing. These transformations will be discussed in detail in Chapter 12.

As A/D converters have become more economical, the transformations to the quantization space are often digital. The original signal is digitized using a very high

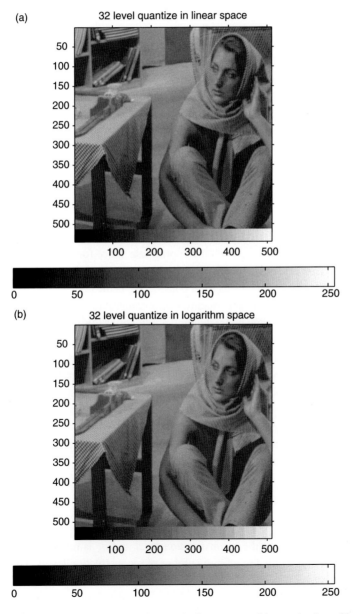

**Figure 4.2.** (a) Quantization of image in linear space; (b) quantization of image in logarithmic space.

number of quantization levels. A transformation to a smaller number of levels, which is used for recording or storage, is done using digital computation or simple look-up tables (LUTs). The use of LUTs is particularly attractive, since it is very fast and very complicated functional transformations can be represented.

A simple example that shows the difference in quantizing in linear and logarithmic spaces is shown in Figs. 4.2a and b. Here the gray levels, normalized to a range of 0 to 1, are quantized to 32 levels using both linear and logarithmic scales. Since the original image data is quantized to 256 levels in linear space, the 32 level quantization in linear space amounts to a subsampling of this space. The quantization in logarithmic space is done by transforming the image data via the logarithm, determining the range in that space, quantizing the data in that space, then transforming back to linear space for the display. We have included the grayscale at the bottom of the image in quantization to show the relative levels more easily. Note that this example is not meant to show an optimum space, but only that the space in which the quantization is done is significant. We will discuss the appropriate spaces for quantization when we discuss photometry and colorimetry in Chapter 8.

## 4.2    Basic quantization

Let us assume that we have chosen the appropriate space for quantization of the image data. There are several decisions that need to be made in creating a quantization scheme. The intent of the image data needs to be considered. Is the image to be used for aesthetic viewing? Are the highlights and shadows important? Are the data to be processed for pattern recognition or image understanding applications? Will the data be processed for enhancement or used in image modeling applications?

A major difference in intent is whether the image needs to be quantitatively accurate for numerical processing or subjectively accurate for aesthetic purposes. Let us deal with quantitative accuracy first. For this purpose, we define the best quantization scheme as the one that produces the smallest error from the original image. The most common error measure is mean square error.

Quantization can be mathematically described as a nonlinear transformation of a signal $x$ to a new signal $y$ defined by

$$y = Q(x) = r_k, \quad \text{if} \quad d_k \leq x < d_{k+1}, \tag{4.3}$$

where $r_k$ is referred to as the *reconstruction level* and $d_k$ is referred to as the *decision level*. The output is limited to a finite number of reconstruction levels. The input values can be continuously varying or can be values that have been previously quantized by another process. It is common to digitize image data to an accuracy of 12 to 16 bits (4096 to 65536 levels) and then requantize the data to eight bits for display or storage.

## 4.2.1 Uniform quantization

The most common quantization scheme is the uniform quantizer. This method divides the range of the input signal into decision intervals of equal length and uses the midpoint of the interval as the reconstruction level. Mathematically, if the input is bounded, $L \le x \le U$, and we wish to use $N$ quantization levels, the decision and reconstruction levels of Eq. (4.3) are found by

$$\Delta = \frac{U - L}{N},$$

$$d_k = k\Delta + L, \text{ for } 0 \le k \le N,$$

$$r_k = (k + 0.5)\Delta + L, \quad \text{for } 0 \le k \le N - 1.$$

Uniform quantization is used most often because it is easy to implement. It is the optimal quantization method if the input signal is uniformly distributed between its limits. In many cases, if the distribution of the input signal is unknown, we choose one that makes the fewest assumptions about the data. This *maximum ignorance assumption* is generally taken to be the uniform distribution. In many cases, we do have some information about the distribution of the input values. In these cases, it will pay to take advantage of that information to create a more optimum quantization scheme.

## 4.2.2 Optimal quantization

The problem of finding the optimal quantizer for a signal with a probability distribution, $p_s(x)$, is given by

$$\text{minimize} \quad \epsilon = E\{[x - \hat{x}]^2\} = \int (x - \hat{x})^2 p_s(x) dx,$$

where $\hat{x}$ is the reconstructed value associated with $x$ and $E\{\cdot\}$ is the expected value operator. Assuming there are $L$ reconstruction levels available, the integral can be written piecewise as

$$\epsilon = \sum_{k=1}^{L} \int_{d_k}^{d_{k+1}} (x - r_k)^2 p_s(x) dx.$$

To find the optimal values of $r_k$ and $d_k$, differentiate the above equation with respect to those variables and set the results equal to zero. This gives the two equations

$$\frac{\partial \epsilon}{\partial d_k} = (d_k - r_{k-1})^2 p_s(d_k) - (d_k - r_k)^2 p_s(d_k) = 0, \tag{4.4}$$

$$\frac{\partial \epsilon}{\partial r_k} = -2 \int_{d_k}^{d_{k+1}} (x - r_k) p_s(x) dx = 0. \tag{4.5}$$

The result of solving these equations gives an implicit solution, where the optimal values of the decision levels are given as functions of the optimal reconstruction levels, and vice versa:

$$d_k = \frac{r_k + r_{k-1}}{2},$$

(4.6)

which is the mean of the reconstruction values,

$$r_k = \frac{\int_{d_k}^{d_{k+1}} x p_s(x) \mathrm{d}x}{\int_{d_k}^{d_{k+1}} p_s(x) \mathrm{d}x},$$

(4.7)

which is the centroid of the probability between the decision values. The solution for this set of equations can be found numerically for any given probability distribution, $p_s(x)$. The solution method for the optimum quantizer levels is iterative. A simple method starts with uniformly placed reconstruction levels, $\{r_k^0\}$, and computes the corresponding decision levels from the above formula, $\{d_k^0 = \frac{r_k^0 - r_{k-1}^0}{2}\}$. From these new decision levels, new reconstruction levels are computed from the corresponding formula for the set, $\{r_k^1\}$. The iteration is repeated until the changes in the levels are very small. This method is crude but works for most well behaved probability distribution functions [177].

The results for common distributions, such as Gaussian and Laplacian distributions, are tabulated in several papers and texts. The result for a uniform distribution is, as you would expect, equally spaced decision levels ([134] pp. 103–111, [217] p. 153). A qualitative description of the results would note that in regions of high probability, the decision levels are more closely spaced than in regions of low probability. Problems 4.11 and 4.12 provide an exercise to see this effect. The next quantizer works on the same principle but is not optimal.

## 4.3 Companding quantizer

The optimum quantizer may be difficult to compute for arbitrary distributions or distributions defined by sample histograms. An alternative quantizer is obtained by transforming the signal to produce a uniform (or nearly uniform) distribution and using a uniform quantizer. The uniformly quantized signal is then passed through the inverse transform to obtain the quantized value of the original signal. This technique is called *companding*, which is a combination of compressing and expanding. The result is a system that approximates the optimum quantizer.

There are several ways of defining the transformation of the signal with probability distribution $p(x)$ to obtain an approximation to the optimal quantizer of Section 4.2.2. The most obvious is

$$y = T[x] = \int_{-\infty}^{x} p(\eta) \mathrm{d}\eta.$$

(4.8)

The transformation is the cumulative probability function. It can be shown that the variable $y$ is uniformly distributed on $[0, 1]$. The exercise is left to the reader [134, 217].

In many cases, the problem may be that of requantizing data that is defined by a very large number of levels. For example, it was mentioned that image data is often recorded at 12 to 16 bits (4096 to 65536 levels). These data are then requantized to 8 bits or 256 levels for storage or display. For such cases, the probability distribution, $p_s(x)$ is replaced by a discrete histogram, $h_s(k)$, where $0 \leq k \leq N - 1$ for $N$ quantization levels in original data. The histogram should be normalized to sum to unity, since it is representing a probability distribution. We wish to reduce the number of levels to $M$. To use the compander, we replace the integral in Eq. (4.8) by the summation

$$T(k) = \sum_{j=0}^{k} h_s(j). \tag{4.9}$$

The decision levels correspond to the inverse images of the equally spaced levels for the uniformly distributed transformed variable. The $m$th decision level would ideally be given by $d_m = T^{-1}(m/M)$. There is a problem, since the functions are discrete and no true inverse exists. Practically, we choose the decision level to be either of the discrete values of the input signal, $k$ or $k + 1$, such that

$$T(k) \leq \frac{m}{M} < T(k + 1). \tag{4.10}$$

The reconstruction value for this interval, $r_m$, is defined by the discrete equivalent of Eq. (4.7),

$$r_m = \frac{\sum_{j=d_m}^{d_{m+1}} j h_s(j)}{\sum_{j=d_m}^{d_{m+1}} h_s(j)}. \tag{4.11}$$

The reconstruction value will probably need to be rounded to the closest integer value.

Within the precision of discrete values, the output values of the transformation $T(k)$ are close to uniformly distributed. Thus, a uniform quantizer is optimal for that random variable. The quantization decision and reconstruction levels in the original space are found by using the approximate inverse mapping. However, it must be remembered that the quantization error is defined in the original space. While the companding operation may give an acceptable quantization scheme, it is not optimal in the sense of the mean square error scheme presented earlier.

## 4.3.1 Visual quantization

The human eye is not a minimum mean square error detector. Thus, the optimum mean square error quantizer may not be the most visually pleasing. This fact has led to the introduction of many subjective weighting functions and transformations. An example of this type of quantization is one that considers the contrast sensitivity of the eye.

It was mentioned that the eye has a roughly logarithmic response to light intensity. Two nonlinear transformations related to the eye's response are

$$T[x] = \alpha \, \log(1 + \beta x),$$

for $0 \leq x \leq 1$ and

$$T[x] = \alpha x^\beta,$$

where $\alpha = 1$ and $\beta = 1/3$ are commonly used [154]. The value for $\beta$ is the same as used for photometric and colorimetric transformations ($L^*a^*b^*$) that are presented in Chapter 8.

### 4.3.2  Color quantization

Since color images are represented as three channels of data, usually red, green and blue bands, it is natural to consider quantizing color images by quantizing the bands independently. This would allow the use of simple quantization schemes on the three channels. Indeed, this is most often done in inexpensive scanners and applications with limited processing capability. Higher end scanners may scan the three channels separately, but will use different minimum and maximum values to determine the quantization step size for each channel.

It is noted that some scanners offer options for the final color space of the image, e.g., sRGB, LCH, CIELAB. In most cases, the original scan takes place using red, green or blue channels. The channels may be the result of filters on the sensors or the characteristic of the illuminants. The transformation to the desired color space is done by computation or a look-up table. In either case, the final quantization error can be no better than that of the original data. If the original data are quantized with a very large number of levels and the quantization in the desired space has many fewer levels the degradation may be acceptable. Furthermore, if a reduction in the number of levels is necessary, the selection of the desired space is important. The discussion of the effects of the selection of the final quantization space is found in Chapter 8.

The three color channels are usually quantized separately for reasons of simplicity of hardware and software. It would seem reasonable that a quantization scheme that takes into account the true vector nature of the color image would have an advantage in fidelity. The next section discusses this approach to quantization.

## 4.4      Vector quantization

It is natural to think of the pixels of a color image as three-dimensional vectors in a color space. However, even monochrome images, and indeed, any signal, can be quantized using a vector approach. In the case of a monochrome image, pairs of adjacent pixels may be grouped together to form a sequence of two-dimensional vectors. Two-by-two groups of pixels could be considered four-dimensional "superpixels." There are many creative ways to form signal vectors. Let us consider the problem of determining the best quantization once a vector signal has been created.

The optimal scalar quantizer can be extended to vector fields. The random signal in this case is a vector, $\mathbf{x} = [x_1, \ldots, x_N]^T$ with probability density function, $p_s(\mathbf{x})$. The mean square quantization error is given by

$$\epsilon = \sum_{k=1}^{L} \int_{D_k} (\mathbf{x} - \mathbf{r}_k)^T (\mathbf{x} - \mathbf{r}_k) p_s(\mathbf{x}) d\mathbf{x},$$

where $D_k$ represents the $N$-dimensional decision region, $\mathbf{r}_k$ represents the reconstruction value for all points within $D_k$ and $L$ is the number of reconstruction levels.

Using the same methods as in scalar quantization, we differentiate the error function with respect to $D_k$ and $\mathbf{r}_k$. The result of differentiation with respect to the reconstruction value yields

$$\mathbf{r}_k = \frac{\int_{D_k} \mathbf{x} p_s(\mathbf{x}) d\mathbf{x}}{\int_{D_k} p_s(\mathbf{x}) d\mathbf{x}}. \qquad (4.12)$$

This can be represented using the conditional probability

$$\mathbf{r}_k = E\{\mathbf{x} | \mathbf{x} \in D_k\}. \qquad (4.13)$$

This should be recognized as the centroid of the region defined by $D_k$, which is the same form as the scalar case.

Differentiation with respect to $D_k$ is not well defined, since the boundaries of the decision region can be complex. While in one dimension the decision regions were linear and had only two endpoints that had to be defined, the decision regions for the $N$-dimensional problem may have arbitrary shapes.

Because the general problem is so complex, there have been many suboptimal methods developed to obtain usable quantizers. Most of these rely on the fact that the data that are to be quantized are already available in a finely quantized form. For example, many vector quantization applications are in image and signal coding. The data are usually available at 8–16 bits per pixel. The *vector quantization* (VQ) problem is to minimize the average bit-rate when transmitting the image. The vectors that are used in this case are usually groups of pixels. Most often pairs of pixels in monochrome images are taken as the units to be requantized. An overview of vector quantization methods is presented in [59]. The next subsections will give a brief overview of the basic approach.

## 4.4.1 Full search vector quantization

The vector quantization process consists of two steps: (1) dividing the input space into decision regions, and (2) assigning the reconstruction levels for each of the regions. The reconstruction levels of scalar quantization are referred to as codewords in most VQ literature. Since the input space is assumed to be quantized, there are only a finite number of ways to divide the space. The output space is also quantized, so there are only a finite number of reconstruction levels. Of course, for any realistic number of quantization levels, it is clearly impossible to test all possible combinations of decision regions and reconstruction levels. Thus, we look for ways to restrict the problem to something that is mathematically tractable.

### 4.4.2    LBG algorithm (generalized Lloyd)

A suboptimal quantizer that produces a local minimum in a reasonable time is described in [59, 166]. The method assumes that a training set of vectors, $\{\mathbf{x}_k\}_{k=1}^{K}$, is available. The method can be modified to be used with a probability density function if desired. The number of reconstruction vectors (quantization levels) is fixed by the user at $N$. An initial set of reconstruction vectors is selected; $R_0 = \{\mathbf{r}_n^0\}_{n=1}^{N}$. The algorithm is given by:

1. Given $R_m$, select the partition of input vectors in the training set, $S_j$, by the rule: $\mathbf{x} \in S_j$ if $d(\mathbf{x}, \mathbf{r}_j^m) \leq d(\mathbf{x}, \mathbf{r}_i^m)$ for all $i$. The function $d(\mathbf{x}, \mathbf{y})$ is a distance measure between the two vector arguments. Most often $d(\mathbf{x}, \mathbf{y})$ is the common Euclidean norm. If the vectors represent color pixels, a measure in a color space, discussed in Chapter 8, is appropriate.
2. For the partitioning, $\{S_j\}_{j=1}^{N}$, compute the average error measure,

$$E_m = \frac{1}{N} \sum_{k=1}^{N} d(\mathbf{x}_k, \mathbf{r}_j^m), \qquad (4.14)$$

where $\mathbf{x}_k \in S_j$.
3. If $\frac{E_{m-1} - E_m}{E_m} \leq \epsilon$, stop the iteration. Use the reconstruction vectors, $R_m$. The convergence factor, $\epsilon$, needs to be set as an initialization parameter.
4. Find the optimal reconstruction vectors for the partition, $S_j$.

$$\mathbf{r}_j^{m+1} = \frac{1}{||S_j||} \sum_{\mathbf{x} \in S_j} \mathbf{x}, \qquad (4.15)$$

where $||S_j||$ represents the number of training vectors in $S_j$. This is the mean of the partition as we expect from Eq. (4.15). With the set $R_{m+1}$ go to step 1.

Since the algorithm reduces the distortion error at each step and the error is bounded below by zero, it is guaranteed to converge. Since all values are quantized at the start, the algorithm will converge in a finite number of steps. The parameter, $\epsilon$, will have an effect on the convergence rate but experience has shown that the algorithm is not very sensitive to changes in $\epsilon$. Values of about 0.0001 are common for 8 bit image values.

### 4.4.3 Color palettization (palette design)

A typical vector quantization problem arises from the need to display color images on a color monitor that uses a color palette. The monitor has only $M$ bits to define a color but it can use any of the colors available in a full 24 bit color space (three 8 bit channels). The number of bits, $M$, is usually 8 or 16. The problem is to choose which colors to put in the $M$ bit look-up table. For this discussion, let us assume that $M = 8$.

The original color image is defined by three 8 bit channels, usually red, green and blue. More recently, owing to the demand for colorimetric imaging, the channels may correspond to one of the uniform color spaces. A common scheme for requantizing the 24 bit image is to take the most significant three bits of red, three bits of green and two bits of blue. This is simple, but as there is no real colorimetric information about red, green and blue, it cannot be expected to be optimal in any sense. Modifying the scheme to work in a more appropriate color space would help, but is still naive.

A more sophisticated approach is presented in [202]. The algorithm produces a binary tree structure where the nodes of the tree are designated $\{C_j\}$ and the leaves are the vectors to be quantized, $\{\mathbf{x}_k\}$. The error that is desired to be minimized is

$$\epsilon = \sum_{\text{all } C_j} \sum_{\mathbf{x}_k \in C_j} ||\mathbf{x}_k - \mathbf{r}_j||^2,$$

where $\mathbf{r}_j$ is the reconstruction vector for all vectors (colors) in node $C_j$. A global minimum is difficult to obtain but, as before, suboptimal methods can yield good results.

The tree is constructed by successively splitting the sets of vectors represented by the nodes. Each split is determined by the plane perpendicular to the direction of maximum variation. Once the division of the space is completed, the reconstruction vectors can be determined from Eq. (4.15). It can be shown that for Gaussian distributions, this strategy produces optimal quantization. It is possible to weight the error in order to account for some characteristics of the human visual system.

## 4.5 Quantization noise

Quantization of a signal creates an error. This error can be considered as adding noise to the original signal. An important result for the uniform distribution is a rule of thumb for determining the number of bits needed to obtain a specified signal-to-noise ratio.

Assuming that the signal has a uniform distribution over a finite range $A$, the variance, or signal power, is given by $A^2/12$.[1] For a quantization of $B$ bits, or $2^B$ levels, the average error is the same on each of the $2^B$ intervals of length $q = A/2^B$, and is given by

$$\epsilon = \int_{-q/2}^{q/2} x^2 \frac{1}{q} dx = \frac{q^2}{12}. \tag{4.16}$$

---

[1] Note that when we discuss signal power, we are usually not interested in the mean, and so compute the variance. There is a further discussion about when this is appropriate in Section 7.2.3.

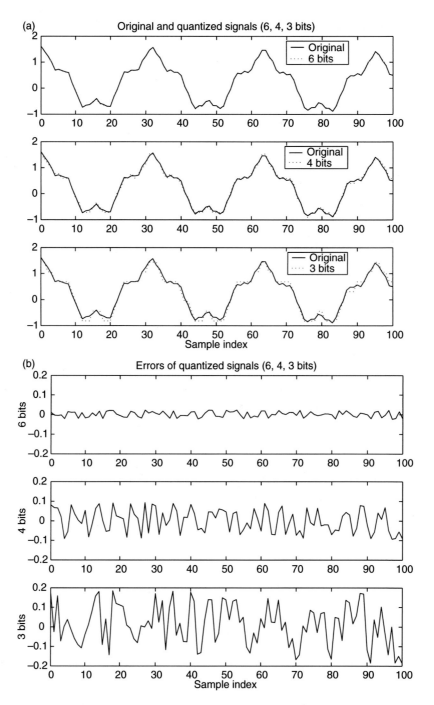

**Figure 4.3.** (a) Original signal and 6, 4, and 3 bit quantized versions; (b) errors for 6, 4, and 3 bit quantized versions.

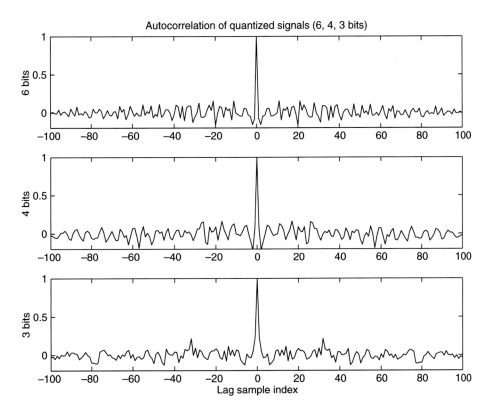

**Figure 4.4.** Autocorrelation of 6, 4, and 3 bit errors.

Note that a substitution is made to make the integral symmetric about the reconstruction value.

The signal-to-noise ratio is given by

$$\text{SNR} = \frac{A^2/12}{(A/2^B)^2/12} = 2^{2B};$$

and in decibels

$$\text{SNR}_{\text{dB}} = 10\log_{10}(2^{2B}) \approx 6B. \tag{4.17}$$

Thus, the rule of thumb is that the SNR improves 6 dB for every bit that is added to the system. A 14 bit audio system has a signal-to-noise ratio of about 84 dB.

Measurements on image scanners show that this ideal limit is rarely achieved. A typical 16 bit per channel scanner will usually perform at about 35–40 dB SNR in tests using uniform fields of varying density [298]. This is significantly below the ideal limit of 96 dB.

The assumption for computing the signal-to-noise ratio for quantization noise was that the noise was signal independent, uncorrelated, zero mean and uniformly distributed over

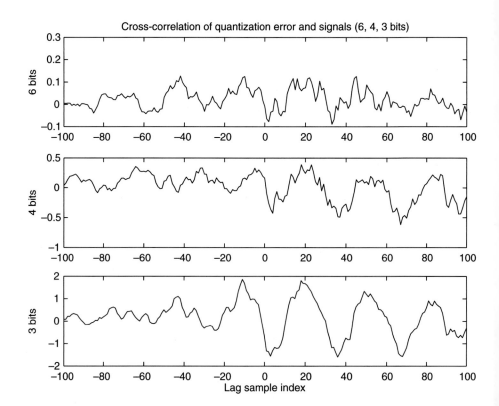

**Figure 4.5.** Cross-correlation of 6, 4, and 3 bit errors with original signal.

the quantizing interval. It is natural to ask under what conditions this assumption is valid. As a rule of thumb, if the signal varies by several quantization levels in each sampling interval, the quantization noise can be modeled as signal independent and uniformly distributed. This implies that finer quantization is more likely to satisfy the assumptions than coarse quantization. Consider the signal defined by

$$s(n) = 0.3\cos(2\pi 0.25n/127) + \cos(2\pi 4n/127)$$

$$+ 0.25\cos(2\pi 16n/127) + 0.0625\cos(2\pi 48n/127).$$

The original signal and quantized versions for 6, 4, and 3 bit quantizers are shown in Fig. 4.3a. The quantization errors for these signals are shown in Fig. 4.3b. To test the uncorrelated assumption, the autocorrelation was computed for each error signal, as shown in Fig. 4.4. Because the magnitudes of the errors differ significantly, the autocorrelations are normalized so that the autocorrelation at zero lag is unity. This allows us to compare the relative peak at zero lag to the other lags for all quantization levels. The autocorrelation for all quantization levels is reasonably close to the expected delta function, which indicates that the error is virtually uncorrelated with itself. Finally, we assumed that the noise was independent of the signal, so the signal and noise should be uncorrelated. The cross-correlation of the signal and quantization noise is shown in Fig. 4.5. Here we see that for 3 and 4 bit quantization, the signal and noise are definitely correlated. This correlation for coarse quantization indicates a failure of the basic assumptions. It is also an indicator that the errors will be visible to the human observer, since the eye is very good at detecting correlations. This type of error can be observed in Fig. 4.2b in the smooth background areas. It is often referred to as *contouring*.

## 4.6    Problems

**4.1**    Define the function $f(x) = x$ on $[0, 1]$. Determine the 2 bit uniform quantizer for this function. Plot the output of the quantizer. Compute the largest error. Compute the average square error.

**4.2**    Define the function $f(x) = x^2$ on $[0, 1]$. Determine the 2 bit uniform quantizer for this function. Plot the output of the quantizer. Compute the largest error. Compute the average square error.

**4.3**    Compare the results of Problems 4.1 and 4.2.

**4.4**    Describe qualitatively how an optimal quantizer would change the results of Problems 4.1 and 4.2. Compute the optimum 2 bit quantizer for Problems 4.1 and 4.2, or create a heuristic approximation to it. Plot the output of your quantizer. Compute the largest error. Compute the average square error. Compare the results with those of Problems 4.1 and 4.2.

**4.5**    Compute the quantization signal-to-noise ratio (QSNR) for the quantized signals in Problems 4.1 and 4.2.

**4.6**    Using the monochrome image *image-one* created in the problems in Chapter 3, requantize the image using a 4 bit uniform quantizer. Compute the QSNR. Display the result such as to make a valid comparison with the original image.

**4.7**    Formulate the algorithm to obtain the optimal quantizer using a histogram instead of the continuous probability distribution.

**4.8**    Using the monochrome image *image-one* created in the problems in Chapter 3, requantize the image using the 4 bit optimal quantizer developed in Problem 4.7. Compute the QSNR. Display the result such as to make a valid comparison with the original image.

**4.9**    Compare the QSNRs obtained in the previous problems with the 6 dB per bit rule of thumb that was developed in this chapter.

**4.10**    Consider the transformation defined by

$$y = \int_{-\infty}^{x} p(\tau) d\tau,$$

where $p(x)$ is the probability density function (PDF) of the random variable $x$. Show that the PDF of $y$ is uniform on $[0, 1]$.

**4.11**   Using the monochrome image *image-one* created in the problems in Chapter 3, requantize the image using a 4 bit companding quantizer using the following:

(a) A companding quantizer of your choice;
(b) The visual companding function of Section 4.3.1;
(c) A companding function based on the function $y = \int_{-\infty}^{x} p(\tau)d\tau$ where $p(x)$ is the PDF of the random variable $x$. Your compander will work with the histogram rather than with the PDF.

Compute the QSNR. Display the result such as to make a valid comparison with the original image.

**4.12**   Consider the 1-D signal of Fig. 4.3. The signal has 100 samples. If the signal is quantized to 2 bits per sample, the total number of bits is 200. Consider a vector quantizer that quantizes pairs of samples, $[s(n), s(n + 1)]$, where $n$ is even. A comparable vector quantizer would use 4 bits per pair.

(a) Show a plausible vector quantizer for this signal, i.e., show a set of reconstruction vectors and a set of boundaries that is consistent with the properties of the signal. Give your reasoning for this quantizer. The point of this problem is to see if you understand the qualitative behavior of vector quantizers, not to test your programming ability.
(b) Generate a vector quantizer by the methods described in the text. This problem requires programming the LBG method.
(c) Quantize the signal using the quantizers. Show the original signal, uniformly quantized 2 bit signal and vector quantized signal on the same graph.
(d) Compare the QSNR of the quantizers.

# 5   Frequency domain representation

Our first encounters with signals were in the time domain for 1-D signals and the spatial domain for 2-D images. We have seen time domain signals as a graph or as a trace on an oscilloscope. Undergraduate engineers have usually used a spectrum analyzer in the laboratory to characterize signals in the frequency domain. However, almost everyone has seen a graphical representation of an acoustic frequency spectrum when they observe the flashing lights on the spectrum displays of graphic equalizers on higher quality stereo systems. The display shows the observer the relative power of the signal in various frequency ranges.

The interpretation in the frequency domain of audio signals is aided by the fact that the ear is basically a spectrum analyzer. It is easy to interpret the terms high and low frequency when applied to audio signals. We have no difficulty thinking of a rumble as a low-frequency sound, or a screech as a high-frequency sound.

We will have to work a bit to achieve the same associations of visual phenomena with frequency bands. However, be assured that the effort is worthwhile. Among the interpretations that will be shown are that edges are associated with higher frequencies; shading is associated with lower frequencies; blurring is basically a low pass filter, while differentiation is a high pass operation.

It is important to be able to understand the characteristics of the signal in both the space and frequency domains. There are properties of the signal that are best described in one domain rather than the other. Generally, structural properties such as space limits (region of support), amplitude bounds, lines and edges are best described in the space domain; global features such as texture, filtering and visual effects are best described in the frequency domain.

The advantages of interpretation are significant, but computation in the frequency domain is also extremely important in image processing. Many operations are computed much more easily in the frequency domain. For example, bandpass filters are reduced to simple term-by-term multiplications in the frequency domain. In addition, the *fast Fourier transform* (FFT) algorithm permits more efficient computation of convolution by performing the operation in the discrete frequency domain.

We assume that the reader is familiar with the one-dimensional continuous Fourier transform from an undergraduate signals and systems course. A brief review is given here before proceeding to two dimensions.

## 5.1          Continuous Fourier transform

All transform operations can be done using the continuous Fourier transform if generalized (delta) functions are allowed. The advantage of using only the continuous transform is that concepts in the various combinations of discrete and continuous domains are easily transferred.

### 5.1.1          One-dimensional transform

Given a one-dimensional, analog signal, $s_a(t)$, where the argument usually represents time,[1] the Fourier transform pair is defined by

$$\tilde{s}_a(F) = \int_{-\infty}^{\infty} s_a(t)e^{-j2\pi Ft}\, dt, \tag{5.1}$$

and

$$s_a(t) = \int_{-\infty}^{\infty} \tilde{s}_a(F)e^{j2\pi Ft}\, dF, \tag{5.2}$$

where $F$ is frequency in units of hertz or cycles per second, and the tilde (˜) indicates the Fourier transform of the corresponding symbol in the time or space domain. We use the tilde to indicate the transform since upper case letters are used to denote matrices. In many signal processing texts, the upper case letter is used to represent the transform of the signal denoted by the lower case letter. There is a problem in imaging texts where upper case, bold face letters represent matrices. Thus, in later chapters, with the tilde, it is easy to denote the discrete transform of a matrix. We will emphasize the analog nature of the signal by using the subscript a. Note that while it is customary to use time as the argument for one-dimensional signals, the argument may represent any desired physical quantity, e.g., distance or wavelength or angle. The frequency can also be represented by radian frequency, as $\omega = 2\pi F$. This will yield a transform pair defined by

$$\tilde{s}_a(\omega) = \int_{-\infty}^{\infty} s_a(t)e^{-j\omega t}\, dt, \tag{5.3}$$

and

$$s_a(t) = \frac{1}{2\pi}\int_{-\infty}^{\infty} \tilde{s}_a(\omega)e^{j\omega t}\, d\omega. \tag{5.4}$$

We will denote Fourier transform pairs with the double arrow

$$s(t) \longleftrightarrow \tilde{s}(F) \quad \text{or} \quad s(t) \longleftrightarrow \tilde{s}(\omega).$$

---

[1] The images that are the subject of this text are usually represented as functions of spatial variables. However, since most signal processing texts treat one-dimensional signals as functions of time, we will continue that notation here.

The advantage of the frequency definition of Eq. (5.1) is the use of the natural units of hertz or cycles per second. The advantage of the second form, Eq. (5.3), is a concise notation.

Since it is assumed that the reader has had an introduction to the one-dimensional Fourier transform, we will present the properties and results that are required to go from one dimension to two dimensions. Some of these results are discussed in more detail in the appendices.

### Properties of Fourier transforms (1-D)

Table 5.1 gives a concise summary of the important properties of the one-dimensional Fourier transform. We elaborate on some of the properties below.

The linearity of the transform is common to all major transforms used in engineering. This property allows us to break the signal into simple component parts and process or analyze the components separately.

Time or space shifting is equivalent to multiplication in the frequency domain by a linear phase factor. The power at each frequency is unchanged; only the phase is modified by the shift.

Multiplication in one domain is equivalent to convolution in the other domain. Multiplication in time is also known as *modulation*.

Parseval's theorem states that the total power in one domain is equal to the total power in the other domain. It is the distribution of power in each domain that is usually of interest. A common use of Parseval's theorem is in the computation of the mean square error of a signal, $s(t)$, and its approximation, $\hat{s}(t)$. We recognize the total square error integral,

$$\epsilon = \int_{-\infty}^{\infty} [s(t) - \hat{s}(t)]^2 \, dt,$$

**Table 5.1.** Properties of Fourier transforms (1-D)

| Property | Time $\longleftrightarrow$ frequency relationship |
|---|---|
| Linearity | $\alpha_1 s_1(x) + \alpha_2 s_2(x) \longleftrightarrow \alpha_1 \tilde{s}_1(F) + \alpha_2 \tilde{s}_2(F)$ |
| Scaling time or | |
| space argument | $s(\alpha x) \longleftrightarrow \frac{1}{|\alpha|} \tilde{s}(\frac{F}{\alpha})$ |
| Shifting in time | |
| or space | $s(x - x_0) \longleftrightarrow e^{-j2\pi(x_0 F)} \tilde{s}(F)$ |
| Convolution | $s(x) * h(x) \longleftrightarrow \tilde{s}(F)\tilde{h}(F)$ |
| Multiplication in time | |
| or space | $s(x)h(x) \longleftrightarrow \tilde{s}(F) * \tilde{h}(F)$ |
| Parseval's theorem | $\int_{-\infty}^{\infty} |s(x)|^2 dx = \int_{-\infty}^{\infty} |\tilde{s}(F)|^2 dF$ |
| Conjugate symmetry | |
| for real signals | $\tilde{s}(F) = \tilde{s}^*(-F)$ |
| Time/space reversal | $s(-x) \longleftrightarrow \tilde{s}(-F)$ |
| | If $s(x)$ is real then |
| | $s(-x) \longleftrightarrow \tilde{s}^*(F)$ |

**Table 5.2.** Common transform pairs (1-D)

| Time/space domain | Fourier transform |
|---|---|
| $\delta(t)$ | $1$ |
| $\delta(\alpha t)$ | $\frac{1}{|\alpha|}$ |
| $\delta(t - t_0)$ | $e^{-j2\pi t_0 F}$ |
| $\mathrm{comb}(t)$ | $\mathrm{comb}(F)$ |
| $\mathrm{comb}(\alpha t)$ | $\frac{1}{|\alpha|}\mathrm{comb}(\frac{F}{\alpha})$ |
| $\mathrm{rect}(t)$, | $\sin(\pi F)/\pi F$ |
| where $\mathrm{rect}(t)$ is defined by | |
| $\mathrm{rect}(t) = \begin{cases} 1 & \text{if } |t| < 1/2 \\ 0 & \text{else} \end{cases}$ | |
| $\sin(\pi t)/\pi t$ | $\mathrm{rect}(F)$, |
| | where $\mathrm{rect}(F)$ is defined by |
| | $\mathrm{rect}(F) = \begin{cases} 1 & \text{if } |F| < 1/2 \\ 0 & \text{else} \end{cases}$ |
| $\cos(2\pi F_0 t)$ | $\frac{1}{2}\delta(F - F_0) + \frac{1}{2}\delta(F + F_0)$ |

as the power or energy of the error signal. Parseval's theorem states that the error power can be measured in either domain. It is often easier to compute in the frequency domain. Since human vision is more sensitive to some spatial frequencies than others, weighting the error in the frequency domain can lead to better visual results.

The conjugate symmetry property is very useful, since it means that we need compute only half of the transform coefficients. The other half can be inferred by the conjugate symmetry property. This also means that we expect to see symmetry in the spectral plots of the signals. In one dimension, it is reasonable to show only the positive half of the spectrum to save space.

The time/space reversal property is useful in analyzing signals with certain symmetries. It is also the basis for relating convolution and correlation.

Table 5.2 lists a number of common one-dimensional transform pairs. The derivation of these transforms is given in most signals and systems texts, e.g., [106, 201].

### 5.1.2 Two-dimensional transform

The two-dimensional Fourier transform is a straightforward extension of the one-dimensional transform. Although the extension is straightforward, the mathematics and the interpretation require additional effort to understand. The definition is

$$\tilde{s}_a(F_x, F_y) = \int_{-\infty}^{\infty} \int_{-\infty}^{\infty} s_a(x, y) e^{-j2\pi(xF_x + yF_y)} \, dxdy, \tag{5.5}$$

$$s_a(x, y) = \int_{-\infty}^{\infty} \int_{-\infty}^{\infty} \tilde{s}_a(F_x, F_y) e^{j2\pi(xF_x + yF_y)} \, dF_x dF_y, \tag{5.6}$$

where $F_x$ and $F_y$ are spatial frequencies in units of cycles per unit distance, e.g., cycles/mm.

Alternatively,

$$\tilde{s}_a(\omega_x, \omega_y) = \int_{-\infty}^{\infty} \int_{-\infty}^{\infty} s_a(x, y) e^{-j(x\omega_x + y\omega_y)} \, dx dy,$$

and

$$s_a(x, y) = 1/(2\pi)^2 \int_{-\infty}^{\infty} \int_{-\infty}^{\infty} \tilde{s}_a(\omega_x, \omega_y) e^{j(x\omega_x + y\omega_y)} \, d\omega_x d\omega_y,$$

where $\omega_x$ and $\omega_y$ are given in terms of radian frequency.

We will denote Fourier transform pairs as

$$s_a(x, y) \longleftrightarrow \tilde{s}_a(F_x, F_y) \quad \text{or} \quad s_a(x, y) \longleftrightarrow \tilde{s}_a(\omega_x, \omega_y).$$

### 5.1.3  Examples of two-dimensional sinusoids

With the brief review of one-dimensional Fourier transforms, we proceed to functions of interest in two dimensions. Examples of two-dimensional sinusoids are shown in Figs. 5.1 and 5.2. Figure 5.1a shows a two-dimensional cosine function as a shaded mesh plot; the values are between 0 and 255 for display purposes. The same function is shown in Fig. 5.1b as a grayscale plot. The high values of Fig. 5.1a appear as white in Fig. 5.1b. The grayscale plot shows the visual frequency that would appear in an image. It is much easier to see the orientation that corresponds to the relative frequencies in the $x$ and $y$ directions in the grayscale plot.

The frequencies in the $x$ and $y$ directions can be obtained by counting the number of cycles (periods) in each direction. For example, in Fig. 5.2d, there are eight periods

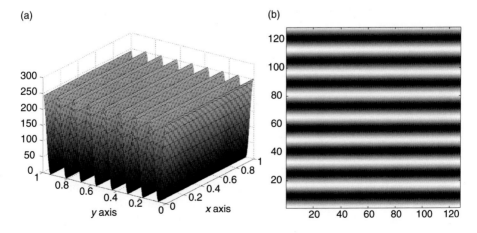

(a)   (b)

**Figure 5.1.** (a) $\cos[2\pi(8y/128)]$ as shaded mesh; (b) $\cos[2\pi(8y/128)]$ as grayscale.

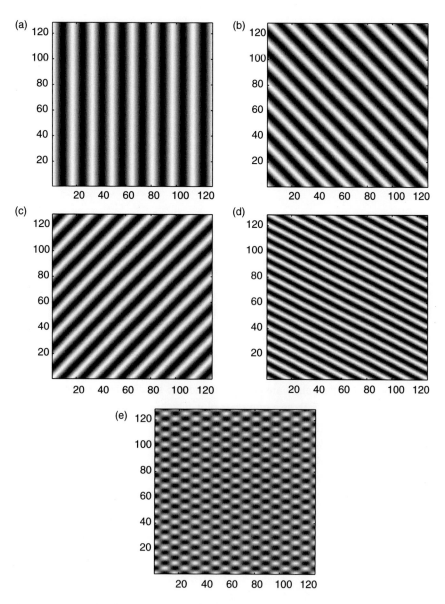

**Figure 5.2.** (a) $\cos[2\pi(8x/128)]$; (b) $\cos[2\pi(8x/128 + 8y/128)]$; (c) $\cos[2\pi(8x/128 - 8y/128)]$; (d) $\cos[2\pi(8x/128 + 16y/128)]$; (e) $\cos[2\pi(8x/128)]\cos[2\pi(16y/128)]$.

along the $x$-axis, which has a length of 128. If we assume a unit sampling interval, the 128 corresponds to the total number of samples. Thus, the frequency in the $x$-direction is $F_x = 8/128 = 1/16$ cycles per unit. If the unit distance were measured in millimeters, the frequency would be $1/16$ cycles/mm. Likewise, it can be seen from the fact that there are 16 cycles in 128 units in the $y$ direction, that the frequency in the $y$ direction is $1/8$ cycles/unit. The sinusoid can be represented by $\cos[2\pi(x/16 + y/8) + \theta]$. From the observation that the value of the sinusoid at $(x, y) = (0, 0)$ is a maximum, the phase of the cosine is $\theta = 0$.

Let us consider the effect of the sign of the frequency in two-dimensional representation. In one dimension, the sign of the frequency can often be ignored, as in the case $\cos(2\pi Ft) = \cos(2\pi(-F)t)$. In two dimensions, the sign of the frequencies gives the relative orientation of the sinusoid. From Figs. 5.2b and 5.2c, we can see that $\cos[2\pi(x/16 + y/16)] \neq \cos[2\pi(x/16 - y/16)]$. However, negation of both terms will yield identical frequencies, e.g., $\cos[2\pi(x/16 + y/16)] = \cos[2\pi(-x/16 - y/16)]$.

Figure 5.2e shows the image defined by $\cos[2\pi(8x/128)]\cos[2\pi(16y/128)]$. This is not a pure sinusoid but the sum of sinusoids. This can be seen by considering the representation of the cosine by Euler's formula. This is the two-dimensional form of modulation.

$$
\begin{aligned}
s(x, y) &= \cos[2\pi(8x/128)]\cos[2\pi(16y/128)], \\
&= \frac{1}{2}\left[e^{j2\pi(8x/128)} + e^{-j2\pi(8x/128)}\right]\frac{1}{2}\left[e^{j2\pi(16y/128)} + e^{-j2\pi(16y/128)}\right], \\
&= \frac{1}{4}\left[e^{j2\pi(x/16+y/8)} + e^{j2\pi(x/16-y/8)} + e^{j2\pi(-x/16+y/8)} + e^{j2\pi(-x/16-y/8)}\right], \\
&= \frac{1}{2}\cos\left[2\pi(8x/128 + 16y/128)\right] + \frac{1}{2}\cos\left[2\pi(8x/128 - 16y/128)\right].
\end{aligned}
$$

## 5.2 Properties of 2-D Fourier transforms

The properties of the two-dimensional Fourier transform are summarized using the two-dimensional notation in Table 5.3.

The first property is unique to 2-D transforms since separability is not defined in one dimension. By definition a two-dimensional function, $f(x, y)$, is *separable* if it can be written as the product of two one-dimensional functions,

$$
f(x, y) = f_x(x)f_y(y).
$$

The transform is implemented by performing one-dimensional transforms in each coordinate direction. The definition is

$$
\tilde{s}(F_x, F_y) = \int_{-\infty}^{\infty}\int_{-\infty}^{\infty} s(x, y)e^{-j2\pi xF_x}e^{-j2\pi yF_y}\,dx\,dy.
$$

This can be rewritten to show the integration in each coordinate,

$$
\tilde{s}(F_x, F_y) = \int_{-\infty}^{\infty}\left[\int_{-\infty}^{\infty} s(x, y)e^{-j2\pi xF_x}\,dx\right]e^{-j2\pi yF_y}\,dy = \int_{-\infty}^{\infty}\tilde{s}_x(F_x, y)e^{-j2\pi yF_y}\,dy.
$$

This implies that if the space domain function is separable, then its Fourier transform is separable also, i.e., if $s(x, y) = s_x(x)s_y(y)$ then

$$\tilde{s}(F_x, F_y) = \tilde{s}_x(F_x)\tilde{s}_y(F_y).$$

This property is often used to simplify computation. There are times when separability is assumed purely for computational convenience, even though this may lead to inaccuracies. The price of the errors is considered worth the benefit of computational speed. Examples of separable functions include the Gaussian functions,

$$f(x, y) = e^{-\frac{1}{2}\left[\frac{(x-\bar{x})^2}{\sigma_x^2} + \frac{(y-\bar{y})^2}{\sigma_y^2}\right]},$$

or the rectangular box functions,

$$\text{rect}(x, y) = \begin{cases} 1 & \text{if } |x| < a/2 \text{ and } |y| < b/2 \\ 0 & \text{else} \end{cases}.$$

Examples of nonseparable functions include the circular pillbox functions of the form

$$\text{pill}(x, y) = \begin{cases} 1 & \text{if } x^2 + y^2 < R \\ 0 & \text{else} \end{cases},$$

or various polynomials, e.g.,

$$p(x, y) = x^2 y + xy^2 = xy(x + y).$$

**Table 5.3.** Properties of Fourier transforms (2-D)

| Property | Time $\longleftrightarrow$ frequency relationship |
|---|---|
| Separability of kernel | $\tilde{s}(F_x, F_y) = \int_{-\infty}^{\infty}\left[\int_{-\infty}^{\infty} s(x, y)e^{-j2\pi xF_x}dx\right]e^{-j2\pi yF_y}dy$ |
| if $s(x, y) = s_x(x)s_y(y)$ | $\tilde{s}(F_x, F_y) = \tilde{s}_x(F_x)\tilde{s}_y(F_y)$ |
| Linearity | $\alpha_1 s_1(x, y) + \alpha_2 s_2(x, y) \longleftrightarrow \alpha_1 \tilde{s}_1(F_x, F_y) + \alpha_2 \tilde{s}_2(F_x, F_y)$ |
| Scaling time or space | $s(\alpha x, \beta y) \longleftrightarrow \frac{1}{|\alpha\beta|}\tilde{s}(\frac{F_x}{\alpha}, \frac{F_y}{\beta})$ |
| argument | |
| Shifting in space | $s(x - x_0, y - y_0) \longleftrightarrow e^{-j2\pi(x_0 F_x + y_0 F_y)}\tilde{s}(F_x, F_y)$ |
| Convolution | $s(x, y) * h(x, y) \longleftrightarrow \tilde{s}(F_x, F_y)\tilde{h}(F_x, F_y)$ |
| Multiplication in space | $s(x, y)h(x, y) \longleftrightarrow \tilde{s}(F_x, F_y) * \tilde{h}(F_x, F_y)$ |
| Parseval's theorem | $\int_{-\infty}^{\infty}\int_{-\infty}^{\infty}|s(x, y)|^2\,dxdy = \int_{-\infty}^{\infty}\int_{-\infty}^{\infty}|\tilde{s}(F_x, F_y)|^2\,dF_xdF_y$ |
| Conjugate symmetry | $\tilde{s}(F_x, F_y) = \tilde{s}^*(-F_x, -F_y)$ |
| for real signals | |
| Time/space reversal | $s(-x, -y) \longleftrightarrow \tilde{s}(-F_x, -F_y)$ |
| | If $s(x, x)$ is real then |
| | $s(-x, -y) \longleftrightarrow \tilde{s}^*(F_x, F_y)$ |

**Table 5.4.** Common transform pairs (2-D)

| Time/space domain | Fourier transform |
| --- | --- |
| $\delta(x,y)$ | $1$ |
| $\delta(\alpha x, \beta y)$ | $\frac{1}{|\alpha\beta|}$ |
| $\delta(x-x_0, y-y_0)$ | $e^{-j2\pi(x_0 F_x + y_0 F_y)}$ |
| $\text{comb}(x,y)$ | $\text{comb}(F_x, F_y)$ |
| $\text{comb}(\alpha x, \beta y)$ | $\frac{1}{|\alpha\beta|}\text{comb}\left(\frac{F_x}{\alpha}, \frac{F_y}{\beta}\right)$ |
| $\text{rect}_2(x/\alpha, y/\beta) = \text{rect}(x/\alpha)\text{rect}(y/\beta)$, where $\text{rect}_2(x,y)$ is defined by $\text{rect}_2(x,y)$ $= \begin{cases} 1 & \text{if } |x| < 1/2 \text{ and } |y| < 1/2 \\ 0 & \text{else} \end{cases}$ | $|\alpha\beta| \left[ \sin(\pi F_x \alpha)/\pi F_x \alpha \right] \left[ \sin(\pi F_y \beta)/\pi F_y \beta \right]$ |
| $\cos[2\pi(xu_0 + yv_0)]$ | $\frac{1}{2}\delta(F_x - u_0, F_y - v_0) + \frac{1}{2}\delta(F_x + u_0, F_y + v_0)$ |
| $\cos(2\pi x u_0)\cos(2\pi y v_0)$ | $\frac{1}{4}\left[\delta(F_x - u_0, F_y - v_0) + \delta(F_x + u_0, F_y - v_0) + \delta(F_x - u_0, F_y + v_0) + \delta(F_x + u_0, F_y + v_0)\right]$ |

The properties of linearity, scaling, shifting, convolution and multiplication are direct extensions of the same properties in one dimension.

Conjugate symmetry is easily written in two dimensions;

$$\tilde{s}(F_x, F_y) = \tilde{s}^*(-F_x, -F_y).$$

Again, this means that only half of the frequency domain information is unique and need be computed. For the 2-D case, the first and third quadrants are conjugate symmetric, as are the second and fourth. When analyzing a one-dimensional signal in the frequency domain, it is common to display only the positive frequency axis. However, for two-dimensional applications, it is common to display the entire two-dimensional plane. The DC frequency, $(F_x, F_y) = (0,0)$, is usually displayed in the center of the spectral display. This convention will be followed in this text. Thus, the conjugate symmetry should be apparent in the spectra of the various examples to follow.

Space reversal is also an easy extension of the one-dimensional property, but some practice is needed in its visualization. Space reversal is equivalent to taking the mirror image of the signal first about one axis, e.g., the $x$ axis, and then taking the mirror image about the other axis, e.g., the $y$ axis. This gives the same symmetry as the conjugate symmetry property for real functions.

Common two-dimensional transform pairs are shown in Table 5.4. The reader should compare these functions with their one-dimensional counterparts in Table 5.2.

## 5.2.1    Relation between analog Fourier transforms and Fourier series

There are several different forms of the Fourier transform depending on whether the signal is analog or discrete, periodic or aperiodic. It is beneficial to understand the relations between the various forms, rather than simply use the mathematical definitions.

**Table 5.5.** Common DFT pairs (1-D and 2-D)

| Time/space domain | Fourier transform |
| --- | --- |
| $\delta(n)$ | $1$ |
| $\delta(n - n_0)$ | $e^{-j2\pi \frac{n_0}{N} k}$ |
| $\delta(m - m_0, n - n_0)$ | $e^{-j2\pi(km_0 + ln_0)}$ |
| $\text{rect}_L(n)$ | $e^{-j\pi k(L-1)/N} \frac{\sin(\pi k L/N)}{\sin(\pi k/N)}$ |

where $\text{rect}_L(n)$ is defined by

$$\text{rect}_L(t) = \begin{cases} 1 & \text{if } 0 \leq n \leq L-1 \\ 0 & \text{if } L \leq n \leq N-1 \end{cases}$$

| | |
| --- | --- |
| $\text{rect}_{K,L}(m, n) = \text{rect}_K(m)\text{rect}_L(n)$ | $e^{-j\pi k(K-1)/M} \frac{\sin(\pi k\, K/M)}{\sin(\pi k/M)} e^{-j\pi l(L-1)/N} \frac{\sin(\pi l\, L/N)}{\sin(\pi l/N)}$ |

note the use of separable functions

| | |
| --- | --- |
| $\cos\left(2\pi \frac{k_0}{N} n\right),$ | $\frac{N}{2}\delta(k - k_0) + \frac{N}{2}\delta(k + k_0)$ |

note that because of periodicity,
$$\delta(k + k_0) = \delta(k - N + k_0) = \delta(k - (N - k_0))$$

| | |
| --- | --- |
| $\cos\left[2\pi\left(\frac{mk_0}{M} + \frac{nl_0}{N}\right)\right]$ | $\frac{N}{2}\delta(k - k_0, l - l_0) + \frac{N}{2}\delta(k + k_0, l + l_0)$ |
| $\cos\left[\left(\frac{2\pi m k_0}{M}\right)\cos\left(\frac{2\pi n l_0}{N}\right)\right]$ | $\frac{1}{N}[\delta(k - k_0, l - l_0) + \delta(k + k_0, l - l_0) +$ |
| | $\delta(k - k_0, l + l_0) + \delta(k + k_0, l + l_0)]$ |

In this section, we will discuss the relationship between the transforms of periodic and aperiodic analog signals. The Fourier transform of a periodic signal can be obtained using the Fourier series definitions, see Section 4.5 of [200]. For brevity, the derivation here will use 1-D signals.

Let $s(t)$ be identical to one period of the periodic signal $s_p(t)$ over a single period and zero outside of that range. If we use the period centered about zero and if the period of $s_p(t)$ is $T$, then

$$s(t) = \text{rect}(t/T)s_p(t),$$

where we use the definition of the rectangular pulse defined in Table 5.2. The analysis and synthesis equations for the Fourier series are given by

$$\tilde{s}_p(k) = 1/T \int_{-T/2}^{T/2} s_p(t)e^{-j2\pi(kt/T)}\, dt, \tag{5.7}$$

and

$$s_p(t) = \sum_{k=-\infty}^{\infty} \tilde{s}_p(k)e^{j2\pi(kt/T)}. \tag{5.8}$$

Note that the above equation holds for all $t$, even those outside the fundamental period used in the definition of Eq. (5.7). From the Fourier transform, we have

$$\tilde{s}(F) = \int_{-\infty}^{\infty} s(t)e^{-j2\pi(Ft)}\,dt. \tag{5.9}$$

Since $s(t)$ is zero outside the single period about zero, we have

$$\tilde{s}(F) = \int_{-T/2}^{T/2} s(t)e^{-j2\pi(Ft)}\,dt, \tag{5.10}$$

and

$$s(t) = \int_{-\infty}^{\infty} \tilde{s}(F)e^{j2\pi(Ft)}\,dF. \tag{5.11}$$

From Eq. (5.7) and Eq. (5.10), we obtain

$$\tilde{s}_{\mathrm{p}}(k) = 1/T\tilde{s}(k/T). \tag{5.12}$$

Thus, the Fourier series coefficients are obtained by sampling, at a frequency $k/T$, the analog Fourier transform of the aperiodic signal defined by a single period of the periodic signal.

Now, let us consider writing the Fourier series in the analog form. If a function in the Fourier domain has the form

$$\tilde{s}(F) = \sum_{k=-\infty}^{\infty} \tilde{s}_{\mathrm{p}}(k)\delta\left(F - \frac{k}{T}\right), \tag{5.13}$$

then substituting the definition of the inverse transform into Eq. (5.11) gives

$$s(t) = \int_{-\infty}^{\infty} \sum_{k=-\infty}^{\infty} \tilde{s}_{\mathrm{p}}(k)\delta\left(F - \frac{k}{T}\right) e^{j2\pi Ft}\,dF = \sum_{k=-\infty}^{\infty} \tilde{s}_{\mathrm{p}}(k)e^{j2\pi(\frac{kt}{T})}. \tag{5.14}$$

This is the form of a Fourier series for a periodic function. It is noted here and later that if a signal has a discrete representation in one domain (either time, space or frequency), it is periodic in the other domain.

To show that the Fourier transform of a comb is a comb, note that the comb in the time domain is a periodic function with unit period. Substitution of the delta function for $s_{\mathrm{p}}$ and $s$ above will yield the result.

In the case of periodic two-dimensional signals, we must define the period in each direction. We will denote the directions of the period by subscripts. The 2-D Fourier series of a periodic signal is defined by

$$\tilde{s}_{\mathrm{p}}(k,l) = 1/(T_x T_y) \int_{-T_x/2}^{T_x/2} \int_{-T_y/2}^{T_y/2} s_{\mathrm{p}}(x,y) e^{-\mathrm{j}2\pi(kx/T_x+ly/T_y)}\, dxdy, \tag{5.15}$$

$$s_{\mathrm{p}}(x,y) = \sum_{k=-\infty}^{\infty} \sum_{l=-\infty}^{\infty} \tilde{s}_{\mathrm{p}}(k,l) e^{\mathrm{j}2\pi(kx/T_x+ly/T_y)}. \tag{5.16}$$

Notice that the periods may be different in the $x$ and $y$ directions.

The above equations are written for a function that is periodic on the common rectangular lattice. Two-dimensional functions can be periodic with oddly shaped periods. The hexagonal lattice is the nonrectangular lattice most often used [68].

## 5.3    Derivation of DFT from Fourier transform

The discrete signals encountered in image processing are usually samples of continuous signals, i.e., $s(n) = s_{\mathrm{a}}(nT)$. The processing of the discrete signals is often done in the frequency domain. The user should understand the implications of the discrete mathematical operations so that informed judgments can be made about the appropriateness of various procedures and algorithms.

The use of the one-dimensional discrete Fourier transform (DFT) assumes that we are given a finite number of samples of a signal, $\{s(n)\}_{n=0}^{N-1}$, which is assumed to represent a single period of a periodic signal. The defining equations are

$$\tilde{s}(k) = \sum_{n=0}^{N-1} s(n) e^{-\mathrm{j}2\pi(kn/N)}, \tag{5.17}$$

$$s(n) = \sum_{k=0}^{N-1} \tilde{s}(k) e^{\mathrm{j}2\pi(kn/N)}. \tag{5.18}$$

Note that both $s(n)$ and $\tilde{s}(k)$ are periodic with period $N$.

To understand the relation of the DFT to the continuous Fourier transform, it is useful to review a derivation of the DFT starting from the definition of the continuous Fourier transform given by Eqs. (5.1) and (5.2).

Assuming a sampling interval of $T$, the sampled signal is represented by sampling the synthesis formula of Eq. (5.2):

$$s_{\mathrm{a}}(n) = s_{\mathrm{a}}(nT) = \int_{-\infty}^{\infty} \tilde{s}_{\mathrm{a}}(F) e^{\mathrm{j}2\pi FnT}\, dF. \tag{5.19}$$

This can be rewritten as the sum of the integrals over successive intervals of length $1/T$.

$$s_{\mathrm{a}}(nT) = \sum_{m=-\infty}^{\infty} \int_{m/T}^{(m+1)/T} \tilde{s}_{\mathrm{a}}(F) e^{\mathrm{j}2\pi FnT}\, dF. \tag{5.20}$$

Writing the integrand as a shifted function, we can write the integral over the normalized interval $[0, 1/T]$.

$$s_a(nT) = \sum_{m=-\infty}^{\infty} \int_0^{1/T} \tilde{s}_a(F + m/T) e^{j2\pi nT(F+m/T)} \, dF. \tag{5.21}$$

Noting that $e^{j2\pi nT(F+m/T)} = e^{j2\pi nTF}$ for all $m$ and interchanging the summation and integral, we have

$$s_a(nT) = \int_0^{1/T} \left[ \sum_{m=-\infty}^{\infty} \tilde{s}_a(F + m/T) \right] e^{j2\pi nTF} \, dF. \tag{5.22}$$

The term in brackets is periodic with period $1/T$ and will be recognized as the aliased spectrum of the analog signal,

$$\tilde{s}_p(F) = \sum_{m=-\infty}^{\infty} \tilde{s}_a(F + m/T). \tag{5.23}$$

If $s_a(t)$ is bandlimited to the frequencies $|F| < \frac{1}{2T}$, then all of the shifted spectra $\tilde{s}_a(F + m/T) = 0$ for $m \neq 0$. This implies no aliasing error.

Note that we have assumed that the summation converges and the integral is defined. Such assumptions are typical in "engineering mathematics," where they are not emphasized for fear of losing the main ideas in a sea of detail. However, it will be beneficial to be aware of such tendencies and recognize it when it occurs, in order to avoid the possible traps.

The duality of the Fourier transform yields the sampled spectrum, which is analogous to Eq. (5.22),

$$\tilde{s}_a(k/NT) = \int_0^{NT} \left[ \sum_{m=-\infty}^{\infty} s_a(t + mNT) \right] e^{-j2\pi kt/NT} \, dt, \tag{5.24}$$

i.e., starting with functions in the frequency domain instead of the time domain as in Eq. (5.19).

The summation in brackets is periodic with period $NT$

$$s_p(t) = \sum_{m=-\infty}^{\infty} s_a(t + mNT).$$

The samples in the frequency domain, $\tilde{s}_a(k/NT)$, are the Fourier series coefficients of the periodic analog signal in brackets in Eq. (5.24). The periodic time domain signal may be considered an aliased version of the original signal. The aliasing has created a periodic signal.

If we approximate the continuous integral in Eq. (5.22) by a simple summation, we have

$$s_a(nT) \approx \sum_{k=0}^{N-1} \tilde{s}_p(F + k/NT)e^{j2\pi knT/NT} 1/NT,$$

or

$$s_a(nT) \approx 1/NT \sum_{k=0}^{N-1} \tilde{s}_p(F + k/NT)e^{j2\pi kn/N},$$

which is the definition of the DFT of $s_a(n) = \frac{1}{NT} s_a(nT)$. Note that the normalizing constant $1/NT$, which relates the energy or power of the analog signal to the sampled signal, may be omitted for computational convenience.

We have considered aperiodic analog signals (Fourier transforms), periodic analog signals (Fourier series) and discrete periodic signals (discrete Fourier transforms). To complete the discussion of Fourier transforms, it remains to discuss aperiodic, discrete signals. This is the domain of most digital signal processing [200, 218]. Such a signal can be thought of as the result of sampling an aperiodic analog signal. For these signals, defined for an infinite number of samples, the discrete-time Fourier transform (DTFT) is defined by the pair

$$\tilde{s}(F) = \sum_{n=0}^{\infty} s(n)e^{-j2\pi Fn}, \tag{5.25}$$

$$s(n) = \int_{-\frac{1}{2}}^{\frac{1}{2}} \tilde{s}(F)e^{j2\pi Fn} \, dF. \tag{5.26}$$

This pair can be obtained from the equations used to derive the DFT. It requires only a little mathematical manipulation to obtain Eq. (5.26) from Eqs. (5.22) and (5.23).

A graphical derivation of the DTFT and DFT is presented here to give another view and additional insight into the interpretation of discrete transforms. For this graphical interpretation, we need to use the basic properties of convolution and multiplication of the continuous Fourier transform. We will also use the common Fourier transform pairs associated with the sampling or comb functions in both time and frequency domains.

Let us begin with the equivalence of the representations in the time and frequency domains: $x(t) \longleftrightarrow \tilde{x}(F)$. The pair of graphs are shown in Fig. 5.3a. Note that we use a symmetric time domain function. This allows us to use a real function in the frequency domain. For nonsymmetric functions, you would have to imagine the same operations represented in the graph of complex valued functions.

The sampling of the signal in the time domain is equivalent to multiplication in time by the comb function and convolution in frequency by the equivalent comb function,

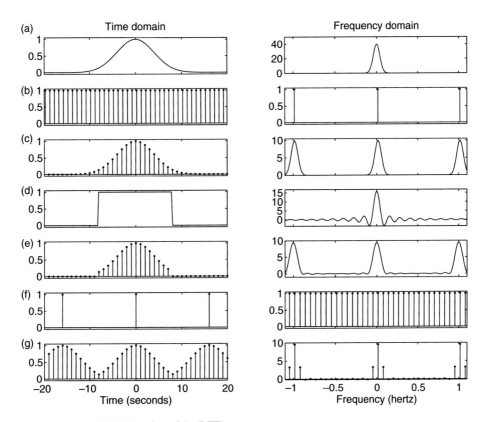

**(a)** Time domain

**Frequency domain**

**Figure 5.3.** Graphical derivation of the DFT.

Fig. 5.3b. The convolution of the comb in the frequency domain yields a periodic function. There is a replication of the original spectrum at each position of the delta functions in frequency, Fig. 5.3c. Note that if the original signal is not bandlimited, there is overlap of the replicated spectra, which gives aliasing. This corresponds to Eq. 5.23. At this point, the signal in the frequency domain is the DTFT. Symbolically, we have

$$x(t)\text{comb}\left(\frac{t}{T}\right) \longleftrightarrow \tilde{x}(F) * \text{comb}(FT),$$

where $T$ is the sampling interval in time.

To consider a DFT, we need a periodic signal. The first step is to create a truncated signal of length $NT$. This is done by multiplying in time by a rectangular pulse of length $NT$. The rectangular function and its transform are shown in Fig. 5.3d. This gives us $N$ nonzero samples in time. Multiplication by the rectangular function in time is equivalent to convolution by the sinc function in frequency. Note that the truncation of the infinite signal in time results in a distortion of the spectrum, Fig. 5.3e. This distortion takes place even if the original signal is bandlimited.[2] Symbolically, we have

$$x(t)\text{comb}\left(\frac{t}{T}\right)\text{rect}\left(\frac{t}{NT}\right) \longleftrightarrow \tilde{x}(F) * \text{comb}(FT) * \text{sinc}(FNT).$$

To produce the periodic signal in the time domain, we sample the signal in the frequency domain with interval $1/NT$. Sampling in frequency is equivalent to multiplying in the frequency by a comb function, Fig. 5.3f. This is equivalent to convolving in time with a corresponding comb function. As we noted previously, the convolution with the comb function produces a periodic signal. Thus, the DFT relationship is shown in Fig. 5.3g. We will leave it to the reader to verify that the sampling intervals and length of the rectangular truncation yield the appropriate functions. Symbolically, we have

$$x(t)\text{comb}\left(\frac{t}{T}\right)\text{rect}\left(\frac{t}{NT}\right) * \text{comb}\left(\frac{t}{NT}\right)$$

$$\longleftrightarrow [\tilde{x}(F) * \text{comb}(FT) * \text{sinc}(FNT)]\text{comb}(FNT).$$

Problems 5.7 and 5.8 give the reader a chance to gain further insight by using this methodology to compute the DFT of some common functions.

## 5.4 Two-dimensional discrete Fourier transform

The 2-D discrete Fourier transform of a discrete periodic signal is defined by

$$\tilde{s}(k,l) = \sum_{m=0}^{M-1}\sum_{n=0}^{N-1} s(m,n)e^{-j2\pi(km/M+ln/N)}, \tag{5.27}$$

$$s(m,n) = \sum_{k=0}^{M-1}\sum_{l=0}^{N-1} \tilde{s}(k,l)e^{j2\pi(km/M+ln/N)}. \tag{5.28}$$

Notice that the periods may be different in the $m$ and $n$ directions. This is useful since images are usually rectangular rather than square.

Since the discrete signal (image) is defined on the rectangle $[0, M-1] \times [0, N-1]$, the summation can be computed by first summing in the $m$ direction and then in the $n$ direction. This is the discrete equivalent of the separable kernel property of continuous two-dimensional transforms of Section 5.2. The resulting $M$ one-dimensional transforms are computed by

$$\tilde{s}(k,l) = \sum_{m=0}^{M-1}\left[\sum_{n=0}^{N-1} s(m,n)e^{-j2\pi ln/N}\right]e^{-j2\pi km/M},$$

---

[2] Note that a signal cannot be both bandlimited and time/space-limited.

where the term in brackets is a 1-D DFT,

$$\tilde{s}_m(m, l) = \sum_{n=0}^{N-1} s(m, n) e^{-j2\pi ln/N}.$$

Thus, the 2-D transform is computed by $(M + N)$ 1-D transforms.

If the function $s(m, n)$ is separable, i.e., $s(m, n) = s_x(m)s_y(n)$, then the DFT of $s(m, n)$ is the product of two 1-D DFTs,

$$\tilde{s}(k, l) = \tilde{s}_x(k)\tilde{s}_y(l).$$

This can be a significant computational saving since only two 1-D transforms are required. The functions that are most often used in separable computations are the constant functions with rectangular support and exponential functions, which include the Gaussian forms.

### 5.4.1 Common DFT pairs

The major differences in the continuous and discrete Fourier transform pairs of common functions is the periodicity requirement. Recall that the use of the DFT implies that the discrete signals are periodic with a period of the length of the transform. If the discrete-time Fourier transform, which does not assume periodic signals, is used, then delta functions are permitted as representations of spectra in the frequency domain. In this case, the transform pairs of discrete signals look very similar to those of continuous signals. For example,

$$x(n) = \cos(2\pi f_0 n) \longleftrightarrow \frac{1}{2}\delta(f - f_0) + \frac{1}{2}\delta(f + f_0) \text{ where } 0 \le f_0 \le \frac{1}{2}.$$

However, for DFT representation, the signals are finite length or are forced to have a finite period. This can be represented by truncation of an infinite sequence, $\{x_d(n)\}$, which is equivalent to multiplication by the finite window:

$$x_d(n) = x(n)\text{rect}_N(n),$$

where

$$\text{rect}_N(n) = \begin{cases} 1 & \text{if } 0 \le n \le N - 1, \\ 0 & \text{else,} \end{cases}$$

and a periodic extension is created;

$$x_p(n) = x_d(n - kN) \quad \text{if } kN \le n < (k + 1)N.$$

If the periodically extended function is the same as the original function, then the delta function characteristic of the transform of the original is preserved, i.e., if $x(n) = x_p(n)$.

It is noted that for this case, the frequency of the original periodic function, $x(n)$, can be represented exactly by the discrete frequencies of the DFT. Consider the sinusoidal signal, $x(n) = \cos(2\pi \frac{k_0}{N} n)$, where $k_0$ is an integer. This function has a period of $N$. An $N$-point DFT has frequencies $\{\frac{k}{N}\}$ for $0 \le k \le N - 1$. Clearly, $\frac{k_0}{N}$ is among those represented. Problems 5.5 and 5.6 illustrate this property.

For our work, let us assume that the signal, $x(n) = x_p(n)$, has an initial region of support of $N$ samples and is periodically extended so that a DFT can be computed. For two-dimensional functions, the periods in the two directions are $M$ and $N$.

## 5.5      Discrete Fourier transform convolution using matrices

It was shown in Chapter 2 how matrix algebra can be applied to represent various operations in the spatial domain. Let us now consider how it can be used to represent operations in the frequency domain. The basis of using matrices in the discrete frequency domain is knowledge of the properties of the DFT. In particular, the convolution with which we are concerned is circular or periodic convolution. This was described in Section 2.7.

We know that since convolution in time is equivalent to multiplication in frequency for all domains of the Fourier transforms, discrete circular convolution can be computed by the DFT. If $h(n)$ and $x(n)$ are discrete signals of length $N$, and represent one period of periodic signals, then the circular convolution of $h(n)$ and $x(n)$ is computed in the time (or space) domain as

$$y(n) = \sum_{k=0}^{N-1} h(n - k)x(k), \tag{5.29}$$

where all indices are computed using mod $N$ arithmetic. In the frequency domain, the computation is done for each index of the DFT;

$$\tilde{y}(k) = \tilde{h}(k)\tilde{x}(k) \quad \text{for} \quad 0 \le k \le N - 1.$$

Consider the DFT definition of Eq. (5.17) and let us determine how to represent this using matrices. Let one period of the signal, $x(n)$, be denoted by the $N$ vector, $\mathbf{x} = [x(0), x(1), \ldots, x(N - 1)]$. A similar notation is used for the convolution kernel, $h(n)$, $\mathbf{h} = [h(0), h(1), \ldots, h(N - 1)]$. Finally, let $\mathbf{W}$ be an $N \times N$ matrix with the DFT coefficients $w_N = \exp(-j2\pi/N)$,

$$\mathbf{W} = \begin{bmatrix} w_N^0 & w_N^0 & w_N^0 & \cdots & w_N^0 \\ w_N^0 & w_N^1 & w_N^2 & \cdots & w_N^{N-1} \\ w_N^0 & w_N^2 & w_N^4 & \cdots & w_N^{2N-2} \\ \vdots & \vdots & \vdots & \vdots & \vdots \\ w_N^0 & w_N^{N-1} & w_N^{N-2} & \cdots & w_N^1 \end{bmatrix}, \tag{5.30}$$

where the term $w_N^k$ is $w_N$ raised to the $k$th power. We can write the matrix in the form $\mathbf{W} = [w_N^{mn}]_{mn}$, where the term in brackets indicates the form of the element in the $m$th row and $n$th column. The inverse of $\mathbf{W}$ is the inverse DFT and is given by $\mathbf{W}^{-1} = \frac{1}{N}[w_N^{-mn}]_{mn}$. See Appendix B for details.

The discrete Fourier transform of the signal vector can be written:

$$\tilde{\mathbf{x}}_{N \times 1} = \mathbf{W}_{N \times N} \mathbf{x}_{N \times 1}.$$

The periodic convolution of the discrete periodic functions $x(n)$ and $h(n)$ can be written in the Fourier domain as

$$\tilde{\mathbf{y}} = \mathbf{Wy} = \mathbf{WH}_c\mathbf{x} = \mathbf{WH}_c\mathbf{W}^{-1}\mathbf{Wx},$$

where $\mathbf{H}_c$ is the circulant matrix discussed in Section 2.7. The terms $\mathbf{Wy}$ and $\mathbf{Wx}$ are recognized as the DFTs of the output and input respectively. The term $\mathbf{WH}_c\mathbf{W}^{-1} = \Lambda_H$ is a diagonal matrix that contains the terms of the DFT of $h(n)$ on the diagonal. The proof of this is shown in Appendix B. Thus, the term $\mathbf{WH}_c\mathbf{W}^{-1}\mathbf{Wx}$ is the element-by-element multiplication of the DFTs of the input signal and impulse response.

There are other special properties to note about the diagonalization of $\mathbf{H}_c$:

- Any circulant matrix is diagonalized by the discrete Fourier transform. This is seen by noting that it is only the circularity of the matrix that is required for diagonalization.
- The DFT matrix of Eq. (5.30) can be modified to yield a unitary transform. A unitary transform, $\mathbf{U}$ has the property that $\mathbf{U}^{-1} = \mathbf{U}^*$, where the superscript * indicates the conjugate transpose. The conjugate is needed for matrices defined in a complex space. This is important since a derived property of unitary matrices is that a unitary transform does not change the norm of the vector, i.e., $||\mathbf{Ux}|| = ||\mathbf{x}||$. This is basically Parseval's theorem for DFTs. The required modification is to distribute the constant $\frac{1}{N}$ between the forward and inverse transform. The result is that $\mathbf{W}_u = \frac{1}{\sqrt{N}}\mathbf{W}$ is a unitary transform. While the unitary form of the DFT matrix is mathematically appealing, computationally, we always use the form of Eq. (5.30).
- The elements of the DFT vector $\mathbf{Wh}$ are the eigenvalues of $\mathbf{H}_c$ corresponding to the eigenvectors that are the Fourier basis functions. This means that all circular matrices of a given size have the same eigenvectors.
- The diagonalization method can be extended to noncirculant matrices by using a circulant approximation to Toeplitz forms.

The two-dimensional discrete Fourier transform matrix is obtained by using the one-dimensional matrix. The two-dimensional matrix form for image processing is obtained by using the stacked notation, see Chapter 2, Eq. (2.26). This results in a block form for the convolution matrices and a block-circulant form for circular convolution. The block circulant is diagonalized by the 2-D DFT.

The 2-D discrete Fourier transform matrix that corresponds to an $N \times N$ image, $\mathbf{W_2}$, is defined by

$$\mathbf{W}_{2N^2 \times N^2} = \mathbf{W}_{N \times N} \otimes \mathbf{W}_{N \times N},$$

where the symbol $\otimes$ represents the Kronecker product (outer product). This product is defined in Appendix B. The 2-D DFT of $\mathbf{x}$ can be written

$$\tilde{\mathbf{x}}_{N^2 \times 1} = \mathbf{W}_{2N^2 \times N^2} \mathbf{x}_{N^2 \times 1},$$

where the $N \times N$ image is represented in stacked notation by the $N^2 \times 1$ vector $\mathbf{x}$. Two-dimensional convolution can be written in the Fourier domain as

$$\tilde{\mathbf{y}} = \mathbf{W_2 y} = \mathbf{W_2 H_c x} = \mathbf{W_2 H_c W_2}^{-1} \mathbf{W_2 x},$$

where the subscript c emphasizes the block circular extension of the point spread function (PSF) $\mathbf{H}$. As in the one-dimensional case, the terms $\mathbf{W_2 y}$ and $\mathbf{W_2 x}$ represent the DFTs of the output and input respectively. Likewise, it can be shown that $\mathbf{H_c}$ can be diagonalized by the operation

$$\mathbf{W_2 H_c W_2}^{-1} = \mathbf{\Lambda_H},$$

where the elements on the diagonal of $\mathbf{\Lambda_H}$ correspond to the 2-D DFT of the base matrix (in the upper left corner) of the block circulant matrix of $\mathbf{H_c}$. Thus, the term $\mathbf{W_2 H_c W_2}^{-1} \mathbf{W_2 f}$ is the element-by-element multiplication of the DFTs of the input signal and PSF.

It is important to note that matrix representation is a powerful tool for deriving results and gaining insight into image processing problems. However, it is not used for actual computation. The matrices are too large for all but the largest supercomputers. Two-dimensional DFTs are computed using efficient algorithms that produce $N \times N$ matrices from $N \times N$ matrices. Multiplications are carried out term-by-term on these matrices.

## 5.6     Computation of 2-D DFT and the FFT

As discussed in Section 5.4, the computation of the 2-D DFT of an $M \times N$ image is accomplished by computing $(M + N)$ 1-D transforms. Since DFTs of signals that are defined on a rectangular grid are computed by using 1-D DFTs, it is necessary to consider fast algorithms for 1-D computation. The fast Fourier transform (FFT) is used to compute all 1-D DFTs. The most commonly used version of the FFT is based on a decomposition of the computation into a series of shorter DFTs. There are two decompositions used for the FFT, denoted decimation in time or decimation in frequency. The largest time savings are obtained when the length of the signal is a power of 2. In this case, the computation time is proportional to $N \log_2 N$, where $N$ is the length of the signal. Direct computation is proportional to $N^2$. This computation saving is particularly important when processing 2-D signals.

A detailed discussion of the FFT computation is found in many digital signal processing texts, e.g., [38, 200, 218]. For the purposes of this text, it is sufficient to know the computational saving of $N \log_2 N$ versus $N^2$ operations.

---

**Example 5.1.** Assume that an $N = 800$ sample signal is to be convolved with an $L = 100$ sample impulse response. Let us use the number of multiplications as the indicator for the time of the convolution. Direct convolution requires $L$ multiplications per sample of output for $N + L - 1$ samples or $L(N + L - 1) = 89\,900$ operations. The FFT method requires padding both signals to the power of two such that $M = 2^k \geq N + L - 1$, computing the FFT of the padded signals, multiplying the FFTs and computing the inverse FFT of the result. This gives

- $2(M \log_2 M)$ operations for the forward transforms,
- $M$ operations for the multiplication of the FFTs,
- $(M \log_2 M)$ operations for the inverse transform,
- $3(M \log_2 M) + M$ total operations.

For the example, $M = 1024$ and $k = 10$, so this yields $31\,744$ operations. The saving, although smaller, holds even if $N = 900$ and $L = 126$, which gives $M = 2048$ and $69\,632$ operations.

See Problem 5.14 for an example in two dimensions.

---

## 5.7 Interpretation and display of Fourier transforms

The computation of Fourier transforms is straightforward mathematics. Given a functional form of the continuous 2-D function, its transform is given by Eq. (5.5). While the actual mathematical manipulation of the equation can be nontrivial, it is conceptually straightforward. In practice, it is rare that a continuous transform is computed. More often, Fourier analysis is done on the sampled image. This requires a discrete Fourier transform, which is computed using a digital computer. The two major aspects of Fourier analysis are computation and interpretation. This chapter will deal with the interpretation and leave the computational details to other texts [38, 200, 218].

To interpret the result of the Fourier transform of 2-D signals associated with imaging, it is necessary to understand the basic one- and two-dimensional continuous transform relationships. For this, we will rely heavily on the knowledge of the common transform pairs presented in Tables 5.2 and 5.4. There is also a need to understand the differences between the continuous and discrete transforms.

### One-dimensional transforms

The first thing to note about analyzing Fourier transforms is that they are actually complex valued functions. A single graph or plot is not sufficient to represent the values. For one-dimensional signals, it is easy to plot the magnitude and phase of the transform. Consider

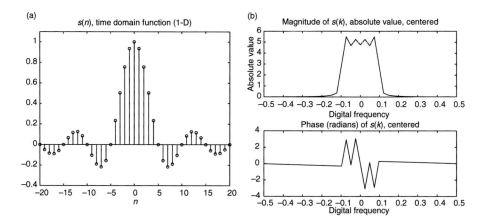

**Figure 5.4.** (a) Discrete sinc function; (b) DFT of discrete sinc, magnitude and phase.

the one-dimensional signal defined by

$$s(n) = \begin{cases} \text{sinc}(n/5) & \text{if } -20 \le n \le 20 \\ 0 & \text{else} \end{cases}, \qquad (5.31)$$

and plotted in Fig. 5.4a. The magnitude and phase of the DFT of the periodic extension of this signal is shown in Fig. 5.4b. Note that since the time domain signal is symmetric, its DFT is real. That means that the phase is either zero or $\pm\pi$. The MATLAB computation yields phase values that are consistent with either $+\pi$ or $-\pi$. The difference is $2\pi$ and is mathematically equivalent for most numerical purposes.[3]

It is necessary to call the reader's attention to the actual computation of the DFT as given in Eq. (5.17). The function given in Eq. (5.31) is obviously symmetric. However, the usual definition of the DFT uses indices that start at $n = 0$. It was noted that a DFT assumes that the signal is periodic. This implies that the computation is done with a signal that can be represented by a single period starting at $n = 0$ as shown in Fig. 5.5.

Recalling the relationship between the DTFT and the DFT, the DFT is the DTFT sampled at the frequencies $\{\frac{k}{N}\}_{k=0}^{N-1}$. It is often of interest to consider the DTFT and examine the interpolation of frequencies between the samples. The DTFT can be estimated by padding the $N$-point signal with additional zeros and computing a longer DFT. The example shown in Fig. 5.6 extends a 41 sample signal to 241 samples with zero-padding. The ripples in the magnitude plot reflect the sinc function associated with the rectangular window of 41 samples. The phase plot has been modified to reflect consistent values of $-\pi$ when the real-valued function is negative.

Note that there is significant detail that is of interest in the region of small magnitude. This can be better observed by plotting the magnitude in decibels instead of absolute

---

[3] An example when the difference is important is a case where the continuity of phase is used. MATLAB provides a function, unwrap(), that attempts to compute phase values that represent a continuous function.

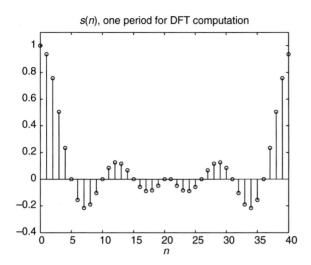

*s(n)*, one period for DFT computation

**Figure 5.5.** Discrete sinc function, period starting at $n = 0$.

value. This has always been the preferred plotting format for 1-D digital signal processing work in filter design and signal analysis. The plot of the spectrum of Fig. 5.6a in decibels is shown in Fig. 5.6b. Note that the choice of phase scaling is independent of the choice for magnitude scaling.

The padding with zeros must be done in such a way as to preserve any symmetries that are important. We saw that the computation is done on a single period starting at $n = 0$. To preserve the symmetry, the padding must effectively add an equal number of zeros on either side of the signal in Fig. 5.4 or in the middle of the signal shown in Fig. 5.5. This type of padding was used to produce Fig. 5.6.[4] If we add 200 zeros to only one side of the signal of Fig. 5.5, the effect on the time-domain signal is shown in Fig. 5.7. Not only has the symmetry been lost, but the functional character has been drastically changed. The result in the frequency domain, shown in Fig. 5.18, demonstrates how completely different is the spectrum of the new function. The phase characteristics of this new function are extremely difficult to determine because of the $2\pi$ wrap around.

### Two-dimensional transforms

As an example of the display of a 2-D transform, let us first consider the simple 2-D sinc function used in Chapter 3. The function is defined on a grid of $41 \times 41$ samples. The $41 \times 41$ sample DFT is computed; the magnitude and phase are shown in Figs. 5.9 and 5.10, respectively. Again the advantage of plotting the magnitude in decibels is shown in Fig. 5.11. The isometric style plots work well with this type of data, owing to the smooth contours of the function. The phase characteristics are similar to those of the 1-D example. The use of the decibel scale is even more apparent when the grayscale display is used.

---

[4] Note that we have used continuous plotting to show the discrete signals. The discrete stems would clutter the display on a figure of this size.

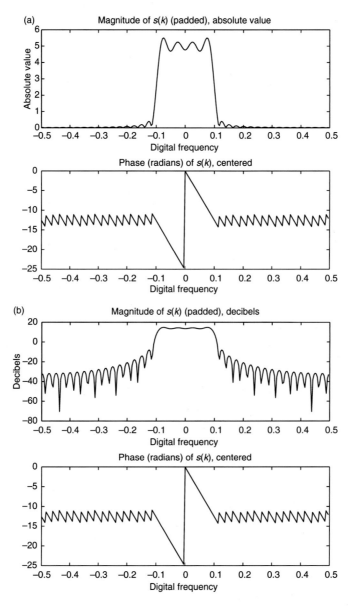

**Figure 5.6.** (a) Discrete Fourier transform of discrete sinc of Fig. 5.5 padded in the middle (magnitude plotted in absolute value and phase), (b) DFT of discrete sinc of Fig. 5.5 padded in the middle (magnitude plotted in dB and phase).

The magnitudes in absolute value and decibels are shown in Figs. 5.12a and 5.12b, respectively. The detail in the central region and in the low magnitude regions is readily apparent in the decibel scale plot of Fig. 5.12b. The pattern for the phase can be seen in Fig. 5.10. It is impossible is determine the linear nature of the phase from the grayscale plot of Fig. 5.13. It may also be of interest to observe the interpolated values of the DFT

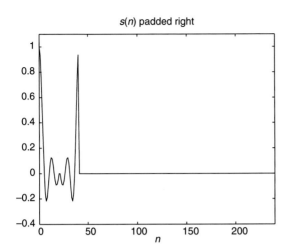

**Figure 5.7.** Discrete sinc function padded on right side.

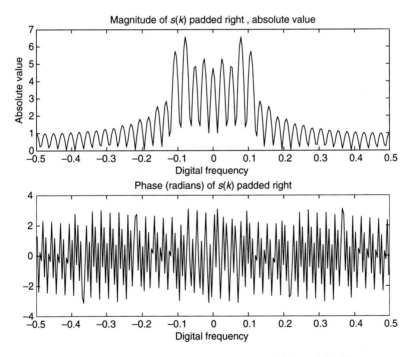

**Figure 5.8.** Discrete Fourier transform of discrete sinc padded on right side.

by using the zero-padding method demonstrated in 1-D. The higher resolution Fig. 5.12c shows the rippling that is caused by the truncation of the function to the finite grid.

Let us now consider the DFT of a monochrome image. The image used in Chapter 3 is particularly good since it has several regions that contain periodic structures of varying frequency and orientation. Before displaying the magnitude and phase of the DFT, a few

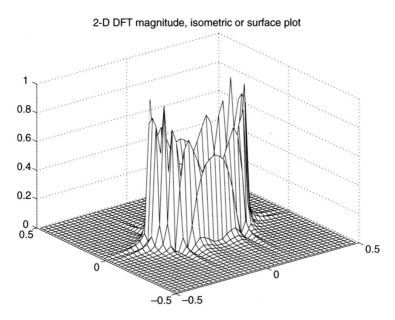

**Figure 5.9.** DFT of 2-D sinc, magnitude (absolute value).

remarks are appropriate. The first thing to consider is the range of values to be displayed. An image is a nonnegative function and, thus, will have a large positive DC term. The DC term is the average value or sum, depending on whether the constant $\frac{1}{N}$ term is placed in the forward or inverse transform in the definition of the DFT. Our definitions place it in the inverse transform, as Eq. (5.17). Because of the nonnegative characteristic, the DC and low-frequency terms of the DFT will usually overwhelm higher frequency terms. For the image in Fig. 3.5, the magnitudes of the first eight terms of the transform along either axis vary by a factor of 100:1. The higher frequencies produce even larger ratios. Even deleting the DC term from the display range calculation, the display of absolute values is totally dominated by a few low frequency terms, as shown in Fig. 5.14a. The low frequency terms represent the overall shading of the image. The light and dark regions determine the dynamic range of the image. Because of this characteristic of pictorial images to have the largest percentage of power in the lowest frequency terms, it is very important to display the DFT using decibel scaling. This is shown in Fig. 5.14b.

When displaying power spectra, we are usually interested in the range of values and not their specific values. For this reason, we will normalize the power spectrum by dividing by its maximum value before computing the logarithm. This will yield a decibel plot that always has 0 dB as the highest value. By using this normalization, we are better able to see the relative distribution of power in the lower and higher frequencies when comparing the spectral characteristics of various images.

A second important characteristic is the DFT phase of the image. The phase is extremely important information. It is the portion of the spectrum that is sensitive to the relative position of objects in the image. However, the phase information of an

2-D DFT phase, isometric or surface plot

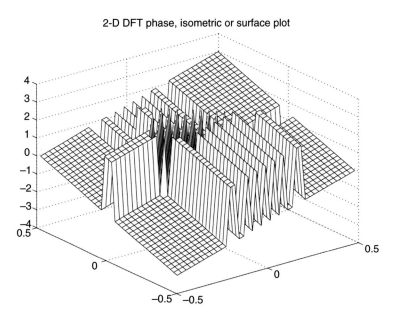

**Figure 5.10.** Discrete Fourier transform of 2-D sinc, phase (radians).

2-D DFT magnitude (dB), isometric or surface plot

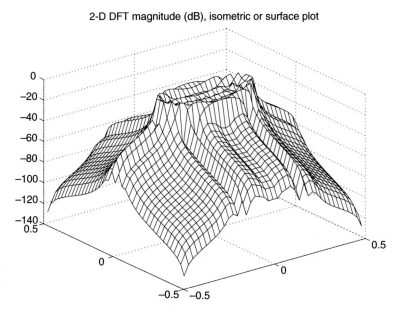

**Figure 5.11.** Discrete Fourier transform of 2-D sinc, magnitude (decibels).

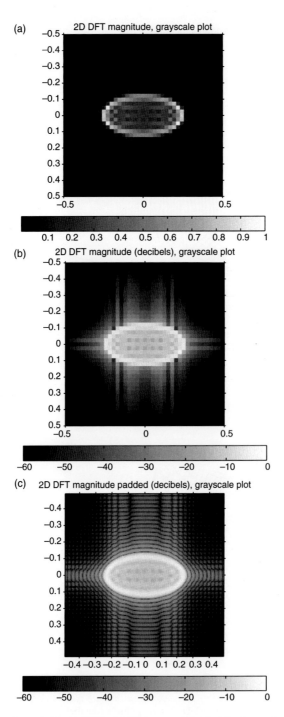

**Figure 5.12.** (a) DFT of 2-D sinc, magnitude (absolute value); (b) DFT of sinc, magnitude (decibels); (c) DFT of sinc padded; magnitude (decibels).

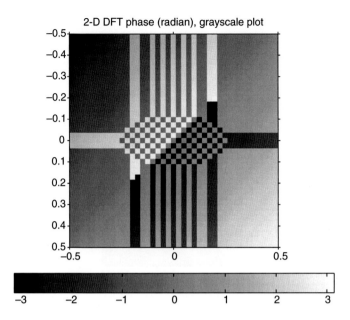

**Figure 5.13.** Discrete Fourier transform of 2-D sinc, phase (radians).

image is almost impossible for the user to interpret. Furthermore, the phase unwrapping algorithms, mentioned in Section 5.7, that are used to detect discontinuities at the $\pm\pi$ boundaries do not work well in two dimensions. This differs considerably from the phase of one-dimensional functions, in particular, point spread functions, which are readily interpreted. However, phase unwrapping algorithms can still be a problem even for well behaved functions in two dimensions. The phase of the image in Fig. 3.5 is shown in Fig. 5.15.

To show the importance of phase, consider the results of maintaining the magnitude of the transform (Fig. 5.14) but setting the phase equal to a constant value. Zero is very convenient. This image is shown in Fig. 5.16a and bears little resemblance to the original. On the other hand, maintaining the phase and setting the magnitude equal to a constant yields the image shown in Fig. 5.16b, which is obviously related to the original. An even better image will result if a magnitude function is used that emphasizes low frequencies, as is the case in most pictorial imagery.

The magnitude information of the DFT can be used to determine the significance of specific frequencies in an image. The magnitude spectrum of Fig. 5.14b indicates the presence of several groups of frequencies. Looking at the original image of Fig. 3.5, it is obvious that there are periodic patterns that should be identifiable in the frequency domain. However, since the image does not consist of pure sinusoids, we should not expect to see pure delta functions at certain frequencies. Indeed the periodic patterns are limited in spatial extent and even change periodicity.

Consider the region of striped cloth as it wraps around the woman's head or body. The effect is similar to a chirp signal where the frequency changes with time. The result is

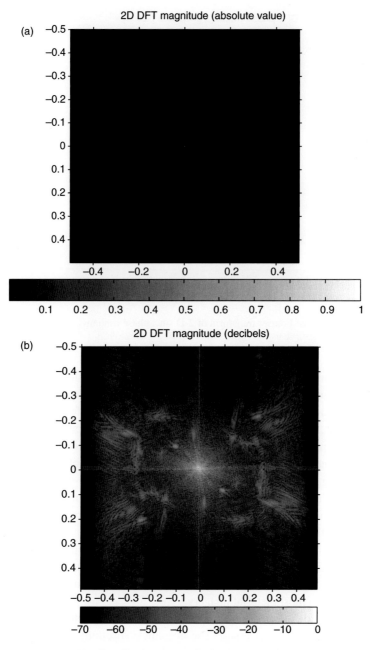

**Figure 5.14.** (a) Discrete Fourier transform of the "bars" image, Fig. 3.5, magnitude (absolute value); (b) DFT of the "bars" image, magnitude (decibels).

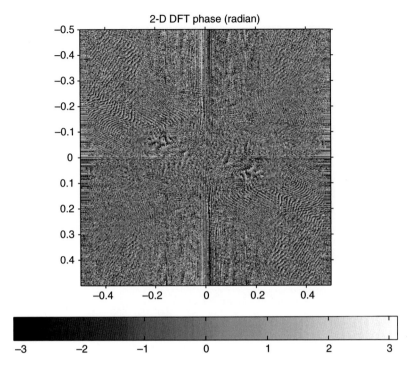

**Figure 5.15.** Discrete Fourier transform of image, phase.

a blurring or smearing of the delta function spike. To demonstrate this effect, consider a small region near the woman's right knee, shown in Fig. 5.17a. The magnitude of the discrete Fourier transform is shown in Fig. 5.17b. The dominant frequency can be estimated by counting cycles of the periodic pattern. From 320 to 350 in the $y$ direction, there are about 5 cycles. From 290 to 310 in the $x$ direction, there are about 6 cycles. Note also that the coordinate axes are reversed in the $y$ direction from the usual increasing from bottom to top. This is typical of the implied coordinates of images where the (0,0) point is at the top left, as opposed to the bottom left for functions. Thus, there should be a peak at about $(6/20, -5/30) = (0.30, -0.17)$ in the frequency domain. Although the peak is not large, it is distinct. The blurring of the peak is clearly obvious.

A secondary characteristic of the magnitude of discrete Fourier transform of pictorial imagery is the strong lines in the horizontal and vertical directions through the origin. The orientation of such lines indicates strong horizontal and vertical edges in the image. There are a few such edges, but these would not be strong enough to produce such lines in the spectrum. The horizontal and vertical spectral lines are produced by the "edge" created by forcing periodicity on the image when the DFT is computed. One way to observe these edges is to shift the original image, as shown in Fig. 5.18. This figure represents a periodic shift in the horizonal and vertical directions of half a period, i.e., half the size of the image. If the artifacts caused by such edge discontinuities interfere with analysis of the spectrum, they can be reduced by windowing, that is, multiplying the image by a window function that goes to zero at the edges of the region of

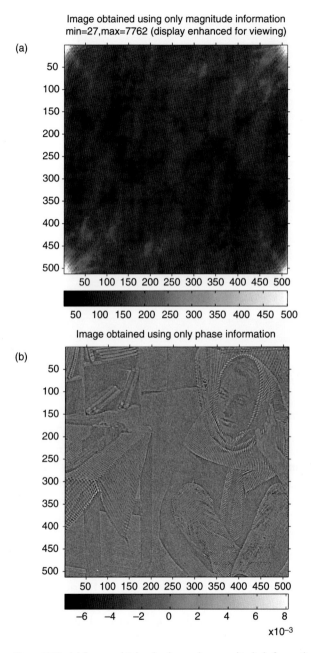

**Figure 5.16.** (a) Image obtained using only magnitude information of Fig. 5.14; (b) image obtained using only phase information of Fig. 5.15.

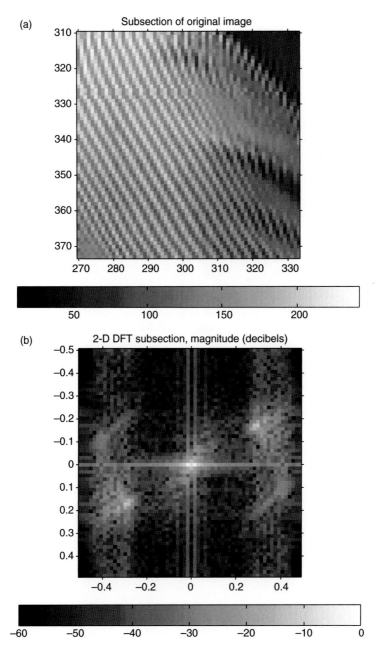

**Figure 5.17.** (a) Subsection of original image (around right knee); (b) DFT of subimage, magnitude (dB).

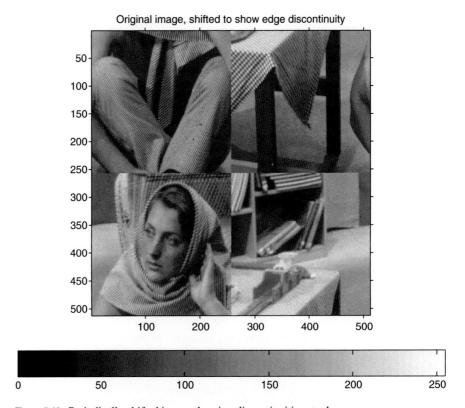

Original image, shifted to show edge discontinuity

**Figure 5.18.** Periodically shifted image showing discontinuities at edges.

support. Alternatively, the image boundaries can be extrapolated using mirror symmetric extrapolation.

The treatment of edges and endpoints is important when modeling continuous systems with computers. The use of discrete signals requires the use of the DFT for efficient computation. As noted previously, the use of the DFT implies the periodicity of the discrete signals. A more detailed discussion and references to methods of handling boundary conditions is given in [225].

## 5.8    Problems

**5.1**   (Review 1-D transforms.) Without using any integrals, determine the Fourier transforms of the following functions. The transform of a periodic function will be defined by Dirac delta functions.

(a) $s_1(t) = 2 + 4\cos(300t)$.

(b) $s_2(t) = 2\cos(3.4t) + 4\sin(5.1t)$.

(c) $s_3(t) = 5.2\cos(2\pi 400t) - 2.6\cos(2\pi 1600t)$.

(d) $s_4(t) = 5.2\cos(2\pi 400t) - 5.2\sin(2\pi 400t)$.

(e) $s_5(t) = 10\cos(2\pi 400t) - 6\cos(2\pi 1200t + \pi/6) + 3\cos(2\pi 2000t - 3\pi/4)$.

**5.2** (Review 1-D transforms.) Plot the magnitude and phase spectra for the signals in the preceding problem.

**5.3** Show that the (1-D) Fourier transform of a Gaussian is a Gaussian. If you are familiar with characteristic functions, this is very easy. Otherwise, this can be shown by completing the square of the terms in the exponentials.

**5.4** Show that the (1-D) convolution of a Gaussian with a Gaussian is a Gaussian. This can be solved easily with the result from the previous problem.

**5.5** Compute the $M$ sample discrete Fourier transform of

$$f(m) = \cos[2\pi(f_x m)] \text{ for } 0 \le m \le M - 1,$$

where $M = 128$, $f_x = 1/16$. This computation should be done by hand. The solution will reduce to a very simple form. You may use MATLAB to check your results.

**5.6** Repeat Problem 5.5 with $M = 128$, $f_x = 1/12$. Note that the solution does not reduce to the same simple form as Problem 5.5. Using the graphical derivation of the DFT, explain the differences in the qualitative forms of the two cases.

**5.7** Using the graphical derivation of the DFT in Fig. 5.3, sketch the graphs for a time-domain signal defined by $s(t) = \cos(2\pi t/5)$ and sampling rate of $T = 1$. Choose other frequencies and sampling rates to see the effects of aliasing.

**5.8** Repeat Problem 5.7 with $s(t) = \text{sinc}(t/4)$ and $T = 1$. Choose other scaling factors and sampling rates to see the effects of aliasing. This approach can be used to explain the result of the sinc operation in Figs. 5.4 and 5.5.

**5.9** Using the definitions of the Fourier transform in Eqs. (5.5) and (5.6), derive the common 2-D transform pair identity

$$\cos[2\pi(xu_0 + yv_0)] \longleftrightarrow \frac{1}{2}\delta(F_x - u_0, F_y - v_0) + \frac{1}{2}\delta(F_x + u_0, F_y + v_0).$$

**5.10** Determine the 2-D Fourier transforms of the following signals. The units of $x$ and $y$ are in mm.

(a) $s_1(x, y) = 2 + 4\cos(20x)$.
(b) $s_2(x, y) = 2\cos(2\pi 20x) + 4\sin(2\pi 20y)$.
(c) $s_3(x, y) = 4\cos(2\pi 40x)\cos(2\pi 20y)$.
(d) $s_4(x, y) = 4\cos[2\pi(40x + 20y)]$.
(e) $s_5(x, y) = 10\cos(2\pi 40x) - 6\cos[2\pi(120x + 40y) + \pi/6]$
$\qquad\qquad + 3\cos[2\pi(200x - 120y) - 3\pi/4]$.

**5.11** Show that if $f(x, y)$ is circularly symmetric, i.e., $f(x, y) = f(\sqrt{x^2 + y^2})$, then its Fourier transform is also circularly symmetric.

**5.12** Compute the $M \times N$ discrete Fourier transform of

$$f(m, n) = \cos[2\pi(f_x m + f_y y)] \text{ for } 0 \le m \le M - 1 \text{ and } 0 \le n \le N - 1,$$

where $M = 128$, $N = 256$, $f_x = 1/8$ and $f_y = 3/32$. This computation should be done by hand. You may use MATLAB to check your results.

**5.13**   How does the result of Problem 5.12 change quantitatively and qualitatively if $M$ and $N$ remain the same and $f_x = 1/7$ and $f_y = 3/31$?

**5.14**   Compute the direct computational cost and FFT computational cost for a $480 \times 480$ image convolved with a $32 \times 32$ kernel. Give the results in terms of the number of both multiplications and additions.

**5.15**   Compute the DFT of the following 2-D functions defined on the square domain $0 \le m \le 127$ and $0 \le n \le 127$, using a $128 \times 128$ DFT. Repeat the computations using zero padding to compute $512 \times 512$ DFTs. Display the magnitude spectra in dB. Scale the frequency axes between $[-0.5, 0.5]$ as shown in the figures in this chapter. Describe the qualitative differences produced by the zero padding for each function.

(a) $s_1(m, n) = \begin{cases} 1 & \text{if } 0 \le m \le 127 \text{ and } 0 \le n \le 127 \\ 0 & \text{else.} \end{cases}$

(b) $s_2(m, n) = \begin{cases} 1 & \text{if } 0 \le m \le 31 \text{ and } 0 \le n \le 127 \\ 0 & \text{else.} \end{cases}$

(c) $s_3(m, n) = \begin{cases} 1 & \text{if } 0 \le m \le 31 \text{ and } 0 \le n \le 31 \\ 0 & \text{else.} \end{cases}$

(d) $s_4(m, n) = \begin{cases} \cos[2\pi(m/8 + n/16)] & \text{if } 0 \le m \le 63 \text{ and } 0 \le n \le 63 \\ 0 & \text{else.} \end{cases}$

(e) $s_5(m, n) = \begin{cases} \sin[2\pi(m/8 + n/16)] & \text{if } 0 \le m \le 63 \text{ and } 0 \le n \le 63 \\ 0 & \text{else.} \end{cases}$

(f) $s_6(m, n) = \begin{cases} \cos[2\pi(m/8 + n/16)][1 - \cos[(2\pi m/64)][1 - \cos[(2\pi n/64)] \\ \quad \text{if } 0 \le m \le 63 \text{ and } 0 \le n \le 63 \\ 0 \qquad\qquad\qquad\qquad\qquad\qquad \text{else.} \end{cases}$

**5.16**   A composite image $s(x, y)$ is given in file patches_cosines_digital.tif in www.cambridge.org/9780521868532. It is made up of five sections. The sections include the following signals:

(a) Several pure sinusoids at various spatial frequencies.
(b) A pure sinusoid that is multiplied by a Hanning (raised cosine) window on that section, i.e., the function goes to zero at the boundaries of the section.
(c) A chirped sinusoid (or FM signal).

For this image,

(a) Display the spatial domain image, $s(x, y)$.
(b) Display the magnitude of the Fourier transform of $s(x, y)$.
(c) Identify the structures in the spectrum with the various portions of the spatial domain image.

**5.17**   Using your image, *gray-one*, select a portion of the image that has a periodic structure, or almost periodic structure. Crop this portion of the image, compute and display the spectrum. Identify the spatial frequency in the spatial domain and spectral images.

**5.18**  Using your image, *gray-one*, select a square section of the image. For this exercise, use an image with the same number of rows as columns for ease of computation of the 2-D DFT.

(a) Compute and display the magnitude spectrum (dB) of your image using a rectangular window, i.e., compute the periodogram directly.
(b) Compute and display the magnitude spectrum (dB) of your image using a Hamming window.
(c) Comment on the differences of the spectra of (a) and (b).

**5.19**  Using your image, *gray-one*, investigate the importance of the magnitude and phase of the DFT. Compute the 2-D DFT of your image.

(a) Compute and display the image obtained by holding the magnitude of the DFT fixed, while setting the phase equal to zero.
(b) Compute and display the image obtained by holding the phase of the DFT fixed, while setting the magnitude equal to a constant. The constant will vary according to your particular image, but the value should keep the total power about the same as the original.
(c) Comment on the results of (a) and (b).

# 6 Spatial sampling

To process images on computers, the images must be sampled to create digital images. This represents a transformation from the analog domain to the discrete domain. This chapter will concentrate on the very basic step of sampling an image in preparation for processing. It will be shown that this step is crucial, in that sampling imposes strict limits on the processing that can be done and the fidelity of any reconstructions.

Images for most consumer and commercial uses are the color images that we see every day. These images are transformations of continuously varying spectral, temporal and spatial distributions. In this chapter, we will address the problems of spatial sampling. Thus, it is sufficient to use monochrome images to demonstrate the principles. In Chapter 9, we will discuss sampling in the spectral dimension. The principles for color spectral sampling are an extension of those that we will cover in this chapter.

All images exist in time and change with time. We are all familiar with the stroboscopic effects that we see in the movies and television that make car wheels and airplane propellers appear to move backwards. The same sampling principles can be used to explain these phenomena as will be used to explain the spatial sampling that is presented here. The description of object motion in time and its effect on images is another rich topic that will be left for other texts, e.g., [32, 83, 262, 302].

When we think of sampling an image, it is usual to think of a transformation from the analog domain to the discrete domain. The visual effect of the image is somewhat the same in both domains, that is, the observer can sense the same objects in the analog and digital versions of the image. We will refer to this type of transformation as direct sampling. Examples of direct sampling include:

1. Television,[1]
2. Still video and camcorders with CCD arrays,
3. Film and paper scanners,
4. Medical (digital X-ray, fluoroscopy, angiography),
5. Remote sensing, (satellite multiband, FLIR),
6. Range imagery (robotics).

---

[1] Vidicon cameras are hybrid devices, producing analog signals in the horizontal direction, but producing sampled signals in the vertical. Many devices sample the analog TV signal to create a completely digital image. Nowadays, direct digital television uses solid-state imaging sensors instead of the vidicon tube.

It is worth noting some examples of indirect sampling. Indirect sampling occurs when the samples that are recorded do not have any visual similarity to the image that is ultimately produced. A common example is computer tomography. The samples are taken of a signal that is the result of X-rays passing through an object. The samples are taken at many different angles around the object. These samples are used as input to a mathematical algorithm that produces the images of a slice through the object that is visually analyzed by the user. While we will not discuss these imaging modalities in this text, the reader should be aware of the common applications of indirect sampling (computed images):

1. X-ray computer tomography (CT),
2. Magnetic resonance imaging (MRI),
3. Positron emission tomography (PET),
4. Synthetic aperture radar (SAR),
5. Radio astronomy,
6. Seismic imaging,
7. Electron microscopy.

Further discussion of these imaging modalities is found in [33, 42, 63, 134, 173, 227, 248, 249].

## 6.1     Ideal sampling

In most cases, the multidimensional process can be represented as a straightforward extension of one-dimensional processes. Thus, it is reasonable to discuss the one-dimensional operations that are prerequisite to the topic and will form the basis of the multidimensional processes.

### 6.1.1     Ideal sampling, 1-D

The mathematical notation for sampling was introduced in Section 2.4. The basic sampling operation is multiplication of an analog signal by the comb function, which was defined as

$$\text{comb}(t) = \sum_{n=-\infty}^{\infty} \delta(t - n). \tag{6.1}$$

In Chapter 5, the Fourier transform of the comb function was given. The fact that the Fourier transform of a comb is another comb plays a central role in the understanding of sampling effects in the time, spatial and frequency domains. This relationship was used to illustrate the derivation of the DFT in Section 5.3.

We follow the same steps as in the graphical derivation of the DFT to illustrate the effects of proper sampling and undersampling. Let us review this graphically by considering the frequency domain representation of sampled signals such as those in

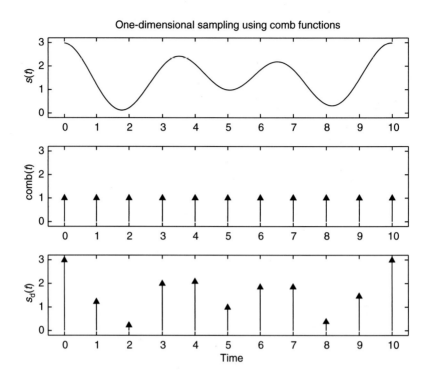

**Figure 6.1.** One-dimensional sampling.

Fig. 6.1. In Chapter 5, we saw that the Fourier transform of comb($t$) is $2\pi$comb($\omega$).[2]
The frequency domain representation of the 1-D sampling process is shown in Fig. 6.2.
The spectra in this figure correspond conceptually to the time domain signals in Fig. 6.1.
The representations in these two figures give the reader a graphical image of the process
of sampling in both domains. The actual spectra of the time domain signals in Fig. 6.1
would be complex and different from those in Fig. 6.2. The most important feature of the
spectrum of the sampled signals is the replication of the analog spectrum. Mathematically,
if the spectrum of $s(t)$ is denoted $S(\omega)$, then the spectrum of the sampled signal, $s_d(t)$,
is given by

$$\tilde{s}_d(\omega) = \sum_{k=-\infty}^{\infty} \tilde{s}(\omega - k\omega_0), \quad \text{where } \omega_0 = 2\pi F_s,$$

where $F_s$ is the sampling rate. See Appendix A for details. Note that reconstruction is
possible only if there is no overlap of the replicated spectra.[3] This corresponds to having

---

[2] The proof of this is also available in undergraduate signals and systems texts, e.g., [201], and in
Appendix A.

[3] Note that in special circumstances the signal may be recovered in the presence of spectral overlap if the
user has special knowledge about the signal. Since these cases are unusual, we will emphasize avoiding
overlap. This is discussed in Section A.6 of Appendix A.

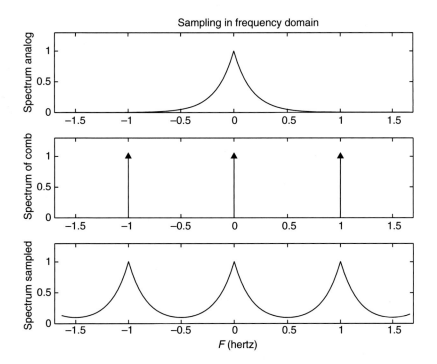

**Figure 6.2.** One-dimensional sampling, frequency domain.

a sampling rate that is greater than twice the highest frequency in the analog signal, $F_{max}$, i.e., $F_s > 2F_{max}$.

From the frequency domain figures, it is easy to see that reconstruction of the original signal requires that the fundamental spectrum, the one centered at zero, be retained, while the replicated spectra be eliminated. In the time domain, this can be accomplished by passing the sampled signal through a low pass filter. While ideal low pass filters are not possible, it is possible to realize sufficiently good approximations such that the reconstruction is close enough to ideal for practical applications. This is a major difference between one-dimensional signal and two-dimensional image reproduction. There is no equivalent analog low pass filter that can be used with optical images. This will be addressed in Section 6.6.

The ideal filtering operation is shown in Fig. 6.3. In this figure, the sampled signal spectrum is shown at the top, the ideal lowpass filter in the middle and the filtered result at the bottom. In this case, one can see that since the original signal is not bandlimited and overlap of the spectra has occurred, the filtered spectrum is not identical to the original spectrum. The result will be a distortion of the original signal.

If the sampling rate is not adequate, then the original signal cannot be reconstructed from the sample values. This is seen by considering the samples of a sinusoid of frequency

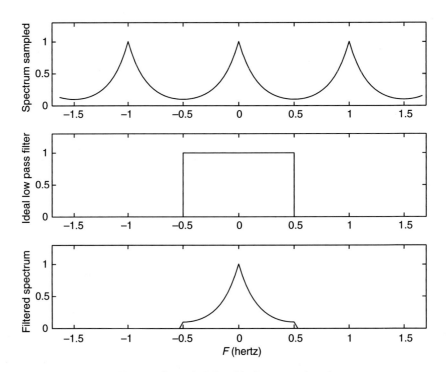

**Figure 6.3.** Low-pass filtering of sampled signal in frequency domain.

$F$, which are given by

$$s_F(n) = \cos(2\pi F n/F_s + \theta) = \cos[2\pi(F_0 + mF_s)n/F_s + \theta],$$
$$= \cos(2\pi F_0 n/F_s + 2\pi nm + \theta) = \cos(2\pi F_0 n/F_s + \theta), \qquad (6.2)$$

where $F_s$ is the sampling rate and $\theta$ is the phase of the sinusoid. We have used the fact that $\cos(\phi + 2\pi k) = \cos(\phi)$ for any integer $k$. A sampling rate of $F_s$ means that the samples are taken at times $t_n = n/F_s$. We see that the samples are the same for all frequencies $F = F_m$ that are related to the sampling frequency by $F_m = F_0 + mF_s$. The samples of these sinusoids are all identical to those of the sinusoid of frequency $F_0$. We will refer to $F_0$ as an alias of the frequencies $F_m$ under the sampling rate of $F_s$. A graphical illustration of this phenomenon is shown in Fig. 6.4. The identical samples, obtained from 100 Hz and 350 Hz sinusoids for a sampling rate of 250 Hz, are shown as circles.

The sampling theorem can be stated as

**Shannon's sampling theorem**: If an analog signal, $s(t)$, contains no power at frequencies greater than $F_{\max}$, then $s(t)$ can be reconstructed exactly from samples of the signal taken at a sampling rate $F_s > 2F_{\max}$.

A graphical illustration of the aliasing of a sinusoidal signal in both the time and frequency domains is shown in Fig. 6.5. In this example, the signal is a cosine with frequency of

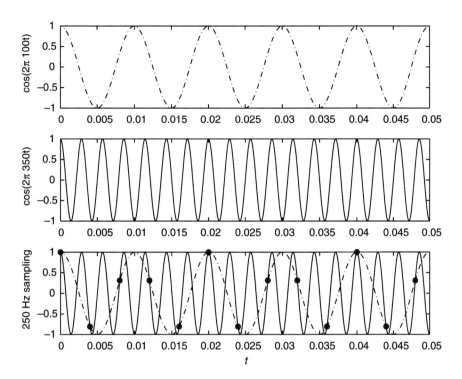

**Figure 6.4.** Example of two cosines of different frequencies (100 and 350 Hz) having the same samples under a sampling rate of 250 Hz.

1 Hz. The sampling interval is 7/8 s, which gives a sampling rate of $F_s = 8/7$ Hz. From the sampling theorem, we see that this sampling rate will allow reproduction of signals with frequencies only up to 4/7 Hz. The replication of the original spectrum occurs every 8/7 Hz. Using the formula for the aliased frequencies given above, frequencies are located at $\{\cdots, -1/7 = 1 - 8/7, 1, 15/7, \ldots\}$ and $\{\cdots, -1, 1/7 = -1 + 8/7, 9/7, \ldots\}$. If we attempt to recover the analog signal by using a low pass filter consistent with the sampling rate, as shown in the figure (lower right), the frequency that will appear in the continuous domain will be 1/7 Hz. This can easily be seen by observing the sampled signal in the lower left. This is the only aliased frequency that occurs within the passband of the filter. The figure is another example of the process that was used in Section 5.3 to derive the discrete Fourier transform.

## 6.1.2   Ideal sampling, 2-D

The two-dimensional Dirac delta function can be defined as the separable product of one-dimensional delta functions, $\delta(x, y) = \delta(x)\delta(y)$, or as the limit of various two-dimensional functions, as shown in Appendix A. The extension of the comb function to two dimensions should probably be called a brush, but we will continue to use the term

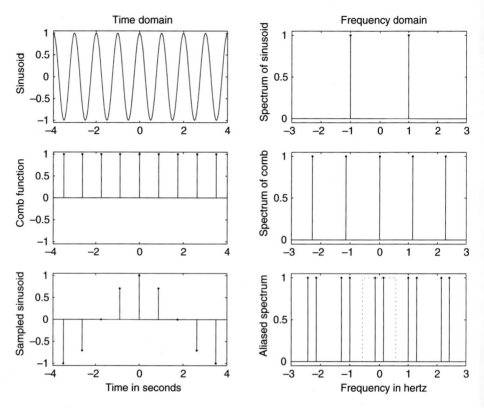

**Figure 6.5.** Aliasing of sinusoid.

comb and define it by

$$\text{comb}(x, y) = \sum_{m=-\infty}^{\infty} \sum_{n=-\infty}^{\infty} \delta(x - m, y - n).$$

The equation for 2-D sampling is

$$s(m, n) = s_d(x, y) = s(x, y)\text{comb}(x, y), \tag{6.3}$$

where a normalized sampling interval of unity is assumed. We have the same constraints on the sampling rate in two dimensions as in one. Of course, the frequency is measured not in hertz, but in cycles per millimeter or inch.[4] Spatial sampling is illustrated in Fig. 6.6. Undersampling in the spatial domain signal results in spatial aliasing. This is easy to demonstrate using simple sinusoidal images. First, let us consider the mathematics.

---

[4] Image processors use linear distance most often, but occasionally use angular measurement, which yields cycles per degree. This is done when considering the resolution of the eye or an optical system.

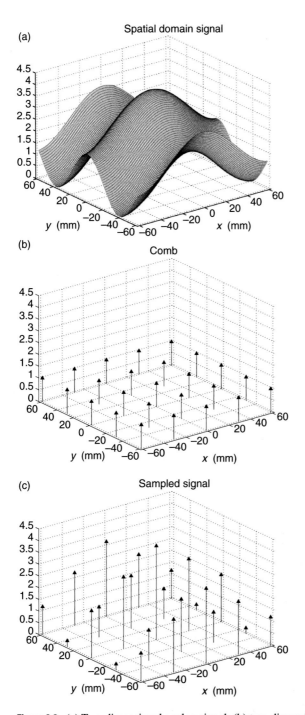

**Figure 6.6.** (a) Two-dimensional analog signal; (b) two-dimensional comb; (c) two-dimensional sampled signal.

Taking Fourier transforms of Eq. (6.3) yields

$$S_d(F_x, F_y) = S(F_x, F_y) * \text{comb}(F_x, F_y) = \sum_{k=-\infty}^{\infty} \sum_{l=-\infty}^{\infty} S(F_x - k, F_y - l), \quad (6.4)$$

where the $*$ denotes convolution. Note that the sampled spectrum is periodic, as in the one-dimensional case.

Consider the effect of changing the sampling interval. Sampling $s(x, y)$, defined by

$$s(m, n) = s(x, y)\text{comb}\left(\frac{x}{\Delta x}, \frac{y}{\Delta y}\right), \quad (6.5)$$

yields

$$S_d(F_x, F_y) = S(F_x, F_y) * \text{comb}(F_x, F_y),$$

$$= \frac{1}{|\Delta x \Delta y|} \sum_{k=-\infty}^{\infty} \sum_{l=-\infty}^{\infty} S(F_x \Delta x - k, F_y \Delta y - l). \quad (6.6)$$

Figure 6.7 shows the spectrum of a continuous analog image. If the image is sampled with intervals of $\Delta x$ in each direction, the sampled image has a spectrum that shows periodic replications at $1/\Delta x$. The central portion of the periodic spectrum is shown in Fig. 6.8. For Fig. 6.8, we have used $\Delta x = 1/30$ mm.

Note that if the analog image, $s(x, y)$, is bandlimited to some 2-D region, then it is possible to recover the original signal from the samples by using an ideal lowpass filter.

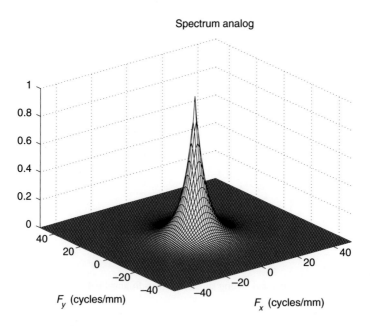

**Figure 6.7.** Analog spectrum.

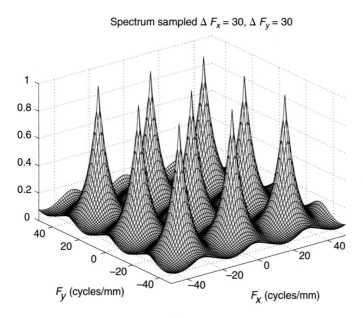

Spectrum sampled $\Delta F_x = 30$, $\Delta F_y = 30$

**Figure 6.8.** Digital spectrum with aliased images of analog spectrum.

The proper sampling intervals are determined from the requirement that the region of support in the frequency domain (bandlimit) is contained in the rectangle defined by

$$|F_x| \leq \frac{1}{2\Delta x} \quad \text{and} \quad |F_y| \leq \frac{1}{2\Delta y}.$$

The effect of sampling can be demonstrated in the following examples. In these examples, aliasing will be demonstrated by subsampling a high resolution digital image to produce a low resolution image. First, let us consider a pure sinusoid; the function

$$s(x, y) = \cos[2\pi(36x/128 + 24y/128)],$$

where $x$ is measured in mm and is sampled at 1 mm spacing in each direction. This produces no aliasing. The function and its spectrum are shown in Fig. 6.9.[5] Note that the frequency of the spectrum is in normalized digital frequency.[6] For this case, the analog frequency, $F$, and the digital frequency, $f$, are the same. This yields $F_x = f_x = 36/128 = 0.28125$ and $F_y = f_y = 24/128 = 0.1875$. The spectrum shows peaks at this 2-D frequency. The image is subsampled by a factor of 4 and shown in Fig. 6.10a. This is equivalent to a sampling of the analog signal with an interval of 4 mm in each direction. The aliased 2-D frequency can be obtained by finding $k$ and $l$ so that

---

[5] The spectra of the sinusoids appear as crosses instead of points because of the truncation of the image to a finite region by using a rectangular window. The full explanation is beyond the scope of this chapter but is basically the same effect observed in 1-D in Fig. 5.3d.
[6] Normalized digital frequency is denoted by $f = F/F_s$, the analog frequency divided by the sampling frequency, and has the constraint $|f| \leq 1/2$, [201].

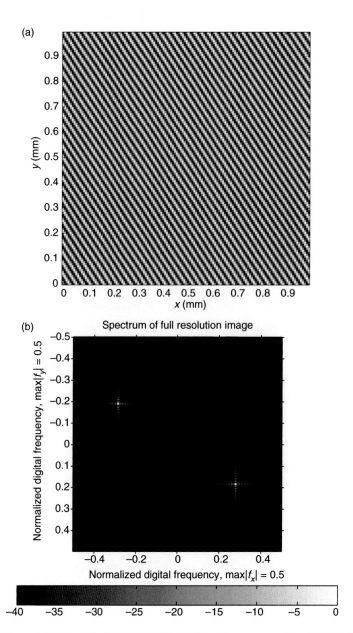

**Figure 6.9.** (a) $\cos[2\pi(36x/128 + 24y/128)]$; (b) spectrum of $\cos[2\pi(36x/128 + 24y/128)]$.

both $|F_x - kF_s| < 0.5F_s$ and $|F_y - lF_s| < 0.5F_s$ hold. For this case, $k = l = 1$ and the aliased analog 2-D frequency is $(F'_x, F'_y) = (0.03125, -0.0625)$. This means that the function,

$$s'(x, y) = \cos[2\pi(0.03125x - 0.0625y)],$$

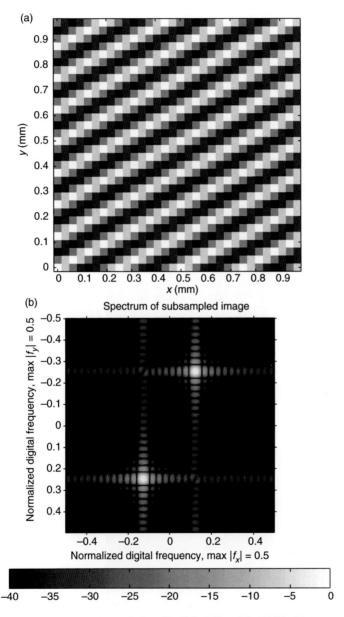

**Figure 6.10.** (a) 4:1 subsampled $\cos[2\pi(36x/128 + 24y/128)]$; (b) spectrum of subsampled $\cos[2\pi(36x/128 + 24y/128)]$.

will yield the same samples as $s(x, y)$ above when sampled at 4 mm intervals in each direction. The spectrum of the sampled signal is shown in Fig. 6.10b. The digital frequencies can be found by normalizing the aliased analog frequency by the sampling rate. For this case, $(f_x', f_y') = (0.03125/0.25, -0.0625/0.25) = (0.125, -0.25)$.

An example of sampling a pictorial image is shown in Figs. 6.11 and 6.12, where Fig. 6.11a is the original; Fig. 6.11b is its spectrum; Fig. 6.12a is a 2:1 subsampling of the original; Fig. 6.12b is the spectrum of the subsampled image. For this case, we can see that the lower frequencies have been preserved but the higher frequencies have been aliased.

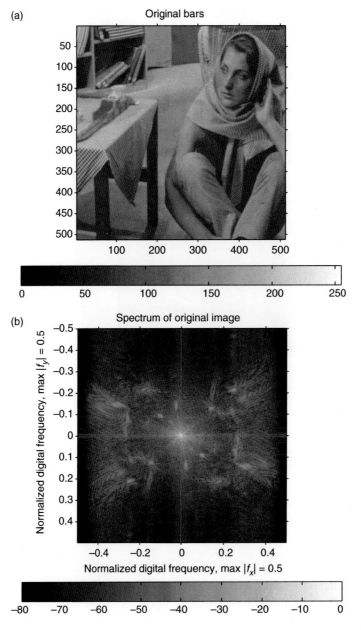

**Figure 6.11.** (a) Original bars image. (b) Spectrum of original bars image.

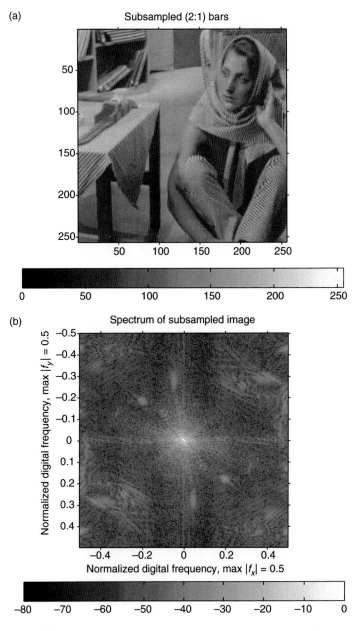

**Figure 6.12.** (a) Sampled bars image 2:1; (b) spectrum of subsampled bars image.

## 6.2    Sampling on nonrectangular lattices

Because images may have oddly shaped regions of support in the frequency domain, it is sometimes more efficient to sample with a nonrectangular lattice. The comparison of a rectangular lattice and a nonrectangular lattice is shown in Fig. 6.13. A thorough

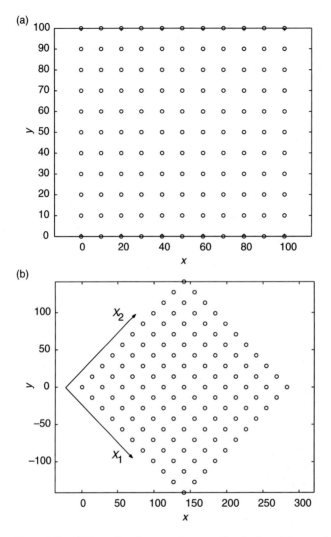

**Figure 6.13.** (a) Example of rectangular sampling lattice; (b) example of nonrectangular sampling lattice.

discussion of this concept is found in [68]. To develop this concept, it is convenient to write the sampling process in vector form. Let $\mathbf{x} = [x, y]$ and the basis vectors for sampling in the space domain be given by $\mathbf{x}_1$ and $\mathbf{x}_2$. The sampling function or comb can be written

$$\text{comb}(\mathbf{r}) = \sum_{m=-\infty}^{\infty} \sum_{n=-\infty}^{\infty} \delta(\mathbf{r} - m\mathbf{x}_1 - n\mathbf{x}_2). \qquad (6.7)$$

This yields the functional form

$$s(m, n) = s(m\mathbf{x}_1 + n\mathbf{x}_2). \qquad (6.8)$$

We can write this in matrix form

$$s(\mathbf{n}) = s(\mathbf{X}\mathbf{n}),$$

(6.9)

where the matrix $\mathbf{X} = [\mathbf{x}_1, \mathbf{x}_2]^T$ and the vector $\mathbf{n} = [m, n]$.

The basis vectors in the frequency domain, $\mathbf{w}_1$ and $\mathbf{w}_2$, are defined by the relation

$$\mathbf{x}_k \mathbf{w}_l^T = \delta(k - l),$$

(6.10)

or using matrix notation

$$\mathbf{X}^T \mathbf{W} = \mathbf{I}.$$

(6.11)

The Fourier transform in matrix notation is written

$$S(\mathbf{w}) = \int_{-\infty}^{\infty} \int_{-\infty}^{\infty} s(\mathbf{x}) \exp(-j2\pi \mathbf{W}^T \mathbf{x}) d\mathbf{x}.$$

(6.12)

The sampled spectrum can be written

$$S(\mathbf{w}) = S(\mathbf{w}) * \mathrm{comb}(\mathbf{w}),$$

$$= \frac{1}{|\mathbf{X}|} \sum_{k=-\infty}^{\infty} \sum_{l=-\infty}^{\infty} S(\mathbf{w} - k\mathbf{w}_1 - l\mathbf{w}_2).$$

(6.13)

The mathematical details of the above equations are found in [134] and [68].

## 6.3    Sampling using finite apertures

Practical imaging devices, such as video cameras, CCD arrays and scanners, must use a finite aperture for sampling. The comb function cannot be realized by actual devices. A finite aperture is required to obtain a finite amount of energy from the scene. The engineering trade-off is one of signal-to-noise ratio (SNR) versus spatial resolution. Large apertures receive more light and, thus, will have higher SNRs than smaller apertures; while smaller apertures permit higher spatial resolution than larger ones. This is true for apertures larger than the order of the wavelength of light. For smaller apertures, diffraction limits the resolution.

The aperture may cause the light intensity to vary over the finite region of integration. For a single sample of a one-dimensional signal at time $nT$, the sample value can be obtained by

$$s(n) = \int_{(n-1)T}^{nT} s(t) a(t - nT) dt,$$

(6.14)

where $a(t)$ represents the impulse response (or light variation) of the aperture. This integral has the form of a simple correlation and assumes that the same aperture is used for every sample. The mathematical representation can be written as convolution if the aperture is symmetric, or we replace the function $a(t)$ by $a(-t)$. The sampling of the signal can be represented by

$$s(n) = [s(t) * a(t)]\text{comb}(t/T), \tag{6.15}$$

where $*$ represents convolution. The model of Eq. (6.15) is interpreted as an analog blur of the analog signal, followed by sampling. This model is reasonably accurate for spatial sampling of most cameras and scanning systems.

The sampling model can be generalized to include the case where each sample is obtained with a different aperture. For this case, the samples, which need not be equally spaced, are given by

$$s(n) = \int_{l_n}^{u_n} s(t)a_n(t)\mathrm{d}t, \tag{6.16}$$

where the limits of integration correspond to the region of support for each aperture. A common application of this representation in two dimensions with uniformly spaced samples is the finite area of a CCD element of an imaging chip. The aperture function $a(t)$ may also take into account the leakage of charge from one cell to another. The form of Eq. (6.16) is also used to represent sampling in the wavelength dimension of the spectral signals.

The two-dimensional aperture in the mathematical model of sampling at unit intervals in each dimension can be written

$$s(m, n) = [s(x, y) * a(x, y)]\text{comb}(x, y), \tag{6.17}$$

where $*$ represents convolution and $a(x, y)$ represents the aperture. Note that using the finite aperture model can be written

$$s(m, n) = \iint_A s(x - m, y - n)a(x, y)\mathrm{d}x\mathrm{d}y, \tag{6.18}$$

where the 2-D integral is taken over the region of the support of the aperture denoted $A$. This equation is actually correlation. The model can be written as convolution with a space reversed aperture, $a_r(x, y) = a(-x, -y)$,

$$s(m, n) = \iint_A s(m - x, n - y)a_r(x, y)\mathrm{d}x\mathrm{d}y. \tag{6.19}$$

For a symmetric aperture, which is most often the case in optical systems, $a_r(x, y) = a(x, y)$. Commonly used apertures include circular disks, rectangles and Gaussians. Note that these have some symmetry that permits the substitution of convolution for correlation.

The Fourier representation of the sampled image is now given by

$$S_d(F_x, F_y) = S(F_x, F_y)A(F_x, F_y) * \text{comb}(F_x, F_y),$$

$$= \sum_{k=-\infty}^{\infty} \sum_{l=-\infty}^{\infty} S_a(F_x - k, F_y - l)A(F_x - k, F_y - l). \tag{6.20}$$

With a finite aperture, the bandlimited function to be sampled is the convolution $s(x, y) * a(x, y)$. The common aperture functions are generally low pass in character; thus, the sampled function is more nearly bandlimited. The aperture is effectively a filter. However, no real aperture exists that is equivalent to the ideal low pass filter. While aliasing caused by undersampling is diminished, the resultant spectrum is still a distorted version of the original.

## 6.4 Ideal reconstruction of deterministic images

From the frequency domain representation, we can easily see that the reconstruction is equivalent to the preservation of the original (*central*) spectrum and the elimination of the replicated spectra. This is accomplished by multiplication in the frequency domain by an ideal low pass filter. The ideal low pass filter is a rectangular function, in one dimension,

$$H_{lp}(F) = \begin{cases} 1 & \text{if } |F| < F_s/2 \\ 0 & \text{else} \end{cases}, \tag{6.21}$$

where $F_s$ is the sampling rate. We assume that the signal has been sampled consistently with the sampling theorem.

From the relationships given in Chapter 5, we know that the low pass filter in the time/space domain has the form of a sinc function

$$h_{lp}(t) = F_s \frac{\sin(\pi F_s t)}{\pi F_s t}. \tag{6.22}$$

The multiplication operation in frequency is equivalent to convolution in time/space. Thus, we have the ideal reconstruction

$$s(t) = s(t)\frac{1}{T}\text{comb}(t/T) * h_{lp}(t), \tag{6.23}$$

where $T = 1/F_s$. The $\frac{1}{T}$ factor occurs because of the scaling property associated with the Dirac delta function; see Appendix A. The analog signal can be written as a summation, as

$$s(t) = \sum_{n=-\infty}^{\infty} s(n)\frac{\sin(\pi(t - nF_s))}{\pi(t - nF_s)}. \tag{6.24}$$

We will refer to the sinc$(\cdot)$ function as the *kernel* of the reconstruction operation. It corresponds to the inverse Fourier transform of the ideal low pass filter of Fig. 6.3.

The two-dimensional case follows the same procedure and uses a separable interpolating function made of one-dimensional sinc functions. The representation for unit sampling in each direction is given by

$$f_a(x, y) = \sum_{m=-\infty}^{\infty} \sum_{n=-\infty}^{\infty} f(m, n) \frac{sin[\pi(x - m)]}{\pi(x - m)} \frac{sin[\pi(y - n)]}{\pi(y - n)}. \qquad (6.25)$$

In the case of real systems, the ideal low pass filter cannot be realized in either one or two dimensions. The methods used for handling these cases are discussed in Section 6.6.

## 6.5      Sampling and reconstruction of stochastic images

An analog stochastic signal is adequately sampled if it can be reconstructed from the samples.[7] The requirements for this are that the signal is a sample from a stationary, ergodic ensemble. The concepts are reviewed in Appendix C. The ensemble must be bandlimited in the sense that the Fourier transform of the autocovariance function is zero outside of some finite range. This is analogous to the signal being bandlimited in the deterministic case.

For a bandlimited, deterministic signal, $f_a(t)$, with unit sampling, the reconstruction of $f_a(t)$ from the samples, $f(k) = f_a(k)$, is

$$f_a(t) = \sum_{k=-\infty}^{\infty} f(k) \frac{sin[\pi(t - k)]}{\pi(t - k)}. \qquad (6.26)$$

As in the case of all Fourier domain representations, convergence of the infinite summation is in the square error sense,

$$f_a(t) = \lim_{N \to \infty} \sum_{k=-N}^{N} f(k) \frac{sin[\pi(t - k)]}{\pi(t - k)}, \qquad (6.27)$$

where it is meant that for every $t$ and for every $\epsilon$, an $N$ can be found such that

$$\left[ f_a(t) - \sum_{k=-N}^{N} f(k) \frac{sin[\pi(t - k)]}{\pi(t - k)} \right]^2 < \epsilon. \qquad (6.28)$$

The process is analogous for the random signal, where convergence is in the mean square sense. For convenience, we assume that the process has zero mean. The random

---

[7] This section requires understanding of stochastic concepts, discussed in Appendix C. It may be skipped without severe damage to the flow of the text.

signal approach indicates the use of the expected value operator, that is, for every $t$ and for every $\epsilon$, an $N$ can be found such that

$$E\left\{\left[f_{\mathrm{a}}(t) - \sum_{k=-N}^{N} f(k)\frac{\sin[\pi(t-k)]}{\pi(t-k)}\right]^2\right\} < \epsilon. \tag{6.29}$$

Let us consider the expected value term and expand it,

$$e(t,N) = E\{[f_{\mathrm{a}}(t)]^2\} - 2\sum_{k=-N}^{N} E\{f_{\mathrm{a}}(t)f(k)\}\frac{\sin[\pi(t-k)]}{\pi(t-k)}$$

$$+ \sum_{k=-N}^{N}\sum_{l=-N}^{N} E\{f(k)f(l)\}\frac{\sin[\pi(t-k)]}{\pi(t-k)}\frac{\sin[\pi(t-l)]}{\pi(t-l)}.$$

It is desired that the error tend to zero as $N \to \infty$.

We note that if $f(t)$ is a stationary process, the autocorrelation is defined by $E\{f(k)f(l)\} = r(k-l)$ and $E\{f_{\mathrm{a}}(t)f(k)\} = r(t-k)$. We need to relate the summation of sinc functions to the first term, which is the variance of a zero mean process. Since we know that the sinc function is an interpolation kernel for bandlimited functions, it is reasonable to require that the autocorrelation of $f(t)$, $r(\tau)$, be bandlimited. Since the Fourier transform of the autocorrelation function is defined as the power spectrum, this gives us the definition of a *bandlimited stochastic signal*. If the autocorrelation is bandlimited, it can be reconstructed from its samples,

$$r(t) = \sum_{k=-\infty}^{\infty} r(k)\frac{\sin[\pi(t-k)]}{\pi(t-k)}. \tag{6.30}$$

Since $f(t)$ is a stationary process, $E\{[f_{\mathrm{a}}(t)]^2\} = r(0)$ and $e(t,N)$ is actually independent of $t$. The error can be written for $t = 0$ and $N = \infty$ as

$$e = r(0) - 2\sum_{k=-\infty}^{\infty} r(-k)\frac{\sin[\pi(-k)]}{\pi(-k)}$$

$$+ \sum_{k=-\infty}^{\infty}\sum_{l=-\infty}^{\infty} r(k-l)\frac{\sin[\pi(-k)]}{\pi(-k)}\frac{\sin[\pi(-l)]}{\pi(-l)}.$$

Now we note the symmetry of $r(\tau)$ and see that the second term is

$$r(0) = \sum_{k=-\infty}^{\infty} r(k)\frac{\sin[\pi(-k)]}{\pi(-k)}. \tag{6.31}$$

To evaluate the double summation in the third term requires the evaluation of two summations. In the first, we note that

$$r(l) = \sum_{k=-\infty}^{\infty} r(k-l) \frac{\sin[\pi(-k)]}{\pi(-k)}. \tag{6.32}$$

Substituting this into the equation results in the third term simplifying to $r(0)$, which yields the result of $e = 0$.

This analysis has shown that the proper sampling of a stochastic signal is determined by the bandwidth of its power spectrum. Heuristically, we know that a bandlimited signal must be correlated. The bandlimit and the interpolation give us the maximum correlation distance. If we know samples of a random signal at intervals less than the *correlation distance*, we can determine the values of the signal anywhere. The correlation distance is the maximum distance $m$ for which the correlation $E\{f(k)f(k+m)\}$ of a stationary random process is significantly different from zero. Of course, "significant" is a subjective term. The basic idea is that the correlation tends to zero as the distance increases. If the samples are taken so that the correlation is "significant," then the values in between can be recovered. Real images do not have power spectra that are zero above a certain frequency. This is discussed in Section 7.2.2.

## 6.6      Modeling practical reconstruction of images

The Shannon theorem of sampling states that a bandlimited signal can be reconstructed if it is sampled properly. The reconstruction requires the infinite summation of a weighted sum of sinc functions. From the practical viewpoint, it is impossible to sum an infinite number of terms and the ideal low pass filter cannot be realized by real electrical devices in one dimension or by incoherent illumination in two dimensions. In one dimension, it is possible to obtain close approximations to the ideal low pass filter. However, good approximations are very expensive since they require precision electrical components. In two dimensions, it is not even possible to obtain a close approximation to the ideal low pass filter, since incoherent illumination cannot generate negative values. It is possible to generalize the sampling theorem to include sampling functions other than comb functions and signals that are not bandlimited. Since this theory is more advanced, it is presented in Appendix A.6. For the basics, it is instructive to consider the one-dimensional reconstruction before turning to the reconstruction of actual images.

### 6.6.1      One-dimensional reconstruction

As noted above, there are two problems that prevent the realization of the ideal low pass filter, the noncausal nature of the infinite summation and accurate representation of the mathematical function that defines the filter. Let us consider the two problems separately.

The ideal reconstruction requires a summation that starts at a time that occurred in the infinite past and goes to a time in the infinite future. This would require a noncausal system to interact with the future values. This cannot be realized. Furthermore, it would require the history of the signal to be known exactly for an infinite past. Thus, we are forced to use an approximation that represents a causal system, as

$$\hat{s}(t) = \sum_{n=0}^{\infty} s(n)g_n(t). \tag{6.33}$$

The function $g_n(t)$ is a weighting of the $n$th sample in the summation. In the time domain, the noncausal nature of the filter can be dealt with by implementing a delay. This delays the output by a time that is equivalent to $N$ samples or $NT$, where $T$ is the sampling interval. The error of the interpolation is obtained by comparing the output of the interpolation with the delayed version of the original signal, i.e.,

$$\epsilon(t) = |s(t - NT) - \hat{s}(t)|^2.$$

The remaining and more difficult problem is creating an analog interpolation function, $g_n(t)$.

In almost all cases of analog interpolation, the interpolation is done by a linear, time-invariant system, which implies that the interpolation is a convolution. In the above notation, this means that $g_n(t) = g(t - nT)$. The compact notation for this operation is now

$$\hat{s}(t) = (s(t)\text{comb}(t/T)) * g(t). \tag{6.34}$$

To get a feel for the effect of the choice of the interpolating function, let us consider some simple forms for $g(t)$.

The simplest form for the interpolation is the rectangular function

$$g_r(t) = \text{rect}_T(t) = \begin{cases} 1 & \text{if } 0 \leq t < T \\ 0 & \text{else} \end{cases}.$$

This can easily be implemented with real hardware by using a sample-and-hold circuit. The result of the convolution of this function with the sampled signal is a series of rectangular pulses that are the same amplitude as the samples. This is illustrated in Fig. 6.14. The analog signal is shown at the top with the sampled signal below it. The rectangular interpolating function is shown next. Note that the length of the rectangular pulse is exactly the same as the sampling interval. The interpolated function is shown at the bottom.

To obtain a better approximation, we can use a triangular interpolating function, defined by

$$g_t(t) = \text{tri}_T(t) = \begin{cases} t/T & \text{if } 0 \leq t < T \\ 2 - t/T & \text{if } T \leq t < 2T \\ 0 & \text{else} \end{cases}. \tag{6.35}$$

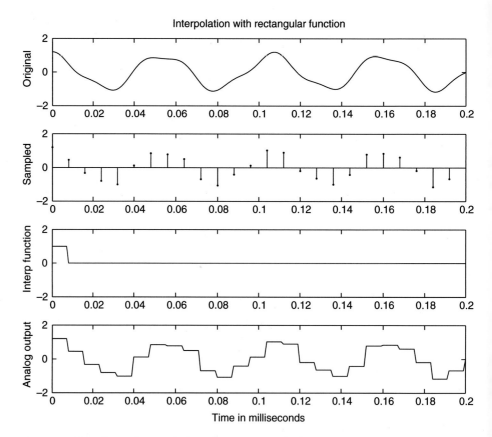

**Figure 6.14.** Sampling and interpolation with rectangular function.

This function is equivalent to a linear interpolation between samples. Note that there is a delay of one sample in the output of the interpolation filter. The graphic illustration of this filter is shown in Fig. 6.15. We have used a scale that makes the delay between the input and output apparent.

The availability of cheap, fast digital hardware opens another avenue for creating accurate and inexpensive reconstructions. If the sampling rate is increased sufficiently, the analog interpolating filter can be replaced by the combination of a high-order digital filter and a simple analog filter. The key to this method is using a sampling rate that is well above the rate needed to reconstruct the signal with the ideal reconstruction filter. Increasing the sampling rate to this extent is called *oversampling*. Let us consider an example of this, as illustrated in both the time and frequency domains.

The process can now be described by

$$\hat{s}(t) = \big[(s(t)\mathrm{comb}(t/T)) * h_{\mathrm{dlp}}(n)\big] * g(t), \tag{6.36}$$

where $h_{\mathrm{dlp}}(n)$ represents a digital low pass filter. The design of $h_{\mathrm{dlp}}(n)$ can be quite exacting. Given the speed of current digital hardware, the accuracy of the filter can be very good. For example, a 96 tap FIR filter is used in some CD players. This filter can

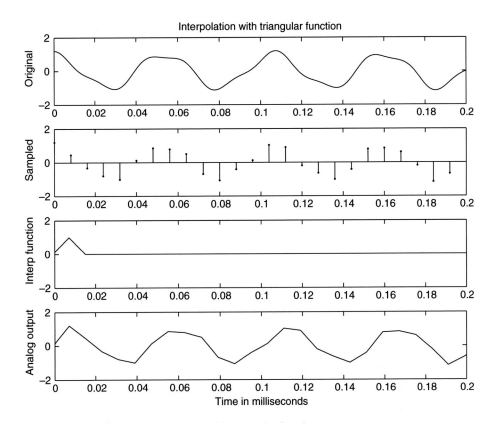

**Figure 6.15.** Sampling and interpolation with triangular function.

have specifications that produce less than one dB distortion in the passband and attenuate the unwanted signal in the stopband at least 60 dB. Furthermore, because of the high degree of oversampling, the errors that are produced are at extremely high frequencies that are above the range of human hearing.

   This process is illustrated in the time domain in Fig. 6.16a and in the frequency domain by Fig. 6.16b. The figures start with a continuous analog function and sample at 44.1 kHz, which is the standard rate for CD quality audio. The samples are shown below the analog signal. The digital interpolation obtained from a digital low pass filter is shown next. The effects of the initial conditions are noticeable on the left side of the graph. This is followed by the reconstruction using a rectangular interpolating function, as is common in CD players. The scale of the figure is such that the stairstep effect of the interpolation can be detected visually. The signal is interpolated using a sampling rate that is four times the original rate. We used an oversampling of four so that we can show the effect on a reasonable graph in the text. Actual oversampling rates are typically 8, 16 and 24.

   Now let us consider the same process in the frequency domain, Fig. 6.16b. The original signal is assumed to be limited to the usual audio band of 20 kHz, as shown in the top graph. The sampled signal reproduces the original spectrum at the sampling rate of 44.1 kHz. The interpolating digital filter has reduced the replicated images in its stopband to below 60 dB of their value in the sampled signal. The digital filter is periodic at the oversampling rate, four times the original in this example. This means that it has a passband at four times the original sampling rate. We see that the replicated image at $4 \times 44.1\,\text{kHz} = 176.4\,\text{kHz}$ is left unchanged. However, the human ear is not sensitive to frequencies this high. While there may be electronic signal power in this range, it does not translate to a distortion that can be heard. There are also other electronic ways to remove or attenuate this high-frequency distortion. The conversion to analog is shown in the bottom graph. The replication at 176.4 kHz has been reduced by the sinc function corresponding to the rectangular pulse used for reconstruction. But, as mentioned before, the signal at this high frequency is not of great consequence.

This text is about image processing and so the presentation of audio methods is only a forerunner to the presentation of interpolating methods for images. It is easy to see the effects of sampling in the time and frequency domains using one-dimensional graphs. We will present the same ideas in the application of two-dimensional image displays. While we will allude to the frequency effects that are shown in Fig. 6.16b, we will not attempt to draw the analogous graphs.

## 6.6.2     Two-dimensional reconstruction

The two-dimensional reconstruction of images from samples follows the same procedure as outlined in the previous section. The general form of the reconstruction from samples taken at unit intervals is

$$\hat{f}(x, y) = [f(x, y)\text{comb}(x, y)] * g(x, y), \qquad (6.37)$$

where $g(x, y)$ represents the form of the physical display spot or aperture used to display the image. Recall that for the ideal case, the ideal low pass filter is given in the time domain by

$$g(x, y) = \frac{\sin(\pi x)}{\pi x} \frac{\sin(\pi y)}{\pi y}. \qquad (6.38)$$

Using the definition of the comb function and assuming unit sampling intervals, we can write Eq. (6.37) as

$$\hat{f_a}(x, y) = \left[ \sum_{m=-\infty}^{\infty} \sum_{n=-\infty}^{\infty} f(m, n)\text{comb}(m - x, n - y) \right] * g(x, y), \qquad (6.39)$$

and using the properties of $\delta(x, y)$, we obtain

$$\hat{f_a}(x, y) = \sum_{m=-\infty}^{\infty} \sum_{n=-\infty}^{\infty} f(m, n)g(x - m, y - n). \qquad (6.40)$$

We encounter the same problems of causality and accurate representation of the interpolating function that we saw in the case of one-dimensional reconstruction. In the

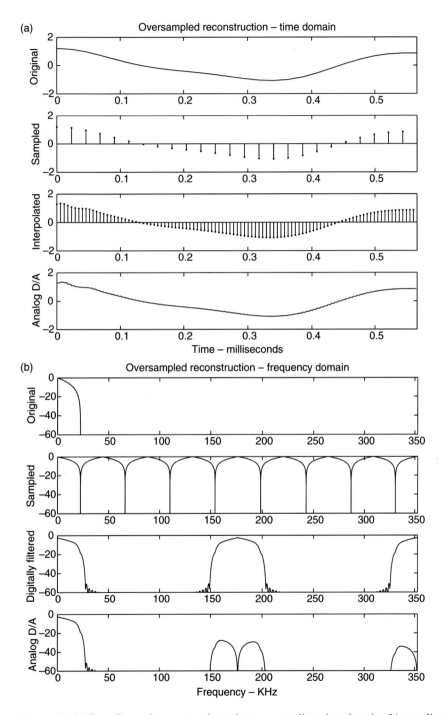

**Figure 6.16.** (a) Sampling and reconstruction using oversampling, time domain; (b) sampling and reconstruction using oversampling, frequency domain.

case of causality, the imaging coordinates do not present a naturally causal system. However, it is the requirement of an infinite number of terms in every direction that prohibits implementation of the ideal filter. Furthermore, the number of terms available to be used for reconstruction are usually far fewer than that of one-dimensional signals. For example, a second of CD quality music contains 44 100 samples, so the result of a 96 tap filter is relatively unaffected by the finite starting point of the signal. However, a digital image has far fewer samples than this in any direction and is finite in all directions. This means that effects at the edges should be explicitly considered.

The finite sum can be modeled as the truncation of the infinite sum,

$$\hat{f}_a(x, y) = \sum_{m=-M}^{M} \sum_{n=-N}^{N} f(m, n) g(x - m, y - n). \tag{6.41}$$

The equivalent operation in the space domain is to truncate the number of samples by the use of the rect$(\cdot)$ function:

$$\hat{f}_a(x, y) = [f_a(x, y) \text{comb}(x, y) \text{rect}(x/M, y/N)] * g(x, y). \tag{6.42}$$

As long as we confine our interest to the center of the image, there are usually enough terms to produce good reconstructions.

Edges can be handled by using estimated values of the samples beyond the edge. Using zeros for these values produces visible artifacts that are to be avoided. Common methods of estimating the samples outside the boundary of the recorded samples are to replicate the edge values or to reflect the image at the boundary. An alternative method is to use a different interpolation function near the edges of the image. This function would use only samples that are within the boundary. In all cases, the estimation near the edges cannot be as accurate as that near the center of the image.

A second problem that is more prominent in image processing is the fact that the samples of the image are not obtained by a good approximation to the delta function. As mentioned in Section 6.3, finite apertures must be assumed when considering real physical systems.

From the frequency domain representation, we recall that sampling produces a periodic replication of the baseband signal. With the inclusion of the finite aperture, we see that the recovery of the original image must not only eliminate the periodic replications of the product $S(F_x, F_y)A(F_x, F_y)$, it must also compensate for the effect of the aperture. The straightforward approach is to filter the sampled image with a kernel of the form

$$G(F_x, F_y) = \frac{1}{A(F_x, F_y)}. \tag{6.43}$$

The problem with this approach is that the spectrum $A(F_x, F_y)$ often has values that are very small or zero, which makes the inverse filter ill-conditioned, i.e., $G(F_x, F_y)$ will have very large values, which will amplify noise. Since most apertures are low pass, the small or zero values usually occur at higher frequencies. A common modification of the above correction is to include a term that will make the filter well conditioned. Such a form is given by

$$G(F_x, F_y) = \frac{H_{lp}(F_x, F_y)}{A(F_x, F_y)}, \tag{6.44}$$

where $H_{lp}(F_x, F_y)$ is a low pass filter.

Of course, the same problem of realizing the analog filter plagues the implementation of the interpolation function $g(x, y)$ corresponding to the representation in Eq. (6.44). The fact that the aperture function, $a(x, y)$ usually covers several samples permits some compensation for the aperture in the digital domain, that is, we can apply a digital filter prior to the conversion of the digital image to analog form. This method is discussed in [123].

One way to allow more exact representation of the aperture function is to increase the sampling rate. This can be done in a manner analogous to the oversampling in one dimension. In imaging, there is another common application where oversampling is used and exactly the same operations are performed as in the case of reconstructing one-dimensional signals.

Image interpolation is often done when a sampled image is enlarged many times its original size. For example, an image may be very small, say 64 × 64. If the image is displayed as one screen pixel for each image pixel, the display device would show a reproduction that is too small, say 1 inch × 1 inch. The viewer could not see this well at normal viewing distances. To use the entire area of the display requires an image with more pixels. For this example, 8× enlargement would produce a 512 × 512 image that would be 8 inches by 8 inches. This type of interpolation reconstruction is very common when using variable sized windows on a monitor, which implies noninteger enlargement of the original. As the physical resolution of monitors increases, even high-definition television formats will be interpolated.

The light distribution of a single screen pixel is represented by $g(x, y)$ in Eq. (6.41). At normal viewing distances, a single pixel cannot be distinguished. Pixels are spaced so that they appear to produce a continuum. In other words, the frequency of the pixel spacing is beyond the resolution of the eye. This is equivalent to the frequency of the sampling rate in one dimension being beyond the range of human hearing. Thus, we can apply the principles of the oversampling in one dimension to the interpolation of images in two dimensions.

In the case of variable sized windows, the interpolation factors are extremely variable. Additionally, the new image must be computed very fast. This means that generating high precision interpolating functions is not practical. Most image interpolation methods are based on simple schemes that have high computational efficiency.

The simplest method of enlarging the image is pixel replication, where each pixel is repeated in each direction some integral number of times. This is equivalent to using a rectangular interpolating function. This is shown in Figs. 6.9a and 6.10a, where the original 128 × 128 image has been sampled at 4:1 and interpolated back to 128 × 128. The square aperture is readily apparent. The figure of the pictorial image, Fig. 6.11a, has more pixels and uses a proportionally smaller reproduction aperture. The aperture is not apparent in this figure. In the case of the sinusoidal images, the purpose of the image was to demonstrate sampling effects. Thus, the obvious image of the aperture helps to make the sampling rate apparent. If we desire to camouflage the sampling and produce a smoother image for viewing, other methods are more appropriate. Of course, replication is used only when increasing the magnification by integral multiples of the original size.

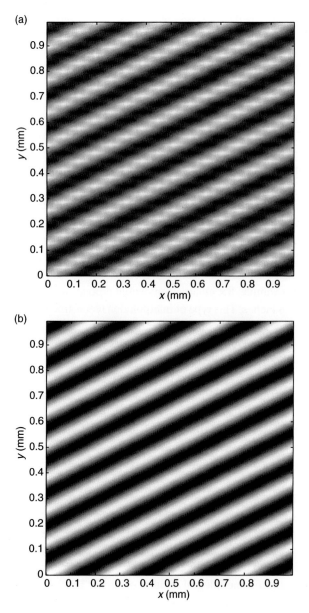

**Figure 6.17.** (a) Bilinear interpolation of subsampled $\cos[2\pi(36x/128 + 24y/128)]$; (b) spline interpolation of subsampled $\cos[2\pi(36x/128 + 24y/128)]$.

For magnifications that are not integral multiples, more sophisticated methods must be used [263, 280].

For images sampled on the usual rectangular grid, *bilinear interpolation* can be used to produce arbitrary sized enlargements. This interpolation is equivalent to using a separable function composed of triangle functions in each coordinate direction. This is an extension of linear interpolation in one dimension. Mathematically, to find the interpolated value of $s(x, y)$, we first find the sample pixels that bound the coordinate of interest, i.e., find the indices $i$ and $j$ such that $x_i \leq x < x_{i+1}$ and $y_j \leq y < y_{j+1}$. Next compute two interpolated values at the desired $x$ coordinate, while keeping the $y$ coordinates fixed at the boundary:

$$z_j = \frac{x - x_i}{x_{i+1} - x_i} s(x_{i+1}, y_j) + \frac{x_{i+1} - x}{x_{i+1} - x_i} s(x_i, y_j),$$

$$z_{j+1} = \frac{x - x_i}{x_{i+1} - x_i} s(x_{i+1}, y_{j+1}) + \frac{x_{i+1} - x}{x_{i+1} - x_i} s(x_i, y_{j+1}).$$

Then we use these results to interpolate the final value linearly:

$$s(x, y) = \frac{y - y_j}{y_{j+1} - y_j} z_{j+1} + \frac{y_{j+1} - y}{y_{j+1} - y_j} z_j.$$

The same value can be obtained by first interpolating in the $y$ direction and then in the $x$ direction. The image of Fig. 6.10a is displayed using bilinear interpolation in Fig. 6.17a. The separability of the interpolation is noticed in the rectilinear artifacts in the image.

A more computationally expensive interpolation is the cubic spline. This method is designed to produce continuous derivatives, in addition to producing a continuous function. The result of this method is shown in Fig. 6.17b. For the smooth sinusoidal image, this method works extremely well. One can imagine that images exist where the increased smoothness of the spline interpolation would produce a result that appears more blurred than the bilinear method. There is no interpolation method that is guaranteed to be optimal for a particular image. There are reasons to use the spline method for a wide variety of images [279]. There are many interpolating functions which have been investigated for many different applications [29, 33, 146, 158, 178, 232, 264, 278, 280].

## 6.7    Problems

**6.1**  1-D aliasing: in the problems below, an analog signal $s(t)$, where $t$ is defined in seconds, is sampled at a rate, $F_s$, defined in Hertz to produce a digital signal, $s_d(n)$. Determine the digital frequencies, $f_x$, represented by the sampled signal and the analog frequencies, $F_y$, that correspond to those digital frequencies. The analog frequencies will be less than $F_s/2$.

(a)  $s(t) = \cos(2\pi 100t)$, $F_s = 500$.
(b)  $s(t) = \cos(2\pi 200t)$, $F_s = 500$.
(c)  $s(t) = \cos(2\pi 300t)$, $F_s = 500$.

(d) $s(t) = \cos(2\pi 400t)$, $F_s = 500$.

(e) $s(t) = \cos(2\pi 50t) + 2\sin(2\pi 150t)$, $F_s = 200$.

(f) $s(t) = \sin(2\pi 50t) + 2\cos(2\pi 100t)$, $F_s = 75$.

**6.2**  1-D ideal reconstruction: in the problems below, an analog signal $s(t)$, where $t$ is defined in seconds, is sampled at a rate, $F_s$, defined in Hertz to produce a digital signal, $s_d(n)$. An analog signal, $r(t)$, is reconstructed according to an ideal reconstruction of Section 6.4. The ideal lowpass filter is identical to that defined by Eq. (6.21). Determine $r(t)$.

(a) $s(t) = \cos(2\pi 750t)$, $F_s = 1000$.

(b) $s(t) = \cos(2\pi 1500t)$, $F_s = 1000$.

(c) $s(t) = \cos(2\pi 300t)$, $F_s = 1000$.

(d) $s(t) = \cos(2\pi 400t)$, $F_s = 1000$.

(e) $s(t) = \cos(2\pi 50t) + 2\sin(2\pi 150t)$, $F_s = 44\,100$.

(f) $s(t) = 2\sin(2\pi 500t) + 3\cos(2\pi 1500t) + 4\cos(2\pi 4500t)$, $F_s = 8000$.

(g) $s(t) = 2\sin(2\pi 500t) + 3\cos(2\pi 2500t) + 4\sin(2\pi 4500t)$, $F_s = 8000$.

(h) $s(t) = 2\sin(2\pi 500t) + 3\cos(2\pi 3500t) - 4\cos(2\pi 4500t)$, $F_s = 8000$.

**6.3**  2-D aliasing: in the problems below, an analog signal $s(x, y)$, where $x$ and $y$ are defined in mm, is sampled using a sampling interval, $\Delta x$ and $\Delta y$ defined in mm, to produce a digital signal, $s_d(m, n)$. Determine the digital frequencies, $(f_x, f_y)$, represented by the sampled signal and the analog frequencies, $(F_x, F_y)$, that correspond to those digital frequencies. The analog frequencies will be less than $\frac{1}{2\Delta x}$ and $\frac{1}{2\Delta y}$ in the respective directions.

(a) $s(x, y) = \cos(2\pi 100x)$, $\Delta x = \frac{1}{500}$, $\Delta y = \frac{1}{500}$.

(b) $s(x, y) = \cos[2\pi(100x + 200y)]$, $\Delta x = \frac{1}{500}$, $\Delta y = \frac{1}{500}$.

(c) $s(x, y) = \cos[2\pi(200x + 300y)]$, $\Delta x = \frac{1}{500}$, $\Delta y = \frac{1}{500}$.

(d) $s(x, y) = \cos[2\pi(200x + 600y)]$, $\Delta x = \frac{1}{500}$, $\Delta y = \frac{1}{500}$.

(e) $s(x, y) = \cos[2\pi(200x + 600y)]$, $\Delta x = \frac{1}{500}$, $\Delta y = \frac{1}{1000}$.

(f) $s(x, y) = \cos[2\pi(600x + 200y)]$, $\Delta x = \frac{1}{500}$, $\Delta y = \frac{1}{1000}$.

(g) $s(x, y) = \cos(2\pi 100x) + \cos(2\pi 200y)$, $\Delta x = \frac{1}{500}$, $\Delta y = \frac{1}{500}$.

(h) $s(x, y) = \cos(2\pi 100x)\cos(2\pi 200y)$, $\Delta x = \frac{1}{500}$, $\Delta y = \frac{1}{500}$.

(i) $s(x, y) = \cos(2\pi 200x) + \cos(2\pi 300y)$, $\Delta x = \frac{1}{500}$, $\Delta y = \frac{1}{500}$.

(j) $s(x, y) = \cos(2\pi 200x)\cos(2\pi 300y)$, $\Delta x = \frac{1}{500}$, $\Delta y = \frac{1}{500}$.

(k) $s(x, y) = \cos[2\pi(100x + 200y)] + 2\cos[2\pi(600x + 200y)]$, $\Delta x = \frac{1}{500}$, $\Delta y = \frac{1}{500}$.

(l) $s(x, y) = \cos[2\pi(100x + 200y)] + 2\sin[2\pi(600x + 200y)]$, $\Delta x = \frac{1}{1000}$, $\Delta y = \frac{1}{500}$.

**6.4**  2-D ideal reconstruction: in the problems below, an analog signal $s(x, y)$, where $x$ and $y$ are defined in mm, is sampled using a sampling interval, $\Delta x$ and $\Delta y$ defined in mm, to produce a digital signal, $s_d(m, n)$. An analog signal, $r(x, y)$, is reconstructed according to an ideal reconstruction of Section 6.4. The ideal low pass filter has a passband defined by $\frac{1}{2\Delta x}$ and $\frac{1}{2\Delta y}$. Determine $r(x, y)$.

(a) $s(x, y) = \cos(2\pi 75x)$, $\Delta x = \frac{1}{100}$, $\Delta y = \frac{1}{100}$.

(b) $s(x, y) = \cos[2\pi(25x + 75y)]$, $\Delta x = \frac{1}{100}$, $\Delta y = \frac{1}{100}$.

(c) $s(x, y) = \cos[2\pi(75x + 150y)]$, $\Delta x = \frac{1}{100}$, $\Delta y = \frac{1}{100}$.

(d) $s(x, y) = \cos[2\pi(150x + 350y)]$, $\Delta x = \frac{1}{100}$, $\Delta y = \frac{1}{100}$.

(e) $s(x, y) = \cos[2\pi(200x + 600y)]$, $\Delta x = \frac{1}{100}$, $\Delta y = \frac{1}{100}$.

(f) $s(x, y) = \sin[2\pi(600x + 200y)]$, $\Delta x = \frac{1}{100}$, $\Delta y = \frac{1}{100}$.

(g) $s(x, y) = \cos(2\pi 140x) + \cos(2\pi 60y)$, $\Delta x = \frac{1}{200}$, $\Delta y = \frac{1}{200}$.

(h) $s(x, y) = \cos(2\pi 140x) \cos(2\pi 60y)$, $\Delta x = \frac{1}{200}$, $\Delta y = \frac{1}{200}$.

(i) $s(x, y) = \cos(2\pi 50x) + \cos(2\pi 30y)$, $\Delta x = \frac{1}{200}$, $\Delta y = \frac{1}{200}$.

(j) $s(x, y) = \cos(2\pi 50x) \cos(2\pi 30y)$, $\Delta x = \frac{1}{200}$, $\Delta y = \frac{1}{200}$.

(k) $s(x, y) = \cos[2\pi(50x + 80y)] + 2 \cos[2\pi(70x + 40y)]$, $\Delta x = \frac{1}{200}$, $\Delta y = \frac{1}{200}$.

(l) $s(x, y) = \cos[2\pi(50x + 150y)] + 2 \sin[2\pi(250x + 350y)]$, $\Delta x = \frac{1}{200}$, $\Delta y = \frac{1}{200}$.

(m) $s(x, y) = \cos[2\pi(50x + 150y)] - 2 \cos[2\pi(250x + 350y)]$, $\Delta x = \frac{1}{200}$, $\Delta y = \frac{1}{200}$.

(n) $s(x, y) = \cos[2\pi(50x + 150y)] + 2 \sin[2\pi(250x + 350y)]$, $\Delta x = \frac{1}{4000}$, $\Delta y = \frac{1}{200}$.

**6.5** Using the patches_cosines_digital.tif image introduced in Problem 5.16 of Chapter 5, subsample the image by a factor of 4:1. From the frequencies that you obtained in that problem, compute the frequencies that can be inferred from the subsampled image. Verify these computations by computing and displaying the spectrum of the subsampled image.

**6.6** Using the monochrome image *gray-one* that you created for use in previous chapters, subsample the image by a factor of 4:1.

(a) Display the original and subsampled images.

(b) Identify any areas of the image that are significantly degraded by the sampling.

(c) Compute and compare the spectra of the original and subsampled images.

**6.7** Using the subsampled image of Problem 6.6, interpolate the image to the size of the original using

(a) Bilinear interpolation.

(b) Any higher-order method of your choice. There are many interpolation methods available in MATLAB. You may use one of them or program something that you can find in the literature or on the web. Be sure to reference the source of your method. Do *not* use a novel method of your own.

Display the original and interpolated images of (a) and (b). Determine if there are areas of the images that are essentially the same and areas that are substantially different.

# 7     Image characteristics

The previous chapters have discussed the various tools and properties that are used to characterize a digital image. The image begins as a reflective or radiant source; a distribution of energy is sensed by a device in one or several bands; the sensed signal is converted from analog to digital format and stored using a finite number of bits. The *characteristics* of an image include properties that are inherent to the content of the image, to the source of the energy distribution and to the sampling and quantization of the image. The characteristics can be deterministic, such as the size of the image, or stochastic, as in the case of the signal-to-noise ratio in a recorded image. In this chapter, we will consider the various characterizations and their effect on the processing of the image.

The characteristics of an image or class of images are important to determine the optimal recording, display, coding and processing. In general, if we are concerned with a specific image, the characteristics are deterministic, since they can be determined by measurements on the image. Such parameters as the mean, minimum and maximum values are examples. If we are concerned with a class of images, it is reasonable to treat the class as a statistical ensemble and characterize it by statistical parameters. Mean, minimum and maximum are examples, but in this case the values are interpreted differently. The mean of the ensemble is an expected value and we would not expect a particular image to have this exact mean. It is the stochastic characterization that is used to determine the hardware properties required to transform an analog image to a digital one. For example, the hardware is usually designed to measure a range of values that will most often be encountered, not the absolute maximum range of values that may exist. Some saturation of the sensors can be allowed if it occurs infrequently.

It is sometimes advantageous to treat parameters of a specific image as if they were stochastic in nature. For example, the histogram of image values for an image is easily computed. It is then used as if it represented a probability distribution of an ensemble to which the specific image belongs. Display parameters are set based on the histogram and even transformations, such as histogram equalization, are computed based on the transformation of probability distributions. The power spectrum of an image is often computed and used in the same way.

## 7.1     Deterministic properties

As mentioned, deterministic parameters are most often associated with a specific image. There are cases where all images in a class are subject to physical limitations that affect every image. In these cases, the relative importance of the property will be considered. We will begin with the most basic and most easily measured properties, then proceed to more complex and theoretical ones.

## 7.1.1    Basic parameters

### Image source

The source that creates the image is important in determining many other properties. An image scanner deals only with reflective or transmissive material, which has a known range of [0, 1]. This makes the quantization process much easier since a fixed range can be used. Images from radiant distributions or ones from reflective sources with widely varying illumination are much more difficult to process. In the case of consumer cameras, both film and digital, the camera must include a device to estimate the amount of light on the scene. In current digital cameras, information about the absolute lighting is often recorded with the image.

Since the major factor for recorded images from cameras is the product of illumination and reflectivity, additional information about the physical objects under investigation is required to separate the two components.[1] Very often this is done by the user. For example, a digital camera knows the characteristics of its flash and can compensate for its light output. In other situations, the user can specify whether the scene is outdoor or indoor. This allows the camera to estimate appropriate color compensations. In many satellite imaging applications, information about the exact relative locations of the satellite, earth and sun provides similar data for making accurate estimates.

In addition to the known range of the values, information about the image formation process can be valuable. In the case of image scanners, information about the source can greatly improve image quality. For example, many copiers have a special setting for scanning halftone images (see Chapter 11). Information about printer inks is valuable since it gives information about the basis functions for color scanning and the gamut of the image. Likewise, information about the film used for transmissive material can be used to improve estimates of the original scene.

### Region of support

The region of support is the set of spatial coordinates or discrete indices outside of which the image values are unknown. For most digital images, this is the entire range of the recorded image, an $M \times N$ rectangular grid. The indices may or may not relate to actual spatial coordinates. There are several cases where the region of support is not so trivial.

In medical images, such as computer tomography or magnetic resonance imaging, the object of interest is known to be bounded within the field of view. In some astronomical images the object of interest is bounded by deep space, which has essentially zero value. This information can be used to improve reconstruction accuracy.

---

[1] Other contributors, such as sensor response and optical properties, as discussed in Chapter 8, are relatively minor. For this chapter, we will concentrate on the major effects.

Images may be partitioned into regions of similar properties or regions of interest, for example, foreground and background. The image may be decomposed into two images: a foreground surrounded by a zero background and a background with a zero foreground. The two components may be processed separately and then recombined to make a final image.

In most images, the values outside the recorded $M \times N$ area are unknown rather than zero. For point processes that address only a single pixel at a time, e.g., tone correction or gamma adjustment, the values outside the recorded region can be ignored. For spatial processing that uses a neighborhood of a pixel, the assumption of zero values outside the recorded area can produce disturbing edge effects. There are various ways of minimizing such effects, such as padding, extrapolation and modifying the estimation process at the edges [4, 225].

## Range and histogram

The range of pixel values is easily measured for a particular digital image. For analog images, cameras or scanners have auxiliary circuits to estimate the proper setting required to produce reasonable recorded images. Of course, if our images are known to come from an $N$-bit analog–digital converter, then we know that the minimum and maximum are zero and $2^N - 1$, respectively. This information may have varying importance depending on the particular image.

The minimum and maximum values are often used to scale the image for display. However, as mentioned in Chapter 3, this is not necessarily optimal. An emphasis on consistent display parameters was presented for the frequent situations when several images are compared. Since we have made the point about consistency, let us concentrate on single images or ensembles.

For both particular images and ensembles, it is often not the maximum and minimum that are important, but the distribution of values. The histogram of an image is an approximation or estimate of the probability distribution of the values. See Appendix C. This should be considered, in order to determine the optimal display settings. As an example, consider the image of Fig. 7.1a. Its histogram is shown in Fig. 7.2. The minimum and maximum values are 25 and 230, respectively. From considering the histogram, it is apparent that there would be little lost in the display if a slightly larger minimum were used and a slightly smaller maximum. We used the true minimum and maximum to map to the range [0, 255] in Fig. 7.1a, while we used 36 and 227 as the minimum and maximum for display of Fig. 7.1b. The overall image contrast of the adjusted scaling should be enhanced compared with the true min/max scaling. Note that relatively few values are truncated by the new mapping. However, it should be noted that such enhancement can only be done legitimately for a single image.

The use of values other than the minimum or maximum is subjective. By choosing display min/max different from the image min/max, some pixel values may be truncated. The importance to the image interpretation is a decision for the user. The rule of Chapter 3 emphasized that all comparisons are to be fairly displayed.

Another use of the histogram of Fig. 7.2 is to show that the digitization of the image is not optimal. The original data of this histogram show that the [0, 255] range has

**Figure 7.1.** (a) Grad student image scaled using true min/max scaling (min = 25, max = 230, expanded to [0,255]); (b) same image scaled using adjusted min/max (min = 36, max = 227, expanded to [0,255]).

been used only moderately well, using 205/255 of the available range, but truncation has been avoided. Truncation would be apparent in the histogram if there were many values at the limits. The image in Fig. 7.3a has *saturated values* in the sky and the water drop reflections. These values exceeded the range of the digitizing device and are set

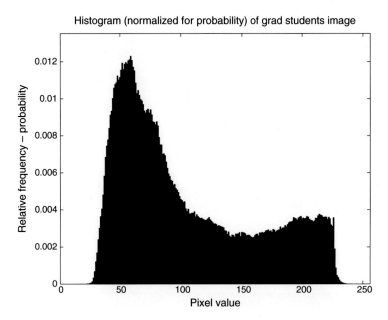

**Figure 7.2.** Histogram of grad student image, Fig. 7.1a.

at the maximum value. This may not be readily apparent in the image, but is obvious in the histogram of Fig. 7.3b.

## Color range and saturation

Since color images are defined by values in a three-dimensional space, the range of colors in an image is hard to define exactly. An easy way to represent the range is by a 3-D box defined by the limits of histograms in each of the three channels that define the image. Of course, this will depend on the color space in which the image is defined. Because of the nonlinear transformations between color spaces, a rectangular box in one space does not map to a rectangular box in another space. An idea of the complexity of the color range of an image may be obtained by considering the range of possible colors that can be produced by a display device. This range is called the *gamut* of the device. Examples of gamuts are shown in Chapter 12, Fig. 12.20, where two output devices are compared.

The effects of saturation or truncation of values of a color can be more severe than in a monochrome image. The truncation can occur in any of the color channels during the digitization process. The color channel characteristics are determined by the particular device. Such characteristics are discussed in detail in Chapter 8. Saturation in color images can change the hue or chroma of the pixel color, in addition to the intensity. Consider the case where one channel is truncated and the others are not. This will produce an obvious hue shift. Another problem that is of interest is the recovery of color when one or more channels are saturated. The interpolation process used in most digital cameras is severely complicated when dealing with saturated pixels.

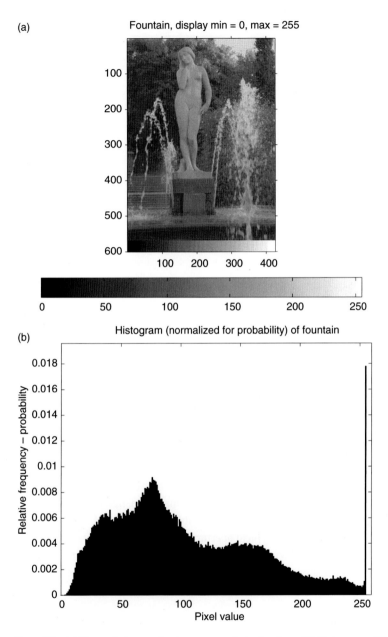

**Figure 7.3.** (a) Fountain image that has saturated pixel values; (b) histogram of fountain.

## 7.1.2 Bandwidth

The basis of all sampling is that the original analog signal can be accurately represented by the samples. This means that the original signal can be reconstructed from the samples. It was shown in Chapter 6 how the sampling rate is related to the bandlimit of the signal. Examples were shown to illustrate the effects of violating the Nyquist sampling rate,

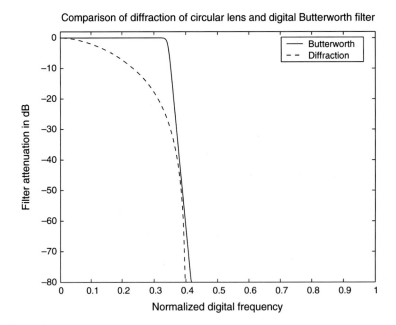

**Figure 7.4.** Comparison of frequency response of diffraction of lens and a Butterworth low-pass filter.

e.g., Fig. 6.12. In the electronic world of one-dimensional signals, it is common practice to bandlimit the signal before sampling. These bandlimiting filters are easily realized with simple electrical circuits. However, in the two-dimensional world of imaging, there is no easy way to bandlimit an analog image with lenses.

Lenses do produce a spatial filtering of the image that attenuates the higher spatial frequencies. This is the result of diffraction effects of the finite aperture and less than perfect lenses. However, the filter characteristics of lenses do not produce the nice bandlimiting cut-offs that are possible with electrical filters. A comparison of the frequency response of a typical aperture–lens combination and a realizable bandlimited electrical filter is shown in Fig. 7.4. It is obvious that the electronic filter can produce a much flatter response in the passband and a much sharper cut-off region than the lens. The frequency scale has been normalized to unity since there is no particular physical system under discussion.

Most images of interest have objects that have sharp edges to some extent. Heuristically, we know that the Fourier transform of a rectangular pulse, which consists of two sharp edges, is a sinc function. This function is clearly not bandlimited. We know from Chapter 5 that the Fourier transform of a unit pulse[2] is a sinc function, $\sin(\pi F)/\pi F$. Ignoring the oscillations of the sinc function, the spectrum falls off as $1/F$, which is not very fast. Thus, images that have sharp edges would have significant

---

[2] We use the pulse to discuss the frequency properties of edges, since an edge represented as a step function, $u(t)$, does not have a Fourier transform.

power at high frequencies. Consider the bars image, Fig. 3.5. This image has several objects that produce sharp edges in the image, e.g., table, bookcase, toys. It also has the striped apparel of the woman to add to the high frequency information. Thus, the spectrum shown in Fig. 5.14b shows significant power at frequencies near the boundaries of the spectral plot that represent the maximum frequencies of the digital image. From this, we can generalize that any image that contains sharp edges contains significant power at higher spatial frequencies. It is not bandlimited, nevertheless, such images must be digitized. The objective for practical sampling of images is to minimize the aliasing effects that we know are a necessary part of sampling nonbandlimited images.

Aliasing errors can be extremely distracting, as shown in Fig. 6.12, where the images contain periodic structures at high spatial frequencies. As the sampling rate is increased, the effects are moved to higher frequencies, which usually occur in fewer objects. When they do occur they are usually lower contrast. There is no way to completely eliminate such problems in the analog-to-digital transformation. When images are subsampled for display, coding and storage, digital bandlimiting filters can be used, as noted in Chapter 6.

The more common aliasing problem is blurring of high contrast edges. This is a significant problem in electrophotographic copiers and scanning of text documents. The problem is easily illustrated by considering that a pixel whose aperture covers a black–white edge contains a variable percentage of black and white. Such a pixel must have some intermediate value between the maximum and minimum associated with the edge. A graphical example of this effect is shown in Fig. 7.5. The sample is represented at the center of an aperture of unit length, e.g., the sample at 4.5 is the average of the signal

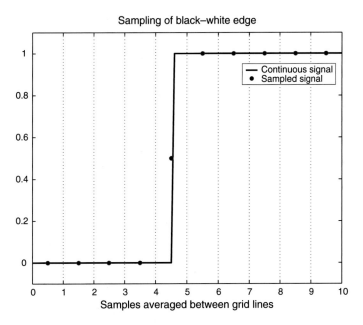

**Figure 7.5.** How intermediate values are created by sampling apertures that contain edges: the value of the sample that contains the edge is the average of the maximum and minimum on either side of the edge.

from 4 to 5. While there is little that can be done to prevent this aliasing in the analog-to-digital conversion step, there are some post-processing techniques that are used to improve text image quality. These will be discussed in Chapter 14.

We saw in Section 7.1.1 how the histogram of an image could be used to indicate the quality of the quantizing part of the analog-to-digital conversion. The examination of the two-dimensional power spectrum of an image can be used to indicate the quality of the spatial sampling of an image. Consider the power spectra of the high-resolution and low-resolution sampling of the cosine function in Figs. 6.9 and 6.10, respectively. It is clear that the low-resolution image has much more power near its Nyquist frequency, the maximum frequency that can be represented at the corresponding sampling rate. The same is true of the pictorial images of Figs. 6.11 and 6.12. A rule of thumb might be: "If there is high relative power at the Nyquist frequencies, then the image was undersampled." We will elaborate on bandwidth in Section 7.2.2.

## 7.1.3　Subspace concepts

The properties of the bandwidth and bandlimit of an image are useful because of our familiarity with the Fourier transform and the frequency domain. The concepts of bandwidth and bandlimit of an image can be generalized to include a subspace of an almost arbitrary vector space. While this may be interesting mathematically, if it were not practically useful for various image processing tasks, it would not be discussed here. Because we are more interested in the uses of the subspace concepts, we will keep the mathematical formalities to a minimum and concentrate on how these concepts may be used to characterize an image or an ensemble of images.

It is necessary to define a vector space in mathematical terms, so that the range of applications is apparent. A *vector space* over a *scalar field* is defined by a collection of objects (vectors) and mathematical operations on those objects. To define a vector space rigorously, a scalar field should be defined, and this may take us too far afield. Thus, let us confine our interest to the scalar fields of the real numbers, $\mathcal{R}$, and complex numbers, $\mathcal{C}$, under operations with which we are already familiar. The simple definition of a vector space is that it is closed under addition and scalar multiplication. Mathematically, for any two vectors $\mathbf{u}$ and $\mathbf{v}$ in the vector space $\mathcal{V}$ and real or complex scalars $a$ and $b$, we have

1. $\mathbf{u} + \mathbf{v} \in \mathcal{V}$. Closed under addition;
2. $\mathbf{u} + (\mathbf{v} + \mathbf{w}) = (\mathbf{v} + \mathbf{u}) + \mathbf{w}$. Associativity of addition;
3. $a\mathbf{u} \in \mathcal{V}$. Closure under scalar multiplication;
4. $a(b\mathbf{u}) = ab\mathbf{u}$. Associativity under scalar multiplication.

The most common vector spaces are the $n$ tuples of real numbers, $[x_1, x_2, \ldots, x_n]$, where $x_i \in \mathcal{R}$. This space is denoted $\mathcal{R}^n$. The $n$ samples of a one-dimensional signal can form a vector space. Taking the discrete Fourier transform of this signal creates an $n$ tuple of complex numbers that can be considered a vector space over the field of complex numbers, $\mathcal{C}$. This space is denoted $\mathcal{C}^n$. We can have infinite-dimensional vector spaces, such as the space defined by real-valued functions defined for all times

$-\infty \leq t \leq \infty$. The space of periodic functions with period $T$, which satisfy the Dirichlet conditions, represents an infinite dimensional space in $\mathcal{C}$. This can be seen by considering the Fourier series of the functions as an infinite-dimensional vector, $[\ldots, X(-2), X(-1), X(0), X(1), X(2), \ldots]$.

### Linear independence and bases

It is clear that vectors in a vector space can be written as the sums of other vectors in the space. We are interested in the cases where we have a special set of vectors that can be used to define the entire vector space, that is, all vectors in the space can be written as the linear combination of these vectors. If this set of vectors is such that there is only one way to write each vector in the space, the set is called a *basis*. To define our terms mathematically, consider a set of vectors, $V = \{v_1, \ldots, v_n\}$:

1. A *linear combination* of vectors is represented by the summation $u = \sum_{i=1}^{n} a_i v_i$, where $a_i$ are in the scalar field of choice.
2. The set $V$ is *linearly dependent* if any one of the vectors in the set can be written as the linear combination of the others, e.g., $v_1 = \sum_{i=2}^{n} a_i v_i$, for some scalars $a_i$ in the scalar field.
3. A set that is not linearly dependent is *linearly independent*.
4. The set of all vectors that can be written as linear combinations of the vectors in $V$ is called the *span* of $V$.
5. If the set $V$ is linearly independent and the span of $V$ is the entire vector space $\mathcal{V}$, then $V$ is called a *basis* of $\mathcal{V}$.

An obvious basis for $\mathcal{R}^N$ is the set,

$$B = \{[1, 0, 0, \ldots, 0, 0], [0, 1, 0, \ldots, 0, 0], \ldots, [0, 0, 0, \ldots, 0, 1]\},$$

where the vectors have $N$ elements. A less obvious example is the basis for $\mathcal{C}^n$ where we take the discrete Fourier transform of the complex-valued samples and define the basis as $B = \{v_0, v_1, \ldots v_{N-1}\}$, where $v_n(k) = [e^{j2\pi kn/N}]$. The relationship between signals and their transformations can be thought of in terms of transformations between vector spaces.

### Subspaces of vector spaces

A subspace of a vector space $\mathcal{V}$ is a vector space $\mathcal{V}_0$ that is totally contained within the original vector space, i.e., $\mathcal{V}_0 \subset \mathcal{V}$. Subspaces are often defined in terms of a basis of the original space. For example, if $B = \{b_1, b_2, \ldots b_N\}$ is a basis of the $N$-dimensional space $\mathcal{V}$, then $B_M = \{b_1, b_2, \ldots b_M\}$, $M < N$, is the basis for an $M$-dimensional subspace of $\mathcal{V}$. In terms of the Fourier transforms of signals, the set of all signals that are bandlimited to frequencies less than $F_{min}$ form a subspace of the set of signals that have a Fourier transform. The set of discrete periodic signals of length $N$ can have a bandlimited subspace defined by all the signals whose discrete Fourier transform values, $X(k) = 0$ for $|k| > M$.

### Inner products and orthonormal expansions

We use a basis, $B$, to write the elements of a vector space as

$$\mathbf{v} = \sum_{i=1}^{N} a_i \mathbf{b}_i. \tag{7.1}$$

It is of interest to show how to compute the scalar coefficients $\{a_i\}$. For an $N$-dimensional vector space, this can usually be accomplished by setting up a linear system of equations, as in the case of spaces that are equivalent to $\mathcal{R}^N$. For infinite dimensional spaces, the answer is not so clear. It is useful in all cases to consider the inner product operation and the orthonormal expansions that can be obtained using that concept.

The *inner product* is a generalization of the dot product that is presented in university physics courses. For two vectors, $\mathbf{u}$ and $\mathbf{v}$ in $\mathcal{R}^N$, the inner product is defined by

$$< \mathbf{u}, \mathbf{v} > = \mathbf{u} \cdot \mathbf{v} = \sum_{i=1}^{N} u(i)v(i). \tag{7.2}$$

For the case of vectors defined on the complex space, $\mathcal{C}^N$, the inner product is defined by

$$< \mathbf{u}, \mathbf{v} > = \mathbf{u} \cdot \mathbf{v} = \sum_{i=1}^{N} u^*(i)v(i), \tag{7.3}$$

where we take the complex conjugate of the first vector. This conjugate operation is important when dealing with complex vectors, such as those derived from the Fourier transform of real vectors. The inner product can be defined for vector spaces that represent continuous, integrable functions, as well as more complicated spaces. An example of such an inner product will be described shortly.

The *norm* of a vector is defined in terms of the inner product,

$$||\mathbf{v}|| = \sqrt{< \mathbf{v}, \mathbf{v} >}. \tag{7.4}$$

For the common Euclidean vector space of $\mathcal{R}^N$, this is

$$||\mathbf{v}|| = \sqrt{\sum_{i=1}^{N} v^2(i)}. \tag{7.5}$$

A vector can be normalized to have a length of unity by dividing by its norm. The vector $\mathbf{e}$, defined by

$$\mathbf{e} = \frac{\mathbf{v}}{||\mathbf{v}||}, \tag{7.6}$$

has unit norm. Unit vectors have several uses in signal and image processing. They will be used in the next section for decomposition of the image to achieve more efficient representations. However, there is another concept that must be described first.

Two vectors, **u** and **v**, are *orthogonal* if their inner product is zero, i.e.,

$$< \mathbf{u}, \mathbf{v} > = 0. \tag{7.7}$$

The orthogonal concept is a generalization of *perpendicular* in Euclidean plane geometry. Combining the several concepts, it is very useful to define an *orthonormal basis* as a set of vectors, $B = \{\mathbf{e}_1, \mathbf{e}_2, \ldots, \mathbf{e}_N\}$, that forms a basis for the vector space, each vector has unit norm, and the vectors are mutually orthogonal, i.e.,

$$< \mathbf{e}_i, \mathbf{e}_j > = \delta_{ij} = \begin{cases} 0 & \text{if } i \neq j \\ 1 & \text{if } i = j \end{cases}. \tag{7.8}$$

The concept of orthonormal bases is valid for infinite dimensional spaces. Indeed, the set of functions

$$V = \left\{ v_n(t) = e^{j2\pi nt/T} \right\}_{n=-\infty}^{\infty} \tag{7.9}$$

form an orthonormal basis for the space of periodic functions with period $T$, where the inner product is defined by

$$< f(t), g(t) >= \int_0^T f^*(t) g(t) dt,$$

where we call attention to the complex conjugate of $f(t)$.

One of the main advantages of an orthonormal basis is the ease of finding the coefficients of a representation of a vector as the linear combination of basis vectors. If the vector **v** can be written in terms of an orthonormal basis

$$\mathbf{v} = \sum_{i=1}^{N} a_i \mathbf{e}_i, \tag{7.10}$$

then the coefficient $a_k$ can be found by using the inner product

$$a_k =< \mathbf{v}, \mathbf{e}_k > = < \left( \sum_{i=1}^{N} a_i \mathbf{e}_i \right), \mathbf{e}_k > = \sum_{i=1}^{N} a_i < \mathbf{e}_i, \mathbf{e}_k > . \tag{7.11}$$

From the last term in Eq. (7.11) and using the definition of an orthonormal basis Eq. (7.8), we see that the only nonzero term in the sum is the $k$th. It can now be recognized that the analysis and synthesis equations of the discrete Fourier transform (DFT) in Section 5.3 use this property.

With these concepts, we can now proceed to define operations of interest and see how those concepts can be interpreted in the description of images.

## Subspace operations

It was shown in the previous section that the space of bandlimited signals is a subspace of a larger vector space of signals. The operation of bandlimiting a signal is an operation that maps a vector in one space into a vector in a subspace. This operation can be generalized to an arbitrary vector space by the use of basis vectors. Let the vector $\mathbf{v}$ have a representation in the basis, $B = \{\mathbf{b}_1, \mathbf{b}_2, \cdots \mathbf{b}_N\}$, as

$$\mathbf{v} = \sum_{i=1}^{N} a_i \mathbf{b}_i. \tag{7.12}$$

The *projection* of $\mathbf{v}$ onto the subspace defined by $B_M = \{\mathbf{b}_1, \mathbf{b}_2, \cdots \mathbf{b}_M\}$, $M < N$, is given by

$$P_M(\mathbf{v}) = \sum_{i=1}^{M} a_i \mathbf{b}_i. \tag{7.13}$$

In other words, we have set all the coefficients of basis vectors not in $B_M$ equal to zero. A *projection operator*, $P(\cdot)$, in this mathematical sense, is a function that gives the same results after multiple operations, i.e., $P(P(\mathbf{v})) = P(\mathbf{v})$. Such an operator is also called *idempotent*. If the basis used to define the projection is orthogonal, such a projection is called an *orthogonal projection*. It has the property that the difference between the original vector and the projection is orthogonal to the projection, i.e.,

$$< P(\mathbf{v}), (P(\mathbf{v}) - \mathbf{v}) > \ = 0. \tag{7.14}$$

The property is very useful in using the projection as a lower dimensional approximation to the original vector or signal, or separating particular properties of an image.

Let us consider an example of the separation of an image into two subspaces by using orthogonal projections. If $P(\cdot)$ represents an orthogonal projection onto a subspace, $V_p$, using an orthogonal basis and definition, such as Eq. (7.13), then a complementary projection operator, $P_c(\cdot)$, can be defined by

$$P_c(\mathbf{v}) = \sum_{i=M+1}^{N} a_i \mathbf{b}_i = \mathbf{v} - P(\mathbf{v}). \tag{7.15}$$

The two projections decompose the vector into two orthogonal components. A simple example of such a decomposition is obtained by low pass and high pass filters in the frequency domain.

The bars image of Fig. 3.5a is decomposed into low and high frequency components, shown in Figs. 7.6a and b, respectively. The power spectra associated with these images are shown in Fig. 7.7. These images are computed by using the DFT and projecting onto the low and high pass regions in the frequency domain. The separation is easily seen in the images of the spectra.

Note that the values of the grayscales on the spatial domain images indicate that min/max scaling is used. The results of performing a projection need not result in an image that has the same range as the original. Indeed, the high pass image has a mean value of zero, since the DC term of the DFT is in the low pass region. To interpret the image as emphasizing the edges of the objects in the image, it is necessary to scale the image appropriately.

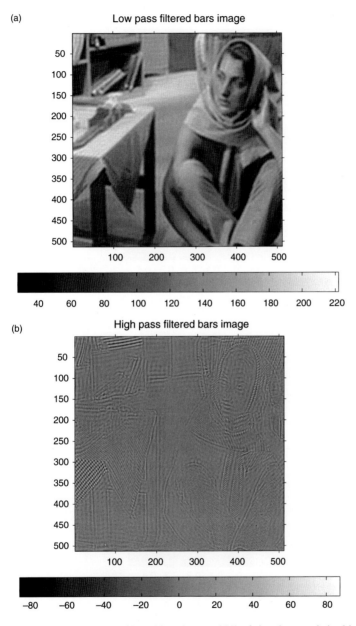

**Figure 7.6.** (a) Low-pass filtered bars image: 95% of signal power is in this region; (b) high-pass filtered bars image: Note rescaling, since average value is zero.

A second characteristic of the images is the obvious ringing around the edges. The ringing is characteristic of truncation of the Fourier transform. To see this, let us modify the figures used to illustrate the derivation of the discrete Fourier transform, Fig. 5.3 of Chapter 5. Consider a rectangular pulse in the time domain, whose Fourier transform is a sinc function. This is shown in Fig. 7.8. If the Fourier transform is truncated, as

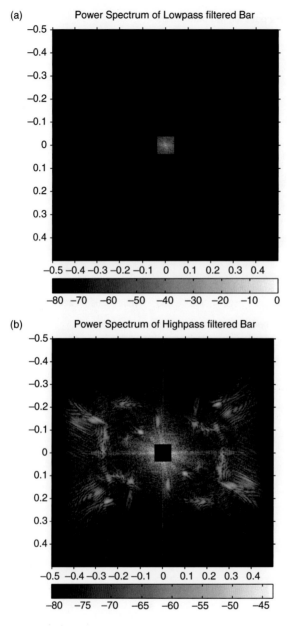

**Figure 7.7.** (a) Spectrum of low pass filtered bars image: 95% of signal power is in this region; (b) spectrum of high pass filtered bars image.

will occur with an ideal low pass filter, the effect is to multiply the Fourier transform of the pulse by a rectangular function in the frequency domain. This is equivalent to convolving the pulse in the time domain by a sinc function, which produces the ringing at the edges of the pulse. This ringing produced by truncation of a Fourier transform is

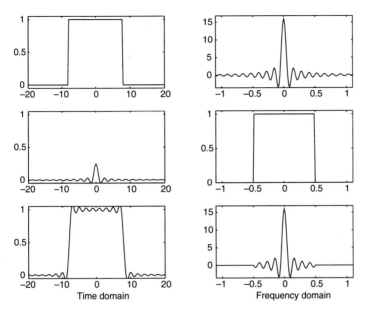

**Figure 7.8.** Graphic demonstration of Gibbs' phenomenon caused by the truncation of the Fourier transform.

a manifestation of an effect called *Gibbs' phenomenon*. The ringing in the image is the two-dimensional analogy of *Gibbs' phenomenon*.

The ringing caused by truncation can be lessened by rolling off the filter at the ends of the passband; that is, instead of having a sharp edge in the frequency domain we can have a smooth transition. An example will be shown later in Fig. 7.9. However, such a filter does not have the projection properties that we wish for subspace decomposition. Other subspaces that can be defined by other transformations, such as, cosine, Walsh–Hadamard, Karhunen–Loeve, wavelet, splines and Legendre polynomials, can be considered if it is necessary to avoid such effects [134, 192, 217, 283].

In the spatial domain, a region of support for an image defines a subspace. For some images, the object of interest is limited to a known region of the total image area. This is true of medical images such as X-ray tomography, but not of great importance for pictorial images. Mathematically, the projection onto the region of support defined by the region, $(i,j) \in \mathcal{R}$, is given by

$$P_{\mathcal{R}}(f(i,j)) = \begin{cases} f(i,j) & \text{if } (i,j) \in \mathcal{R} \\ 0 & \text{if } (i,j) \notin \mathcal{R} \end{cases}. \tag{7.16}$$

The subspaces of interest do not have to represent contiguous areas in either the spatial or frequency domains. Thresholds related to signal power can be used to define the regions of interest. This is commonly done in image coding applications where the power in the frequency domain is used to define which frequencies will be retained.

The subspace concepts that have been introduced here will become even more useful as we introduce statistical characteristics of images in the next section.

2D Gaussian (σ = 3) blurred image

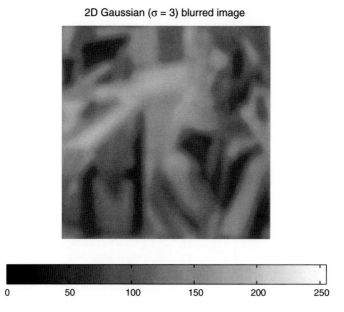

| | | | | |
|---|---|---|---|---|
| 0 | 50 | 100 | 150 | 200 | 250 |

**Figure 7.9.** Estimated mean of ensemble containing bars images.

## 7.2     Stochastic properties

Images can be viewed as a deterministic process of recording a specific scene or object. This is usually the case when dealing with a single image that has no external context. Even then, we use some statistical notions to describe the images, such as the mean and histogram, discussed previously. It is often useful to consider a class of images or even a single image as a representative member of an image ensemble. By describing the characteristics of the ensemble, we also describe the characteristics of the image.

Consider the bars image that we have used for many examples. It may be considered as an example of informal portrait photography, or indoor residential photography. Using a more general classification, it might be considered an example of photographs of people, of furniture, or just an example of photographs. In each case, we would need to decide how representative this image was, relative to the ensemble of interest.

From a practical point of view, there are many statistical image processing techniques that are used to perform various tasks. These include noise reduction, blur restoration, segmentation and classification. These techniques are based on statistical models of the image and require estimates of statistical parameters for implementation. If we decide that we will use such methods, then we estimate the necessary parameters using the best means available to us. Often, this requires that we obtain the estimates from a single image. While this may appear to be based on shaky theoretical grounds, the results are usually useful and acceptable for the applications of interest. We will point out the assumptions and their violations in the following sections.

In the next section, we assume that the reader is familiar with basic statistical characterization of signals. A brief review of the common statistical and probability concepts that are assumed are presented in Appendix C. Here, we will concentrate on the interpretation of these properties in the context of image processing.

### 7.2.1 Basic statistics: mean, variance, correlations

#### Mean

The mean of an image, defined as the average value of a pixel anywhere in the image, can be obtained directly from the histogram of the image. If the mean refers to an ensemble of images, then only an estimate can be obtained from a single image. Let us consider a digital image, $f(m,n)$. The mean at each pixel is denoted $E\{f(m,n)\}$ and may vary with the indices $(m,n)$. If the image has a *stationary* mean,[3] then the mean is the same for all pixels, i.e., $E\{f(m,n)\} = \mu$. Such a situation is reasonable for some image ensembles, e.g., aerial or satellite photos. For many common ensembles, we would expect certain variations. For example, a collection of landscape images would probably be lighter or tending to blue at the top, reflecting the fact that the sky is usually, but not always, in the image and at the top. An ensemble of driver's license photos for a particular state would be nonstationary, since there would be common background with faces centered in the image.

If it is necessary to work with a stationary process, it is easy to subtract a nonstationary mean from the image, leaving a stationary residual. The new image, $g(m,n) = f(m,n) - E\{f(m,n)\}$, has a zero mean at each pixel, and so clearly has a stationary mean. Of course, it remains to obtain an estimate for the mean, $\hat{\mu}(m,n) \approx E\{f(m,n)\}$. If a real collection of images exists, $\{f_i(m,n)\}_{i=1}^{K}$, e.g., if we have an actual collection of driver's license images, the mean can be estimated by an arithmetic average,

$$\hat{\mu}(m,n) = \frac{1}{K}\sum_{i=1}^{K} f_i(m,n). \tag{7.17}$$

Often, such a collection does not exist for a one-of-a-kind image. In these cases, we imagine the ensemble and construct a reasonable mean. In the cases of examples that we know, such as the driver's license collection, we can imagine that the mean of such an ensemble resembles a blurry version of the image of interest. With this in mind, we can construct an estimate of the mean by blurring the image of interest. For the ensemble of images of women wearing striped outfits sitting beside a table, the mean might look like Fig. 7.9. Note that the extent of the blur is a personal choice. This image was blurred using a Gaussian blur with a standard deviation of three pixels in the spatial domain. The Fourier transform of a Gaussian is a Gaussian and does not have the sharp edges of the ideal bandpass filter used to demonstrate projections. This filter avoids the ringing at the edges, which would not be consistent with our idea of a mean image.

---

[3] See Appendix C for a review of the stationary property of stochastic processes.

## Variance

The variance of the image ensemble, as the mean, is also defined as a function of the pixel position. If the image is assumed to be a stationary process, we have $\text{Var}\{f(m, n)\} = E\{(f(m, n) - \mu)^2\} = \sigma^2$. In the case of the variance, it is harder to imagine an image with stationary variance than it is for a stationary mean. Consider the ensemble for which the estimated mean is shown in Fig. 7.9. The variation in the images might be caused by varying camera positions and model poses. For such a scenario, we would expect the variation in the region of the striped clothing to be much higher than in the region of the carpet or wall.

Creating a new image with a truly stationary variance is much more difficult than creating one with a stationary mean. This can be done only by spatially varying processing, for example, amplifying the zero mean process locally to obtain a constant variance. A straightforward way to approximate a constant variance image is to estimate the local variance by averaging the square of the zero mean image. Dividing the zero mean image pixel-by-pixel by the square root of this average gives an image with an approximate variance of unity. This image can be scaled to any range desired. An example of such an image is shown in Fig. 7.10. The main use for such images is a normalizing step in pattern recognition and image analysis applications. Visually, one can see that areas of small variance, e.g., the carpet, are greatly amplified in contrast, while regions of high variance, e.g., the striped clothing, are reduced in contrast.

## Autocovariance, autocorrelation and power spectrum

The relationship between autocovariance and autocorrelation is one of inclusion of the mean of the process. As noted in Appendix C, the autocovariance subtracts the mean

Constant variance image

**Figure 7.10.** Constant variance approximation of bars image.

before taking the expected value. If the mean is known, it can be subtracted to produce a zero mean process, where autocovariance and autocorrelation are identical. With this in mind, we will consider only the autocorrelation.

The other relationship of great importance is between the autocorrelation and the power spectrum. The power spectrum of a stationary random process is the Fourier transform of the autocorrelation of the process. We have used the term *power spectrum* previously as simply the absolute value squared of the Fourier transform of a deterministic signal. Unfortunately, this is common usage in the image processing profession, so it will be continued here. But let us give some justification for this.

To use many of the statistically based processing methods, it is necessary to assume stationarity of the process that forms the image. It was shown in the previous two sections that this assumption is rarely justified for real images. It is possible to create an image that has approximately stationary mean and variance, as shown in Fig. 7.10. However, if the autocorrelation were the same in all local regions of the image, the characteristics of the various objects in the image would disappear. For example, the distinctive pattern of stripes in the clothing of the bars image, implies a periodicity that is manifested by periodicity in the autocorrelation and an isolated peak in the power spectrum; the low-contrast area of the carpet does not show these characteristics. There is no transformation that would make these areas have similar statistical properties and retain anything of their visual identity. So, for all practical purposes, actual images will never be stationary.

From a practical viewpoint, this does not mean that we cannot use statistically based methods that assume stationarity. It means only that when we use such methods, we recognize that they will be suboptimal. When we use such methods, the statistical parameters must be estimated. Since the only data that are available are for the image with which we are working, we have few options except to estimate the parameters using those data. In this case, the estimate of the power spectrum is obtained by computing the Fourier transform of the image, taking the absolute value and squaring it. This is the *periodogram* of the image. This estimate is easy to compute but has several disadvantages.

The most problematic shortcoming of the periodogram is that it is not a *consistent* estimator. An estimator is consistent if the variance of the estimator decreases when more data are used in the computation. It is shown in many statistical and digital signal processing texts that this is not the case for the periodogram. The practical problem with an estimator with a high variance is that it magnifies the variance of the output of the image processing method in which it is used. For example, the minimum mean square error (MMSE) estimator of the original image in the deblurring problem requires a division by the estimate of the power spectrum of the blurred and noisy image. Division by a small estimate can greatly distort the output of the MMSE method.

There are several ways to modify the periodogram to ameliorate this problem. All of these techniques can be found in digital signal processing texts that cover spectral estimation, e.g., [200, 218]; texts on spectral estimation cover the topic in great depth, e.g., [144, 176, 254]. The two most common techniques are *Welch's method* of averaging windowed periodograms from various parts of the image and autoregressive modeling (AR), which has a small number of coefficients to estimate. Both of these methods produce an estimate with a smaller variance. Of course, the price for this smaller variance is a bias that makes the estimate less accurate. As we have noted, since the image is not a stationary process, any estimate that we make of the autocorrelation or power spectrum will be inaccurate.

The power spectra of the images shown in Chapter 5 are computed using the periodogram. This could be done since the estimate was not to be used for further processing. Using only a Hamming window on the subimage of Fig. 5.17a, we obtain the power spectral estimate of Fig. 7.11. This simple addition eliminates the strong frequency components on the horizonal and vertical axes that are the result of the edge discontinuities. These discontinuities were emphasized in Fig. 5.18. The basic frequency components are emphasized without this clutter. The estimate is also noticeably smoother. The frequency components are emphasized by the fact that we choose a section of the image with a single periodic pattern. If we used the Welch method to average spectra over the entire image, Fig. 3.5, the effects would not be so dramatic, as shown in Fig. 7.12. Autoregressive methods of spectral estimation are discussed in Section 7.3.1.

## 7.2.2    Bandwidth

From communications, we speak of a high bandwidth signal as one that contains a wide range of frequencies. In particular, we expect such signals to have a significant portion of high frequency information. This high frequency information is represented as rapid transitions of amplitudes. In images, this means sharp, high contrast edges or areas of fine detail.

The most common example of an edge is a rectangular pulse, as was mentioned in Section 7.1.2. It was noted that the edges caused by the discontinuities at the image

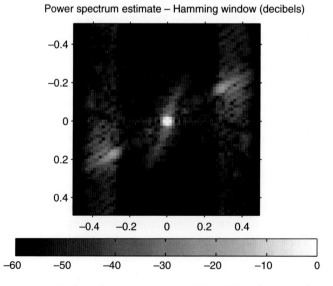

**Figure 7.11.** Estimated power spectrum of Fig. 5.17a using Hamming window.

Power spectrum estimate – Welch–Hamming window (decibels)

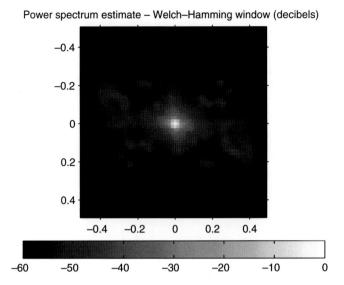

**Figure 7.12.** Estimated power spectrum of Fig. 3.5 using Welch method and Hamming window (averaged over entire bars image).

edges produce much of the high frequency power. Using windows can help eliminate the high frequency power in the spectral estimate that is caused by the artificial edges at the image boundaries. However, it is apparent from Fig. 7.11 that, after eliminating such artificial high frequency power by windowing, there remains much actual high frequency information in the image, as expected.

Images of text have high bandwidths because of the high contrast edges. Text images also have periodic characteristics associated with line and character spacing that show up in the frequency domain. An example of a text image and its spectrum is shown in Figs. 7.13a, 7.13b, respectively. Note the effect of the periodicity of the line spacing. Portraits, such as Fig. 7.14a, do not have a lot of sharp edges and thus would not have significant power at high frequencies. Figure 7.14b shows the power spectrum of this portrait.

It is difficult to quantify the bandwidth of an image since there is rarely, if ever, a maximum frequency, above which there is no signal power. As we have seen in the examples of Figs. 7.11, 7.13b and 7.14b, the image power simply tends toward zero as frequencies increase. As a result, we will often speak of the 95% or 99% power bandwidth. The power of the image contained within this finite region is 95% or 99% of the total power in the image. For example, the region defined by the low pass filter of Fig. 7.7a contains about 95% of the total power in the bars image. While this may seem like a very large amount of power, it is clear that the remaining 5% contains a significant amount of image information. It should also be noted that the decibel scale used in the power spectrum display may be misleading to the novice in judging the percentage of power beyond a certain limit.

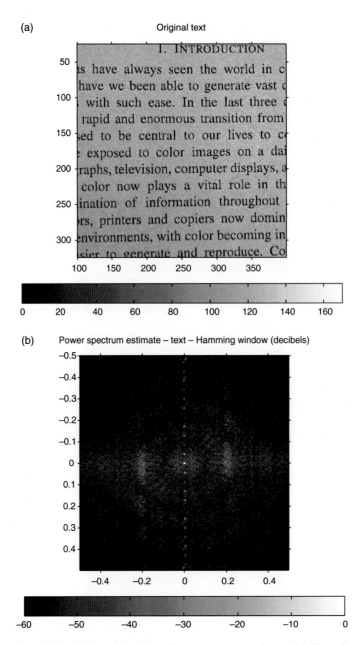

**Figure 7.13.** (a) Text; (b) estimated power spectrum of text with Hamming window.

## 7.2.3 Noise

Any measurable quantity is subject to noise. There is always uncertainty caused by the finite precision of the measuring device. In the digital world, there is uncertainty caused by the finite number of bits that are used to represent the quantity. In the case of light,

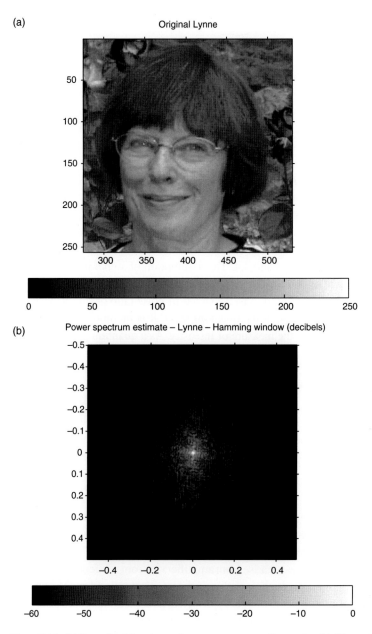

**Figure 7.14.** (a) Portrait; (b) estimated power spectrum of portrait with Hamming window.

there is an inherent uncertainty caused by the nature of light itself. The intensity of light is directly related to the number of photons received in a unit of time. The exact number of photons is a random variable as a result of the quantum nature of photons. We will leave the mathematics of noise processes to Appendix C. In this section, we will concentrate on basic modeling and examples.

The usual model of noise in an image is an additive system:

$$g(m, n) = f(m, n) + \eta(m, n), \tag{7.18}$$

where $f(m, n)$ is the ideal image and $\eta(m, n)$ is the noise. It is usual that the noise process is assumed to be independent of the image. For example, a photodiode is subject to dark current noise, that is, there is some electrical activity caused by random movements of electrons. Since this activity often depends on temperature, it is also referred to as *thermal noise*. This type of noise does not depend on the amount of light that hits the diode, so the independence assumption is reasonable.

*Quantization noise* is usually modeled as a signal independent, white, additive process with a uniform distribution. This is a good assumption for signals that vary by several quantization levels between samples. The variance of the quantization noise depends on the number of bits per pixel, which is directly related to the number of quantization levels. The white noise assumption can be seen by the examples of quantization error in Chapter 4, Figs. 4.3 and 4.4. The assumption of signal independence can be seen to be dependent on the number of bits, as shown in Fig. 4.5. It is shown in Chapter 4 that under reasonable assumptions, the signal-to-noise ratio of a $b$-bit system is about $6b$ dB.

If we consider light at the quantum level, it is the number of photons detected in a certain time that is the measure of intensity. As a quantum phenomenon, the number of photons is usually modeled as a Poisson random process. This is termed *Poisson noise* or *shot noise*. As discussed in Appendix C, the variance of a Poisson process is equal to the mean of the process. So the variance of the noise at a detector is clearly dependent on the average intensity of the light, and the noise is signal dependent. If the number of photons is large, that is, the light intensity is high, the Poisson process can be well approximated by a Gaussian process. The additive model can be used but with the addition of a signal dependent term

$$g(m, n) = f(m, n) + \eta[m, n, f(m, n)], \tag{7.19}$$

where $\eta[m, n, f(m, n)]$ is a random variable drawn from a Gaussian distribution with zero mean and variance $f(m, n)$. *Film grain noise* is typically modeled as image dependent Gaussian, where the dependence is on the film density [217].

Other noise processes arise from amplifiers or from semiconductor properties. In many cases the number of photons reaching a detector is small and must be amplified to produce a measurable current or voltage. Typically, in *amplifier noise*, each photon that is absorbed causes the re-emission of an average of $K$ electrons or other particles. The actual number is a random variable and is usually modeled as a binomial distribution. The combination of a Poisson input signal with binomial amplification can be shown to yield another Poisson distribution. Only the mean is changed by the simple multiplicative factor $K$.

A phenomenon that is observed in semiconductor circuits is *flicker* or $1/f$ (pronounced "one over f") noise. There is presently no generally accepted theory for this type of noise, but it is observed to have a power spectrum that can be approximated by

$$H(f) = \frac{CI^2}{|f|},$$

where $f$ is temporal frequency in hertz, $I$ is current and $C$ is a constant related to the particular circuit materials and geometry. The noise is introduced when sampling one-dimensional signals associated with images. For example, two-dimensional CCD arrays are read by "clocking out" each line of the array, and this produces a one-dimensional analog signal to be sampled. This type of noise can be the dominant noise source at low frequencies. Of course, the model cannot hold at $f = 0$.

There are many ways for noise to enter the imaging process. In fact, whenever, we introduce uncertainty, we tend to describe that uncertainty as noise. For example, it is often convenient to model an image formation process as a simple convolution of the image and the point spread function of the lens, as described in Chapter 2. Since there is uncertainty about the exact form of the point spread function, we might model the image formation as

$$g(m, n) = [h(m, n) + \Delta h(m, n)] * f(m, n), \qquad (7.20)$$

where $*$ represents convolution and $\Delta h(m, n)$ represents the uncertainty in the estimate of the point spread function, $h(m, n)$. The problem of recovering $f(m, n)$ from $g(m, n)$ is very difficult, so the easy approach is to modify the problem and define $\eta(m, n)$ of Eq. (7.18) as

$$\eta(m, n) = \Delta h(m, n) * f(m, n). \qquad (7.21)$$

This noise is clearly signal dependent, but since that problem is difficult to solve, image scientists often proceed with an assumption of independence for computational convenience. The result is suboptimal but often adequate.

### Signal-to-noise ratios

The most common way to measure the effect of noise on a signal is the signal-to-noise ratio (SNR). This is usually defined as the ratio of signal power, $\sigma_f^2$, to noise power, $\sigma_\eta^2$,

$$\text{SNR} = \frac{\sigma_f^2}{\sigma_\eta^2}; \qquad (7.22)$$

or in decibels

$$\text{SNR}_{dB} = 10 \log_{10} \left( \frac{\sigma_f^2}{\sigma_\eta^2} \right). \qquad (7.23)$$

For an $M \times N$ image, the image power is usually estimated by the simple summation

$$\sigma_f^2 = \frac{1}{MN} \sum_{m=0}^{M-1} \sum_{n=0}^{N-1} (f(m, n) - \mu_f)^2, \qquad (7.24)$$

where $\mu_f$ is the mean of the image. The mean is subtracted since images are not zero mean processes. We are interested in the variation of the signal within its range and not its absolute amplitude. For the case of noise in an image, we are interested in any bias or mean value. To estimate the noise power, the mean should not be subtracted in a formula analogous to Eq. (7.24). If samples of the noise are not available, it is common to insert a best guess. This formula for SNR gives a reasonable measure of image quality for images and noise that are widely distributed over the region of interest.

An important application of this SNR formula is the case of a Poisson process, such as light. The signal in this case is the mean of the number of photons. As such, the mean should not be subtracted. In this case, the signal power is the mean squared, $\sigma_f^2 = \mu^2$. The variance of the noise is the mean, so that $\sigma_\eta^2 = \mu$. The SNR of a Poisson process is

$$\text{SNR}_{\text{Poisson}} = \frac{\mu^2}{\mu} = \mu. \tag{7.25}$$

From this, we see that while the variance of the noise increases with the mean, the signal-to-noise ratio also increases. This makes heuristic sense since we can obtain better images with more light. This, of course, neglects any saturation effects of the light detector.

In the case that the region of interest within an image is concentrated in a small region of the image, the above definition of SNR may be misleading. Consider an image of a star against the black background of space. In this case, integrating the signal power over the entire image gives an artificially low value, since the star is readily visible. If the same image power were distributed across the entire extent of the image, it would be very difficult to distinguish the difference from the black background. For such cases, a better measure is the peak signal-to-RMS-noise power, defined by

$$\text{SNR}_{\text{peak}} = \frac{\max\{f(m, n)\}}{\sigma_\eta}. \tag{7.26}$$

A text image would have similar properties that would make $\text{SNR}_{\text{peak}}$ a preferable measure of the effect of noise. While we use the symbol $\text{SNR}_{\text{peak}}$ to make easy comparison with other noise measures, the term PSNR is more often used. The measure is frequently used when measuring image distortion caused by coding, restoration or demosaicking, even though there is debate over whether this is the best measure.

### Examples of noise in images

Having defined two types of signal-to-noise ratio, let us observe their qualitative properties and get some feel for what a given SNR means in terms of image quality and target detectability. Let us begin with the usual bars image. We will assume the additive noise model and that the noise is zero mean, signal independent, white Gaussian. This is the most common noise model. It should be noted that image noise cannot be truly Gaussian, since an image is a nonnegative signal, and the result of adding noise cannot produce a negative value. However, if the image values are high and the noise variance small, the probability of producing a negative value is vanishingly small, and the Gaussian assumption is practical.

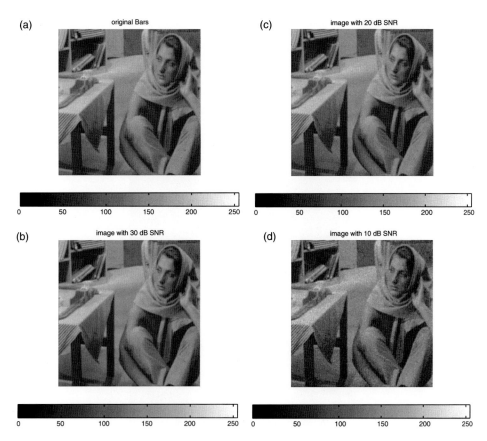

**Figure 7.15.** (a) Bars image original, same as Fig. 3.5; (b) noisy bars image with white Gaussian noise at 30 dB SNR; (c) noisy bars image with white Gaussian noise at 20 dB SNR; (d) noisy bars image with white Gaussian noise at 10 dB SNR.

Let us consider the standard bars image that we have used many times, reproduced here in Fig. 7.15a to allow easy comparison with the noisy versions. Figures 7.15b, c and d show the effects of additive, white Gaussian noise with SNRs of 30 dB, 20 dB and 10 dB, respectively. We see that noise at the 30 dB level is barely visible and that at the 10 dB level it is very distracting.

The same image is reproduced assuming Poisson noise. Since Poisson noise depends on the mean value of the pixel, we assume that the value of the pixel in the original 0–255 range represents the average number of photons detected at that pixel. This is a very small number of photons and we would expect a very noisy image, which is shown in Fig. 7.16a. The SNR computed by Eq. (7.22) is 15.43 dB. This gives an approximate comparison with the additive noise images, but note that the Poisson noise is signal dependent. If the light is increased by a factor of 100, the image is in the range of 0–25 500. The variance of the noise increases, but the SNR increases also. We generate an image based on the value of the pixel being 1/100 of the number of photons detected and scale the resulting image to the original range for display, Fig. 7.16b. The SNR

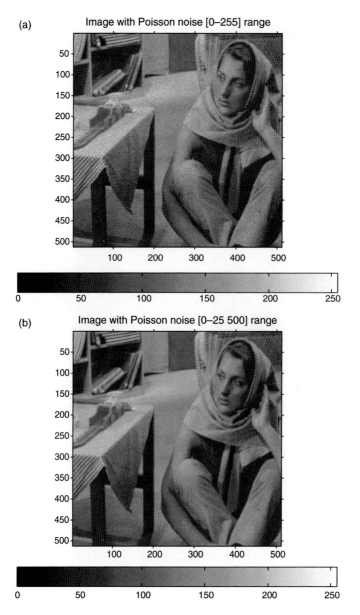

**Figure 7.16.** (a) Noisy bars image with Poisson noise and image in [0–255] range
(SNR = 15.43 dB); (b) noisy bars image with Poisson noise and image in [0–25 500] range 100
times more light than the image in (a) above (SNR = 34.53 dB).

computed by Eq. (7.22) is 34.53 dB. This number gives us the insight that most noise in
photographic images that are taken with normal lighting comes from the dark current,
not from quantum effects. Images taken at low light and many images taken with special
high precision scientific instruments may be subject to Poisson noise.

### 7.2.4     Stochastic subspaces

Stochastic signals are characterized by the statistics of the ensembles to which they belong. The bandwidth of a stochastic signal is determined by the power spectrum, the Fourier transform of the autocorrelation function. As was noted previously, if we are given an image, an estimate of the power spectrum is the periodogram or a windowed version of it. Thus, in many cases, there is little practical difference in characterizing deterministic and stochastic images in the frequency domain. There are two cases of interest where stochastic characterization is extremely useful. The first is the characterization of noise; the second is characterization using nonFourier basis functions.

#### Noise subspaces

In the case of noise, the goal of a subspace decomposition is to find a subspace where the image power dominates the noise power. As mentioned, it is rare that a signal has absolutely no power in a given band. We noted that the power in most images decreases with increasing frequency. Likewise, noise power is usually present in all bands to some extent. Thus, it is the SNR within a band that is of interest.

The most common noise model is white noise that is independent of the image signal. By definition, white noise has an autocorrelation function, $r(m, n)$, that is a multiple of the delta function, $r(m, n) = \sigma^2 \delta(m, n)$. From our knowledge of Fourier transforms, we see that the power spectrum of white noise is a constant. Indeed, the term *white noise* is derived from the analogy to white light, which contains all wavelengths of light at roughly equal power. The power of white noise is equally spread across all spatial frequencies. In the case of white noise, the noise cannot be localized to a subspace. However, since the image has varying power over the frequency bands, the SNR will change across the spectrum. This is the basis for Wiener filtering, discussed in Chapter 14.

There are other types of noise that do have characteristic frequencies. Since images are often the result of a scanning process, noise is often found that is related to the scanning frequency. For example, if an image is formed from a vertical sequence of horizonal scan lines, a slight offset of the vertical spacing can produce periodic banding. Another common example of periodic noise occurs in the scanning of halftoned images. The halftoning process is presented in Chapter 11. Many halftoning methods rely on a periodic dot pattern, which is modulated to produce the displayed image. The periodicity of the dot pattern will be apparent in the spectrum of the scanned image. The effect is an interaction of the scanning frequency and halftone frequencies that results in a *moire* pattern. The detection of such noise patterns is the basis of many algorithms to dehalftone (or descreen) such images. The pattern of noise in the frequency domain will yield a subspace for the noise signal. Eliminating or reducing the power in this subspace will attenuate the visual moire effect.

#### NonFourier basis functions

The use of the frequency domain is facilitated by the fact that the sinusoids that form the basis functions of the Fourier decomposition are familiar to everyone. While the Fourier decomposition is common, it is not necessarily the optimal decomposition for many purposes. There are many transformations used with digital images, including Fourier, cosine, Walsh–Hadamard and wavelets of various types. We will outline the Karhunen–Loeve (K–L) transformation in this section as an example of an optimal transform. This will give the reader insight into reasons to explore this and various other transformations.

The K–L transform is optimal in the sense that it allows the most signal power to be compressed into the smallest dimensional subspace. To make this more precise, let us use one-dimensional signals. Consider the ensemble of stationary, zero-mean $N$-dimensional signals in $\mathcal{R}^N$, where the signal is represented by

$$\mathbf{v} = \sum_{i=1}^{N} a_i \mathbf{b}_i, \tag{7.27}$$

where the set $B = \{\mathbf{b}_i\}_{i=1}^{N}$ represents an arbitrary orthonormal basis.[4] The K–L transform finds a new orthogonal basis, $E = \{\mathbf{e}_i\}_{i=1}^{N}$, such that for any $M$-dimensional subspace of $\mathcal{R}^N$, the expected value of the power of a signal in the subspace, defined by $\{\mathbf{e}_i\}_{i=1}^{M}$, is maximal. Mathematically, if the signal is represented exactly by

$$\mathbf{v}_N = \sum_{i=1}^{N} a_i \mathbf{b}_i = \sum_{i=1}^{N} c_i \mathbf{e}_i, \tag{7.28}$$

and the $M$-dimensional approximations are given by

$$\mathbf{v}_{Mb} = \sum_{i=1}^{M} a_i \mathbf{b}_i \tag{7.29}$$

and

$$\mathbf{v}_{Me} = \sum_{i=1}^{M} c_i \mathbf{e}_i, \tag{7.30}$$

then the mean square error of the K–L representation is no larger than any other approximation,

$$E\{||\mathbf{v}_{Me} - \mathbf{v}||^2\} \le E\{||\mathbf{v}_{Mb} - \mathbf{v}||^2\}. \tag{7.31}$$

Since the total power of the signal for an orthonormal basis is given by

$$P_N = \sum_{i=1}^{N} |a_i|^2 = \sum_{i=1}^{N} |c_i|^2, \tag{7.32}$$

the expected power of the K–L representation in the $M$-dimensional subspace is not less than that of any other orthonormal representation,

$$\sum_{i=1}^{M} |a_i|^2 \le \sum_{i=1}^{M} |c_i|^2. \tag{7.33}$$

---

[4] It can be shown that representations using nonorthonormal bases are less efficient than those using orthonormal ones.

The basis vectors of the K–L transform are actually the eigenvectors of the autocorrelation matrix of the 1-D signal defined by the basis $B$. The autocorrelation is defined as

$$R_a = E\{\mathbf{aa}^T\}. \tag{7.34}$$

The proofs of these statements are found in Appendix C. We should emphasize that since the basis for the K–L transform depends on the autocorrelation of the ensemble, it is unique for each ensemble.

The value of the K–L transformation is to create a representation of the signal such that the signal power is concentrated in the first few dimensions of a vector space. For the case of a signal in white noise, this allows an increase in the SNR in these dimensions, since the noise power is white and has equal power in all dimensions, regardless of the representation.

To generalize the K–L transformation to two dimensions is not straightforward. The easiest mathematically rigorous method requires the use of stacked notation to vectorize the image matrix and the assumption of separability of the two-dimensional autocorrelation matrix. We will leave this manipulation to Appendix C, also. It is of interest to see the effect of such a transformation, which is visually very small. The Fourier approximation using the first 20 terms produces an approximation with SNR of 7.42 dB, while the K–L transform using the same number of terms produces 7.64. Using the first 40 Fourier terms the SNR increases only to 9.20 dB and the K–L to 9.34 dB. The images corresponding to the 40 term reproductions are shown in Fig. 7.17. Note that the K–L method retains the ringing associated with the Gibbs' phenomenon of the Fourier method.

While it is noted that the gain of using the K–L transformation is small, consider the assumptions that were required to make the mathematical implementation tractable. It was necessary to assume a stationary, ergodic random process, in order to estimate the covariance (correlation) matrix from the single image. In addition, the covariance was assumed to be separable, which is another unlikely situation. Nevertheless, the method produced a better compression of energy than the standard Fourier transform.

## 7.3 Models for generation of images

Since we often think of images as members of an ensemble that is characterized by its statistical properties, it is natural to consider how such images might arise from stochastic assumptions. In other words, we would like to determine the nature of the stochastic process that could generate such an ensemble. Most image processing methods require the use of first and second order statistics. This is called *wide-sense stationarity*: we assume a stationary mean and autocovariance. For this case, we need to determine methods that can generate the appropriate mean and autocovariance.

Stochastic signals are usually modeled as the result of the input of a stochastic random process to a deterministic system. Most often the random process is white noise and the deterministic system is a linear filter. From our knowledge of linear, shift-invariant

(a)  First 40 Fourier terms in both horizontal and vertical bars image

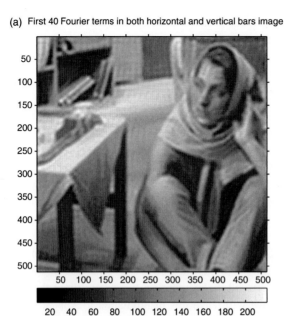

(b)  First 40 K−L terms in both horizontal and vertical bars image

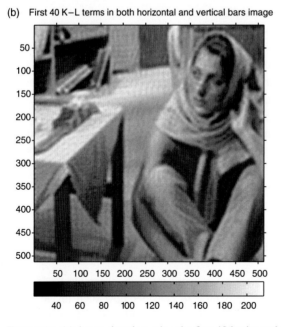

**Figure 7.17.** (a) Approximation using the first 40 horizontal and vertical frequency components of the 2-D Fourier transform (SNR = 9.20 dB); (b) approximation using the first 40 horizontal and vertical frequency components of the K–L transform (SNR = 9.34 dB).

systems, the output of such a model is given by

$$s(x, y) = h(x, y) * w(x, y) = \int_{-\infty}^{\infty} \int_{-\infty}^{\infty} h(r, t) w(x - r, y - t) \, dr dt,$$

where, $w(x, y)$ is white noise and $h(x, y)$ is the impulse response of the system. We show in Appendix C that the power spectra of the input and output are related by

$$P_{ss}(u, v) = |H(u, v)|^2 P_{ww}(u, v) = \sigma^2 |H(u, v)|^2,$$

where $P_{ww}(u, v)$ is the power spectrum of the white noise with variance $\sigma^2$, $P_{ss}(u, v)$ is the power spectrum of the output image and $H(u, v)$ is the Fourier transform of the point spread function. Recall that the power spectrum of white noise is a constant. Under this definition, the constant is the variance of the noise. Since the power spectrum is the Fourier transform of the autocorrelation function, the above relation defines the autocorrelation function as well.

Given a desired autocorrelation function, the process of finding a filter $H(u, v)$ that realizes a stochastic process with those characteristics is called *spectral factorization*. Determining this filter is usually an approximation process. A rational polynomial is assumed for the functional form of $H(u, v)$. In two dimensions, the point spread function may be assumed to be separable in order to further simplify the problem. Details of these methods can be found in digital signal processing texts that discuss least squares filter design, and spectral estimation texts [144, 176, 200, 218, 254].

While we can create systems that can produce sample signals that have the statistical characteristics of the ensemble that are desired, this task is used mostly for running simulations of systems. It is more common to attempt to determine the statistical characteristics of the ensemble from sample signals or, most often, from a single sample image. With this in mind, let us briefly describe some models and the estimation of their parameters.

### 7.3.1 One-dimensional models

We will start with one-dimensional models because of their simple mathematical descriptions. After getting a heuristic feel for the process, we will move to two-dimensional systems.

#### Finite impulse response models
For digital systems, the simplest filter representation is an FIR system. The model for a filter of length $p$ is

$$x(n) = h(n) * w(n) = \sum_{k=0}^{p-1} h(k) w(n - k).$$

An advantage of this model is that the autocorrelation function can be matched exactly for the first $p$ values. This requires a solution to the nonlinear system of equations defined by

$$r(n) = h(-n) * h(n).$$

This system can be solved easily using a recursive algorithm that begins by setting $h(0) = 1$ and solving for $h(p)$, using the last nonzero term in the autocorrelation, $r(p) = h(0)h(p)$.

Alternatively, we can take the fast Fourier transform of the autocorrelation to obtain the power spectrum, $P_{xx}(u)$. Assuming white noise input, we have $P_{xx}(u) = |H(u)|^2$. We can choose the phase of the $H(u)$ to yield a causal filter, $h(n)$. This is virtually equivalent to computing the periodogram as the estimate for the spectrum of the image ensemble. Thus, it suffers from the same problems of inconsistency as the periodogram.

### Infinite impulse response models

The most common signal model is an autoregressive (AR) model. This is the standard all-pole filter. It is a recursive system given by

$$x(n) = \sum_{k=1}^{p} a(k)x(n-k) + w(n).$$

The advantage of this model is that the $P$ terms that define the model are easily determined. The mathematics of this computation are given in Appendix C. The estimates with this model are consistent. The disadvantage is that the model cannot be used to model complex random processes. This model can be considered a predictor for the random process, since the current value of the process, $x(n)$, differs from the "predicted" value, $\hat{x}(n)$, defined by

$$\hat{x}(n) = \sum_{k=1}^{p} a(k)x(n-k),$$

by the noise term, $w(n)$. The quantity $\hat{x}(n)$ is a predictor of the actual signal based on the last $p$ values of the signal. This model is appropriate for $p$th order Markov processes.

The power spectrum of the random process defined by such a model is easily obtained by the discrete Fourier transform of the AR coefficients and is given by

$$P_{xx}(u) = \sigma_n^2 \left| \sum_{k=0}^{P} a(k) e^{j2\pi ku} \right|^2.$$

The demonstration of this fact is shown in Appendix C. Advantages and disadvantages of the autoregressive model are also discussed in that appendix.

## 7.4        Two-dimensional stochastic image models

A major difference in the one- and two-dimensional models is that the concept of *causality* cannot be naturally extended from one to two dimensions. Otherwise, the mathematical methods are virtually identical. The general form of the 2-D autoregressive image formation model is

$$x(m, n) = \sum_{(k,l) \in S_x} a(k, l)x(m - k, n - l) + w(m, n), \tag{7.35}$$

where $a(k, l)$ are the prediction coefficients, $S_x$ is a subset of indices in the 2-D lattice that defines the *prediction region* and $w(m, n)$ white noise. This can be interpreted as the linear predictor, where $w(m, n)$ is the prediction error. We use the notation of the set of indices, $S_x$, to represent the many different shapes of the regions that can be used in two dimensions.

## 7.4.1 Prediction regions

The region for causal prediction is obtained from an analogy to a scanning sequence:

$$S_1 = \{l \geq 1, \forall k\} \cup \{l = 0, k \geq 1\}.$$

This is also known as the nonsymmetric half plane, shown in Fig. 7.18a. A subset of this region would be the quarter plane, which results in a *strongly causal* predictor, Fig. 7.18b. This is defined by

$$S_2 = \{l \geq 1, k \geq 0\} \cup \{l = 0, k \geq 1\}.$$

Note that, in practice, only a finite subset of the prediction region is used,

$$W_1 = \{1 \leq l \leq q, \ -p \leq k \leq p\} \cup \{l = 0, \ 1 \leq k \leq p\}.$$

It is possible to describe a *semicausal* predictor that is causal in one index and noncausal in the other. A typical prediction region, shown in Fig. 7.18c, is given by

$$S_3 = \{l \geq 1, \forall k\} \cup \{l = 0, k \neq 0\}.$$

Likewise, a *noncausal* predictor can be a function of all indices except the index that is predicted, Fig. 7.18d,

$$S_4 = \{\forall(k, l) \neq (0, 0)\}.$$

The noncausal regions of support, $S_3$ and $S_4$, are rarely used in practice.

## 7.4.2 Determining prediction coefficients

The problem of determining the prediction coefficients can be written as a typical least squares minimization

$$\min_{a(k,l)} \ \epsilon^2(m, n) = E\left\{\left[x(m, n) - \sum_{(k,l) \in S_x} a(k, l)x(m - k, n - l)\right]^2\right\}.$$

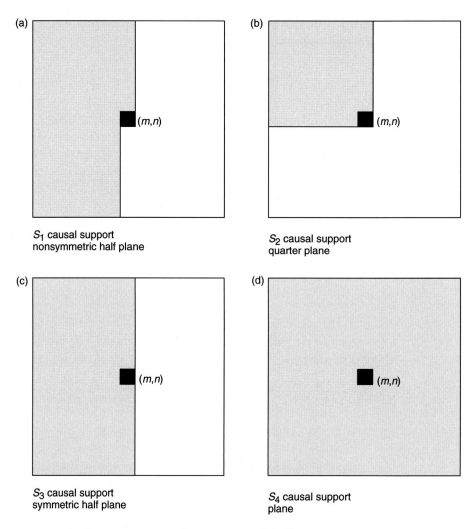

**Figure 7.18.** (a) $S_1$ causal support region, nonsymmetric half plane; (b) $S_2$ causal support region, quarter plane; (c) $S_3$ noncausal (semicausal) support region, symmetric half plane; (d) $S_4$ noncausal support region, plane.

The solution is obtained by differentiating $\epsilon^2(m, n)$ with respect to $a(k, l)$ and setting the result equal to zero or by using the orthogonality principle directly (see Appendix C). The result is called the *minimum variance representation* (MVR). The result is a set of equations given by

$$
E\left\{\left[y(m, n) - \sum_{(k,l) \in S_x} a(k, l)y(m - k, n - l)\right] y(m - p, n - q)\right\} = \beta^2 \delta(p, q),
$$

for $(p, q) \in S_x \cup (0, 0)$.                                                  (7.36)

The $\beta^2$ term represents the minimum error. It can also represent the variance of the white noise input that drives the image model. In practice, we use only a finite number of terms in the prediction support region, $S_x$. We will continue to denote this finite region as $S_x$. This system yields a solution similar to that of the one-dimensional case,

$$\sum_{(k,l)\in S_x} a(k,l)r_{yy}(m-k,n-l) = r_{yy}(m,n),$$

where $\beta$ is obtained from computing the prediction error. The details of this computation are shown in Appendix C. It is shown there that the autocorrelation of the prediction error is the same as that of the white noise,

$$r_{ww}(m,n) = \beta\delta(m,n),$$

for the nonsymmetric half plane or quarter plane models. Because of their noncausal support, the other models yield correlated errors. We will concentrate on the nonsymmetric half plane model, as it is the most commonly used. It is shown that by using the normalization procedure and letting $a(0,0) = 1$, as in the case of 1-D prediction, the dependence on $\beta$ is eliminated. The value of $\beta$ can be obtained by computing the estimation error, $\epsilon^2(m,n)$.

Note that some texts mention a solution method that uses initial values of the random process. If initial conditions of $y(n)$ and the input $x(n)$ are known, then solving the system,

$$x(n) = \sum_{k=1}^{p} a(k)x(n-k) + w(n),$$

is possible. The problem is that most signal models assume a white noise input that cannot be known. Furthermore, the recursive solution is very sensitive to noise. Thus, these methods are rarely used.

There are several theoretical properties of two-dimensional recursive models, such as stability and spectral factorization, that are discussed in Appendix C. These properties are of only minor interest for most image processing needs. The major application of the model is in obtaining spectral estimates of the random process that characterizes the image ensemble. To demonstrate the utility of the model, let us generate spectra for the bars image, Fig. 3.5, and the more periodic subimage of that image, Fig. 5.17a. Their spectra are shown in Figs. 7.19a and 7.19b, respectively. One should compare these spectral estimates with those estimated by the periodogram in Figs. 5.14b for the original image and 5.17b or 7.11 for the subsection.

One of the obvious differences in the qualitative appearance of the spectral estimates is the relative smoothness. The AR spectra are smoother and so will have an advantage when used in computations that are sensitive to noise. This includes most inverse operations, such as deblurring or image restoration.

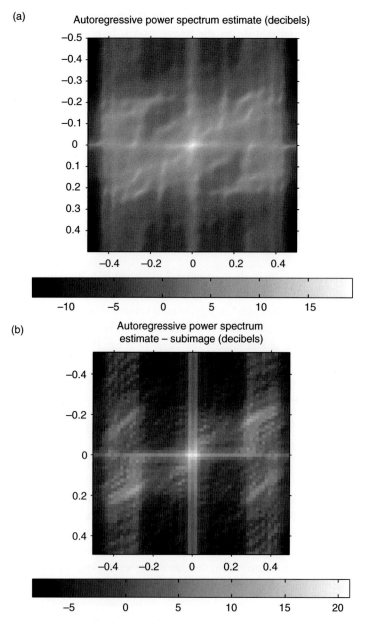

**Figure 7.19.** (a) Autoregressive power spectrum of bars image; (b) autoregressive power spectrum of section of striped pants in bars image.

## 7.4.3    Filtered noise

The basis for most of the stochastic characterizations of images is passing white noise through a linear filter. In the previous section, we have shown the estimates of the power spectra obtained by several of these methods. It is useful to consider

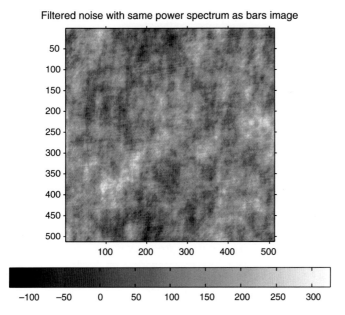

Filtered noise with same power spectrum as bars image

**Figure 7.20.** Filtered white Gaussian noise with same power spectrum as bars image: note the wider range of values.

the appearance of images that are actually generated by these methods. In particular, seeing the effects of the filter on actual noise helps the image processing scientist make reasonable judgments about the characteristics of pictorial images. By correctly characterizing the images, the scientist is better able to select the proper processing methods.

First, let us consider generating an image with the same power spectrum as the bars image, using white Gaussian noise as input. This image is shown in Fig. 7.20. Note that filtered noise with the same power as the pictorial image has a much larger dynamic range of values. We have noted that pictorial images have most of their power at lower frequencies. If the white noise is filtered using a low pass filter of Gaussian form, we obtain an image that has different visual properties, Fig. 7.21a. The low pass noise image is much more uniform in appearance and it lacks the large blotch areas of the image, which have been filtered to replicate the more complicated form of the image power spectrum.

To complete the demonstration, let us show an example of high pass filtered noise. The high pass filter is generated from the low pass Gaussian filter used for Fig. 7.21a by simply subtracting unity from each term of the Fourier transform. The result is shown in Fig. 7.21b. The result of a high pass filter has a mean of zero, so the image must be scaled for viewing. Again, we have generated an image with the same total power as the bars image. The fine texture of the image is a characteristic of high frequency noise.

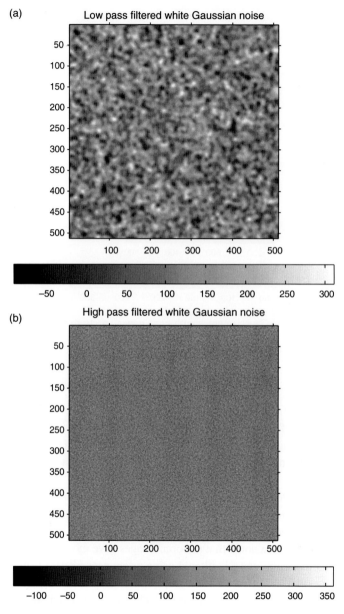

**Figure 7.21.** (a) Low pass filtered white Gaussian noise; (b) high pass filtered white Gaussian noise.

## 7.5 Problems

**7.1** Consider the image of Fig. 7.1.

(a) Assume that the values of the image represent radiance measured in candela. What range of values would be reasonable for this image?

(b) Assume that the values of the image represent reflectance. What range of values would be reasonable for this image?

**7.2**   Consider the image of Fig. 7.3a.

(a) Assume that the values of the image represent radiance measured in candela. What range of values would be reasonable for this image?
(b) Assume that the values of the image represent reflectance. What range of values would be reasonable for this image? Be careful on this answer.

**7.3**   Consider the histograms of images given in Fig. 7.22. Identify the recorded images with the following properties. Justify your answers.

(a) The histogram indicates that the image was recorded well within the range of values that were quantized.
(b) The histogram indicates significant saturation.
(c) The histogram indicates an image that was not quantized well. State the type of problem that could result in the histogram that you choose.
(d) The histogram indicates an image of a page of text.

**7.4**   Consider the power spectra of the 1-D signals in Fig. 7.23, where the power is plotted in decibels and the frequency is in cycles per mm. For each of the signals, determine a reasonable sampling interval, $\Delta x$, that will yield a digital signal with acceptable aliasing.

**7.5**   Consider the spectra of Figs. 5.14b and 5.17b. These show spectra for different size images but with exactly the same sample spacing. Discuss whether the spectra indicate that the sampling is sufficient to accurately record the image content.

**7.6**   Determine if the following sets of images are subspaces.

(a) Images with no spectral power above $F_x = F_y = 10$ cycles/mm,
(b) Images with pixels $x(m, n) = 0$ for $m$ odd and $n$ even,
(c) Images that are piecewise constant,
(d) Images that are bounded by $0 \leq x(m, n) \leq 255$,
(e) Images that can be represented by the summation
   $x(m, n) = \sum_{k=0}^{4} \sum_{l=0}^{5} \alpha_{k,l}(m + n)^{k+l}$, where $\alpha_{k,l}$ are real constants,
(f) Images with pixel values equal to zero outside of the certain range, e.g., $x(m, n) = 0$ if $m^2 + n^2 \geq 10$,
(g) Images with a mean of zero.

**7.7**   Consider the ensemble of all images obtained by sampling the color TV in your home. Assume that the range of values is $[0, 255]$ with a fixed brightness and contrast setting. Discuss the statistics of the ensemble, the mean, the variance and covariance. Describe the mean in common graphic terms. Are the mean and variance stationary?

**7.8**   Answer the questions of Problem 7.7 with respect to the ensemble of images taken from your computer monitor.

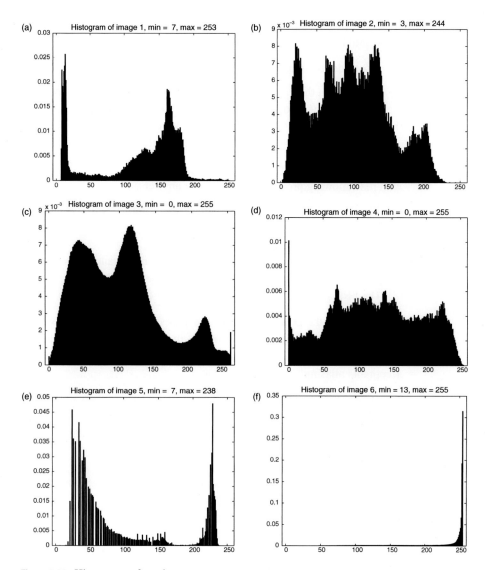

**Figure 7.22.** Histograms of test images.

**7.9** Compute the histogram of *gray-one*, the image you selected previously for many exercises. Determine if the image was quantized appropriately.

**7.10** Compute the mean and variance of *gray-one*. Compute the mean and variances of $N \times N$ nonoverlapping subsections of the image for $N = 40, 50, 100$. From these statistics, determine how nearly stationary the image is.

**7.11** Compute the power spectrum of *gray-one*. From this, determine if the image was sampled appropriately.

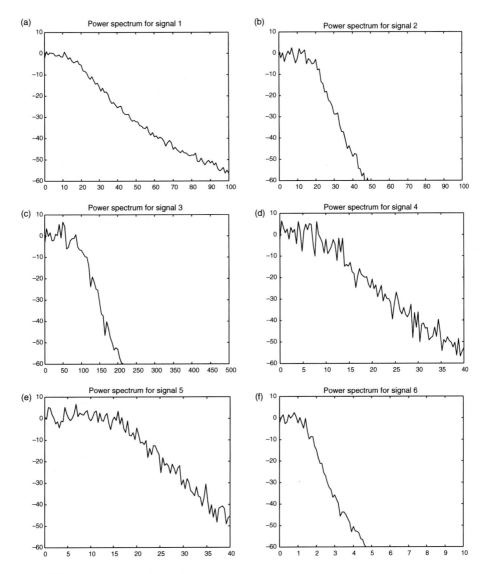

**Figure 7.23.** Power spectra of 1-D signals.

**7.12**  Filter *gray-one* to show the image that contains 90%, 95% and 99% of the original image power. Remember to display the sequence for accurate comparisons.

**7.13**  Assume that the recorded signal is modeled by $r(n) = s(n) + \epsilon(n)$, where the signal $s(n)$ and noise $\epsilon(n)$ are defined below. Compute the signal-to-noise ratio (SNR) in decibels for each case.

(a) $s(n) = 2\cos(2\pi n/15)$ and $\epsilon(n)$ is zero mean, white Gaussian with variance $\sigma^2 = 0.16$. This is abbreviated $\epsilon(n) \in N(0, 0.16)$.

(b) $s(n) = 2\cos(2\pi n/15)$ and $\epsilon(n)$ is white and uniformly distributed on $[-0.4, 0.4]$. This is abbreviated $\epsilon(n) \in U([-0.4, 0.4])$.

(c) $s(n) = \text{rect}_{10}(n) = \begin{cases} 1 & \text{if } n \bmod(20) < 10 \\ 0 & \text{else} \end{cases}$, and $\epsilon(n) \in N(0, 0.16)$.

(d) $s(n) = \text{rect}_{10}(n) = \begin{cases} 1 & \text{if } n \bmod(20) < 10 \\ 0 & \text{else} \end{cases}$, and $\epsilon(n) \in U([-0.4, 0.4])$.

**7.14**   An image has mean, $\mu = 120$, in a range of $[0, 255]$, and variance, $\sigma^2 = 64$. We wish to add white, Gaussian noise to the image to create a SNR of 30 dB. Compute the variance of the noise that is required to obtain this SNR. Repeat the computation for SNRs of 20 dB, 10 dB and 0 dB.

**7.15**   For your *gray-one* image, compute the variance for zero mean, white, Gaussian noise to be added to the image to create a SNR of 30 dB, 20 dB, 10 dB. Create the noisy images and display the results. Be careful about possible saturation effects or values above the usual $[0, 255]$ range.

**7.16**   For your *gray-one* image, compute the range for zero mean, white, uniformly distributed noise to be added to the image to create a SNR of 30 dB, 20 dB, 10 dB. Create the noisy images and display the results. Be careful about possible saturation effects or values above the usual $[0, 255]$ range. Compare the results with the previous problem.

**7.17**   Create a filtered white noise image that has the same power spectrum as *gray-one* image.

**7.18**   For your *gray-one* image, compute the coefficients of the 2-D AR model of Eq. (7.35), using the nonsymmetric half plane. Use only the four adjacent pixels for this model. Using these coefficients, compute the power spectrum of the image and compare it with the power spectrum obtained using the periodogram.

# 8 Photometry and colorimetry

The purpose of photometry and colorimetry is to measure quantitatively the radiation and the derived quantities that determine what is seen by a human observer, a camera, or some other image recording device. The goal of this chapter is to lay a foundation so that the reader will understand what is required to record an image accurately, that is, so that accurate information can be obtained from the recorded data. While the accurate information is often used to present a display of the image, it may also be used to derive information about objects in the scene that is used for computer vision or target tracking. Of course, the accurate display of an image is impossible without accurate data. However, to produce an accurate display requires much more. It requires accurate information about the display device and the intent of the observer, who will be judging the image.

Because densitometry is closely associated with quantitative imaging, it is discussed in this chapter. The fundamental difference of densitometry from photometry and colorimetry is that densitometry is concerned with the measurement of physical quantities of display media. The density of a colorant on paper or dyes on film can be related to the appearance of the image that is produced using these means. The relationship is usually approximate. However, since it is so commonly used in the printing and film industries, it is appropriate to discuss its uses here.

Since this book is concerned primarily with accurate recording and display of images, we will start with a brief description of the eye. This will lead us to the quantitative measurement of light. First radiometric, then photometric concepts will be reviewed. Radiometry is more general, in that it is concerned with the measurement of all types of radiation, whether visible or not. Photometry is concerned with the relation of radiant and reflective properties as they relate to a human observer. Colorimetric concepts, within the context of color matching, will be described in some detail, since they are the basis of determining exactly what will be measured by the instrumentation. Before making a colorimetric or photometric measurement, there must be something to measure. A brief mathematical description of additive and subtractive color reproduction is given to describe the physical objects that are to be measured. Finally, the instrumentation used to make measurements is described.

The purpose of this chapter is to give an overview of the basics of photometry and colorimetry for the novice in the area of color image processing. We will introduce the major topics and direct the reader to sources for more in-depth discussions and more comprehensive presentations that deal with the special cases and extremes of color measurement and reproduction. Such texts include [87, 125, 160, 199, 313].

## 8.1     Fundamentals of the eye

To understand what measurements to make and how to use them to reproduce images, it is necessary to have a basic understanding of the human eye. What is presented here is intended to give the reader a basic understanding of the major components of the eye and their relationship to the perception of images. This is needed to determine the appropriate measurements to make, the limitations of measurements that are made, the selection of display devices and materials, and the limitations of any particular display modality. This section concentrates on only the basics. Additional information is given in Appendix E. The eye and human vision is a fascinating subject in its own right. Recommended texts include those by Wandell [300] for an overall study of psychovisual phenomena, Barlow and Mollon [17] for physiology, Bartleson and Grum [20] for both physiology and colorimetric measurements and Wyszecki and Stiles [313] for a brief description of physiology and how it relates to photometric requirements.

The three major components of the eye that are important for the study of image recording and display are the lens, pupil and retina. Each of these is directly related to various aspects of the physical recording and display processes. The light enters the eye through the pupil, which limits the amount of light that is transmitted through the lens; the light is focused by the lens onto the retina, where it is sensed and converted into signals that are passed to the visual cortex of the brain. There are many components that have indirect effects, such as the cornea, vitreous and aqueous humors; but an understanding of these is not needed to understand the basics of image recording and display.

The major function of the lens is to focus the image on the retina. It is a remarkable device that can change its focal length on demand. Of course, as we age, the range of focus decreases and we wear glasses to help extend the range. Because the eye uses a single lens, it can focus only at a single wavelength of light; that is, if the eye is focused on a red object, a blue object right beside it will be slightly out of focus. This can lead to interesting visual illusions, such as a blue object will appear farther away than a red object. See Fig. E.2.

The major function of the pupil is to limit the amount of light transmitted to the retina. This avoids saturating the sensors. While the pupil reacts very quickly to changes in illumination, we have all experienced a white out when coming from a dark environment into bright light. The diameter of the pupil can vary from about 7 mm to 1 mm. This gives about a 50:1 ratio of brightness control, from the ratio of areas. While that provides a great deal of control in the amount of light reaching the retina, it is not the only factor that allows sensitivity over a range of illumination that is often as much as four orders of magnitude. To obtain this latitude, other factors, such as neural interconnectivity and contrast sensitivity, account for most of the sensitivity range.

A side effect of the pupil is its influence on focus. Smaller apertures, corresponding to smaller pupil diameters, permit a greater depth of field of focus, that is, objects over a larger range of distances from the viewer appear in focus. Small apertures also cause increased diffraction, which limits the resolution.[1]

The retina contains the rods and cones that act as sensors for the human imaging system. The rods and cones operate in different ways and at different light levels. The rods are monochromatic sensors and are used at low light levels. This environment is referred to as *scotopic* vision. It takes more radiant energy to excite the three types of cones. In bright light, the rods are saturated and the cones are used to give us our color vision. The operation at this higher light level is called *photopic* vision. The fact that we have three types of cones that differ in sensitivity to the wavelength of light is the reason for color vision and will explain much about proper recording and display of color images. The sensitivity responses and their implications will be discussed in Section 8.3.

When determining the sampling required for an input image (recording) or an output image (display), it is necessary to consider the limitations of the resolution of the eye. The combination of the discrete sensors on the retina, their neural interconnection, the focus of the lens and the diffraction of the pupil can be analyzed in terms of the frequency response of the eye. Typically, the neural interconnections are modeled as differential operators [17]. A consequence of this effect is that human beings are spatially more sensitive to edge information than large area information. The differential operator is equivalent to a high pass filter. The optical characteristics of focus and diffraction lead to a low pass filter. Thus, the combination of the low pass optical effect and the high pass neural effect results in a bandpass system. In fact, the response of the visual system is not linear, as would be implied by the frequency model. There are many stages in the psychovisual process. Adaptation and interpretation of content are two phenomena that play a significant role in determining what we "see." The linear model does give good qualitative results and allows a reasonable model for visual error. It is used in many applications for optimization of recording or display parameters for an imaging system.

A frequency response of a linear, shift-invariant system is composed of a magnitude response and a phase response. Because of the incoherent nature of the light that is used for virtually all imaging, the phase response is not of interest. The magnitude response is called the *modulation transfer function* (MTF) for optical systems and that term will be used here. A useful model for the MTF is given by the radially symmetric function

$$H(\omega) = A \left[ \alpha + \frac{\omega}{\omega_0} \right] \exp \left[ - \left( \frac{\omega}{\omega_0} \right)^\beta \right],$$

where, for the general case, the frequency, $\omega$, is measured in cycles per degree. Angular frequency makes sense, since it characterizes the eye and is not dependent on the distance of the target from the observer. Angular frequency can be transformed to spatial frequency in cycles/mm for a fixed viewing distance. For example, at a viewing distance of $d$ mm the spatial frequency of $r$ cycles per degree transforms to $r/d$ cycles/mm. Constants that

---

[1] A thorough discussion of optical effects, such as focus and diffraction, is beyond the scope of this text. The presentation in any college level physics text is sufficient for the material in this section.

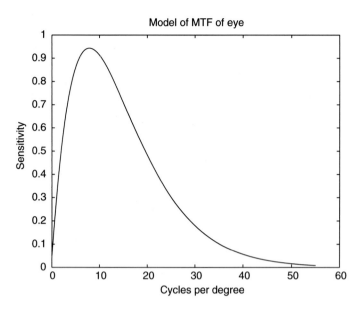

**Figure 8.1.** Modulation transfer function of eye.

have been found useful are: $A = 2.5$, $\alpha = 0.0192$, $\omega_0 = 8.772$ and $\beta = 1.1$ [134, 217]. This results in a peak at about 8 cycle/degree, (see Fig. 8.1). A qualitative method of observing the visual effect of the MTF of the eye is with a chart that varies contrast in one direction and spatial frequency in the other. Such a chart is shown in Fig. 8.2. The response is also dependent upon the color of the variation. This is discussed in Appendix E.

The properties of the pupil and the retina that affect the accurate measurement of images will be discussed in this chapter where appropriate.

## 8.2     Radiometry and photometry

Since we are interested in measuring the quantities that are of importance to the eye, we need to determine the transformation from external radiometric quantities to quantities that are meaningful physiologically. The first step is to characterize the radiation source, $f(\lambda)$. Qualitatively, the function is described in terms of intensity or brightness. However, the term brightness indicates a human response. For this work, the units of $f(\lambda)$ need to be stated more precisely. There is a need to distinguish between the quantities sensed and measured by an instrument and those related more directly to human perception. The major distinction between radiometry and photometry is that radiometry measures absolute quantities, while photometry measures or computes quantities as they relate to the human observer. Furthermore, there is a need to define precisely what is the quality of interest and what is actually being measured. More in-depth discussions on radiometry and photometry are found in texts such as [19, 20, 160, 168, 199, 313].

**Figure 8.2.** Demonstration of MTF of the eye. The viewer should look for the positions in the image where the contrast between black and white bars is no longer visible. These points should trace a rough curve that is a minimum somewhere near the center of the horizonal axis. This gives a qualitative impression of the MTF of the eye.

From a physical point of view, the radiant power emitted by a source is measured in watts. Likewise the power received by a detector is measured in watts. Since the power is a function of wavelength, the unit should be watt/nm. The total power integrated over all wavelengths is called *radiant flux* or radiant power and is measured in watts. We denote radiant flux per nm by $f_r(\lambda)$. Because radiant flux does not indicate how the power is distributed in space, the measurement in watts does not indicate how bright a source appears to the observer. For example, an automobile headlamp may look very bright if you look directly into it, but will be invisible if viewed from the rear of the vehicle.

The luminous efficiency function, $v(\lambda)$, shown in Fig. 8.3, is a dimensionless weighting that indicates the apparent brightness of equally radiant monochrome sources as a function of wavelength. It is noted that the function plotted in Fig. 8.3 is valid for photopic conditions. There is another function tabulated for scotopic conditions that has a similar shape but is shifted toward the blue. The peak of the luminous efficiency function for photopic conditions is 555 nm, while for scotopic conditions it is 507 nm [125, 160, 313]. Since our interest is in viewing images in relatively high light levels, the photopic data are sufficient. The curve has been normalized so that the peak value at 555 nm is unity. It is clear that, given the same viewing conditions, a source of 40 W at 550 nm will appear much brighter than one of the same wattage at 430 nm. For this reason, we define *luminous flux* as the weighted quantity $f_l(\lambda) = v(\lambda)f_r(\lambda)$ integrated over all

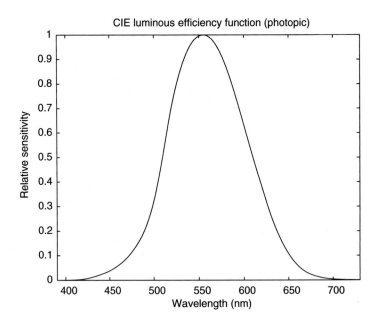

**Figure 8.3.** CIE luminous efficiency function (photopic), usually denoted $v(\lambda)$.

wavelengths,

$$C = K \int_0^\infty v(\lambda) f_r(\lambda) \, d\lambda.$$

Since $v(\lambda)$ is dimensionless, the quantity $C$ has the same units as the radiant flux, watts. It can be thought of as a measure of *perceived* power and this weighted power is measured in *lumens* (lm). One lumen is defined as the intensity of a narrowband (delta function) source at 555 nm of one watt that would give $C = 683$ lm in the above equation, or $K = 683$ lm/watt [47]. The lumen rating of a radiant source is an integrated weighted power that relates the total spectrum to the perceived brightness. The lumen ratings of various lamps and their wattages are shown in Table 8.1. Note the relationship between the power consumed by the lamp (watts) and lumen rating. A lamp that produces more lumens for the same power is more efficient. Table 8.2 shows the relative efficiencies of various types of lamps.

Recently, there has been more use of LEDs as lighting sources. The use of red LEDs in traffic lights and vehicle tail lights are common. Large screen displays use arrays of red, green and blue LEDs. Light emitting diodes are directional sources. They are commonly packaged with a plastic lens that focuses the light output along a narrow solid angle. White LEDs are also available. These are made from an LED that creates blue wavelengths. The blue light is used to excite a phosphor that fluoresces into the other visible wavelengths. Individual LEDs on the market today can currently produce above 60 lumens for white light. Efficiency for current LEDs are at about 50 lumens per watt, with claims in the laboratory of well over 100 lumens per watt. This technology is

**Table 8.1.** Comparison of wattages and lumens for common lamps

| Type | Watts (average) | Lumens (average) |
| --- | --- | --- |
| Incandescent (frosted, clear) | 25 | 230 |
| Incandescent (frosted, clear) | 40 | 480 |
| Incandescent (frosted, clear) | 60 | 890 |
| Incandescent (frosted, clear) | 75 | 1 220 |
| Incandescent (frosted, clear) | 100 | 1 750 |
| Incandescent (soft white) | 100 | 1 660 |
| Incandescent (rough service) | 100 | 1 230 |
| Incandescent (yellow bug away) | 100 | 1 000 |
| Incandescent (silicon coated, shatterproof) | 100 | 1 660 |
| Incandescent (floodlamp) | 100 | 1 250 |
| Incandescent (floodlamp) | 150 | 1 730 |
| Fluorescent (desklamp 8 inch) | 18 | 1 250 |
| Fluorescent (desklamp 16 inch) | 36 | 2 900 |
| Fluorescent (cool white 48 inch) | 40 | 3 150 |
| Fluorescent (daylight 48 inch) | 40 | 2 100 |
| Fluorescent (warm white 48 inch) | 40 | 3 200 |
| Low pressure sodium (display) | 90 | 13 500 |
| Metal halide (outdoor) | 100 | 8 500 |
| Metal halide (outdoor) | 250 | 20 500 |
| Metal halide (outdoor) | 1 000 | 110 000 |
| Mercury vapor (outdoor) | 100 | 4 300 |
| Mercury vapor (outdoor) | 1 000 | 63 000 |

**Table 8.2.** Representative efficiencies (source: various manufacturers' specifications from internet pages)

| Lamp type | Efficiency (lumens/watt) |
| --- | --- |
| Light emitting diode | 10–60 |
| Incandescent | <20 |
| Mercury vapor | 50 |
| Fluorescent | 80 |
| Metal halide | 90 |
| High pressure sodium | 120 |
| Low pressure sodium | 150 |

rapidly changing and the above numbers will probably be outdated by the time this book is published. We suggest checking the internet for the latest performance figures. When considering colored LEDs, the lumen rating may be misleading. Red LEDs for traffic signals have low lumen ratings because of the weighting by the luminous efficiency curve. However, they are more efficient than filtered incandescent bulbs.

The sources of interest for imaging have a directionality property that needs to be taken into account. It is not the total power that is of interest but the power that is emitted in the direction of the eye or sensing instrument. The energy or power measured by a detector

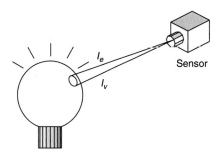

**Figure 8.4.** Measurement geometry for radiant intensity, $I_e$, (W/sr) and luminant intensity, $I_v$, (cd).

will depend on the fraction of the emitted energy or power that is captured. It is the power per solid angle in the direction of the optical system or detector that characterizes the brightness of the source. This quantity, integrated over all wavelengths, is called *radiant intensity* and has units of watts per steradian (W/sr). The concept of solid angle is quite general, as noted in [160], but for this introduction, it is sufficient to think of it as a cone radiating from the light source. Radiant flux is the total radiant intensity integrated over a measured solid angle, and thus has units of watts. The photometric quantity that is obtained by weighting the radiant intensity by the luminous efficiency function is called *luminous intensity* and is measured in *candela* (cd). The geometry for measuring radiant or luminous flux is shown in Fig. 8.4. Here we are concerned with the energy distribution as a function of the solid angle of the source. If we are interested in spectral measurements, then the quantities of interest are given as a function of wavelength and the units are W/sr/nm or cd/nm. These are functions that can be used as $f(\lambda)$ to describe images. The relation between radiant flux and radiant intensity can be described by the qualitative equation

$$\text{radiant flux} = \int \text{radiant intensity } d\omega,$$

where the integral is taken over a solid angle, $\omega$.

When we illuminate a surface area, we may wish to determine how much light is falling on the area. For this we would use an omnidirectional detector. Power measured at the detector is referred to as *irradiance*. Irradiance indicates the total amount of light at a given wavelength that falls on a given area. The sources of the illumination are irrelevant to this measurement. Irradiance is measured in watts per square meter (W/m$^2$). The photometric quantity is *illuminance* and is measured in lumens per square meter (lm/m$^2$). This quantity is of interest to lighting engineers who design systems to illuminate specified areas, such as offices or parking lots [43]. The unit of (lm/m$^2$) is called *lux* (lx). The Imperial unit for illuminance is *footcandles* (lm/ft$^2$).[2] The exact conversion is one lux equals 0.0929 footcandles. The configuration of this measurement is shown in Fig. 8.5. A common instrument for measuring illuminance is the hand-held light meter

---

[2] Note the mix of Imperial (ft) and SI (lm) quantities in footcandles.

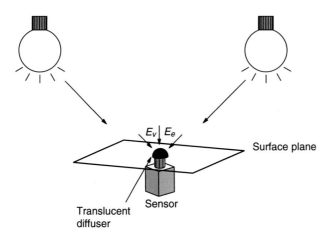

**Figure 8.5.** Measurement geometry for irradiance, $E_e$, (W/m$^2$) and illuminance, $E_v$, (lm/m$^2$).

used by photographers. To make this measurement, the light meter has a translucent diffuser placed over the sensor, to accept light from all directions. Table 8.3 gives some approximate illuminance values for various common environments. The values in the table are approximations that give a feel for the values of different lighting conditions. Such tables can vary widely and should not be regarded as absolute [125, 160, 224].

Now, consider the fact that most objects in images are reflective. We see them because they reflect light from a source. To characterize an object and its reflective properties accurately, we must know its reflective properties as a function of the direction and solid angle characteristics of the receiver (or viewer), and the angular orientation of the object and receiver (or viewer) relative to each other. The configuration of this measurement is shown in Fig. 8.6. The orientation of the surface relative to the detector is important, since viewing the surface from an angle normal to the surface would allow more light to reach the detector, than viewing the surface almost parallel to it.[3] When these geometrical factors are taken into account, we have the radiometric quantity of *radiance* measured in watts per square meter per steradian (W/(m$^2$sr)) or the photometric quantity *luminance* measured in candela per square meter per steradian (cd/(m$^2$sr)). Table 8.3 gives approximate values for the luminance of a 20% reflective surface illuminated by the sources at the corresponding illuminance level. The relation between illuminance and luminance is given by [199]

$$\text{luminance} = \frac{\text{illuminance} \times (\text{reflectance fraction})}{\pi}. \tag{8.1}$$

When an image is recorded, we measure the energy received at our detector. We know the time of the exposure and the solid angle subtended by our detector. Thus we can assume that we are measuring either radiant or luminous intensity for emissive

[3] In fact, the exact geometrical factor is the cosine of the viewing angle. This fact is used to derive the equation that transforms illuminance to luminance, Eq. (8.1).

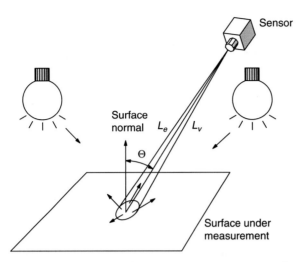

**Figure 8.6.** Measurement geometry for radiance, $L_e$, (W/(m$^2$sr)) and luminance, $L_v$, (cd/m$^2$).

sources or radiance or luminance for reflective sources. In an image, it is impossible to determine if the energy associated with a pixel comes from emissive or reflective objects. Furthermore, it is impossible, without much auxiliary information, to determine the orientation of the surface relative to the viewer. In fact, for image recording purposes, this is not needed. Since most of the scene is composed of reflective objects, it is reasonable to assume that everything is reflective. This means that our visual scene is characterized in terms of luminance. Common instruments for measuring luminance are the light meters on cameras that measure the light that comes through the lens. A summary of the common radiometric and photometric quantities, with their symbols and units, is given in Table 8.4.

The eye is able to adapt to varying brightness levels by adjusting the size of the pupil. On a bright day, the pupil is contracted to about 1–2 mm in diameter; in a dark room, the pupil expands to about 6–7 mm. In the office environment, the pupil is about 3–4 mm in diameter. Thus, the amount of light that reaches the retina is not a direct function of the intensity of the source. Figure 8.7 gives an approximate function of pupil diameter versus light intensity [77]. Other graphs of this relationship are found in [66, 313]. When it is necessary to account for the effect of the pupil, the light is measured in *trolands*, which measures retinal illuminance. The units are equivalent to candela. The conversion is given by

$$T = Lp,$$

where $L$ is the photopic luminance and $p$ is the area of the pupil. One troland is equivalent to a one candela source seen through a pupil of 1 mm$^2$ [20, 313].

Relating the adaptation of the eye to Table 8.3, we note that photopic vision occurs in the range of $L > 10$ cd/m$^2$; scotopic vision occurs in the range $L < 10^{-3}$ cd/m$^2$. The term *mesopic* vision refers to the transition region. In the photopic range, the rods are

**Table 8.3.** Qualitative description of illuminance and luminance levels: 1 lux = 0.0929 footcandle; 1 lux = 15.71 sr × (cd/m$^2$) and assumes 20% reflectance surface, see Eq. (8.1)

| Description | Lux (lm/m$^2$) | Footcandles | Luminance (cd/m$^2$) |
|---|---|---|---|
| Moonless night | $\sim 10^{-5}$ | $\sim 10^{-6}$ | $\sim 6.4 \times 10^{-7}$ |
| Full moon night | $\sim 10^{-3}$ | $\sim 10^{-4}$ | $\sim 6.4 \times 10^{-5}$ |
| Restaurant | $\sim 100$ | $\sim 1\,100$ | $\sim 6.4$ |
| Office | $\sim 300$ | $\sim 3\,200$ | $\sim 20$ |
| Overcast day | $\sim 25\,000$ | $\sim 465$ | $\sim 1.6 \times 10^3$ |
| Sunny day | $\sim 100\,000$ | $\sim 10\,000$ | $\sim 6.4 \times 10^3$ |

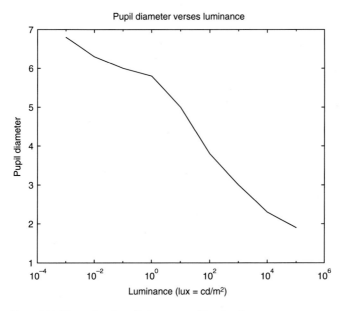

**Figure 8.7.** Example of pupil size versus illumination.

saturated and the signal is dependent on only the cones for color vision. In the scotopic range, the light is below the threshold of the cones and only the rods are active. Both rods and cones are active in the mesopic region.

## 8.3 Mathematics of color matching

The fundamentals of photometry have been covered briefly in the previous sections. Photometry can be considered a subset of colorimetry, since luminance measurement is one of the three colorimetric measurements that are introduced in this section. The material on colorimetry will be used in all aspects of accurate recording and display of images. Thus, this material will be covered with greater attention to mathematical detail.

**Table 8.4.** Summary of radiometric and photometric quantities: note that the subscript $e$ indicates a radiometric quantity; the subscript $v$ indicates a photometric quantity, i.e., multiplication by the luminous efficiency function of Fig. 8.3

| Quantity | Radiometric or photometric | Symbol | Units |
|---|---|---|---|
| Radiant flux | Radiometric | $P_e$ | W |
| Luminant flux | Photometric | $P_v$ | lm |
| Radiant intensity | Radiometric | $I_e$ | W/sr |
| Luminant intensity | Photometric | $I_v$ | lm/sr = cd |
| Irradiance | Radiometric | $E_e$ | W/m$^2$ |
| Illuminance | Photometric | $E_v$ | lm/m$^2$ |
| Radiance | Radiometric | $L_e$ | W/(m$^2$sr) |
| Luminance | Photometric | $L_v$ | cd/m$^2$ |

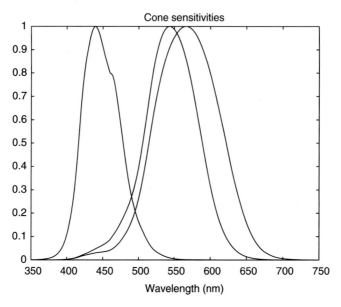

**Figure 8.8.** Cone sensitivities of the human eye.

It has been mentioned that the retina contains three types of cones. Each type is maximally sensitive to a different part of the spectrum. An example of the cones' response curves is shown in Fig. 8.8. Commonly, they are referred to as the red, green and blue regions of the spectrum. More accurately, they are often referred to as long, medium and short wavelength regions since the peaks occur at wavelengths that actually correspond to blue, green and yellow-green. Cone sensitivities are related, but not directly, to the absorption sensitivity of the pigments in the cones. The absorption sensitivities of the different cones have been measured by several researchers. Long before the technology was available to measure the sensitivity curves directly, they were estimated from a clever color matching experiment.

### 8.3.1    Background

Grassmann formulated a set of laws for additive color mixture in 1853 [93, 94]. Additive in this sense refers to the addition of two or more radiant sources of light. These laws can be concisely written with the help of modern notation. Let A,B,C and D be color stimuli; $\beta$ is a scalar representing relative intensity and the symbol $\leftrightarrow$ represents the term "matches the color of." The laws are given by

(1) If A $\leftrightarrow$ B, then B $\leftrightarrow$ A.
(2) If A $\leftrightarrow$ B and B $\leftrightarrow$ C, then A $\leftrightarrow$ C.
(3) If A $\leftrightarrow$ B, then $\beta$A $\leftrightarrow$ $\beta$B.
(4) If any two of the following hold
   - A $\leftrightarrow$ B,
   - C $\leftrightarrow$ D,
   - (A + C) $\leftrightarrow$ (B + D),
   then (A + D) $\leftrightarrow$ (B + C), where the '+' denotes additive mixture.

In addition, Grassmann conjectured that any additive color mixture could be matched by the proper amounts of three primary stimuli (radiant spectra). Considering what was known about the physiology of the eye at that time, these laws represent considerable insight.

Grassmann's laws remain essentially unchanged as printed in recent texts on color science [87, 160, 199, 313]. With our current understanding of the behavior of the physiology of the eye and a basic background in linear algebra, Grassmann's laws can be stated more concisely. Furthermore, extensions of the laws and additional properties are easily derived using the mathematics of matrix theory. There have been several papers that have taken a linear systems approach to describing color spaces as defined by a standard human observer [52–54, 118, 269, 299]. This section will briefly summarize these results and relate them to simple signal processing concepts.

The basis for the vector space approach is the fact that the human retina contains three types of color sensors (cones). The spectral sensitivity of these elements has been measured by both direct and indirect methods. References that contain a good review of these methods are [17, 160, 313]. For the purposes of this work, it is sufficient to note that the spectral responses of the three types of sensor are sufficiently different as to define a three-dimensional vector space (see Sec 7.1.3).

It has been assumed in most research and standards work that the visual frequency spectrum can be sampled finely enough to allow the accurate use of numerical approximation of integration. A common sample spacing is 10 nanometers over the range 400–700 nm, although ranges as wide as 360–780 nm have been used. This sample spacing is used for many color tables and lower priced instrumentation. Precision color instrumentation produces data at 2 nm intervals. Even finer sampling is required for some illuminants with line emitters. Reflective surfaces are usually smoothly varying and can be accurately sampled more coarsely. Sampling of color signals is discussed in detail in Chapter 9.

Proper sampling follows the same bandwidth restrictions that govern all digital signal processing. Following the assumption that the spectrum can be adequately sampled, the space of all possible visible spectra lies in an $N$-dimensional vector space, where $N = 31$ if 400–700 nm is used with 10 nm sampling. The spectral response of each of the eye's sensors can be sampled as well, giving three linearly independent $N$-vectors that define the visual subspace; see Section 7.1.3. In the case of defining color matching properties of the eye, it is not necessary to know exactly what the spectral responses of the sensors are, only that they are linearly independent. However, the exact form of responses may be useful in analyzing the sensitivity of the eye to color errors.

### 8.3.2    Mathematical definition of color matching

The response of the eye can be represented by a matrix, $\mathbf{S} = [\mathbf{s}_1, \mathbf{s}_2, \mathbf{s}_3]$, where the $N$-vectors, $\mathbf{s}_i$, represent the response of the $i$th type sensor (cone). Any visible spectrum can be represented by an $N$-vector, $\mathbf{f}$. The response of the sensors to the input spectrum is a 3-vector, $\mathbf{c}$, obtained by

$$\mathbf{c} = \mathbf{S}^T \mathbf{f}. \tag{8.2}$$

Two visible spectra are said to have the same color if they appear the same to the human observer. In our linear model, this means that if $\mathbf{f}$ and $\mathbf{g}$ are two $N$-vectors representing different spectral distributions, they are equivalent colors if

$$\mathbf{S}^T \mathbf{f} = \mathbf{S}^T \mathbf{g}. \tag{8.3}$$

It is clear that there may be many different spectra that appear to be the same color to the observer. Two spectra that appear the same are called *metamers*. Metamerism (meh **tam** er ism) is one of the greatest and most fascinating problems in color science. It is basically color "aliasing" and can be described by generalizing the sampling theorem of Chapter 6. The topic will be discussed in detail in Chapter 9.

It is noted here that most physical models of the eye include some type of nonlinearity in the sensing process. This nonlinearity is often modeled as a logarithm. In any case, it is always assumed to be monotonic within the intensity range of interest. The nonlinear function, $\mathbf{v} = V(\mathbf{c})$, transforms the 3-vector, $\mathbf{c}$, in an element independent manner; that is,

$$[v_1, v_2, v_3]^T = [V(c_1), V(c_2), V(c_3)]^T. \tag{8.4}$$

Since equality is required for a color match by Eq. (8.3), the function $V(\cdot)$ does not affect our definition of equivalent colors. Mathematically, the equation

$$V(\mathbf{S}^T \mathbf{f}) = V(\mathbf{S}^T \mathbf{g}) \tag{8.5}$$

is true if, and only if, $\mathbf{S}^T \mathbf{f} = \mathbf{S}^T \mathbf{g}$. This nonlinearity does have a definite effect on the relative sensitivity in the color matching process and is one of the causes of much searching for the *uniform color space* to be discussed later.

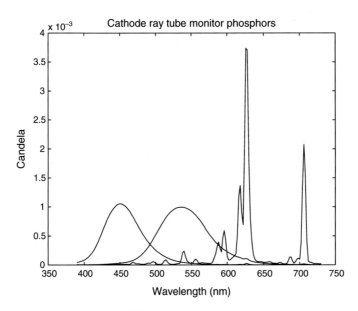

**Figure 8.9.** Example of CRT monitor phosphors.

It is difficult to find the matrix, **S**, that defines the response of the eye. However, there is a conceptually simple experiment that is used to define the human visual space defined by **S**. Consider the set of monochromatic spectra $e_i$, for $i = 1, 2, \ldots, N$. The $N$-vectors, $e_i$, have a one in the $i$th position and zeros elsewhere. The goal of the experiment is to match each of the monochromatic spectra with a linear combination of primary spectra according to Grassmann's conjecture. Construct three lighting sources, called *primaries*, that are linearly independent in $N$-space. Let the matrix, $\mathbf{P} = [\mathbf{p}_1, \mathbf{p}_2, \mathbf{p}_3]$, represent the spectral content of these primaries. The spectra of the phosphors of a color television monitor, shown in Fig. 8.9, are a common example.

The matching of colors using the primaries of the CRT is an example of the usefulness of metamerism. The spectra that are produced by the CRT cannot possibly match the spectra of most reflective objects that have any red component. The physical properties of most materials produce smoothly varying spectra. The red phosphor, shown in Fig. 8.9, has many narrow peaks. However, the basis of color television is that colors can be matched relatively well even though the observed spectra differ significantly.

An experiment is conducted where a subject is shown one of the monochromatic spectra, $e_i$, on one half of a visual field. On the other half of the visual field appears a linear combination of the primary sources, see Fig. 8.10a for grayscale version. The subject attempts to match visually an input monochromatic spectrum by adjusting the relative intensities of the primary sources.

Physically, it may be impossible to match the input spectrum by adjusting the intensities of the primaries. When this happens, the subject is allowed to change the field of one of the primaries so that it falls on the same field as the monochromatic spectrum, see Fig. 8.10b for grayscale version. This is mathematically equivalent to subtracting

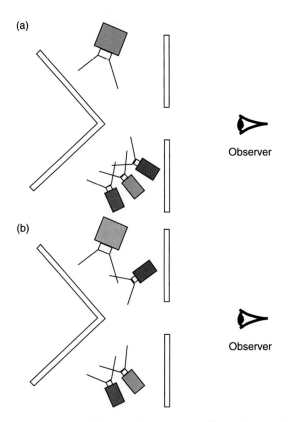

**Figure 8.10.** (a) Color matching, three positive primaries; (b) color matching, two positive primaries, one negative primary (see Plate 1).

that amount of primary from the primary field. Denoting the relative intensities of the primaries by the three-vector $\mathbf{a}_i = [a_{i1}, a_{i2}, a_{i3}]^T$, the match is written mathematically as

$$\mathbf{S}^T \mathbf{e}_i = \mathbf{S}^T \mathbf{P} \mathbf{a}_i. \tag{8.6}$$

Combining the results of all $N$ monochromatic spectra, Eq. (8.6) can be written

$$\mathbf{S}^T \mathbf{I} = \mathbf{S}^T \mathbf{P} \mathbf{A}^T, \tag{8.7}$$

where $\mathbf{I} = [\mathbf{e}_1, \mathbf{e}_2, \ldots, \mathbf{e}_N]$ is the $N \times N$ identity matrix. Thus, the sensitivity matrix can be written as

$$\mathbf{S}^T = \mathbf{S}^T \mathbf{P} \mathbf{A}^T, \tag{8.8}$$

which shows that $\mathbf{S}$ is a linear transformation of the *color matching matrix*, $\mathbf{A}^T = [a_1, a_2, \ldots, a_N]$. Note that because $\mathbf{S}$ and $\mathbf{P}$ are both rank[4] three and the primaries are

---

[4] See Appendix B for the definition of rank.

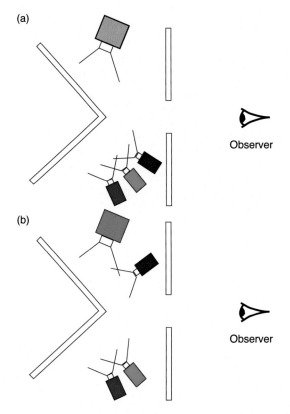

**Plate 1** (a) Color matching, three positive primaries; (b) color matching, two positive primaries, one negative primary (for grayscale version, please see Fig. 8.10).

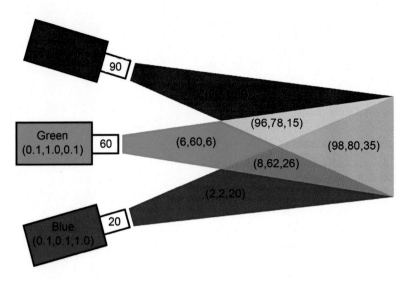

**Plate 2** Additive color system (for grayscale version, please see Fig. 8.15).

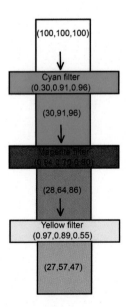

**Plate 3** Subtractive color system (for grayscale version, please see Fig. 8.16).

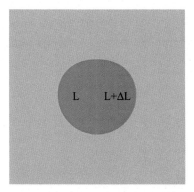

**Plate 4** MacAdam's color comparison experiment (for grayscale version, please see Fig. 8.17).

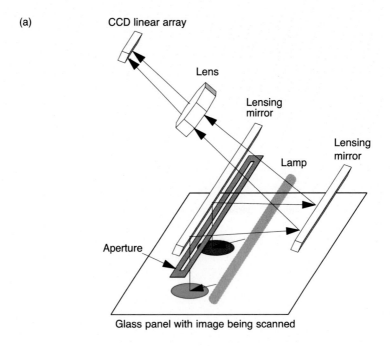

(a)

CCD linear array

Lens

Lensing mirror

Lensing mirror

Lamp

Aperture

Glass panel with image being scanned

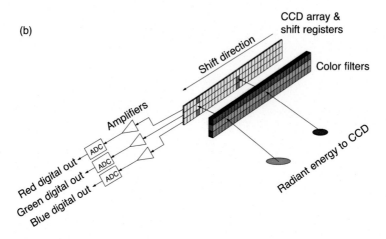

(b)

CCD array & shift registers

Shift direction

Color filters

Amplifiers

Radiant energy to CCD

Red digital out

Green digital out

Blue digital out

ADC

ADC

ADC

**Plate 5** (a) CCD optical path for flat-bed reflectance scanner; (b) CCD sensor details (for grayscale version, please see Fig. 10.1).

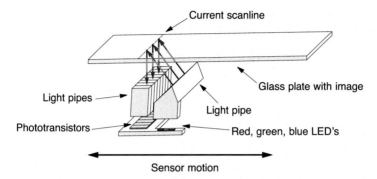

**Plate 6** Contact image sensor (CIS) optical path: the red, green and blue LEDs are time multiplexed to illuminate a single scan line (for grayscale version, please see Fig. 10.2).

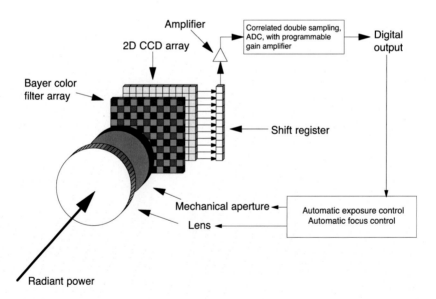

**Plate 7** Imaging front end of digital still camera (for grayscale version, please see Fig. 10.8).

**Plate 8** The Bayer color filter array (for grayscale version, please see Fig. 10.13).

(a)  (b)

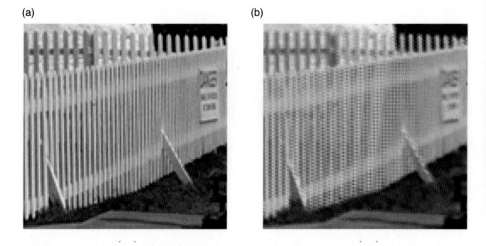

**Plate 9** Bicubic interpolation used for color filter array interpolation results in noticeable artifacts: (a) original image; (b) bicubic spline interpolation; figure from [99] used with permission of the authors and IEEE, ©2005 IEEE (for grayscale version, please see Fig. 10.14).

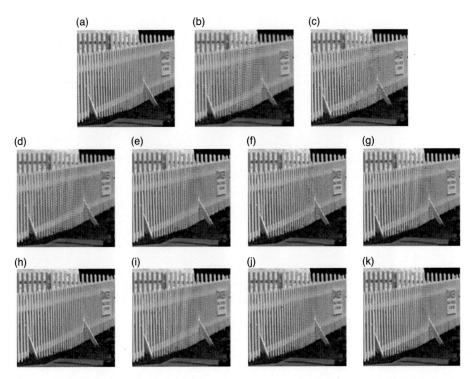

**Plate 10** Result images for Lighthouse image: (a) original image; (b) bilinear interpolation; (c) edge-directed interpolation in [111]; (d) constant-hue-based interpolation in [1]; (e) weighted sum in [150]; (f) second-order gradients as correction terms in [2]; (g) Bayesian approach in [188]; (h) homogeneity-directed in [113]; (i) pattern matching in [46]; (j) alias cancelation in [88]; (k) POCS in [98]; figure is from [99], and used with permission of the authors and IEEE, ©2005 IEEE (for grayscale version, please see Fig. 10.15).

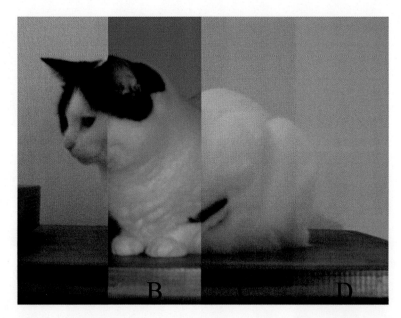

**Plate 11** The conditions and settings of the camera were as follows (a) tungsten illumination with fluorescent white balance; (b) flash illumination with tungsten white balance; (c) tungsten illumination with tungsten white balance; (d) tungsten illumination with daylight white balance (for grayscale version, please see Fig. 10.16).

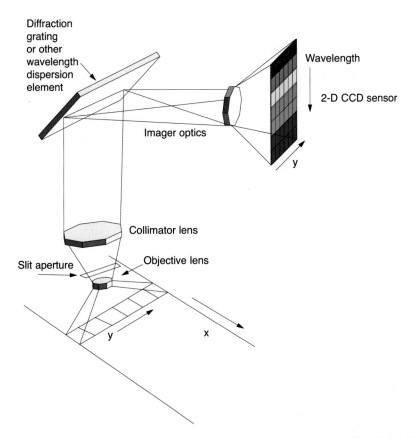

**Plate 12** Example of a hyperspectral camera: the camera moves in the *x* direction, collecting scan lines along the *y* direction; each scan line pixel is dispersed into its spectral components and sampled with a 2-D CCD array (for grayscale version, please see Fig. 10.18).

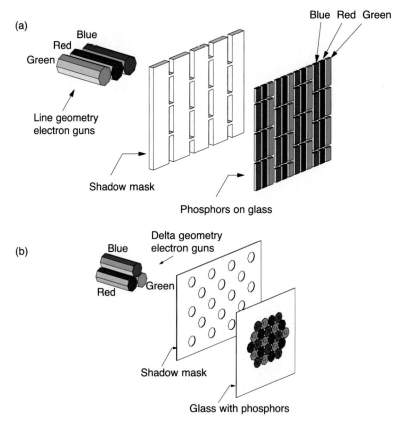

**Plate 13** (a) CRT geometry with in-line electron guns; (b) CRT geometry with delta electron guns (for grayscale version, please see Fig. 11.1).

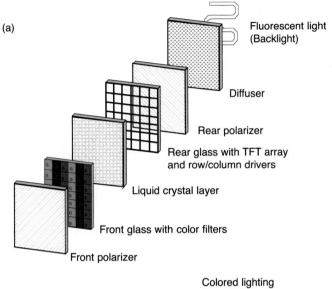

(a)

Fluorescent light (Backlight)

Diffuser

Rear polarizer

Rear glass with TFT array and row/column drivers

Liquid crystal layer

Front glass with color filters

Front polarizer

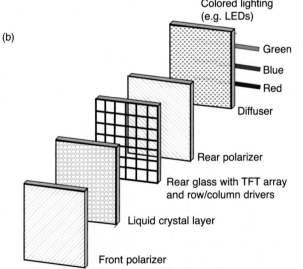

Colored lighting (e.g. LEDs)

(b)

Green

Blue

Red

Diffuser

Rear polarizer

Rear glass with TFT array and row/column drivers

Liquid crystal layer

Front polarizer

**Plate 14** (a) Typical components for active matrix LCD display with white backlighting; (b) example of an LCD display with three colored lights which are time multiplexed (for grayscale version, please see Fig. 11.4).

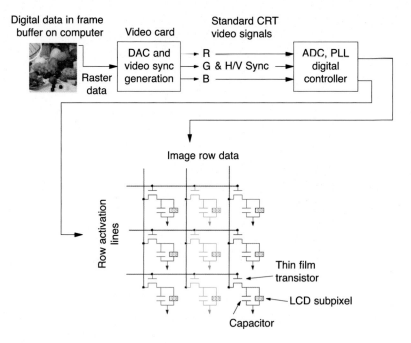

**Plate 15** A once common interface for LCD displays (for grayscale version, please see Fig. 11.7).

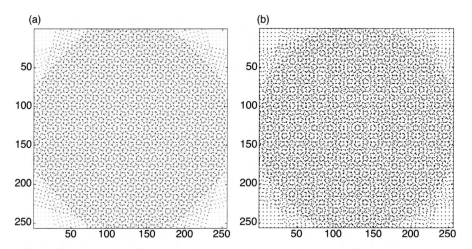

**Plate 16** (a) Color rosette patterns formed by combining screens from Figs. 11.36; (b) black image to accentuate the rosette patterns (for grayscale version, please see Fig. 11.37).

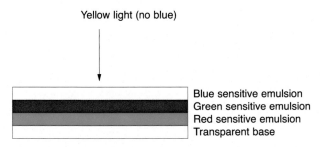

Yellow light (no blue)

Blue sensitive emulsion
Green sensitive emulsion
Red sensitive emulsion
Transparent base

**Plate 17** Color negative film exposed to yellow light (for grayscale version, please see Fig. 11.12).

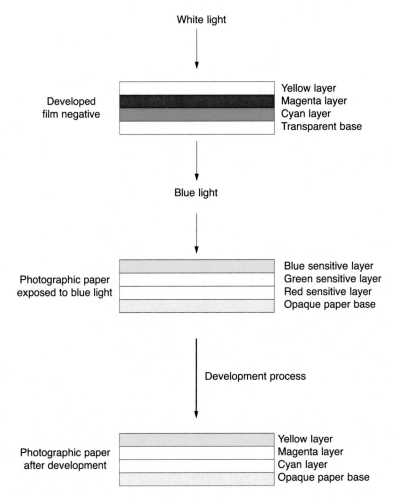

White light

Developed
film negative

Yellow layer
Magenta layer
Cyan layer
Transparent base

Blue light

Photographic paper
exposed to blue light

Blue sensitive layer
Green sensitive layer
Red sensitive layer
Opaque paper base

Development process

Photographic paper
after development

Yellow layer
Magenta layer
Cyan layer
Opaque paper base

**Plate 18** Color print created from film in Fig. 11.12 (for grayscale version, please see Fig. 11.13).

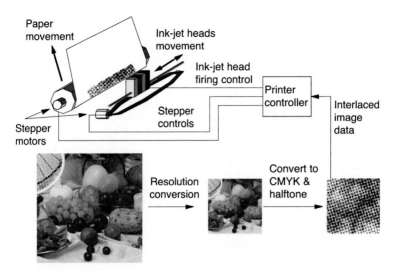

**Plate 19** Ink-jet printing process (for grayscale version, please see Fig. 11.41).

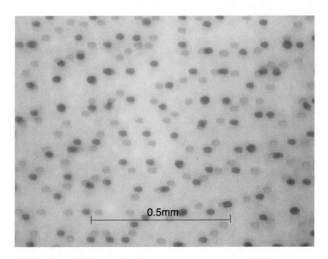

**Plate 20** Magnification of dots created by an ink-jet engine on glossy paper: note that only single dots are created with this print engine (for grayscale version, please see Fig. 11.42).

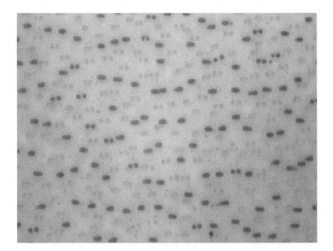

**Plate 21** Magnification of dots created by another ink-jet engine on glossy paper: note that single dots as well as double dots are created with this engine (for grayscale version, please see Fig. 11.43).

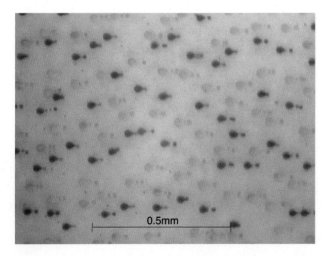

**Plate 22** Magnification of dots created by yet another ink-jet engine on glossy paper: note that an occasional satellite dot occurs (for grayscale version, please see Fig. 11.44).

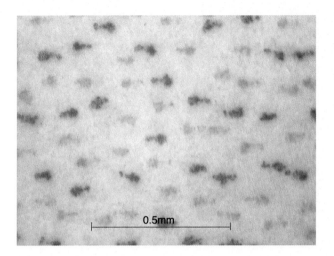

**Plate 23** Magnification of dots created by same engine used to create the dots in Fig. 11.44: the difference is that now ink-jet coated paper is used instead of ink-jet glossy paper (for grayscale version, please see Fig. 11.45).

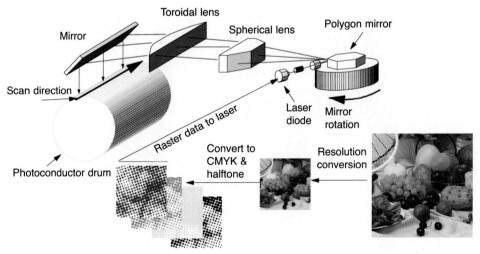

**Plate 24** From digital RGB data to exposing the photoconductor drum (for grayscale version, please see Fig. 11.46).

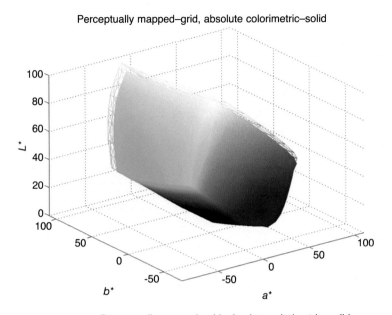

Perceptually mapped–grid, absolute colorimetric–solid

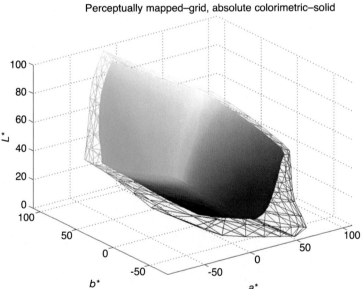

Perceptually mapped–grid, absolute colorimetric–solid

**Plate 25** (a) Gamut (solid) and apparent gamut (grid) of printer with perceptual adjustment of data using method 1; (b) gamut (solid) and apparent gamut (grid) of printer with perceptual adjustment of data using method 2 (for grayscale version, please see Fig. 12.17).

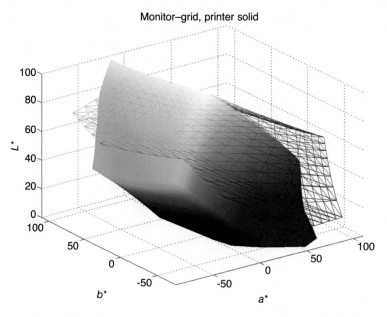

**Plate 26** Monitor gamut given by grid and printer gamut given by solid figure (for grayscale version, please see Fig. 12.20).

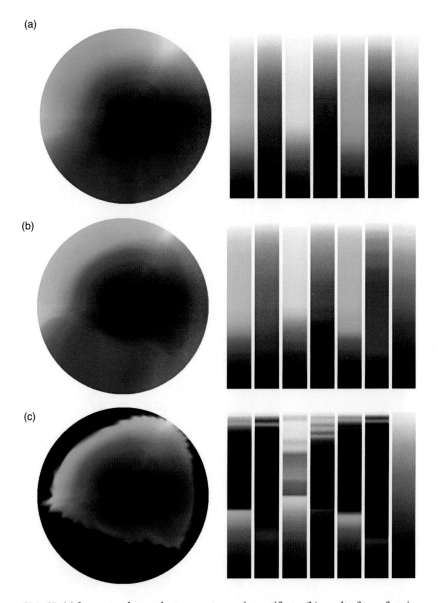

**Plate 27** (a) Image used to evaluate gamut mapping artifacts; (b) result of transforming image in (a) through $\mathcal{F}_{\text{print}}^{-1} (\mathcal{D}(\mathcal{F}_{\text{monitor}} (.)))$; (c) result of transforming image in (a) through $\mathcal{F}_{\text{print}}^{-1} (\mathcal{U}(\mathcal{F}_{\text{monitor}} (.)))$ (for grayscale version, please see Fig. 12.19).

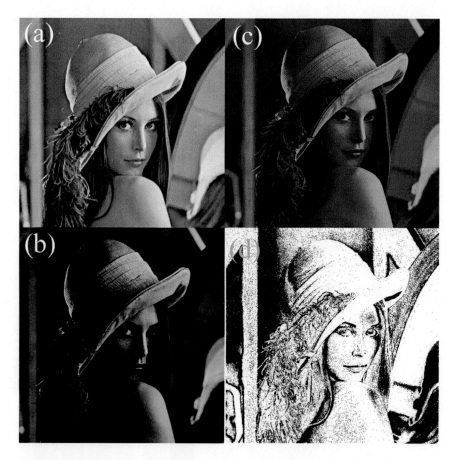

**Plate 28** Lena color images: see text for description (for grayscale version, please see Fig. 12.21).

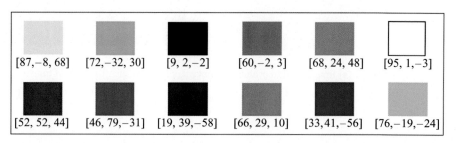

| | | | | | |
|---|---|---|---|---|---|
| [87,−8, 68] | [72,−32, 30] | [9, 2,−2] | [60,−2, 3] | [68, 24, 48] | [95, 1,−3] |
| [52, 52, 44] | [46, 79,−31] | [19, 39,−58] | [66, 29, 10] | [33,41,−56] | [76,−19,−24] |

**Plate 29** Color squares for quantifying publishing reproduction accuracy (for grayscale version, please see Fig. 12.22).

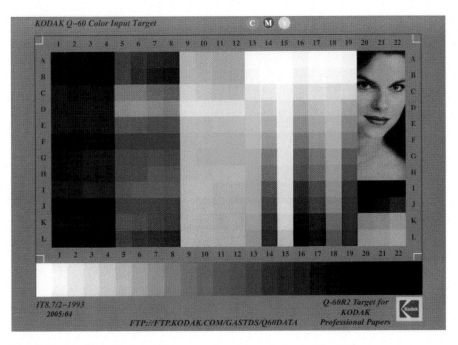

**Plate 30** Kodak Q60 color target (for grayscale version, please see Fig. D.2).

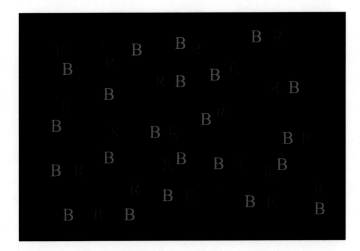

**Plate 31** This image can be used to demonstrate an effect caused by the fact that the HVS is a single lens system and can only focus one wavelength exactly: when viewed closely, it should appear that the red letters are closer than the blue letters even though they are in the same spatial plane (for grayscale version, please see Fig. E.2).

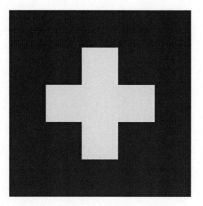

**Plate 32** Figure that can be used to demonstrate the effects of neural fatigue: stare at the yellow cross for 10 to 15 seconds and then stare at the white square; an "after image" of a blue cross in a yellow square will appear (for grayscale version, please see Fig. E.6).

**Plate 33** Example of the effects of simultaneous contrast: spectrally the red areas are the same, but the areas on the right appear to be more yellow (for grayscale version, please see Fig. E.7).

**Plate 34** An example of a frequency pattern in the blue-yellow direction at a constant luminance (for grayscale version, please see Fig. E.10).

**Plate 35** Demonstration of MTF of eye in blue region modulating towards yellow: spatial frequency varies on horizontal axis, magnitude of variation in a blue-yellow direction varies along the vertical axis, and the image is constant luminance (for grayscale version, please see Fig. E.11).

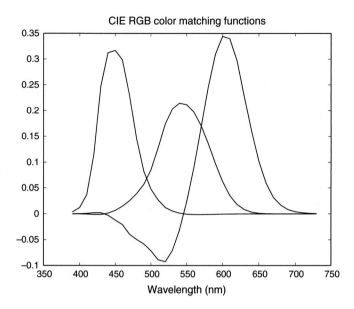

**Figure 8.11.** CIE RGB color matching functions, 1931, 2°.

linearly independent under the cone responses, the product matrix is nonsingular, i.e., $(\mathbf{S}^T \mathbf{P})^{-1}$ exists. The *human visual subspace* (HVSS) in the $N$-dimensional vector space is defined by the column vectors of $\mathbf{S}$; however, this space can be equally well defined by any nonsingular transformation of those basis vectors. The matrix,

$$\mathbf{A} = \mathbf{S}(\mathbf{P}^T \mathbf{S})^{-1}, \tag{8.9}$$

is one such transformation. This equation clearly shows that the color matching matrix, $\mathbf{A}$, is determined solely by the primaries and the human color sensitivity. The columns of the matrix $\mathbf{A}$ are called the *color matching functions associated with the primaries* $\mathbf{P}$. The Commission Internationale de l'Eclairage (CIE) has tabulated a standard set of color matching functions corresponding to a standard set of primaries [48]. The primaries used for the CIE RGB color matching functions shown in Fig. 8.11 are monochromatic lines at 435.8 nm, 546.1 nm and 700 nm.

To avoid the problem of negative values that cannot be realized with transmission or reflective filters, in 1931 the CIE developed a standard transformation of the color matching functions that have no negative values [48]. These are reprinted in [160, 313]. These functions are based on a 2-degree field of vision and were first defined in 1931. In addition to being physically realizable, one of the functions was chosen to be the luminous efficiency function, Fig. 8.3. This is convenient, since both color and monochrome information can be obtained from the same measurements. This set of color matching functions is known as the 1931 *standard observer* or the CIEXYZ color matching functions. These functions are shown in Fig. 8.12. These color matching functions are based on a 2° field of view. The CIE published a set of color matching functions for a 10°

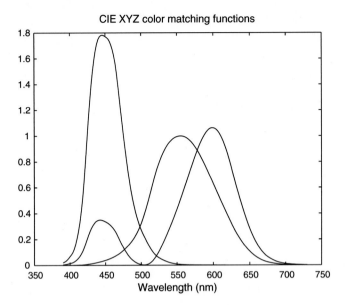

**Figure 8.12.** CIE XYZ color matching functions, 1931, 2°.

field of view in 1964 [48]. Note that there are no realizable primaries associated with these all-positive functions. For the remainder of this chapter, the matrix, $\mathbf{A}$, can be thought of as this standard set of functions. However, the theory and properties presented here are not limited to a particular set of color matching functions. The value of the CIE standard is in precisely defining colorimetric quantities, such as tristimulus values and chromaticity.

### 8.3.3    Properties of color matching functions

Having defined the human visual subspace, it is worthwhile to examine some of the common properties of this space. Because of the relatively simple definition of color matching given in the last section, Eq. (8.3), the standard properties enumerated by Grassmann are easily derived by simple matrix manipulations.

#### Property 1 (existence of color match)

For any visible spectrum, $\mathbf{f}$, there is a unique 3-vector, $\mathbf{c}$, which modulates the primary sources to produce a spectrum that appears the same to the human observer. Mathematically, there exists $\mathbf{c}$ such that

$$\mathbf{S}^T\mathbf{f} = \mathbf{S}^T\mathbf{P}\mathbf{c}. \tag{8.10}$$

Existence can be seen by letting $\mathbf{c} = (\mathbf{S}^T\mathbf{P})^{-1}\mathbf{S}^T\mathbf{f}$ and making the substitution. Uniqueness is also easily demonstrated. The interpretation of negative elements in $\mathbf{c}$ is the same as in the color matching experiment. Given the results of the color matching experiment, see Fig. 8.11, it is impossible to match all possible spectra with nonnegative combinations of nonnegative primaries. See Problem 8.3 for the exercise.

## Property 2 (additivity of colors)

If **c** and **d** are the 3-vectors associated with the visible spectra, **f** and **g** respectively, then **c** + **d** is the 3-vector associated with **f** + **g**.

This is a consequence of the linearity of the vector space model for color matching that has been assumed. An application of this is in the calibration of color CRT monitors. If the color guns are independent, then each color can be calibrated separately. Any mix of colors can be obtained by solving a simple $3 \times 3$ linear system of equations.

## Property 3 (dependence of color on **A**)

Two visual spectra, **f** and **g**, appear the same, if and only if $\mathbf{A}^T\mathbf{f} = \mathbf{A}^T\mathbf{g}$. Writing this mathematically, $\mathbf{S}^T\mathbf{f} = \mathbf{S}^T\mathbf{g}$ iff $\mathbf{A}^T\mathbf{f} = \mathbf{A}^T\mathbf{g}$.

This is a direct consequence of the fact that $\mathbf{A} = \mathbf{S}(\mathbf{P}^T\mathbf{S})^{-1}$.

The importance of this property is that any linear transformation of the sensitivities of the eye or the CIE color matching functions can be used to determine a color match. This gives more latitude in choosing color filters for cameras and scanners, as well as for color measurement equipment.

A note on terminology is appropriate here. When the color matching matrix is the CIE standard [313], the elements of the 3-vector defined by $\mathbf{c} = \mathbf{A}^T\mathbf{f}$ are called *tristimulus values* and are usually denoted by $X, Y, Z$; i.e., $\mathbf{c}^T = [X, Y, Z]$. The $Y$ value corresponds to the luminance defined in Section 8.2. The *chromaticity* of a spectrum is obtained by normalizing the tristimulus values,

$$x = X/(X + Y + Z),$$
$$y = Y/(X + Y + Z),$$
$$z = Z/(X + Y + Z).$$

Since the chromaticity coordinates have been normalized, any two of them are sufficient to characterize the chromaticity of a spectrum. The $x$ and $y$ terms are the standard for describing chromaticity. A chromaticity diagram is often used to describe the possible range of colors that can be produced by a color output device. The mathematically largest range is given by the chromaticities of monochromatic colors. This maximum range is plotted as a horseshoe or shark fin shaped curve in two dimensions, as shown in Fig. 8.13. It is noted that the convention of using different variables for the elements of the tristimulus vector may make mental conversion between the vector space notation and notation in common color science texts more difficult, but the $X, Y, Z$ convention is established.

The CIE has chosen the $\mathbf{a}_2$ sensitivity vector to correspond to the luminous efficiency function of the eye. This function, shown in Fig. 8.3 and as the middle curve in Fig. 8.12, gives the relative sensitivity of the eye to the energy at each wavelength. The $Y$ tristimulus value is luminance and indicates the perceived brightness of a radiant spectrum. The chromaticities $x$ and $y$ indicate the hue and saturation of the color. Often the color is described in terms of $[x, y, Y]$ because of the ease of interpretation. Other color coordinate systems will be discussed in Section 8.5.

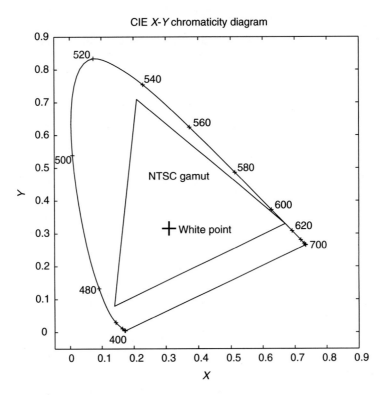

**Figure 8.13.** CIE chromaticity diagram: the boundary is the chromaticity of monochromatic sources at wavelengths between 400 nm and 700 nm; the inner triangle is the color gamut of NTSC television, with the NTSC white marked with a +.

### Property 4 (transformation of primaries)

If a different set of primary sources, $\mathbf{Q}$, is used in the color matching experiment, a different set of color matching functions, $\mathbf{B}$, is obtained. The relation between the two color matching matrices is given by

$$\mathbf{B}^T = (\mathbf{A}^T \mathbf{Q})^{-1} \mathbf{A}^T. \tag{8.11}$$

This transformation is fundamental for corrections when displaying a single image on several different additive devices. It is embedded in all television receivers.

This relation is shown by first considering the fundamental color matching Eq. (8.8) for each set of primaries,

$$\mathbf{S}^T = \mathbf{S}^T \mathbf{P} \mathbf{A}^T = \mathbf{S}^T \mathbf{Q} \mathbf{B}^T, \tag{8.12}$$

and noting, that $\mathbf{A}^T = (\mathbf{S}^T \mathbf{P})^{-1} \mathbf{S}^T$, from Eq. (8.9). Multiplying on the left by $(\mathbf{S}^T \mathbf{P})^{-1}$ gives

$$(\mathbf{S}^T \mathbf{P})^{-1} \mathbf{S}^T \mathbf{P} \mathbf{A}^T = (\mathbf{S}^T \mathbf{P})^{-1} \mathbf{S}^T \mathbf{Q} \mathbf{B}^T. \tag{8.13}$$

Simplifying the first term and using Eq. (8.9), we obtain

$$\mathbf{A}^T = \mathbf{A}^T \mathbf{Q} \mathbf{B}^T. \tag{8.14}$$

Noting that the matrix, $\mathbf{A}^T \mathbf{Q}$, must be nonsingular, multiply Eq. (8.14) on the left by $(\mathbf{A}^T \mathbf{Q})^{-1}$ to get the desired result.

The more common interpretation of the matrix $\mathbf{A}^T \mathbf{Q}$ is obtained by a direct examination. The $j$th column of $\mathbf{Q}$, denoted $\mathbf{q}_j$, is the spectral distribution of the $j$th primary of the new set. The element $[\mathbf{A}^T \mathbf{Q}]_{i,j}$ is the amount of the primary $\mathbf{p}_i$ required to match primary $\mathbf{q}_j$. It is noted that the above form of the change of primaries is restricted to those that can be adequately represented under the assumed sampling discussed previously. In the case that one of the new primaries is a Dirac delta function located between sample frequencies, the transformation $\mathbf{A}^T \mathbf{Q}$ must be found by interpolation.

---

**Example 8.1 (Characterization of CRTs by white point).**     One of the uses of this property is in determining the optimal color separation filters for color television cameras. The color matching functions associated with the primaries used in the television monitor are the ideal filters. In this case, the recorded values obtained by such filters would directly give the values to drive the color guns in the television display. There would be no need for a linear transformation of the recorded values. The common $[R, G, B]$ values used to describe images are usually related to these color matching functions associated with the television primaries. The common $[Y, I, Q]$ values that are actually transmitted are used for coding purposes [134].

Unfortunately, since the TV primaries are realizable, the color matching functions that correspond to them are not. This means that the filters that are used in TV cameras are only an approximation to the ideal filters. These filters are usually obtained by simply clipping the part of the ideal filter that falls below zero. This clipping introduces an error that cannot be corrected by post-processing.

The phosphors of a CRT display are not standardly described by their tristimulus values, since the brightness can be adjusted over a wide range. The chromaticity of the phosphors is sufficient to determine the transformation if a normalizing constant is included in the specification. The normalizing constraint is usually the *white point*; that is, the chromaticity of the color produced when all three phosphors have equal intensity.

Consider the specifications for a CRT where the chromaticities of the phosphors are given by $x_r, y_r$ (red), $x_g, y_g$ (green), $x_b, y_b$ (blue) and the chromaticity of the white point is $x_w, y_w$. The white point is often specified by a *color temperature*, which can be related to a chromaticity. This relation will be discussed in Section 8.6.

Since the chromaticity values of the phosphors are given, the tristimulus values associated with the phosphors are known to within a constant, that is,

$$\mathbf{A}^T \mathbf{Q} = \mathbf{T} \Lambda = \begin{bmatrix} X_r & X_g & X_b \\ Y_r & Y_g & Y_b \\ Z_r & Z_g & Z_b \end{bmatrix} \begin{bmatrix} \lambda_r & 0 & 0 \\ 0 & \lambda_g & 0 \\ 0 & 0 & \lambda_b \end{bmatrix}, \tag{8.15}$$

where the values of the diagonal matrix are to be determined. The color matching functions for the CRT are given by

$$A_{CRT}^T = (A^T Q)^{-1} A^T.$$

Substituting for $A^T Q$ from Eq. (8.15), we obtain

$$A_{CRT}^T = (T\Lambda)^{-1} A^T.$$

Using the constraint on the white point, we map the tristimulus values of the white point, which are known to within a constant, to the equal amplitudes of the primaries,

$$\begin{bmatrix} 1 \\ 1 \\ 1 \end{bmatrix} = \Lambda^{-1} T^{-1} \begin{bmatrix} x_w \\ y_w \\ z_w \end{bmatrix} \mu_w, \tag{8.16}$$

where the constant $\mu_w$ can be used to compensate for any gain on the equal amplitude vector. The value of $\mu_w$ can be set to any convenient value, say 1, to obtain a numerical solution. In effect, $\mu_w$ is only a scaling factor, which can be considered part of the gain control of the CRT. It can be used to normalize the new color matching functions according to the user's desires.

Multiplying Eq. (8.16) on the left by $\Lambda$, the values of $\Lambda$ are determined by

$$\begin{bmatrix} \lambda_r \\ \lambda_g \\ \lambda_b \end{bmatrix} = T^{-1} \begin{bmatrix} x_w \\ y_w \\ z_w \end{bmatrix} \mu_w,$$

and $A_{CRT}$ is determined to within a constant. It is the shape of the color matching functions that is important; the gain can be easily adjusted. These functions determine the filters used for scanning images that are to be reproduced on the CRT. The NTSC standards are shown in Table 8.5 [24, 125].

As an example, the color matching functions for NTSC television are computed as follows:

(1) Solve for $[\lambda_r, \lambda_g, \lambda_b]$ by

$$\begin{bmatrix} \lambda_r \\ \lambda_g \\ \lambda_b \end{bmatrix} = \begin{bmatrix} 0.670 & 0.210 & 0.140 \\ 0.330 & 0.710 & 0.080 \\ 0 & 0.080 & 0.780 \end{bmatrix}^{-1} \begin{bmatrix} 0.310 \\ 0.316 \\ 0.374 \end{bmatrix} = \begin{bmatrix} 0.2863 \\ 0.2610 \\ 0.4527 \end{bmatrix}.$$

(2) Solve for vectors that represent $A_{NTSC}$

$$A_{NTSC}^T = \begin{bmatrix} 0.2863 & 0 & 0 \\ 0 & 0.2610 & 0 \\ 0 & 0 & 0.4527 \end{bmatrix}^{-1} \begin{bmatrix} 0.670 & 0.210 & 0.140 \\ 0.330 & 0.710 & 0.080 \\ 0 & 0.080 & 0.780 \end{bmatrix}^{-1} A^T.$$

**Table 8.5.** Defining chromaticities for NTSC television

|             | x     | y     |
|-------------|-------|-------|
| Red         | 0.670 | 0.330 |
| Green       | 0.210 | 0.710 |
| Blue        | 0.140 | 0.080 |
| White point | 0.310 | 0.316 |

**Table 8.6.** Defining chromaticities for HDTV television

|             | x     | y     |
|-------------|-------|-------|
| Red         | 0.640 | 0.330 |
| Green       | 0.300 | 0.600 |
| Blue        | 0.15  | 0.060 |
| White point | 0.313 | 0.329 |

(3) A plot of the NTSC color matching functions is shown in Fig. 8.14a. Note that there are significant negative portions in these functions. Truncation of these portions to permit building filters for cameras will produce significant color errors. A more accurate method is discussed later.

As a comparison, the HDTV specifications are shown in Table 8.6 and yield the color matching functions shown in Fig. 8.14b. The different chromaticities were chosen because of changes in the phosphors used in modern televisions, which provide a larger gamut.

### Property 5 (transformation of color vectors)

If **c** and **d** are the color vectors in 3-space associated with the visible spectrum, **f**, under the primaries **P** and **Q** respectively, then

$$d = (A^T Q)^{-1} c, \tag{8.17}$$

where **A** is the color matching function matrix associated with primaries **P**. This states that a $3 \times 3$ transformation is all that is required to go from one color space to another. An obvious application is the transformation of recorded NTSC color to HDTV color. The CIE tristimulus values of objects could be transformed to either television format. Of course, a problem is the fact that the recorded values of television color are approximate because filters are not available to match exactly the space defined by the color matching functions.

### Property 6 (metamers and the human visual subspace)

The $N$-dimensional spectral space can be decomposed into a 3-dimensional subspace known as the human visual subspace (HVSS) and a subspace of dimension $N-3$ that is

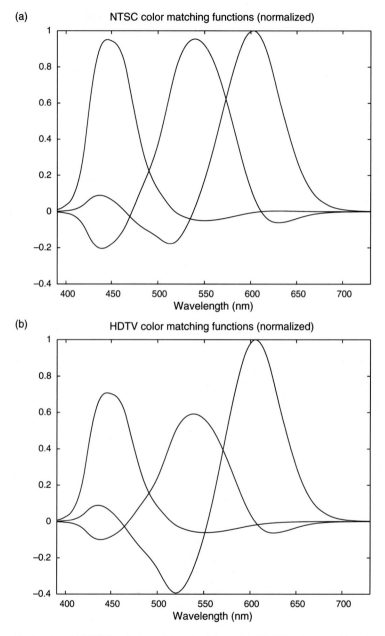

**Figure 8.14.** (a) NTSC color matching functions; (b) HDTV color matching functions.

known as the black space. The visual system is dependent only on the component of the spectrum that lies in the visual space. All metamers of a particular visible spectrum, $\mathbf{f}$, are given by

$$\mathbf{x} = \mathbf{P}_v \mathbf{f} + \mathbf{P}_b \mathbf{g}, \tag{8.18}$$

where $\mathbf{P_v} = \mathbf{A}(\mathbf{A}^T\mathbf{A})^{-1}\mathbf{A}^T$ is the orthogonal projection operator to the visual space, $\mathbf{P_b} = [\mathbf{I} - \mathbf{A}(\mathbf{A}^T\mathbf{A})^{-1}\mathbf{A}^T]$ is the orthogonal projection operator to the black space, and $\mathbf{g}$ is any vector in $N$-space.

It should be noted that humans cannot see (or detect) all possible spectra in the visual space. Since it is a vector space, there exist elements with negative values. These elements are not realizable and thus cannot be seen. All vectors in the black space have negative elements. While the vectors in the black space are not realizable and cannot be seen, they can be combined with vectors in the visible space to produce realizable spectra.

An application of Property 6 may be in designing color reflectances using dyes, inks or other colorants. The user wishes to produce a match to a certain color. If only the fundamental spectra of the components, defined by $\mathbf{P_v f}$, is considered, it may be possible to see a combination of the components that will yield the fundamental of the desired color. Whereas, by considering the entire spectra of the components, the black space portions may camouflage the correct combination.

### Property 7 (effect of illumination)

The effect of an illumination spectrum, represented by the $N$-vector $\mathbf{l}$, is to transform the color matching matrix $\mathbf{A}$ by

$$\mathbf{A}_l = \mathbf{LA}, \tag{8.19}$$

where $\mathbf{L}$ is a diagonal matrix defined by setting the diagonal elements of $\mathbf{L}$ to the elements of the vector $\mathbf{l}$.

The emitted spectrum for an object with reflectance vector, $\mathbf{r}$, under illumination, $\mathbf{l}$, is given by multiplying the reflectance by the illuminant at each wavelength. This is described by the equation

$$\mathbf{g} = \mathbf{Lr}. \tag{8.20}$$

The tristimulus values associated with this emitted spectrum are obtained by

$$\mathbf{c} = \mathbf{A}^T\mathbf{g} = \mathbf{A}^T\mathbf{Lr}, \tag{8.21}$$

which can be simplified to

$$\mathbf{c} = \mathbf{A}_l^T\mathbf{r}, \tag{8.22}$$

by the substitution of Eq. (8.19). The substitution shows that the illumination can be thought of as modifying the human visual subspace of Property 6. The matrix $\mathbf{A}_l$ will be called the color matching functions under illuminant $\mathbf{l}$.

Metamerism under different illuminants is one of the greatest problems in color science [41]. A classic example is matching buttons to a fabric. Comparison of samples under the fluorescent lights of the store may indicate a match, but the samples no longer appear the same when viewed out of the store in daylight. As mentioned before, this effect can be described as color aliasing.

The mismatch can be expressed mathematically by the relations

$$\mathbf{A}^T \mathbf{L}_f \mathbf{g}_1 = \mathbf{A}^T \mathbf{L}_f \mathbf{g}_2, \tag{8.23}$$

$$\mathbf{A}^T \mathbf{L}_d \mathbf{g}_1 \neq \mathbf{A}^T \mathbf{L}_d \mathbf{g}_2, \tag{8.24}$$

where $\mathbf{L}_f$ and $\mathbf{L}_d$ are diagonal matrices representing standard fluorescent and daylight spectra respectively; and $\mathbf{g}_1$ and $\mathbf{g}_2$ represent the reflectance spectra of the fabric and button respectively. The ideal objects would have $\mathbf{g}_2$ matching $\mathbf{g}_1$ under all illuminations, which would imply they are equal. This is virtually impossible since the fabric and button are made of different materials. It may be sufficient to have the two match under a limited number of illuminants. The solution to this problem will be discussed below.

### Property 8 (ideal color recording)

The goal of image recording is to obtain data that will allow a user to determine how the image would appear to a standard observer. Once this is known, the image may be displayed on any of several devices or just used for analysis. If the appearance of the image under a particular illuminant is to be recorded, then the recorder must have sensitivities that are within a linear transformation of the color matching functions under that illuminant. For most cases, the recorder is a scanner or camera, which consists of an illumination source, a set of filters, an optical path and a detector. The product of the four must be within a nonsingular transformation of the desired color matching functions. Mathematically, this is written

$$\mathbf{A}_l = \mathbf{L}\mathbf{A} = \mathbf{B}\mathbf{L}_r \mathbf{D}\mathbf{O}\mathbf{M}, \tag{8.25}$$

where $\mathbf{L}_r$ is a diagonal matrix defined by the recorder illuminant, $\mathbf{D}$ is the diagonal matrix defined by the spectral sensitivity of the detector, $\mathbf{O}$ is the diagonal matrix defined by the spectral transmission of the optics, $\mathbf{M}$ is the $N \times 3$ matrix defined by the transmission characteristics of the scanning filters, and $\mathbf{B}$ is a $3 \times 3$ transformation. In some modern scanners, three colored lamps are used instead of a single lamp and three filters. In this case, the $\mathbf{L}_r$ and $\mathbf{M}$ matrices can be combined.

In most applications, the scanner illumination is a high intensity source, to minimize scanning time. The detector is usually a standard CCD or photodiode array or photomultiplier tube. The design problem is to create a filter set $\mathbf{M}$ that brings the product in Eq. (8.25) to within a linear transformation of $\mathbf{A}_l$. Since creating a perfect match with real materials is a problem, it is of interest to measure the goodness of approximations to a set of scanning filters. This is discussed in [65, 70, 75, 194, 285, 311].

It is often the case that the matrix $\mathbf{L}_r \mathbf{D}\mathbf{O}\mathbf{M}$ is not within a linear transformation of the desired $\mathbf{A}_l$. In such cases, $\mathbf{B}$ is usually found by solving a least squares problem. In setting up the least squares problem, a data set is either chosen or generated. This data set should be representative of the type of images and materials being used. The resulting transformations are optimal only for that set of imaging conditions.

Another aspect of color recording is the limitation to a single viewing illuminant. The matrix $\mathbf{B}$ is clearly a function of $\mathbf{A}_l$. A typical problem arises in the design of a color copier. The filters and correction are designed for one illuminant, e.g., office fluorescence lighting. The customer changes the location of the copier so that it is near a window, which permits a strong daylight component. Since the illumination has changed, the copies, which may have been optimal for one illuminant, are no longer accurate under the new illuminant. The problem of multiple illuminants can be addressed by a least squares problem. For this, we simply change the cost function to be an error that is averaged over all of the illuminants in question. In addition, it is possible to add filters and record additional channels of data, which will permit better correction to all viewing conditions [292, 293].

## 8.4    Mathematics of color reproduction

To reproduce a color image, it is necessary to generate new vectors in $N$-space from vectors obtained by some multispectral sensor. Since the eye can be represented as a 3-channel sensor, it is most common for the multispectral sensor to use three scanning filters. It was noted in the previous section that this limits the reproduction to the viewing environment specified by the color matching functions, $\mathbf{A}_l$, associated with the recording illuminant. By using methods from signal processing, it has been shown that under many practical conditions additional channels can produce more accurate reproductions [292, 293]. However, the trade-off is one of the cost in time and money for the extra data versus the increased accuracy of the reproduction. It is clear that the quality of the reproduction is limited by the accuracy of the recorded data.

The characteristics of the response functions associated with the multispectral display device form a critical aspect of color reproduction. This may be a nearly additive device, such as a CRT, or a highly nonlinear device, such as an ink-jet printer. Display devices can be characterized as being additive or subtractive. Additive devices, such as monitors, produce light of varying spectral composition that is directly received by the human observer, see Fig. 8.15. Subtractive devices, such as ink-jet printers, produce filters which attenuate portions of an illuminating spectrum, as shown in Fig. 8.16. The details of these figures will be discussed in the appropriate sections. The additive system is simpler to analyze and will be considered first. For the present, it will be assumed that the sensor used with the reproduction system is a linear transformation of the color matching function of the human eye and the illuminant is uniform. This means that the information is available to match the input color exactly.

Physical limitations of the electronics and chemicals must also be considered in color reproduction. These limits will be the source of many constraints in the mathematical description of color systems. In color matching, the assumed linearity of the system is not of great consequence since equalities are considered. As mentioned earlier, any monotonic, pointwise, nonlinear function can be ignored in color matching. In practical situations, the relative sensitivity of regions of the visible spectrum is important. In these cases, nonlinearities are of great concern and must be taken into account in evaluating the color system. This will be discussed shortly.

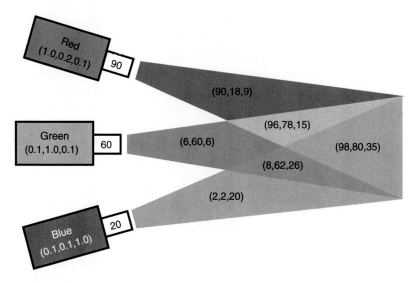

**Figure 8.15.** Additive color system (for color version, please see Plate 2).

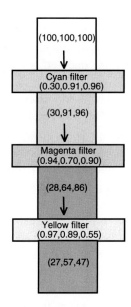

**Figure 8.16.** Subtractive color system (for color version, please see Plate 3).

## 8.4.1    Additive color systems

The additive reproduction system is dependent on both its input sensor and its output response. It is assumed here that the input sensor is equivalent to the color matching matrix, $\mathbf{A}$; thus, $\mathbf{A}$, itself, can be used as the sensitivity function. The multispectral output response is given by the $N \times 3$ matrix, $\mathbf{E}$, which serves the same purpose as the primaries in the color matching experiment. The goal of color reproduction can be stated as follows.

A spectral distribution is recorded by the input sensor. An output spectrum is produced by adjusting the amplitudes on each of the output response functions such that the visual appearance of the output spectrum matches that of the input spectrum. Referring to Fig. 8.15, we will use a simple three-band spectral representation or its output spectra. A 31-band system would be too cumbersome. The characteristic spectra for each of the three primaries are given in the colored box, e.g., the red primary has most of its power in the first spectral component, corresponding to the red of red, green, blue. Like all actual primaries, the red primary has some nonzero power in the other spectral bands. The intensity of each spectrum is controlled by the gain indicated by the number in the white rectangle associated with the colored box. Thus, the intensity of the spectrum produced by the red primary is obtained by multiplying the characteristic spectra by the gain, e.g., for the $90 * (1.0, 0.2, 0.1) = (90, 18, 9)$. The spectral values in the various color combinations show that the bands are additive.

Mathematically, the recorded input is given by

$$c = R^T f, \tag{8.26}$$

where $R$ is the response of the input sensor; the output is given by

$$g = Ed, \tag{8.27}$$

and the problem is to choose the input to the display, $d$, such that,

$$A^T f = A^T Ed, \tag{8.28}$$

where $d$ is determined from the recorded 3-vector $c$. If the system is assumed to be linear, then the problem is to choose a matrix, $M$, such that,

$$A^T f = A^T EMR^T f. \tag{8.29}$$

Since the spectral response of the sensor is within a linear transformation of the color matching functions, $R$ can be written as $AB$, where $B$ is an invertible $3 \times 3$ matrix. The equality becomes

$$A^T f = A^T EMB^T A^T f. \tag{8.30}$$

The solution is

$$M = (B^T A^T E)^{-1}. \tag{8.31}$$

This inverse exists if the output response functions are linearly independent, which is always the case in practical applications.

The mathematical formalism above indicates that almost any set of output response functions will work equally well for color reproduction. Unfortunately, in the real world, the output response functions must be nonnegative functions, since negative light sources do not exist for incoherent light. (Negative light is effectively generated by coherent sources by adjusting the phase.) Furthermore, the coefficients of these functions, **d** of Eq. (8.27), must also be nonnegative. There are also physical limits on the magnitude of the driving functions; for example, a monitor has a maximum voltage that can be used to produce light from the screen. The range of color that is physically obtainable by a color system is called the *gamut* of the device.

For an additive system like a monitor, the gamut is easily described. Since the colors are linear combinations of three primaries, the possible colors are those obtained from the relation

$$\mathbf{c} = \mathbf{C}_{\max}\beta, \tag{8.32}$$

where $\mathbf{C}_{\max}$ is the matrix of tristimulus values for the maximum control value (usually 255) of each color gun and $\beta$ is a vector whose values vary independently between zero and unity. The graphical representation of the gamut is most often done using the chromaticity coordinates for a fixed luminance. Figure 8.13 shows the gamut of a typical CRT monitor as a triangle. If the CRT is significantly nonlinear or the color guns are not nearly independent, the gamut may be a more complicated function. Fortunately, high quality monitors can be well approximated by this simple model. Another complicating factor is the use of multiple primaries in some recent solid-state monitors.

### 8.4.2    Subtractive color systems

Subtractive systems are characterized by the property that color is obtained by removing selected portions of a source spectrum. Color film and hard-copy printing are examples of such systems. While the colorants for subtractive systems may be inks, dyes, waxes, or toners, the same mathematical representation can be used to approximate them. The color may be presented on a transmissive medium like slides or on a reflective medium, such as paper.

Consider a simple printing process. Each of the cyan, magenta and yellow colorants removes an amount of its complementary color, red, green and blue, respectively, related to the concentration of the colorant. The amount of light removed, by blocking or absorption, is determined by the material properties of the colorant. The main property of interest for imaging is the optical density. This is discussed in Chapter 4, where it is of interest because it provides an alternative space for quantizing an image. We reiterate that the *transmission* of an optically transmissive material is defined as the ratio of the intensity of the light that passes through the material to the intensity of the source, as shown in Fig. 4.1. The equation is given by

$$T = \frac{I_{\text{out}}}{I_{\text{in}}}. \tag{8.33}$$

The transmission can be thought of as either the fraction of photons that pass through the material or the probability that a photon will pass through the material. Referring to Fig. 8.16, we will use the same three-band representation as in the additive example of Fig. 8.15. In this case the light entering the system is white, with equal intensities in all three bands. Each filter layer transmits a fraction of the light that enters it. The cyan filter passes mostly blue and green; thus it has high values for the second and third components of the spectrum. As in the case of real filters, it also passes some power in the other bands. The spectrum that exits the cyan filter and enters the magenta filter is obtained by multiplying the intensity of the light entering by the fraction of the light passed in each band. In this case, the light entering the magenta filter is $(100 * 0.30, 100 * 0.91, 100*0.96) = (30, 91, 96)$. This spectrum is multiplied by the transmission of the magenta filter as it passed through it. The light entering the yellow filter is $(30 * .94, 91 * 0.70, 96 * 0.90) = (28, 64, 86)$.

*Optical density* is defined by

$$d = -\log_{10}(T), \tag{8.34}$$

and is related to the physical density of the material. To get a feel for the concept of optical density, consider the transmission of a material made of $n$ layers of the same material. Assume that the layers have thicknesses $dx$ and that for this thickness the material has transmission $1 - dT$, where $dT$ is a small positive value for very thin layers. The transmission through a thickness of $x = ndx$, $T(x)$, is given by

$$T(x) = (1 - dT)^n = (1 - dT)^{x/dx} = [(1 - dT)^{1/dx}]^x.$$

If the material is such that the limit of $(1 - dT)^{1/dx}$ is a constant as $dx \to 0$, then the idea of using the logarithm is established. See Problem 8.7 to explore this relationship. The derivation of the meaning of optical density is beyond the scope of this text. It is easy to show that if the transmission function has the form $T(x) = Ae^{-cx}$, then the limit is a constant. It is sufficient here to demonstrate the usefulness of density.

We have used the spatial concept of thickness to demonstrate the use of the logarithm. A little reflection will indicate that spatial thickness may be replaced by material concentration. In other words, if one puts the same optical density of two thicknesses of material into a single thickness, one has increased the material density or the material concentration. If we assume that there is a maximum amount of material that can be put in a given thickness, we can base our description on this maximum. Using this concept, we will define the concentration of a colorant as a fraction, between 0 and 1, that represents the fraction of the maximum density of the colorant that is present.

The use of density for film is straightforward since film is a transmissive medium. For reflective media, the concept is analogous where the transmission of Eq. (8.34) is replaced by reflectance. In cases of reflection media produced by toners or dye sublimation, we can consider the total reflection of an area as related to the transmission of the light through the colorant, reflecting off the paper, and retransmission through the colorant. While this model is a reasonable concept to begin to understand the various properties of hard-copy media, the actual process is much more complicated. However, with this model we can give a useful description of the subtractive image formation.

The inks can be characterized by their density spectra, the $N \times 3$ matrix $\mathbf{D}$. The spectrum that is seen by the observer is the product of an illumination source, the transmission of the ink and the reflectance of the paper. Since the transmissions of the individual inks each reduce the light proportionately, the output at each wavelength, $\lambda$, is given by

$$g(\lambda) = l(\lambda)t_1(\lambda)t_2(\lambda)t_3(\lambda), \tag{8.35}$$

where $t_i(\lambda)$ is the transmission of the $i$th ink and $l(\lambda)$ is the intensity of the illuminant. This is an extension of the simple example of Fig. 8.16. For simplification, the reflectance of the paper is assumed to be perfect, i.e., 1.0. The transmission of a particular colorant is related logarithmically to the concentration of ink on the page. The observed spectrum is obtained mathematically by

$$\mathbf{g} = \mathbf{L}[10^{-\mathbf{Dc}}], \tag{8.36}$$

where $\mathbf{L}$ is a diagonal matrix representing an illuminant spectrum and $\mathbf{c}$ is the concentration of the colorant. The concentration values must be between zero and unity and the matrix of density spectra, $\mathbf{D}$, represents the densities at the maximum concentration. The exponential term is computed componentwise, i.e.,

$$10^{\mathbf{r}} = [10^{r_1} 10^{r_2} \ldots 10^{r_N}]^T. \tag{8.37}$$

This simple model ignores nonlinear interactions between the colorant layers. For a reflective medium, the model requires an additional diagonal matrix that represents the reflectance spectrum of the surface. For simplicity, this can be conceptually included in the illuminant matrix $\mathbf{L}$.

One way of simplifying the problem is to restrict the form of the matrix $\mathbf{D}$. If the three columns of $\mathbf{D}$ have only unity and zero values and no nonzero elements in the same index locations, i.e., $D(i,j) = 1$ implies $D(i,k) = 0$ for $k \neq j$, then the matrix $\mathbf{D}$ can be carried through the exponentiation. This is usually extended to assuming that the unity values are contiguous within their respective columns of $\mathbf{D}$. This is known as the *block dye* assumption. If uniform illumination is also assumed, the observed spectrum can be written

$$\mathbf{g} = \mathbf{D}_b 10^{-\mathbf{c}}, \tag{8.38}$$

where $\mathbf{D}_b$ represents the rectangular functional forms of the block dyes. This limited case can be expanded slightly to the use of linear combinations of the block dyes. If the dye responses, $\mathbf{D}$, can be modeled by

$$\mathbf{D} = \mathbf{D}_b \mathbf{Z}, \tag{8.39}$$

where $\mathbf{Z}$ is a $3 \times 3$ matrix, the observed spectrum can be written

$$\mathbf{g} = \mathbf{D}_b 10^{-\mathbf{Zc}}. \tag{8.40}$$

Under these conditions, the control values, $\mathbf{c}$, can be obtained using a scanning filter matrix, $\mathbf{M}$, that approximates the $\mathbf{A}_l$ of Eq. (8.25), by

$$\mathbf{c} = -\mathbf{Z}^{-1} \log(\mathbf{M}^T \mathbf{D_b})^{-1} \mathbf{M}^T \mathbf{g}. \tag{8.41}$$

While the block dye model may seem extremely restrictive, it has proven very useful in many industrial applications. The actual process is so complex that an adequate physical model has never been found. Recent work that uses such models includes [16, 242].

## 8.5 Color spaces

It has been shown that color can be described by many different vectors. The spectral space of $N$-vectors is the highest dimensional space and most complete. That is, if one knows the spectrum of the radiant source or the reflectivity of an object, one can compute its color coordinates for all practical uses. However, in most cases, the complete spectrum is not needed and only the tristimulus values for a radiant source, or a limited set of tristimulus values under a few illuminants for a reflective object are required. The restriction to tristimulus values greatly reduces the dimensionality of the problem. It also changes the color space used to describe the objects.

There are practical reasons for choosing to describe a color in a particular space. Any color space is adequate for computing a color match, as long as it can represent all of the perceptual colors in the CIE spaces uniquely. There are two additional criteria for a color space that can make it more or less desirable. It is desirable for the computation of the transformation to the color space to be fast. Since perfect matches are almost impossible to achieve, it is desirable for distances of color vectors in the space to correspond to perceptual distances, that is, if two colors are far apart in the color space, they look significantly different. Unfortunately, these two criteria are antagonistic. The color spaces that can best be used to measure perceptual difference require heavy computation. We will examine several color spaces and investigate the trade-offs involved. The history and greater details of color spaces can be found in [28, 74].

### 8.5.1 Uniform color spaces

It has been mentioned that the psychovisual system is known to be nonlinear. The problem of color matching can be treated by linear systems theory since the receptors behave in an almost linear mode and exact equality is the goal. In practice, an engineer can seldom produce an exact match to any specification. The nonlinearities of the visual system play a critical role in the determination of a color sensitivity function. Color vision is too complex to be modeled by a simple function. The sensitivity of the system depends on what is being observed and the purpose of the observation. A measure of sensitivity that is consistent with the observations of arbitrary scenes is well beyond present capability. However, much work has been done to determine human color sensitivity in matching two color fields that subtend only a small portion of the visual field.

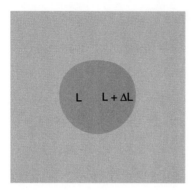

**Figure 8.17.** MacAdam's color comparison experiment (color version, please see Plate 4).

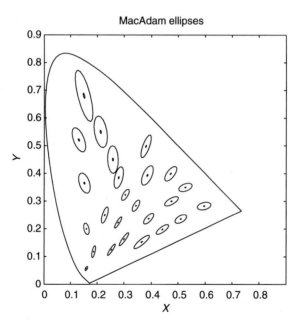

**Figure 8.18.** MacAdam ellipses: small ellipses are actual size, large ellipses are 10 times actual size for better viewing.

Some of the first controlled experiments in color sensitivity were conducted by MacAdam [171]. The observer viewed a disk made of two hemispheres of different colors on a neutral background, Fig. 8.17. One color was fixed; the other could be adjusted by the user. The observer tried to match the fixed color by controls that changed the variable color along a path in tristimulus space that included the fixed color. In the original work, the luminance was held constant so that only the chromaticity changed. The error in the color match yielded the sensitivity ellipses shown in Fig. 8.18. The ellipses represent a *just noticeable difference* in chromaticity.

Since MacAdam's pioneering work, there have been many additional studies of color sensitivity. Most of these have measured the variability in three dimensions, which yields sensitivity ellipsoids in tristimulus space., i.e., the space defined in Property 3 of Section 8.3.3. The work by Wyszecki and Fielder [312] is of particular interest as it shows the variation between observers and between a single observer at different times. The large variation of the sizes and orientation of the ellipsoids in Fig. 8.18 indicates that mean square error in tristimulus space is a very poor measure of color error. Of course, it has been long known that mean square error is usually a poor measure of error in any phenomenon involving human judgment. A common method of treating the nonuniform error problem is to transform the space into one where the Euclidean distance is more closely correlated with perceptual error. The CIE recommended two transformations in 1976 in an attempt to standardize measures in the industry.

Neither of the CIE standards achieve the goal of a uniform color space. Given the variability of the data, it is unreasonable to expect that such a space could be found. The transformations do reduce the variations in the sensitivity ellipses by a large degree. They have another major feature in common: the measures are made relative to a reference white point. By using the reference point, the transformations attempt to account for the adaptive characteristics of the visual system. The CIELAB (see-lab) space is defined by

$$L^* = 116f\left(\frac{Y}{Y_n}\right) - 16, \tag{8.42}$$

$$a^* = 500\left[f\left(\frac{X}{X_n}\right) - f\left(\frac{Y}{Y_n}\right)\right], \tag{8.43}$$

$$b^* = 200\left[f\left(\frac{Y}{Y_n}\right) - f\left(\frac{Z}{Z_n}\right)\right], \tag{8.44}$$

where $f(x) = x^{1/3}$ for $x > 0.008856$ and $f(x) = 7.787x + 16/116$ otherwise. The values $X_n, Y_n, Z_n$ are the CIE 1931 tristimulus values of the reference white under the reference illumination, and $X, Y, Z$ are the tristimulus values that are to be mapped to the CIELAB color space. This maps the reference white to $(L^*, a^*, b^*) = (100, 0, 0)$. The boundary transition at normalized values of about 0.01 is an attempt to account for the fact that at low illumination the cones become less sensitive and the rods (monochrome receptors) become active. This is the reason why "all cats look gray in the dark." A linear model is used at low light levels.

The CIELUV (see-luv) space is defined by

$$L^* = \begin{cases} 116\left(\frac{Y}{Y_n}\right)^{\frac{1}{3}} - 16, & \text{if } \frac{Y}{Y_n} > 0.008856, \\ 903.3\left(\frac{Y}{Y_n}\right), & \text{if } \frac{Y}{Y_n} \leq 0.008856, \end{cases} \tag{8.45}$$

$$u^* = 13L^*(u - u_n), \tag{8.46}$$

$$v^* = 13L^*(v - v_n), \tag{8.47}$$

where

$$u = \frac{4X}{X + 15Y + 3Z}, \tag{8.48}$$

$$v = \frac{9Y}{X + 15Y + 3Z}, \tag{8.49}$$

$$u_n = \frac{4X_n}{X_n + 15Y_n + 3Z_n}, \tag{8.50}$$

$$v_n = \frac{9Y_n}{X_n + 15Y_n + 3Z_n}, \tag{8.51}$$

and the subscripted tristimulus values represent a reference white. Note that the $L^*$ values are the same as for CIELAB if the normalized values $Y/Y_n$ are above the 0.008856 threshold.

Color errors between two colors $\mathbf{c}_1$ and $\mathbf{c}_2$ are measured using

$$\Delta E^*_{ab} = \left[ (L^*_1 - L^*_2)^2 + (a^*_1 - a^*_2)^2 + (b^*_1 - b^*_2)^2 \right]^{1/2}, \tag{8.52}$$

$$\Delta E^*_{uv} = \left[ (L^*_1 - L^*_2)^2 + (u^*_1 - u^*_2)^2 + (v^*_1 - v^*_2)^2 \right]^{1/2}. \tag{8.53}$$

A useful rule of thumb is that two colors cannot be distinguished in a scene if their $\Delta E^*_{ab}$ value is less than 3.

The CIE has since updated $\Delta E^*_{ab}$ with a new weighted version, which is designated $\Delta E^*_{94}$ [49]. The measure was designed for use in manufacturing environments to compare two colors, where one is the standard and the other is to be compared to the standard. The new measure weights the hue and chroma components in the $\Delta E^*_{ab}$ measure by a function of chroma. In addition the users can alter parameters to weight the relative importance of hue, chroma and lightness differences for their applications.

The measure is given by

$$\Delta E^*_{94} = \left[ \left( \frac{\Delta L^*}{k_L S_L} \right)^2 + \left( \frac{\Delta C^*_{ab}}{k_C S_C} \right)^2 + \left( \frac{\Delta H^*_{ab}}{k_H S_H} \right)^2 \right]^{1/2} \tag{8.54}$$

where

$$S_L = 1$$
$$S_C = 1 + 0.045 C^*_{ab} \tag{8.55}$$
$$S_H = 1 + 0.015 C^*_{ab}$$

$$C^*_{ab} = \sqrt{(a^*)^2 + (b^*)^2} \quad \text{(chroma)} \tag{8.56}$$

$$\Delta H^*_{ab} = \sqrt{(\Delta E^*_{ab})^2 - (\Delta L^*)^2 - (\Delta C^*_{ab})^2} \quad \text{(hue difference)} \tag{8.57}$$

and for equal relative weighting of hue, chroma and lightness we have

$$k_L = k_C = k_H = 1. \tag{8.58}$$

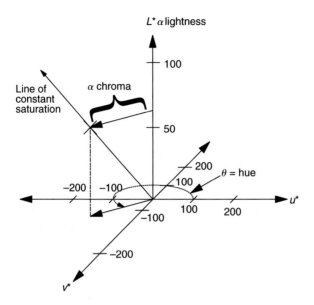

**Figure 8.19.** CIELUV color space and its relationship to commonly used color perception terms.

The chroma in Eq. (8.55) is computed using the $a^*b^*$ values of the color standard. If neither color is designated as the color standard, then the chroma is computed for both colors and the geometric mean of the two chromas is used for $C_{ab}^*$ in Eq. (8.55). Note that on the neutral axis (i.e., $a^* = b^* = 0$) that $\Delta E_{ab}^* = \Delta_{94}^*$ (for $k_L = k_C = k_H = 1$). Off the neutral axis we have $\Delta E_{ab}^* > \Delta E_{94}^*$.

The $\Delta E_{ab}^*$ and $\Delta E_{94}^*$ just-noticeable-difference threshold is much lower in the experimental setting of Fig. 8.17 than in pictorial scenes. It is noted that the sensitivities discussed above are for flat fields. The sensitivity to modulated color is a much more difficult problem. This is discussed further in Appendix E.

There is also a color difference measure designated CIE2000 [170, 245]. It has so far not been widely adopted due to the complexity of calculation as well as problems with discontinuities.

The CIELAB and CIELUV color spaces can be used to visualize color attributes such as hue, chroma and lightness. These perceptual color terms, as well as saturation (which is frequently confused with chroma), are defined in Wyszecki and Stiles [313, pp 168–196, 487]. Figure 8.19 displays a 3-D plot of the CIELUV space and quantities that correlate with these attributes. The figure for CIELAB would be similar. A note on the hue error term, $\Delta H_{ab}^*$, is helpful, since the term is defined in terms of a distance in CIELAB space, but Fig. 8.19 shows hue as an angle. The distance is an approximation to the distance between the two colors that is attributed to the difference in hue angle, $\Delta\theta$. This distance is dependent on the magnitude of the errors in lightness and chroma, as shown in the formula for $\Delta H_{ab}^*$.

### 8.5.2 Device independent and dependent spaces

The terms *device independent* and *device dependent* color spaces are frequently used in problems dealing with accurate color recording and reproduction. A color space is defined to be device independent (DI) if there exists a nonsingular transformation between the color space and the CIEXYZ color space. If there is no such transformation, then the color space is a device dependent (DD) color space.

Device dependent spaces are typically related to some particular output or input device. They are often used for the simple reason that most output and input devices report or accept values that are in a device dependent space. A simple example is the 8-bit/channel RGB scanner that provides values that are contained in a cube defined by the points $[0, 0, 0]$ and $[255, 255, 255]$. This cube is a device dependent color space. The space however is still useful since the device dependent RGB values can be sent directly to a monitor or printer for image display. No device independent color space needs to be used. However, it is often the case that the output image will not look like the original scanned image. Methods for correcting this problem are addressed in Chapter 12.

Many algorithms have been developed that process in an "RGB" color space without defining this space in terms of the CIE color matching functions, or even in terms of the spectral responses of R, G and B. Such algorithms are nothing more than multichannel image processing techniques applied to a three band image, since there is no accounting for the perceptual aspect of the problem. To obtain some relationship with the human visual system, many color image processing algorithms operate on data in hue, saturation, lightness (HSL) spaces. Commonly these spaces are transformations of the above mentioned "RGB" color space, and hence have no visual meaning until a relationship is established back to a CIE color space. To confuse the issue further, there are many variants of these color spaces including hue, saturation, value (HSV), hue, saturation, intensity (HSI), and hue, chroma, intensity (HCI), some of which have multiple definitions in terms of transforming from "RGB." To avoid confusion, developers of color algorithms should take care to define the color spaces in which they are working by defining their relationships to the CIE color matching functions.

### 8.5.3     Pseudo-device independent spaces

To maintain the simplicity of the device dependent space, but provide some degree of matching across input and output devices, standard device dependent color spaces have been defined. These spaces will be referred to as *pseudo-device independent* spaces and they include sRGB and Kodak's PhotoYCC space. These spaces are well defined in terms of a device independent space. As such, a device manufacturer can design an input or output device such that when given sRGB values, the proper device independent color value is displayed. However, there do exist limitations with this approach and those are discussed in Chapter 12.

The sRGB space is the most common as it is related directly to monitors [7, 196, 256].[5] The sRGB values are related to the CIEXYZ values by a nonlinear transformation that

---

[5] The website of [256] gives the most complete description. However, websites change frequently. Look for the base organization site of the International Color Consortium, www.color.org/.

begins with the linear matrix transformation

$$
\begin{bmatrix} R' \\ G' \\ B' \end{bmatrix} = \begin{bmatrix} 3.2410 & -1.5374 & -0.4986 \\ -0.9692 & 1.8760 & 0.0416 \\ 0.0556 & -0.2040 & 1.0570 \end{bmatrix} \begin{bmatrix} X \\ Y \\ Z \end{bmatrix}. \tag{8.59}
$$

The range of output values for the elements of the vector is $[0,1]$. Values outside this range are clipped to the nearest boundary. Each of the values $R'$, $G'$, $B'$ is then transformed using a "gamma correction" if the values are above a threshold of $0.0031308$. Otherwise, there is a linear scaling. For example, consider the $R_{sRGB}$ value obtained from $R'$ by

$$
R_{sRGB} = \begin{cases} 1.055(R')^{(1.0/2.4)} - 0.055, \text{if } R' > 0.0031308, \\ 12.92R', \text{ else.} \end{cases} \tag{8.60}
$$

The final finite precision digital value is obtained by linearly scaling to the appropriate digital range and rounding to the nearest integer. The green and blue sRGB values are found using Eq. (8.60) with appropriate substitutions of $G'$ and $B'$.

The relation of the sRGB values to display monitors is that the values represent the tristimulus values associated with the primaries of HDTV. The transformation of Eq. (8.59) is exactly the one obtained by the transformation of primaries (Property 4) described in Section 8.3.3.

The transformation from sRGB to XYZ follows the mathematical inverse. For example, $R' = R_{sRGB}/255$, assuming that the digital range is $[0,255]$, then

$$
R = \begin{cases} [(R' + 0.055)/1.055]^{2.4}, \text{if } R' > 0.04045, \\ R'/12.92, \text{ else.} \end{cases} \tag{8.61}
$$

The $G$ and $B$ values are obtained from Eq. (8.61) using the appropriate substitutions. Finally, the XYZ values are obtained by

$$
\begin{bmatrix} X \\ Y \\ Z \end{bmatrix} = \begin{bmatrix} 0.4124 & 0.3576 & 0.1805 \\ 0.2126 & 0.7152 & 0.0722 \\ 0.0193 & 0.1192 & 0.9505 \end{bmatrix} \begin{bmatrix} R \\ G \\ B \end{bmatrix}. \tag{8.62}
$$

## 8.6  Color temperature

It is clear from Eq. (8.19) that the characteristics of the illumination affect the appearance of colored objects. While the exact effect can be computed if all of the spectra are known, it is impossible to compute every color shift in a complex scene. The lighting industry devised a rule of thumb to estimate the change in qualitative appearance of a color using a single number to characterize the illuminant. This number is the *color temperature* [199, 313].

The color temperature of an illuminant is related to the color of the spectrum emitted by a black body radiator at a given temperature. Generally, the hotter an object, the

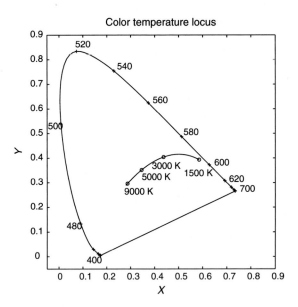

**Figure 8.20.** Color temperature locus.

whiter its spectrum will appear. The defining properties of color temperature are hue and saturation, not brightness. In other words, it is the chromaticity of the color that specifies the color temperature. Two lamps can emit different spectra but have the same chromaticity and, thus, the same color temperature. They may not be metamers since they may have different luminances. The range of color temperatures is shown in Fig. 8.20.

Note that since the spectra of different lamps with the same color temperature are different, the appearance of objects under the two may be different. This can be a problem when evaluating images that demand high quality color matching at different viewing locations.

While the color temperature of the black body radiator is a well defined curve on the chromaticity diagram, not many lamps fall exactly on the curve. To account for this, a lamp is given the correlated color temperature, that is, the closest point on the color temperature curve to the actual chromaticity of the lamp. The closest distance is measured with respect to visual sensitivity; that is, the direction from the locus of black body radiators on the chromaticity diagram is determined by the MacAdam ellipses. A diagram of this closest correlated color temperature is shown graphically in [145] and reproduced in [199, 313].

## 8.7 Color measurement instruments

The accurate measurement of color is a difficult task. While cameras and image scanners record color information, they are not suitable for the most accurate color measurements. For the accurate measurement of color, the instrument must have carefully controlled sensors (filters and detectors) and optical geometry. If the color of reflective material is to be measured, the illumination must be precisely known and matched with the sensors. There are physical problems with the color media that further complicate the task. Properties such as specular reflectance and translucence should be taken into account. These properties will be discussed in the follow sections.

If only the tristimulus values or some derivative of them, such as $L^*a^*b^*$ values, are desired, a *colorimeter* can be used. This device uses filters to match the vector space defined by the eye. Thus, a measurement is limited to one set of viewing conditions. The colorimeter need measure only the quantities that can be transformed into tristimulus values. The minimal system consists of three filters and three detectors or changeable filters and a single detector. These devices are much less expensive than the devices designed to measure the entire spectrum.

The most complete information is obtained by measuring the entire visible spectrum. A *spectroradiometer* measures radiant spectra; a *spectrophotometer* measures reflective spectra. Having the spectrum allows the user to compute tristimulus values under any viewing condition. To measure the spectrum requires that the spectrum of the light be spread physically. This can be done with a prism, following Newton's famous early experiments. However, to make accurate measurements, the exact spreading of the spectrum must be known and controlled. This is done with optical gratings, which can be made more precisely and are much less bulky than prisms. A system of lenses is used to focus the spectrum onto the detector. The high-quality optics required for this task greatly increase the cost of these color measurement instruments.

After the spectrum is spread, the intensity of the light at each wavelength must be measured. This can be achieved in several ways. The most common method currently is to use a linear CCD array. A movable slit can also be used to limit the wavelength band being measured. The exact spread of the spectrum on the array is determined by measuring a known source. Interpolation methods are used to generate the data at the specified wavelengths.

The range of wavelengths and their sampling interval varies among the instruments. Higher precision instruments record data over a larger range and at a finer sample spacing. The CIE recommends a range of 360–830 nm with a sample spacing of 1 nm for computation of color [48]. However, there are few instruments that actually take data at this specification. Most high-end instruments sample at 2 nm over a range of about 360 nm to 760 nm. The most popular instruments sample at 10 nm over 400 nm to 700 nm.

Devices that measure radiant and reflective spectra must use larger areas. This is done to eliminate adjacency effects or mixing of colors. Many reflective media have some translucent properties that make it difficult to prevent some contribution from outside the sample area or light escaping to the outside. Typical measurement areas for spectrophotometers are circular with a diameter between 4 and 8 mm. Spectroradiometers are specified in receptive angle, which are usually between 0.5 and 2 degrees. The apertures for spectroradiometers are usually circular or rectangular.

The various instruments used in color measurement will be briefly described. The purpose of the description is to allow the reader to understand the basic principles and

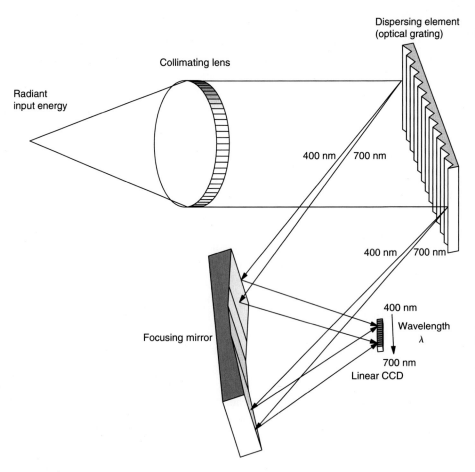

**Figure 8.21.** Spectroradiometer.

understand some characteristics and limitations of the devices. The details can be found in more specialized texts [128, 199, 313].

### 8.7.1    Spectroradiometer

The task of the spectroradiometer is to measure the intensity (power) of light at discrete wavelengths in the visible band. The units of intensity are candela, as discussed in Section 8.2. A simple diagram of a spectroradiometer is shown in Fig. 8.21. In this illustration, the light is spread onto a linear CCD array. The major problem is to interpolate the values obtained by the array into intensity values of the spectrum at evenly spaced intervals. The grating does not spread the spectrum so that equal wavelength intervals are spread to equal linear distances. Furthermore, minor changes in the physical position of the optics can change the mapping of the wavelengths onto the detector elements.

The wavelengths are mapped to the elements by measuring a calibrated, known source or set of sources. These sources are chosen to have well defined line spectra. Mercury lamps are often used for this purpose because of their well known spectral lines. The most difficult part of the calibration is to determine the absolute gain factors needed for the interpolation. For this computation to be accurate, the exact amplitude of the source must be known. To obtain this accuracy, power to the source lamp must be carefully controlled and the lamp kept in good condition. These calibration procedures demand precision equipment. For this reason, calibration is often done by the manufacturer on a periodic basis.

The detector is often cooled to give good signal-to-noise ratios (SNRs). Since there is noise in the system, most spectroradiometers make a measurement with the aperture closed (dark signal) after the measurement of the object. This gives an estimate of the background noise. The noise measurement is subtracted from the object measurement to obtain a better estimate of the radiant spectrum of the object. In these devices, the signal is measured in photon counts. This implies that the signal is naturally Poisson distributed. The noise that is measured with the closed aperture is thermal noise. However, since the measurement is in integer counts,[6] this noise cannot be Gaussian as is often assumed. Since the dark signal is a random variable, it is possible to generate negative counts after the subtraction. The usual treatment of this case is a simple truncation to zero.[7]

The measurements have to account for the intensity of the light. Whether the instrument uses CCD arrays or photomultiplier tubes, the exposure should be adjusted to avoid saturation of the detector, while keeping the signal-to-noise ratio as high as possible. Exposure is normally controlled by the integration time of the measurement. Changing the apertures, as in cameras, would require the added expense and complexity of a set of precision apertures.

The measurements will have a limited dynamic range. If the intensity is measured in photon counts, the device will have an upper limit to avoid saturation. The SNR will be signal dependent. Since the noise is thermal, it will be almost the same at each wavelength for instruments that use CCD arrays, and the same for those that use photomultiplier tubes. Thus, the wavelengths with higher counts will have higher SNRs. This can cause a problem when using the measured spectrum to compute other quantities, such as reflectance.

Having measured the radiant spectrum, many derived quantities can be computed with the data from a spectroradiometer. The reflectance of an object can be obtained by measuring the spectrum of the illuminant, measuring the spectrum of the light reflected from the object and dividing the two measurements wavelength-by-wavelength.[8] The luminance can be obtained by multiplying the spectrum by the luminous efficiency function. The tristimulus values can be computed by multiplying the spectrum with

---

[6] The counts are converted to candela for output.

[7] Some devices truncate to one since this avoids problems if the log of the spectrum is to be computed.

[8] While this is conceptually simple, it is very difficult in practice because of problems in controlling the illumination and geometry.

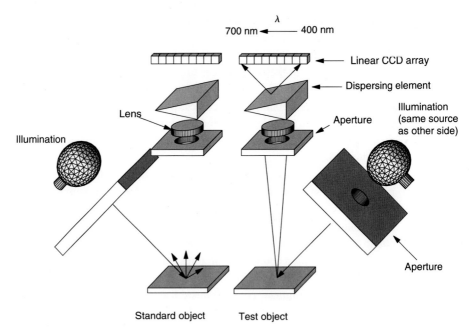

**Figure 8.22.** Spectrophotometer.

stored spectra of illuminants and the color matching functions. The color temperature can be computed from the tristimulus values and auxiliary tables.

## 8.7.2    Spectrophotometer

The spectrophotometer measures the reflectance (or transmittance) of an object. The basic process can be thought of as making two spectroradiometric measurements and taking their ratio. The spectrophotometer has its own light source and a standard reference reflector whose spectra are known and given by $l_s(k)$ and $r_s(k)$, respectively. It is assumed that the standard reflectance does not change, whereas the internal lamp may change with age and operating conditions.

The basic elements of a spectrophotometer are shown in Fig. 8.22. We will use the reflectance mode in this section and discuss the transmission mode in the section on densitometry. The reference reflectance is measured for each wavelength along with the object under investigation. The reference measurement is $m_r(k) = l_s(k)r_s(k)$; the object measurement is given by $m_o(k) = l_s(k)r_o(k)$. The relative reflectance is found by

$$r_o(k) = \frac{m_o(k)r_s(k)}{m_r(k)}.$$

The spectrum can be separated in several ways.

A monochromometer can create nearly monochromatic bands of light by time-sequentially separating the spectral bands by moving, optically or physically, a slit

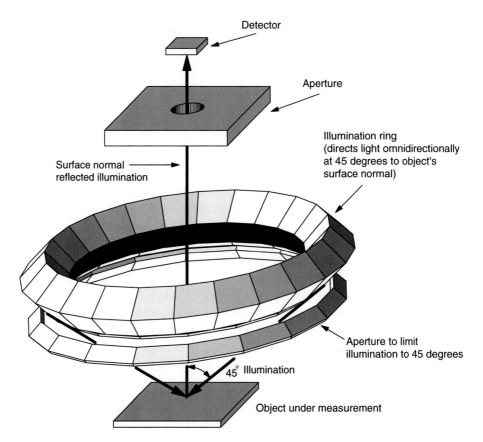

Detector

Aperture

Illumination ring
(directs light omnidirectionally
at 45 degrees to object's
surface normal)

Surface normal
reflected illumination

Aperture to limit
illumination to 45 degrees

45° Illumination

Object under measurement

**Figure 8.23.** 45–0 degree reflection geometry.

across the spectrum that is spread by a prism or grating. This monochromatic light illuminates both reference and object. The measurement is made with a single detector and the ratio is computed as before. Alternatively, white light is used to illuminate both reference and object and the resulting spectra are detected using a solid-state array. The trade-off that was discussed between single and multiple detectors is applicable here. However, the cost and bulk of a monochromometer makes the solid-state array more popular.

The reflection measurement can be made in several different ways depending on the relative geometry of the illuminant and the detector. The measurement can also be a function of the collection mode as in the case of the transmission measurements. The 45–0 degree specular geometry is one of the most common and is illustrated in Fig. 8.23. The 45–0 refers to the illuminant being at an angle of 45 degrees and the measurement being taken at 0 degrees. Note that it is common when using 45–0 degree geometry to use a ring of illumination rather than a few point sources. This avoids problems with directionality of the source and the texture of the surface.

A significant problem in measuring surface reflectance occurs because of the surface properties of the object. There are two extremes of surface reflectance. A *Lambertian surface* reflects incident light in all directions. This is much like a matte finish for paint. A *specular surface* reflects incident light only at the complementary angle to the incident direction. This is like a perfect mirror. Glossy surfaces have a large specular component. Most surfaces encountered in imaging are somewhere between these extremes.

The spectrophotometer design must account for a compromise measurement of different surfaces. A 45–0 degree reflectance measurement of a mirror would indicate a black object. This may or may not be what the user wishes to know about the object. Thus, instruments can be made to measure in several modes. They may gather all the light that is reflected by using an integrating sphere (diffuse geometry). They may measure only the specular component by placing the detector at the complementary angle to the incident illumination (specular geometry). The modes are similar to those of the transmission devices illustrated in Fig. 8.24. They may exclude the specular component by putting a hole in the integrating sphere at the complementary angle. Detailed illustrations are presented in [128, 199, 313].

There does not appear to be any perfect measurement geometry for imaging. The user must be aware of the peculiarities of the application for which the measurement is to be made. Currently, the 45–0 degree geometry is the most common measurement for printed images. A note on the reciprocity of angles is that from a theoretical viewpoint, a 0–45 degree geometry should be equivalent to a 45–0 geometry. Unfortunately, due to various nonlinear effects of many reflective surfaces, this is not exactly true. While the differences are usually very small, there can be specific cases where the difference is substantial.

### 8.7.3     Colorimeter

The colorimeter is designed to determine the defining color parameters of an object under a specific illumination. This usually means determining the CIE tristimulus values or some derivative of them. The instrumentation is very much like a digital color camera with the CCD array replaced by a simple photodetector. The optics do not need the same precision since pixel size resolution is not required. However, the filter–sensor combination is more precise than cameras. Colorimeters that are used to calibrate color monitors may not have any optical elements but are placed directly on the screen. The filters may be placed directly over the detectors.

The combination of detector sensitivity and color filters must give a response that is within a linear transformation of the CIE color matching functions. This was demonstrated in Property 3 of Section 8.3.3.

The relationship between colorimeters and image scanners and digital cameras is quite strong. To record true color, the device must have suitable filters. Color scanners are basically pixel-level colorimeters. Color cameras can be designed with CCD sensors that record three filtered images. Currently, most cameras are designed with a mosaicked array of color filters. This is covered later in Chapter 10. There are many reasons why

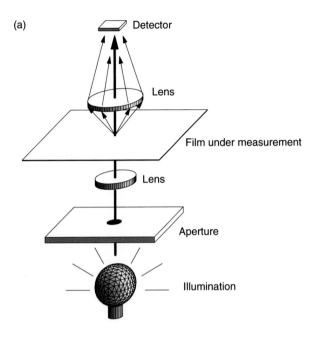

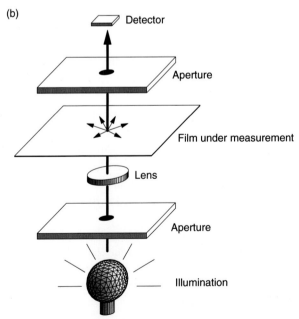

**Figure 8.24.** (a) Transmission densitometry: diffuse density geometry; (b) transmission densitometry: specular density geometry.

the scanners and cameras cannot record color as well as a colorimeter, which is specially designed for the task. Aside from the control of the geometry, most of the reasons are related to cost and will be discussed later.

## 8.7.4    Densitometer

In Section 8.4.2, optical density was defined and related to the amount of colorant used to form the reflection properties of a pixel. In this sense, the amount of colorant is measured in terms of mass, e.g., milligrams of ink, toner or silver. Densitometry is concerned with measuring the amount of colorant used. It is indirectly related to the color of the area being measured. In the ideal case, described by the equations of Section 8.4.2, the relation is complicated but known. In practice, the relation is obtained from experimental measurements and correlation of photometric and densitometric quantities. This often involves compiling large amounts of tabular data. The printing industry has historically relied much more on densitometry than photometry.

Transmission and reflection are two common measurement modes in densitometry. The transmission measurement can be made by either diffuse or specular methods. The two methods are illustrated in Fig. 8.24. The diffuse method attempts to collect all the light that passes through the medium; the specular method collects only that which passes straight through it.

Reflection densitometry is often used for monitoring image reproduction processes in press printing and photography, with the goal of keeping the process in some known state. Reflection densitometers are similar in design to 45–0 colorimeters. Recall that the intent of densitometry is to determine the amount of colorant present. To do this, the filters used for measuring densities are tuned to the peak densities of the colorants of interest. It is assumed that the peaks of the cyan, magenta and yellow colorants are sufficiently different to allow this separation. Remember, the transmission regions of cyan, magenta and yellow overlap substantially, but the density peaks do not. For example, a high density in the green region of the spectral measurement would indicate the presence of a large amount of magenta colorant. Black ink, used in four color printing, will overlap all of the other three colorants.

Since four color printing is common, there are four values reported by the densitometer and only three reported by the colorimeter. The four channels in the densitometer are often referred to as $C, M, Y$ and $K$. The $C, M$, and $Y$ channels are measured, respectively, by filters in the red, green and blue portion of the visible spectrum. The $K$ channel is the luminous efficiency function of Fig. 8.3.

Because the colorants used for different media have different material properties, different sets of filters are used to characterize the densities. A common standard used for photographic film and prints is given by the Status A density functions shown in Fig. 8.25a. Status T, shown in Fig. 8.25b, is commonly used in the printing industry. Note that the $K$ channel is the same for all status filter sets. A list of status filter sets for film is given in [125]. The actual specification is given in [132].

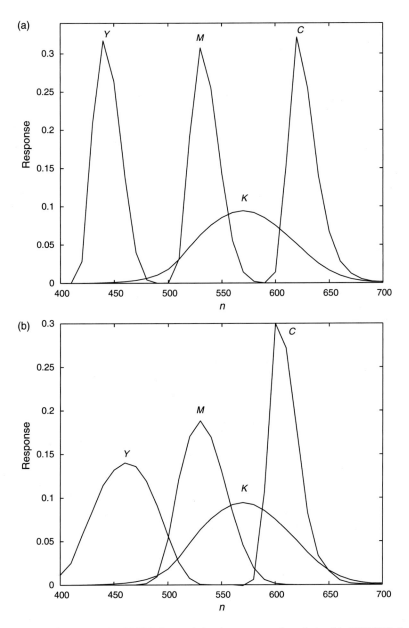

**Figure 8.25.** (a) The ANSI/ISO Status A density response functions; (b) ANSI/ISO Status T density response functions.

The Status T response of the magenta ($M$) channel is shown in Fig. 8.26a superimposed on the reflectance spectra of varying magenta ink amounts from a web offset printing process. The spectra represent a range of 10% to 100% coverage in steps of 10%. The partial coverage is done by a halftoning process, which is described in detail in

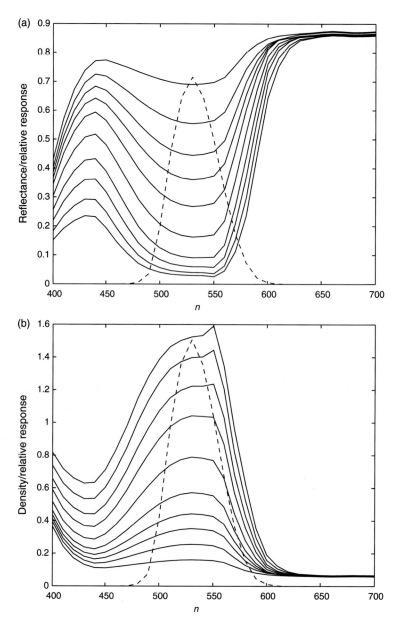

**Figure 8.26.** (a) Web offset magenta spectra shown in reflectance space with scaled Status T magenta response function; (b) web offset magenta spectra shown in density space with scaled Status T magenta response function, dashed line in magenta (M) filter of Fig. 8.25.

Section 11.5. The same information is shown in Fig. 8.26b as density spectra. The measured values are modeled by

$$t = \mathbf{m}^T \mathbf{r},$$

(8.63)

**Table 8.7.** Status T density values for magenta spectra

| Measured | Density | Percentage |
|----------|---------|------------|
| 0.04 | 1.36 | 100 |
| 0.06 | 1.24 | 90 |
| 0.08 | 1.08 | 80 |
| 0.12 | 0.92 | 70 |
| 0.20 | 0.71 | 60 |
| 0.30 | 0.52 | 50 |
| 0.39 | 0.41 | 40 |
| 0.47 | 0.33 | 30 |
| 0.58 | 0.24 | 20 |
| 0.70 | 0.15 | 10 |

where $\mathbf{m}$ is the instrument response in the $M$ channel and $\mathbf{r}$ is the reflectance under measure. The density reported is given by

$$d = -\log(\mathbf{m}^T \mathbf{r}). \tag{8.64}$$

Table 8.7 shows the relation between the measured values, computed density and percentage coverage for a typical halftone printing system.

Recall that the log operation was discussed earlier as a common model for nonlinearity in the human visual system. For this reason, the reflectance densitometer is often touted to provide visually related measurements, even though the response functions are not a linear transformation of the CIE color matching functions.

## 8.8     Problems

**8.1**   A viewer sits 40 cm from a computer monitor. She observes an image in the center of the screen that measures 10 cm on each side. The image is represented in the computer by $1000 \times 1000$ pixels. We will assume optimal but unspecified viewing conditions. From the MTF graph of Fig. 8.1, answer the following questions.

(a) The MTF of Fig. 8.1 is given as a function of cycles per degree. For what spatial frequencies (in cycles/mm) on the screen is the apparent intensity reduced by 50% from the maximum?

(b) What digital frequency used in the function $f(x, y) = \cos(2\pi f_0 x)$ will produce these frequencies?

(c) How does the answer to the previous question change if $f(x, y) = \cos(2\pi f_0 y)$?

(d) How does the answer to the previous question change if $f(x, y) = \cos[2\pi(f_x x + f_y y)]$?

**8.2**   Color matching functions (CMFs) are always referenced to a specific set of primaries. Recall that the standard CIE RGB color matching functions are referenced to monochromatic lines at 435.8 nm, 546.1 nm and 700 nm. The transformation of CMFs from one set of primaries to another was developed using matrix algebra in Section 8.3.3.

However, color matching functions are tabulated with wavelength spacing ranging from 1 nm to 10 nm. Given the CIE CMFs, $\mathbf{A}$, that are tabulated at 1 nm intervals, available on the text website, describe how to obtain the $3 \times 3$ matrix $[\mathbf{A}^T\mathbf{Q}]^{-1}$ that is needed to compute the CMFs, $\mathbf{B}$, that correspond to the primaries, $\mathbf{Q}$, where the primaries are monochromatic lines at 432.5 nm, 555.5 nm and 680.3 nm. Plot and compare the CMFs of $\mathbf{B}$ to those of $\mathbf{A}$.

Hint: start from the physical interpretation of the matrix $\mathbf{A}^T\mathbf{Q}$.

**8.3** It was noted in Section 8.3.3 that, given the color matching functions associated with the human eye of Fig. 8.10, for any transformation of these functions that corresponds to realizable (nonnegative) primaries, the color matching functions will have some negative values.

(a) Verify this statement mathematically.
(b) Verify the corollary, that if the color matching functions are nonnegative, then the associated primaries are not realizable, i.e., they have negative values.

**8.4** Use the method discussed in Section 8.3.3 to characterize monitors by the chromaticities of their phosphors and the white point to determine the color matching functions for HDTV. Your graph of these functions should match that of Fig. 8.14b.

**8.5** To get a basic idea of the relation of reflectance spectra and metamers, consider a four-dimensional spectral space, e.g., spectra sampled with 100 nm bands from 360 nm to 760 nm. Assume a fictitious set of color matching functions given by

$$\mathbf{A}^T = \begin{bmatrix} 1/2 & 1 & 1/2 & 0 \\ 0 & 1/2 & 1 & 1/2 \\ 0 & 0 & 1/2 & 3/2 \end{bmatrix}.$$

Let the illuminant be given by $\mathbf{l}_1 = [1, 1, 1, 1]$. The tristimulus values associated with the reflectance spectra $\mathbf{r}_1 = [1/2, 1/2, 1/2, 1/2]$ under illuminant $\mathbf{l}_1$ are $\mathbf{t}_1 = [1, 1, 1]$.

(a) Starting with the reflectance form $\mathbf{r}_2 = [p, q, \frac{5}{8}, \frac{11}{24}]$, find values $p$ and $q$ so that $\mathbf{r}_2$ is a metamer of $\mathbf{r}_1$ under illuminant $\mathbf{l}_1$.
(b) Find the formula for all metamers of $\mathbf{l}_1$. Show that the vector $\mathbf{r}_2$ found above satisfies this formula.
(c) Determine if the vectors $\mathbf{r}_1$ and $\mathbf{r}_2$ are metamers under illuminant $\mathbf{l}_2 = [1/2, 3/4, 1, 5/4]$.

**8.6** Let us modify the exercise in Problem 8.5 by using the 31-band spectral space and the CIE CMFs at that resolution. These CMFs are available at the text website: www.cambridge.org/9780521868532. Let $\mathbf{r}_1$ be the uniform reflectance spectrum with value 0.5, and $\mathbf{l}_1$ be the uniform illuminant with all values equal to unity.

(a) Find a reflectance $\mathbf{r}_2 \neq \mathbf{r}_1$ that is a metamer of $\mathbf{r}_1$ under illuminant $\mathbf{l}_1$.
(b) Find the formula for all metamers of $\mathbf{l}_1$. Show that the vector $\mathbf{r}_2$ found above satisfies this formula.

(c) Determine if the vectors $r_1$ and $r_2$ are metamers under illuminant $l_2$ defined as illuminant A, available on the text website.

**8.7** Let us consider the exponential relationship presented for subtractive color. Show that if the transmission of a material is related to the thickness of the material by

$$T(x) = Ae^{-cx},$$

where $x$ is the thickness, then the conditions for density are satisfied, i.e.,

$$\lim_{x \to 0} (1 - dT)^{1/dx} = \text{constant.}$$

**8.8** We have seen how uniform color spaces are used to measure color differences. This problem gives you the opportunity to study the effect of the choice of white point. Define the XYZ tristimulus values for several measurements as

$$t_1 = [100, 100, 100]; \quad t_2 = [101, 101, 100];$$
$$t_3 = [1, 1, 1]; \quad t_4 = [1.01, 1.01, 1];$$
$$t_5 = [100, 50, 50]; \quad t_6 = [101, 51, 49];$$
$$t_7 = [1.00, .50, .50]; \quad t_8 = [1.01, .51, .49];$$

Two white points are given for the CIELAB transformation
$$w_1 = [100, 100, 100]; \quad w_2 = [1, 1, 1].$$

Compute the CIELAB values for the tristimulus values and white point specified along with the $\Delta E^*_{ab}$ between the two:

(a) $t_1$, $t_2$ and $w_1$,
(b) $t_1$, $t_2$ and $w_2$,
(c) $t_3$, $t_4$ and $w_1$,
(d) $t_3$, $t_4$ and $w_2$,
(e) $t_5$, $t_6$ and $w_1$,
(f) $t_5$, $t_6$ and $w_2$,
(g) $t_7$, $t_8$ and $w_1$,
(h) $t_7$, $t_8$ and $w_2$.

**8.9** Given the results of Problem 8.8, determine if the following rule for choosing a white point is reasonable. *The white point used for computing color errors in images should be a point near the equal chromaticity point with a luminance value near the maximum of the tristimulus values of the pixels in the image.*

**8.10** Choose a reasonable white point value to measure color differences for a computer monitor, assuming the XYZ tristimulus values of the image are approximately uniformly distributed between 0 and 255 in each variable for the following conditions:

(a) The chromaticity of the white point corresponds to the NTSC white point (0.310,0.316);
(b) The chromaticity of the white point corresponds to the HDTV white point (0.313,0.329);

(c) The chromaticity of the white point corresponds to cool white fluorescent lamps (0.372,0.375);

(d) The chromaticity of the white point corresponds to tungsten lamps (D50) (0.346,0.353).

**8.11**    Discuss the problems that would be encountered by using status A filters, Fig. 8.25, in a digital still camera.

# 9 Color sampling

Spatial and temporal sampling has a long history and much has been written in signal processing texts. Color sampling has not been treated with as much rigor, even though the CIE formalized a set of color matching functions in 1931, long before the era of digital signal processing. One reason for the neglect of a formal approach to color sampling is that the goal of color measurements was not to recreate the color spectrum but to describe colors in a consistent quantitative way. Recently, as digital processing of color images has become common, there has been more work that requires that the signals associated with color images be sampled appropriately. Let us consider the problem of sampling color signals and look at the difference between the goal of sampling color and that of sampling spatially or temporally. We will see that the same basic theory can be applied to both problems, but the color sampling requires a more general approach.

Sampling of the radiant power signal associated with a color image can be viewed in at least two ways. If the goal of the sampling is to reproduce the spectral distribution, then the same criteria for sampling the usual electronic signals can be applied directly. An accurate representation of the spectrum is required for modeling the performance of color capture and reproduction devices. However, the goal of color sampling is often not to reproduce the spectral distribution but to allow reproduction of the color sensation. Since this case is more common, let us describe it in detail. In succeeding sections, we will describe the more exacting process of capturing the color spectrum.

## 9.1 Sampling for color reproduction

To illustrate the color reproduction problem, let us consider the case of a television system. The goal is to sample the continuous color spectrum in such a way that the color sensation of the spectrum can be reproduced by the monitor. This discussion will rely heavily on material presented in Section 8.3.3. We will concentrate only on the color aspects of the signal and not the spatial dimensions, so we will consider only a single pixel. A scene is captured with a television camera that uses three sensors with sensitivities $\mathbf{M}$ to sample the radiant spectrum. The measurements are given by

$$\mathbf{v} = \mathbf{M}^T \mathbf{r}, \tag{9.1}$$

where $\mathbf{r}$ is a high resolution sampled representation of the radiant spectrum and $\mathbf{M} = [\mathbf{m}_1, \mathbf{m}_2, \mathbf{m}_3]$ represent the high resolution sensitivities of the camera. We use high resolution signals instead of continuous ones to allow the use of matrix notation. The same conclusions could be obtained using continuous signals and integration instead of summation, but the mathematics would be more complicated.

These values are used to reproduce colors at the television receiver. Let us represent the reproduction of color at the receiver by a linear combination of the radiant spectra of the three phosphors on the screen, denoted $\mathbf{P} = [\mathbf{p}_1, \mathbf{p}_2, \mathbf{p}_3]$, where $\mathbf{p}_k$, $k = 1, 2, 3$, represent the spectra of the red, green and blue phosphors. We will also assume the driving signals, or control values, for the phosphors to be linear combinations of the values measured by the camera. The reproduced spectrum is

$$\hat{\mathbf{r}} = \mathbf{Pc}, \tag{9.2}$$

where the elements of $\mathbf{c}$ are a linear combination of the measured values

$$\mathbf{c} = \mathbf{Bv}, \tag{9.3}$$

and $\mathbf{B}$ is a $3 \times 3$ linear transformation. Nonlinear transformations are possible, but most television receivers are designed to use linear circuits.

The appearance of the radiant spectra is determined by the response of the human eye. Thus, if the cones of the eye have sensitivities $\mathbf{S}$, the "sensed" values of the original scene are computed for the eye by

$$\mathbf{t} = \mathbf{S}^T \mathbf{r}. \tag{9.4}$$

These tristimulus values are sufficient to describe the color seen by the human eye. Recall the relation to the CIE color matching functions described in Section 8.3.2.

The tristimulus values of the spectrum reproduced by the television are obtained by

$$\hat{\mathbf{t}} = \mathbf{S}^T \hat{\mathbf{r}} = \mathbf{S}^T \mathbf{PBM}^T \mathbf{r}. \tag{9.5}$$

If the sampling is done correctly, the original tristimulus values can be reproduced, that is, $\mathbf{B}$ can be chosen so that $\mathbf{t} = \hat{\mathbf{t}}$. We recall from the *ideal color recording* property of Section 8.3.3 and Eq. (8.25) that this means that the sensitivities of the camera are within a linear transformation of the sensitivities of the eye, or equivalently, the color matching functions. The matrix $\mathbf{B}$ represents the ideal transformation.

In the above case, it was assumed that the camera sensitivities were within a linear transformation of the color matching functions. However, the creation of such a set of physical sensor sensitivities is extremely difficult. In most cases, the recording sensitivities are optimized with respect to the limitations of the system. The transformation from sensor values to tristimulus values must be treated as a stochastic optimization problem. As usual in such cases, the mean square error is used to find a matrix $\mathbf{B}$,

$$\min_{\mathbf{B}} E\{||\mathbf{S}^T \mathbf{r} - \mathbf{S}^T \mathbf{PBM}^T \mathbf{r}||^2\}, \tag{9.6}$$

where the expected value is taken over the ensemble of possible radiant spectra. The result, using the vector differentiation reviewed in Appendix B, is given by

$$\mathbf{B} = \left(\mathbf{P}^T \mathbf{S} \mathbf{S}^T \mathbf{P}\right)^{-1} \mathbf{P}^T \mathbf{S} \mathbf{S}^T \mathbf{K_r} \mathbf{M} \left(\mathbf{M}^T \mathbf{K_r} \mathbf{M}\right)^{-1}, \tag{9.7}$$

where $\mathbf{K_r} = E\{\mathbf{r}\mathbf{r}^T\}$, the autocorrelation matrix of the reflectance ensemble. The expected value of the least squares formulation can be replaced with a summation over samples that are representative of the ensemble,

$$\min_{\mathbf{B}} \sum_{k=1}^{K} ||\mathbf{S}^T \mathbf{r}_k - \mathbf{S}^T \mathbf{PBM}^T \mathbf{r}_k||^2.$$

This will mean replacement of the autocorrelation matrix $\mathbf{K_r}$ with an estimate obtained from the summation of samples. By using numerical methods, the problem can include the transformation to CIELAB space or other uniform color spaces, where the error is more aligned with the sensitivity of the eye.

A second problem with the implementation is that while a linear transformation $\mathbf{B}$ may exist in theory, the values may not be realizable with physical hardware. Typical limitations include maximum and minimum limits on the driving circuits and quantization of values in the transformation matrix. Finding solutions to these problems is complicated and beyond the scope of this text.

The colorimetry discussed in Chapter 8 notes the dependence of the color that is sensed by the eye on the illumination of the scene. A television camera or digital camera attempts to capture the scene under whatever light is illuminating the scene at the time. This illumination is usually not known with precision. In the case of the color sampling of scanners and copiers, the illumination is known but may have properties that make color reproduction problematic.

The reproduction of reflective color presents a more difficult problem since the illumination must be taken into account. In the case of television, the original image is a radiation field and the output is a radiation field. In the case of scanners and copiers, the original is a reflection print or transmissive film that is illuminated by an internal lamp. If the output is a print, then the viewing illuminant must be taken into account. The color matching problem for a reflective sample $\mathbf{r}$ can be written mathematically,

$$\mathbf{S}^T \mathbf{L_v} \mathbf{r} = \mathbf{BM}^T \mathbf{L_r} \mathbf{r}, \tag{9.8}$$

where $\mathbf{L_r}$ is a diagonal matrix defined by the recorder illuminant, $\mathbf{L_v}$ is a diagonal matrix defined by the viewing illuminant, and $\mathbf{B}$ is a $3 \times 3$ transformation. The matrix $\mathbf{M}$ is the $N \times 3$ device sensitivity matrix that combines the elements used in Eq. (8.25): the scanning filters, optics and sensor responses. Note that in Eq. (9.8), we could use the color matching matrix $\mathbf{A}$ instead of $\mathbf{S}$, the matrix of sensitivities of the eye.

The practical problem with reflectance scanning is that several elements have to be adjusted to obtain the device sensitivity matrix $\mathbf{M}$. In practice, the filter sensitivities are the elements that have the most flexibility in design. Given that the matrix $\mathbf{M}$ has been defined, the optimal value of **B** can be determined in a manner analogous to that of Eq. (9.7). With this formula for **B**, the optimization can done to find the best **M**. The details of this operation are given in [294].

The viewing illuminant must be considered to solve the problem of optimal capture of reflectance or transmissive media as shown in Eq. (9.8). In practice, reflectance images may be viewed under many different illuminations. The copy that is produced by a printer may be viewed under the fluorescent lamps of the office, the incandescent lamp of a desk or the daylight that comes through a window. While it is mathematically possible to design a three-filter set that could capture color accurately for a reproduction that is to be viewed under a single illuminant, it is generally impossible for three filters to match colors under multiple illuminants.

Dealing with multiple illuminants increases the dimensionality of the problem. In the worst case, each illuminant adds three dimensions to the problem, since the color matching functions under a single illuminant define a three-dimensional space. Of course, it is possible that the spaces of two illuminants overlap, so that the increase in dimensionality is only one or two. The obvious solution to handling multiple illuminants is to increase the dimension of the recorded color data. Instead of recording only three channels, we could record four, five or six channels. While we could record three more channels for each illuminant that we wish to consider, this is clearly not a practical solution. The question of how many channels are needed when recording to produce images under several illuminants has been treated in depth in [241, 292–294, 309]. Let us consider this more general problem briefly.

Consider the case where the number of sensors in the camera or any color measuring device is now $Q$, larger than three. The condition for accurate sampling is that each of the sets of color matching functions associated with the illuminants, $\{\mathbf{A}_i = \mathbf{L}_i \mathbf{A}, i = 1, \ldots, P\}$, must be represented by a linear combination of the sampling device sensitivities. In this case, for illuminant $i$,

$$\mathbf{A}_i^T = \mathbf{B}_i \mathbf{M}^T, \tag{9.9}$$

where the sensor matrix **M** is now $Q \times N$ and $\mathbf{B}_i$, the transformation associated with the $i$th illuminant, is $(3 \times Q)$. The increase in the number of basis functions used in the measuring device allows more freedom to the designer of the instrument. From the vector space viewpoint, the sampling is accurate if the range space of the augmented matrix formed by combining the $P$ color matching functions associated with the illuminants, $[\mathbf{A}_1, \mathbf{A}_2, \ldots, \mathbf{A}_P]$, is contained in the range space of the sensor matrix **M**. Since it is unlikely that perfect containment can be obtained, approaches to minimize the error of the mismatch have been used. The process of optimizing the sensitivities of the capture device has also been carried out for the case of noisy data and filter fabrication errors [287, 294].

## 9.2    Color aliasing

The emphasis on correct sampling of color is on obtaining the tristimulus values. Visual aliasing occurs when the sensitivities of the sampling device are not linear combinations of the sensitivities of the eye. This means that there are spectra that would yield the same tristimulus values but do not give the same measurement values. Recall that spatial aliasing results in signals at one frequency appearing as another frequency after sampling. The same is true of color aliasing. A signal that is one color appears to have values associated with a different color after sampling. To be more precise, let us write the effect mathematically.

Consider two unequal radiant spectra, $\mathbf{r}_1$ and $\mathbf{r}_2$, that yield the same tristimulus values under a given illumination, $\mathbf{A}_L^T \mathbf{r}_1 = \mathbf{A}_L^T \mathbf{r}_2$, but yield different measurements from the instrument, $\mathbf{M}^T \mathbf{r}_1 \neq \mathbf{M}^T \mathbf{r}_2$. This occurs when the combined sensor–filter matrix $\mathbf{M}$ is not within a linear transformation of $\mathbf{A}_L$, that is, there is no $\mathbf{B}$ for which $\mathbf{A}_L = \mathbf{MB}$. For any nonsingular transformation $\mathbf{B}$ that can be used to transform measured values to the tristimulus space, $\mathbf{t}_1 = \mathbf{BM}^T \mathbf{r}_1 \neq \mathbf{BM}^T \mathbf{r}_2 = \mathbf{t}_2$. In other words, the reflectances $r_1(\lambda)$ and $r_2(\lambda)$ should appear the same, but since the measured values are different, the estimates of the tristimulus values are different.

It can also be shown that there exist reflectances, $\mathbf{r}_1$ and $\mathbf{r}_2$, that yield different tristimulus values under a given illumination, $\mathbf{A}_L^T \mathbf{r}_1 \neq \mathbf{A}_L^T \mathbf{r}_2$, but yield identical measurements from the instrument, $\mathbf{M}^T \mathbf{r}_1 = \mathbf{M}^T \mathbf{r}_2$. In this case, colors that should appear to be different will be measured as appearing to be the same. This is analogous to different analog frequencies appearing the same after sampling in the time or spatial domains.

Consider measurements that are taken under one illuminant that indicate a match of two objects. It is possible that the objects when viewed under a second illuminant appear different. This frequently occurs when matching fabrics or accessories in a store and finding out upon leaving the store that the two do not match under daylight or home illumination. This is another example of color aliasing.

There is a related problem that may occur in the reconstruction process. Here, a problem occurs when control values associated with different measured colors produce the same output color. This can be described by considering the control values obtained from nonmetameric reflectances, $\mathbf{r}_1$ and $\mathbf{r}_2$,

$$\mathbf{c}_1 = \mathbf{BM}^T \mathbf{r}_1 \neq \mathbf{c}_2 = \mathbf{BM}^T \mathbf{r}_2,$$

but the output of the display gives equality,

$$\mathbf{S}^T \mathbf{Pc}_1 = \mathbf{S}^T \mathbf{Pc}_2.$$

## 9.3    Sampling for color computation

One of the major applications of the theory presented in this text is accurate modeling of color imaging devices. We wish to predict how well a device will perform or we may wish to design components, such as filters, that will increase the accuracy of the device. Since the device will probably be required to work in the analog world, we need to approximate digitally the continuous system using sampled color spectra. In Section 9.1, we saw what was required to reproduce the sensation of color. The problem now becomes more difficult, since we need to measure exactly what errors occur in various designs or realizations of color systems.

In all of the presentations in past chapters, it has been assumed that the radiant or reflective spectrum of the color signal can be accurately represented by discrete samples, $\mathbf{r} = [r_1 r_2 \ldots r_N]^T$. We have not explicitly stated what sampling intervals are adequate for numerical modeling. To determine this, let us consider the computations that need to be approximated. The basis for this presentation is given in [156, 273]. The basic operation is the spectral capture of a sensor,

$$c_i = \int_0^\infty r(\lambda) m_i(\lambda) \mathrm{d}\lambda, \tag{9.10}$$

where $r(\lambda)$ is the power of the radiant spectrum as a function of wavelength that reaches the sensor and $m_i(\lambda)$ is the spectral sensitivity of the $i$th sensor. Because the sensitivity of the human observer is limited to a finite range of wavelengths, the limits on the integral can be assumed to be between 360 nm and 760 nm. As we have done previously, we would like to approximate this integral by a summation, denoted by a matrix-vector operation $c_i = \mathbf{m}_i^T \mathbf{r}$. It is not required that we reproduce the radiant spectrum, only that we accurately compute the integral of the product of the continuous functions. Recall the basic color matching equation,

$$\mathbf{t} = \mathbf{A}^T \mathbf{L}_\mathbf{v} \mathbf{r} = \mathbf{B} \mathbf{M}^T \mathbf{ODL}_\mathbf{r} \mathbf{r}, \tag{9.11}$$

where $\mathbf{A}$ is the CIE color matching functions, $\mathbf{M}$ is the filter set, $\mathbf{L}_\mathbf{v}$ is the diagonal matrix that defines the viewing illuminant, $\mathbf{L}_\mathbf{r}$ is the diagonal matrix that defines the recording illuminant, $\mathbf{D}$ is the diagonal matrix whose elements define the detector sensitivity, $\mathbf{O}$ is the diagonal matrix whose elements represent the transmission of the optical path and $\mathbf{B}$ is the $3 \times 3$ transformation to obtain the CIE tristimulus values under illuminant $\mathbf{L}_\mathbf{v}$. For most applications, the optical sensitivities, detector sensitivities and the filter transmissivities are combined in a single matrix. We should define the appropriate sampling for each of these elements, so that the summation of the discrete product will accurately approximate the integral of the product of continuous functions.

## 9.3.1     Characteristics of color signals

From Eq. (9.11), it is seen that there are three basic types of color signals to consider: reflectances, illuminants and sensors. The transmission properties of optical systems are usually quite uniform and can be combined with the sensors. Note that transmissions can be substituted for reflectances if the images are presented on film rather than paper. It should be noted that Eq. (9.11) neglects the phenomenon of fluorescence, where radiation at one wavelength is absorbed and re-emitted at another wavelength. Reflectances usually characterize common everyday objects, but occasionally man-made items with special properties such as filters and gratings are of interest. Illuminants vary a great deal from natural daylight or moonlight to special lamps used in imaging equipment. The sensors most often used in color evaluation are those of the human eye. However, with increasing use of digital devices the effects of CCDs, photodiodes and photomultiplier tubes are of interest. Each of these classes of signals is considered below.

The adequacy of sampling will be determined by the inspection of the power spectra of the various signals. We will use the same criteria for sampling the signals in the wavelength domain as we did for judging the adequacy of spatial sampling in Chapter 7. We will examine the relative power of the signal at the Nyquist limits associated with the various sampling rates.

The highest resolution sampling for most color signals is 2 nm. We will see this is more than sufficient for all but a few special illuminants. The Nyquist frequency for 2 nm sampling is 0.25 cycles per nm. It is very common for color instruments to sample spectra at a 10 nm interval. This implies a Nyquist frequency of 0.05 cycles/nm. These are the points on the frequency graphs at which the reader should be looking to make the decision about adequate sampling.

## Sensors

The most important sensor characteristics are the cone sensitivities of the eye. Along with the cone sensitivities are the various color matching functions that are approximately linear transformations of the cone sensitivities. These were discussed in detail in Section 8.3.2. It is seen in Fig. 9.1 that these functions are very smooth and have limited bandwidths.

A reminder on bandwidth is appropriate here. The color matching functions represent continuous functions with finite support. Because of the finite support constraint, they cannot be bandlimited. However, they are clearly smooth and have very low power outside of a very small frequency band. Using 2 nm representations of the functions, the power spectra of the CIE XYZ color matching functions are shown in Fig. 9.1. The spectra represent the Welch estimate where the data are first windowed, then the magnitude of the DFT is computed. The windowing is not critical for these estimates, since they naturally tend to zero. For other signals, the windowing will be significant. The fact that 2 nm sampling is sufficient is evident from the fact that there is no significant signal power close to the 0.25 cycle/nm limit. In fact, we see that all of the curves have power reduced by more than 60 dB at 0.05 cycles/nm. This indicates that 10 nm sampling is sufficient for reconstruction of the spectra.

To obtain accurate estimates of the tristimulus values for a particular illuminant, the sensor responses must be within a linear transformation of the color matching functions. The linear transformation does not alter the maximum bandwidth of the three functions. Thus, the bandwidth of the narrow blue function defines the bandwith of the CIE functions. Since the cone sensitivities are approximately a linear transformation of the CIE color matching functions, the maximum bandwidth of the cone functions can be no greater than that of the color matching functions.

In the context of Eq. (9.11), the actual photo-electric sensor should be considered. Fortunately, most sensors have very smooth sensitivity curves that are a function of the material properties of the sensors. The bandwidths are comparable to those of the color matching functions. Reducing the range of sensors to be studied can also be justified by

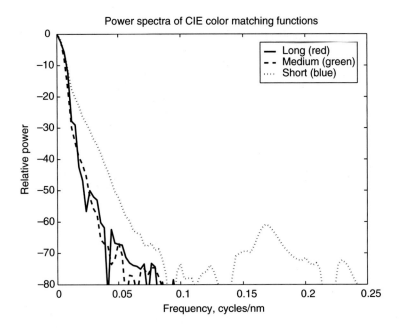

**Figure 9.1.** Power spectrum of CIE XYZ color matching functions.

the fact that filters can be designed to compensate for the characteristics of the sensor and bring the combination within a linear combination of the CMFs. A sensitivity function of a typical photodiode is shown in Fig. 9.2. Note that the curve is from data taken at 10 nm sampling. This means that we cannot compute a meaningful power spectrum to any higher frequency than 0.05 cycle/nm. It is obvious that the function is relatively smooth and we would not expect significant power above this frequency. Indeed, since the photodiode responses are characteristically so smooth, they are almost always sampled at 10 nm or greater intervals.

### Reflectances and transmissivities

The function $r(\lambda)$, which is sampled to give the vector **r** of Eq. (9.11), can represent either reflectance or transmission. Desktop scanners usually work with reflective media. There are, however, several film scanners on the market that are used in this type of environment. The larger dynamic range of the photographic media implies a larger bandwidth. Fortunately, there are not large differences over the range of everyday objects and images.

Several ensembles were used for a study of the reflectance properties of materials in an attempt to include the range of spectra encountered by image scanners and color measurement instrumentation [291]. The reflective spectra were obtained with a spectroradiometer using a sampling interval of 2 nm. The actual resolution of the device was somewhat greater than this but, as will be seen in the results, it is of little consequence for this part of the study. A collection of spectra from 170 natural objects was obtained. The objects included skin, hair, cloth, leaves, wood, brick, plastics, etc. Several types of

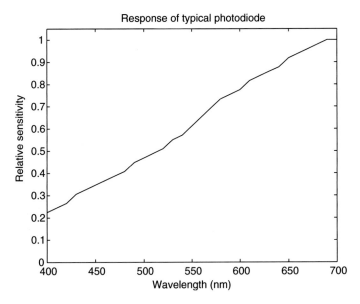

**Figure 9.2.** Sensitivity function of a typical photodiode (10 nm sampling).

printed material were recorded, including samples of gravure, offset and ink-jet printers, thermal dye transfer devices and color copiers. To obtain more saturated colors that were not the result of a three or four color process, a collection of automotive paint samples was recorded. Another common set of pigment based samples was obtained by recording a set of Munsell color chips.

The reflectance spectra with the maximum bandwidth for the natural objects and automotive paint samples are shown in Fig. 9.3a. The frequency spectra corresponding to these reflectances are shown in Fig. 9.3b. In these cases, it is obvious that the 2 nm sampling is adequate to represent the signal. An interesting note is that the natural object with the maximum bandwidth is a leaf. Such foliage usually has its peak reflectances in the near infrared. The other samples have bandwidths that are smaller than those shown. We can see that 2 nm sampling is adequate for this analysis and that 10 nm sampling would be adequate for most purposes.

## Illuminations

There are three major types of viewing illuminants of interest for imaging: daylight, incandescent lighting and fluorescent lighting. There are many more types of illuminants used for scanners and measurement instruments. The properties of the three viewing illuminants can be used as a guideline for sampling and signal processing that involves other types. It will be shown that the illuminant is the determining factor for the choice of sampling interval in the wavelength domain.

Incandescent lamps and natural daylight can be modeled as black body radiators at various color temperatures [313]. Color temperature is discussed in Section 8.6. The black body spectra are relatively smooth and have relatively small bandwidths. The CIE

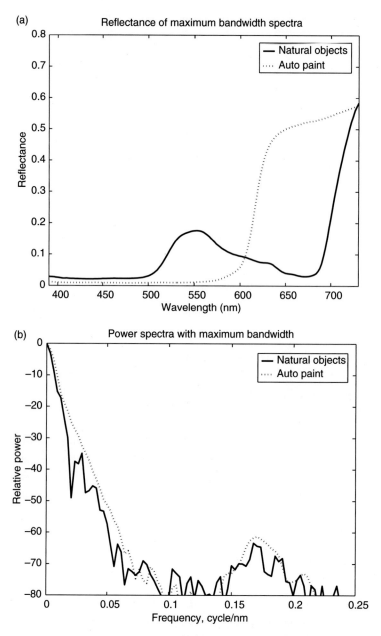

**Figure 9.3.** (a) Reflectivities of the natural object and paint sample that have the largest bandwidths; (b) maximum bandwidth spectra of natural objects and paint samples.

has standard spectra that are used to represent these sources [48]. The relative power in the wavelength domain for CIE illuminants A (incandescent) and D65 (daylight) are shown in Fig. 9.4a. The frequency power spectra associated with these sources are shown in Fig. 9.4b.

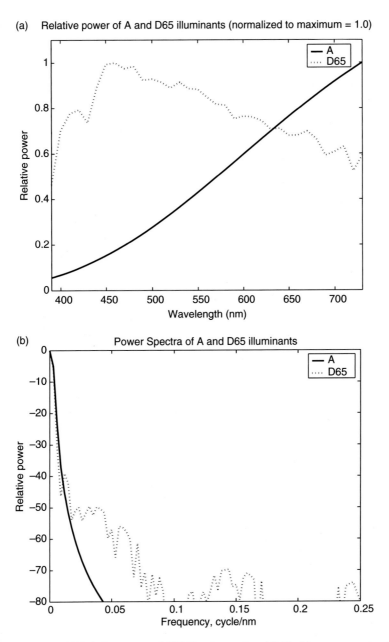

**Figure 9.4.** (a) Relative power of CIE illuminants A and D65; (b) power spectra of CIE illuminants A and D65.

Office lighting is dominated by fluorescent lamps. These are usually characterized by their color temperature. It may seem semantically odd that "cool white fluorescent" is more bluish and has a higher color temperature than "warm white fluorescent." Typical wavelength spectra and their frequency power spectra are shown in Figs. 9.5a and b, respectively.

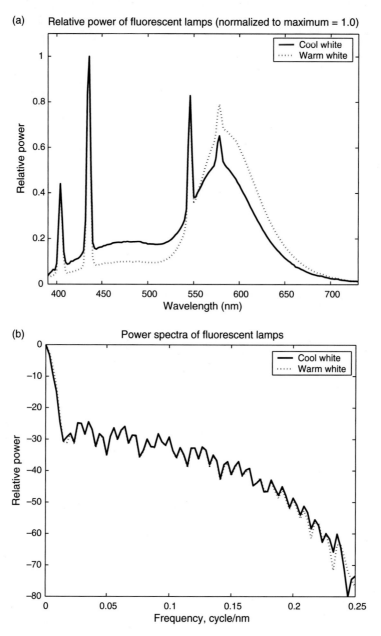

**Figure 9.5.** (a) Relative power of cool white fluorescent and warm white fluorescent lamps: (b) power spectra of cool white fluorescent and warm white fluorescent lamps.

It is with the fluorescent lamps that the 2 nm sampling becomes suspect. The peaks that are seen in the wavelength spectra are characteristic of mercury and are delta function signals at 404.7 nm, 435.8 nm, 546.1 nm and 578.4 nm. The fluorescent lamp can be modeled as the sum of a smoothly varying signal and a delta function series:

$$l(\lambda) = l_d(\lambda) + \sum_{k=1}^{q} \alpha_k \delta(\lambda - \lambda_k), \tag{9.12}$$

where $\alpha_k$ represents the strength of the spectral line at wavelength $\lambda_k$. It is the mercury line at 253.7 nm that is most useful in causing the phosphors in the lamp to fluoresce.[1] The wavelength spectra of the phosphors are relatively smooth, as seen from Fig. 9.5a.

It is clear that the fluorescent signals are not bandlimited in the sense used previously. The amount of power outside of the "bandlimit" is a function of the positions and strengths of the line spectra. Since the lines occur at known wavelengths, it remains only to estimate their power. This can be done by signal interpolation methods that can use the information of the spectrum at samples on either side the wavelength of the fluorescent line. The methods are similar to the interpolation methods used in Section 6.6. Using such methods, the frequency spectrum of the lamp may be estimated by combining the frequency spectra of its components,

$$L(\omega) = L_d(\omega) + \sum_{k=1}^{q} \alpha_k e^{j\omega(\lambda_0 - \lambda_k)}, \tag{9.13}$$

where $\lambda_0$ is an arbitrary origin in the wavelength domain. The bandlimited spectra $L_d(\omega)$ can be obtained from the sampled restoration and are easily represented by 2 nm sampling [273].

## 9.3.2 Color operations

Sampled spectra are used in many applications. Measurements of the CIE tristimulus values under a variety of illuminants can be obtained from an estimate of the reflectance spectrum of an object. Filters for scanners are designed by compensating for the effects of illuminants and detectors. The effect of illuminants on the appearance of colors (color rendering) can be estimated by using sampled spectra. For a large number of these applications, 10 nm sampling is common. The appropriateness of this sampling rate depends on the application and the values to be computed.

The most common quantity computed is the tristimulus vector associated with a particular object as seen under a particular illuminant, Eq. (9.11). The sampling problem is to determine under what circumstances can the continuous integral be adequately approximated by a summation, that is,

$$\int_0^\infty r(\lambda)l(\lambda)a_i(\lambda)d\lambda \approx \Delta\lambda \sum_{k=0}^{\infty} r(k\Delta\lambda)l(k\Delta\lambda)a_i(k\Delta\lambda), \tag{9.14}$$

---

[1] We do not show this line on our usual graphs from 400 nm to 700 nm. The interested reader is referred to [313] or to the lamp manufacturers' data on the internet.

for $i = 1, 2, 3$. The sampling theorem discussed in Chapter 6 states that a continuous signal, $s(\lambda)$, can be reconstructed from discrete samples taken at an interval $\Delta\lambda$, if the signal is bandlimited to $F_{max} < \frac{1}{2\Delta\lambda}$. If the continuous signal can be reconstructed, then the continuous integral can be computed numerically with arbitrary accuracy. For this case, the product in the integral, $r(\lambda)l(\lambda)a_i(\lambda)$, is the function that should be bandlimited.

In standard signal processing theory, the system of interest is linear-invariant and time-invariant, which is represented by convolution. However, the basic operation of color systems is not convolution but multiplication. Let us consider how this operation affects signal bandwidth.

Consider the simple computation of the tristimulus values in the continuous domain;

$$t_i = \int_0^\infty a_i(\lambda)l(\lambda)r(\lambda)d\lambda. \tag{9.15}$$

Assume for the moment that the illuminant is uniform and can be neglected. The product

$$p_i(\lambda) = a_i(\lambda)r(\lambda), \tag{9.16}$$

is represented in the frequency domain by convolution

$$P_i(\omega) = \int_{-\infty}^\infty A_i(\alpha)R(\omega - \alpha)d\alpha. \tag{9.17}$$

It is easily shown that the worst case condition (both functions are rectangular) results in doubling the bandwidth. This shows that for the approximation of Eq. (9.14) to be valid each of the signals must be sampled at the rate determined by the bandwidth of the product, which is, in general, larger than the bandwidth of the individual signals.

Fortunately, the CIE color matching functions and most reflectance spectra are low bandwidth signals, as has been shown. For the case of the color matching functions and typical reflectance signals, this increase is still well within the usual 10 nm sampling representation. The effect of multiplying the blue CMF by an illuminant is illustrated in Fig. 9.6, which shows the frequency power spectra of the product of the blue CIE color matching function with three illuminants, CIE A, D65 and F2. The blue CIE color matching function is used since it has the widest bandwidth. We can see the increase in bandwidth caused by the illuminant when we compare the results with Fig. 9.1. It is clear that 2 nm sampling is inadequate for fluorescent lamps and 10 nm sampling is suspect for high-precision work.

Since accurate color evaluation requires a controlled environment, special lamps are used to view color samples and images. These lamps are constructed to simulate the daylight spectrum and are designated by their color temperature. Since color temperature is derived from the chromaticity values, there can be many different spectra that have the same color temperature. Because the spectra are different, the visual effect

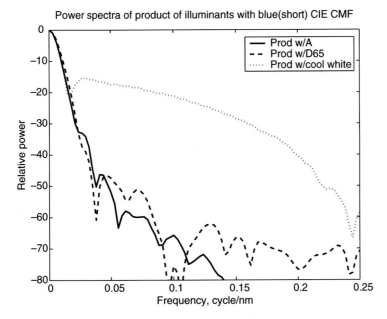

**Figure 9.6.** Power spectra of the product signals of standard illuminants and the blue CMF.

is often noticeably different; mathematically,

$$\int_{-\infty}^{\infty} r(\lambda) l_1(\lambda) a_i(\lambda) \mathrm{d}\lambda \neq \int_{-\infty}^{\infty} r(\lambda) l_2(\lambda) a_i(\lambda) \mathrm{d}\lambda, \qquad (9.18)$$

even though

$$\int_{-\infty}^{\infty} l_1(\lambda) a_i(\lambda) \mathrm{d}\lambda = \int_{-\infty}^{\infty} l_2(\lambda) a_i(\lambda) \mathrm{d}\lambda. \qquad (9.19)$$

The differences in the tristimulus values under the two illuminations are used to compute the color rendering index [313].

To compute the index accurately, the spectra must be sampled appropriately. Lamps may be designed to yield certain spectra that have good color rendering properties. The computations that are used with these designs should be carried out with the proper sampling. The task is further complicated by the fact that most daylight simulators are fluorescent. The line spectra associated with these lamps indicate that methods that take the delta function form of this signal into account should be used when designing such lamps and color viewing booths.

In the design of a color scanner or color copier, Eq. (9.14) would be used to compute the performance in simulations. The optical path, detector sensitivities and reflectances are usually smooth functions and have small bandwidths. The lamps for scanners are usually fluorescent or high intensity gas-discharge types. Both of these types have the line spectra that yield a higher bandwidth. To get accurate simulation values, the delta function form must be considered.

### 9.3.3    Signal processing for accurate computation

The previous section described several applications where proper sampling and computation were critical to computing accurate color values. This section will analyze the problems from a signal processing point of view and suggest methods for solving them.

#### Aliasing

It was noted that it is not the entire frequency spectrum of the product of Eq. (9.10) in which we are interested. It is the integral that is of interest. This value is the DC or $\omega = 0$ term of the Fourier transform,

$$t_i = \int_0^\infty a_i(\lambda)l(\lambda)r(\lambda)e^{-j\omega\lambda}d\lambda \mid_{\omega=0} . \tag{9.20}$$

The effect of aliasing caused by undersampling on color measurements is interesting and informative. Since the tristimulus value is the DC term of the Fourier transform of the product in Eq. (9.17), it is only this term that needs to be studied. This term is obtained by integrating the product of the Fourier transform of the color matching functions and the spectrum to be measured. Substituting $\omega = 0$ into Eq. (9.17) gives

$$t_i = P_i(0) = \int_{-\infty}^\infty A_i(\alpha)R(-\alpha)d\alpha = \int_{-\infty}^\infty A_i(\alpha)R^*(\alpha)d\alpha. \tag{9.21}$$

Since the color matching function is a very low bandwidth signal, its energy is concentrated heavily about $\omega = 0$ in the frequency domain. This means that only the frequencies around zero affect the tristimulus vector. The tristimulus vector obtained from the aliased signal is corrupted only by power in the frequency domain around multiples of the sampling rate. In the case of 10 nm sampling, the aliasing errors come from the power around $F = 0.1\,\text{nm}^{-1}, 0.2\,\text{nm}^{-1}, \ldots$ as shown in Fig. 9.7. The magnitude of the error in the tristimulus vector computed at 10 nm sampling is directly related to the power around these frequencies.

To represent the aliasing error mathematically, it is easier to work with a product of two signals rather than three. For ease of representation, let us combine the CMF and the illuminant as in Section 8.3.3, $g_a(\lambda) = a(\lambda)l(\lambda)$, where the indices for the three CMFs have been dropped. The bandwidth of this signal is dominated by the bandwidth of the illuminant as shown in Section 9.3.2. The aliased signal has a frequency spectrum represented by

$$G(\omega) = \sum_{m=-\infty}^{\infty} G_a(\omega - mF_s), \tag{9.22}$$

where $F_s$ is the sampling rate, $G_a(\omega)$ represents the analog spectrum and $G(\omega)$ the sampled spectrum. An example of $G_a(\omega)$ is shown as the top curve in Fig. 9.7. The sampling at 10 nm intervals causes the values around frequencies of $F = 0.1\,\text{nm}^{-1}, 0.2\,\text{nm}^{-1}, \ldots$ to be added to the values around $F = 0$. These values are

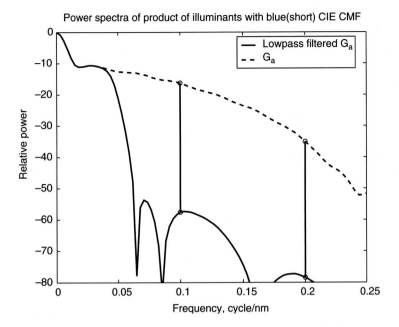

**Figure 9.7.** Source of aliasing errors due to subsampling and bandlimiting.

indicated in the figure. The computation from the discrete samples is obtained by substituting the aliased signal forms of $G(\omega)$ and $R(\omega)$, e.g., Eq. (9.22), into Eq. (9.21). This gives

$$\hat{P}(0) = \int_{-F_s/2}^{F_s/2} \sum_{m=-\infty}^{\infty} G_a(\omega - mF_s) \sum_{n=-\infty}^{\infty} R_a^*(\omega - nF_s)d\omega. \qquad (9.23)$$

If the reflectance is bandlimited, which can be assumed from Section 9.3.1, the aliasing error can be approximated by

$$\epsilon_a = \int_{-F_s/2}^{F_s/2} \sum_{m\neq0} G_a(\omega - mF_s)R_a^*(\omega)d\omega. \qquad (9.24)$$

By bandlimiting the signals with a lowpass filter before sampling at 10 nm, the aliasing error can be significantly reduced. The spectrum of the bandlimited signal is shown as the lower curve in Fig. 9.7. The values that are added to the frequencies around $F = 0$ are much smaller in magnitude than without filtering.

### Lowpass filtering

From the description of the error above, a larger bandwidth of the signal to be sampled indicates a larger error when computing the tristimulus vector from an undersampled signal. The aliasing errors can be eliminated by the standard digital signal processing method of lowpass filtering the wavelength signal prior to sampling. In many cases, a finely sampled signal is subsampled prior to computation of color quantities. The tristimulus error obtained from the bandlimited signal is the integrated product of the spectrum of the nonbandlimited signal and the spectrum of the color matching function. Since the spectrum of the color matching function is so small in this portion of the frequency spectrum, the error is relatively small. This error is much smaller than the aliasing error from undersampling and is given by

$$\epsilon_B = 2 \int_B^\infty |G_a(\alpha)R(-\alpha)|^2 d\alpha. \tag{9.25}$$

For computation of errors, the bandlimiting filter is most easily computed in the digital frequency domain using the DFT. Since the signals of interest may not be zero within the visible range of wavelengths, windowing is necessary. This is not a problem since the CMFs do tend to zero. Care should be taken to pad the signals appropriately to avoid wraparound effects caused by the DFT, see Section 5.7. The bandlimiting filters can be computed in the wavelength domain with care taken to pad to avoid truncation effects.

When using instruments that measure color signals with larger sampling intervals, the user should be aware of how the signal is processed. Simple averaging by optical spreading of the spectrum is a low pass operation, but it is not well controlled in the sense of a good lowpass filter. This is analogous to the effects of optical lenses as "anti-aliasing" filters.

### Computation with delta functions

Bandlimiting the signals is a natural way for a signal processor to approach the problems caused by aliasing. However, since the portion of the signals that cause the aliasing are sums of delta functions, special methods may be used to obtain more accurate values. Substituting the decomposition of Eq. (9.12) into Eq. (9.15) gives

$$t_i = \int_{-\infty}^\infty a_i(\lambda)l_d(\lambda)r(\lambda)d\lambda + \sum_{k=1}^q \alpha_k a_i(\lambda_k)r(\lambda_k). \tag{9.26}$$

The integral of the product of bandlimited signals can be accurately computed using the discrete samples. There is no reason to assume that the lines in the wavelength domain at $\lambda_k$ lie on sample points. However, since the signals $a_i(\lambda)$ and $r(\lambda)$ are bandlimited, an accurate interpolation can be obtained for the estimation of $a_i(\lambda_k)$ and $r(\lambda_k)$.

### 9.3.4　Significance of the errors

In the work on which this section is based, it is assumed that 2 nm sampling is adequate for all bandlimited signals that were described in the ensembles of natural objects, paint samples and Munsell[2] samples [273]. The sampled versions of CIE illuminants A, D65

---

[2] The American artist A. H. Munsell developed one of the first quantitative color scales in 1905. He published the *Munsell Book of Color* that contained samples spaced at "subjectively uniform" increments in his hue, value, chroma space. The book is now available from GretagMacbeth LLC.

and F2 were obtained from standard tables [48, 313]. The decomposition of F2 was obtained from the tabular data by least squares fitting methods.

The tristimulus errors were computed for the reflectance ensembles under the three standard illuminants. From these values the errors in CIELAB space were computed. Three methods were used to estimate the tristimulus values under a given illuminant. These methods were:

1. Sample the signals at a given rate, $F_s$, and compute the values by Eq. (9.14). The samples at intervals greater than 2 nm are subsamples of the 2 nm recorded data (direct method).
2. The recorded data of both reflectances and illuminants are bandlimited to $F_s/2$, then subsampled at that rate. The values are computed with the modified signals using Eq. (9.14) (bandlimited method).
3. The values for the F2 illuminant are obtained from the 2 nm data using method 2 for the bandlimited part and interpolation for the delta function part, Eq. (9.26) (decomposition method).

The results of [273] show that errors are small and not visually significant for computations using illuminants A and D65 when using sampling intervals up to 10 nm. Visually significant here means that a maximum $\Delta E_{ab}^*$ value was less than three. Recall the rule of thumb of Section 8.5.1. Using this criterion, it is seen that the problem lies with the computation of the values for the fluorescent illuminant. Unfortunately, it is this type of illuminant that is used in most color evaluation work. The errors that resulted from computations with the F2 illuminant were much larger and quite significant visually, with maximum $\Delta E_{ab}$ values exceeding seven for all but the smallest sampling intervals.

Since it is apparent that proper sampling can make a difference in color computation, it is important for the user of color instrumentation to investigate the details of the devices with which he or she is working. Taking the appropriate precautions in dealing with the sampled signals can avoid problems caused by incorrect assumptions.

## 9.4 Problems

**9.1** Assume that the recording filters of Eq. (9.5) satisfy the ideal sampling criteria. Show that $\mathbf{S}$ can be replaced by the CIE color matching functions $\mathbf{A}$ and still achieve perfect color reproduction.

**9.2** Assume that $\mathbf{M}$ represents the recording Gaussian-shaped filters denoted by *scanning_set_1_2nm.asc* in the online text database (www.cambridge.org/9780521868532). This set is not ideal but simulates a practical set of filters. Let $\mathbf{P}$ be the primaries associated with red, green and blue LEDs, denoted by *RGB_LEDS_2nm.asc* in the online text database. Use the sensor as $\mathbf{S} = \mathbf{A}$. Assume the reflectances of interest have a correlation matrix $\mathbf{K}r = \sigma^2\mathbf{I}$.

(a) Compute the $3 \times 3$ correction matrix $\mathbf{B}$, assuming that $\sigma^2 = 1$.

(b) Compute the mean square error for $\sigma^2 = 1$.

(c) For the 170 natural object database of [291], which is available on the text website, compute the mean square error of the reproduction.

(d) For the 170 natural object database of [291], compute the mean $\Delta E^*_{ab}$ error, using an appropriate white point.

**9.3** Derive the result given in Eq. (9.7) from the mean square error minimization problem of Eq. (9.6).

**9.4** Equation (9.7) gives the correction matrix **B** in terms of known recording filters and primaries. Since the primaries are usually fixed by the user's output device, the only components that a scanner manufacturer may be free to modify are the recording filters. Assuming that the users will use the optimal correction matrix **B** once the filters are determined, write the equations to obtain the optimal scanning filters.

**9.5** Demonstrate the color aliasing properties of Section 9.2 using a four-dimensional spectral space. Define a $4 \times 3$ color matching matrix, **A**; a $4 \times 3$ sensor matrix, **M**; two $4 \times 4$ diagonal illuminant matrices, $\mathbf{L}_1$ and $\mathbf{L}_2$; and two $4 \times 1$ reflectance spectra $\mathbf{r}_1$ and $\mathbf{r}_2$, such that

(a) $\mathbf{A}_L^T \mathbf{r}_1 = \mathbf{A}_L^T \mathbf{r}_2$ and $\mathbf{M}^T \mathbf{r}_1 \neq \mathbf{M}^T \mathbf{r}_2$ .

(b) $\mathbf{A}_L^T \mathbf{r}_1 \neq \mathbf{A}_L^T \mathbf{r}_2$ and $\mathbf{M}^T \mathbf{r}_1 = \mathbf{M}^T \mathbf{r}_2$ .

**9.6** Use the 2 nm sampled natural object database, illuminants and color matching functions as the basis for this problem and the next.

(a) Compute XYZ tristimulus values for the natural objects under the D65 illuminant. Compute the CIELAB values of this set using the D65 illuminant as the white point. For this part use the full 2 nm data.

(b) Repeat the above computation for 6 nm sampling; that is, subsample the 2 nm data by a factor of three and repeat the computation. Compute the $\Delta E^*_{ab}$ between these values and the 2 nm values.

(c) Repeat the above computation for 10 nm sampling; that is, subsample the 2 nm data by a factor of five and repeat the computation. Compute the $\Delta E^*_{ab}$ between these values and the 2 nm values.

(d) Repeat the above computation for 20 nm sampling; that is, subsample the 2 nm data by a factor of ten and repeat the computation. Compute the $\Delta E^*_{ab}$ between these values and the 2 nm values.

(e) Determine the objects that have the largest $\Delta E^*_{ab}$ values. What are their characteristics?

**9.7** Repeat Problem 9.6 using the F2 illuminant.

**9.8** There is a problem with using only color temperature to define an illuminant. Consider the illuminant spectra available in the text website. The file *d65_2nm.asc* contains the standard D65 illuminant. The file *fluor_d65_2nm.asc* contains a simulated fluorescent illuminant that has the same color temperature as the daylight spectrum.

(a) Compute the $(x, y)$ chromaticities of each of the illuminants and verify they are nearly identical.

(b) Compute the CIELAB values of the 170 natural objects under each illuminant.

(c) Determine the largest $\Delta E_{ab}^*$ difference. If the fluorescent lamp were a good approximation to the daylight spectrum, there would be little difference.

(d) What are the characteristics of the reflectance spectra that correspond to the larger differences?

# 10 Image input devices

The primary digital image recording devices are the digital scanner and the digital still camera. In recent years, these devices have become commonplace, leading to a proliferation of digital images. In this chapter, we discuss these devices in detail, focusing on their limitations and variations. In addition, we will discuss hyperspectral imaging, which makes use of more than three bands to obtain information that can be used in multiple illuminant color reproduction and image segmentation and classification.

## 10.1 Scanners

To process images from scanners and digital cameras effectively, it is necessary to understand the transformations that affect these images during recording. There are several approaches to sampling the two-dimensional image. The first scanners used a single sensor and moved the medium in both orthogonal directions. With the advent of the CCD array, it was possible to project a scan line onto the sensor and move the medium (or sensing array) in the direction orthogonal to the linear array. Finally, it is possible to use a 2-D sensor array to sample the medium without movement during the scan. The most common desktop scanners record the image data using a row of sensors. Thus, we will concentrate on that technology.

The "paper moving" designs consist of both sheet-fed and flat-bed scanners. The "sensor moving" designs include hand-held scanners, which require the user to move the instrument across the paper, as well as flat-bed scanners. The primary sensor types are charge-coupled device (CCD) arrays and contact image sensor (CIS) arrays. Currently, CCD arrays provide higher signal-to-noise ratio (SNR) levels, while CIS arrays result in scanners of very low cost due to simplistic optical designs. We will discuss both types.

Figures 10.1a and b display the optical path and the initial processing of a CCD desktop scanner, respectively. In the system shown in Fig. 10.1a, a lamp illuminates the image being scanned. The lamp consists of a small fluorescent tube that is mounted spatially close to the image and designed to emit a diffuse light. The illumination and detection geometry are usually designed to approximate the 45–0 degree sensing of Fig. 8.23 . The reflectance from the image is passed through an aperture and focused onto the CCD array through a series of mirrors and lenses. Typically, a full page width (21.5 cm) is focused on a CCD array that may be only 28 mm wide. The mirrors, lens and CCD elements are generally housed in a single enclosure, designed to move with a stepper motor. Most

(a)

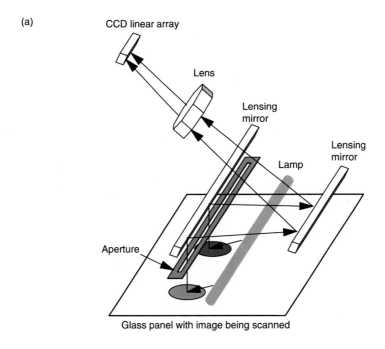

(b)

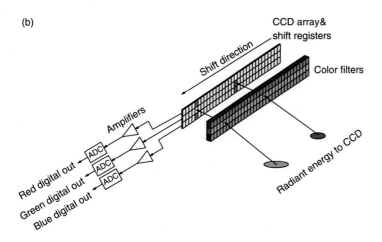

**Figure 10.1.** (a) CCD optical path for flat-bed reflectance scanner; (b) CCD sensor details (for color version, please see Plate 5 ).

color scanners contain a single light source and a CCD array consisting of three rows, where each row is covered with red, green or blue filters. However, there is a variant that consists of three colored lamps (typically red, green and blue) and a single row CCD array.

The CIS design is displayed in Fig. 10.2. In a typical CIS design, red, green and blue LEDs are time multiplexed to illuminate an image row at an angle of 45 degrees. The

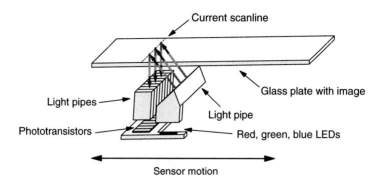

**Figure 10.2.** Contact image sensor (CIS) optical path: the red, green and blue LEDs are time multiplexed to illuminate a single scan line (for color version, please see Plate 6).

radiant power of the LEDs is directed to the image through the use of a plastic light pipe. The diffuse reflectance from the image is passed through a collection of plastic light pipes, which are spaced across the row. These light pipes limit the viewing angle seen by each photoelement.[1] The spatial resolution is controlled by the spacing of the light pipes and the number of photoelements (these photoelements could be photodiodes or phototransistors). Since there are no mirrors or lenses involved, this type of sensor is very inexpensive compared with its CCD counterpart, which requires expensive optical elements to reduce the scan line to the CCD array size.

In the CCD design, the sensor values are read into a shift register (see Fig. 10.1b), amplified and then converted to digital values by an analog-to-digital converter (ADC). The sensor performance is generally specified in terms of its dark noise, saturation level, noise variation and *photoresponse nonuniformity* (PRNU). A typical model of data recording for the sensor is given by

$$m_i = g_i \mathbf{d}^T \mathbf{r}_i + n(\mu_i, \sigma_i^2),$$

where $i$ indicates the spatial location of the pixel on the sensor, $g_i$ represents the photoresponse spatial nonuniformity, which varies from sensor to sensor, $\mathbf{d}$ represents the sensor's spectral sensitivity,[2] $\mathbf{r}_i$ is the diffuse spectral reflectance of the image at spatial location $i$, and $n(\mu_i, \sigma_i^2)$ is additive noise with mean $\mu_i$ and variance $\sigma_i^2$. Image noise is discussed further in Chapter 7.

The ADC in the system is primarily specified in terms of the number of bits used for quantization, the *differential nonlinearity* (DNL), *integral nonlinearity* (INL) and sampling rate [9, 18, 39]. Each of these have a significant effect on the quality of the scanned image. In the ideal ADC, the quantization step sizes do not vary across the full scale of the device. This is the assumption of the discussion of quantization in Chapter 4. The differential nonlinearity is a measure of the difference between the actual transition

---

[1] These light pipes are usually made in one piece.

[2] A more general model would be to make $\mathbf{d}$ vary with spatial location. Since all the sensor elements are from the same silicon wafer and have very similar properties, this is usually not necessary.

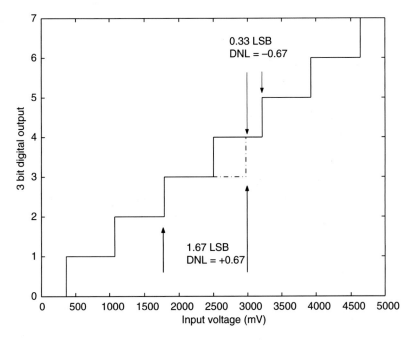

**Figure 10.3.** A 3 bit ADC with differential nonlinearity: the ideal quantizer is the solid line; the area where the actual ADC response differs from the ideal response is shown as a dashed line.

and the ideal transition. It is usually specified as a worst case value. Figure 10.3 displays an example of a DNL in a 3 bit ADC. The integral nonlinearity is a measure of the departure of the ADC from an ideal linear response. Figure 10.4 displays how it is quantified. Note that DNL and INL are related. The INL is dependent upon how the DNL is distributed. Also, note that if the differential nonlinearity is large, ADC code values can be missing, that is, they will never occur.

In addition to the reflectance scanners discussed above, there are transmittance scanners used for digitizing slides, negatives and transparencies. The major difference in these devices is that the illumination and sensor are mounted on opposite sides, allowing the light to travel through the media. The remaining components are the same as those discussed above for reflectance scanners. The geometries of these devices attempt to approximate the instrumentation of Chapter 8.

Once the digital data are obtained, several processing steps are performed before recording the final values. From Fig. 10.1b, it is clear that the red, green and blue linear arrays are spatially displaced with respect to one another. Hence, the red pixel at location $[x, y]$ will be read at the same time as the green pixel at location $[x, y + y_o]$ and the blue pixel at location $[x, y + 2y_o]$, where the magnitude and sign of $y_o$ depend upon the size of the displacement and the scan direction, respectively. It is necessary for the scanner firmware or driver software to re-order or interpolate the recorded data in order to compensate for this displacement. For the CIS scanner, the scan engine may be

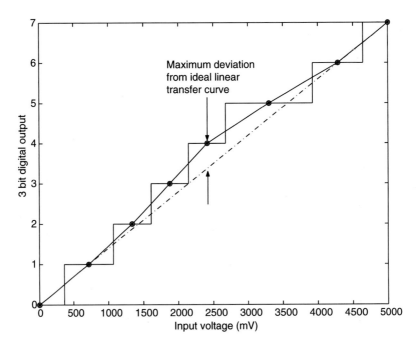

**Figure 10.4.** A 3 bit ADC showing integral nonlinearity, which is the maximum departure of the ADC response from a full scale linear curve.

moving continuously during the acquisition process. In this case, the time-multiplexed acquisition of the bands results in a $\frac{1}{3}$ vertical displacement between the color bands. Figure 10.5 presents an example of this displacement.

### 10.1.1 Optical issues

In the design of a CCD scanner, the optics can be a costly part of the system. The optics are responsible for accurately focusing and evenly distributing the light across the field of view. Of these two tasks, the more difficult is that of evenly illuminating the object. As in most engineering problems, there is a trade-off between the complexity and cost of the scanner optics and the irradiance fall-off at the edges of the detector. Figure 10.6 defines the variables associated with the optical geometry. Assuming an ideal lens and a Lambertian source, which implies that the radiance of the source (the image) is independent of the angle (or that the source is completely diffuse), then the irradiance at a point on the detector can be expressed as a function of the on-axis irradiance $I_o$ and the off-axis angle $\theta$ (the axis in this case is the optical axis). Recall the discussion of photometric measurements in Section 8.2. The value of the irradiance at the off-axis angle $\theta$ is given by

$$I_\theta = I_o \cos^4(\theta). \tag{10.1}$$

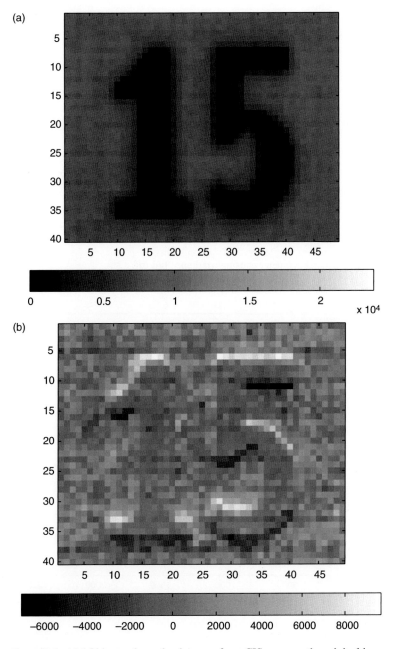

**Figure 10.5.** (a) 16 bit per channel color scan from CIS scanner: the original image was black text on a white background; (b) difference image between red and blue bands (red–blue) of the image above.

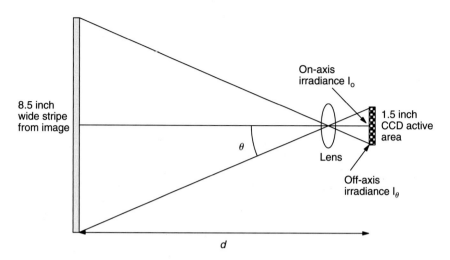

**Figure 10.6.** Optical geometry causing irradiance fall-off.

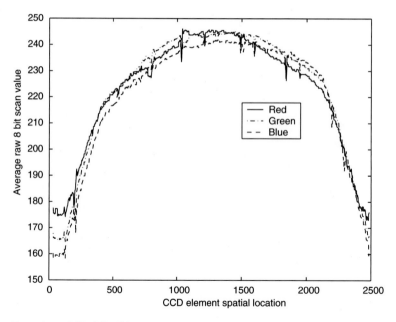

**Figure 10.7.** CCD fall-off in a real CCD scan engine.

To reduce the fall-off, it is necessary to make $\theta$ as small as possible. This is achieved by increasing the optical path, thereby increasing the size or optical complexity of the scanner.

To demonstrate the level of a typical fall-off, a constant white region was scanned with a CCD scanner and the average computed along the columns. The average is shown in Fig. 10.7. The fall-off, at its worst, is a 35% loss from the on-optical axis region.

To correct this fall-off, most scanners start by measuring a white stripe that is built into the scanner; then making a dark measurement (light off) prior to scanning the image. This helps define the dynamic range and noise properties. The bias and scale of the recorded sensor values are then digitally adjusted to compensate for the optical fall-off, as well as any changes in the bias and gain of the system.

### 10.1.2  Spectral response and color characterization

Owing to the effect of metamerism, which is defined in Section 8.3.2, it is quite possible that spectra that appear the same to the standard human observer may look quite different to the digital scanner. This is because the spectral response of the color scanner is not related by a linear transformation to the CIE color matching functions. This has led to a significant amount of research over the past decade on the design of color filters [241, 285, 286, 293, 309]. At best, a three-band scanner could provide true standard color values for only one type of illuminant. However, recent design methods have shown that it is possible to provide reasonable color accuracy for a number of illuminations by adding additional filter bands (that is more than three) [293]. In the limit of adding filters, the device will become a spectral scanner. Currently, digital still camera versions of such devices are used for research and art archival purposes [288]. We will discuss hyperspectral devices further in Section 10.3.

The characterization of a desktop scanner involves the measurement of a color target by both the scanner and a colorimeter. From these measurements, the scanner output values are mapped to device-independent color values by utilizing model-based techniques whose parameters are optimized or by multidimensional look-up tables (LUT) [11, 138, 296]. Color characterization is discussed in detail in Chapter 12.

## 10.2  Digital still cameras

Compared with a scanner, the electronics of the digital still camera (DSC) are smaller, use less power, and are required to work in more demanding environments with various illuminations. The basic image formation and digitization process is shown in Fig. 10.8. The radiant energy passes through the lens and aperture, through the color filter array and is measured by the 2-D sensor array. As mentioned in Section 7.1.2, the lens has properties that are like an anti-aliasing filter. The reader is referred back to Fig. 7.4, which displays the diffraction roll-off of a lens and aperture system. Finally, note that most cameras will include an infrared blocking filter to compensate for the high sensitivity of silicon imaging elements to radiation in the near infrared band, see Fig. 9.2.

### 10.2.1  Pipeline

The standard issues of noise sources, optical limitations, and quantization are of importance when quantifying the DSC image data. In addition, the DSC image data can be affected by the interpolation of the demosaicking algorithm, interpolation for

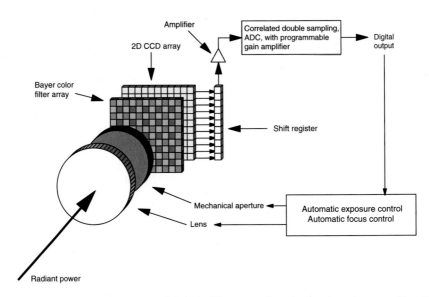

**Figure 10.8.** Imaging front end of digital still camera (for color version, please see Plate 7).

image size, possible data compression, color balance adjustments that depend on camera settings and the lighting environment. Most cameras allow the adjustment of exposure time and system gain (similar to the ISO film speed). These settings will also affect the dynamic range and noise level of the recorded image. A typical pipeline for a DSC is shown in Fig. 10.9. The pipeline is discussed in more detail in [222].

Most cameras have modes where the aperture size, exposure time, system gain, color balance and focus are adjusted automatically from the imaging scene data. These algorithms tend to be proprietary. In the case of exposure time and system gain, the typical approach is to divide the image into several subimages. Luminance statistics, such as the mean, minimum and maximum values, are then computed in these subimages. These statistics are used to determine system exposure and gain. During the design of the DSC, functional forms that are used to compute the exposure and gain are determined by first computing the statistics for a large number of images (ideally representative of the type for which the camera will be used). The manufacturer then manually determines the optimal exposure and gain settings for those images. The parameters for the functional forms or multidimensional look-up tables (MLUT) are used to create a mapping from the image statistics to the camera settings.

There are many techniques to achieve automatic focus on cameras. One approach is for the camera to emit a signal, like infrared illumination or ultrasound, and determine the distance of the closest object from properties of the reflected signal. Other approaches look at the properties of the image to determine the optimal focal setting. One common approach is for the camera to adjust the focal setting to achieve the greatest contrast in the sensor. A measure of contrast can be obtained by an analysis of an image histogram [23]. For example, the blurred image in Fig. 7.9 clearly has less contrast than the nonblurred image shown in Fig. 7.1a. A histogram for the nonblurred image is shown in

Image in

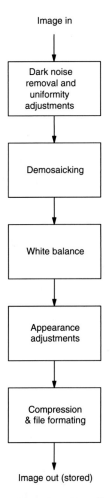

Dark noise
removal and
uniformity
adjustments

Demosaicking

White balance

Appearance
adjustments

Compression
& file formating

Image out (stored)

**Figure 10.9.** Typical digital still camera processing steps after digitization.

Fig. 10.10a.[3] A histogram for the image in Fig. 7.9 is shown in Fig. 10.10b. Note that more of the data are contained in the mid-gray range compared with the histogram in Fig. 10.10a. The minimum and maximum values of the image usually change as well. In this example, it is obvious that the maximum value in the blurred image is significantly less than the maximum in the original, while the minimum value is only slightly greater.

Blurring reduces the high frequency content in the image. This relationship leads to another autofocus approach in which adjustments are made to the focal length to maximize the high frequency content of the image data. This approach requires the implementation of a high pass digital filter in the camera. This can be done by using

[3] This is the histogram of the original image. The image used in Chapter 3 was scaled to a smaller range to allow the addition of noise and still keep the result within [0, 255].

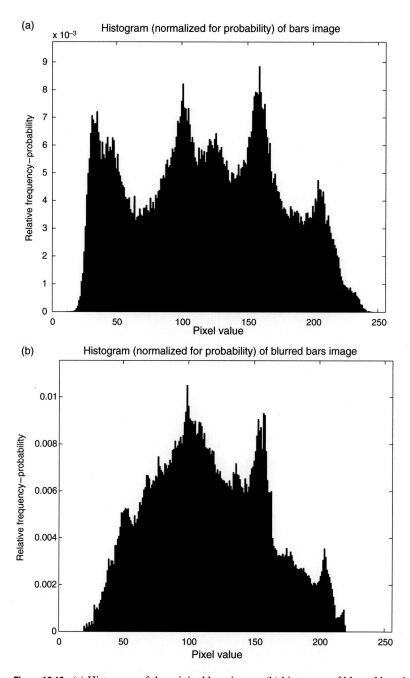

**Figure 10.10.** (a) Histogram of the original bars image; (b) histogram of blurred bars image.

a small 2-D FIR filter to limit computation time. Additional autofocus methods are reviewed in [222].

## 10.2.2 The sensor

Most digital still cameras (DSCs) utilize either CCD or CMOS 2-D sensor arrays. In a 2-D CCD, the charges in the sensor elements are clocked to vertical shift registers. These charges are then shifted to a horizontal shift register. At this point, the charges are shifted out of the horizontal shift register and converted to voltages, which are provided to an external analog-to-digital converter (ADC). Note that the shifting rate of the horizontal shift register is faster than the shifting rate of the vertical shift registers. If the array is of size $M \times N$ ($M$ vertical by $N$ horizontal), then the horizontal shift register would need to operate at $N$ times the rate of the vertical registers. An example is shown in Fig. 10.11, where the horizonal shift register operates at five times the rate of the vertical shift registers. Obviously the vertical shift registers take up space that could be used for imaging. Some 2-D CCDs eliminate the vertical shift registers and shift the charges across the actual sensing elements. While these devices will have more area for sensing light, and thereby either more resolution or greater sensitivity, no image sensing can occur during the shifting. This reduces frame rate for video applications. CCDs are designed using fabrication processes that have been optimized for image quality and optical properties. As is possible in the CMOS device, this fabrication process is not readily used for integrating other electronics onto the CCD chip.

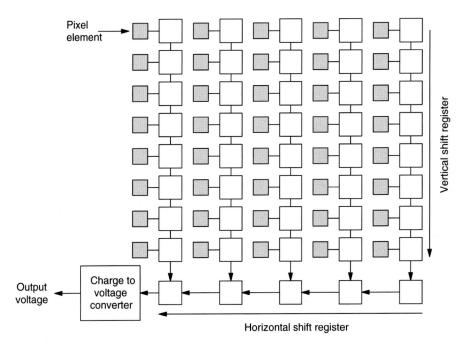

**Figure 10.11.** Diagram of a 2-D CCD sensor.

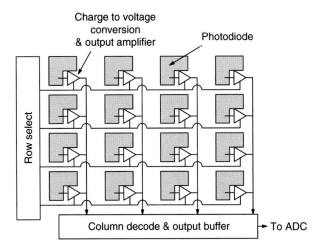

**Figure 10.12.** Diagram of a 2-D CMOS sensor.

The CMOS sensors are designed using the same fabrication process used for typical integrated circuits. This makes possible the design of a *system on a chip* (SoC), which could include the imaging sensor, timing circuits and an ADC. The integration of these components can lead to a reduction in system cost. The cost of this integration is that the CMOS sensor is typically noisy compared with an equivalent CCD sensor. Most CMOS sensors are designed with matrix-like read-out, where any subregion of the image can be read independently of any other, in contrast to the sequential read-out of the CCD. Figure 10.12 shows an example of the CMOS architecture where the charge is converted to a voltage at each sensor element. This process can result in greater sensor nonuniformity than for a CCD sensor. Today, CCDs tend to be used in high-end imaging applications, which require lower noise, e.g., high end consumer cameras, while CMOS sensors are used in high-volume, low-cost designs, e.g., cell phone cameras.

## 10.2.3     Color separation

For both CMOS and CCD based systems, color images are usually created by using a color filter array (CFA) so that each pixel records the output of only one of the color filters. Hence, at each spatial location, the resulting color channels have a single recorded value (red, green or blue for an RGB camera) and must be further processed using appropriate interpolation schemes to generate an image, where each pixel location is defined by three color values. This process is called demosaicking and is discussed in detail in [99] and below in Section 10.2.4. A common CFA is the Bayer pattern [22], which is shown in Fig. 10.13 [22]. Note that the green channel is sampled at twice the spatial rate of the red and blue channels. The rationale of this design is that the green channel spectral response is close to that of the human visual system's (HVS) luminance response (luminous efficiency function of Fig. 8.3). The human luminance channel is more sensitive to high spatial frequencies compared with the HVS chrominance response. This characteristic of the HVS is discussed briefly in Appendix E and in more detail in [300, pp. 326–329]. Some devices use cyan, magenta and yellow filters in an array. The advantage of this approach is that more photons reach the photodetector due to the lower density of these filters compared with the red, green and blue filters. There are digital color sensors that achieve color separation by using the fact that the photon penetration depth into silicon is wavelength dependent [180]. Silicon has the property that long wavelengths penetrate deeper than short wavelengths. These sensors do not require demosaicking. However, some processing is required for the usual noise suppression, color correction and compensation for the fact that the spatial resolution is not the same for all depths (color channels) [81, 170].

## 10.2.4    Demosaicking

The color filter array used by virtually all consumer cameras records a single color band at each spatial location of the Bayer array as indicated in Fig. 10.13. The values of the other bands at a location must be estimated from the surrounding information. The goal of such interpolation methods is to obtain both color accuracy and high spatial resolution. These goals are somewhat complementary and cannot both be obtained simultaneously with equal accuracy.

   The straightforward approach is to treat each channel separately and compute the interpolations as we did the reconstructions of Section 6.6. However, the Nyquist rate of an array like that of Fig. 10.13 is, at best, half the resolution of the sensor, that is, the green channel is sampled at half the maximum rate of the sensor and the other channels are at a quarter of the maximum. This simple approach would severely limit the spatial resolution of the reconstructed image. For example, using spline interpolation on all three channels of a Bayer array results in good color reproduction of smoothly varying areas but extreme color artifacts in regions of high spatial activity. An example of this is shown

**Figure 10.13.** The Bayer color filter array (for color version, please see Plate 8).

(a)                                          (b)

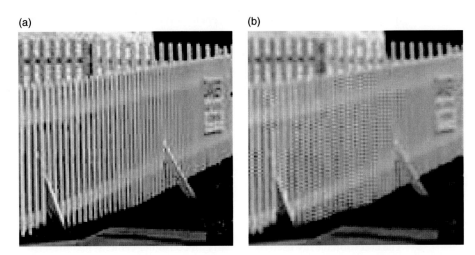

**Figure 10.14.** Bicubic interpolation used for color filter array interpolation results in noticeable artifacts: (a) original image; (b) bicubic spline interpolation; figure from [99] used with permission of the authors and IEEE, ©2005 IEEE (for color version, please see Plate 9).

in Fig. 10.14. The picket fence is an excellent example of varying spatial frequency as it goes from low frequency in the foreground to high frequencies above the Nyquist rate as the distance from the camera increases. The color aliasing problems are evident in the middle frequencies of the fence.

It is obvious that the three or more color channels of a CFA are not independent. The channels are significantly correlated. Thus, it makes sense to use this correlation to reconstruct the color image. In addition to the statistical correlation of the signal channels, the characteristics of the human visual system should be taken into account. These simple observations have led to a vast amount of work on the demosaicking problem, with many approaches yielding results that far exceed the simple independent channel approach. A good review of demosaicking methods is given by [99]. We will give only a brief description of the various approaches.

From the results of Fig. 10.14, we see that the major color aliasing problems occur in the regions with edges. With this insight, the basic idea behind all effective demosaicking methods is to identify the presence of edges and their orientation. If the orientation of the edge can be determined, then the interpolation should be done along the edge, in the direction of high correlation. Interpolation across the edge, where values are uncorrelated, can be avoided. The edges should be identified using the information in all channels, but the choice of the color space in which to perform the interpolation is important. This choice is usually based on models of the human visual system.

The edges that we see are most often the result of differences in luminance. In fact, it is very difficult to find an edge in an actual pictorial image that is only a difference in chrominance. For this reason, the green channel of the CFA, which approximates the CIE luminance efficiency function, provides the main information that is used to determine the presence and orientation of edges. The presence of an edge is indicated by significant differences in the local values. To obtain good resolution, the neighborhood that is used to detect the edge must be relatively small. To obtain a good estimate of the presence of an edge and its direction, the neighborhood should be larger. Again, these are conflicting requirements. In practice, most demosiacking methods use a minimal $3 \times 3$ pixel neighborhood to estimate edge properties.

Having estimated the presence and direction of a local edge, the information is used to interpolate the green values in the adjacent pixels where only a red or blue measurement exists. This will give a full-resolution image in the green (G) or luminance channel. This data can be used to determine how to interpolate the other channels. As mentioned previously, the interpolation may operate directly on the red (R) and blue (B) channels or one of the color difference channels, since the $R - G$ and $B - G$ values are available after the interpolation of the green channel.

Several algorithms use a multistep approach, where the images in each of the channels are successively refined by using information from the previous step. Often, correlation between the color channels is used in the multistep methods. This allows testing of the interpolated values to determine if the high-resolution image could have reasonably been subsampled to yield the original recorded mosaicked data. Most demosaicking algorithms use an interpolation scheme that does not alter the original data, although minor deviations within the range of the measurement noise would be reasonable. The multistep methods also allow the imposition of various constraints, such as smoothness of hue, that the designer feels are important. In addition, multistep methods can use information in both the spatial domain and frequency domain. Using the frequency domain allows the algorithm to exploit directly the high pass and low pass nature of various features in the image.

It is beyond the scope of this text to describe in detail many of the demosaicking methods that have been published. Fig. 10.15 shows a sampling of the results of such methods by reproducing the examples presented in the review [99].

## 10.2.5    White balance

Colorimetrically, the primary difference between a digital still camera and a scanner is that the camera has limited control over the illumination source. Figure 10.16 shows an example of a real image captured with different illuminations and white balance settings. Note that a huge variation in the color of the cat is recorded. With the automatic white balance turned off, the recorded color is dependent upon the actual illumination and the expected illumination. To the human observer, the cat will appear black and white for standard illumination conditions. This is the adaptive nature of the HVS and the reason for the white normalization of the CIE transformation from CIEXYZ to CIELAB. The automatic white balance control in a DSC is designed to perform a similar compensation.

The automatic adjustments for white balance are typically proprietary. One approach is to have an additional sensor on the camera that obtains an estimate of the color of the average scene illumination. Alternatively, the estimate can be made from the imaging sensor data. Most camera images are recorded under a limited number of illuminations such as daylight (with and without clouds and at different times of the day),

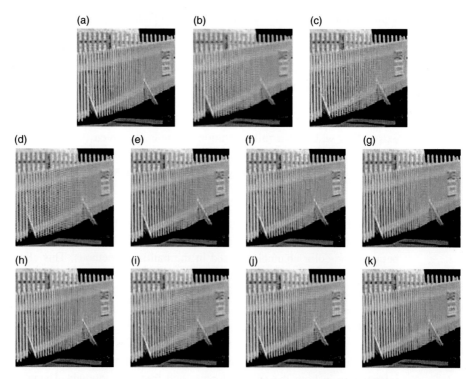

**Figure 10.15.** Result images for Lighthouse image: (a) original image; (b) bilinear interpolation; (c) edge-directed interpolation in [111]; (d) constant-hue-based interpolation in [1]; (e) weighted sum in [150]; (f) second-order gradients as correction terms in [2]; (g) Bayesian approach in [188]; (h) homogeneity-directed in [113]; (i) pattern matching in [46]; (j) alias cancelation in [88]; (k) POCS in [98]; figure is from [99], and used with permission of the authors and IEEE, ©2005 IEEE (for color version, please see Plate 10).

tungsten, fluorescent and flash.[4] One approach is to correlate the data with these various illumination conditions.

The problem of determining how to adjust the white balance is related to the problem of illumination estimation [270]. In illumination estimation, the ideal goal is to estimate the spectral power distribution of the illumination. It is easier and usually sufficient to estimate the chromaticity values of the illumination. For proper white balance, the goal is to ensure that a reference white in the image is white in the digital image, that is, the measured device-dependent camera values that are obtained from a "white" object are transformed to visually "white" values in a device-independent color space. An accurate estimate of the illumination will usually enable the creation of a mapping that achieves proper white balance.

---

[4] Obviously, there could be combinations of these and, while the list is not exhaustive, it does apply for the majority of digital photography applications. Compensation for variations in the lighting on Mars by the NASA Mars Rover was determined by periodically imaging samples of known reflectances (red, green, blue and yellow).

Some white balance methods apply simple scaling to the red, green and blue image bands to compensate for illumination changes [209, 222], similar to the mapping that is used from CIEXYZ to CIELAB. This method, which is mathematically represented as the multiplication of the tristimulus values by a diagonal matrix, can result in significant color errors [289]. An approach that results in fewer color errors is to use a mapping with additional parameters, which are determined by spectrally modeling the camera system and the imaging process. For example, similarly to what was discussed in Chapter 9, the camera recording process can be modeled as

$$\mathbf{c} = \mathbf{M}^T \mathbf{L} \mathbf{r}, \tag{10.2}$$

where $\mathbf{c}$ is a three element RGB value, the columns of matrix $\mathbf{M}$ are the spectral transmittances of the three types of color filters combined with the transmittance of the optical elements and the sensor spectral sensitivity, $\mathbf{L}$ is a diagonal matrix representing the spectral power distribution of the scene illumination and $\mathbf{r}$ represents diffuse spectral reflectance.

If the illumination is tungsten, the spectral power distribution will be heavily weighted towards red and hence the recorded RGB values will be biased towards red. When printed on white paper, this color cast will be very noticeable. The goal is to map the recorded RGB values to remove this bias. Such a mapping can be determined by estimating the value that would have been recorded independent of the scene illumination $\mathbf{L}$, or with a more uniform illumination. In this case, the goal is to map the recorded values in Eq. (10.2) to the values

$$\mathbf{d} = \mathbf{M}^T \mathbf{r}. \tag{10.3}$$

One approach is to use a simple affine transformation and a least squares estimator in the camera RGB color space. The problem then is to solve

$$\min_{\mathbf{B}, \mathbf{b}} E \left\{ \| \left( \mathbf{B}\mathbf{M}^T \mathbf{L} \mathbf{r} + \mathbf{b} \right) - \mathbf{d} \|^2 \right\}, \tag{10.4}$$

where the expected value operation is usually approximated using an ensemble of typical reflectances. The estimate in this case is given by

$$\hat{\mathbf{d}} = \mathbf{M}^T \mathbf{K}_r \mathbf{L} \mathbf{M} [\mathbf{M}^T \mathbf{L} \mathbf{K}_r \mathbf{L} \mathbf{M}]^{-1} [\mathbf{c} - \mathbf{M}^T \mathbf{L} \mathbf{m}_r] + \mathbf{M}^T \mathbf{m}_r, \tag{10.5}$$

where $\mathbf{K}_r$ is the covariance matrix of the reflectance spectra of the image, and $\mathbf{m}_r$ is the mean of the reflectance spectra. The equation subtracts the current mean of $\mathbf{c}$, multiplies by a $3 \times 3$ matrix and adds a mean for the ensemble of estimates. A more sophisticated method involves characterizing the DSC (see Chapter 12), and performing the above optimization in a more perceptually meaningful color space, such as CIELAB.

We can see the qualitative effects of the color balance algorithm in the camera used to produce Fig. 10.16. The third section from the left is taken with correct white balance and produces an accurate white for the cat. The first section is taken with a fluorescent white

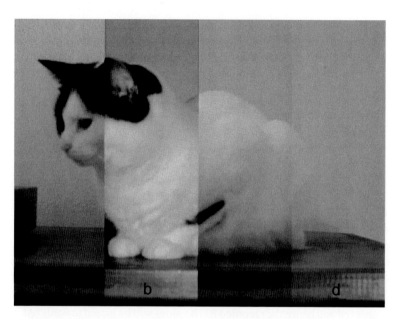

**Figure 10.16.** The conditions and settings of the camera were as follows: (a) tungsten illumination with fluorescent white balance; (b) flash illumination with tungsten white balance; (c) tungsten illumination with tungsten white balance; (d) tungsten illumination with daylight white balance (for color version, please see Plate 11).

balance setting. Since fluorescent lamps are heavily weighted in the green because of the spectral lines (see Fig. 9.5a), the white balance algorithm will attempt to deemphasize the green. The result of using tungsten lighting instead of fluorescent is an image with more red from the illuminant and more magenta from the compensation by reducing the green content. The second section assumed a tungsten illuminant, so the algorithm sought to deemphasize the red or boost the blue content. Since the actual illumination was a flash, which has a relatively flat spectrum, the resulting compensation produces a blue image. The appearance of the fourth section can be explained similarly (see Problem 10.13).

## 10.2.6 Appearance

Colorimetric accuracy is not the usual goal in consumer digital still cameras. Rather, the typical goal is obtaining an image that is "pleasant to look at." For the engineer, who is used to dealing with exact solutions, the technical translation of "this image doesn't feel right" can be difficult to determine. In addition, human judgment of the "goodness" of a set of images can be fraught with inconsistencies.

In most cases, the luminance and chrominance dynamic ranges of the reproduced image will be much less than the dynamic range of the original scene, owing to limitations in the display technology. To compensate for this loss in dynamic range, the contrast is typically increased, which leads to a loss of image information in the highlights and shadows. The increase in contrast is typically achieved with a mapping similar to that

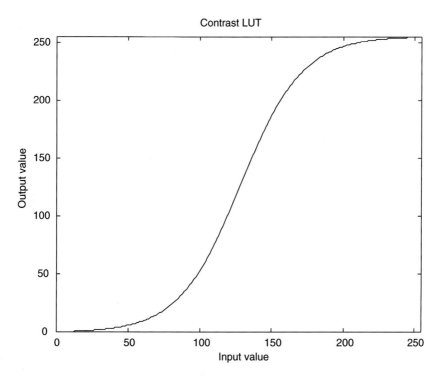

**Figure 10.17.** Example mapping to increase image contrast.

shown in Fig. 10.17. Consider the effect of this mapping with respect to the principles presented in Chapter 3 for image display.

In addition, viewers tend to prefer vivid colors, even when they do not accurately reflect the original scene [209]. Typically, these adjustments are determined by having a group of viewers select the "best" image from a set of images that differ only in their contrast setting and chroma enhancement. In such a study, it is obviously critical to select a distribution of color samples that reflects the relative importance of the various objects to be recorded. For example, it is important to include certain colors such as skin tones of people of various ethnic backgrounds in the set of images. A complete presentation of appearance issues is presented in [74].

## 10.3 Multispectral and hyperspectral imaging

While the majority of digital still cameras and scanners record the image data using three separation bands, some commercial digital still and video cameras use color filter arrays that consist of four different types of filter. The devices that use more than three relatively broad spectral bands will be referred to as *multispectral* imaging devices. Modeling these devices is a straightforward extension of Eq. (10.2). As discussed in Chapter (9, these devices are better at correcting for illumination variations. NASA's

Mars Rovers' cameras contain 11 unique color filters for imaging, in addition to a blue and infrared filter pair for solar imaging and tracking.

Cameras that measure using many evenly spaced narrow wavelength bands are referred to as *hyperspectral* imaging devices. The bands can be within or outside the visible range. Hyperspectral imaging is used heavily in remote sensing imagery, where the primary application is detection and classification of objects and terrain features.

The technology used to achieve color separation in hyperspectral and multispectral devices is varied. There are, of course, extensions of the standard color separation methods using color filter wheels [288] or spatial mosaics with more than three filter types. The more unique methods make use of specialty devices like the acousto-optic tunable filter (AOTF) [233]. The AOTF consists of a piezo-electric transducer attached to a birefringent material.[5] A varying electrical signal (typically an RF signal) applied to the transducer induces a periodic redistribution of the refractive index through the material, which causes it to behave like a transmission diffraction grating. Changes in the frequency of the transducer signal vary the period of the refractive index variation and thus the wavelength of light that is diffracted.

Another approach to hyperspectral imaging, especially for airborne systems, is shown in Fig. 10.18. In this figure, the camera is in motion in the $x$ direction and it captures a line of the image along the $y$ direction similar to a flat-bed scanner, as discussed in Section 10.1. Here however, the light is sent to a dispersing element and separated into its spectral components. For each scan line, a 2-D signal is captured, whose dimensions are the spatial direction $y$ and the spectral wavelength. At the completion of a scan, a 3-D data structure, called an image cube, is obtained, consisting of the two spatial dimensions and a wavelength dimension.

## 10.4    Problems

**10.1**    Compare the advantages and disadvantages of image scanners that use a single sensor with those that use solid-state array sensors.

**10.2**    Consider the CCD scanner system that uses the 3-row RGB linear array described in Section 10.1. Write a matrix equation that models the data measurement process. Identify all components of the system with their corresponding matrix. Identify all sources of noise and indicate plausible density functions for them.

**10.3**    Consider the CCD scanner system that uses a 3-row RGB linear array, described in Section 10.1. Indicate the possible optical distortions of the device and give plausible mathematical models.

**10.4**    Consider the CIS scanner system that uses a 1-row linear array with colored LEDs, described in Section 10.1. Write a matrix equation that models the data measurement process. Identify all components of the system with their corresponding matrix. Identify all sources of noise and indicate plausible density functions for them.

---

[5] This is crystal material, which has two indices of refraction, each associated with different polarizations.

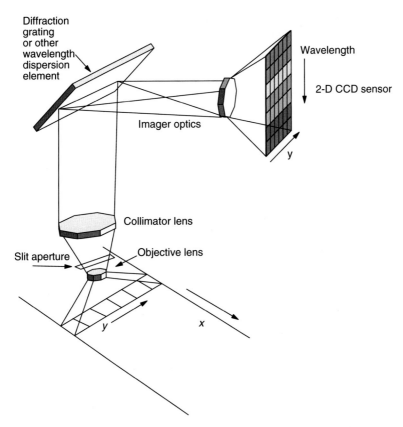

Diffraction grating or other wavelength dispersion element

Wavelength

2-D CCD sensor

Imager optics

$y$

Collimator lens

Slit aperture

Objective lens

$y$       $x$

**Figure 10.18.** Example of a hyperspectral camera: the camera moves in the $x$ direction, collecting scan lines along the $y$ direction; each scan line pixel is dispersed into its spectral components and sampled with a 2-D CCD array (for color version, please see Plate 12).

**10.5**   Consider the CIS scanner system that uses a 1-row linear array with colored LEDs, described in Section 10.1. Indicate the possible optical distortions of the device and give plausible mathematical models.

**10.6**   Create an 8-bit ADC differential nonlinearity using a uniform random number generator. Assume that the ADC digitizes the voltage range 0–5V. You should justify the range you use for the uniform distribution.

(a) Plot the function indicating the error between the actual ADC output and the ideal output.
(b) Use the actual and ideal ADC output to generate monochrome versions of your chosen example image, *gray-one* (See Problem section of Chapter 3). You can create a simulated continuous (nonquantized) version of your digital image by adding uniform white noise with a range equal to one quantization interval. Compare the two images visually, noting places where they differ noticeably.
(c) Use the actual and ideal ADC output to generate color versions of your chosen example image, *gray-one*.

**10.7**   Using the $\cos^4(x)$ model of irradiance fall-off, find a range of angles that approximates Fig. 10.7. How well does the mathematical approximation match the actual measurements? Visual examination is sufficient.

**10.8**   It was noted in the discussion of autofocusing of cameras that a histogram could be used. Show that in general, we can expect

(a) the minimum of the in-focus image to be less than the minimum of a blurred version of the same image;
(b) the maximum of the in-focus image to be greater than the maximum of a blurred version of the same image;
(c) the mean of the in-focus image to be the same as that of a blurred version of the same image.

Note that we are not asking for a mathematical proof. There exist cases where all three statements are not true.

**10.9**   Using your chosen image, *image-one*, compare the histograms for a single channel for the original and three blurred versions of various severity.

**10.10**   Using the color version of *image-one*, create simulated mosaicked data by subsampling the R, G and B channels using a Bayer pattern.

(a) Create an interpolated approximation to the original by using bilinear interpolation on each channel.
(b) Compare the original and interpolated images. Note any color artifacts.
(c) Use other mosaic patterns that use only RGB filters combined with bilinear interpolation. Compare the results with the Bayer result.
(d) Note that patterns that use CMY filters would require transformation from your RGB data to CMY data before subsampling. Write a flow chart to describe the steps required to simulate a CMYG array.

**10.11**   Derive the estimate for **d**, in Eq. (10.5), using the matrix differentiation of Appendix B.

**10.12**   A reasonable project, but not homework, would be to compare several demosaicking methods.

**10.13**   Explain in detail the reason for the appearance of the fourth (right-most) section of Fig. 10.16, which represents an image processed using compensation for daylight illumination when the image was actually taken under tungsten light.

**10.14**   Using your chosen image, *image-one*, create a $3 \times 3$ diagonal transform that would simulate the following color balance mismatches:

(a) Flash illumination with tungsten white balance,
(b) Tungsten illumination with fluorescent white balance,
(c) Fluorescent illumination with daylight (D65) white balance,
(d) Daylight (D65) illumination with tungsten white balance,
(e) Flash illumination with daylight (D65) white balance.

# 11 Image output devices and methods

In the previous chapter, input devices were discussed. The methods and problems of converting an analog image to a digital form that can be stored and processed in a computer were presented. In this chapter, we explore the devices and methods for displaying this digital image data. The ideal method for displaying a digital image depends upon the user's intent. That intent may be information transfer, analysis or aesthetics. The requirements for each of these purposes determine the necessary modality and quality of the reproduction.

The important characteristics of an output image include:

- Permanence,
- Cost,
- Accuracy,
- Display conditions,
- Size,
- Number of copies.

These characteristics should be considered as the following output technologies are discussed: CRT monitors, LCD displays, photography, electrophotography, commercial printing, e.g., gravure, offset, ink-jet printing and thermal transfer devices.

## 11.1    Cathode ray tube monitors

The cathode ray tube (CRT) was invented in 1897 by Karl Ferdinand Braun. Today, color CRT monitors are a common soft-copy output device. While black and white monitors are used for some text and document applications, color has become so economical that almost all imaging applications use color monitors.

Most color CRTs use three independent electron guns for each of the three primary phosphors. The guns can be arranged in line or in a triangle (delta) geometry, the geometries of which are shown in Figs. 11.1a and b. The Trinitron$^{TM}$ gun actually uses three cathodes in a single gun. All systems require a control grid, acceleration grid, focusing coil, and deflection coil, as shown in Fig. 11.2 [96]. The three beams are modulated in intensity, and as the electron beams hit the screen phosphors, the energy is converted to visible light.

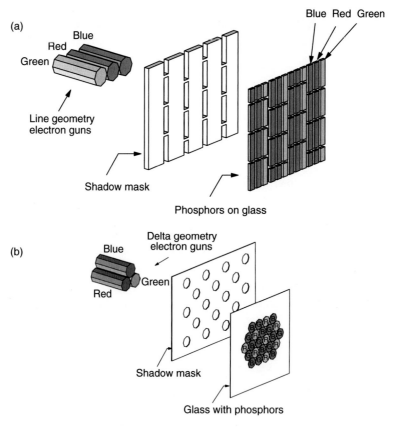

**Figure 11.1.**  (a) CRT geometry with in-line electron guns; (b) CRT geometry with delta electron guns (for color version, please see Plate 13).

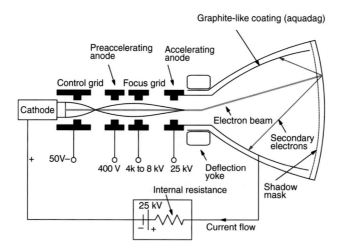

**Figure 11.2.**  Basic CRT components.

The intensity of the light is a nonlinear function of the electron beam current. The current is a linear function of the control grid voltage, which is determined by the sample values in the image memory. The nonlinear function, $l_\lambda(\cdot)$, for screen radiance at a particular wavelength, $\lambda$, versus input voltage is usually modeled as a power law device,

$$l_\lambda(V_{cg}) = K_\lambda(V_{cg} - V_0)^\gamma,$$

where $V_{cg}$ is the control grid voltage, $V_0$ is the cut-off (or minimum) voltage, $\gamma$ models the exponential nonlinearity and $K_\lambda$ is a constant to account for the radiometric dimensionality. Since the image memory contains discrete quantized values, $n\Delta V$, the model can be written

$$l_\lambda(n) = K_\lambda(ak\Delta V \frac{n}{n_{max}} + akV_{min} + b - V_0)^\gamma, \qquad (11.1)$$

where $V_{min}$ is the voltage of the black pixels in the image ($n = 0$); $\Delta V = V_{max} - V_{min}$; $V_{max}$ is the maximum voltage ($n = n_{max}$); the constant $k$ accounts for the voltage drop due to the resistance of the transmission path; the constant $a$ is the video amplifier gain determined by the contrast control; the constant $b$ is the offset determined by the brightness control; and to avoid using too many symbols, the function $l_\lambda(\cdot)$ is used with the discrete value $n$. Analysis and characterization can be simplified by using the ratio [25, 26, 175],

$$\frac{l_\lambda(n)}{l_\lambda(n_{max})} = \left(\frac{n - x_0}{n_{max} - x_0}\right)^\gamma, \qquad (11.2)$$

where

$$x_0 = \frac{n_{max}(V_0 - b - akV_{min})}{ak\Delta V},$$

instead of Eq. (11.1). The use of Eq. (11.2) for calibration of the monitor will be discussed in Chapter 12.

For high ambient lighting conditions, the light reflected off the display may affect the perceived image. This effect is called *flare* and it can be included in the above model as an additive term that depends upon the illumination and the reflectance properties of the display.

The screen of the color CRT is made of small areas of red, green and blue phosphors. The colorimetric properties of these phosphors are discussed in Chapter 8. The area patterns most common are vertical strips or triads of the dots, depending on the geometry of the electron guns (see Fig. 11.1). The electron beams for each color need to be directed to only the appropriate phosphor. This is done using a shadow mask. The principle of the shadow mask for two color guns is shown in Fig. 11.3. Shadow masks vary in their design, as shown in Fig. 11.1.

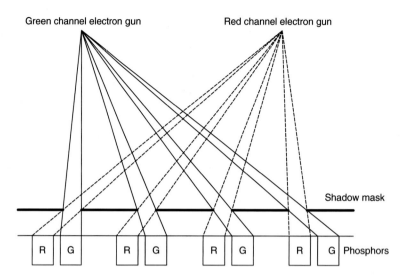

**Figure 11.3.** Shadow mask illustration.

The modulation transfer function (MTF) of the CRT changes with the displayed light level [190]. As the brightness increases, the MTF becomes more low pass. The blurring effect at the high brightness levels is often called *blooming*.

The persistence of the phosphors, which is the duration they emit visible light after excitation, affects the quality of video display and the required refresh rate for quality display. If the persistence is too low, then the display may flicker. If the persistence is too high, then there may be smearing artifacts when video is displayed, i.e., moving objects leave trails. For color displays, the persistence of the three phosphor types is usually different, which can lead to the appearance of chromatic artifacts in video.

It is clear that the monochrome monitor does not need a shadow mask and, thus, can produce a higher resolution image. The elimination of the shadow mask and the use of white phosphors on a monochrome monitor also produce a brighter picture.

## 11.2     Flat panel displays

The term *flat panel display* refers to various systems that use solid-state elements to control the pixel color and brightness. This eliminates the bulky CRT and allows a relatively flat display. Early flat panel displays suffered from low luminance, poor color and significant dependence on viewing angle. Flat panel technology is rapidly changing [179, 243, 247, 305, 306] and, with the solution of these problems, it is likely that flat panel displays will cause the demise of CRT displays. Most flat panel displays have the advantage of being thinner, lighter, and less power hungry than a CRT. In addition, in typical viewing conditions, flat panel displays have a larger dynamic range than CRT displays [243].

A common flat panel technology in laptop PCs is the liquid crystal display. Liquid crystals were discovered by Friedrich Reinitzer in 1888, but were not considered to be of much use until 1963 when Robert Williams discovered their electro-optic features. Two years later, George Heilmeier invented an LCD [143].

The active matrix version of the LCD is shown in Fig. 11.4. The system of Fig. 11.4a consists of:

- A backlight, typically a fluorescent source, which may be at the top, side or directly behind the display screen;
- A diffusing element, which scatters the light from the lamp to produce a more uniform illumination;
- A rear polarizing element, which transmits light of only one polarization;
- A glass element with thin film transistors (TFTs);
- A liquid crystal layer, which provides control for the amount of light that will reach the viewer;
- A front glass element with color filters;
- A front polarizer element, which transmits only light that is perpendicular in polarization to that of the rear polarizer (see Fig. 11.5).

To reduce power consumption, and improve efficiency, the backlight typically has peaks in the red, green and blue spectral regions. Ideally, these peaks should be matched to the red, green and blue filters of the screen. To obtain a reasonable image when driven by the same digital signals that produce an image on a CRT, the combination of backlight and color filters are designed to produce chromaticities close to those of the CRT phosphors [243].

Less common today is also a passive matrix LCD display.[1]

The purpose of the liquid crystal element is to change the polarization of the light. This change in polarization is illustrated in Fig. 11.5, where in one state the crystal changes the light's polarization (it actually twists the light) allowing it to be transmitted to the viewer. In the other state, it does not change the polarization, which causes it to be blocked by the front polarizer. Gray (or color) gradations are created by partial voltage application to the crystal. There are several methods used to modulate the light polarization. Early devices used twisted nematic[2] (TN) liquid crystals. This approach is quickly being replaced by multidomain vertical alignment (MVA) and in-plane switching (IPS) technologies, which offer improvements in terms of brightness, contrast, response time and viewing angle [260].

The amount of light that reaches the output is a nonlinear function of voltage. For a large nonspatially varying color region, a colorimetric model for the system shown in

---

[1] The nonactive or passive LCD lacks the thin film transistors of the active version. Instead, to apply current to the crystal, a voltage is applied along a selected row (column) and a ground is applied along a selected column (row). The resulting current directly powers the selected LCD element. Such a system is much slower than the active system and is rarely used today, owing to its limitations for video applications.

[2] The terms nematic, smectic and cholesteric refer to different molecular orientations.

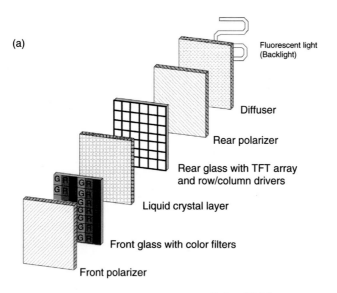

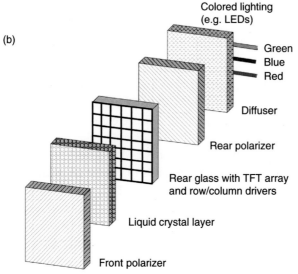

**Figure 11.4.** (a) Typical components for active matrix LCD display with white backlighting; (b) example of an LCD display with three colored lights which are time multiplexed (for color version, please see Plate 14).

Fig. 11.4 is given by

$$\mathbf{t} = \mathbf{A}^T \mathbf{LDPTF}(\mathbf{Rc}(V_r) + \mathbf{Gc}(V_g) + \mathbf{Bc}(V_b)), \tag{11.3}$$

where the parameters are as follows:

- **t**: CIEXYZ value shown on display,
- **A**: CIEXYZ color matching functions,

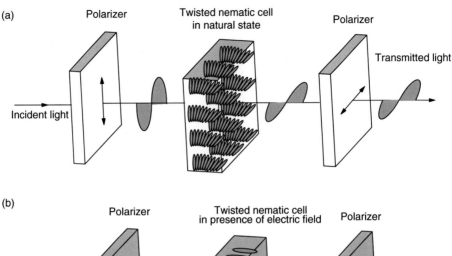

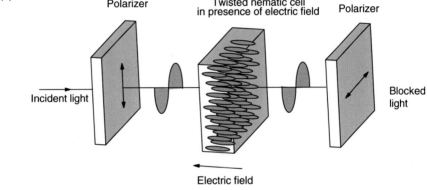

**Figure 11.5.** (a) In its natural state, the crystal rotates the light to change its polarization by 90 degrees, and the light then passes through the output polarizer; (b) an electric field is applied to the crystal and the liquid crystals align with the electric field, causing no change in the passing light's polarization: the polarized light is then blocked by the front polarizer.

- **L**: Diagonal matrix containing the spectral power distribution of the lamp,
- **D**: Diagonal matrix containing the spectral transmittance of the diffusing element,
- **P**: Diagonal matrix containing the spectral transmittance of the rear polarizer,
- **T**: Diagonal matrix containing the spectral transmittance of the TFT layer,
- **F**: Diagonal matrix containing the spectral transmittance of the front polarizer,
- **R**: Diagonal matrix containing the spectral transmittance of the red filters,
- **G**: Diagonal matrix containing the spectral transmittance of the green filters,
- **B**: Diagonal matrix containing the spectral transmittance of the blue filters,
- $\mathbf{c}(V)$: Vector containing the spectral transmittance of the liquid crystal at a voltage level $V$,
- $V_r$: Voltage level for liquid crystals associated with red pixels,
- $V_g$: Voltage level for liquid crystals associated with green pixels,
- $V_b$: Voltage level for liquid crystals associated with blue pixels.

The nonlinearity $\mathbf{c}(V)$, which defines the crystal transmittance as a function of voltage, depends upon the type of crystals that are used in the display. Figure 11.6 displays the relationship for twisted nematic crystals. The large voltage difference between on and off voltages shown in Fig. 11.6 is difficult for high speed switching systems to achieve in display applications. This problem is overcome through the use of super-twisted nematic crystals, which have much smaller on–off voltage differences. Since gray (or color gradations) are achieved by partial voltage application, close on–off voltages can affect the number of achievable grayscale levels or addressable color values, owing to the system's extreme sensitivity.

Often, the spectral transmittance of the LCD is approximated by a constant spectrum, **s**, that is scaled by a nonlinear function of applied voltage $G(V)$ [243]. In this case, the voltage dependent transmittance is modeled as

$$\mathbf{c}(V) = \mathbf{s}G(V),$$

where $G$ is a scalar monotonic function. As shown in Fig. 11.6, the system will have some transmission of light even at high voltages. The nonlinearity is significantly different from the power law model for a CRT given in Section 11.1. For this reason, the CRT model works poorly as a model for an LCD display [243]. The LCD software driver may contain 1-D look-up tables, which make the overall system (driver and display) have a nonlinearity similar to a CRT. Alternatively, it is possible to achieve the same effect by introducing a nonlinearity in the system's digital-to-analog converter (DAC). The nonlinearity in the DAC can be implemented using nonuniform resistor ladders or multiple reference voltages.

In the active matrix LCD display, each color element of a pixel is controlled by a single thin film transistor (TFT). The use of a transistor with a capacitor for holding the charge enables creation of larger displays, since the refresh cycle can be longer. Faster switching liquid crystal materials enable the viewing of video on LCD displays. Arising from the legacy of CRT displays, a once common interface of an LCD display with a desktop computer is shown in Fig. 11.7, where the image is converted from digital data to an analog video signal and then back to a digital signal for the LCD controller. The sampling rate of the ADC is dependent upon the refresh rate of the incoming video signal and the number of pixels in the LCD. The conversion from digital to analog and back to digital will create distortions. Standards for direct digital interface to the display digital controllers have been established [67].[3]

One variant of the above system is to cycle in time between red, green and blue LED light sources (in place of the single light source) and have no color filters. Figure 11.4b shows such a system. Light emitting diodes are ideal for this application due to their long life, low power consumption and the variety of color choices. An engineering challenge is to obtain a uniform illumination on the display with the large number of LEDs, which often vary significantly in their efficiency. This approach has the obvious advantage of improved resolution over the color filter approach. Prototype

---

[3] The standards are (high-definition multimedia interface) HDMI and (digital video interface) DVI, the latter of which comes in a variety of flavors and is a source of confusion for nontechnical consumers (and some technical ones!) setting up a home theater.

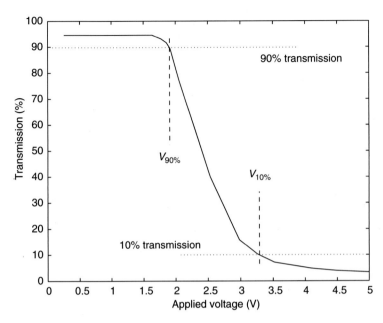

**Figure 11.6.** Relationship between transmission and voltage for twisted nematic pixel cell (on axis viewing).

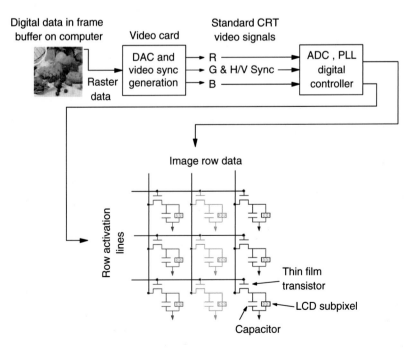

**Figure 11.7.** A once common interface for LCD displays (for color version, please see Plate 15).

hybrid systems that use multiple illuminant colors and multiple colored filters have also been designed, which provide improvements in the display gamut and luminous efficiency [247].

It is possible to create displays with very large gamuts by using more than three LED colors. Besides the illumination uniformity issue, using more than three colors of LEDs complicates the design of the transformation to the display control values. This is because different control values can create the same color. This problem is related to one of halftoning with more than three color inks, which will be discussed in Section 12.3.8. There are also prototype displays that combine LED arrays and an LCD display [237]. Each element of the LED array can be controlled with 8 bits, as can each LCD element, making for a high dynamic range system. With today's LED technology, the spatial resolution of the LED array is much lower than the LCD display.

The fast switching times of current LCD displays presents an interesting problem for video of moving objects. The CRT displays relied on phosphor persistence to make smooth transitions from frame to frame. The LCD units behave more like sample-and-hold circuits, which can give the appearance of discontinuous jumpy movements (judder), or blur [151, 156, 203]. Perceived blur on LCDs is actually caused by a combination of two different phenomena. The first is the slow response time of the liquid crystal material. The second and more dominant source is due to the fact that a quickly moving object is held stationary on screen between frames, but the eye naturally tracks the motion smoothly. In this case, the perceived blur is caused by image smearing on the retina [156, 204]. Considering the eye like any sensor, the effect is similar to motion blur (where the sensor is moving but the object is still), which is discussed in Section 13.5.2.

Other flat panel technologies include field-emission displays [133], organic LED displays [80] and plasma displays [275]. Each of these have their own advantages, which may be in manufacturability, flexibility, efficiency, CRT-like images or resolution. Although some of the above displays create a color image by subtracting (or filtering) portions of a white light source, they are all additive color systems. Those that begin with a white light source are optically equivalent to a system with three light sources that have the spectral distributions of the filtered light sources.

There are flat panel systems that are not emissive devices like the above systems, but are reflective. These systems have the advantage of working well in bright environments, e.g., outdoors. They are often used in mobile devices, where power consumption is a major design concern [149]. Some of these display systems are being developed as alternatives to hard copy [62]. There are also transreflective displays that mix reflective and emissive elements within each pixel. These displays have the advantage of working well in a variety of lighting conditions, while saving power in bright lighting conditions [131, 149, 306].

Figure 11.8 displays a diagram model for one pixel of a cholesteric LCD color reflective display. Each layer has reflectance properties that lie between two extreme states. In one state, the layer will reflect a spectral range of energy, e.g., a blue band,

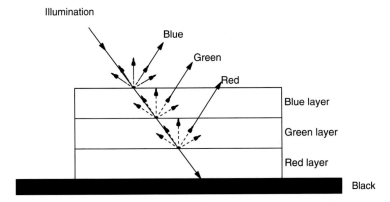

**Figure 11.8.** Reflective cholesteric LCD flat panel system.

while letting energy in other parts of the spectral range continue to the next layer. In its other state, the layer will be transparent to the spectral band that it previously reflected.

By using three layers that respectively reflect and transmit red, green and blue, a full color display can be created. Like printed images, the color reflected from this display depends upon the illumination. Tonal qualities are achieved by using voltage levels on the cholesteric LCD that are between the two extreme states (similar to the active matrix LCD previously discussed). Once the voltage level has been applied, the cholesteric LCD is stable and power can be removed without losing the image. This stability has the unfortunate aspect of causing long refresh times, making the cholesteric LCD unsuitable for video.

Unlike the other flat panel systems discussed, the system shown in Fig. 11.8 is not a simple additive color system. In one sense, the system is similar to a subtractive system, but instead of absorbing a color, e.g., yellow absorbing blue, blue is reflected. A mathematical model for the CIEXYZ value of a single pixel could be expressed as

$$\mathbf{t}(\beta, \gamma, \rho) = \mathbf{A}^T \mathbf{L}[\mathbf{b}(\beta) + \mathbf{F}_b(\beta)\mathbf{B}_b(\beta)(\mathbf{g}(\gamma) + \mathbf{F}_g(\gamma)\mathbf{B}_g(\beta)$$

$$(\mathbf{r}(\rho) + \mathbf{F}_r(\rho)\mathbf{B}_r(\rho)\mathbf{k}))], \tag{11.4}$$

where $\beta$, $\gamma$ and $\rho$ are the voltage levels that are applied to the blue, green and red layers respectively; $\mathbf{b}$, $\mathbf{g}$ and $\mathbf{r}$ are the reflectance spectra of the blue, green and red layers; $\mathbf{B}_b$, $\mathbf{B}_g$ and $\mathbf{B}_r$ are the diagonal matrices representing the backward (coming back to the viewer) transmission spectra of the blue, green and red layers; $\mathbf{F}_b$, $\mathbf{F}_g$ and $\mathbf{F}_r$ are the diagonal matrices representing the forward (going away from the viewer) transmission spectra of the blue, green and red layers; and $\mathbf{k}$ is the reflectance spectrum of the absorbing black backing.

## 11.3    Photographic film and paper

The world's first photograph was made by Joseph Nicéphore Niépce in 1827. The exposure lasted eight hours and Niépce had difficulty permanently fixing the latent image. Louis Jacques Mandé Daguerre partnered with Niépce in 1829 and is credited with determining a method for permanently fixing the latent image in 1837. The method created a positive image on a metal support and was called a daguerreotype. The process was time consuming and difficult for the average consumer. The introduction of flexible film in 1884 by George Eastman was a significant improvement. The real mass market breakthrough occurred in 1888 with the introduction of the film roll by George Eastman.[4]

Today, photographic images are the often selected choice for high quality. Film provides high resolution, a wide selection of exposure ranges, longevity and readily available processing options. The most common film is used to produce color prints as the final product. Before this process can be studied, it is necessary to review monochromatic film recording.

### 11.3.1    Monochromatic film

The film is basically an emulsion spread on a transparent base as shown in Fig. 11.9. The emulsion is made of silver halide grains in a gelatin. A halide is an element in the 7th column of the periodic table, e.g., chlorine, bromine and iodine. Silver bromide is the compound most often used. The base may consist of several sublayers for special purposes. It is common to have an anti-halation layer to reduce the reflection of light from the base back into the emulsion and an anti-static layer to reduce electrical discharges that can expose the film.

When light strikes a silver halide grain, a photochemical reaction causes a development center to be formed. The development center will cause the entire grain to be converted to metallic silver in the chemical development process. Note that a single

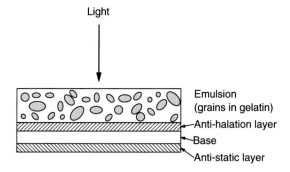

**Figure 11.9.** Monochrome negative film.

---

[4] Although George Eastman provided the masses with film rolls and cameras, the patent for the film roll was awarded to Rev. Hannibal Goodwin and infringed upon for many years by the Eastman Kodak Company.

photon hitting a single grain will not cause development. It normally takes at least three photons within a given time to produce a development center. The image is created by removing all of the undeveloped grains.

The exposure, $e$, of the film is the product of the intensity of the light, $i$, times the time the film is exposed to light, $t$,

$$e = i \times t.$$

From this equation, we obtain the reciprocity property of film. The exposure remains constant as long as the intensity and time produce the same product. If the intensity is doubled by opening the aperture to allow twice as much light, the time must be halved to retain the same exposure. Reciprocity failure occurs at low intensities and long time exposures, when the three photon hits do not occur within the critical time.

The conversion of exposure to optical density is based on the following assumptions:

1. The number of grains of silver exposed is proportional to the number of photons allowed to strike the film (intensity $\times$ time).
2. The mass of silver present after development is proportional to the number of grains exposed.
2. The density of silver is proportional to the number of grains exposed.

The transmission of the film is the ratio of the intensity of the light that passes through the film to the intensity of the source. As discussed in Section 8.4.2, transmission can be either diffuse or specular and is given by

$$T = \frac{I_{\text{out}}}{I_{\text{in}}}.$$

Since optical transmission is related exponentially to the density of the silver, we have

$$T = e^{-\alpha dx},$$

where $d$ is the density of the silver, $x$ is the thickness of the film or emulsion and $\alpha$ is a constant relating the physical properties of the silver to the probability that a photon will pass through the film. Recalling the relationship in 8.4.2, we note here that optical density is proportional to physical density as

$$D = -\log_{10}(T) = [\log_{10}(e^{\alpha dx})] = Kd.$$

A photographic print would be characterized by reflectivity instead of transmission. Density would be defined analogously. The same concepts can be applied to any printed medium, e.g., prints from a thermal writer, pages from an offset press.

The optical density as a function of exposure is the relation of interest for photography. A typical curve of density versus exposure for black and white films is shown in Fig. 11.10. The curves are sometimes called H and D curves after Hurter and Driffield,

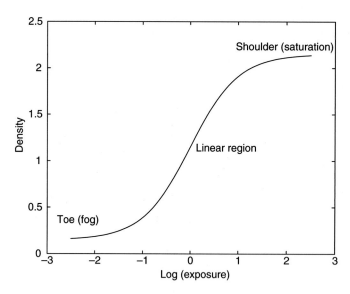

**Figure 11.10.** Typical density versus log(exposure) curve for negative film.

who developed the method for their determination. The linear portion of the curve is represented by

$$d = \gamma[\log_{10}(E)] + K,$$

where $\gamma$ represents the slope of the curve and $K$ is the linear offset value. High values of $\gamma$ correspond to high contrast film.

### 11.3.2    Color film

Color film is a sandwich of layers of emulsions. Instead of metallic silver, the final layers consist of varying densities of dyes. The layers for color negative film are shown in Fig. 11.11. Each of the layers has a $D$–$\log E$ curve similar to that of black and white film, but each curve may have a unique shape.

Figure 11.12 displays a color negative film after exposure to yellow (red plus green) light. In this case, the green and red sensitive layers react to the exposure, but the blue sensitive layer does not react. The development of the exposed negative in Fig. 11.12 creates an image on the film that contains magenta (green absorbing) dye and cyan (red absorbing) dye but no yellow (blue absorbing) dye. The negative will appear blue, the complementary color to the yellow light that exposed the film.

### 11.3.3    Photographic prints

As mentioned, most people have their photographic images printed upon color photographic paper. The conventional process for creating prints from color negative

Before development

| Blue sensitive emulsion |
| Yellow filter |
| Green sensitive emulsion |
| Red sensitive emulsion |
| Base (transparent) |
| Anti-halation layer |

After development

| Yellow (blue absorbing) dye |
| Clear |
| Magenta (green absorbing) dye |
| Cyan (red absorbing) dye |
| Base (transparent) |
| Clear |

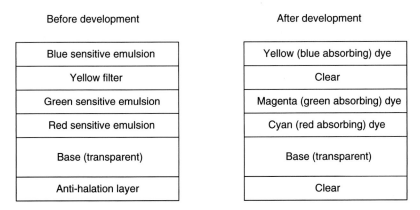

**Figure 11.11.** Color negative film.

Yellow light (no blue)

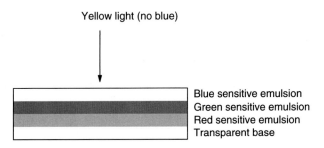

Blue sensitive emulsion
Green sensitive emulsion
Red sensitive emulsion
Transparent base

**Figure 11.12.** Color negative film exposed to yellow light (for color version, please see Plate 17).

film is to project white light through the developed film onto the unexposed color print paper. The light passes through a projection system to enlarge or reduce the image size. In Fig. 11.13, the negative film created in Fig. 11.12 is used to create the yellow input image on a color print. When white light is illuminated through the film, red and green portions are absorbed and blue light is transmitted. In Fig. 11.13, this blue light is imaged to expose the photographic paper, where only the blue sensitive layer reacts. When the photographic paper is developed, only yellow dye will be present, which is the color of the original exposing light.

Today, it is more common to create photographic prints directly from digital images. In this case, there is no developed film negative. The positive digital image, recorded in RGB, is electronically converted to a negative to expose the paper. The modern digital lab (the large machine behind the counter at the photo store) exposes the color print media by controlling red, green and blue lasers. The lasers are modulated by the image pixels as they scan the print media. Alternatively, liquid crystal displays can be used to control the amount of blue, green and red light that reaches the paper. Note that the same chemical process of the photographic paper still takes place as described above.

The small photo kiosks that are customer operated often use a dye-sublimation print process (see Section 11.8) to produce prints at the kiosks. A variation on this is a kiosk

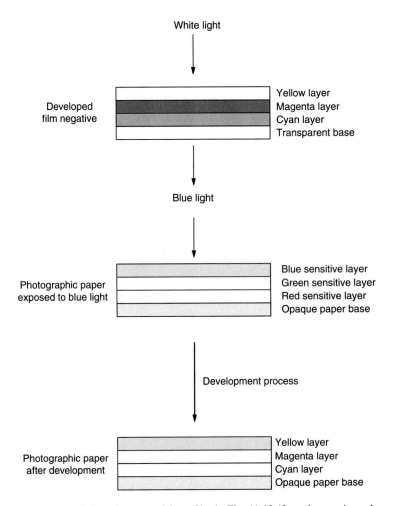

**Figure 11.13.** Color print created from film in Fig. 11.12 (for color version, please see Plate 18).

that allows the customer to manipulate the image and then send a file to the lab behind the counter. The dye-sublimation prints can be of photographic quality. However, for high-volume printing, the digital lab is faster and more cost effective.

## 11.4    Commercial printing

Printing is by far the oldest method of mass image reproduction. Of course, painting is the oldest imaging method, but it cannot be used for the reproduction of large numbers of images. The Chinese block printing methods are the oldest form of printing, dating to the seventh century (T'ang Dynasty). The Chinese actually developed a movable type in the

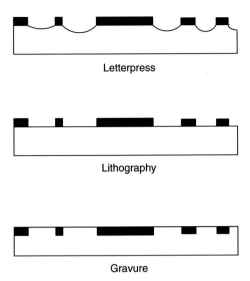

**Figure 11.14.** Printing technologies illustration.

tenth century prior to Gutenberg's invention in the middle 1400s. The Koreans invented a phonetic alphabet that could take advantage of the new printing method. Unfortunately, because of the high status of the Chinese style, the new method did not become popular.

Printing is a binary display technology. The ink is either present or absent. Tonal qualities are achieved by halftoning, which will be addressed shortly. There are three basic types of printing technologies: letterpress, lithography and gravure. In letterpress printing, the spaces of the printing plate are engraved, leaving a raised surface to carry the ink. In lithography, the surface of a printing plate is treated so that the ink is attracted to only certain parts of the plate. In gravure printing, the part of the plate to contain the ink is engraved. The three technologies are illustrated in Fig. 11.14.

The ink is transferred to the paper by pressure in the case of letterpress and lithography. In gravure printing, the plate is actually a cylinder that is rotated at high speed. The ink is transferred by centrifugal force. Letterpress is used for single color printing and usually for printing runs of 500–10 000 copies.

Lithography and gravure are used for multiple color printing. Four inks are common: usually cyan, magenta, yellow and black, but presses are made to use as many as eight to ten inks. The additional inks are used for printing special objects, such as company logos. In some ink-jet printing systems, which will be discussed in detail later, hi-fidelity versions exist that use up to eight inks including the standard cyan, magenta, yellow and black inks. There are also several desktop ink-jet printers, which include a light cyan and light magenta ink, in addition to the standard cyan and magenta inks. The purpose of these lighter inks is to reduce halftone artifact visibility in the image highlights. In some recently developed systems, a gray ink is used to give a more pleasing reproduction of light neutral areas.

The lithographic process uses the offset method for most applications. In offset printing, the image on the plate is transferred to a flexible sheet and then to the paper. This transfer saves wear on the plate so that it lasts longer. Press runs for lithography are from 5000–200 000 copies. The gravure cylinders are engraved and then chromed for use on very large jobs. Press runs are from 100 000–2 000 000 copies.

## 11.5    Halftone reproduction

Since printing is an all-or-nothing method, gray tones and color tones are obtained by halftoning. This method assumes that the image will be viewed from a distance and that the parameter of interest is the average color in an area of the printed image. Figure 11.15 displays a typical view that one would see when viewing a halftoned image under magnification.

Although the fundamental concepts of halftoning have been used for years in weaving and engraving, William Henry (Fox) Talbot is credited with introducing the photomechanical halftoning process in 1852. The earliest halftones were produced by photographing a sandwich of the image of interest and a halftone mask onto high contrast film. The process can be illustrated in one dimension.

Referring to Fig. 11.16, consider the original image denoted by $f(x)$ and the halftone mask denoted by $h(x)$. The halftone mask is a periodic continuous tone function. The

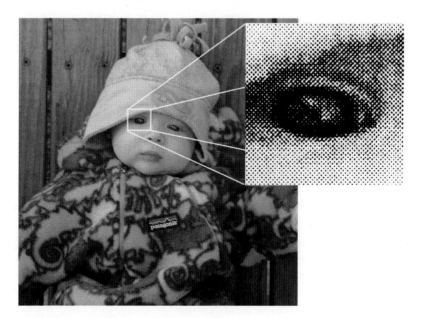

**Figure 11.15.** Magnification of halftoned image.

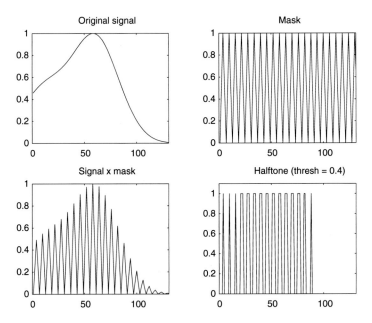

**Figure 11.16.** Halftone example (one dimension).

sandwich is the product of the two, $s(x) = f(x)h(x)$. The halftone image is obtained by thresholding the sandwich:

$$s_h(x) = \begin{cases} d_{\max} & \text{if } s(x) \geq \alpha \\ d_{\min} & \text{if } s(x) < \alpha. \end{cases}$$

For the example of Fig. 11.16, the original signal and mask are normalized to unity, $d_{\min} = 0.2$ and $d_{\max} = 1.8$.

In the actual printing process, the mask may be either binary or continuous tone. The tonal effect produced by the binary screen is caused by "blooming," which is the result of adjacency effects in the over-exposed image, or by diffraction. The binary mask can be photographed by a slightly out-of-focus lens to produce a "vignetted dot," which has continuous tone.

Two-dimensional masking can produce moire patterns. These effects are basically frequency aliasing. The halftone mask can be thought of as a sampling function. No spatial frequency can be recorded in the halftone image that is greater than half the frequency of the mask. This is the result of the sampling theorem of Chapter 6. The moire patterns can result from high spatial frequencies in the original image or halftoning an image that is already halftoned. This is frequently a problem with graytone reproduction in electrophotographic copying. An example of this effect is shown later in Fig. 11.30. Figure 11.17 shows an example of a moire pattern that was created from two screens of the same frequency. The screens were rotated 12 degrees relative to one another. Note that there are both higher and lower frequencies present in Fig. 11.17. Problem 11.10 gives

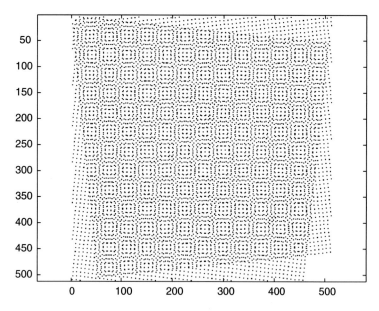

**Figure 11.17.** Moire pattern produced by overlapping two screens that were rotated 12 degrees from one another.

an exercise to explore the mathematics of moire patterns based on the use of sampling functions.

### Digital halftone

With the advent of digital computers and desktop publishing, most digitally controlled printers print on a rectangular grid (or raster). Each dot is approximately the same size and shape. The positions of the dots are spaced so that the printed dots overlap slightly. This overlap allows the approximation of a continuous line on the paper.

While many devices allow variation in dot size, let's start our discussion assuming a fixed dot size. In this case, the halftone effect is achieved by varying the number of dots within a given area. This process produces a trade-off between the output device's resolution and the number of apparent tonal levels. It is clear that for the same screen frequency, the continuous halftone mask will produce better results than the digital printer. For the digital printer to be competitive, it must have a higher raster frequency than the continuous halftone mask. Usually, a factor of four to eight is sufficient to achieve similar quality. The digital printer can simulate the varying size of the halftone dots on its sampling raster. However, there can be many more and varied dot patterns than a simple size progression of solid dots.

The fundamental idea of digital halftone is the same as continuous halftone, that is, simulate a gray tone by using the average value of the area of binary dots. With analog halftone methods, the only way to vary the average graytone is to vary the size of a single dot within that area. Digital halftoning allows the average to be obtained by many different patterns. The average is obtained by the fraction of available positions filled by

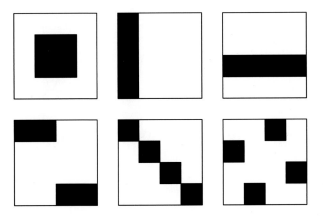

**Figure 11.18.** Examples of 0.25 average halftone reflectance.

dots. If there are $N$ positions and $n$ are filled, the average reflectance is

$$r_a(\lambda) = \frac{n}{N} r_b(\lambda) + \frac{N-n}{N} r_w(\lambda),$$

where $r_b(\lambda)$ is the reflectance of the ink on paper and $r_w(\lambda)$ is the reflectance of the paper alone. For example, an average reflection of 0.25 can be obtained by any of the patterns in Fig. 11.18. The aesthetic quality produced by the patterns can vary greatly, and is the subject of much research.

The above calculation of reflectance is based on the assumption that the dots completely fill an area and do not overlap. In practice, the dots are nominally circular or elliptical and must overlap to produce a continuous line. The actual reflectance depends on:

1. Amount of overlap,
2. Spatial pattern (determines number of overlapped dots),
3. Variation in dot position,
4. Variation in dot size,
5. Variation in dot shape.

There are many algorithms for determining what dot pattern will be used to represent a particular gray-level pixel. One simple approach is to map every pixel within a certain range to a fixed pattern with the appropriate reflectance. A problem with such an approach is that such repeated patterns are readily visible to the eye. To reduce visible artifacts, more complicated patterns can be used. Several patterns with the same nominal reflectances may be selected at random to break up the repetition. Alternatively, the randomness may be obtained by adding noise to the image or the threshold.

*Dithering* is defined as a quantization method in which a "noise" signal is added to the input signal prior to quantization. The noise signal may be:

- Random,
- Periodic,

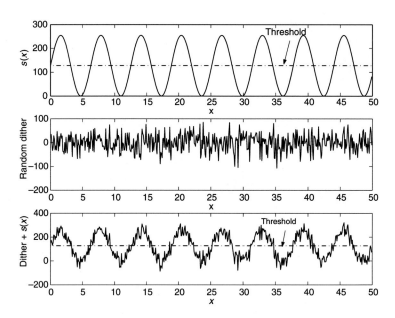

**Figure 11.19.** An input signal (top) and random dither pattern (middle) and their sum (bottom).

- Correlated with the input signal,
- Combinations of the above.

Dithering decreases the signal-to-noise ratio of the signal but improves the perceived quality of the quantized signal, by reducing contouring effects. An example of the effects of 1-D dithering with a purely random signal is given in Figs. 11.19 and 11.20.

An example of 2-D dithering with a purely random signal is shown in Fig. 11.21, where the continuous image in Fig. 11.21a is quantized directly to four levels in Fig. 11.21b, and is quantized to four levels in Fig. 11.21c after the addition of noise. The human visual system is sensitive to the abrupt edges in Fig. 11.21b. For this reason, the dithered image is typically preferred.

The process of adding a "noise" to a signal and using a fixed threshold is equivalent to adding "noise" to the threshold and not to the image. Like the case for the dithering noise, the threshold can vary randomly, be periodic, be correlated with the signal, or any combination.

Ordered periodic dithering methods using a periodic threshold pattern work similarly to a digital screen. For the 2-D case, a periodic digital matrix of threshold values is overlaid on the digital image. Each point of the image is compared with the corresponding point on the threshold matrix. If the value of the image pixel is greater than the threshold pixel, the halftone image pixel is set to the maximum; if the image pixel is less than the threshold pixel, the halftone image is set to the minimum.

To emulate an analog halftone mask, a spiral-dot screen is used. A 5 × 5 example is illustrated below. The periodicity is shown by including the previous side and edge,

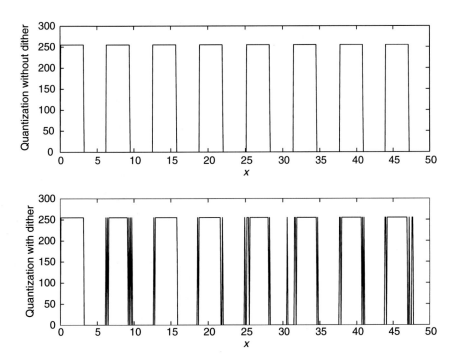

**Figure 11.20.** Thresholded signal from Fig. 11.19 without dithering (top) and with dithering (bottom).

giving the $6 \times 6$ matrix in Eq. (11.5):

$$\mathbf{M} = \begin{bmatrix} 21 & 22 & 23 & 24 & 25 & 21 \\ 20 & 7 & 8 & 9 & 10 & 20 \\ 19 & 6 & 1 & 2 & 11 & 19 \\ 18 & 5 & 4 & 3 & 12 & 18 \\ 17 & 16 & 15 & 14 & 13 & 17 \\ 21 & 22 & 23 & 24 & 25 & 21 \end{bmatrix}. \tag{11.5}$$

The $5 \times 5$ screen matrix is tiled over the entire image. Associated with each element of the screen is a threshold value. If a linear threshold step is to be used, then for the screen above, and assuming 8 bit/pixel (value range from 0 to 255), the threshold values would be given by the sequence

$$\{5 \quad 15 \quad 26 \quad 36 \quad 46 \quad 56 \quad 67 \quad 77 \quad 87$$
$$97 \quad 108 \quad 118 \quad 128 \quad 138 \quad 148 \quad 159 \quad 169 \quad 179$$
$$189 \quad 200 \quad 210 \quad 220 \quad 230 \quad 241 \quad 251\}.$$

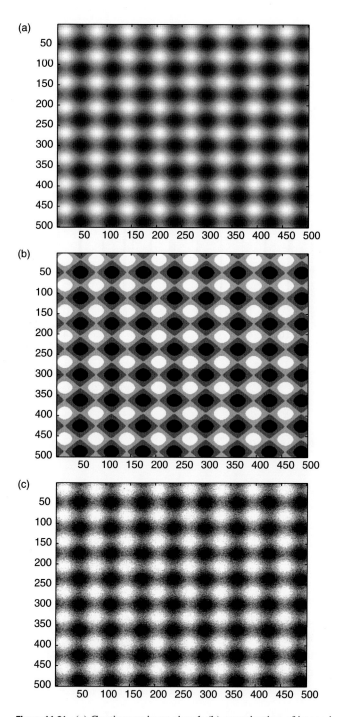

**Figure 11.21.** (a) Continuous input signal; (b) quantization of image in (a) to four levels without dithering; (c) quantization of image in (a) to four levels after the addition of a random noise signal.

In this case, the threshold matrix is given by

$$\mathbf{T} = \begin{bmatrix} 210 & 220 & 230 & 241 & 251 \\ 200 & 67 & 77 & 87 & 97 \\ 189 & 56 & 5 & 15 & 108 \\ 179 & 46 & 36 & 26 & 118 \\ 169 & 159 & 148 & 138 & 128 \end{bmatrix} . \tag{11.6}$$

In general, it is not necessary for the threshold steps to be linear over the value range.

While the center-growing dot emulates the analog halftone dots, it may not produce the most visually pleasing image. Dispersed dot patterns have some advantages in producing halftones with the screen pattern not as readily visible to the observer as the spiral mask. Examples of the dispersed dot masks are shown below for both rectangular, $\mathbf{M}_{4\times4}$, and diamond patterns, $\mathbf{M}_{5\times5d}$. The diamond pattern gives the appearance of a $45°$ screen pattern,

$$\mathbf{M}_{4\times4} = \begin{bmatrix} 2 & 16 & 3 & 13 & 2 \\ 10 & 6 & 11 & 7 & 10 \\ 4 & 14 & 1 & 15 & 4 \\ 12 & 8 & 9 & 5 & 12 \\ 2 & 16 & 3 & 13 & 2 \end{bmatrix} ,$$

$$\mathbf{M}_{5\times5d} = \begin{bmatrix} & & & & 2 & & & & \\ & & & 16 & 18 & 10 & & & \\ & & 3 & 32 & 6 & 26 & 4 & & \\ & 13 & 19 & 11 & 22 & 14 & 20 & 12 & \\ 2 & 29 & 7 & 27 & 1 & 30 & 8 & 28 & 2 \\ & 10 & 23 & 15 & 17 & 9 & 24 & 16 & \\ & & 4 & 31 & 5 & 25 & 3 & & \\ & & & 12 & 21 & 13 & & & \\ & & & & 2 & & & & \end{bmatrix} .$$

As mentioned, the digital halftone screen is implemented by tiling the image with the screen pattern. Once the threshold matrix is determined, the operation is simple to perform as shown below, where we have shown one screen period, the first $5 \times 5$ pixels of the image shown in Fig. 11.21a, and the resulting binary output.

$$\begin{bmatrix} 210 & 220 & 230 & 241 & 251 \\ 200 & 67 & 77 & 87 & 97 \\ 189 & 56 & 5 & 15 & 108 \\ 179 & 46 & 36 & 26 & 118 \\ 169 & 159 & 148 & 138 & 128 \end{bmatrix} \quad \begin{bmatrix} 127 & 133 & 140 & 146 & 152 \\ 133 & 140 & 146 & 152 & 158 \\ 140 & 146 & 152 & 158 & 164 \\ 146 & 152 & 158 & 165 & 170 \\ 152 & 158 & 164 & 170 & 176 \end{bmatrix} \longrightarrow \begin{bmatrix} 0 & 0 & 0 & 0 & 0 \\ 0 & 1 & 1 & 1 & 1 \\ 0 & 1 & 1 & 1 & 1 \\ 0 & 1 & 1 & 1 & 1 \\ 0 & 0 & 1 & 1 & 1 \end{bmatrix} .$$

Thresholds        Image pixels        Halftone

Figure 11.22a displays a spiral dot screening of the Bars image and Fig. 11.23 displays a dispersed screening of this image. While simple to compute, note the patterns in the images. These are caused by the repetitive patterns in the grid. These patterns are easily

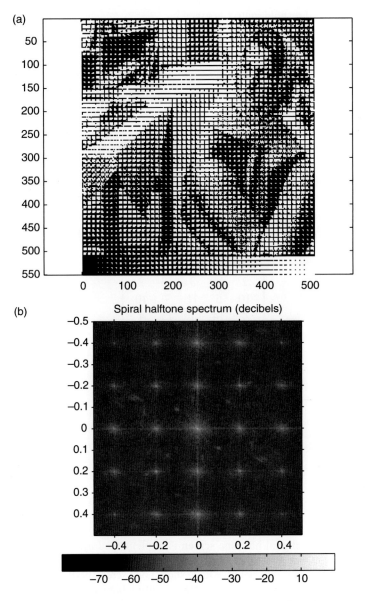

**Figure 11.22.** (a) Digital halftoning using a spiral dot screening; (b) power spectrum of digital halftoning using a spiral dot screening.

detected using the power spectrum, shown in Fig. 11.22b. The magnitude peaks in the power spectrum are often used as a measure of quality for halftoned images. The location of the spectral peaks is also of interest, since the eye is more sensitive to power along the horizontal and vertical axes. These effects can be reduced by using more sophisticated methods outlined below.

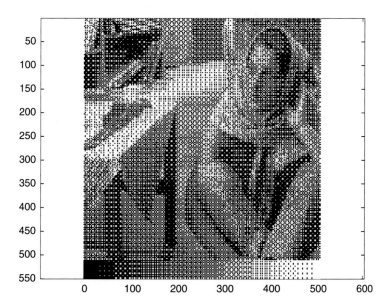

**Figure 11.23.** Digital halftoning using a dispersed screening.

### Error diffusion

One of the problems with any halftoning algorithm that uses a periodic mask is the visibility of periodic patterns. The human observer easily detects such patterns and finds them distracting, particularly rectilinear patterns. To avoid such periodic patterns and to respond to variations in the image, adaptive techniques were developed. The most popular of these techniques are the variations of error diffusion. The methods are based on using the characteristics of the human visual system (HVS) and reducing the average visual error. The simple algorithm is shown in the block diagram of Fig. 11.24, where the operator $Q(.)$ is a threshold operation and $h(n)$ is the error diffusing filter.

The process can be illustrated in one dimension for an input signal, $s(n)$. Assume that the input is normalized so that $0 \leq s(n) \leq 255$. The output halftone signal, $t(n)$, takes only the values 0 and 255. The error signal is the difference between the signal that is thresholded and its halftone approximation, $e(n) = s(n) - t(n)$. The error is passed through a filter, $h(n)$, and added to the input image. The filter diffuses the error and lets the algorithm "remember" past errors and, thus, create a halftone area that is closer to the average area of the original signal. The function $f(\cdot)$ will be used to denote this memory. The algorithm is given by:

1. Set $e(0) = 0, f(0) = 0$ and $n = 0$;
2. $r(n) = s(n) + f(n)$;
3. $t(n) = \begin{cases} 0 & \text{if } r(n) \leq \mu \\ 255 & \text{if } \mu < r(n); \end{cases}$
4. $e(n) = r(n) - t(n)$;
5. $f(n) = h(n) * e(n)$, where $*$ represents convolution;
6. $n = n + 1$ and go to step 2.

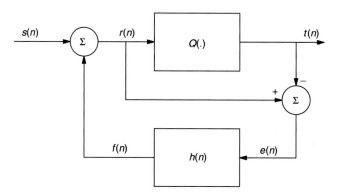

**Figure 11.24.** Error diffusion algorithm.

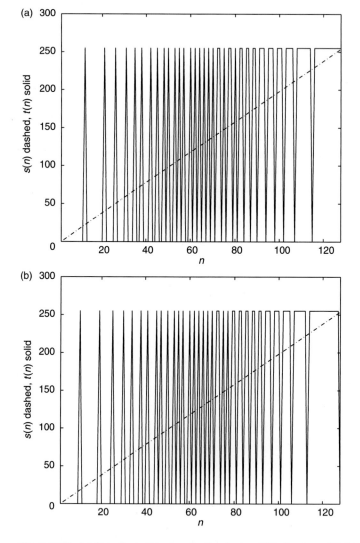

**Figure 11.25.** (a) One-dimensional example of error diffusion ($\alpha = 0$); (b) one-dimensional example of error diffusion ($\alpha = 0.5$).

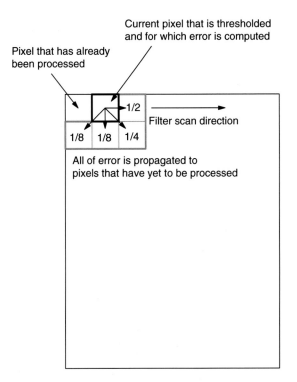

Current pixel that is thresholded
and for which error is computed

Pixel that has already
been processed

1/2

Filter scan direction

1/8  1/8  1/4

All of error is propagated to
pixels that have yet to be processed

**Figure 11.26.** Two-dimensional error diffusion.

Examples of 1-D error diffusion with the simple error filter, $h(n) = \alpha h(n-1) + (1-\alpha) \delta(n)$, are shown in Fig. 11.25. The result in Fig. 11.25a uses $\alpha = 0$; that of Fig. 11.25b uses $\alpha = 0.5$. Both figures use a threshold of $\mu = 128$. The differences are minor and occur around $n = 75$ and $n = 90$. Error diffusion is an example where the dithering "noise" is correlated to the image data.

The extension of the above algorithm to two dimensions requires determining a two-dimensional filter with which to diffuse the error as well as a scanning path for the filter to follow. Figure 11.26 displays an example where the scanning path is row by row (raster scanning) and there are four filter weights. One half of the error is added to the next pixel to be processed. The remaining half is divided by the weights 1/8, 1/8, 1/4 and added to the three pixels below the current pixel being processed.

There are a number of filters that are commonly used in 2-D error diffusion. Most are based on an approximation of the PSF of the human eye. Two common error diffusion filters are shown in Fig. 11.27. The choice of filter can have a significant effect on the spatial frequencies in the printed image, as shown in Fig. 11.28. In these images, the lines in the woman's clothing are more visible in Fig. 11.28a, which uses a Jarvis–Judice–Ninke filter [135], compared with Fig. 11.28b, which uses a Floyd–Steinberg filter [79]. The power spectra of the two methods are shown in Fig. 11.29. The differences between the two are small, but slightly in favor of the Jarvis–Judice–Ninke filter. The differences between the two and that of the spectrum associated with the spiral dot method of

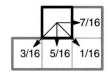

Floyd–Steinberg error diffusion filter

Jarvis–Judice–Ninke error diffusion filter

**Figure 11.27.** Two commonly used error diffusion filters.

Fig. 11.22b are obvious. It is clear by comparison with the spectrum of the original, Fig. 5.14b, that much of the spectral detail of the original image is apparent in the spectra of the error diffusion methods, whereas that detail is completely lost in the spectrum of the spiral dot method.

The grid used for these images is the same as that used for the dither patterns in Figs. 11.22 and 11.23. The resolution and tonal qualities are obviously superior to the digital screen methods. It should be noted, however, that electrophotography of error diffused halftone images typically results in a larger degradation than electrophotography of ordered dithered images, owing to the creation of moiré fringes from the high frequencies contained in the error diffused image. An example of aliasing that can occur is shown in Fig. 11.30. This image is the result of subsampling the Floyd–Steinberg error diffused image of Fig. 11.28. Note the low frequency aliasing artifacts introduced by this process.

Error diffusion suffers from several artifacts, the most common of which are often referred to as snakes. An example of snake artifacts is shown in Fig. 11.31b, which is a 2-D error diffusion halftone of the image shown in Fig. 11.31a. The artifact occurs in low contrast image areas and is a result of the cyclic behavior of the algorithm. Several methods have been investigated to reduce error diffusion artifacts including:

- Random filter coefficients [276],
- Random thresholds [153],
- Input dependent filter coefficients [71],
- Input dependent thresholds [152],
- Adaptive error diffusion [310],
- Alternate scanning strategies [276, 307],
- Incorporation of printer models [206].

(a)

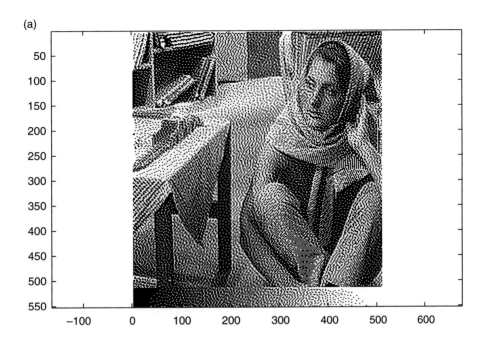

(b)

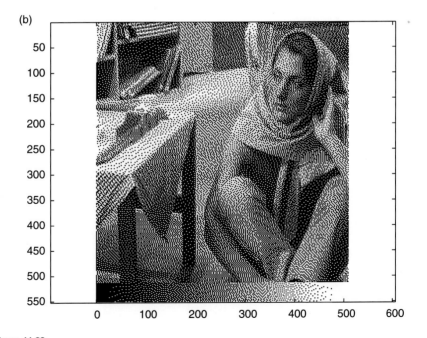

**Figure 11.28.**
(a) Error diffusion using a Jarvis–Judice–Ninke filter;
(b) error diffusion using a Floyd–Steinberg filter.

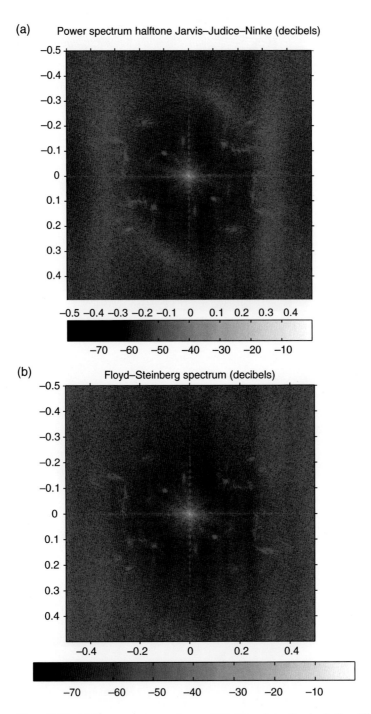

**Figure 11.29.** (a) Power spectrum of error diffusion using a Jarvis–Judice–Ninke filter; (b) power spectrum of error diffusion using a Floyd–Steinberg filter.

**Figure 11.30.** Result of subsampling the image in Figure 11.28b with no anti-aliasing filter.

## Iterative and search-based methods

Like most digital halftone methods, search-based halftone methods attempt to minimize the visual error between the continuous input image and the halftone image [164, 207, 319]. These methods make use of a model of the human visual system [148] and of the printer system [206]. The methods work through the image using two basic operations, toggle and swap. A toggle changes a halftone dot from on to off or vice versa. A swap interchanges a pair of adjacent on–off dots. The methods evaluate the visual error function with each operation and keep the change if the error decreases. This type of algorithm may not be optimal, but it is guaranteed to decrease the visual error.

Figure 11.32 displays a block diagram for a search-based halftone algorithm, where HVS refers to a model for the human visual system and $||\mathbf{e}||$ represents the visual error between the continuous tone ideal image and the halftoned image. Figure 11.33 displays the results of performing a direct binary search (DBS) algorithm [164] for ten iterations starting with the image shown in Fig. 11.23. Note that the resulting output does not contain snakes or other artifacts that occur in error diffusion. The dispersed dot method of Fig. 11.23 was designed to use a fixed set of patterns, which can result in repetitive patterns in low contrast areas. The iterative toggle and swap method is effective at eliminating such patterns.

While computationally expensive, iterative methods provide a technique for the design of digital screens, as well as the selection of error diffusion filter coefficients and thresholds [163].

In the design of large digital screens, attempts are often made to emulate the characteristics of error diffusion or minimize some visual error [253]. The sizes of the

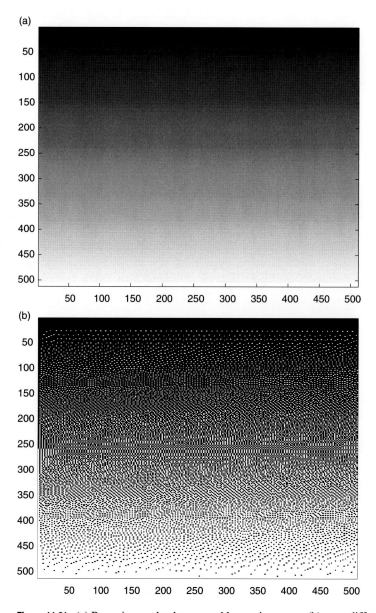

**Figure 11.31.** (a) Ramp image that has smoothly varying tones; (b) error diffusion of image above: note the snake horizontal periodic dot patterns at the top of the image as well as the snake artifacts at the bottom.

screens in these cases are quite large (64 × 64, 128 × 128, 256 × 256). Figure 11.34 displays the results of applying a 64 × 64 screen to the bars image. Note the significant improvements over the other screening results shown in Figs. 11.22a and 11.23. In this example, the dot profile (a representation of the dots that are turned on for each gray level) was designed using a void and cluster approach [277], where new dots are added or removed based upon the largest void or clusters that appear at the current gray level.

Original image

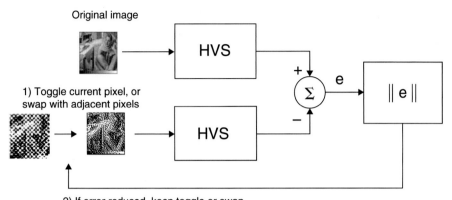

1) Toggle current pixel, or
swap with adjacent pixels

2) If error reduced, keep toggle or swap.
After testing all possible adjacent swaps
move to next pixel.

**Figure 11.32.** Block diagram of search based halftone method.

**Figure 11.33.** Halftone image created through iterative dot toggle and swap.

A low pass filter is applied to the dot pattern at a particular gray level $n$ to determine
the location of the largest void and dot clusters. Using the low pass image in the design,
dots are added to gray level $n$ to reduce the voids and create the gray level $n - 1$ (the
next darker gray level). Similarly, dots are removed from the gray level $n$ to remove the
clusters and create gray level $n + 1$.

Figure 11.35 illustrates this process for a $16 \times 16$ screen where we assume that we have
an initial dot pattern for level 128. A Gaussian filter is applied to this pattern to create

**Figure 11.34.** Digital halftoning using a 64 × 64 void-cluster designed screen.

the low-pass image. The maximum point of the low-pass image at index $[x, y] = [5, 16]$ is the largest void, so a dot is added at this location to create the dot pattern for level 127 (added dot is shown in gray). Similarly, the minimum point for the low-pass image at index $[x, y] = [5, 12]$ is the largest cluster, so a dot is removed at this location (shown in gray) to create the dot pattern for level 129.

Once the dot profile is constructed, the threshold matrix is easily computed. With 64 × 64 locations, the threshold values, which range from 0 to 255, each appear approximately 16 times within the threshold matrix. A clear advantage of the large screens is that the simple threshold operation is very fast, compared with an error diffusion algorithm. This is important for an embedded system with limited computational resources.

## Color halftone

As with monochrome halftoning, the goal of color halftone reproduction is to match the average color over an area of the image. The monochrome problem attempted to match the average reflectance. The color problem must try to match the tristimulus values of the color image under a specified illumination. The printing process remains binary in each of the colorants but the combinations of colors are greatly increased. There are hybrid printing processes that use halftoning in combination with control for the colorant concentration placed in a dot. While requiring more complex driving algorithms, such printing processes will have a higher resolution than the pure halftone system due to the ability to achieve a larger combination of average colors in a small fixed area as compared with a pure halftone system.

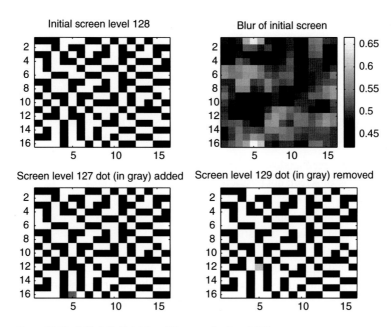

**Figure 11.35.** Initial digital $16 \times 16$ screen for level 128.

Consider a simple three color printing process with cyan, magenta and yellow inks. There are eight possible colors that can be produced:

1. white: the reflectance of the paper with no ink, $r_w(\lambda)$;
2. cyan: the reflectance of the cyan ink alone on the paper, $r_c(\lambda)$;
3. magenta: the reflectance of the magenta ink alone on the paper, $r_m(\lambda)$;
4. yellow: the reflectance of the yellow ink alone on the paper, $r_y(\lambda)$;
5. red: the reflectance of the magenta and yellow inks on the paper, $r_{my}(\lambda)$;
6. green: the reflectance of the cyan and yellow inks on the paper, $r_{cy}(\lambda)$;
7. blue: the reflectance of the magenta and cyan inks on the paper, $r_{cm}(\lambda)$;
8. black: the reflectance of all inks on the paper, $r_{cmy}(\lambda)$.

The average tristimulus value of an area is determined by the proportion of each of these colors in the area. The eight tristimulus values of the possible colors are denoted by

$$\mathbf{t}_k = \mathbf{A}^T \mathbf{L}_v \mathbf{r}_k, \quad k = 1, \dots, 8;$$

where $\mathbf{r}_k$ is the vector of sampled reflectance values of the $k$th ink and paper combination, $\mathbf{L}_v$ is the diagonal matrix representing the viewing illuminant and $\mathbf{A}$ is the matrix of CIE color matching functions. The tristimulus value of an area where the colors are mixed is determined by

$$\mathbf{t} = \mathbf{T}^T \mathbf{p},$$

where $\mathbf{T} = [\mathbf{t}_1, \dots, \mathbf{t}_8]$ and $\mathbf{p} = [p_1, \dots, p_8]$ is the proportion of the area covered by the corresponding color. The definition of $\mathbf{p}$ implies:

$$\sum_{k=1}^{8} p_k = 1.$$

As in any real system, there will be various sources of noise to make the above equations less than exact. Some factors affecting the variability include:

1. Relative screen angles;
2. Variation of screen dot positions;
3. Variation in dot size;
4. Variation in dot shape;
5. Interaction between layers:
   - Chemical,
   - Physical (spreading, mixing, penetration, etc.);
6. Variation in the interaction of colorants with the paper or other media.

For any practical system, it is necessary to determine how much of each color ink to print in a given area. There is a problem in not knowing exactly how the various inks will overlap and, thus, not knowing the exact proportion of the area covered by each color. Neugebauer addressed this problem by assuming a probabilistic mix of the colors [125, 193, 226]. Consider the case of a mix of cyan and yellow ink on paper. Let us assume that the cyan ink by itself covers proportion $P_c$ of the area ($0 \le P_c \le 1$) and the yellow ink covers proportion $P_y$ of the area. If the dispersions of the inks are random and independent of each other, the expected fraction of the area covered by no ink is $p_w = (1 - P_c)(1 - P_y)$, the expected fraction covered by cyan is $p_c = P_c(1 - P_y)$; the expected fraction covered by yellow is $p_y = P_y(1 - P_c)$; the expected fraction covered by green is $p_g = P_c P_y$. The other combinations of colors can be found in a similar manner.

For a specified tristimulus value, the amount of each color can be obtained by solving the system of equations

$$\mathbf{t} = \mathbf{T}^T \begin{bmatrix} (1 - P_c)(1 - P_m)(1 - P_y) \\ P_c(1 - P_m)(1 - P_y) \\ (1 - P_c)P_m(1 - P_y) \\ (1 - P_c)(1 - P_m)P_y \\ (1 - P_c)P_m P_y \\ P_c(1 - P_m)P_y \\ P_c P_m(1 - P_y) \\ P_c P_m P_y \end{bmatrix}.$$

This equation is obviously nonlinear and must be solved by numerical methods. This would be too time consuming for printing an entire image, even if the equations represented the physical model well.

Commercial and many desktop printing systems use four colors of ink instead of three. Black ink can be substituted for the overprinting of cyan, magenta and yellow inks to produce a more pleasing and more economical black. In addition, the black ink produces a more visually pleasing black for printing text.[5] The Neugebauer equations can be easily extended to a four color printing system. However, since there are now four unknowns and three equations required to match a specific tristimulus value, there is some additional freedom in how the desired color can be matched. The problem is basically one of determining how much black ink to substitute for the combination of overprinting cyan, magenta and yellow. This problem is called *undercolor removal* and has been addressed in many ways over a long period of time, as is expected for a technology that has been around as long as color printing. Many of these methods are discussed in [11]. A brief explanation and examples are given in Section 12.3.8.

The reader should note the underlying problem of an overcomplete basis, that is, there are several ways to represent an object in a vector space. This occurs in halftoning, in high-fidelity color where multiple densities of the same inks are used and display systems that use more than the three basic red, green and blue LEDs.

A simple approach to the problem is to solve for the three colors, cyan, magenta and yellow, then remove the portion represented by the equal portions of the three. Suppose $P_c$, $P_m$ and $P_y$ are the proportions of cyan, magenta and yellow that are required to match a specified tristimulus value, $t$. This implies that

$$t = T[P_c, P_m, P_y]^T.$$

If the black ink can be reproduced by the three colored inks, the proportion can be found by

$$t_k = T[P_{cb}, P_{mb}, P_{yb}]^T,$$

where $t_k$ is the tristimulus value of the black ink. This would ideally be $P_{cb} = P_{mb} = P_{yb} = 1$. In practice, the black ink is not usually the same as the combination of the three colors. Assuming this to be the case, the same color can be reproduced by varying amounts of black ink. This is written

$$t = T[P_c - \alpha P_{cb}, P_m - \alpha P_{mb}, P_y - \alpha P_{yb}]^T + \alpha t_k.$$

It would appear that the most economical solution would be to replace as much of the three inks as possible, that is, choose $\alpha$ as large as possible. In practice, it has been found that between 50% to 80% undercolor removal produces the most pleasing visual results.

For commercial printing processes, the basic assumption that the primary colors are randomly dispersed and independent is false. The color halftone processes use different masks for the different colors. The screens are oriented in different directions to minimize the visibility of moire effects. Typical screen angles are cyan at 75°, magenta at 15°, yellow at 90° and black at 45°. Each of these screens is shown in Fig. 11.36.

---

[5] The black ink is often denoted as K (giving the notation CMYK for traditional four color printing with cyan, magenta, yellow and black). The K stands for key, which denoted the key plate in traditional printing. The key plate was used to add additional contrast detail to the color image by adding black ink.

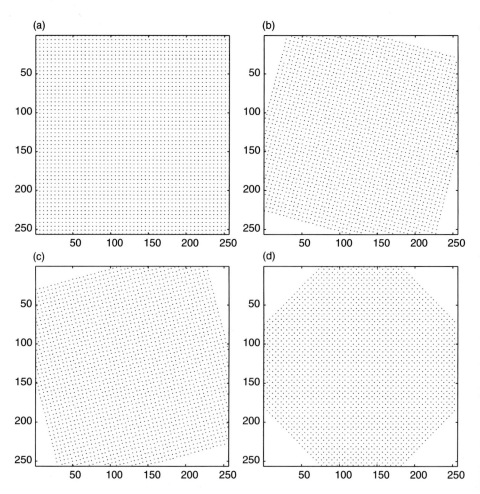

**Figure 11.36.** (a) Yellow halftone screen at 90°; (b) magenta halftone screen at 15°; (c) cyan halftone screen at 75°; (d) black halftone screen at 45°.

Since the screens are fixed, the relative dispersion of the colors is clearly not independent and not uniformly distributed over the area, as required by the Neugebauer model. Nevertheless, the model has proved useful in the printing industry and has been modified many times to give improved performance, e.g., [213, 317]. An artifact of fixed screen angles is rosette patterns. These circular artifacts are visible in the CMYK image shown in Fig. 11.37.

The assumptions of the Neugebauer model may be most nearly satisfied by the ink-jet printers used in desktop publishing. These printers print all colors on the same rectangular grid. While the colored dots are concentrated in the center, they are more random in their coverage of the area than the dots generated by lithography or gravure. Because error diffusion is used for each of the ink colors, there are no screen angles to cause moiré or rosette patterns.

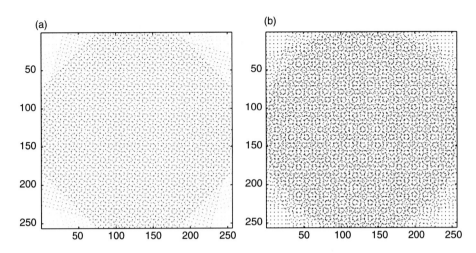

**Figure 11.37.** (a) Color rosette patterns formed by combining screens from Figs. 11.36; (b) black image of (a) to accentuate the rosette patterns (for color version, please see Plate 16).

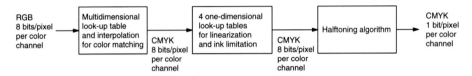

**Figure 11.38.** Common flow of image data for CMYK halftone device.

Figure 11.38 displays a common transformation process used in halftone print devices. The input data are usually 8 bits/pixel per color channel RGB data. These data are processed by a color transformation that is often implemented as a multidimensional look-up table combined with an interpolation method. The undercolor removal or creation of the black data channel is handled by this step. The design of this transformation and the interpolation methods are discussed in detail in Chapter 12 and Appendix D. The output of this block is a CMYK 8 bits/pixel per color channel representation of the image data. These data are often sent through four one-dimensional tables that will limit the amount of colorant that can be placed upon the paper as well as *linearize* the output device. Linearization and the creation of these tables is described in detail in Section 12.3.3. The output of this block is provided to a halftoning algorithm that determines where colorant dots should be placed upon the paper.

While it is clear that the CMYK color planes could be error diffused independently, the halftoning problem can be formulated in a vector approach, where the color error is diffused across the primary colors [282]. There are many variants of vector error diffusion. Here we discuss the obvious extensions from traditional error diffusion. Figure 11.39 displays a block diagram of a system with a continuous tone input vector

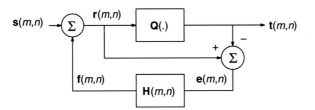

**Figure 11.39.** Vector error diffusion in a color space.

$s(m, n)$ (8 bits/pixel per color channel), where the algorithm is given by the equations:

$$\mathbf{r}(m, n) = \mathbf{s}(m, n) + \mathbf{H} * \mathbf{e}(m, n), \tag{11.7}$$

$$\mathbf{e}(m, n) = \mathbf{r}(m, n) - \mathbf{t}(m, n), \tag{11.8}$$

$$\mathbf{t}(m, n) = \mathbf{Q}(\mathbf{r}(m, n)), \tag{11.9}$$

and $\mathbf{Q}(\cdot)$ is the quantization function that selects the appropriate color dot. For a CMY system, the quantization function chooses from among the eight combinations of the three inks. The combinations are represented by the matrix

$$\mathbf{C} = 255 \begin{bmatrix} 0 & 1 & 0 & 1 & 0 & 1 & 0 & 1 \\ 0 & 0 & 1 & 1 & 0 & 0 & 1 & 1 \\ 0 & 0 & 0 & 0 & 1 & 1 & 1 & 1 \end{bmatrix}. \tag{11.10}$$

The value of $\mathbf{Q}(\mathbf{r}(m, n))$ is determined by

$$\mathbf{Q}(\mathbf{r}(m, n)) = \mathbf{c}_I, \tag{11.11}$$

$$I = \arg(\min_i ||\mathbf{c}_i - \mathbf{r}(m, n)||^2), \tag{11.12}$$

and $\mathbf{c}_i$ is the $i$th column of the matrix $\mathbf{C}$.

The convolution given by $\mathbf{f}(m, n) = \mathbf{H} * \mathbf{e}(m, n)$ is a vector-matrix sequence convolution, which is computed as

$$\mathbf{H} * \mathbf{e}(m, n) = \sum_{[j,k] \in S} \mathbf{H}(j, k)\mathbf{e}(m - j, n - k), \tag{11.13}$$

where $S$ is the support size of the matrix $\mathbf{H}$. The above formulation assumes three primary colorants, e.g., cyan, magenta and yellow, and diffuses the error in the device coordinate space. The design of the filter $\mathbf{H}$ is difficult and should be performed using a color visual model [153]. One method using sCIELAB [321] (see Section E.4.3) is described in [282]. For the CMYK error diffusion case, the dimension of the vectors simply increases by one, making $\mathbf{C}$ a $4 \times 16$ dimension matrix. In this case, the matrix sequence $\mathbf{H}$ must be carefully designed to ensure that the errors are propagated in an appropriate manner between the color channels. For example, there should be little diffusion between the yellow and black channels, since a yellow dot creates very little change in luminance while a black dot results in a large change in luminance.

Another approach to vector color error diffusion is to perform the diffusion in a perceptual meaningful color space such as CIELAB. The algorithm in this case would be the same as that shown in Fig. 11.39. The above equations remain the same except that the columns of the matrix **C** contain the CIELAB values of the primary colorants. To maintain the errors within a certain boundary, it may be necessary to gamut map the incoming colors to colors that can be reproduced by the colorants of the device.

There are vector color error diffusion methods that are hybrid in nature, in that they process the yellow channel independently as a scalar and combine only the cyan, magenta and possibly black channels in a vector [76]. These methods are typically designed with the idea of using one vector component to determine if a dot should be placed at a location, while the other component(s) specify the dot color. This approach has also been used in iterative search methods [161].

At the current ink-jet printer resolutions, there is usually very little difference in quality between vector-based methods and methods that error diffuse each colorant independently. Considering the added complexity, vector-based methods are rarely worth the cost to implement them.

For some devices that can create different sized dots, multilevel halftoning is implemented. For example, the output of the halftoning algorithm in Fig. 11.38 could be CMYK 2 bits/pixel per color channel to represent three different dot sizes (and one more code for the case of no dot). The error diffusion algorithm is implemented using multiple threshold levels that quantize the data to the proper number of bits.

Finally, there are the cases of hi-fidelity printing that use more than the traditional four inks. For example, many ink-jet devices use light and dark magenta and cyan inks to reduce the visibility of halftone artifacts. Creation of the continuous tone CMYKcm image data for input into the halftoning algorithm is often achieved through the use of one-dimensional look-up tables that map the cyan colorant output of the multidimensional table in Fig. 11.38 to light and dark cyan continuous tone values [198]. High fidelity printing that uses unique inks like green or orange for expanded gamuts have more complex color separations that are typically handled through carefully designed multidimensional look-up tables.

Historically, the printing industry has not attempted to produce accurate tristimulus values from scanned material. The original image that is scanned is usually a photographic transparency. The scanner is set up by a technician, who from experience and continued discussions with each customer, manually adjusts the scanner responses for each of the three bands. The image is not scanned with filters that replicate the CIE color matching functions since the goal is to produce a visually pleasing image for the customer. The filters are more closely associated with the Status A filters used for densitometry, mentioned in Section 8.7.4. This usually means that the color seen on the film is not the color that the customer wants in the final print. Thus, measuring the image color precisely has limited utility.

(a)

Piezo crystal deforms

Drop forced out by deformation

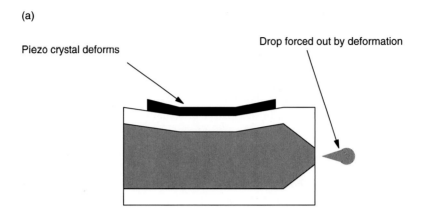

(b)

Drop forced out by bubble

Bubble formed by heating

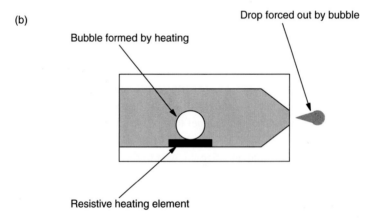

Resistive heating element

**Figure 11.40.** (a) Pressure scheme for ink-jet printing; (b) thermal scheme for ink-jet printing.

## 11.6    Ink-jet devices

Commercial printing methods rely on pressing the ink onto the paper. Ink-jet devices spray the ink onto the paper. The control of the ink in such small amounts is a difficult problem. The various solutions are truly ingenious. Pressure and thermal schemes are currently the two primary approaches for drop-on-demand[6] ink-jet printing heads. These methods are illustrated in Fig. 11.40. In the pressure scheme, a piezo crystal is electrically stimulated, causing a deformation of the micro-chamber and thereby forcing a drop of ink out onto the paper. In the thermal scheme, a heating element causes the formation of a bubble, which forces ink from the micro-chamber onto the paper.

---

[6] We will not discuss continuous flow printers, since they are not used for printing images.

The printers are designed with the ink-jet heads mounted in line on a movable stage. Depending upon the design and the settings, the heads may spray ink when going from left to right or right to left. The direction in which the head is moving at the time the dot is sprayed can affect the dot shape and placement and is typically corrected for in the printer firmware.

Each head contains a number of micro-nozzles, where each micro-nozzle corresponds to one of the units in Fig. 11.40. The line spacing is fixed mechanically, and the timing of the spray of each dot, as the heads move along the line, is such that each color is printed on the same rectangular grid. In practice, the ink-jet head passes each pixel location more than once. This occurs so that only a portion of the required ink needs to be placed on the paper in each pass, thereby reducing ink coalescence problems. Ink coalescence occurs when the ink has not had sufficient time to be absorbed into the paper before additional ink is placed on the same or nearby location. Hence, the ink viscosity, ink surface tension and paper type greatly affect the rate at which dots can effectively be placed on the paper. This process of printing in multiple passes is often referred to as *shingling* or *weaving* and each pass is called a *swath*. The shingling process also has the effect of reducing visible artifacts caused by nonuniformity in the nozzle locations or reducing artifacts caused by nonfunctioning nozzles.

Ink-jet engines are bi-level, that is, they can either place a dot on the paper or not. To create the appearance of a continuous tone image, it is necessary to perform halftoning. There are also multilevel devices that use the bi-level engines. These printers will place a second dot on top of a dot with the same color or have different sized drops. This has the effect of making a darker or larger dot. In this case, multilevel halftoning methods are necessary. In practice, ink-jet engines typically use error diffusion as a halftoning technique, owing to the well defined and repeatable dot shape [64].

Color ink-jet engines commonly use three or four colors: cyan, magenta, yellow and black CMY(K). However, six color engines are prevalent, where a light magenta and light cyan are introduced. These light colors reduce the visibility of halftone artifacts in high reflectance regions, where the lower reflectance magenta and cyan dots would be highly visible. The transition between light and dark colorants can be handled by the design of 1-D look-up tables. There are also ink-jet printers that include green and red colorants. The purpose of these inks is to expand the gamut of the printer.

Figure 11.41 displays a conceptual diagram of the transformation from the digital source image to an ink-jet print. In this process, the image is first adjusted to the proper resolution for the printer, converted to CMY(K) values, and halftoned. The data are interlaced since the printer will be using all colors at the same time. Hence, the print driver must indicate to the controller the image dimensions as well as factors which will control the number of passes the heads should make over the same image area to avoid coalescence problems. With this information and the binary halftone data, the controller can determine if it should place a dot on the paper as it moves the ink-jet heads and advances the paper.

Note that the resolution conversion step is not necessarily to scale the continuous tone image at the resolution of the ink-jet dot placement, e.g., 4800 dpi by 4800 dpi. Instead,

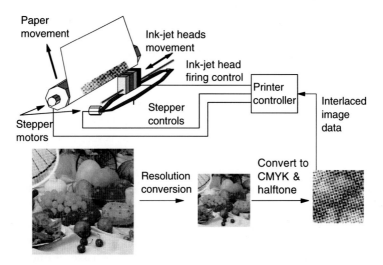

**Figure 11.41.** Ink-jet printing process (for color version, please see Plate 19).

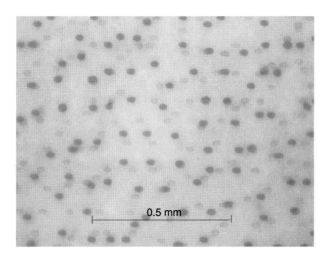

**Figure 11.42.** Magnification of dots created by ink-jet engine #1 on glossy paper: note that only single dots are created with this print engine (for color version, please see Plate 20).

it is typical to scale the continuous tone image (8 bits/pixel per color channel) to 300 or 600 dpi. This image is then halftoned on a grid at the ink-jet engine's dot placement resolution.

Most engines are capable of printing at a variety of dot placement resolutions. The one that is used depends upon the quality settings made in the driver by the user as well as the paper type. For example, an engine may print at 600 dpi by 600 dpi for plain paper but at 4800 dpi by 4800 dpi for photo glossy paper. In both cases, the dot size may be the same. Since the dots overlap in the 600 dpi case, they must greatly overlap in the 4800 dpi case. While the photo paper is designed to handle much more ink than plain

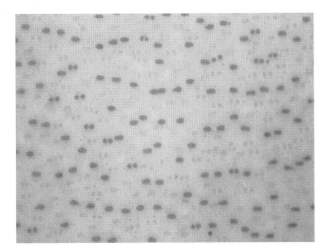

**Figure 11.43.** Magnification of dots created by ink-jet engine #2 on glossy paper: note that single dots as well as double dots are created with this engine (for color version, please see Plate 21).

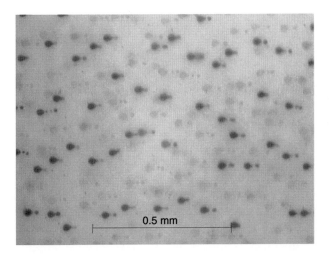

0.5 mm

**Figure 11.44.** Magnification of dots created by ink-jet engine #3 on glossy paper: note that an occasional satellite dot occurs (for color version, please see Plate 22).

paper, it is often necessary to limit the ink amounts in the color conversion process, i.e., the RGB to CMYK mapping.

In any real system, there will be various sources of noise that affect the quality of the printing process. Some factors affecting the variability include: the halftoning method, variation in dot size, shape and location, as well as chemical and physical interaction of the inks and media. Obviously, the ink must have a consistency that permits it to be sprayed through a small opening. This type of ink has had problems with fading. However, newer, more expensive archival inks are becoming available.

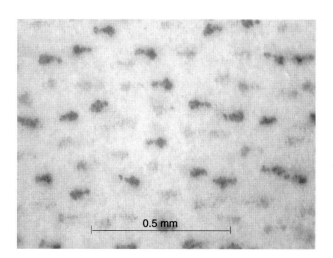

0.5 mm

**Figure 11.45.** Magnification of dots created by engine #3 used to create the dots in Fig. 11.44: the difference is that now ink-jet coated paper is used instead of ink-jet glossy paper (for color version, please see Plate 23).

Figures 11.42–11.45 show dot distributions from three different ink-jet devices, imaginatively denoted printers 1, 2 and 3. Figures 11.42 and 11.45 show the difference in the dot patterns for printers 1 and 2, when using the same paper. The effect of the paper is shown in Figs. 11.44 and 11.45 by using printer 3 to generate identical patterns on two types of paper. In this example, the shape of the dot has obviously changed as a result of the properties of the paper. Note that the shape of the dots, primarily the larger dots, shown here is asymmetric. The dots are wider along the axis parallel to the movement of the ink-jet cartridge across the paper. This is caused by the carriage motion as the ink drop is expelled.

Upon exiting the nozzle, the drop is often made of multiple droplets. The break up of the drop into droplets is undesirable and ideally the droplets should coalesce into a single drop on their way to the paper. In some cases, such as shown in Figure 11.44, the drops fail to coalesce. The smaller drops are referred to as a satellite drops. The physics that create the satellite drops is complex, involving the properties of the ink, e.g., viscosity and surface tension, the cartridge firing rate and the capillary filling of the micro-chamber from the reservoir.

Knowledge of the dot shape of a particular printer–paper combination can be used in the model of error diffusion [162] or other halftone methods to obtain improved performance.

## 11.7     Electrophotographic imaging

Chester F. Carlson created the first electrophotographic image in 1938 [108]. It was over ten years before a commercial system was created. The system required over 14 steps and

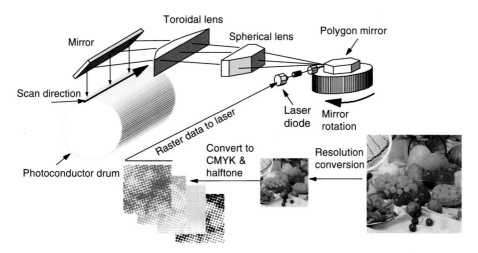

**Figure 11.46.** From digital RGB data to exposing the photoconductor drum (for color version, please see Plate 24).

was very slow. In the original document copiers, the device used an optical formation of the image to expose the photoconductor. High intensity lamps were used with a complex optical system to project the image of the page onto the photosensitive drum or belt. The development of the laser allowed digital control of the exposure of the photosensitive medium. This was first utilized on laser printers. Today, it is common for a digital scanner to be used to record the data and a laser print engine to be used to create the copy. This newer design makes it possible to manipulate the image data digitally for operations such as color characterization, resolution conversion, digital halftoning and segmentation. Today, the electrophotographic process (also known as xerography[7]) is used in laser printers and copiers.

As in the ink-jet printing process, the digital image must be halftoned. Traditionally, digital screen halftoning methods have been used for laser printing. The transformation from digital data to print is shown conceptually in Figs. 11.46 and 11.47. In Fig. 11.46, the RGB image data are spatially scaled to the output resolution of the printer, converted to CMYK color space and halftoned. The halftoned data are utilized to modulate the laser. The polygon mirror and the lens assembly cause the laser to scan across the photoconductor drum as shown. Unlike the ink-jet engine, which prints all four colors at the same time, the laser engine processes each color plane in a sequential manner. Figure 11.47 displays each of the primary steps, which are as follows:

1. Initial charging of the photoconductive material (there may also be a cleaning step, which is not shown);
2. Exposing the photoconductive material with a laser, spatially related to the negative of the image to be printed – exposure to light removes the positive charge;

---

[7] Xerography comes from the Greek and means "dry writing." The Haloid Company purchased the rights to Carlson's invention and eventually changed their name to the Xerox Corporation.

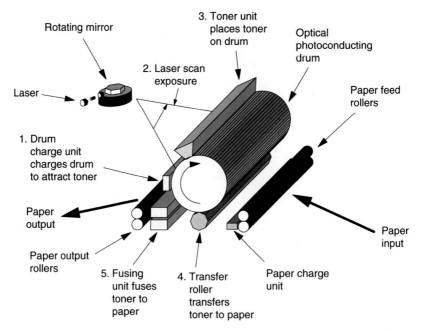

**Figure 11.47.** Details of using charge on photoconductor drum to pick up toner, transfer toner to paper and fuse toner to paper.

3. Presenting negatively charged toner particles to the photoconductive material – those areas that were not illuminated will now have toner;
4. Electrostatic transfer of the toner from the photoconductive material to paper;
5. Heat fusion of the toner to the paper.

The first four steps listed above are performed for each toner color, e.g. CMYK, prior to fusing the toners to the paper. This repeated application of each of these steps can introduce distortions in the printed image.

There are a number of variants to the system shown in Fig. 11.47. These include devices that image all four color planes on the photoconductive drum prior to the paper transfer and devices that transfer all four toners to an intermediate belt (transfer belt) prior to a one-time transfer onto paper. Both of these methods will have better registration between the color planes, as compared with the system that performs four individual toner transfers to paper. There are also variants that have the laser add charge to the photoconductor, instead of removing charge, at the locations that require toner.

Although rarely used today, electrofax is a variant of electrophotography where the photoconductive material is a dielectric embedded in the paper. The charging, exposing, and toner transfer are all carried out directly on the paper [108]. There are also electrographic printing processes in which the exposure step is performed once, and then multiple copies are printed from the single exposure [40]. This process is used for high volume printing.

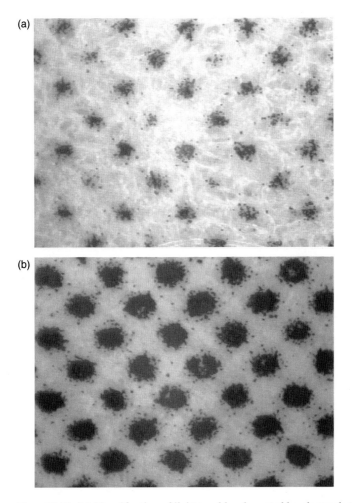

**Figure 11.48.** (a) Magnification of light tonal level created by electrophotographic printer; (b) magnification of tonal level slightly darker than that shown in the image above.

Figure 11.48 displays magnified dot patterns for two different tonal levels from a monochrome electrophotographic printer. Compared with the ink-jet samples in Section 11.6, the dot shape from the laser device does not have a well defined edge. This poor dot shape, and its unstable nature at small resolutions, is the reason why error diffusion halftone algorithms are rarely used for laser engine applications.

From these images, it is clear that the parameters of interest in modeling an electrophotographic system include the dot's location (position), shape and splatter. Such a model may require the estimation of dot statistics. Values such as mean location and variation can be estimated by printing samples on paper that contains well placed fiducial markers. The printed image is then imaged with a digital microscope (or scanned with a high resolution scanner), and the fiducial markers are used to register the printer dots, allowing the estimation of dot statistics.

## 11.8     Dye sublimation

The methods of hard-copy image reproduction that use inks or toners are basically binary processes. The ink is present or absent. There is little control over the density of the ink from pixel to pixel. Thermal methods such as dye transfer and hot wax have the advantage of allowing continuous variation of density of the colorant. The dye transfer method will be described here as an example.

The basic thermal dye transfer process consists of sublimating[8] the dye, which is on a carrier ribbon. The ribbon is made with successive strips of yellow, magenta and cyan dyes. The yellow image is laid down first; the paper is repositioned; the magenta image is then laid down; the paper is repositioned and the final cyan image is laid down. The paper and ribbon are moved simultaneously over a thermal head, which vaporizes the dye. The vaporized dye diffuses into the paper surface and then returns to solid form. The printing head consists of one individually controlled heating element for each column of pixels. Thermal printers produce high resolution images of almost photographic quality. Figure 11.49 graphically displays this process. For some systems, there is often a fourth layer, which is a clear coat.

The hardware used to produce the dye-sublimation image requires a high degree of precision. There are problems that originate from the fundamental physics of the process as well as from limitations of the manufacturing process. Some of these problems include:

1. Variability of the heating elements,
2. Variable warm-up time and behavior of the heads,
3. Variation caused by ambient conditions,
4. Hysteresis of the heating elements,

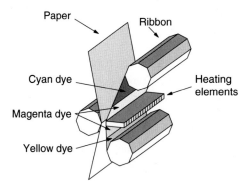

**Figure 11.49.** Dye-sublimation printing process.

---

[8] Sublimation is a material state change from a solid state directly to a gaseous state without passing through a liquid state.

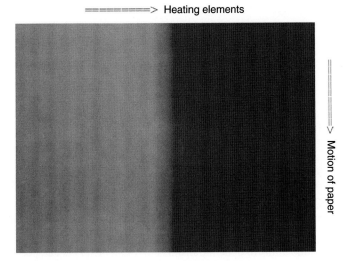

===========> Heating elements

Motion of paper

**Figure 11.50.** Magnification of two different tonal levels created by monochrome sublimation printer.

5. Dye inhibition; a dye laid down on top of another dye does not adhere as well as it would to paper,
6. Resublimation; the heating for a subsequent dye can resublime the dye that has been previously laid down.

In addition, there is usually significant dependency of what is diffused at the current row of pixels based upon the image content of the previous rows. The previous rows affect the current row because the heating element's current temperature depends upon its previous heating history. For example, if the previous rows were white, the head would be cooler than if the previous rows were 100% density and the heating element had been used continuously.

Figure 11.50 displays a magnification of two different tonal levels created by a monochrome sublimation printer. The vertical lines in the image are related to each of the heating elements. This effect is repeatable and can be corrected. It is related to the type of correction that is done for nonuniform lighting in scanners that is discussed in Section 10.1.1.

# 11.9    Problems

**11.1**   Consider a simulation of a new proposed active matrix LCD display.

(a) Discuss the measurements that would be needed to make an accurate simulation.
(b) Describe the tests that you would recommend in order to evaluate the proposed system.

**11.2**   Assume a voltage versus transmission function for a twisted nematic cell that is defined by the function

$$
t(v) = \begin{cases}
0.95 & \text{if } v \le 1.0 \\
1.05 - 0.1v & \text{if } 1.0 \le v \le 1.5 \\
1.50 - 0.4v & \text{if } 1.5 \le v \le 3.5 \\
1.45 - 0.1v & \text{if } 3.5 \le v \le 4.0 \\
0.05 & \text{if } 4.0 \le v.
\end{cases}
$$

(a) Define the continuous function, $s(t)$, that would give the best linearization, i.e., $s(t(v))$ is approximately linear over the largest possible range.
(b) Assuming uniform 8-bit quantization of the input values for the desired transmission, construct a look-up table to generate the voltage values that best linearize the output. You may assume uniform optical transmission of all elements and perfect additivity of the color channels.

**11.3**   Using the monochrome version of your chosen image, *gray-one*, create a halftone representation using the $5 \times 5$ spiral dot pattern of Eq. (11.5).

**11.4**   Color halftone processes are virtually always CMY or CMYK systems. Using a simple $3 \times 3$ matrix transformation, we can transform the RGB representation to a CMY representation. One such transformation is given by

$$
\begin{bmatrix} C \\ M \\ Y \end{bmatrix} = \begin{bmatrix} 0 & 0.5 & 0.5 \\ 0.5 & 0 & 0.5 \\ 0.5 & 0.5 & 0 \end{bmatrix} \begin{bmatrix} R \\ G \\ B \end{bmatrix}.
$$

(a) Using the spiral dot pattern for halftoning each of the CMY layers, create a color halftone image of the color version of your chosen image, *image-one*.
(b) Convert the CMY to RGB and display it.
(c) Compare the color halftone with the original. Discuss the quality and the appearance of any artifacts.
(d) This is an example of a simulation of a halftone printing process. Discuss the strengths and weaknesses of this simulation.

**11.5**   Develop a flow chart for the generation of a halftone screen of $15°$ for simulating the offset or gravure process.

**11.6**   Using the monochrome version of your chosen image, *gray-one*, generate a halftone by error diffusion using the Floyd–Steinberg filter

$$
\mathbf{H} = \begin{bmatrix} 0 & 0 & 7/16 \\ 3/16 & 5/16 & 1/16 \end{bmatrix}.
$$

**11.7** Use the RGB to CMY transformation to generate a halftone by error diffusion using the Jarvis–Judice–Ninke filter,

$$\mathbf{H} = \begin{bmatrix} 0 & 0 & 0 & 7/48 & 5/48 \\ 3/48 & 5/48 & 7/48 & 5/48 & 3/48 \\ 1/48 & 3/48 & 5/48 & 3/48 & 1/48 \end{bmatrix},$$

for each channel separately.

Note that this is a simplistic approximation for color error diffusion. The actual cases would use vector methods and filters closely related to the human visual system. Implementation of a full-color error diffusion method would make a good project.

**11.8** Develop a flow chart for a method to simulate dot variability in an ink-jet printer using a computer monitor for display.

**11.9** Develop a flow chart for a method to simulate dot variability in an electrophotographic printer using a computer monitor for display.

**11.10** The moiré effect can be described as the result of sampling a sampled image, or halftoning a halftoned image. We'll explore the former approach in this problem, as it can be described in a more straightforward manner. Let us do this with a one-dimensional example. Let the original continuous signal be denoted by $f(x)$; the two sampling grids are denoted by

$$h_1(x) = \sum_{n=-\infty}^{\infty} \delta(x - nT_1),$$

$$h_2(x) = \sum_{n=-\infty}^{\infty} \delta(x - nT_2).$$

The first sampling is given by $s_1(x) = f(x)h_1(x)$ and the second sampling by $s_2(x) = f(x)h_1(x)h_2(x)$. Using the properties of the Fourier transform and the transform of the comb function, determine the frequencies present in $s_2(x)$.

# 12 Characterization of devices

Having discussed the common devices used to obtain and display images, we now focus on achieving accuracy in the recording and reproduction process through device characterization. Device characterization is the problem of determining the relationship between device-dependent values and photometric values. Device-dependent values include the control values sent to an output device, e.g., CMYK, RGB, and values received from an input device, e.g., RGB. Photometric values include CIE colorimetric or photometric values and ANSI or ISO status density values.

The methods for characterization can be divided into parametric and nonparametric based approaches. The parametric based methods require the estimation of model parameters using data collected from a photometric or colorimetric instrument. The nonparametric based methods require the estimation of look-up table (LUT) entries or artificial neural network coefficients. In this chapter, the problem of device characterization is presented in a general framework, which can be applied to a wide variety of devices.

## 12.1 Goal of characterization

The need for device characterization is best illustrated by a simple example, in which the goal is to record and display a copy of an image such that a "best" visual match is made to the original image. There are essentially two approaches to this problem. One approach would be to determine a mapping from the recorded values directly to the reproduction device control values as shown in Fig. 12.1. This approach is often defined as being a closed loop solution [239], since the mapping will work only for that specific input and output device. The other approach involves the characterization of the input and output devices as shown in Fig. 12.2. This approach is often defined as being an open loop solution [239], since image data from any device that is characterized can be communicated to any other characterized device. With $N$ recording devices and $M$ reproduction devices, the closed loop solution would require the determination of $M \times N$ mappings, while the open loop solution would require the determination of only $M + N$ mappings.

To obtain the best visual match in the open loop approach, it is necessary to map the recorded values of the input device to values that are visually meaningful, e.g., CIELAB values. Similarly, it is necessary to map these visual descriptors to control

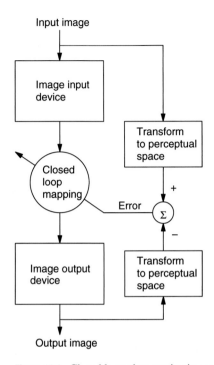

**Figure 12.1.** Closed loop characterization approach.

values for output devices. In this case, the characterization problem for image recording and reproduction devices can be viewed as a problem of determining a mapping between the digital control or recorded values and the visual descriptors of the samples that are reproduced or recorded. The determination of these mappings is the focus of this chapter.

## 12.2    Monochrome

The characterization of a monochrome or grayscale reproduction or recording device can be viewed as a 1-D mapping problem. The problem is to determine a mapping between the grayscale digital value and some grayscale visual descriptor of the corresponding physical sample. This process is frequently referred to as *linearization*, the reason for which will be discussed in an example below.

The grayscale visual descriptor of a sample is determined by performing a measurement of the sample with a photometric instrument. Instruments that are commonly used include densitometers, photometers, colorimeters and spectrophotometers. These instruments are reviewed in Chapter 8. These instruments are produced with various optical geometries and aperture sizes. Depending upon the characteristics of the samples, the geometry and aperture size can significantly affect the measurements that are obtained. For example, when measuring a halftoned sample, the aperture must be large enough to include a statistically significant number of dots.

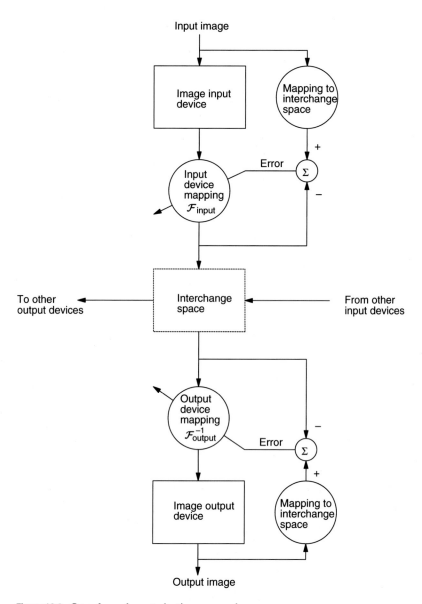

**Figure 12.2.** Open loop characterization approach.

There are a variety of visual descriptors that are used for the monochrome characterization problem including ANSI/ISO visual density, CIE Y luminance, and CIE $L^*$ luminance (see Chapter 8). The ANSI/ISO visual density and $L^*$ descriptors are correlated to the human visual perception of the sample, while CIE Y is proportional to the sample reflectance.

Different input and output devices will usually have different *white points, black points* and *dynamic ranges*. For monochrome devices, the terms are easily defined. The white point of an output device is the descriptor of the brightest value that can be produced. For a monochrome device, this would correspond to the highest $L^*$ value. For an input device, the white point is the brightest value that can be recorded without saturating the detector. The black point of a monochrome output device is the darkest value that can be produced. For an input device, the black point is the lowest value that can be recorded above the noise floor of the detector, i.e., the point at which a signal can be distinguished from noise. For output devices the black and white points correspond to the output of the device when the input is the minimum and maximum, respectively, usually 0 and 255. The dynamic range of a display device is defined by the gamut of the device, which represents the range of gray levels the device can recreate. This range is defined by the properties of the ink, toner or illumination used by the reproduction process.

To account for these differences in devices, a perceptual normalization is often performed such that the white point of a monochrome device always maps to the maximum value defined by the device descriptor value, e.g., $L^* = 100$. This normalization ensures that the display white on a CRT will be mapped to the paper white of the printer. A similar adjustment can be performed at the black end of the scale. This process is referred to as *perceptual mapping* and will be discussed further for color in Section 12.3.9.

## 12.2.1 Input devices

Monochrome input devices can be characterized by measuring a target grayscale ramp such as that shown in Fig. 12.3. The physical ramp is produced by a continuous-tone process, so the scanning aperture is less critical. This is similar to the 32 step grayscale ramp that was used for visual calibration discussed in Chapter 3. To characterize an input device, the ramp is measured with the input device and with a photometric instrument that will provide the visual descriptor values.

### Scanners
Let the model for a monochrome scanner be given by

$$g_i = \mathcal{H}(s^T r_i) + \epsilon_i, \tag{12.1}$$

where $g_i$ is the recorded grayscale value at pixel $i$, $r_i$ is the spectral reflectance of the sample at pixel $i$, and $\epsilon_i$ is additive noise. The vector $s$ represents the spectral sensitivity of the scanner (including the illumination and optics),[1] and $\mathcal{H}$ denotes the scanner

**Figure 12.3.** Monochrome (grayscale) characterization target.

---

[1] Since the scanner is monochromatic, $s$ is a vector.

nonlinearity. To reduce the effect of noise ($\epsilon_i$), the ramp in Fig. 12.3 is usually scanned at a sufficiently high resolution to allow an averaging of pixels within each sample square. Alternatively, if available, a larger aperture can be used with the device to reduce the level of noise.

If the visual descriptor value obtained from the photometric instrument for the grayscale reflectance $\mathbf{r}_i$ is given by the scalar $d_i$, then the characterization problem is to determine a 1-D function $\mathcal{F}_{\text{input}}$ such that

$$d_i = \mathcal{F}_{\text{input}}(g_i). \tag{12.2}$$

We will use the notation $\mathcal{F}_{\text{input}}: \Omega_{\text{DD}} \rightarrow \Omega_{\text{P}}$ to make it clear that the function $\mathcal{F}_{\text{input}}$ maps device-dependent values, $g$, to photometric values, $d$. In the case that noise is a significant problem or that the function is required to be smooth, least squares methods may be used. In these cases, we will not have the equality of Eq. (12.2).

## Cameras

Although most consumer digital cameras provide color images, there are many industrial and military applications that use monochrome digital cameras. A model for a monochrome digital camera can be given by

$$g_i(t) = \mathcal{H}(\mathbf{s}^T \mathbf{L}(t)\mathbf{r}_i) + \epsilon_i(t), \tag{12.3}$$

which is similar to the scanner model of Eq. (12.1) with the inclusion of a time dependent diagonal illumination matrix $\mathbf{L}(t)$.

Many digital cameras have automatic gain controls (AGCs) that adjust the recorded values based upon the current light level. This adjustment, which may be linear or nonlinear, is performed to increase the dynamic range of the camera. This adjustment may depend on only $\mathbf{L}(t)$ or on $\mathbf{L}(t)\mathbf{r}_i$, $i = 1, \ldots, N$, where there are $N$ pixels in the recorded image.

It is difficult to characterize a camera that has this automatic control, especially if the changes are a function of the image reflectances $\mathbf{r}_i$. To characterize such a camera, it is necessary either to turn off the automatic control, thereby reducing the flexibility of the camera, or to determine what adjustments are being applied to the recorded values, thereby allowing a mathematical correction.

Another problem is the temporal dependency of the illumination $\mathbf{L}(t)$. The illumination could be changing in relative spectral content or only in absolute amplitude. In some situations, the camera is used only under constant known illumination conditions. In this case, the characterization of a monochrome digital camera is made under these specific illumination conditions, e.g., $\mathbf{L}(t) = \mathbf{L}_j$, $j = 1, \ldots, P$, and is similar to that of the scanner characterization problem. First, a grayscale ramp is recorded under each illuminant $\mathbf{L}_j$, $j = 1, \ldots, P$, providing the values $g_{ij}$, $i = 1, \ldots, M$, $j = 1, \ldots, P$. Second, the descriptor values for the grayscale ramp are determined using the photometric instrument. If the descriptor value for the grayscale reflectance $\mathbf{r}_i$ is given by the scalar $d_i$, then the characterization problem is to determine the 1-D functions $\mathcal{F}_{\text{input}_j}$ such that

$$d_i = \mathcal{F}_{\text{input}_j}(g_{ij}), \text{ for } j = 1, \ldots, P. \tag{12.4}$$

Since it is usually impossible to match all values exactly with a well behaved function, least squares methods are used.

## 12.2.2 Output devices

Given a particular grayscale level, $g_i$, a monochrome printing device will place a specific amount of colorant on the print medium, creating a sample that has a specific visual descriptor value $d_i$. Similarly, a radiant output device will radiate a specific amount of light, which has a certain visual descriptor value. Both types of monochrome output devices are characterized by creating a target grayscale ramp with the output device. This is similar to that shown in Fig. 12.3, but may not be continuous tone, depending on the output device. The ramp is measured with an instrument that provides the visual descriptor values. If $g_i$ is the control value necessary to create a visual descriptor $d_i$, then the characterization problem is to determine the mapping $\mathcal{F}_{\text{output}}^{-1}: \Omega_P \to \Omega_{\text{DD}}$, where

$$g_i = \mathcal{F}_{\text{output}}^{-1}(d_i). \tag{12.5}$$

---

**Example 12.1 (Monochrome characterization).**    In the following example, an image was created on a monochrome laser printer, scanned with a monochrome desktop scanner and then printed using a second monochrome laser printer from a different manufacturer. This entire process is displayed in Fig. 12.4. The image printed by the first laser printer was defined to be the ideal image. The goal was to characterize the scanner and the second laser printer such that a transformation, $\mathcal{F}_{\text{output}}^{-1}(\mathcal{F}_{\text{input}}(.))$, could be applied on the scanned image data prior to printing on the second laser printer, resulting in a close match with the ideal image. This composite function represents a mapping, $\mathcal{F}_{\text{output}}^{-1}(\mathcal{F}_{\text{input}}(.))$: $\Omega_{\text{DD}} \to \Omega_{\text{DD}}$, which is a remapping of the device-dependent values onto themselves. Recall that in order to preserve meaningful graytone definition with halftone images, it is necessary to scan the image and target ramp at a resolution well below the resolution of the printers. In this case, the images were produced using 1200 dpi, while the scanning was done at 300 dpi.

First consider the problem of determining $\mathcal{F}_{\text{output}}^{-1}$, which is the printer characterization problem. A block diagram of the laser printer characterization process is shown in Fig. 12.5a.

- Using laser printer 2 (the second laser printer), a grayscale ramp like that shown in Fig. 12.3 is printed. The printer uses control values, $\{g_1, g_2, \ldots, g_N\}$.
- The output grayscale samples are measured to obtain $L^*$ values for D50 illumination to obtain the visual descriptor values, $\{d_1, d_2, \cdots, d_N\}$.

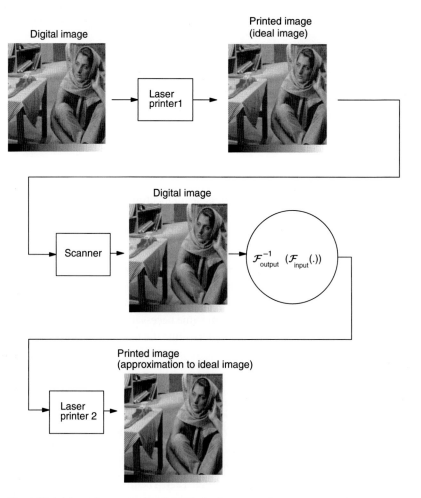

**Figure 12.4.** Monochrome device characterization example.

- The visual descriptor values are perceptually normalized ($d_i^{\text{scaled}}$).
- Linear interpolation is used to compute the mapping, $\mathcal{F}_{\text{output}}^{-1}: \Omega_P \rightarrow \Omega_{\text{DD}}$, which maps visual descriptor values to digital control values.

As mentioned, the perceptual normalization of the visual descriptor values is performed to account for visual adaptation to the reproduction white point and black point. In this example, the visual descriptors will be scaled using

$$d_i^{\text{scaled}} = 100 \left( \frac{d_i - d_{\min}}{d_{\max} - d_{\min}} \right), \quad i = 1, \ldots, N, \tag{12.6}$$

where there are $N = 33$ unique grayscale levels in the ramp shown in Fig. 12.3. The $d_i^{\text{scaled}}$ values represent normalized visual descriptor values. Equation (12.6) will scale the descriptors between 0 and 100 where $d_{\min}$ and $d_{\max}$ are the minimum and maximum visual descriptor values that can be produced by the output device.[2] Using linear

---

[2] The range 0–100 is arbitrary.

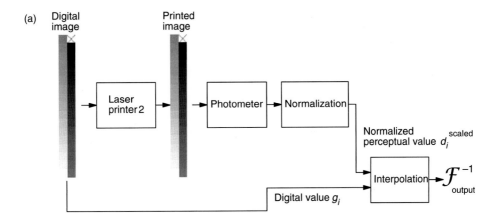

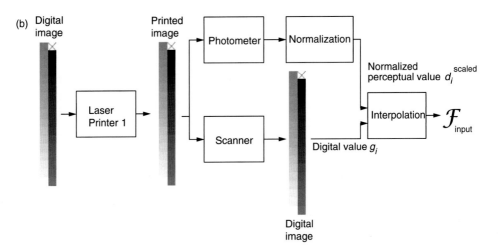

**Figure 12.5.** (a) Process for characterizing monochrome laser printer 2; (b) process for characterizing monochrome scanner.

interpolation to compute values for all $0 \leq d_i \leq 100$. Figure 12.6a shows a plot of the device characterization function $\mathcal{F}_{\text{output}}^{-1}$.

The process of determining $\mathcal{F}_{\text{output}}^{-1}$ is often called *device linearization*. The reason for this terminology is that $\mathcal{F}_{\text{output}}^{-1}$ can be used to determine steps in control values $g_i$ that will result in linear steps in visual descriptor values. For example, consider the linearly spaced control values $d_i$, defined by

$$d_i = \frac{i}{N}(d_{\max} - d_{\min}) + d_{\min}, \text{ for } i = 0, 1, \ldots, (N-1).$$

The control values obtained from

$$g_i' = \mathcal{F}_{\text{output}}^{-1}(d_i), \tag{12.7}$$

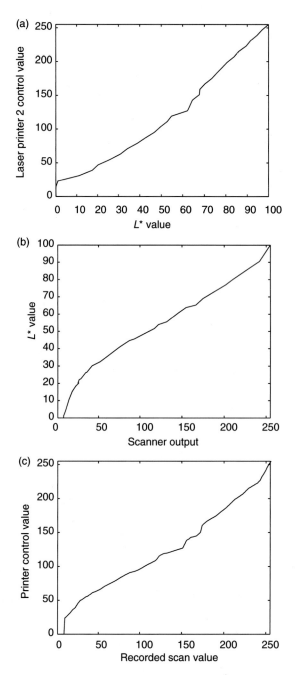

**Figure 12.6.** (a) Characterization mapping $\mathcal{F}_{\text{output}}^{-1}$ for laser printer 2; (b) characterization curve $\mathcal{F}_{\text{input}}$ for scanner; (c) composite function $\mathcal{F}_{\text{output}}^{-1}(\mathcal{F}_{\text{input}}(\cdot))$.

will produce the resulting visual descriptors,

$$d_i = \mathcal{F}_{\text{output}}(g_i'), \tag{12.8}$$

which are linearly spaced in the visual descriptor space by definition. See Problems 12.2–12.4 for exercises related to monochrome device characterization.

It remains to determine the scanner characterization $\mathcal{F}_{\text{input}}$. A block diagram of the scanner characterization process is shown in Fig. 12.5b. The process is as follows:

- A scan is made of an $N$-step grayscale ramp that was created using laser printer 1.
- The average scanned grayscale value for each square in the scanned grayscale wedge is computed, providing the values $g_i$ of Eq. (12.2).
- The same grayscale ramp is measured with a photometer to obtain the $L^*$ values for D50 illumination, which are the values $d_i$ of Eq. (12.2).
- As for the printer, the values $d_i$ are mapped to normalized perceptual values using Eq. (12.6).
- Linear interpolation is used to compute values for the entire output range of the scanner, giving the mapping shown in Fig. 12.6b.

Note that, ideally, the black in the grayscale ramp measured by the scanner should be at least as black as that which will occur in the images to be scanned. Similarly the white in the grayscale ramp should be at least as white as that which will occur in the images to be scanned. As was done here, creating the ramp from the process that created Fig. 12.7a (laser printer 1) insures that the black and white points of the grayscale ramp meet this requirement.

To demonstrate the effectiveness of the characterizations, the ideal image created by laser printer 1, shown in Fig. 12.7a, was scanned. The scanned data were then printed on laser printer 2 with no corrections. The scanned output of laser printer 2 is shown in Fig. 12.7b. Note that the contrast in the scanned image is significantly different from that of Fig. 12.7a. To display the scanned data properly, it is necessary to perform the composite function $\mathcal{F}_{\text{output}}^{-1}(\mathcal{F}_{\text{input}}(\cdot))$ prior to printing, as shown in Fig. 12.4. This composite function is shown in Fig. 12.6c. It should be noted that performing the perceptual normalization corrections to the visual data in determining $\mathcal{F}_{\text{output}}^{-1}$ and $\mathcal{F}_{\text{input}}$ has the advantage that the range space of the mapping $\mathcal{F}_{\text{input}}$ is within the domain of the mapping $\mathcal{F}_{\text{output}}^{-1}$. Without the perceptual normalization mapping, this may not occur since some devices can create darker visual descriptors than others and white points will vary according to the medium used. After applying the composite mapping to the scanned data, the resulting output from laser printer 2 was scanned and is shown in Fig. 12.7c. The corrected image from laser printer 2 is very close to that of the original image.

## 12.3    Color

The characterization of color devices is more difficult than monochrome characterization, primarily owing to the increase in dimension. As discussed in Chapter 8, the visual

(a)

(b)

(c)

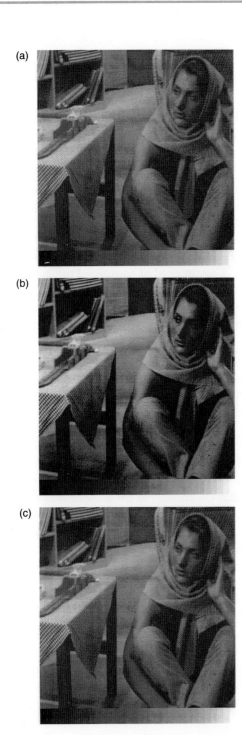

**Figure 12.7.** (a) Original image created on laser printer 1 and scanned; (b) image shown in (a) printed on laser printer 2 and scanned for display; (c) image corrected for output on laser printer 2.

description of color requires at least three values and many output devices use four or more control values to specify the amount of colorant to place on the paper. In spite of the dimension increase, the concept of color device characterization is the same as the monochrome device characterization problem discussed in Section 12.2. The goal is to determine a mapping between the digital vector value of the recorded or reproduced sample and some color visual descriptor of the sample. In color device characterization, color visual descriptors are commonly referred to as *device-independent* (DI) values. The reason for this terminology is that the device-independent values are not tied to a physical device. Instead, the device-independent values are related only to the human visual system. In the monochrome characterization problem of the previous section, the device-independent values were denoted by the scalar $d_i$. For color, the device-independent values are denoted by vectors, $\mathbf{d}_i$. Here we will expand on the color space definitions introduced in Chapter 8.

For describing device-independent color, it is useful to use the following terminology: Consider two spaces $\Omega_1$, $\Omega_2$, and a mapping $\mathcal{F}$.

- The mapping $\mathcal{F}$ is from $\Omega_1$ *into* $\Omega_2$ if for every value $\mathbf{c}$ in $\Omega_1$ the value $\mathbf{d} = \mathcal{F}(\mathbf{c})$ is in $\Omega_2$.
- The mapping $\mathcal{F}$ from $\Omega_1$ into $\Omega_2$ is a mapping *onto*[3] $\Omega_2$ if for every value $\mathbf{d}$ in $\Omega_2$ there is a value $\mathbf{c}$ in $\Omega_1$ for which $\mathbf{d} = \mathcal{F}(\mathbf{c})$.
- The mapping $\mathcal{F}$ from $\Omega_1$ into $\Omega_2$ is *one-to-one* if for every value $\mathbf{c}_1$ and $\mathbf{c}_2$ in $\Omega_1$, the relation $\mathcal{F}(\mathbf{c}_1) \neq \mathcal{F}(\mathbf{c}_2)$ implies $\mathbf{c}_1 \neq \mathbf{c}_2$, and $\mathcal{F}(\mathbf{c}_1) = \mathcal{F}(\mathbf{c}_2)$ implies $\mathbf{c}_1 = \mathbf{c}_2$.

Using the above terminology, a *device-independent color space* (DICS) is defined as any space for which there is a *one-to-one* mapping *onto* the CIEXYZ color space. Device-independent values describe color for the CIE standard observer. Examples of device-independent color spaces include CIEXYZ, CIELAB, CIELuv, and Yxy.

By definition, there cannot be a one-to-one mapping onto a device-independent color space from a *device-dependent color space* (DDCS). In the case of a recording device, e.g., a scanner or digital camera, the device-dependent (DD) values describe the response of that particular device to radiant (or reflected) energy. Recording devices are usually limited by having sensors that are not within a linear transformation of the CIE color matching functions (see Section 8.3.3). The sensors are also subject to saturation, which limits the range. Quantization is usually not a problem if the number of bits is large.

For a reproduction device, e.g., a printer or monitor, the device-dependent values describe only those colors the device can produce. Thus, for the reproduction device there may exist a one-to-one mapping ($\mathcal{F}_{output}$ in Example 12.1) from the device-dependent color space *into* the device-independent color space but not *onto* it. For CMYK (4-color) printers, the mapping from device-independent colors to device-dependent values is not one-to-one. The CMYK printer can place different combinations of ink concentrations on the paper (different device-dependent values), giving different reflectance spectra, which look the same visually (same device-independent values). Recall that this aliasing effect was introduced in Section 8.3.2 and is called metamerism.

---

[3] In other words, *onto* here implies that every point in $\Omega_2$ can be obtained using a value $\mathcal{F}(\mathbf{c})$ where $\mathbf{c}$ is in $\Omega_1$.

There are color spaces that will be defined as *pseudo-device independent color spaces* (PDICS). A pseudo-device independent color space is designed such that there will exist mappings between a number of device-dependent color spaces *into* the pseudo-device independent color space. Note however that there need not exist a mapping from a pseudo-device independent color space *onto* a device-independent color space, which implies that the pseudo-device independent color space is truly a device-dependent color space. Examples of pseudo-device independent color spaces include a number of standard RGB spaces [7, 258]. The usefulness of these spaces will be discussed later.

When transferring color image data between various devices, the color space used to communicate the color is of great importance. Communicating color using device-dependent values presents a problem in the world of networked computers and printers. Sending the same RGB value to different monitors can result in different colors. Similarly, sending the same CMYK value to different printers can result in different colors. To obtain the same output regardless of the display device, the user must know the characteristics of the device for which the original image is defined, in addition to the characteristics of the device on which the image is to be displayed. This is the previously mentioned closed loop design. This can work well for limited systems; for example, a copier can contain a scanner and a printer.

As discussed in Section 12.1, a better approach is the open loop design since it is necessary to know only the mappings between the *interchange color space* (ICS) and the device-dependent values of the display device. The interchange color space is typically selected to be a device-independent color space or a pseudo-device independent color space. The advantages of using a pseudo-device independent color space versus a device-independent color space as the interchange color space will be discussed later. In the above example of a copier, the manufacturer may have several different combinations of scanners and printers from which to choose.

For the open loop design, it is necessary to determine a function $\mathcal{F}_{device}: \Omega_{DD} \rightarrow \Omega_{ICS}$ that will provide a mapping from device-dependent values to the interchange color space. The notation with the function indicates the source and destination spaces. If the device records images, then the mapping $\mathcal{F}_{device}$ is sufficient to characterize the device. In the case of a display device, it is necessary to determine a transformation, $\mathcal{F}_{device}^{-1}$: $\Omega_{ICS} \rightarrow \Omega_{DD}$. This denotes that $\mathcal{F}_{device}^{-1}$ is a mapping from the interchange color space into a device-dependent color space. Finally, for soft-copy display devices, $\mathcal{F}_{device}$ and $\mathcal{F}_{device}^{-1}$ may be needed since such devices are commonly used as both a source of image data, e.g., creation of graphics images that are subsequently printed, and as a display device for viewing recorded images.

We need the concepts of white point, black point and dynamic range that were used in the section on monochrome devices. In the color world, the definitions of these terms become more complex. There are differences in definition of these terms depending on whether the device is additive or subtractive. For additive devices, such as soft-copy displays, the white point is usually defined as the color with all primaries at their maximum values, e.g., $[R, G, B] = [255, 255, 255]$, and the black point as the color with all zero input, e.g., $[R, G, B] = [0, 0, 0]$. However, we also use the terminology to denote the white point of an image transformation. The two should not be confused. The white point of the display device is characteristic of that device. The white point of a transformation refers to how the device is being used.

The white point of a subtractive color output device is defined as the color obtained when there are no colorants placed on the material. For a printer, the white point of the device depends on the reflectivity characteristics of the paper. This can correspond to the definition for additive systems if the input is [R, G, B], since [R, G, B] = [255, 255, 255] corresponds to no colorant on the paper. However, for subtractive devices, the black point is defined as the neutral color ($a^* = 0$, $b^* = 0$) with minimum $L^*$ that the device can create. This is needed since putting the maximum concentration of all inks or toners on the paper may not yield a neutral color. The black point is determined after other operations, such as undercolor removal (see Section 12.3.8) have been completed.

The dynamic range of a display device is defined by the gamut of the device, which represents the range of colors the device can create. This range is defined by the properties of the colorants or primaries used in the color reproduction process. It is represented as a three-dimensional solid in any color space of interest.

In the end, the performance of a methodology can be only as good as the relationship of the CIE color space to actual human visual perception space. Experiments are still carried out studying perceptual differences and observer variability [5]. Note that as improvements to the CIE color space are made, the mathematics described here will remain valid and just as useful.

## 12.3.1  Device gamut

Modern printers and display devices are limited in the colors they can produce. This limited set of colors is defined as the *gamut* of the device. If $\Omega_{\mathrm{DICS}}$ is the range of numerical values in the selected device-independent color space and $\Omega_{\mathrm{DD}}$ is the numerical range of the device-dependent values, then the set

$$\Omega_{\mathrm{gamut}} = \{\, \mathbf{t} \in \Omega_{\mathrm{DICS}} \mid \text{there is a } \mathbf{c} \in \Omega_{\mathrm{DD}} \text{ where } \mathcal{F}_{\mathrm{device}}(\mathbf{c}) = \mathbf{t} \,\} \qquad (12.9)$$

defines the gamut of the color output device. Similarly, the complement set,

$$\Omega_{\mathrm{gamut}}^{c} = \{\, \mathbf{t} \in \Omega_{\mathrm{DICS}} \mid \text{there is not a } \mathbf{c} \in \Omega_{\mathrm{DD}} \text{ where } \mathcal{F}_{\mathrm{device}}(\mathbf{c}) = \mathbf{t} \,\}, \qquad (12.10)$$

defines colors outside the device gamut. For colors in the gamut, there will exist a mapping between the device-dependent values and the device-independent color space. Colors that are in $\Omega_{\mathrm{gamut}}^{c}$ cannot be reproduced and must be *gamut mapped* to a color that is within $\Omega_{\mathrm{gamut}}$. The gamut mapping algorithm, $\mathcal{D}$, is a mapping from $\Omega_{\mathrm{DICS}}$ to $\Omega_{\mathrm{gamut}}$, that is $\mathcal{D}(\mathbf{t}) \in \Omega_{\mathrm{gamut}}$ for every $\mathbf{t} \in \Omega_{\mathrm{DICS}}$. Figure 12.8 shows a conceptual 2-D picture of this 3-D process, where an out-of-gamut vector $\mathbf{t}$ is first mapped into the device gamut to a vector $\mathbf{t}_{g}$, at which point the desired control value $\mathbf{c}$ is determined ( $\mathbf{t} \rightarrow \mathbf{t}_{g} \rightarrow \mathbf{c}$ ). Gamut mapping is discussed in detail in Section 12.3.10.

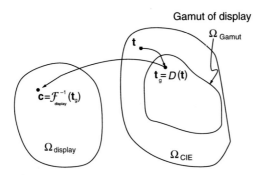

**Figure 12.8.** The mappings $\mathcal{F}_{\text{display}}$ and $\mathcal{D}$.

## 12.3.2    Selection of interchange color space

The 2-D graphical representation in Fig. 12.9a illustrates how a pseudo-device independent color space could be effectively used as an interchange color space. In this figure, the gamuts of two devices are denoted by $G_1$ and $G_2$. Since the gamuts of the two devices are completely inside the gamut of the pseudo-device independent color space, the device-dependent data from one device could be colorimetrically communicated to the other device without ever having to transfer data to the device-independent color space.

An advantage of using a pseudo-device independent color space as the interchange color space as opposed to a device-independent color space is that there may be less quantization error introduced if a pseudo-device independent color space is used. The reason for the reduced error can be visualized by Fig. 12.10. In representing the colorimetric data with digital samples, it is necessary to sample the interchange color space. In Fig. 12.10a, $N$ bits are used to quantize the entire device-independent color space. In Fig. 12.10b, the same number of bits are used to quantize the pseudo-device independent color space. Note that the step size in Fig. 12.10b is smaller than in Fig. 12.10a, which will result in less quantization error. Essentially, using the pseudo-device independent color space as the interchange color space will provide improved quantization in the colors that the devices can reproduce, since codes are not used to represent colors the devices are unable to reproduce.

Quantization errors are also affected by the uniformity of the interchange color space [141, 255]. Clearly, uniform sampling of the color space is optimal only when the Euclidean difference between two points is related to a specific perceptual difference regardless of where the points are located. The concept of uniformity in a color space was introduced in Chapter 8.

When two new devices are introduced with gamuts that are outside the gamut of the pseudo-device independent color space a problem can occur. In this case, color information that could be communicated using a device-independent color space is lost since it must be gamut mapped into the gamut of the pseudo-device independent color space. This problem is illustrated in Fig. 12.9b.

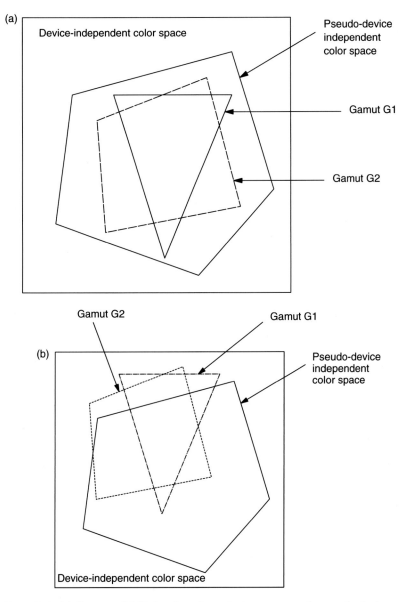

**Figure 12.9.** (a) Conceptual 2-D drawing of two device gamuts and a pseudo-device independent color space; (b) conceptual 2-D drawing of two device gamuts and a pseudo-device independent color space: device gamuts have values outside the allowable range of values in the pseudo-device independent color space.

An additional problem with using a pseudo-device independent color space is that the space may not be well suited for gamut mapping. Unlike CIELAB, the Euclidean difference between two nearby points in the pseudo-device independent color space may not relate to any notion of perceptual difference. In addition, a common practice for

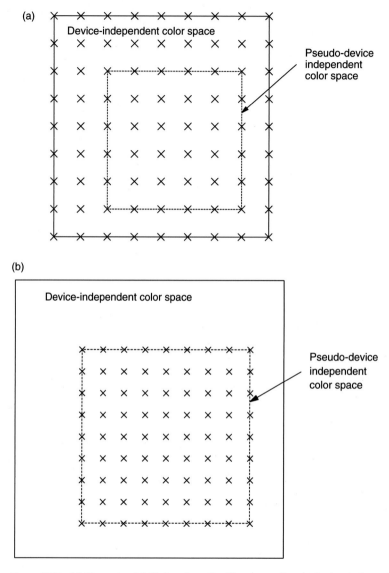

**Figure 12.10.** (a) Conceptual 2-D drawing of uniform sampling in device-independent color space; (b) conceptual 2-D drawing of uniform sampling in pseudo-device independent color space.

gamut mapping is to preserve the hue at the expense of lightness and chroma. These terms are described in Figure 8.19. For CIELAB, lines of constant hue have been empirically determined [122]. For many pseudo-device independent color spaces, it is unclear how to map along lines of constant hue, and such a mapping may be very complex. One approach would be to convert the data to a device-independent color space such as CIELAB, but this negates one of the often proclaimed advantages of a pseudo-device independent color space by introducing additional computations.

### 12.3.3    Calibration and profiling

As verbs, the terms *characterize* and *profile* are frequently used to mean the same thing in the world of digital color science. The technical terms *profile* and *calibrate*, however, are often improperly interchanged.

A *device profile* (or simply *profile* as a noun) is defined by the mappings $\mathcal{F}_{\text{device}}$, $\mathcal{F}_{\text{device}}^{-1}$, and $\mathcal{D}$. These mappings describe the transformation between an interchange color space and the device-dependent values. Therefore, a profile completely characterizes a reproduction or recording device. The profile for certain devices such as scanners and digital cameras needs only $\mathcal{F}_{\text{device}}$. The International Color Consortium (ICC) has suggested a standard format for describing a profile. This standard profile can be based on a physically based mathematical model (common for monitors) or a look-up table (LUT) (common for printers and scanners) [129, 210]. An ICC profile can be fairly simple, or quite complex. Figure 12.11 displays an example of the information that is often contained within an ICC profile for a printer. In this profile, there is the header information and the tag table that is used to locate the data in the file. In addition, there are three distinct mapping types denoted by the mapping pairs $\{\mathcal{F}_i(.), \mathcal{F}_i^{-1}(\mathcal{D}_i(.))\}, i = 1, 2, 3$. The ability to provide different mapping types for a single device enables the incorporation

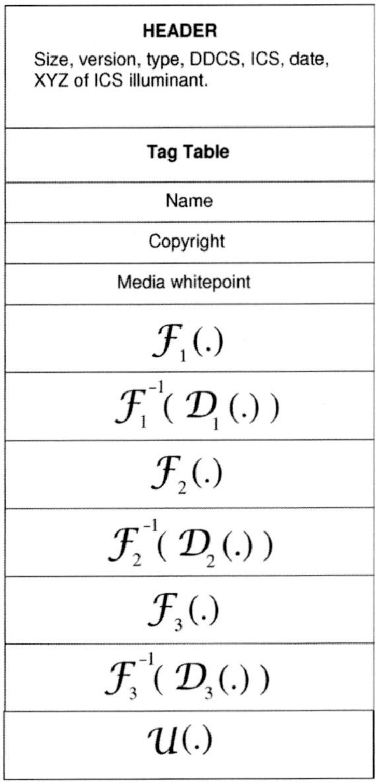

| HEADER<br>Size, version, type, DDCS, ICS, date,<br>XYZ of ICS illuminant. |
| --- |
| **Tag Table** |
| Name |
| Copyright |
| Media whitepoint |
| $\mathcal{F}_1(.)$ |
| $\mathcal{F}_1^{-1}(\mathcal{D}_1(.))$ |
| $\mathcal{F}_2(.)$ |
| $\mathcal{F}_2^{-1}(\mathcal{D}_2(.))$ |
| $\mathcal{F}_3(.)$ |
| $\mathcal{F}_3^{-1}(\mathcal{D}_3(.))$ |
| $\mathcal{U}(.)$ |

**Figure 12.11.** Simplified diagram of the ICC format for a color printer: the functions are defined in Section 12.3; the function $\mathcal{U}$ is an out-of-gamut indictor.

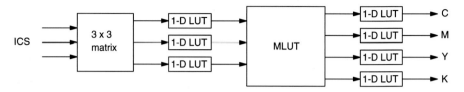

**Figure 12.12.** Functional form used in the ICC format for describing printer mappings: this is the mapping from interchange color space to the device-dependent color space; note, per specification, if the interchange color space is not CIEXYZ then the $3 \times 3$ matrix must be the identity matrix [129].

of multiple gamut mapping methods, as well as rendering effects. These functional mappings are described using matrices, multidimensional look-up tables (MLUTs), and 1-D look-up tables (LUTs), as shown in Fig. 12.12. The function $\mathcal{U}$ in Fig. 12.11 is an out-of-gamut function from the interchange color space to a binary value of 255 if the point is in-gamut and 0 if the point is out-of-gamut. This function is useful for comparing the gamuts of devices.

*Calibration* is different from profiling, in that the goal of calibration is to place the recording or reproduction device into a known state. This may be achieved by adjusting specific controls on the device or through software. Depending upon the device and the level of control desired, calibration is performed periodically or only when there are significant changes in the device, for example when the device is moved to a new environment, the medium is changed or colorants are replaced.

Mathematically, the calibration problem can be described by considering two mappings from the device-dependent color space to a device-independent color space. One mapping is the current state of the device, $\mathcal{F}_{\text{curr}}: \Omega_{\text{DD}} \to \Omega_{\text{ICS}}$, and the other mapping is the desired state, $\mathcal{F}_{\text{des}}: \Omega_{\text{DD}} \to \Omega_{\text{ICS}}$. If the calibration is achieved through the use of software, then the goal is to determine a mapping $\mathcal{G}$, from the device-dependent color space into the device-dependent color space, such that

$$\mathcal{F}_{\text{curr}}(\mathcal{G}(\mathbf{c})) = \mathcal{F}_{\text{des}}(\mathbf{c}), \tag{12.11}$$

for all device-dependent values $\mathbf{c}$. Assuming that the mapping $\mathcal{F}_{\text{curr}}^{-1}$ exists, $\mathcal{G}$ is given by

$$\mathcal{G}(\cdot) = \mathcal{F}_{\text{curr}}^{-1}(\mathcal{F}_{\text{des}}(\cdot)). \tag{12.12}$$

A direct approach to calibration would be to determine the mappings $\mathcal{F}_{\text{curr}}^{-1}$ and $\mathcal{F}_{\text{des}}$. Of course, determining $\mathcal{F}_{\text{curr}}^{-1}$ would be equivalent to determining the device profile.

Typically, a *channel independent* form is used for the function $\mathcal{G}$. This form significantly lowers complexity and is adequate for most devices. If the device-dependent values are $N$-tuplets, usually $N=3$ or $N=4$, then $\mathcal{G}$ is expressed as

$$\mathcal{G}(\mathbf{c}) = [\mathcal{G}_1(c_1), \ldots, \mathcal{G}_N(c_N)]^T, \tag{12.13}$$

where $\mathbf{c} = [c_1, \ldots, c_N]^T$ is a device-dependent vector, and the functions $\mathcal{G}_i, i = 1, \ldots, N$, are scalar valued mappings. Calibration is achieved by determining the mappings,

$\mathcal{G}_i, i = 1, \ldots, N$. In this case, $\mathcal{F}_{curr}$ and $\mathcal{F}_{des}$ are replaced by a current state and desired state for each of the $N$ channels giving

$$\mathcal{F}_{curr}(\mathbf{c}) = [\mathcal{F}_{curr_1}(c_1), \ldots, \mathcal{F}_{curr_N}(c_N)]^T, \qquad (12.14)$$

$$\mathcal{F}_{des}(\mathbf{c}) = [\mathcal{F}_{des1}(c_1), \ldots, \mathcal{F}_{des_N}(c_N)]^T. \qquad (12.15)$$

At this point, the procedure of calibration becomes similar to the method used for characterizing monochrome devices shown in Section 12.2. Note that interchannel compensations cannot be made with this calibration method.

---

**Example 12.2.** As an example, consider channel $k$ of an $N$ channel color display device. A set of $M$ control values $\{\mathbf{c}_i\}_{i=1}^M$ is sent to the device. These values step from no colorant to full colorant for channel $k$. An example sequence for a CMYK printer may be

$$\{[0, 0, 0, 0], [15, 0, 0, 0], [31, 0, 0, 0], \ldots, [255, 0, 0, 0]\},$$

where $[0, 0, 0, 0]$ places no colorant on the paper and $[255, 0, 0, 0]$ places 100% cyan on the paper, but no other colorant. The resulting set of reflection spectra, $\{\mathbf{r}_i\}_{i=1}^M$, produced by the control sequence is measured using an instrument that provides visual descriptors. As in the case of the monochrome characterization problem of Section 12.2, the visual descriptors could be various standard types, including ANSI/ISO Status density values (see Section 8.7.4) or CIE values. In any case, these measurements provide the current state of the $k$th channel.

---

### Densitometric approach

If a Status reflection densitometer (see Section 8.7.4) is used to quantify the current state, then the measuring instrument reports a four-element CMYK vector for each of the $M$ samples. Typically, only one element of each of the $M$ four-element vectors is used to describe the current state of channel $k$. If the yellow channel is being measured, then the yellow element of the CMYK vector reported by the instrument is used to describe the state of the channel. Some high-fidelity printers have nontypical colorants such as green or orange. For these colorants, the CMYK element used to describe the state of the channel is the one that provides the largest difference between no colorant and maximum colorant.

In the case of the cyan colorant, the set of cyan elements of the $M$ measurement vectors is used to describe the current state of the cyan channel for the reproduction device. These values will be denoted by $\{C_j\}_{j=1}^M$. It is necessary to determine a desired state of the device in terms of density values, which will be denoted by $\{D_j\}_{j=1}^M$. The $\{D_j\}_{j=1}^M$ may be a set of equally spaced density values from the no colorant value to the maximum colorant value. In this case, the sequence $\{D_j\}_{j=1}^M$ will be given by

$$D_j = \frac{(j-1)(C_M - C_1)}{M - 1} + C_1. \qquad (12.16)$$

In the monochrome calibration example of Section 12.2, it was pointed out that the monochrome calibration process was often referred to as linearization. The same term is often used to describe the color calibration problem also, since the desired state can readily be defined by a set of equal steps in density as given in Eq. (12.16).

### Colorimetric approach

If a CIE color space, such as CIELAB, is used to quantify the samples, then the instrument reports a three-element vector for each of the $M$ samples, as opposed to the four-element vector reported by the Status densitometer. While we are still operating in a channel independent model, a question occurs as to how to use this information to calibrate the instrument. For example, if only the $L^*$ value of the three-element CIELAB vector is used to calibrate the device, then sensitivity to noise and quantization may occur since for colorants, such as yellow, there is very little difference between the $L^*$ value at maximum colorant and the paper white. There is, however, a large difference in $b^*$ between maximum yellow colorant and paper white. This information can be used in the calibration process by looking at the change in $\Delta E_{ab}^*$ between adjacent samples as we go from no colorant to maximum colorant for each of the colorant channels. In this case, if the CIELAB values for the $M$ samples are given by the vectors $\{\mathbf{t}_j\}_{j=1}^M$, then the values used to describe the current state of the device for that channel are given by

$$C_j = \sum_{i=1}^{j-1} ||\mathbf{t}_i - \mathbf{t}_{i+1}||, \quad j = 2, \ldots, M, \tag{12.17}$$

$$C_1 = 0.$$

The values, $C_j$, can be interpreted as the distance along the curve in the color space that is traced as the printer lays down no colorant to maximum colorant. Again relating calibration to linearization, it is often desired to have uniform steps occur in $\Delta E_{ab}^*$ as the control values are stepped uniformly along the path from no colorant to maximum colorant. In this case, the desired $M$ values are given by

$$D_j = \frac{j-1}{M-1} \sum_{i=1}^{M-1} ||\mathbf{t}_i - \mathbf{t}_{i+1}||, \quad j = 1, \ldots, M. \tag{12.18}$$

### Calibration mapping

For both the colorimetric and densitometric approaches, there are three sets of values that are used: the control values, the measured values, and the desired values. The control values drive the particular channel of the device, e.g., the cyan values mentioned above of $\{0, 15, 31, \ldots, 255\}$, which will be denoted by $\{v_{jk}\}_{j=1}^M$ for the $k$th channel. Note that since we are looking at the $k$th channel, $v_{jk}$ relates to the device-dependent control vector $\mathbf{c}_j$ of Eqs. (12.13)–(12.15) by

$$v_{jk} = [\mathbf{c}_j]_k, \tag{12.19}$$

where $[\mathbf{c}]_k$ selects the $k$th element of the vector $\mathbf{c}$. The measured and desired sets are given respectively by $\{C_j\}_{j=1}^M$ and $\{D_j\}_{j=1}^M$ (Eqs. (12.16)–(12.18)). To calibrate the channel, it is necessary to determine a mapping from the control values to new control values (i.e., $\mathbf{c} \rightarrow \mathbf{c}'$.) (See Eqs. (12.12)–(12.13).) If the current relationship between the control value and the descriptor value for the $k$th channel is given by the mapping

$$\mathcal{F}_{\text{curr}_k}(v_{jk}) = C_j, \tag{12.20}$$

and the desired state is given by

$$\mathcal{F}_{\text{des}_k}(v_{jk}) = D_j, \tag{12.21}$$

then the correction mapping is given by a function, $\mathcal{G}_k$, a component of the vector in Eq. (12.13), where

$$\mathcal{F}_{\text{curr}_k}(\mathcal{G}_k(v_{jk})) = \mathcal{F}_{\text{des}_k}(v_{jk}) = D_j. \tag{12.22}$$

Assuming the inverse $\mathcal{F}_{\text{curr}_k}$ exists, $\mathcal{G}_k$ is given by

$$\mathcal{G}_k(\cdot) = \mathcal{F}_{\text{curr}_k}^{-1}(\mathcal{F}_{\text{des}_k}(\cdot)). \tag{12.23}$$

In other words, calibration of the $k$th channel of the device is achieved by applying the function $\mathcal{F}_{\text{curr}_k}^{-1}(\mathcal{F}_{\text{des}_k}(\cdot))$ to that channel's control value, prior to sending it to the output device.

The problem of determining the mapping $\mathcal{F}_{\text{curr}_k}^{-1}(\mathcal{F}_{\text{des}_k}(.))$ is equivalent to the monochrome example given in Example 12.1. This equivalence is a result of the channel-independent assumption mentioned earlier in this Section.

If the density values of the device in the desired state are outside the range of the device in the current state, then the mapping $\mathcal{F}_{\text{curr}_k}^{-1}$ is creating control values that are outside the range of allowable values. In this case, these values must be mapped to values that are within the device range. This mapping can be performed using a simple clipping operation, or using something similar to the gamut mapping methods discussed in Section 12.3.10.

Calibration is often used in combination with profiling. Creating an accurate profile is usually measurement intensive and therefore time consuming. In contrast, calibration is often performed using very few measurements. For this reason, a calibration procedure is often used to return a device to a state in which a previously computed profile is a valid characterization.

## 12.3.4    Color management systems

A color management system (CMS) is the system that applies the various profiles and gamut mapping algorithms to transform the image data from one device-dependent color space to another. Figure 12.13 shows an overview of the entire process of recording, mapping and reproducing an image. The transformations implemented by the color management system can be performed in several different levels including: in a device, e.g., Adobe Postscript™ level 2 and 3; in a device driver, e.g., Canon Colorgear™; in an

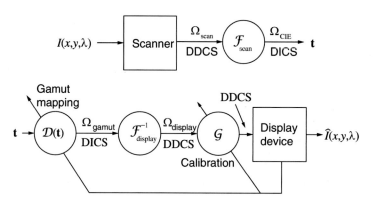

**Figure 12.13.** Color management block diagram.

application, e.g., Adobe Photoshop™; or in an operating system, e.g., Apple ColorSync™ or Microsoft Windows Color System™ (WCS) [239].

It is interesting to note that the Microsoft Windows Color System™ can either use ICC profiles created for a device or create a mapping using the colorimetric measurements that are typically used to create an ICC profile. These measurements are stored within an ICC profile through the use of a private tag in the profile file. In this case, WCS will use the colorimetric measurements to fit a suitable device model, color appearance model and gamut mapping model. While offering flexibility over the standard ICC work flow, this approach may require more device driver code development, especially for those devices that provide embedded solutions.

Many of these systems use multidimensional look-up tables (MLUTs) to describe the functional mapping between the interchange color space and the device-dependent color spaces. To reduce the effect of noise, the systems rarely map the image data to the interchange color space. Instead, all the operations to be performed are linked into a new MLUT that transforms the image data directly to the output device control values. In other words, for the color management system in Fig. 12.13, an MLUT is computed that approximates the composite function $G(\mathcal{F}_{display}^{-1}(\mathcal{D}(\mathcal{F}_{scan}(\cdot))))$. This composite function is the only operation performed on the recorded data.

Many image file formats, e.g., XPS, PDF and JPEG, currently provide options for embedding a source profile within the image file. This source profile contains the information on how to convert from the device-dependent values of the image data to device-independent values. Again, the color management system will typically take this profile and combine it with any other operations that will be performed on the image data.

## 12.3.5    Models

In constructing the mapping between the interchange color space and the device-dependent color space, there are two primary approaches; a parametric or model-based method and a nonparametric method. The model-based approach uses a functional form characterized by a limited number of parameters. One example is the colorimetric or spectral Neugebauer model for a printer [14, 193, 231, 284]. The model parameters are often determined by collecting a few measurements and performing a least squares fit. Unfortunately, there is no single device model that works well for the large variety of devices. Many models that are used are nonlinear, which may affect the processing speed. To increase the processing speed, an MLUT approximation of the functional mapping is often computed. In this case, the continuous nonlinear function is approximated by a fast tetrahedral or trilinear interpolation of the MLUT entries. Multidimensional look-up table interpolation computations are reviewed in Appendix D.

The nonparametric approach relies upon a dense sampling of the device-dependent color space, such that MLUT entries can be accurately determined by interpolation and extrapolation from the measured values. An artificial neural network method would be classified as a nonparametric approach. The advantage of a nonparametric approach is that no physical model is required. A disadvantage of the nonparametric approach is that collecting the large number of measurements can be time consuming. In addition, it is difficult to know how to update the mapping if a minor change in conditions occurs, e.g., paper lot or ink lot changes.

### 12.3.6 Profiling of capture devices

Profiling or characterizing an input device requires the determination of a function that will map the recorded values to device-independent values. The most common input devices are scanners and digital cameras. As in the monochrome case, the primary difference between these two devices is that the camera image can be recorded under various illuminants while the scanner illuminant does not change.

#### Scanners
Mathematically, the recording process of a scanner can be expressed as

$$\mathbf{z}_i = \mathcal{H}(\mathbf{M}^T \mathbf{r}_i), \tag{12.24}$$

where the matrix $\mathbf{M}$ contains the spectral sensitivity of the three (or more) bands of the device, $\mathbf{r}_i$ is the spectral reflectance at spatial point $i$, $\mathcal{H}$ models any nonlinearities in the scanner, and $\mathbf{z}_i$ is the vector of recorded values. The matrix $\mathbf{M}$ includes the effects of optics and the illuminant. The function $\mathcal{H}$ is invertible within the range of interest.

*Colorimetric scanning* is defined as the process of scanning or recording an image such that the device-independent values of the image can be recovered from the recorded data. Recall from Section 8.3.3 that this means that the sensor functions are within a linear transformation of the CIE color matching functions. This means that image reflectances that appear different to a standard observer under a given illuminant will be recorded as different device-dependent values. Mathematically, this implies

$$\mathbf{A}^T \mathbf{L}_v \mathbf{r}_k \neq \mathbf{A}^T \mathbf{L}_v \mathbf{r}_j \;\Rightarrow\; \mathbf{M}^T \mathbf{r}_k \neq \mathbf{M}^T \mathbf{r}_j, \tag{12.25}$$

for all $\mathbf{r}_k, \mathbf{r}_j \in \Omega_r$ $k \neq j$ where $\Omega_r$ is the set of physically realizable reflectance spectra. This is essentially Property 8 (ideal color recording), discussed in Section 8.3.3.

Given such a scanner, the characterization problem is to determine the continuous mapping $\mathcal{F}_{\text{scan}}$ that transforms the recorded values to a device-independent color space. In other words, determine the function $\mathcal{F}_{\text{scan}}$ such that

$$\mathbf{t} = \mathbf{A}^T \mathbf{L}_v \mathbf{r} = \mathcal{F}_{\text{scan}}(\mathbf{z}), \tag{12.26}$$

for all $\mathbf{r} \in \Omega_r$. If the sensors are colorimetric, the transformation is a simple $3 \times 3$ matrix multiplication. Unfortunately, most scanners are not colorimetric. This is caused by physical limitations on the scanner illuminants and filters that prevent them from being within a linear transformation of the CIE color matching functions.

For the noncolorimetric scanner, there will exist spectral reflectances that look different to the standard human observer, but when scanned produce the same recorded values. These colors are defined as being metameric to the scanner. Likewise, there will exist spectral reflectances that give different scan values, but look the same to the standard human observer. While the latter can be corrected by the transformation $\mathcal{F}_{\text{scan}}$, the former cannot.

On the upside, there will often exist a set of reflectance spectra over which a transformation from scan values to device-independent values will exist. Most hard-copy images, including printed images and photographs, are produced with a limited set of colorants. Reflectance spectra from such processes have been well modeled with very few (3–5) basis vectors [51, 114, 291, 299]. When limited to such data sets, it may be possible to determine a transformation $\mathcal{F}_{\text{scan}}$ such that

$$\mathbf{t} = \mathbf{A}^T \mathbf{L}_v \mathbf{r} = \mathcal{F}_{\text{scan}}(\mathbf{z}), \tag{12.27}$$

for all $\mathbf{r}$ contained in the data set. The idea of using a limited data set to determine such a mapping is discussed in [118].

Look-up tables as well as nonlinear and linear models for $\mathcal{F}_{\text{scan}}$ have been used to characterize color scanners [11, 102, 121, 136, 137, 295, 296]. In all of these approaches, the first step is to select a collection of color patches that span the colors of interest. The reflectance spectra of these $M_q$ color patches will be denoted by $\{\mathbf{q}_k\}_{k=1}^{M_q}$. Ideally, these colors should not be metameric in terms of the scanner sensitivities or to the standard observer under the illuminant for which the profile is being produced. This constraint assures a one-to-one mapping between the device-dependent values and the device-independent values across these samples. In practice, this constraint is easily obtained. The standards IT8.7/1-1993 and ISO 12641:1997(E) define a standard for scanner characterization targets. The standards define layout and color range of the samples. Most of the major color film manufacturers have such targets available. A Kodak version is shown in Fig. D.2.

For the target supplied by the film manufacturer, the CIELAB values of the patches are often provided. It should be realized however that each individual target is not measured by the manufacturer. Instead, a batch of targets is created and a nominal measurement for the batch is determined. To achieve the best results, it is recommended that the patches on the target be measured using a spectrophotometer or a colorimeter, rather than using the nominal batch measurements. These sample device-independent values will be denoted by

$$\left\{ \mathbf{t}_k = \mathbf{A}^T \mathbf{L}_v \mathbf{q}_k \right\}_{k=1}^{M_q}. \tag{12.28}$$

Without loss of generality, $\{\mathbf{t}_k\}_{k=1}^{M_q}$ could represent any colorimetric or device-independent values, e.g., CIELAB and CIELUV, in which case $\{\mathbf{t}_k = \mathcal{L}(\mathbf{A}^T \mathbf{L}_v \mathbf{q}_k)\}_{k=1}^{M_q}$, where $\mathcal{L}(\cdot)$ is the transformation from CIEXYZ to the appropriate device-independent color space. The scanner to be characterized is used to measure the patches, which provides the device-dependent values $\{\mathbf{z}_k = \mathcal{H}(\mathbf{M}^T \mathbf{q}_k)\}_{k=1}^{M_q}$.

Mathematically, the characterization problem is a classic least squares minimization problem: find a transformation $\mathcal{F}_{\text{scan}}$ where

$$\mathcal{F}_{\text{scan}} = \arg \left( \min_{\mathcal{F}} \sum_{i=1}^{M_q} ||\mathcal{F}(\mathbf{z}_i) - \mathcal{L}(\mathbf{t}_i)||^2 \right), \tag{12.29}$$

and $|| \cdot ||^2$ is the error metric in the device-independent color space. Other metrics may be used if desired.

In practice, it may be necessary and desirable to incorporate constraints on $\mathcal{F}_{\text{scan}}$. Constraints of interest include the following:

data consistency:

$$\mathcal{F}_{\text{scan}} \in \{ \mathcal{G} \mid ||\mathcal{G}(\mathbf{u}_i) - \mathcal{L}(\mathbf{t}_i)|| \le \delta_v, \quad i = 1, \ldots, M_p \}, \tag{12.30}$$

where $\delta_v$ is a just-noticeable-difference (JND) threshold.

smoothness:

$$\mathcal{F}_{\text{scan}} \in \{ \mathcal{G} \mid ||(\nabla \mathcal{G})(\mathbf{u})|| \le \delta_{\text{smooth}}, \quad \forall \mathbf{u} \in \Omega_{\text{scan}} \}, \tag{12.31}$$

where $\Omega_{\text{scan}}$ is the range of numerical values produced by the scanner, and $\nabla \mathcal{G}$ is the gradient of the function $\mathcal{G}$. The motivation for requiring smoothness is that the underlying physical reproduction process of the scanner is usually well behaved. The smoothness constraint is a way to *regularize* the solution to keep from overfitting the data (see Section 14.1.7). Details of how to create an MLUT based characterization for a scanner are given in Appendix D.

### Digital cameras

The characterization of a color digital camera can be formulated in the same manner as that of a color scanner with the addition of a variable recording illuminant into the model. Unfortunately the illumination under which an image is recorded can vary among daylight, tungsten, fluorescent, with flash, without flash or combinations of these. Figure 10.16 illustrates some effects of illumination on the recorded image data.

Another problem is that the class of reflectance spectra cannot be as readily limited for the camera as for the desktop scanner. For example, the desktop scanner can be easily profiled for a particular film/paper type, but the digital camera will be used for recording images with a more varied selection of reflectance spectra, as well as radiant sources.

A profile for the digital color camera is valid for only one recording illuminant. To avoid the need for a large number of separate profiles, one for each possible illuminant, we can estimate the profile for a new illuminant based on an existing profile for the camera for a known illuminant. To do this, it is necessary first to determine the illumination under which the image was recorded [31, 89, 159, 269]. Once an estimate of the illumination has been determined, changing the profile for the recording illumination can be done using a common least squares approach.

Mathematically, this illumination correction problem can be described as follows: let there exist a profile $\mathcal{F}_{\text{camera}}$ for the digital camera for images recorded under illuminant $\mathbf{L}_v$. This profile was created for images recorded as

$$\mathbf{d}_i = \mathbf{N}^T \mathbf{L}_v \mathbf{r}_i. \tag{12.32}$$

Owing to limited control, an image is recorded under illuminant $\mathbf{L}_r$ giving recorded values of

$$\mathbf{c}_i = \mathbf{N}^T \mathbf{L}_r \mathbf{r}_i, \tag{12.33}$$

where the columns of $\mathbf{N}$ are the spectral sensitivity of the camera.

The question is: what transformation should be performed on the values $\mathbf{c}_i$ prior to using the mapping $\mathcal{F}_{\text{camera}}$? For example, if no transformation is performed and $\mathbf{L}_v$ is D50, while $\mathbf{L}_r$ is F2 fluorescent, then the images will appear to have a green cast when later viewed. This effect implies that an illumination correction on the values $\mathbf{c}_i$ is needed. The relation to the white balance problem of Section 10.2.5 is noted. To correct for this problem, one approach is to find a mapping $\mathcal{B}_{\text{r2v}}$ such that

$$\mathcal{B}_{\text{r2v}} = \arg(\min_{\mathcal{B}} E\{||\mathcal{B}(\mathbf{c}) - \mathbf{N}^T \mathbf{L}_v \mathbf{r}||^2\}). \tag{12.34}$$

The solution to this problem is often achieved using ensemble statistics for the reflectance spectra. Once a mapping is determined, the profile for the camera under illuminant $\mathbf{L}_r$ can be expressed as $\mathcal{F}_{\text{camera}}(\mathcal{B}_{\text{r2v}}(\cdot))$. Note that the camera white point setting is designed to perform this correction.

## 12.3.7    Profiling of display devices

Characterization of a display device requires the determination of a mapping from the device-independent color space to the device-dependent color space. In this section, soft and hard-copy devices are discussed.

## Cathode ray tubes

The profile for a CRT is almost always based on a physical model of the device [25, 26, 34, 60, 175, 215]. Problems such as spatial variation of the screen or electron gun dependence are typically ignored, but have been considered [58, 61]. For more complex relationships, an MLUT can also be used to characterize the CRT [257].

A typical model is

$$\mathbf{t} = \mathbf{H}[r', g', b']^T + \mathbf{t}_{bp}, \tag{12.35}$$

where

$$r' = \left( \frac{r - r_0}{r_{\max} - r_0} \right)^{\gamma_r},$$

$$g' = \left( \frac{g - g_0}{g_{\max} - g_0} \right)^{\gamma_g}, \tag{12.36}$$

$$b' = \left( \frac{b - b_0}{b_{\max} - b_0} \right)^{\gamma_b},$$

and:

- $\mathbf{t}$ is the CIEXYZ value produced by driving the monitor with the device-dependent control value $\mathbf{d} = [r, g, b]^T$;
- The parameters $\gamma_r$, $\gamma_g$, $\gamma_b$, $r_0$, $g_0$, $b_0$, $r_{\max}$, $g_{\max}$, $b_{\max}$, $\mathbf{t}_{bp}$, and $\mathbf{H}$ are defined in the profile: this standard model is often used to provide an approximation to the mapping $\mathcal{F}_{\text{monitor}}(\mathbf{d}) = \mathbf{t}$;
- $\mathbf{t}_{bp}$ is the *black point* of the output device;
- $r_{\max}$, $g_{\max}$, $b_{\max}$ are the maximum values of the control values, e.g., 255.

To determine the parameters, a series of color patches is displayed on the CRT and measured with a colorimeter. This will provide pairs of CIE values $\{\mathbf{t}_k\}_{k=1}^M$ and control values $\{\mathbf{d}_k\}_{k=1}^M$.

Values for $\gamma_r$, $\gamma_g$, $\gamma_b$, $r_0$, $g_0$, and $b_0$, used in Eq. (12.36), are determined such that the elements of $[r', g', b']$ are linear with respect to the elements of $XYZ$ and scaled between the range $[0, 1]$ [175].[4] The matrix $\mathbf{H}$ is then determined from the tristimulus values of the CRT phosphors at maximum luminance. Specifically, Eq. (12.35) is represented by

$$\begin{bmatrix} X \\ Y \\ Z \end{bmatrix} = \begin{bmatrix} X_{\text{Rmax}} & X_{\text{Gmax}} & X_{\text{Bmax}} \\ Y_{\text{Rmax}} & Y_{\text{Gmax}} & Y_{\text{Bmax}} \\ Z_{\text{Rmax}} & Z_{\text{Gmax}} & Z_{\text{Bmax}} \end{bmatrix} \begin{bmatrix} r' \\ b' \\ g' \end{bmatrix}, \tag{12.37}$$

where $[X_{\text{Rmax}}, Y_{\text{Rmax}}, Z_{\text{Rmax}}]^T$ is the CIEXYZ tristimulus value of the red phosphor for control value $\mathbf{d} = [r_{\max}, 0, 0]^T$ and we have ignored the display black point $\mathbf{t}_{bp}$. The green and blue phosphors are similarly defined. In practice, the device-independent values of

---

[4] The scaling between 0 and 1 is arbitrary, but useful to allow the use of Eq. (12.37).

the phosphors are mapped to account for perceptual effects and a viewing illumination. Perceptual effects are discussed in Section 12.3.9.

### Modern display technologies

There are many different types of flat panel display systems and new technologies will certainly be developed in the future [112, 304, 315, 316]. These systems are related to the CRT device by the fact that they are all additive color reproduction systems (see Sections 8.4.1, 11.1, 11.2). While most current systems use three primaries, it is possible to use more than three to increase the display gamut of the device. Such overcomplete systems exist in hard-copy reproduction systems including high-fidelity (six-color) and CMYK printers.

A model for the mapping of the device-dependent values to device-independent values for a generic additive system that has $N$ primaries is given by

$$\mathcal{F}_{\text{display}}(\cdot) = \mathbf{H}(\mathcal{H}(\cdot)) + \mathbf{b}, \tag{12.38}$$

where the columns of the $3 \times N$ matrix $\mathbf{H}$ are the CIEXYZ values of the device primaries (see Eq. (12.37)), $\mathbf{b}$ is the CIEXYZ value of the device *black point*, and the vector valued mapping $\mathcal{H}$ is from the device-dependent color space to the set of $N$ element vectors with elements bounded between 0 and 1.

If the channels are independent, then the mapping $\mathcal{H}$ can be expressed as $N$ scalar valued mappings. This independence assumption greatly simplifies the process of determining $\mathcal{H}$. As for the CRT case, it may be possible to parameterize the $N$ 1-D mappings. The specific model used is dependent upon the technology used to create the radiant light.

A common problem occurs in obtaining accurate radiometric measurements of the wide variety of soft-copy displays. The source of the problem is visible to the human observer by simply varying the viewing angle of the soft-copy display. For a CRT, there is a relatively small change in radiant energy to the viewer as the viewer moves from the optimal (front center) viewing location. For many older flat screen displays, there is a large change in the radiant energy to the viewer as the viewer moves only a small distance from the optimal viewing location. This variation in energy causes problems with many of the radiant measuring colorimetric instruments on the market. To compensate for the viewing angle dependency, the measuring device may need to know, via some control, the type of display that is under measure.

### Printers

Printer characterization is difficult, owing to the inherent nonlinearity of the printing process, and the wide variety of methods used for color printing, e.g., lithography, ink-jet, dye sublimation. Because of these difficulties, printing devices are often profiled with a multidimensional look-up table (MLUT) and interpolation [15, 45, 104, 105, 121, 138, 197, 221, 257]. In other words, the continuum of values for any function in the profile is found by interpolating between points in the MLUT. For particular printing methods, model based methods are also used for characterizing printers [11, 13, 14, 27, 147, 284, 314, 320].

To produce a profile of a printer, a subset of $M_p$ values spanning the space of allowable control values for the printer is first selected. Denote these device-dependent values by $\{\mathbf{c}_k\}_{k=1}^{M_p}$. In the printing process, these values produce a set of reflectance spectra that are denoted by $\{\mathbf{p}_k\}_{k=1}^{M_p}$.

The printed samples are measured using a colorimeter, as for the scanner characterization, and this provides the values

$$\{\mathbf{t}_k = \mathbf{A}^T \mathbf{L}_v \mathbf{p}_k\}_{k=1}^{M_p}. \tag{12.39}$$

Again, $\mathbf{t}_k$ could represent any colorimetric or device-independent values, not just CIEXYZ.

The problem is to determine a mapping $\mathcal{F}_{\text{print}}$ that is the solution to the optimization problem

$$\mathcal{F}_{\text{print}} = \arg \left( \min_{\mathcal{F}} \sum_{i=1}^{M_p} ||\mathcal{F}(\mathbf{c}_i) - \mathcal{L}(\mathbf{t}_i)||^2 \right), \tag{12.40}$$

where $\mathcal{L}$ is the transformation to a selected interchange color space. As in the scanner characterization problem, there may be constraints that $\mathcal{F}_{\text{print}}$ must satisfy.

Constraints of interest include:

- Data consistency:

$$\mathcal{F}_{\text{print}} \in \{ \mathcal{G} \mid ||\mathcal{G}(\mathbf{c}_i) - \mathcal{L}(\mathbf{t}_i)|| \le \delta_v, \quad i = 1, \ldots, M_p \}, \tag{12.41}$$

where $\delta_v$ is a just-noticeable-difference (JND) threshold.
- Ink limit:

$$\mathcal{F}_{\text{print}} \in \{ \mathcal{G} \mid ||\mathcal{G}^{-1}(\mathbf{t})|| \le \delta_{\text{ink}}, \quad \forall \mathbf{t} \in G \}, \tag{12.42}$$

where $\delta_{\text{ink}}$ is the maximum amount of ink that should be placed on the media.
- Smoothness:

$$\mathcal{F}_{\text{print}} \in \{ \mathcal{G} \mid ||(\nabla\mathcal{G})(\mathbf{c})|| \le \delta_{\text{smooth}}, \quad \forall \mathbf{c} \in \Omega_{\text{print}} \}, \tag{12.43}$$

where $\nabla\mathcal{G}$ is the gradient of the function $\mathcal{G}$ and $\Omega_{\text{print}}$ is the range of control values for the printer.

In practice, the function that is of interest is the inverse function $\mathcal{F}_{\text{print}}^{-1} : \Omega_{\text{ICS}} \to \Omega_{\text{DD}}$. Details on creating MLUTs for output devices are contained in Appendix D. Note that the profile created is valid for only one viewing illuminant, $\mathbf{L}_v$. However, it is possible to alter the profile for one illuminant to create a profile for another illuminant [290]. This problem is similar to the problem of changing source illumination for the digital color camera in Eq. (12.34). Details on creating output mappings are contained in Section 14.4.

## 12.3.8     Undercolor removal

The common use of a black colorant in color printing complicates the printer characterization process. Black colorant is used in color printing for several reasons including:

- Neutral colorants are less expensive than wavelength selective colorants,
- Less total colorant is needed to create the dark colors,
- The black of the black ink is usually blacker than that achievable with the wavelength selective inks,
- Many media are unable to absorb large amounts of ink, in which case black is more easily achieved with the use of a black ink,
- Shadow details are usually significantly improved when a black colorant is included [318].

*Undercolor removal* (UCR), *black generation*, and *gray component replacement* (GCR) are all terms used to denote a method of using less wavelength selective colorants by including a black colorant [116, 117, 318]. Regardless of the terminology, UCR is often considered to be a problem restricted to the design of a color printing process. In fact, UCR is of great importance to the characterization of a four-color printer, and at this time, this problem has received only limited research effort [117, 130, 138, 216].

For a four-color, CMYK, digital printer, there exists a mapping from the device-dependent four element vectors into a device-independent color space. Since the system of equations is overdetermined, different device-dependent values can create the same device-independent value (metamerism). In other words, the mapping is not one-to-one within the device gamut. A question arises as to which device-dependent value should be used to create a specific device-independent value. The device-independent value can be created in many ways. The table needs to reflect a consistent approach that does not use significantly different input values to create slightly different output values. If significantly different values are used for adjacent entries in the MLUT, then because of the highly nonlinear nature of the printing process, entry interpolations may introduce significant errors. Enforcing a smoothness constraint during the construction of the MLUT may lessen this problem. Another approach is to limit the allowable device-dependent values used in the MLUT. This approach is where UCR enters into the process of characterizing a four-color digital printer.

Traditional UCR is often expressed as a mapping from a three-element CMY vector to a four-element CMYK vector. Most UCR algorithms can be mathematically expressed using a set of five scalar valued mappings, $g_c$, $g_m$, $g_y$, $f_k$, and $h$, in the form

$$\mathcal{H}([c, m, y]^T) = [c + g_c(\alpha), m + g_m(\alpha), y + g_y(\alpha), f_k(\alpha)]^T, \qquad (12.44)$$

where $\alpha = h([c, m, y]^T)$.

To make it clear how a UCR algorithm can be expressed by Eq. (12.44), consider a UCR algorithm that will be referred to as *max UCR*. In *max UCR*, equal amounts of the CMY inks are removed, or rather not placed on the paper. Black colorant equal in blackness to the total ink removed is placed on the paper. The amount of each colorant

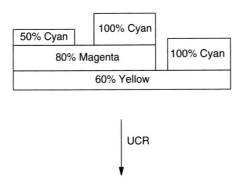

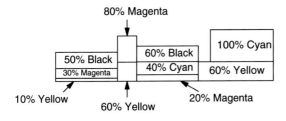

**Figure 12.14.** Undercolor removal example.

that is removed at a particular location in the image is the minimum of the original CMY colorant concentrations. This example assumes that equal amounts of C, M, and Y create a neutral color. Figure 12.14 provides a graphical display of this process. In this case, at every pixel location in the max UCR CMYK image, one of the elements of the CMYK vector is always equal to 0. In other words, the set of allowable CMYK values has been restricted to a specific region in the hypercube defined by all CMYK values. This specific mapping can be expressed with Eq. (12.44) by using

$$g_c(\alpha) = g_m(\alpha) = g_y(\alpha) = -\alpha,$$ (12.45)

$$f_k(\alpha) = \alpha,$$ (12.46)

$$\alpha = h([c, m, y]^T) = \min(c, m, y).$$ (12.47)

A value of $c = 0$ denotes no ink from colorant $c$ placed on the paper. The same is true for the values $m$, $y$, and, $k$.

The UCR mapping given by Eq. (12.44) can be used to define a set $H$ that can be used to constrain the mapping from the device-independent values to the device-dependent values. For example, a set $H$ could be defined as

$$H = \{[c + g_c(\alpha), m + g_m(\alpha), y + g_y(\alpha), f_k(\alpha)] \mid \alpha = h(c, m, y) \},$$ (12.48)

where $c, m, y \in [0, 255]$. With $H$ defined, the constraint of undercolor removal on the function that maps from the device-independent color space to the device-dependent

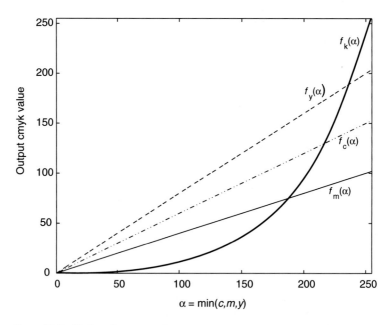

**Figure 12.15.** Undercolor removal curves.

color space is given by:

$$\mathcal{F}_{\text{print}}^{-1} \in \{\, \mathcal{G} \mid \mathcal{G}(\mathbf{t}) \in H, \ \forall \mathbf{t} \in G \,\}, \tag{12.49}$$

where $G$ is the set of device-independent colors within the device gamut.

There are a variety of mapping functions, $\mathcal{H}$, that are used for UCR. One example that is used in Adobe Photoshop™ is displayed by the curves of Fig. 12.15, where $g_i(\alpha) = f_i(\alpha) - \alpha$, for $i = (c, m, y)$. In this plot, white is at the origin and black is at the far right side. At $\alpha < 50$, the highlight region of the printer, there is little black colorant added. At $\alpha = 150$, the gray mid-tone region of the printer, there is a moderate amount of black colorant added. Finally, at $\alpha = 255$, the black point of the printer is achieved with 100% black colorant and moderate amounts of the CMY colorants.

From the above discussion, it is clear that UCR can be implemented in the color management system within the mapping $\mathcal{F}_{\text{print}}^{-1}$ by limiting the range of this function, i.e., certain CMYK values will not be allowed.

## 12.3.9     Perceptual issues

Color is a psychophysical phenomenon and is subject to extensive processing by the visual cortex. Appendix E discusses properties of the human visual system. The appearance of a color stimulus is mainly affected by changes in illumination and surrounding colors. In practice, it is necessary to consider these effects when constructing profiles. For example, often a CIELAB value of $[100, 0, 0]$ is mapped to the white point of a monitor and the white point of the printer even if neither the paper or monitor white have a CIELAB value of $[100, 0, 0]$. This white point correction is similar to the process used to characterize monochrome devices in Example 12.1. If this matching of white points is not performed, then the printed image may have an undesired color cast compared to the monitor, or vice versa. Note that the CIELAB transformation has a white point correction that is defined by the CIEXYZ value of the illumination as discussed in Chapter 8.

Typically, a perceptual color space accounts for white point adaptation, color constancy, and other viewing conditions. These effects can be included in the device characterization problem. As before, the patches $\{\mathbf{p}_k\}_{k=1}^M$ are measured using a colorimetric device giving

$$\{\mathbf{t}_k = \mathbf{A}^T \mathbf{L}_v \mathbf{p}_k\}_{k=1}^M. \tag{12.50}$$

These values are then mapped to the perceptual values $\{\mathbf{v}_k = \mathcal{M}(\mathbf{t}_k)\}_{k=1}^M$, where $\mathcal{M}$ maps the CIE values to a perceptual color space, such as CIELAB, CIELUV and others in [72, 126, 191]. The profile is then constructed between the values $\{\mathbf{v}_k = \mathcal{M}(\mathbf{t}_k)\}_{k=1}^M$ and the device-dependent values $\{\mathbf{c}_k\}_{k=1}^M$.

---

**Example 12.3.** Perceptual mappings often affect the apparent gamut of the output device. To demonstrate this effect, the following two perceptual mapping examples are discussed:

- A $9 \times 9 \times 9$ RGB sequence (729 samples - see below for definition of this sequence) was sent to a three-color CMY dye-sublimation [103] printer.
- The resulting 729 samples were measured with a colorimeter to obtain CIELAB D50 2 degree values.
- The actual gamut of the printer was estimated from these CIELAB values.
- The 729 CIELAB values were adjusted such that the CIEXYZ value of the paper white mapped to the CIEXYZ value of the illuminant used in the transformation to CIELAB (in this case D50 illumination), and a perceptually adjusted gamut was calculated.
- The 729 CIELAB values were adjusted such that the CIEXYZ value of the paper white mapped to the CIEXYZ value of the illuminant used in the transformation to CIELAB and the printer *black point* (RGB $[0, 0, 0]$) mapped to the CIEXYZ value $[0, 0, 0]$. Using this data a perceptually adjusted gamut was calculated.

The term $9 \times 9 \times 9$ RGB sequence denotes a sequence of 729 equidistant values in the 3-D device-dependent color space. For example, a $3 \times 3 \times 3$ RGB sequence would be given by (from left to right and then top to bottom – black to white):

0, 0, 0      0, 0, 127      0, 0, 255      0, 127, 0      0, 127, 127      0, 127, 255
0, 255, 0    0, 255, 127    0, 255, 255    127, 0, 0      127, 0, 127      127, 0, 255
127, 127, 0  127, 127, 127  127, 127, 255  127, 255, 0    127, 255, 127    127, 255, 255
255, 0, 0    255, 0, 127    255, 0, 255    255, 127, 0    255, 127, 127    255, 127, 255
255, 255, 0  255, 255, 127  255, 255, 255.

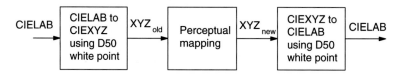

**Figure 12.16.** Block diagram of one approach to perceptual mapping.

The first perceptual mapping is achieved by transforming the data from CIELAB to CIEXYZ using the CIEXYZ value of the D50 illumination as the white point and then scaling the CIEXYZ data using the equations:

$$X_{new} = \frac{X_{old} * X_{d50}}{X_{wp}},$$

$$Y_{new} = \frac{Y_{old} * Y_{d50}}{Y_{wp}},$$

$$Z_{new} = \frac{Z_{old} * Z_{d50}}{Z_{wp}},$$

where $[X_{old}, Y_{old}, Z_{old}]$ is the measured CIEXYZ D50 value of a sample, $[X_{d50}, Y_{d50}, Z_{d50}]$ is the CIEXYZ value of the D50 illumination, $[X_{wp}, Y_{wp}, Z_{wp}]$ is the CIEXYZ D50 value of the paper, which corresponds to $[R, G, B] = [255, 255, 255]$ and $[X_{new}, Y_{new}, Z_{new}]$ is the sample's perceptually adjusted CIEXYZ value. These perceptually adjusted CIEXYZ values can then be mapped back to CIELAB space using the D50 2 degree white point, i.e., $[X_{d50}, Y_{d50}, Z_{d50}]$. This entire process is illustrated in Fig. 12.16. Note that the same result can be achieved by using the value $[X_{wp}, Y_{wp}, Z_{wp}]$ as the white point in the transformation to CIELAB for the $[X_{old}, Y_{old}, Z_{old}]$ values. In Fig. 12.16, the magnitude of the CIEXYZ D50 white point is arbitrary but should be consistent through all transformation steps.

For the second perceptual mapping, the data were adjusted such that the CIEXYZ value of the paper mapped to $[X_{d50}, Y_{d50}, Z_{d50}]$ and the printer black point mapped to a CIEXYZ value of $[0, 0, 0]$. Mathematically, this can be achieved by transforming the data from CIELAB to CIEXYZ using the white point $[X_{d50}, Y_{d50}, Z_{d50}]$ and then adjusting the CIEXYZ data using the equations:

$$X_{new} = \frac{(X_{old} - X_{bp}) * X_{d50}}{X_{wp} - X_{bp}},$$

$$Y_{new} = \frac{(Y_{old} - Y_{bp}) * Y_{d50}}{Y_{wp} - Y_{bp}},$$

$$Z_{new} = \frac{(Z_{old} - Z_{bp}) * Z_{d50}}{Z_{wp} - Z_{bp}},$$

where $[X_{bp}, Y_{bp}, Z_{bp}]$ is the CIEXYZ D50 value of the printer black point.

Figure 12.17 provides a visualization of the real gamuts and the apparent gamuts in CIELAB space for the two perceptual mapping methods. Three-dimensional

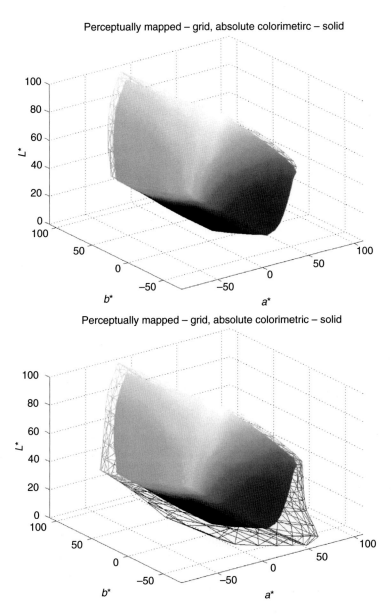

**Figure 12.17.** (a) Gamut (solid) and apparent gamut (grid) of printer with perceptual adjustment of data using method 1; (b) gamut (solid) and apparent gamut (grid) of printer with perceptual adjustment of data using method 2 (for color version, please see Plate 25).

animations of these figures are available at the text's website (www.cambridge.org/9780521868532). The solid object is the printer gamut as determined from the measured output values of the printer. The mesh grid is the apparent gamut of the printer after the perceptual adjustment. Note that in addition to the adjustment of the white and black points, there is a significant change to the highly saturated colors with an even more dramatic change for the case of method 2.

The above perceptual transformations are just one example of how such a transformation can be performed. There are a variety of methods including the Von Kries [313, p. 431] and Bradford [157] transformations. The Bradford transformation, named after the University of Bradford, is used in the CIECAM97s color appearance model [74, Chapter 15] and for illumination adaptation in ICC profile computations [129, 196]. Most of these methods are variants of the above transformation with the inclusion of a $3 \times 3$ matrix mapping from CIEXYZ into another color space prior to the scaling operation, followed by a $3 \times 3$ matrix mapping to return to CIEXYZ.

### 12.3.10   Gamut mapping

As discussed, color reproduction devices are limited in the colors they can produce. These colors define the device gamut. Gamut mismatch is a problem that occurs when two devices have different gamuts, and it is desired to reproduce an image displayed with one device using the other device. Consider two gamuts $G_{monitor}$ and $G_{print}$. It is desired to print an image that is displayed on the monitor. Assuming that $\mathcal{F}_{monitor}$ is known, we can map from the monitor RGB values to device-independent values. At this point, it is necessary to map these device-independent values to device-dependent values for the printer. The problem is that there may be colors that the monitor can display but that the printer cannot print. As mentioned in Section 12.3.1, the mapping $\mathcal{D}$ is used for this purpose. In this case, the printer control value for the device-independent value $\mathbf{t}$ is given by $\mathcal{F}_{printer}^{-1}(\mathcal{D}(\mathbf{t}))$.

Certain problems that occur in gamut-mapping are well illustrated graphically. Consider Fig. 12.18, which displays a 2-D simplification of the 3-D gamut mapping problem. The gamut $G$ of the device is clearly outlined and all points that are outside of this gamut must be assigned a value within $G$. A simple approach would be to assign the point outside $G$ to the closest value within $G$. Note, however, that for point A, there is no single closest point in $G$. This is because gamut $G$ is *nonconvex* in the device-independent color space. In this case, two points that are very near point A will be mapped to significantly different points. Note also that the entire region B is assigned to a single value C. In this case, points that are significantly different will be mapped to points that are very close.

These problems introduce trade-offs that exist when designing a gamut mapping method. Some issues that must be considered are:

- Should colors in gamut be mapped exactly?
- What is the desired appearance, e.g., saturated colors, lightness preservation, primary reproduction?
- What is the most appropriate point to assign for out-of-gamut colors?

Depending upon the desired effect and the medium in use, the function $\mathcal{D}$ may or may not be the identity operator on the colors within $G$. The reason for using a function $\mathcal{D}$ that is not the identity operator can be illustrated by the example in which there are smoothly varying regions in the image that are outside the printer gamut. These colors will be gamut mapped to the same color on the gamut boundary, which will result in a solid color in the previously varying region. This is the problem shown in Fig. 12.18 for

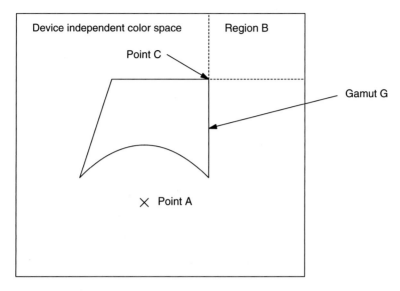

**Figure 12.18.** Two-dimensional illustration of gamut mapping problems.

region B. To reduce this artifact, a gamut mapping can be used that compresses all the colors in the image to reduce the colorimetric dynamic range in the image while ensuring that all the colors can be reproduced. For example, all the colors in the image could be moved toward one point, such as a mid-gray, until all the colors in the image are within the device gamut. Mathematically this problem can be posed as

$$\min |\alpha|, \quad \forall \mathbf{t}_k \in I, \tag{12.51}$$

such that

$$\hat{\mathbf{t}}_k = \mathbf{t}_k + \alpha \mathcal{J}(\mathbf{t}_0 - \mathbf{t}_k) \in G,$$

where $\hat{\mathbf{t}}_k$ is the updated tristimulus value, $\mathbf{t}_0$ is the mid-gray color, $G$ is the device gamut, $I$ is the set of color values in the image, and $\mathcal{J}$ is a nonlinearity. Unlike a simple clipping approach in which out-of-gamut colors are mapped to the closest in-gamut color, this method will retain some of the variation in smoothly varying image regions that are beyond the device gamut. Note that the above operation is image dependent.

All color reproduction devices are limited in the colors they can reproduce. Gamut mapping provides the opportunity to decide how those limitations affect the final output. In the end, it must be decided if it is better to retain the variation in the image or if it is better to maintain good color accuracy of those colors that can be reproduced.

In practice, gamut mapping is performed in a color space in which the Euclidean distance has a perceptual meaning, e.g., CIELAB [172]. Other work [69, 119] has noted that a method that maps to the closest in-gamut color in a perceptual color space such as CIELAB produces color differences that are less acceptable than an algorithm that maintains *lightness* and the *hue angle*, $h = \arctan(b^*/a^*)$. Note however that hue angle as defined with the CIELAB and CIELUV color spaces relates poorly with perceptual hue in certain regions of the color space [122]. Other work has noted that there should be a trade-off between *chroma* and lightness [186]. For detailed gamut mapping experiments, the reader is referred to [35, 69, 86, 119, 185, 187, 250, 308]. It is doubtful that there is a universally optimal solution to this problem, owing to the large variety of devices and the varied perceptual effects that are often desired. For example, a different mapping may be desired when printing business graphics versus pictorial images [35, 36, 142].

---

**Example 12.4.**    To demonstrate artifacts from gamut mapping and the effect from gamut mismatch, an RGB image was created on a monitor. The image, shown in Fig. 12.19a, consists of two figures. One figure is a color wheel that displays a continuum of RGB values such that one of the values is always 0, e.g., $RGB = [0\ 240\ 120]$). The other figure is a series of color bars each of which smoothly step from black to a primary color, e.g., red, green, blue, cyan, magenta, yellow, and then to white. For example, the red bar was created by stepping through the RGB vector sequence $\{[0\ 0\ 0], [1\ 0\ 0], \ldots, [255\ 0\ 0],$ $[255\ 1\ 1], \ldots, [255\ 255\ 255]\}$. The smooth transitions between highly saturated colors make these figures ideal for demonstrating gamut mapping artifacts.

A monitor profile was created between the monitor RGB values and CIELAB D50, i.e., $\mathcal{F}_{\text{monitor}}$ was determined, using the procedure described in Section 12.3.7. A dye-sub RGB printer, a 3-color CMY printer that accepted RGB input values, was also profiled from CIELAB D50, i.e., $\mathcal{F}_{\text{print}}^{-1}$ was determined, to printer RGB space. As discussed in Section 12.3.7, this profile was created by measuring a series of color patches with a colorimeter and creating a multidimensional look-up table (MLUT). The specific method used to create the MLUT is discussed in Appendix D. Out-of-gamut colors were mapped, via $\mathcal{D}$, to the closest in gamut value, along a constant hue angle while preserving lightness in CIELAB space. For comparison, the gamuts of both devices are shown in Fig. 12.20 where the monitor gamut is the grid and the printer gamut is the solid figure. Some regions of mismatch are clearly visible in the figure.

Two images that illustrate out-of-gamut effects were printed and are shown in Figs. 12.19b and 12.19c. The images are as follows:

Figure 12.19b: Image created by sending the values $\mathcal{F}_{\text{print}}^{-1}(\mathcal{D}(\mathcal{F}_{\text{monitor}}(\mathbf{m}_k)))$ to the printer, where $\mathbf{m}_k$ is the $k$th pixel in the image shown in Fig. 12.19a.

Figure 12.19c: Image created by sending the values $\mathcal{F}_{\text{print}}^{-1}(\mathcal{U}(\mathcal{F}_{\text{monitor}}(\mathbf{m}_k)))$ to the printer, where $\mathcal{U}$ maps colors outside of the printer's gamut to black and is the identity operator on the in-gamut colors.

As can be seen in Fig. 12.19c, a significant number of colors are outside of the gamut of the printer. In the bar figure of Fig. 12.19c, the banding, especially in the yellow bar, indicates that the values are going in and out of the printer gamut as the monitor device-dependent control values are stepped from black to a primary color and then to white. In addition, blocking artifacts are visible in Fig. 12.19b where previously smoothly varying regions, as shown in Fig. 12.19a, are mapped to the same area on the gamut boundary. Note also that the monitor pure red does not map to a pure red on the printer.

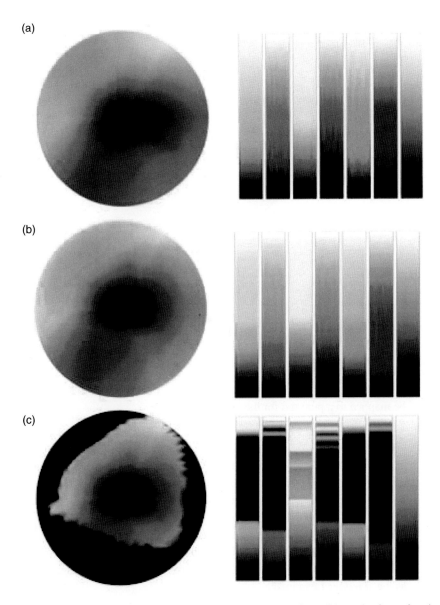

**Figure 12.19.** (a) Image used to evaluate gamut mapping artifacts; (b) result of transforming image in (a) through $\mathcal{F}_{\text{print}}^{-1}(\mathcal{D}(\mathcal{F}_{\text{monitor}}(.)))$; (c) result of transforming image in (a) through $\mathcal{F}_{\text{print}}^{-1}(\mathcal{U}(\mathcal{F}_{\text{monitor}}(.)))$; (for color version, please see Plate 27).

It is possible to alter the gamut mapping method such that the primary colors on the monitor are mapped to primary colors at the printer output. Such a mapping is a closed loop design however, since it will be valid only for a particular monitor and printer combination. For example, the monitor maximum red value of $[255, 0, 0]$ will create a particular device-independent value of $\mathbf{t}_1$. Unfortunately, a different monitor may very

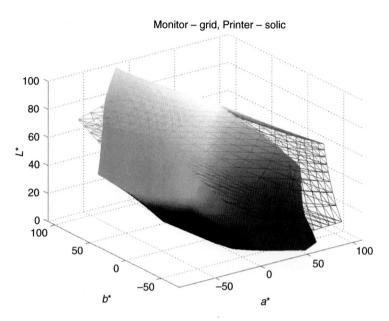

**Figure 12.20.** Monitor gamut given by grid and printer gamut given by solid figure (for color version, please see Plate 26).

well create a value $t_2 \neq t_1$. In such situations, it is necessary to know if $t_2$ or $t_1$ should be mapped to a pure red for the printer.

**Example 12.5 (Color management).** As an example of the usefulness of color management, an original printed version of the commonly used Lena image was scanned on a desktop scanner. The scanned image will be referred to as the *newly scanned* Lena image. In addition, a color target was scanned that contained 276 color patches. The target patches were measured with a colorimeter and an MLUT mapping was determined from scanned RGB values to CIELAB D50, i.e., $\mathcal{F}_{scan}$ was created. For comparison, the commonly used digital color Lena image was obtained. This image will be referred to as the *standard* Lena image.

The MLUT for the dye-sub printer that was used for the gamut mapping example was used to map from the CIELAB D50 values to printer control values. Four images were printed and are shown in Fig. 12.21 for comparison. The images are described below, where $l_k$ is the RGB value of the $k$th pixel for the standard Lena image and $ls_k$ is the RGB value for the $k$th pixel in the newly scanned Lena image:

(a) Image created by sending the RGB values $l_k$ directly to the printer with no processing.
(b) Image created by sending the values $ls_k$ directly to the printer with no processing.
(c) Image created by sending the values $\mathcal{F}_{print}^{-1}(\mathcal{D}(\mathcal{F}_{scan}(ls_k)))$ to the printer.
(d) Binary image to display out of gamut areas. The white regions are in gamut while the black regions are outside the dye-sub printer gamut.

**Figure 12.21.** Lena color images: see text for description (for color version, please see Plate 28).

It is worthwhile to compare the Lena images in Fig. 12.21 with other color printed versions of the Lena image [90, 195, 211, 259, 296, 301].[5] A quick look at the various versions of Lena color images provides an appreciation for the difficulty in accurately reproducing and even specifying a color image.

The image shown in Fig. 12.21c is a close match to the original printed image, which appeared in the November 1972 issue of *Playboy*. Simply providing the scanned RGB values directly to the printer produces a much different image, as shown in Fig. 12.21b. One should realize, however, that the commonly displayed Lena image 12.21a is just that, a scanned RGB image which is often provided directly as input to the available color printer. Comparison of 12.21a and 12.21b gives an indication of the differences in the raw scanner data. The large differences between Fig. 12.21a, 12.21b and 12.21c demonstrate that widely different results can occur depending upon how an image is scanned, processed and printed. This is a significant problem when attempting to convey the results of a color image processing algorithm, and to compare those results with previously archived material. Figure 12.21d displays those areas of the image that are outside the printer gamut, where the black regions in this difference image are out-of-gamut. Finally, note that in Fig. 12.21c the shoulder and arm region of Lena contains minor artifacts due to quantization problems in the MLUT.

In the publication process, the color images in this book are processed by a printer that will introduce artifacts and loss of accuracy due to problems like lack of control

---

[5] We selected the Lena image for this example to allow a comparison with many other printed versions. See [189] for a history of the image.

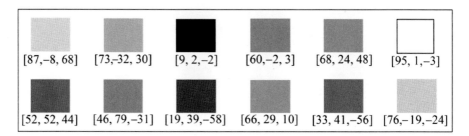

**Figure 12.22.** Color squares for quantifying publishing reproduction accuracy (for color version, please see Plate 29).

and gamut differences. To quantify this effect, we have provided an additional image containing color squares in Fig. 12.22. The CIELAB D50 values are given for each square on the original dye-sub print. Readers are encouraged to measure the color squares to test the accuracy of the process if they have access to a colorimeter. If not, then the measured values after publication are available at the text's website www.cambridge.org/9780521868532. All images produced in these examples, data used to create the ICC profiles and the ICC profiles are also available at this website.

## 12.4    Problems

**12.1**    This chapter describes procedures for characterizing several input and output devices. Input devices include desktop scanners and color cameras; output devices include desktop printers, both monochrome and color; CRTs; LCD displays; and halftone printing, both desktop and commercial. For each of these devices, determine which of the measurement instruments described in Chapter 8 is appropriate to characterize the device.

**12.2**    The linearization of effect of Eqs. (12.7) and (12.8) is ideal. Discuss the problems with achieving exact linearization for practical monochrome systems.

**12.3**    Assume a monochrome input device, e.g., a scanner, that is being characterized using eight levels, for ease of computation. The input levels, $g_k$, representing density, with measurement values, $\mathcal{F}(g_k)$, are given in Table 12.1. We have assumed that the input device has 8-bit resolution.

**Table 12.1.** Data for Problem 12.3

| $d_k$ | 0.05 | 0.41 | 0.70 | 0.95 | 1.26 | 1.53 | 1.88 | 2.20 |
|---|---|---|---|---|---|---|---|---|
| $\mathcal{F}(d_k)$ | 3 | 40 | 72 | 101 | 138 | 171 | 214 | 255 |

(a) Create an 8-bit look-up table (LUT) using linear interpolation to represent the function $n = \mathcal{F}(d)$.

(b) Approximate the function $\mathcal{F}^{-1}(n)$ as a LUT.
(c) For 256 equally spaced density values in $[0, 2.20]$, compute the composite function $\mathcal{F}^{-1}(f(d))$.
(d) Repeat the above three steps using a nonlinear interpolation method of your choice.

**12.4** Assume a monochrome output device, e.g., printer, that is being characterized using eight levels, for ease of computation. The levels, $n_k$, are control values that produce the measured reflectance values, $\mathcal{F}(g_k)$, given in Table 12.2

**Table 12.2.** Data for Problem 12.4

| $g_k$ | 0 | 30 | 65 | 95 | 130 | 200 | 225 | 255 |
|---|---|---|---|---|---|---|---|---|
| $\mathcal{F}(g_k)$ | 0.03 | 0.25 | 0.40 | 0.57 | 0.67 | 0.82 | 0.85 | 0.96 |

(a) Create an 8-bit look-up table (LUT) using linear interpolation to represent the function $r = \mathcal{F}(n)$.
(b) Approximate the function $\mathcal{F}^{-1}(r)$ as a LUT.
(c) For 256 equally spaced reflection values in $[0, 1]$, compute the composite function $\mathcal{F}(\mathcal{F}^{-1}(r))$. Remember to round the control values to integers.
(d) Repeat the above three steps using a nonlinear interpolation method of your choice.

**12.5** This problem considers extension of interpolation using LUTs to two dimensions. Here we will use a known function that we can sample, then interpolate and measure the error. Let our system device be defined on the unit square $[0, 1] \times [0, 1]$ by

$$f(x, y) = x - xy + x^{1/2}y^{1/2} + y^3 + \sin\left(\frac{\pi}{2}x\right)\sin^2(\pi y^2).$$

(a) Create a 2-D, 4-bit look-up table (LUT) in each dimension, i.e., an equally spaced $16 \times 16$ grid, using bilinear interpolation to represent the function $f(x, y)$.
(b) Using the approximation, find the mean square error on an equally spaced $1024 \times 1024$ grid.
(c) Create a 2-D 6-bit look-up table (LUT) in each dimension, i.e., an equally spaced $64 \times 64$ grid, using bilinear interpolation.
(d) Using the approximation, find the mean square error on an equally spaced $1024 \times 1024$ grid. Compare the results with the 4-bit LUT of step (a).
(e) Repeat the above using a nonlinear interpolation method of your choice.

**12.6** Data from a printer is found in the text's website (www.cambridge.org/9780521868532). The CIELAB values under D50 were measured for a $9 \times 9 \times 9$ grid of control values, given by $\{0, 32, 64, 96, 128, 196, 228, 255\}$ in each of the R, G and B dimensions. A usual task would be to construct a high resolution LUT from this data, e.g., $32 \times 32 \times 32$. However, we will use the same principle and design a lower resolution LUT that can be checked for accuracy using the real data. We will create a look-up table that will approximate $\mathcal{F}_p(\mathbf{n})$, where $\mathbf{n}$ is a control value and output is a CIELAB value.

(a) Create a $9 \times 9 \times 9$ look-up table (LUT) from a $3 \times 3 \times 3$ equally spaced subset of the data. Use linear interpolation and compute the mean and maximum $\Delta E^*_{ab}$ for the $9 \times 9 \times 9$ result.

(b) Create a $9 \times 9 \times 9$ look-up table from a $5 \times 5 \times 5$ equally spaced subset of the data. Use linear interpolation and compute the mean and maximum $\Delta E^*_{ab}$ for the $9 \times 9 \times 9$ result.

(c) Create a $9 \times 9 \times 9$ look-up table from a $3 \times 3 \times 3$ equally spaced subset of the data. Use your choice of a nonlinear interpolation method and compute the mean and maximum $\Delta E^*_{ab}$ for the $9 \times 9 \times 9$ result.

(d) Create a $9 \times 9 \times 9$ look-up table from a $5 \times 5 \times 5$ equally spaced subset of the data. Use your choice of a nonlinear interpolation method and compute the mean and maximum $\Delta E^*_{ab}$ for the $9 \times 9 \times 9$ result.

**12.7**   Using the most accurate $9 \times 9 \times 9$ LUT produced in Problem 12.6, extract a $5 \times 5 \times 5$ subtable.

(a) From these data, construct a $9 \times 9 \times 9$ LUT for the inverse function, $\mathcal{F}_p^{-1}(\mathbf{t})$ that maps CIELAB values, $\mathbf{t}$, to control values, $\mathbf{n}$.

(b) The accuracy of this mapping can be used to determine how well colors can be reproduced by the printer. For the CIELAB values in the original data, first map the values to the control values using the LUT just constructed. These values will usually not correspond exactly to the control values of the original data. Round the values obtained by $\mathcal{F}_p^{-1}(\mathbf{t})$ to the closest control value of the original data, $\hat{\mathbf{n}}$, then use the LUT that approximates $\mathcal{F}_p(\mathbf{n})$ to obtain the output CIELAB value, $\hat{\mathbf{t}}$. Compute the average and maximum $\Delta E^*_{ab}$ error between $\mathbf{t}$ and $\hat{\mathbf{t}}$.

**12.8**   In the conceptual example of undercolor removal in Fig. 12.14, we replaced the maximum amount of C, M and Y colorants with black. The curves for replacement for an actual color management system, shown in Fig. 12.15, do not begin to replace the colorants until about a quarter (64/256) of the colorant coverage is used. Furthermore, each colorant has a distinct curve.

(a) Give plausible explanations for why the curves in Fig. 12.15 represent a reasonable strategy.

(b) Explain how you would simulate on a soft-copy display, e.g., a computer monitor, the effects of various undercolor removal algorithms.

**12.9**   Consider the problems of gamut mapping illustrated in Fig. 12.18. One method for avoiding the problem of mapping all colors in region B to a single point is to map out-of-gamut colors inside the device gamut, instead of to the boundary.

(a) Construct a 1-D example of such a gamut mapping by mapping the range $[-4,4]$ to the range $[-1,1]$.

(b) Construct a 2-D example of such a gamut mapping by mapping the range $[-4, 4] \times [-4, 4]$ to the range $[-1, 1] \times [-1, 1]$.

(c) Gamuts are usually rather oddly shaped. Construct a 2-D example of such a gamut mapping by mapping the range $[-4, 4] \times [-4, 4]$ to the gamut defined by the vertices $\{(-1, 0.75), (-0.5, 1), (0.75, 1), (1, -1)\}$.

**12.10**   Consider the gamut of Fig. 12.18. It was noted that two points near point A would be mapped to very different colors if out-of-gamut colors are mapped to the nearest boundary point. Develop a gamut mapping algorithm that avoids this problem. Illustrate the effectiveness of your method by using it on the simple 2-D gamut, defined by the vertices $\{(-2, 0), (-2, 2), (0, 1), (2, 2), (2, 0)\}$.

# 13 Estimation of image model parameters

The basis for much of this text is the premise that the physical imaging process can be modeled by a mathematical representation. The models are defined by parameters, whose values must be determined in order for the model to be accurate. In this chapter, we will discuss methods for estimating many of the parameters that define an imaging system. Note that this is different from modeling the image itself, as in Section 7.4. Appendix C on stochastic images also addresses that problem. We will begin by considering a hierarchy of models, and then we will discuss the estimation of the various functions and parameters that define each model.

## 13.1 Image formation models

Image formation models can be written with varying degrees of accuracy and complexity. For this chapter, we will use the simplest hierarchy of models that is needed to illustrate the methods of parameter estimation. We will note the assumptions and simplifications in the following descriptions. The models presented below will be for monochrome images. The extension to multispectral and hyperspectral images requires an additional step of applying stacked notation on the wavelength bands in addition to the stacked notation on the columns in the spatial domain. The algebraic equations remain unchanged. For most parameter estimation work, dealing with a single image band is sufficient.

1. $\mathbf{g} = \mathbf{f} + \epsilon$, where $\epsilon$ is signal independent noise from measurement or quantization. The simplest case is white noise, which is usually a good approximation for thermal noise, quantization noise, background radiation and some coding errors. The case of correlated noise includes harmonic noise, e.g., 60 Hz crosstalk, interfering signals and filtered white noise, e.g., the remaining noise after demosaicking. Here it is assumed that the recording has perfectly focused optics and perfectly linear sensors.

2. $\mathbf{g} = \mathcal{S}(\mathbf{f}) + \epsilon$, where $\mathcal{S}(\cdot)$ represents a nonlinear sensor response. In the case of photographic film, the transformation is usually modeled by $\mathcal{S}(x) = \gamma \log_{10}(x)$. The noise is multiplicative after exponentiating to obtain signals in the intensity domain. This case would also be appropriate to include the sensor response of a digital scanner or camera, where the transformation includes the spectral effect of the optics on the image. We still assume that the spatial focus is perfect.

3. $\mathbf{g} = \mathbf{f} + \epsilon(\mathbf{f})$, where the noise is signal dependent. Such cases include Poisson noise (photon) and film grain noise. Note that "signal dependent" does not imply that the noise is correlated with the signal in a statistical sense.

4. $\mathbf{g} = \mathbf{Hf} + \epsilon$, where $\mathbf{H}$ represents the spatial point spread function (PSF) and the noise is signal independent. This is a simple model for optical blurs recorded with a linear sensor and is the one most often used. We will develop restoration methods based on this model in Chapter 14.

5. $\mathbf{g} = \mathcal{S}(\mathbf{Hf}) + \epsilon$ is a simple model for optical imaging with electronic or film grain noise. Note that most digital cameras include a linearization step prior to recording the data.

6. $\mathbf{g} = \mathcal{S}(\mathbf{Hf}) + \epsilon[\mathcal{S}(\mathbf{Hf})]$ is a more accurate model for optical imaging on film, since the noise is signal dependent.

Let us consider the characteristics of the elements of the models. The functions and parameters may be either deterministic, stochastic or mixed. For example, in the model $\mathbf{g} = \mathcal{S}(\mathbf{Hf}) + \epsilon$, the parameters that define the model are discussed below.

$\mathcal{S}(\cdot)$ is usually deterministic. The transformation of the image energy into a measurable value that is quantized to a digital value can usually be determined by repeated experiments using known input quantities and measured output values. Since any measurement is subject to noise, averaging multiple measurements increases the accuracy.

$\mathbf{H}$ is usually deterministic. The blurring or interaction of spatial locations is usually determined by the optical system of the imaging device. Stochastic blurring is present when imaging through a turbulent atmosphere and in some low-light sensors that use intensifying screens. Variations of stochastic blurs are often included in the noise term for simplicity. The method of *total least squares* can be used to produce a solution that can account for the variation in $\mathbf{H}$ [91, 223, 281].

$\epsilon$ is noise and, by definition, is stochastic. Any deterministic bias can be removed, so noise is usually modeled as having a zero mean. The noise may have a variety of distributions as noted in Chapter 7.

## 13.2    Estimation of sensor response

For most applications, the characterization of the sensor will include the effect of the optical path, since it cannot be easily separated. The discussion of the characterization of devices in Chapter 12 covered this aspect in detail. In that chapter, the emphasis is on characterization of the sensor response as defined by tristimulus values for color and luminance for monochrome devices. In addition to those characteristics, it may be of interest to estimate the spectral sensitivity of color sensors if they are not known. The discussion in that chapter was also limited to devices over which the user had complete control. There are some applications where the user has less control, e.g., a camera that has been carried into space to survey a distant planet or a consumer camera that is using an autoexposure setting. In general, the common ways of estimating the sensor response include:

1. Measuring the response when the system is constructed or prior to utilization, e.g., digital cameras and space telescopes. Here the manufacturers use well calibrated equipment and controlled conditions. The linearization of the scanners discussed in Section 12.2 uses data of this type. For monochrome devices, a simple step chart is sufficient. For color devices where we are interested in the tristimulus response, a chart with relatively few colors is usually adequate, since sensors usually have smoothly varying responses. If the spectral sensitivity is desired, a more complete covering of the color space is needed. We will delay the discussion of estimation of spectral sensitivity until Section 14.1.10, after the mathematical tools for this task have been presented in Chapter 14.

2. Approximating the sensor response using known characteristics of similar sensors. Manufacturers usually include a nominal sensor response curve with their documentation. Such information might include a graph of voltage output versus luminance input or of quantized values versus reflectance. The spectral sensitivities of the sensors are rarely available for consumer devices, as they are regarded as proprietary. In these cases, the effect of the optics is assumed to be negligible, since the manufacturer's data would not include optics.

3. Including a monochrome step chart with known values or a known object in the image, e.g., science applications or surveillance. For color work, it is not feasible to use a large color chart, but charts containing 20–30 samples are common. This method assumes some prior information about the illumination. A standard daylight spectrum is often used. The absolute intensity is not usually critical in these applications. This method is used in the case of cameras with automatic exposure control, where the user cannot know the exact setting of the sensor at the time that the image is recorded.

4. For many visual tasks, the human visual sensitivity must be included. Measurement of the human eye's response is a psychovisual experiment. See Section 8.3.2.

5. For cases requiring a high degree of accuracy, the spectral sensitivity of the sensor can be obtained by measuring its response to the output of a wavelength adjustable monochromatic light source, called a monochromometer, which is usually implemented with an optical grating. The source is also measured with a spectroradiometer (see Section 8.7.1) to get a calibration reading. Measurements are made at a sequence of discrete wavelengths. The complete spectral sensitivity at all wavelengths is determined using the interpolation methods described in Chapter 9. Extreme care is required in this process to ensure that the radiant flux (see Section 8.2) viewed by the spectroradiometer is the same as viewed by the device under measure. This is especially true if the spatial distribution of the source varies as a function of the selected wavelength.

Note that determination of the limits of the sensor is important. Saturation and low light response can fundamentally limit the ability to recover information. In Chapter 7, the use of histograms for the identification of problems with the sensor limits was discussed.

## 13.3    Estimation of noise statistics

The statistical form of the noise is usually obtained from a priori knowledge of the imaging system and assumptions. Several types of noise model were discussed in Section 7.2.3. Here, we are concerned with estimation of the noise parameters of an unknown system. In many cases, the noise characteristics can be determined by experiment and testing prior to the actual recording of data. The noise can be classified by several characteristics:

1. Additive vs. multiplicative: electronic noise at sensors is usually modeled as additive with zero mean. Film grain noise is a multiplicative process. In some scanners, where log amplifiers are used, the multiplicative model is more appropriate. Finally, since additive noise is simply easier to work with, it is often used in the model for tractability.

2. Signal independent vs. signal dependent: electronic noise is usually signal indepen-dent. Because of this, many systems include a preprocessing step to subtract such noise prior to subsequent processing. This is possible in photon counting systems where the signal is nonnegative. Such noise can only add to the signal, so subtraction of a minimum value is helpful. See Problem 13.3 for an exercise related to this concept. It is noted that Poisson noise, which is characteristic of photon counters, is signal dependent. Special methods are required to deal with this type of noise, particularly, at low signal levels where the Poisson distribution cannot be well approximated by a Gaussian.

3. Gaussian vs. nonGaussian: since the Gaussian process is completely determined by its mean and variance, it is the most popular noise model. Even in the case of nonGaussian noise, many of the processing techniques are based on mean square error minimization, which require only knowledge of the noise variance. These methods are usually theoretically optimal for Gaussian signals. While they may be suboptimal for nonGaussian signals, the increased complexity of handling nonGaussian assumptions makes such assumptions unattractive for most practical systems.

4. White vs. colored: many noise processes can be reasonably assumed to be white, uncorrelated from pixel to pixel. Electronic measurement noise and quantization noise for highly variable signals are examples where the white assumption is reasonable. Colored noise is more difficult to characterize, but when it can be, it is fairly easy to include that characterization in the subsequent processing. An example of this is minimum mean square error restoration, which is discussed in Chapter 14. When the correlated characteristics of colored noise are caused by unwanted signals of unknown origin, taking them into account is much more difficult.

5. Stationary vs. nonstationary: if the noise is stationary, then the characteristics are the same in all regions of the image. This makes estimation of the characteristics easier, since averaging methods can be used. Signal dependent noise would not be stationary and, thus, is more difficult to characterize.

For most image processing tasks, the noise is assumed to be additive and signal independent. If the noise is assumed to be white, then the only parameter of interest is the variance. For colored noise, the estimated the spectrum is usually obtained by measuring the spectrum of images of uniform radiation fields that are taken during separate experiments with the same or similar sensors. The following methods can be used to determine the variance of additive, signal independent noise. The characterization of other noise types is left for more advanced texts.

There are two cases of interest. To determine the noise variance of a device over which we have control, it is possible to set up an experiment to make the estimate. This is true of scanners or cameras that are to be characterized. However, in many cases, the image has been recorded, and the noise variance must be estimated from the recorded data, in what ever form it is in. This is the case for images that are obtained from sources where the recording device is not available to the analyst.

## 13.3.1    Estimation of noise variance from experiments

Frequently, it is desired to determine the signal-to-noise ratio of a recording device, e.g., a scanner or camera that is currently being manufactured or used in a lab or office. Let us consider a scanner first, since it is simpler and measures reflectances under controlled lighting. Since the device is available, it is reasonable to have it scan a test image and analyze the results.

The test image should have several different reflectances, which span the range of practical values. The image should have these reflectance levels in patches of sufficient size so that the values of many pixels can be averaged to obtain a good estimate of the variance within each patch. A monochrome test image is adequate for characterizing the noise on color devices, since the average value in each channel will be removed. The important property of the test image is that it should have negligible variability within each of the patches of constant reflectance. It would not be advised to generate a custom test image with a printer owing to the limited spatial resolution and the use of halftoning. High quality photographic methods are recommended. Such images can be readily purchased.

The results of such tests usually show that the noise variance is uncorrelated with the signal and much higher than that expected from quantization alone. For example, a desktop scanner was characterized for a survey paper on digital color devices [298]. This 16-bit per band scanner had an SNR of about 38 dB. This is well below the expected 96 dB SNR that would have resulted from quantization alone, under the rule of thumb of 6 dB per bit (see Chapter 4).

For cameras, the determination of noise properties is more difficult. Not only does the test object have to be well controlled, but the lighting must also be uniform. The other factor is that the signal from the sensor for most cameras is difficult to isolate. The processing that is done for color images includes many software steps, including demosaicking. However, the manufacturer can create special hardware and invest in special labs where such characterization can be done. While consumers can test their scanners, the same cannot be easily done for cameras.

## 13.3.2 Estimation of noise variance from recoded data

For the cases where the noise must be estimated from the degraded recorded image, there are several methods to estimate the necessary parameters. We will assume stationary, white, signal independent noise for the models discussed here. Since we have assumed stationarity, any portion of the recorded signal may be used to estimate the variance.

Since the noise is assumed signal independent, the relation

$$\text{Var}(f + \epsilon) = \text{Var}(f) + \text{Var}(\epsilon)$$

is fundamental to the estimation methods. To estimate the variance of the noise, the user needs to locate a region in the signal where there is relatively little signal power. This region can be in either the space or frequency domains.

1. Choose a low contrast area of the image. Since contrast is a measure of variation, this implies that the signal power is small, $\text{Var}(f) \approx 0$. Compute the variance of the recorded image, $\text{Var}(g) = \text{Var}(f + \epsilon) \approx \text{Var}(\epsilon)$. There is a practical problem of a user being able to identify sufficiently low contrast areas.
2. An automated approach to the space domain method is to section the image into small regions. For example, a $12 \times 12$ section contains 144 samples and can give a statistically significant result. To obtain an estimate, the variance of each section is computed and the smallest variance is used as the estimate of $\text{Var}(\epsilon)$. This is theoretically appropriate since the variance of the section is the sum of the variance of the image and the variance of the noise. We assume that noise variance is constant and the image variance of the section with the smallest total variance is near zero.
3. Transform the image to the frequency domain where it is hoped that the noise and signal can be separated. The power spectrum of the recorded signal is given by

$$P_g(\omega) = P_f(\omega) + P_\epsilon(\omega).$$

If the noise is white, then $P_\epsilon(\omega) = K\sigma_\epsilon^2$ is a constant. If the signal is sampled properly, $P_f(\omega) = 0$ for $|\omega| > \omega_c$, where $\omega_c$ is the bandlimit for the signal. In the frequency range $\omega_c < |\omega| < \omega_{\max} = \pi/T$, where $T$ is the sampling interval, we have $P_g(\omega) = P_\epsilon(\omega)$.

Using the periodogram and expected values, we take the DFT of the recorded image, assuming the linear model, $\mathbf{g} = \mathbf{Hf} + \epsilon$. This gives

$$E\{|\tilde{g}(k)|^2\} = |\tilde{h}(k)|^2 E\{|\tilde{f}(k)|^2\} + E\{|\tilde{\epsilon}(k)|^2\}.$$

It can be shown that $E\{|\tilde{\epsilon}(k)|^2\} = M\sigma^2$, where $M$ is the dimension of the vectors $\mathbf{g}$, $\mathbf{f}$ and $\epsilon$.

Choose a region in the frequency domain where the noise power dominates the signal power, usually in the higher frequencies, and estimate the noise power as the power of the recorded image power.

4. The singular value decomposition (SVD) is an orthogonal transformation that can often be used to obtain better separation than a Fourier decomposition. The set of basis functions for the SVD is derived based on the characteristic statistics of the particular signal [236]. The higher indexed components of the SVD should be dominated by the noise. Thus, the problem looks like the frequency domain decomposition described above.

5. If the noise is correlated, the correlation properties of the image and noise must be known in order to separate them.

6. If the signal and noise cannot be separated in either the spatial or frequency domains, sometimes an adaptive filter can be used to remove the correlated portions of the signal from the noise [106]. This depends on having a stationary model for the image over an area large enough so that adaptation is nearly complete.

**Example 13.1 (Noise estimation).**  The examples of noisy images in Fig. 7.15 in Section 7.2 provide a good testing set for the methods introduced above. Table 13.1 shows the results of three of the methods: variance on a selected low contrast area, minimum variance on blocks over the whole image, and variance estimated from the high frequency part of the power spectrum.

The low contrast area method was tested using two $16 \times 16$ areas of the image: (1) a section of the table leg nearest to the camera in the foreground and (2) the dark area in the top center. The relatively poor estimates show the difficulty for the user in locating a sufficiently smooth portion of the image. For higher noise levels the problem is not as bad, but there are better, more consistent methods.

The estimation by using the minimum variance of all $16 \times 16$ blocks in the image gives good "ballpark" approximations, except for the 30 dB case. In this case, it is clear that the noise variance is of the same order as the image power in the lowest contrast areas. The variance estimate that we use for each block is itself a random variable. Thus, even in the absence of a signal, the estimate of the variance would vary according to a statistical distribution. By choosing the minimum estimate, we are biasing the estimate. This is why the estimates for the higher two noise levels are low.

**Table 13.1.** Comparison of noise estimation methods

| SNR (dB) | 30 | 20 | 10 |
|---|---|---|---|
| Noise variance | 1.967 | 19.67 | 196.7 |
| Est. low contrast (1) | 17.22 | 34.22 | 208.3 |
| Est. low contrast (2) | 9.685 | 29.07 | 240.0 |
| Est. min. $16 \times 16$ block | 3.499 | 18.26 | 175.6 |
| Est. high freq. spectrum (high 5%) | 7.645 | 25.34 | 205.3 |

The power spectral method estimated the noise power as the power in the highest 5% of the frequency range. From the spectrum in Fig. 5.14, we note that there is little visible power near the edges, which is where the highest 5% estimate is being made. Even with this, the estimate of the lowest noise level shows significant error. The other two estimates for the higher noise levels are usable for most processing purposes.

## 13.4     Estimation of the point spread function

Many modern digital cameras record the aperture and focal length settings that are used for each recorded image. Even with this information, there is some uncertainty about the exact range of the object of interest in the image. Still, most cases require that we treat a recorded image as having been blurred by an unknown point spread function (PSF) that is unique to that particular image. In addition to the common cases of unknown focus of the camera, examples of blurring include that caused by atmospheric turbulence and the relative motion of the camera and subject. Estimation of the PSF from the degraded image is still an open research area.

The estimation of the point spread function for scanners is a simpler problem, since the optical path is fixed. Nevertheless, adjacent regions on the image will have some effect on an individual pixel. The fact that the system is fixed permits experimentation, such as recording test patterns, that can be used to characterize the PSF.

Methods for estimating PSF usually assume the linear model $\mathbf{g} = \mathbf{H}\mathbf{f} + \epsilon$. Some of the methods that have proved useful are:

1. Locate the image of a point source in the image. This gives the PSF directly. The first problem is in locating such a point, since they are rare, and isolating the response from the rest of the image. A second problem is that images of bright objects give a good qualitative impression of the PSF but such objects are rarely single points; there may be several pixels in any dimension.
2. Locate an image of a line and relate the line spread function to the point spread function. Problems include finding an appropriate line. Edges can be more readily found, but must be differentiated to obtain the line response. The theoretical bases for these approaches are discussed in Sections 13.4.1–13.4.2.
3. Use white noise input to an imaging system and measure the output. White noise is far easier to generate and measure than a specific known image. If the system is noiseless, the input can be divided out in the frequency domain. If noise is a problem, which it usually is, the power spectrum can be obtained by averaging sections of the image. This gives the modulation transfer function (MTF) and not the optical transfer function (OTF). The difference is that the OTF is the Fourier transform of the PSF, whereas the MTF is the magnitude of the OTF.
4. Use spectral signatures, usually characteristic zeros, to determine the parameters of a blur with a known model. This works well with motion and focus blurs. This is discussed in Section 13.4.3.

## 13.4.1　Estimation of the point spread function from a line spread function

Given a line on the $x$ axis (if the line is at another orientation simply rotate the image), that is, represented by

$$f(x, y) = \delta(y),$$

we wish to estimate the point spread function, $h(x, y)$ of an imaging system. The image of the line is given by the convolution $g = h * f$,

$$g(x, y) = \int_{-\infty}^{\infty} \int_{-\infty}^{\infty} \delta(t) h(x - s, y - t) \, ds \, dt.$$

The output image is a function of only $y$,

$$g(y) = \int_{-\infty}^{\infty} h(x - s, y) \, ds.$$

This function can be thought of as the projection of $h(x, y)$ in the direction of the $y$ axis. This projection is the basis of X-ray computerized tomographic (CT) systems used for medical imaging. Sometimes the term computer assisted tomography or computerized axial tomography (CAT) is used.

To convert the line spread function to a point spread function, consider the 1-D Fourier transform of the projection,

$$\tilde{g}(v) = \int_{-\infty}^{\infty} g(y) e^{-jvy} \, dy.$$

Consider how this is related to the 2-D Fourier transform of the image,

$$\tilde{g}(u, v) = \int_{-\infty}^{\infty} \int_{-\infty}^{\infty} g(x, y) e^{-j(ux+vy)} \, dx \, dy.$$

We see that the 1-D transform is the 2-D transform evaluated at $u = 0$,

$$\tilde{g}(v) = \tilde{g}(0, v) = \int_{-\infty}^{\infty} \int_{-\infty}^{\infty} g(x, y) e^{-jvy} \, dx \, dy.$$

The Fourier transform of the image of a line in the $x$ direction is the Fourier transform of the PSF evaluated along the $v$ direction.

For a line at an arbitrary angle, $\theta$, the Fourier transform of the image of a line at angle $\theta$ relative to the $x$ axis is the Fourier transform of the PSF evaluated along a line at an angle $\theta$ relative to the $v$ axis. This result is known as the *slice-projection theorem*.

The problem is to obtain lines in all directions, so as to fill in the Fourier transform data, then take the inverse transform to obtain the PSF. If the number of lines is sparse, then the Fourier transform values must be interpolated from the polar grid to the rectangular grid. Note that, in practice, there will always be some interpolation error, and this error will be nonstationary. If the PSF is known to be circularly symmetric, then only one line is needed to define the PSF. This assumption is generally used to evaluate optical systems.

### 13.4.2 Estimation of the line spread function from an edge spread function

Consider a 1-D edge, which is represented as a step function,

$$u(t) = \begin{cases} 0 & t < 0 \\ 1 & t > 0. \end{cases}$$

The Dirac delta can be defined as

$$\delta(t) = \frac{\partial u(t)}{\partial t}.$$

The edge spread function of a linear, time-invariant system is defined as

$$g(t) = \int_{-\infty}^{\infty} h(\tau)u(t-\tau)d\tau.$$

Differentiating the edge spread function in 1-D, we obtain

$$\frac{\partial g(t)}{\partial t} = \int_{-\infty}^{\infty} h(\tau)\frac{\partial u(t-\tau)}{\partial t}d\tau;$$

$$\frac{\partial g(t)}{\partial t} = \int_{-\infty}^{\infty} h(\tau)\delta(t-\tau) = h(t).$$

The method can be applied in 2-D by noting that the step function can be considered an edge and the derivative in the direction perpendicular to the edge is a line. Averaging along the edge will reduce noise and give a better estimate of the line spread function.

If the PSF is assumed to be a separable function, then there are only two measurements that need to be made. A line spread function in each of the orthogonal directions is sufficient to characterize the PSF. If the PSF is assumed to be radially symmetric only one edge need be used.

### 13.4.3 Estimation of the point spread function by spectral analysis

From the properties of the Fourier transform, we know that the power spectrum of an image formed by the linear model

$$\mathbf{g} = \mathbf{Hf} + \epsilon$$

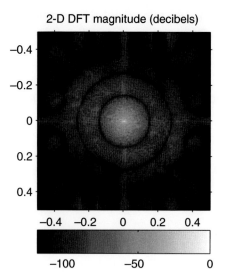

**Figure 13.1.** Spectrum of image blurred by a focus blur of 9 pixels in diameter (very low noise).

is given by

$$P_{gg}(\omega) = |\tilde{h}(\omega)|^2 P_{ff}(\omega) + P_{\epsilon\epsilon}(\omega).$$

If the transfer function has a spectral signature that is significantly different from that of the image, then there is the possibility of separating the two. In the case of creating an experiment with a white noise input image, the power spectrum, $P_{ff}(\omega)$, is a delta function and the power spectrum of the recorded image, $P_{gg}(\omega)$, is a noisy version of the MTF. In particular, many optical blurs have characteristic patterns of zeros that are unique for a class of distortion. For example, it can be shown that the Fourier transform of an out-of-focus lens PSF, modeled by a disk, is a Bessel function [92]. The radii of the zeros in the frequency domain uniquely identify the radius of the disk.

One way to identify the blur is to identify the first zero in the frequency domain. This may be hard to do if the noise is large. In low noise situations, like Fig. 13.1, it is obvious. A second way is to try to identify the periodic zero pattern. Since the zeros are periodic in the case of a linear motion and almost periodic in the case of an out-of-focus lens (zeros of the Bessel function of the first kind, $J_1(r)$, are at $r = 2.40$, 5.52, 8.65, 11.79, 14.93 ...), a periodic analysis seems reasonable. This implies a Fourier transform.

### Definition of the cepstrum

The cepstrum of a signal, $f(x, y)$, is defined by

$$C_f(x, y) = \mathcal{F}^{-1}\{\log[\mathcal{F}\{f(x, y)\}]\},$$

where the log of a complex number is given by

$$\log[\tilde{f}(u, v)] = \log[|\tilde{f}(u, v)|] + j \, \arg[\tilde{f}(u, v)].$$

The *power cepstrum* is frequently used in the estimation of signal parameters:

$$C_f(x, y) = \mathcal{F}^{-1}\{\log[|\mathcal{F}\{f(x, y)|^2\}]\}.$$

This yields a real-valued function, which can be easily plotted.

The terminology for using the cepstrum is derived from a paper by Bogert, Healy and Tukey, "The Quefrency Alansyis of Time Series for Echoes: Cepstrum, Pseudo-Autocovariance, Cross-Cepstrum and Saphe Cracking," [30]. The authors must have had a great time thinking up the terminology for this work. The cepstrum is discussed in the usual digital signal processing texts [200, 218].

Heuristically, the cepstral method works by changing zeros into poles via the log function and determining the period of these dominant signals. Note that the logarithms of near zero values are large negative values; thus, it is the periodic structures with negative components that are of interest. It is usually advantageous to clip the power cepstrum above zero and invert it for visual and numerical analysis. In practice, the standard noise reduction techniques of data averaging should be used. Often overlapping segments of the signal can be used effectively.

Examples of the spectral and cepstral signatures of common blurs can be instructive. Figure 13.1 shows the power spectrum of an image that has been blurred with a focus blur of 9 pixels in diameter. The grayscale has been expanded so the nearly circular pattern of zeros is easily seen. The cepstrum of this image is shown in Fig. 13.2. The plots are limited to a small range in order to display the peaks better. Note that the cepstral plots use inversion and clipping to display the peaks. In the grayscale image, we have displayed the high values as black, instead of the usual white, since the peaks are isolated and black points on a white background are easier to see. Figure 13.3 shows the spectrum for an image with a 9-pixel horizonal motion blur. Figure 13.4 shows the corresponding cepstrum.

## 13.5    Modeling point spread functions

Because we will need to simulate blurred images and test various methods of estimating blur parameters, it is appropriate to introduce the digital representation of continuous point spread functions. We will also use this capability to generate the degraded images that would be used to test the restoration methods discussed in Chapter 14.

In Section 2.3, we used several figures to show the approximate linearity of optical systems and introduced the point spread function (PSF). The PSFs of interest have finite extent and can be represented by a matrix operation. For most imaging applications, there are three types of blurring of interest. The blurring caused by optical misfocus or

(a)

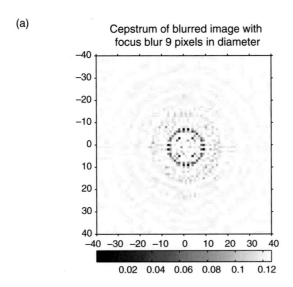

(b)     Cepstrum of blurred image with focus blur 9 pixels in diameter

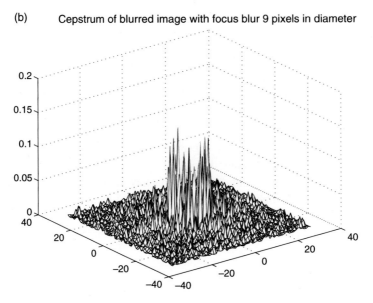

**Figure 13.2.** (a) Cepstrum of image blurred by a focus blur of 9 pixels in diameter (grayscale); (b) cepstrum of image blurred by a focus blur of 9 pixels in diameter (isoplot).

depth-of-field problems is modeled by representing the PSF as an image of the optical aperture of the system. There is frequently blurring caused by relative motion of the sensor and the object being imaged. Finally, there is blurring caused by dispersion in the medium through which the imaging takes place. Since the blurs must be represented by discrete matrices, we include a brief discussion on the requirements for the numerical approximation of these functions.

2-D DFT magnitude (decibels)

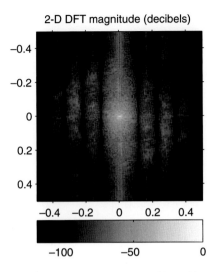

**Figure 13.3.** Spectrum of image blurred by a horizonal motion blur of 9 pixels in length.

## 13.5.1 Optical apertures

In common optical systems, the aperture is primarily responsible for the shape of the PSF and the focusing lenses are primarily responsible for the size or scaling of the PSF. The pinhole camera illustrated in Fig. 2.1 can be used to illustrate this effect. The image formed by a point is a scaled version of the aperture. The scale factor is $d_a + d_i/d_a$, where $d_a$ is the distance from the point to the aperture and $d_i$ is the distance from the aperture to the image plane. Focus can be a problem in scanners as well as cameras. Furthermore, the focus is also important when modeling output devices, where it is necessary to generate a finite-sized image of a pixel. The PSF of the laser that writes the image in an electrophotographic system is important. The dot shapes associated with ink-jet printers, although actually stochastic, can be approximated by deterministic PSFs. Common aperture shapes include:

1. Circular (disk): note that in digital simulation of continuous systems the circular aperture can be only approximated. The approximation improves as the radius of the circle increases,

$$a(x, y) = \begin{cases} \frac{1}{\pi R^2} & \text{if } \sqrt{x^2 + y^2} \le R, \\ 0 & \text{else.} \end{cases}$$

This is the common PSF associated with an out-of-focus lens. It is a good approximation. The actual PSF for the lens is an Airy disk [92]. This model can be modified to an elliptical shape to model printer output dots or the shapes of scanning lasers or CRT beams. Elliptical PSFs are obtained by an easy modification of this model.

(a)

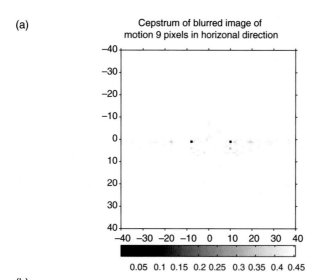

(b)

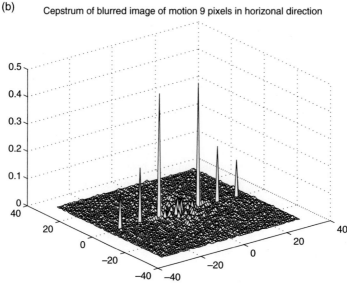

**Figure 13.4.** (a) Cepstrum of image blurred by a horizonal motion blur of 9 pixels in length (grayscale); (b) cepstrum of image blurred by a horizontal motion blur of 9 pixels in length (isoplot).

2. Rectangular: this type is often used in flat-bed scanners or digital camera sensors. For output devices, the pixels of LCD displays are often modeled using this shape. It is the shape of the two-dimensional sample-and-hold reconstruction method analogous to the 1-D method discussed in Section 6.6.1,

$$
a(x, y) = \begin{cases} \frac{1}{RS} & \text{if } -R/2 \le x \le R/2 \text{ and } -S/2 \le y \le S/2, \\ 0 & \text{else.} \end{cases}
$$

3. Hexagonal: this type is found in most high quality 35 mm cameras. For many digital applications, the hexagonal aperture can be well approximated by the circular aperture.
4. Diamond (parallelogram): this type is often used in lower quality film cameras.

### 13.5.2    Motion point spread functions

Motion is a common distortion in many applications, e.g., moving scanners or cameras, fast moving objects. It is often assumed that the shutter speed is fast enough or the imaging time is short enough so that the relative motion of the object and aperture is negligible. Unfortunately, there are many cases when this assumption is not satisfied. The case for arbitrary motion is too complex for mathematical analysis with common techniques. Most studies have been restricted to constant velocity linear motion. There is some work on the extension to motion trajectories that can be easily parameterized. For now, let us consider the simplest case.

Consider a perfect optical system whose point spread function is a delta function. Since it is only the relative motion of the object, aperture and image plane that is important, let us assume the image plane is moving. To further simplify the study, let us assume that the motion is restricted to one of the coordinate axes. This allows us to use a 1-D model. Since the optical system is perfect, the image at the image plane, $g(x)$, is a perfect replica of the object, $f(x)$, i.e., $g(x) = f(x)$. Actually, the image may be reversed depending on the lens system. For this presentation, we will neglect any nonblurring transformations without loss of generality. Assume that the image plane is moving with velocity $v_x$ and that the aperture is open from time $t = 0$ to $t = T$. The image plane at coordinate $x = 0$ is exposed to different portions of the object at different times. For example, at $t = 0$ it is exposed to $f(0)$, while at $t = T$ it is exposed to $f(v_x T)$, as illustrated in Fig. 13.5.

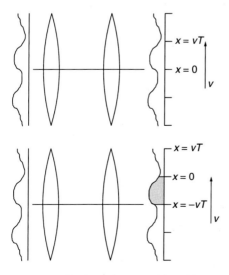

**Figure 13.5.** Motion point spread function.

The cumulative effect at $x = 0$ is the integral of all object values that passed the point during the exposure,

$$g(0) = \int_0^{v_x T} f(x) \mathrm{d}x.$$

By a transformation of variables, we can write the result as a function of time

$$g(0) = \int_0^T f(v_x t) \mathrm{d}t.$$

The image for any $x$ is given by

$$g(x) = \int_0^T f(x + v_x t) \mathrm{d}t.$$

To make the point spread function explicit, we can rewrite this result:

$$g(x) = \int_{-\infty}^{\infty} \int_0^T f(\xi)\delta(x + v_x t - \xi) \mathrm{d}t \mathrm{d}\xi,$$

which indicates that the point spread function is given by

$$h(x) = \int_0^T \delta(x + v_x t) \mathrm{d}t.$$

For the general two-dimensional case, the constant velocity linear motion PSF is given by

$$h(x, y) = \int_0^T \delta(x + v_x t, y + v_y t) \mathrm{d}t,$$

where $v_x$ and $v_y$ indicate the velocities in the $x$ and $y$ directions respectively.

Some cases of spatially varying motion can be treated by a geometric warping of the image as used in the case of circular motion [229, 230]. In these cases, it is necessary to parameterize the trajectory of the motion. If motion vectors can be obtained for different regions of the image, for example when sequential frames of a sequence are available, the processing can be treated as locally linear [271].

### 13.5.3     Distortions by imaging medium

The medium through which the image is recorded may have a profound effect on the quality of the result. Astronomical images are a classic example of a system limited by atmospheric distortions. Underwater photography is another common example. For many of the applications in this text, we could consider dispersions caused by dust or vapor in the optical path or on the optical components. We will use the atmospheric model, since it is well known and results in a form that can be applied to other phenomena.

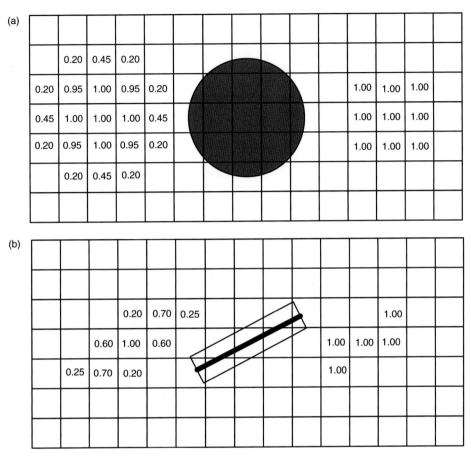

**Figure 13.6.** (a) Digital approximations to circular (out-of-focus lens) point spread function; (b) digital approximations to linear motion point spread function.

Atmospheric turbulence is a time varying phenomenon as demonstrated by the twinkling of the stars. The small differences in the density of the air cause phase shifts as the light passes through it. For images taken with short exposure times, the PSF associated with the atmosphere must be regarded as a stochastic process [120]. For longer time exposures, such as those obtained using a tracking camera, the average PSF can be used. The model that has been suggested is based on experimental data and is given by [120]

$$h(x, y) = K_1 \exp\left[-(K_2 x^2 + K_3 y^2)^{5/6}\right],$$

where the $K_i$ are determined by fitting experimental data. For most applications, the 5/6 exponent is replaced by unity and $K_2$ is set equal to $K_3$ to yield a symmetric

Gaussian form,

$$h(x, y) = K_1 \exp\left[-\frac{1}{2\sigma^2}(x^2 + y^2)\right].$$

### 13.5.4 Numerical approximation of point spread functions

The functional forms are easy to write mathematically, but need to be approximated in a matrix form for numerical computation. For PSFs with small spatial extent, this can create a sampling problem, similar to that of sampling any two-dimensional signal. A rigorous mathematical treatment of this aliasing is beyond the scope of this text and would be of little value. It is important to note that care should be taken to use interpolation as in the case of reconstructing images (see Section 6.6). A discussion of the sampling accuracy of the PSF is given in [228].

Let us consider two examples, where we emphasize the interpolation needed for the approximations. In all cases, the final matrix approximation should have values that sum to one, since this is required for lossless optical systems, i.e., the DC values of the original and blurred images are the same. Our examples use unity as the maximum value for simplicity rather than the fraction that would be required in the final version that would sum to one. The final version is obtained by dividing by the sum of the elements.

A circular disk of diameter 4 pixels could be approximated by several $5 \times 5$ matrices. The disk is shown in Fig. 13.6a with a grid. Two representations are shown on either side. The one on the right uses a binary representation that is one if most of a pixel area is covered by the PSF, and zero if less than half of the pixel area is covered. The other uses approximately the area of the pixel area that is covered by the PSF. It is clear that the smoother approximation is superior because it will produce a more nearly circular pattern in both the spatial and frequency domains. A linear motion blur that coincides with the horizonal or vertical axes is easily approximated by unit values for the number of pixels corresponding to the length of the motion. The end values may be fractions depending on the exact length. However, for other orientations, the approximation is more complex. A linear motion blur of length 4 pixels at $30°$ is shown on a grid in Fig. 13.6b. We superimpose a rectangle of one pixel width. This lets us use the same covering method as for the disk. Again, the better approximation is obviously the smoother one. The MATLAB function *fspecial* can be used to create standard point spread functions with appropriate numerical approximations.

## 13.6 Problems

**13.1** Consider the problem of determining the sensor response of a camera that was used to take images of the Martian landscape from a robotic probe. Describe a procedure for calibrating the sensor response for a series of images taken during a short time interval. What information would be required? What would be the sources of inaccuracies?

**13.2**  Obtaining the sensor response for each pixel in a large CCD array is impractical. What approximations can be made to obtain estimates of the sensor characteristics over the 2-D area? What tests or experiments would be needed to make such estimates?

**13.3**  Consider the method of noise reduction that subtracts a noise level from the recorded values of an image. Frequently, noise is measured for an input device by recording data with zero input, e.g., by taking a picture with the lens cap on. These values are averaged and then subtracted from the values obtained when the document or scene is recorded. Assuming the additive noise model of $\mathbf{g} = \mathbf{f} + \epsilon$, under what assumptions will this noise subtraction produce a more accurate estimate of the image data?

**13.4**  Consider the 1-D signals generated in Problem 7.13. For each of the signals, estimate the noise variance using at least two of the methods described in Section 13.3.2. Compare the accuracy of the methods with the known noise variance. Determine the effect of the characteristics of the signal and the noise variance estimation.

**13.5**  Consider the images generated in Problem 7.15, using your image, *gray-one*. Estimate the noise variance using at least two of the methods described in Section 13.3.2. Compare the accuracy of the methods with the known noise variance.

**13.6**  Consider the images generated in Problem 7.16, using your image, *gray-one*. Estimate the noise variance using at least two of the methods described in Section 13.3.2. Compare the accuracy of the methods with the known noise variance.

**13.7**  Show that a linear motion blur of length $N$ pixels produces peaks in the cepstral domain at a distance $N$ from the origin and multiples of $N$ in the same direction as the blur in the spatial domain.

**13.8**  Using the green band of your *image-one*, simulate a horizonal linear motion blur of $N$ pixels in length, by convolving the PSF defined by the vector of equal weights of length $N$, i.e., $\mathbf{h} = [1/N, 1/N, \ldots, 1/N]$. Be sure to note any shifting of the origin of the image matrix.

(a) Display the result for $N = 9, 13, 19$.
(b) Estimate the length of the blur using the edge spread function. Note any difficulties in defining an edge precisely.
(c) Estimate the length of the blur using the spectral or cepstral methods. Note any problems encountered using this method.

**13.9**  Simulate a 45° motion blur of 9 pixels in length using the green band of your image, *image-one*. Your simulation should result in no shifting of the image, only a blur. Compute the blurred image by convolving your image with a simulated PSF using conv2 in MATLAB. This is NOT circular convolution, as would be done if you used the FFT methods.

(a) Extract a small central portion, e.g., $256 \times 256$, $512 \times 512$, of the blurred image that has no pixels within 9 pixels of the edge. This will eliminate any edge effects, caused by the fact that the image outside the original recorded area is assumed to be zero. Display this image. This represents what physically occurs in cameras when an image is captured. Let us call this blurred image *blur_a*.

(b) Extract a $256 \times 256$ portion of the original unblurred image at the same position as the portion defined in (a). Use the FFT to compute the circular convolution of the blur with the image. Let us call this blurred image *blur_b*.

(c) Using a single band of your image, *image-one*, and the 2-D DFT, convolve a simulated circular aperture with your image. This convolution will be circulant or periodic. Thus, there will be edge effects. The point spread function (PSF) of the pinhole aperture (or out-of-focus lens) is well modeled by a circular disk,

$$h(x, y) = \begin{cases} 1/\pi R^2 & \text{if } x^2 + y^2 \le R^2 \\ 0 & \text{else} \end{cases}.$$

The resulting blurred image is obtained by convolution

$$g(x, y) = \iint f(\xi, \eta) h(x - \xi, y - \eta) \mathrm{d}\xi \mathrm{d}\eta.$$

i. Depending on the size of your image, let $R$ be about 4 to 7 pixels. Create an image of the PSF. Be sure to normalize your discrete approximation of the PSF so that the elements sum to one. Display the image of the PSF.

ii. Perform the 2-D convolution using the DFT. Display the result. Be sure to use the methods discussed in the chapter on elementary display. Note any obvious edge effects caused by the periodicity of the Fourier processing.

iii. Compute and display the spectrum of the original and blurred images.

(d) Repeat Problem 13.9c using the following PSFs

$$h_1(x, y) = \begin{cases} \frac{1}{4XY} & \text{if } |x| \le X \text{ and } |y| \le Y \\ 0 & \text{else} \end{cases}.$$

Choose a value of $X$ and $Y$ that is comparable to your $R$.

$$h_2(x, y) = \begin{cases} \frac{1}{2X} & \text{if } |x| \le X \text{ and } y = 0 \\ 0 & \text{else} \end{cases}.$$

$$h_3(x, y) = \begin{cases} \frac{1}{2Y} & \text{if } |y| \le Y \text{ and } x = 0 \\ 0 & \text{else} \end{cases}.$$

(e) Add Gaussian white noise to the image obtained in part (a) to produce SNRs of 30, 20 and 10 dB. The SNR is computed as the ratio of the blurred image power to the noise power. Display these images. Remember to use the proper display methods of Chapter 3. This should give you a feel for the visual effect of various SNRs and should be in agreement with your previous homework experiences. Repeat the creation of noisy images for those of part (b). Display these images and compare them with those of *blur_a*. They should look almost identical to the results from using *blur_a*.

Note: The images generated in this problem will be used in the problems in Chapter 14 on image restoration.

**13.10**   Consider the blurred, noisy images that were generated in Problem 13.9e using the image *blur_a*. For each SNR, estimate the noise variance by both spatial domain and frequency domain methods. Compare your estimates with the variance of the actual noise that you added.

Note: Using the *blkproc* routine in MATLAB will make the block averaging much easier.

**13.11**   For each SNR of the images generated using *blur_a* in Problem 13.9e, estimate the blur type and parameter. Compare your estimate with the actual value. Display the spectrum and cepstrum, if you use those methods.

**13.12**   Repeat Problems 13.9, 13.10 and 13.11, using a blur that approximates an out-of-focus lens, a disk of diameter 9 pixels.

**13.13**   Repeat Problems 13.9, 13.10 and 13.11, using a blur that approximates atmospheric turbulence, a Gaussian with standard deviation of 4 pixels.

**13.14**   A blurred noisy image named mystery_image.mat has been created and is available on the text's website (www.cambridge.org/9780521868532). The file is saved as a *.mat file instead of a tif file to preserve the SNR. We use the *.mat file to avoid problems caused by quantization after the blur and additive noise. A TIFF version of the image is available for visual inspection. Determine the noise variance and the blur type and parameter.

# 14   Image restoration

Since any real image recording system must use a finite aperture and is subject to measurement noise, we are naturally interested in methods of correcting imperfections in the recorded image. The goal of image restoration is to estimate the original appearance of an image that has been degraded in some way. Typical degradations include optical blurring, geometric warping, sensor transformations, quantization and electronic noise. Even halftoning in the reproduction process can be considered a degradation that may be corrected by some later operation. It is important to distinguish between restoration and enhancement, which also tries to improve the appearance of an image. The restoration methods discussed here are applied to both spatial degradations (blurring and noise) and spectral degradations (color distortions and noise).

Restoration is a mathematically well defined process that estimates the original signal from recorded data. To restore an image much quantitative information is required, in particular:

1. Image formation model with known parameters. The models and their parameters are discussed in Chapter 13. Of course, the accuracy with which the parameters are known affects the quality of the restoration.
2. Restoration criterion. This is usually an optimization criterion of some type. The minimum mean square error is the one most frequently used. This is done for ease of analysis and mathematical tractability. However, with the advent of faster computers, more visually meaningful cost functions are being used, such as $\Delta E_{ab}^*$ for color images. In addition, constrained problems can be formulated that account for a priori knowledge and physical constraints, such as lower and upper bounds on the image values.
3. Computation algorithm. Ultimately, the mathematical problem defined by the restoration criterion must be solved to obtain a numerical solution. A restored image must be generated. It is this step that may produce the fundamental limits on the quality of the restoration. Chapter 5 introduced the discrete Fourier transform as a fast algorithm to compute convolution and deconvolution. The cost of this speed is the circularity assumption that prevents high quality restoration near the edges of the image. In Chapter 7 and Appendix C we note the need for the assumption of stationary random processes for mathematical tractability, while noting that real images are not really stationary. In other cases, the use of constrained optimization methods results in

iterative methods that have practical limits on the number of iterations. The *projection onto convex sets* (POCS) methods used for demosaicking in Chapter 10 is an example.

Enhancement is an algorithmic process whose goal is to make an image look better to an observer. There does not need to be any degradation of an original for enhancement to be used. The enhancement process requires qualitative information, such as:

1. Intent of the observer or user of the processed image. The image may be used for informational purposes, such as surveillance or forensic images. In such cases, the intent may be to make text readable, count various objects or measure areas. Processing for this intent would be quite different from processing to make a pictorial scene more pleasing. Artistic modifications include color transformations, edge sharpening and noise suppression.
2. Type of image information or characteristics that are most important. For informational processing, the type of characteristics of interest include spatial size and frequencies of objects, while for pictorial processing, the user might be more interested in color saturation, or highlight versus shadow detail enhancement.
3. Viewing conditions: physical and temporal. The characteristics of the viewing mode and variability are important in pictorial applications. The dynamic range of the display modality affects the perception. The gamut mapping of Chapter 12 demonstrates this. If a printed image is to be viewed under varying illumination, it will be treated differently than if it is to be viewed in a single controlled environment.

This chapter will concentrate on restoration. In this case, restoration is defined as attempting to recover the original image from recorded data. It is assumed that the parameters of the image formation process that resulted in the data are known. The estimation of these parameters is discussed in Chapter 13. Many of the mathematical methods of restoration can be used or easily modified to obtain enhancement algorithms. Let us begin with the restoration of spatially blurred images.

## 14.1 Restoration of spatial blurs

For this brief introduction to restoration, we will concentrate on the linear model presented in Chapter 13, which we will assume can be accurately represented by sampled data and written algebraically

$$\mathbf{g} = \mathbf{H}\mathbf{f} + \boldsymbol{\epsilon}. \tag{14.1}$$

In the frequency domain, we have in the continuous domain

$$\tilde{g}(\omega_x, \omega_y) = \tilde{h}(\omega_x, \omega_y)\tilde{f}(\omega_x, \omega_y) + \tilde{\epsilon}(\omega_x, \omega_y),$$

and using the discrete Fourier transform,

$$\tilde{g}(k, l) = \tilde{h}(k, l)\tilde{f}(k, l) + \tilde{\epsilon}(k, l).$$

For the linear model, we need to define the blurring function, $\mathbf{H}$ and the statistics of the noise, $\epsilon$. The noise is discussed in Chapters 7 and 12 and Appendix C.

We will begin our discussion of restoration methods with the simplest ones, which have the fewest and most naive assumptions. We will see that these methods have shortcomings that can be overcome at the cost of additional assumptions and a priori knowledge, as well as, increased computation. Recalling that a restoration method requires an image formation model, a restoration criterion and a computational algorithm, we begin the sections on each method with the definition of the restoration criterion. Since this chapter is limited to the model of Eq. (14.1), there is no need to repeat it.

The mathematics for deriving the restoration estimates is the same for both monochrome and color images. The monochrome image is represented as a vector by using stacked notation, where the columns of the image are stacked on each other (see Section 2.7). The color image is represented as a vector by extending the stacking to include the bands of the image. This approach was used in [274] to derive a minimum mean square error demosaicking method. As we have noted previously, the matrix algebraic approach is excellent for deriving results, but is never used for numerical computation.

### 14.1.1    Inverse filter

Restoration criterion: find the linear estimate, $\hat{\mathbf{f}} = \mathbf{Q}\mathbf{g}$, that best fits the data in the mean square sense. The mathematical problem is defined by

$$\min_{\hat{\mathbf{f}}} ||\mathbf{g} - \mathbf{H}\hat{\mathbf{f}}||^2.$$

Note the use of the caret, ^, to indicate the estimate of the quantity. Rewriting the above norm as

$$\Phi(\hat{\mathbf{f}}) = (\mathbf{g} - \mathbf{H}\hat{\mathbf{f}})^T(\mathbf{g} - \mathbf{H}\hat{\mathbf{f}}),$$

$$\Phi(\hat{\mathbf{f}}) = \mathbf{g}^T\mathbf{g} - 2\mathbf{g}^T\mathbf{H}\hat{\mathbf{f}} + \hat{\mathbf{f}}^T\mathbf{H}^T\mathbf{H}\hat{\mathbf{f}}.$$

Minimizing $\Phi(\hat{\mathbf{f}})$ requires the derivative of the scalar function with respect to the vector, $\hat{\mathbf{f}}$. Taking the derivative of $\Phi(\hat{\mathbf{f}})$ (see Appendix B) and setting it equal to zero, we obtain

$$\frac{\partial \Phi(\hat{\mathbf{f}})}{\partial \hat{\mathbf{f}}} = -2\mathbf{H}^T\mathbf{g} + 2\mathbf{H}^T\mathbf{H}\hat{\mathbf{f}} = 0,$$

$$\mathbf{H}^T\mathbf{H}\hat{\mathbf{f}} = \mathbf{H}^T\mathbf{g}.$$

We note that since the matrix $\mathbf{H}$ may not be square, much less have an inverse, we need to apply a theorem from linear algebra that allows us to deal with such cases. This is also discussed in Appendix B.

THEOREM. The consistent equations $\mathbf{Ax} = \mathbf{b}$ have a solution $\mathbf{x} = \mathbf{Gb}$, if and only if $\mathbf{A} = \mathbf{AGA}$.

For a proof, see [236, Section 9.4]. From this, it is seen that the pseudoinverse $\mathbf{G} = \mathbf{A}^+$ will yield a solution. Applying the theorem to our problem,

$$\hat{\mathbf{f}} = (\mathbf{H}^T\mathbf{H})^+\mathbf{H}^T\mathbf{g}. \tag{14.2}$$

Note that if $\mathbf{H}$ is invertible, then

$$\hat{\mathbf{f}} = \mathbf{H}^{-1}\mathbf{g}.$$

Assuming that the system can be adequately approximated by circular convolution, the matrix $\mathbf{H}$ can be represented by a circulant and the system diagonalized by the DFT.

$$\mathbf{Wg} = \mathbf{WHW}^{-1}\mathbf{Wf} + \mathbf{W}\boldsymbol{\epsilon}.$$

This solution in the frequency domain is

$$\hat{\tilde{f}}(k,l) = [\tilde{h}^*(k,l)\tilde{h}(k,l)]^+\tilde{h}^*(k,l)\tilde{g}(k,l), \tag{14.3}$$

where

$$[\tilde{h}^*(k,l)\tilde{h}(k,l)]^+ = \begin{cases} \frac{1}{|\tilde{h}(k,l)|^2} & if \quad \tilde{h}(k,l) \neq 0, \\ 0 & if \quad \tilde{h}(k,l) = 0. \end{cases}$$

The superscript $+$ indicates a *pseudoinverse* that is discussed in Appendix B. An exercise relating that concept to this solution is given in Problem 14.4. A problem arises because of the amplification of the noise

$$\hat{\tilde{f}}(k,l) = [\tilde{h}^*(k,l)\tilde{h}(k,l)]^+\tilde{h}^*(k,l)[\tilde{h}(k,l)\tilde{f}(k,l) + \tilde{\epsilon}(k,l)], \tag{14.4}$$

for the frequencies for which $\tilde{h}(k,l) \neq 0$, we have

$$\hat{\tilde{f}}(k,l) = \tilde{f}(k,l) + \frac{\tilde{\epsilon}(k,l)}{\tilde{h}(k,l)}. \tag{14.5}$$

For small but nonzero values of $\tilde{h}(k,l)$, the noise term can dominate the first term of the restoration. This could be avoided by setting a nonzero threshold, above which we would use the inverse form and below which we would set the result to zero. This would be rather heuristic and, as we shall see shortly, there are better formulations of the restoration problem that avoid this pitfall in a more elegant manner.

A second derivation of the inverse filter can be obtained from a stochastic formulation or *Bayesian* approach of the problem. The case of zero-mean, white Gaussian noise leads to the *likelihood function* that is derived from the probability distribution of the noise

$$p(\mathbf{g}|\mathbf{f}) = \frac{1}{(2\pi\sigma_n)^{N/2}} \exp\left[-\frac{1}{\sigma_n^2}(\mathbf{g} - \mathbf{Hf})^T(\mathbf{g} - \mathbf{Hf})\right],$$

where $\sigma_n^2$ models the variance of $\epsilon$, and $\mathbf{Hf}$ represents the recorded signal mean. The restoration criterion is to find the image $\mathbf{f}$ that makes the recorded data $\mathbf{g}$ the most likely data to have been obtained. In this case, it is desired to maximize the above probability as a function of $\mathbf{f}$. This leads to minimizing the argument of the exponential, which gives the identical equation as before in Eq. (14.2).

### 14.1.2    Minimum mean square error (MMSE) filter

The inverse filter requires knowledge only about the blurring function, $\mathbf{H}$. Its drawback was the likely amplification of the noise. It seems intuitive that if we have some information about the noise and the signal, we should be able to produce a better restoration. The heuristic about choosing a nonzero threshold in the last section is generalized by the minimum mean square error filter, named for Norbert Wiener, who was a major contributor to the solution of many classical communication problems. It should be noted that Wiener's problem formulation was much more complex than the simple matrix problem presented here.

#### Wiener filter

Restoration criterion: assume that the image is generated by a zero-mean random process; find the linear estimate that minimizes the expected square error between the estimate, $\hat{\mathbf{f}} = \mathbf{Qg}$, and the original image, $\mathbf{f}$. Since images are usually not zero mean, the mean should be subtracted to produce a zero-mean process. The restoration problem can be stated mathematically as

$$\min_{\mathbf{Q}} E\{||\hat{\mathbf{f}} - \mathbf{f}||^2\}.$$

Substituting $\hat{\mathbf{f}} = \mathbf{Qg}$ and expanding the terms, we get

$$\Phi(\mathbf{Q}) = E\{(\mathbf{Qg} - \mathbf{f})^T(\mathbf{Qg} - \mathbf{f})\},$$

$$\Phi(\mathbf{Q}) = E\{\mathbf{g}^T\mathbf{Q}^T\mathbf{Qg} - 2\mathbf{f}^T\mathbf{Qg} + \mathbf{f}^T\mathbf{f}\},$$

$$\Phi(\mathbf{Q}) = E\{\mathbf{g}^T\mathbf{Q}^T\mathbf{Qg}\} - 2E\{\mathbf{f}^T\mathbf{Qg}\} + E\{\mathbf{f}^T\mathbf{f}\}.$$

Taking the derivative with respect to $\mathbf{Q}$ (see Appendix B), we obtain

$$\frac{\partial \Phi(\mathbf{Q})}{\partial \mathbf{Q}} = 2\mathbf{Q}E\{\mathbf{gg}^T\} - 2E\{\mathbf{fg}^T\}.$$

Setting the derivative equal to zero and solving for $\mathbf{Q}$, we have

$$\mathbf{Q} = E\{\mathbf{fg}^T\}E\{\mathbf{gg}^T\}^{-1}.$$

Making the substitution that $\mathbf{g} = \mathbf{Hf} + \epsilon$, we have

$$\mathbf{Q} = (E\{\mathbf{ff}^T\mathbf{H}^T\} + E\{\mathbf{f}\epsilon^T\})[E\{\mathbf{Hff}^T\mathbf{H}^T\} - 2E\{\mathbf{Hf}\epsilon^T\} + E\{\epsilon\epsilon^T\}]^{-1}.$$

We make the usual assumption that the noise is zero mean and signal-independent, which gives

$$\mathbf{Q} = E\{\mathbf{ff}^T\}\mathbf{H}^T[\mathbf{H}E\{\mathbf{ff}^T\}\mathbf{H}^T + E\{\boldsymbol{\epsilon}\boldsymbol{\epsilon}^T\}]^{-1},$$

$$\mathbf{Q} = \mathbf{R}_{ff}\mathbf{H}^T[\mathbf{H}\mathbf{R}_{ff}\mathbf{H}^T + \mathbf{R}_{\epsilon\epsilon}]^{-1}, \tag{14.6}$$

where we denote the correlation of the image and noise ensembles by $\mathbf{R}_{ff}$ and $\mathbf{R}_{\epsilon\epsilon}$, respectively.

To compute the estimate with reduced computational cost, we usually transform to another domain where the matrices are diagonal. Under the proper assumptions of Section 5.5, this is the frequency domain via the 2-D DFT, and the transformation is given by

$$\mathbf{W}\mathbf{Q}\mathbf{W}^{-1} = \mathbf{W}\mathbf{R}_{ff}\mathbf{W}^{-1}\mathbf{W}\mathbf{H}^T\mathbf{W}^{-1}[\mathbf{W}\mathbf{H}\mathbf{W}^{-1}\mathbf{W}\mathbf{R}_{ff}\mathbf{W}^{-1}\mathbf{W}\mathbf{H}^T + \mathbf{W}\mathbf{R}_{\epsilon\epsilon}\mathbf{W}^{-1}]^{-1}.$$

Recall that $(\mathbf{ABA}^{-1})^{-1} = \mathbf{AB}^{-1}\mathbf{A}^{-1}$. Thus, in the frequency domain we have

$$\tilde{q}(k,l) = \frac{\tilde{h}(k,l)^* P_{ff}(k,l)}{\tilde{h}(k,l) P_{ff}(k,l)\tilde{h}(k,l)^* + P_{\epsilon\epsilon}(k,l)}. \tag{14.7}$$

Another convenient form of this filter is

$$\tilde{q}(k,l) = \frac{H(k,l)^*}{|\tilde{h}(k,l)|^2 + P_{\epsilon\epsilon}(k,l)/P_{ff}(k,l)}, \tag{14.8}$$

where we can see the equivalence to the inverse filter in Eq. (14.3) when the term $P_{\epsilon\epsilon}(k,l)/P_{ff}(k,l)$ is small. Writing the estimate in the frequency domain as

$$\hat{\tilde{f}}(k,l) = \frac{\tilde{h}(k,l)^* \tilde{g}(k,l)}{|\tilde{h}(k,l)|^2 + P_{\epsilon\epsilon}(k,l)/P_{ff}(k,l)}, \tag{14.9}$$

we can make a direct comparison to the inverse result of Eq. (14.5). In either form, one can see that when the noise dominates the signal in the ratio $P_{\epsilon\epsilon}(k,l)/P_{ff}(k,l)$, the filter naturally tends to zero (the mean), avoiding the instability of the inverse filter.

### Practical aspects

Note that the amount of a priori knowledge required for implementation of this method is significantly greater than that required for the inverse filter. In addition to the knowledge of the PSF, we now need the power spectra of both the signal and the noise.

If the noise is assumed to be white, then the spectrum is flat and only the variance is needed. The spectrum of the ensemble from which the original signal is a member is more difficult to estimate. This estimate also involves some philosophical decisions about the amount of knowledge that is assumed. Often the power spectrum is estimated from an undegraded image that is thought to be statistically similar to the one under investigation. If maximum ignorance is assumed, then the image can be modeled by a flat spectrum and the filter reduces to

$$\tilde{q}(k,l) = \frac{\tilde{h}(k,l)^*}{|\tilde{h}(k,l)|^2 + \alpha}, \qquad (14.10)$$

which is convenient because the signal restoration method now is a function of only the signal-to-noise ratio, $\alpha$.

In the case where there is no blurring function, i.e., $\mathbf{H} = \mathbf{I}$,

$$\mathbf{Q} = \mathbf{R}_{ff}[\mathbf{R}_{ff} + \mathbf{R}_{\epsilon\epsilon}]^{-1}.$$

Note that if the image ensemble has a nonzero mean, the form of the MMSE estimate should reflect that fact. The form should be

$$\hat{\mathbf{f}} = \mathbf{Qg} + \mathbf{b}.$$

### Finite impulse response implementation

Most frequently, the MMSE filter is implemented in the frequency domain. One problem is that the filter usually requires a large region of support if it is to be represented accurately. However, sometimes hardware and time constraints make an FIR implementation necessary. The problem can be formulated as an optimal FIR filter problem

$$\min_{\mathbf{Q}_{\mathrm{FIR}}} E\{||\mathbf{f} - \mathbf{Q}_{\mathrm{FIR}}\mathbf{g}||^2\}.$$

In this case, there are many elements of $\mathbf{Q}_{\mathrm{FIR}}$ that are restricted to zero and the transformation to the frequency domain is not helpful. The nonzero elements of $\mathbf{Q}_{\mathrm{FIR}}$ can be found by solving a set of equations based on the autocorrelation and cross-correlation matrices as in the case of 1-D AR modeling. The equations are given by

$$r_{fg}(m,n) = \sum\sum q(k,l)r_{ff}(m-k,n-l),$$

where the sums are taken over the region of support for the FIR filter. However, this is a computationally intensive method and so suboptimal methods that are more tractable for obtaining FIR restoration filters are often used.

One computationally simple method for generating useful FIR filters is similar to the window method of filter design studied in basic digital signal processing [200, 218]. The filter is created in the frequency domain with high accuracy, transformed to the space domain and windowed to the size required by the implementation. The 2-D windows are separable versions of the 1-D windows used in a basic DSP course. The errors caused by this manipulation can be analyzed in a similar manner to the truncation error caused by using finite data in spectral estimation, as is discussed in Section 5.3.

### 14.1.3    Spatially varying FIR filters

In practice, nonstationary image models are extremely difficult to characterize accurately. Simple characterization can include parametric models of the blur or image spectrum. Estimating the image spectrum as white noise and trying to determine its variance is sometimes useful. Spatially varying means are often used. However, the estimate for the mean is usually obtained from the degraded image and leads to a certain bias in the estimate.

### 14.1.4    Parametric Wiener filters

To allow more user interaction (tweaking) to the theoretical filter, a parametric form was developed:

$$\tilde{q}(k,l) = \frac{\tilde{h}(k,l)^*}{|\tilde{h}(k,l)|^2 + \alpha P_{\epsilon\epsilon}(k,l)/P_{ff}(k,l)},$$

where $\alpha$ is determined by the user according to whether it is desired to increase or decrease the high frequency power in the estimate. It should be noted that the addition of such parameters takes the filter out of the class of restoration and into the class of enhancement.

### 14.1.5    Power spectral estimation

Since the MMSE filter calls for the power spectrum of the original image and of the noise, these quantities must be estimated. We will limit our discussion here to the monochromatic case. The extension to color is discussed in Section 14.1.11. The noise spectrum is usually considered to be flat, that is, representing white noise. Thus, the only parameter of interest is the variance of the noise. The estimation of the noise variance is discussed in Chapter 13.

The spectrum of the original image must be obtained by making an assumption about the ensemble of images from which the original image came. There are several ways to estimate the spectrum given this assumption.

1. Choose a prototype image that is believed to have similar characteristics to the image that is being restored. Compute the periodogram of this image. Windowing is advisable to reduce variations in the spectrum arising from peculiarities of the prototype image.
2. Choose a prototype image that is believed to have similar characteristics to the image that is being restored. Compute the AR model for the image and compute the spectrum from the model. This produces a very smooth estimate that has shown good results in applications.
3. Compute the AR model of the degraded image and use this to estimate the power spectrum of the original. This results in a biased estimate and has some very bad properties.

4. If the PSF, $\mathbf{H}$, and the spectrum of the noise are assumed to be known, the spectrum of the image ensemble may be estimated by

$$P_{ff}(k, l) = \frac{P_{gg}(k, l) - P_{nn}(k, l)}{|\tilde{h}(k, l)|^2}.$$

This method is very sensitive to the estimates of the parameters used for the "known" quantities.

### 14.1.6    Maximum a posteriori (MAP) restoration

Restoration criterion: find the estimate that is most likely to have generated the recorded data; maximize the probability of the estimate given the data. Mathematically, this is

$$\hat{\mathbf{f}} = \arg\ \max_{\mathbf{f}} p(\mathbf{f}|\mathbf{g}).$$

We use Bayes' theorem,

$$p(\mathbf{f}|\mathbf{g}) = \frac{p(\mathbf{g}|\mathbf{f})p(\mathbf{f})}{p(\mathbf{g})},$$

to rewrite the problem in terms of the a priori densities, $p(\mathbf{g}|\mathbf{f})$ and $p(\mathbf{f})$.

Since most probability distributions used to describe images are based on exponentials, e.g., Gaussian, Poisson or Laplacian, it is standard to take the log of the conditional density. This produces an additive problem instead of a multiplicative one. Taking the derivative with respect to $\hat{\mathbf{f}}$ and setting it equal to zero we have

$$\frac{\partial \log[p(\mathbf{g}|\mathbf{f})]}{\partial \mathbf{f}} + \frac{\partial \log[p(\mathbf{f})]}{\partial \mathbf{f}} = 0. \qquad (14.11)$$

Note that

$$\frac{\partial \log[p(\mathbf{g})]}{\partial \mathbf{f}} = 0,$$

since the recorded data has been determined and does not depend on the estimate.

If we assume the linear model, $\mathbf{g} = \mathbf{H}\mathbf{f} + \boldsymbol{\epsilon}$, with noise that has a symmetric distribution and the mean of the ensemble for the original image is constant (stationary), then the MAP estimate is identical with the MMSE estimate. The power of the MAP methods is the variety of probability distribution with which it can be effectively applied.

The MAP estimate has been used successfully with the nonlinear model

$$\mathbf{g} = \mathcal{S}(\mathbf{H}\mathbf{f}) + \boldsymbol{\epsilon}.$$

Let us consider the case where the probability density functions in Eq. (14.11) have Gaussian forms,

$$p(\mathbf{g}|\mathbf{f}) = \frac{1}{(2\pi)^{N/2}} \frac{1}{|\mathbf{R}_{\epsilon\epsilon}|^{1/2}} \exp\left[(\mathbf{g} - \mathcal{S}(\mathbf{H}\mathbf{f}))^T \mathbf{R}_{\epsilon\epsilon} (\mathbf{g} - \mathcal{S}(\mathbf{H}\mathbf{f}))\right],$$

and

$$p(\mathbf{f}) = \frac{1}{(2\pi)^{N/2}} \frac{1}{|\mathbf{R}_{ff}|^{1/2}} \exp\left[(\mathbf{f} - \bar{\mathbf{f}})^T \mathbf{R}_{ff} (\mathbf{f} - \bar{\mathbf{f}})\right],$$

where $N$ is the dimension of the vectors, and $\bar{\mathbf{f}}$ is the mean of the a priori distribution for $\mathbf{f}$. If we assume simple covariance forms for the distributions, $\mathbf{R}_{\epsilon\epsilon} = \sigma_\epsilon^2 \mathbf{I}$ and $\mathbf{R}_{ff} = \sigma_f^2 \mathbf{I}$, then the equation to be solved has the form

$$\frac{1}{\sigma_\epsilon^2} \|\mathbf{g} - \mathcal{S}(\mathbf{Hf})\|^2 + \frac{1}{\sigma_f^2} \|\mathbf{f} - \bar{\mathbf{f}}\|^2 = 0. \tag{14.12}$$

Note that we could use a full covariance matrix for the term based on $p(\mathbf{g}|\mathbf{f})$ in the equation, but this is rarely done. To handle the nonlinearity, an iterative method is used. The details of the solution are given in [265]. An interesting principle is given by the form of Eq. (14.12). The solution is the one that balances the error in matching the recorded data, the first term of Eq. (14.12), and the weighted distance from the a priori mean, the second term. In the next approach, we will generalize the meaning of the second term to include a wider range of a priori knowledge.

## 14.1.7   Constrained least squares (CLS) restoration

The objective of constrained restoration is to eliminate some of the artifacts that accompany other restoration methods. One of the most noticeable and objectionable artifacts is ringing around edges.

Restoration criterion: find the smoothest image that could have generated the recorded image. This is written mathematically as

$$\min_{\mathbf{f}} \mathbf{f}^T \mathbf{C}^T \mathbf{C} \mathbf{f},$$

subject to: $\|\mathbf{g} - \mathbf{Hf}\|^2 = N\sigma_n^2,$

where $N$ is the number of samples in the image and $\sigma_n^2$ is the variance of the noise. The matrix $\mathbf{C}$ is usually a differential operator, e.g., Laplacian, but can be any operator that increases in norm as the roughness of the image $\mathbf{f}$ increases. This allows many definitions of the term "smooth." It is possible to use the expected value $E\{\mathbf{f}^T \mathbf{C}^T \mathbf{C} \mathbf{f}\}$ if necessary or desirable.

The problem is solved using Lagrange multipliers [101]:

$$\min_{(\mathbf{f},\lambda)} \mathbf{f}^T \mathbf{C}^T \mathbf{C} \mathbf{f} + \lambda[\|\mathbf{g} - \mathbf{Hf}\|^2 - N\sigma_n^2],$$

where the parameter $\lambda$, the Lagrange multiplier, multiplies the constraint term that must be zero. Let

$$\Psi(\mathbf{f}) = \mathbf{f}^T \mathbf{C}^T \mathbf{C} \mathbf{f} - 2\lambda \mathbf{g}^T \mathbf{Hf} + \lambda \mathbf{g}^T \mathbf{g} + \lambda \mathbf{f}^T \mathbf{H}^T \mathbf{Hf} - \lambda N\sigma_n^2.$$

Differentiate with respect to $\mathbf{f}$ and $\lambda$ then set the resulting derivatives to zero. First, we consider the derivative with respect to $\mathbf{f}$,

$$\frac{\partial \Psi(\mathbf{f})}{\partial \mathbf{f}} = 2\mathbf{C}^T \mathbf{C} \mathbf{f} + 2\lambda \mathbf{H}^T \mathbf{H} \mathbf{f} - 2\lambda \mathbf{H}^T \mathbf{g} = 0.$$

Solving for $\mathbf{f}$ we obtain

$$\mathbf{f} = [\mathbf{H}^T \mathbf{H} + \gamma \mathbf{C}^T \mathbf{C}]^{-1} \mathbf{H}^T \mathbf{g},$$

where $\gamma = 1/\lambda$. Next, we consider the derivative with respect to $\lambda$,

$$\frac{\partial \Psi(\mathbf{f})}{\partial \lambda} = ||\mathbf{g} - \mathbf{H}\mathbf{f}||^2 - N\sigma_n^2 = 0.$$

Differentiating with respect to $\lambda$ yields the constraint. This means simply that the Lagrange multiplier, $\lambda$, is chosen so that the solution satisfies the original constraint.

As is often the case, the solution can be obtained efficiently by transforming into the frequency domain using the DFT. In the frequency domain, this estimate can be written

$$\hat{\tilde{f}}(k,l) = \frac{\tilde{h}^*(k,l)\tilde{g}(k,l)}{|\tilde{h}(k,l)|^2 + \gamma|\tilde{c}(k,l)|^2}. \tag{14.13}$$

Consider the behavior of the filter in the frequency domain. The term $\gamma|\tilde{c}(k,l)|^2$ appears in the same position as the term $P_{\epsilon\epsilon}(k,l)/P_{ff}(k,l)$ in the MMSE filter of Eq. (14.9). This term may be considered as *regularizing* the solution and preventing the ill-conditioned behavior of the inverse filter. We have seen several different forms of this term. It is of interest to consider what other matrices, $\mathbf{C}$, might be useful in addition to differential forms. See Problem 14.6 for exercises on this topic.

## 14.1.8    Projection onto convex sets

The previous sections have formulated the restoration problem as one of optimization. We have seen that the solution is often a balanced weighting of satisfying the data equation and satisfying another piece of a priori knowledge or constraint. The set theoretic approach is somewhat different in that it seeks to find a *feasible solution*. In this sense, a feasible solution is one that could have generated the recorded data, while satisfying all known constraints on the solution. Note that we wish to find a feasible solution, not *the* feasible solution. There may be many such solutions and all are acceptable under this problem formulation. Philosophically, this can be disturbing to some image scientists, since the solution is not unique. On the other hand, if the solution satisfies all conditions that we have put on the solution, why should it not be acceptable? Conversely, if we find a solution unacceptable, then we need to ask ourselves what property of the solution have we not included in the constraints that has been violated to render this solution unacceptable?

The set theoretic approach is based upon defining various properties of the solution as sets. A feasible solution is any member of the intersection of all of the sets we have defined. Thus, we have defined our restoration criterion. This criterion is quite versatile and allows the maximum amount of information about the solution to be applied to the problem. Some sets that are of interest in image processing include:

$$C_n = \{\mathbf{f} \mid f(m,n) \geq 0\}; \tag{14.14}$$

the set of nonnegative vectors (realizable images);

$$C_\sigma = \{\mathbf{f} \mid \|\mathbf{Hf} - \mathbf{g}\|^2 \leq N^2\sigma^2\}; \tag{14.15}$$

the set of images that, when blurred and subtracted from the recorded image, produce a noise variance that is less than or equal to the known variance. This is often called the residual set, since it is based on the statistics of the residual error, $\mathbf{Hf} - \mathbf{g}$;

$$C_0 = \{\mathbf{f} \mid |[\mathbf{Hf} - \mathbf{g}]_{(m,n)}| \leq 3\sigma_n\}; \tag{14.16}$$

the set of images that, when blurred and subtracted from the recorded image, produce no differences outside of the $3\sigma$ bound (eliminates outliers);

$$C_C = \{\mathbf{f} \mid \mathbf{f}^T \mathbf{C}^T \mathbf{C} \mathbf{f} \leq \delta_C\}; \tag{14.17}$$

the set of images that are smooth (defined by the operator $\mathbf{C}$);

$$C_d = \{\mathbf{f} \mid f(m,n) = \{v_1, v_2, \ldots v_K\}\}; \tag{14.18}$$

the set of images that assume only the values in the set $\{v_1, v_2, \ldots v_K\}$ (finite number of gray levels).

It remains to determine an algorithm to obtain a solution. For this, we will rely on the theory of *projection onto convex sets* (POCS). The obvious restriction to this theory is that the set must be *convex*. A set is convex if for two points, $\mathbf{x}$ and $\mathbf{y}$, in the set, all points on the line connecting the two points are also in the set. Mathematically, if $\mathbf{x} \in \Omega$ and $\mathbf{y} \in \Omega$, then $(\alpha\mathbf{x} + (1-\alpha)\mathbf{y}) \in \Omega$, for all values of $0 \leq \alpha \leq 1$. Of the sets defined above, only $C_d$ is not convex.

The fundamental theorem on which POCS rests is based on the concept of **closed convex** sets. A set is **closed** if it contains all of its boundary points. The interval defined by $0 < x < 1$ is open, the interval $0 \leq x \leq 1$ is closed. While it is necessary to prove the sets that we are working with are closed, it is not difficult. Since our sets are usually defined by continuous functions, such as the norm operator, we can apply the definition of a continuous function to verify that the set is closed. One of the definitions of a continuous function is that a function $f: \mathcal{R}^n \to \mathcal{R}$ is continuous if the inverse image of a closed set is closed. Let us consider the example of the set defined by Eq. (14.15).

The function of interest here is $\phi(\mathbf{f}) = ||\mathbf{Hf} - \mathbf{g}||^2$. This function is obviously a continuous function of $\mathbf{f}$, since it is a quadratic form in linear algebra. The set of interest is the inverse image of the closed set $[0, N^2\sigma_n^2]$. Since $\phi(\mathbf{f})$ is continuous, the inverse image of a closed set is closed. Thus, the set defined by Eq. (14.15) is closed. Now the basic theorem can be stated. For details, see [37, 56, 97].

**Projection onto convex sets theorem**: given a collection of closed convex sets, $\{C_i\}_{i=1}^n$, with projection operators, $\{P_i(\cdot)\}_{i=1}^n$, the iteration

$$\mathbf{x}_{k+1} = P_M (P_{M-1}(...P_1(\mathbf{x}_k)...)) \qquad (14.19)$$

converges to a point in $\cap C_i$.

The projection of $\mathbf{y}$ onto $C_i$, $P_i(\mathbf{y})$, is defined as the point in $C_i$ that is closest to the point $\mathbf{y}$. If $\mathbf{y}$ is in $C_i$, then the projection is itself. The restriction that the sets be closed and convex is necessary for the projection to be uniquely defined.

The projection operator is usually obtained using Lagrange multipliers. For example, consider the projection onto the set $C_\sigma$ from an initial image, $\mathbf{f}_0$. The problem is formulated as

$$\min_{\mathbf{f}_p} ||\mathbf{f}_p - \mathbf{f}_0||^2,$$

subject to: $\mathbf{f}_p \in C_\sigma$.

The problem of finding the projection, $\mathbf{f}_p$, is reformulated as a minimization using the Lagrange multiplier, $\lambda$, as

$$\min_{(\mathbf{f}_p, \lambda)} ||\mathbf{f}_p - \mathbf{f}_0||^2 + \lambda \left( ||\mathbf{g} - \mathbf{Hf}_p||^2 - N\sigma_n^2 \right).$$

The equality constraint can be used since the closest point to a point outside the set must lie on the boundary of the set. If the initial point is already in the set, there is nothing to compute. The details of this and other projections are found in [266, 267]. It is of interest that the projection can be done in the frequency domain with the usual computational efficiency.

The next aspect to consider is the iteration of sequential projections. The point of convergence depends on both the initial estimate and the order of the projections. This is illustrated in Fig. 14.1. Starting at initial point $X_0$ and projecting in the order of sets, 1, 2, 3, we obtain the estimate $Z_1$. Keeping the same initial point but changing the order

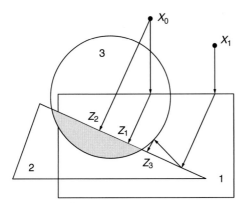

**Figure 14.1.** Varying convergence points of POCS; final point depends on initial point of iteration and order of projections.

of projections to 2, 1, 3, we obtain the estimate $Z_2$. Remember, there was no promise of a unique solution.

The theorem states that it is only in the limit that the sequence of projections converges. There is no reason to believe that the sequence will converge in a finite number of steps. This is illustrated in Fig. 14.1, using the initial point $X_1$ and the projection order 1, 2, 3. The iteration will produce a sequence of points that, in the limit, converge to $Z_3$. In practice, a bound can be set to terminate the iteration if the current estimate is within a specified distance from each of the constraint sets. This is equivalent to checking for convergence on slightly larger sets than the ones onto which we are projecting.

There has been some work done on methods to accelerate the convergence rate of the algorithm. The most successful has been [57] where all projections are computed and weighted to obtain the next iteration, instead of successively projecting. Some work has also been done on extending the method to nonconvex sets but this approach is dependent on the particular characteristics of the specific problem [55].

## 14.1.9  Examples of restoration of blurred images

Having presented the most common restoration methods for recovering images from blurred and noisy data, let us consider the visual results as a function of blur type and noise. Figure 14.2 shows images that have been blurred by an out-of-focus lens (9 pixels in diameter) and by linear motion (9 pixels in length) with a signal-to-noise ratio (SNR) of 30 dB. These simulations were created using the DFT for both image formation and restoration. This avoids the edge effects that are discussed in Section 5.7. Problem 14.11 gives the reader a chance to explore these effects. An artificial constant square has been added to the image to insert a very sharp edge and make it easy to observe the effects of the blurs. The linear motion blur does not blur the square in the vertical direction. This effect may be seen with more effort in the stripes on the woman's clothing. The out-of-focus lens blurring is more isotropic, blurring in all directions.

Since many of the restoration methods use the power spectrum at some point in the processing, and since methods to estimate the PSF from the power spectrum of the recorded image are discussed in Section 13.4.3, we present the spectra of the images in Fig. 14.3. The Wiener filter (minimum mean square error criterion) is the classic standard with which other methods are most often compared. We will present the Wiener restorations for several examples and leave most of the others for exercises. A reason for this approach is that the differences in performance are usually slight and may depend on the characteristics of the images under investigation. For example, the POCS method is very effective on recovery of images that have large areas near the limits of the dynamic range because it can use the nonnegativity constraint. High contrast images of text or astronomical images are images of this type. Linear filters, like the Wiener, constrained least squares and their cousins, will generate values outside the range that manifests itself in a ringing phenomenon. Ringing, although not severe, can be seen on the restorations of the motion blur presented here. Look to the left of the inserted square. The spectra with noise should be compared to the noiseless spectra of Figs. 13.1 and 13.3.

The Wiener filter results, using Eq. (14.9), for the images of Fig. 14.2 are shown in Fig. 14.4. This represents the upper limit on restoration quality using this method, since the parameters for the model are known exactly. It is worth an exercise to study how the variation in parameter estimates affects the quality of the restoration. A study of this type was done in [261, 268]. The effect of noise will be shown below. For the restorations in Fig. 14.4, it is easy to see that the noise has been controlled and does not dominate the image as would have occurred for an inverse filter. We have omitted the "restoration" obtained by the inverse filter of Eq. (14.5), since it would have shown nothing but a noise field for this SNR.

The same sequence of blurred images, spectra and Wiener restorations is repeated for the same blurs, but with a SNR of 20 dB, in Figs. 14.5–14.7. From this, it can be seen that the Wiener filter trades noise control for deblurring. The restorations are not as sharp but the noise, which had more power in these images, is not amplified. It is also instructive to compare the spectra at this noise level with those at the 30 dB SNR. Detecting the blurs from the spectral signatures will be more difficult in this case.

It was noted that a simplification can be obtained by estimating the original image power spectrum as a white noise process. This makes the filter a function of a simple SNR, as shown in Eq. (14.10). This has the advantage of omitting the estimation of the power spectrum as described in Section 14.1.5. It does substantially change the character of the estimate. Since most of the power in the spectrum of the image is concentrated at low frequencies, as noted in Sections 5.7 and 7.1.3, this changes the emphasis of the filter. The simplified filter of Eq. (14.10) will pass less power in the low frequencies and more power in the higher frequencies than the usual Wiener filter. This is shown for the 30 dB SNR case in Fig. 14.8. The restorations appear to be lower contrast and noisier than those of Fig. 14.4. A simple improvement of this method would be to include a simple spectral shape that decreases at the high frequencies. This is one of the characteristics of the AR estimates of Section 7.3.1. These models were used in [268], among many, to good effect.

(a) Image blurred by 9 pixel diameter focus blur
with noise added at 30 dB SNR

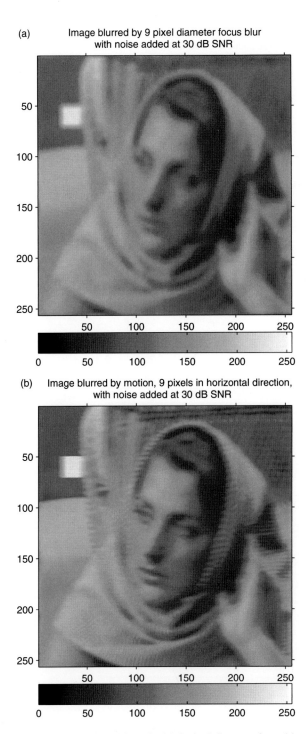

(b) Image blurred by motion, 9 pixels in horizontal direction,
with noise added at 30 dB SNR

**Figure 14.2.** (a) Image blurred with 9 pixel diameter focus blur with SNR 30 dB; (b) image blurred with 9 pixel horizontal linear motion blur with SNR 30 dB.

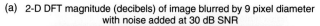

(a)  2-D DFT magnitude (decibels) of image blurred by 9 pixel diameter
with noise added at 30 dB SNR

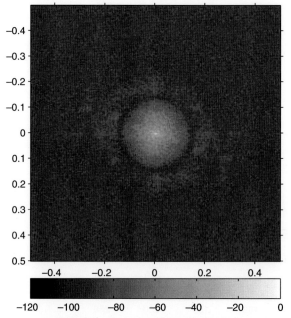

(b) 2-D DFT magnitude (decibels) of image blurred by motion, 9 pixels in
horizontal direction, with noise added at 30 dB SNR

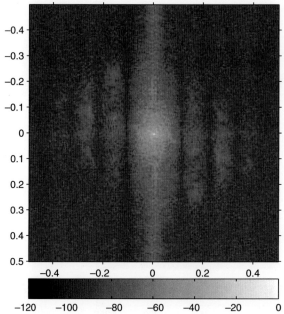

**Figure 14.3.** (a) Spectrum of image blurred with 9 pixel diameter focus blur with SNR 30 dB;
(b) spectrum of image blurred with 9 pixel horizontal linear motion blur with SNR 30 dB.

(a)  Wiener restoration of focus blur 9 pixels in diameter
with noise added at 30 dB SNR

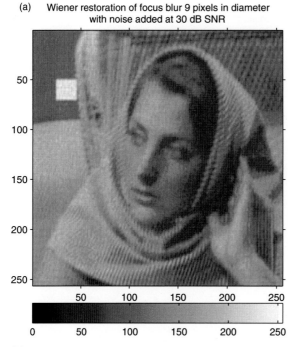

(b)  Wiener restoration of image blurred by motion, 9 pixels in
horizontal direction, with noise added at 30 dB SNR

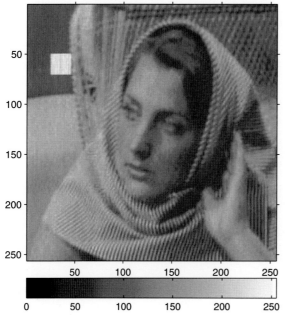

**Figure 14.4.** (a) Wiener restoration of 9 pixel diameter focus blur with SNR 30 dB; (b) Wiener restoration of 9 pixel horizontal linear motion blur with SNR 30 dB.

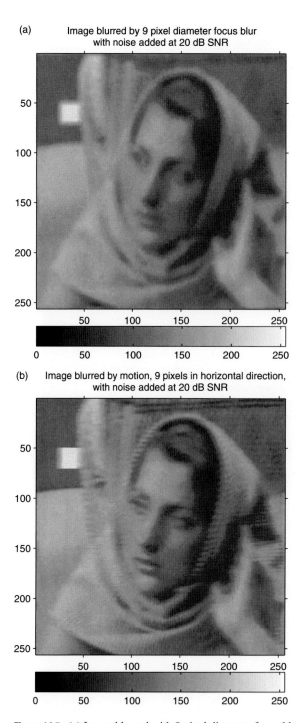

**Figure 14.5.** (a) Image blurred with 9 pixel diameter focus blur with SNR 20 dB; (b) image blurred with 9 pixel horizontal linear motion blur with SNR 20 dB.

(a) 2-D DFT magnitude (decibels) of image blurred by 9 pixel diameter with noise added at 20 dB SNR

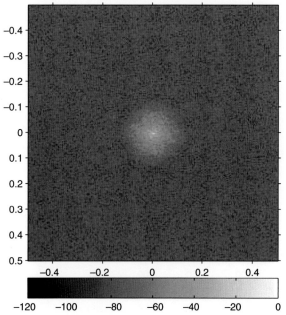

(b) 2-D DFT magnitude (decibels) of image blurred by motion, 9 pixels in horizontal direction, with noise added at 20 dB SNR

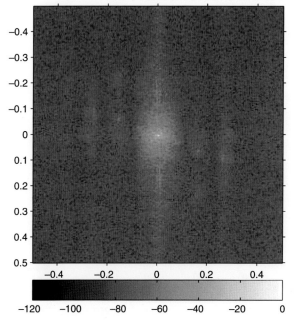

**Figure 14.6.** (a) Spectrum of image blurred with 9 pixel diameter focus blur with SNR 20 dB; (b) spectrum of image blurred with 9 pixel horizontal linear motion blur with SNR 20 dB.

(a)     Wiener restoration of focus blur 9 pixels in diameter
with noise added at 20 dB SNR

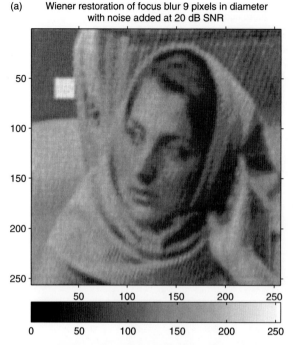

(b)     Wiener restoration of image blurred by motion, 9 pixels in
horizontal direction, with noise added at 20 dB SNR

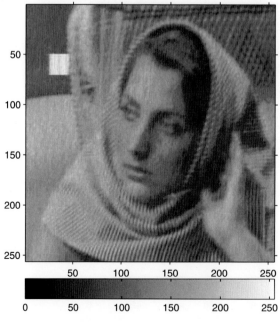

**Figure 14.7.** (a) Wiener restoration of 9 pixel diameter focus blur with SNR 20 dB; (b) Wiener restoration of 9 pixel horizontal linear motion blur with SNR 20 dB.

(a) Wiener restoration (const. $P_{ff}$) of focus blur 9 pixels in diameter
with noise added at 30 dB SNR

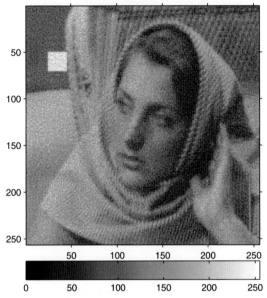

(b) Wiener restoration (const. $P_{ff}$) of image blurred by motion, 9 pixels in
horizontal direction, with noise added at 30 dB SNR

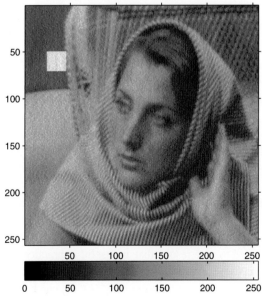

**Figure 14.8.** (a) Wiener restoration using only signal power instead of frequency dependent spectrum for the 9 pixel diameter focus blur with SNR 30 dB; (b) Wiener restoration using only signal power instead of frequency dependent spectrum for the 9 pixel horizontal linear motion blur with SNR 30 dB.

## 14.1.10   Estimation of scanner response

In Section 13.2, we introduced a few methods of estimating the response characteristics of a scanner. Having introduced estimation methods in the previous sections, we can review their use in estimating scanner responses. We can represent the measured responses of any of the scanner's channels to a collection of $M$ reflectances, $\{\mathbf{r}_k\}_{k=1}^{M}$, as

$$c_k = \mathbf{m}^T \mathbf{r}_k + \epsilon_k,$$

where $\mathbf{m}$ is the vector representing the sampled sensitivity of the scanner, including sensor, illuminant, filter and optics; $\epsilon_k$ represents the measurement noise; and $c_k$ is the recorded value. The mathematical model for the entire system is given in Section 8.3.3, Eq. (8.25). The various components of the scanner, filters, optics, detector sensitivity and illuminant, cannot be separated using only the recorded measurements. This is not necessary, since the components can be grouped under the designation of scanner spectral response.

The equations above can be arranged to form a matrix-vector equation. Let the set of reflectance samples be grouped to form the matrix $\mathbf{R} = [\mathbf{r}_1, \mathbf{r}_2, \ldots, \mathbf{r}_M]$. The measured values form the vector $\mathbf{c} = [c_1, c_2, \ldots, c_M]^T$. The noise vector is similarly formed, $\epsilon = [\epsilon_1, \epsilon_2, \ldots, \epsilon_M]^T$. The system can now be written

$$\mathbf{c} = \mathbf{R}^T \mathbf{m} + \epsilon. \tag{14.20}$$

This is exactly the same form as the spatial blurring model of Eq. (14.1). Thus, all of the methods that were developed for restoration of spatial blurs can be applied to the problem of estimation of scanner responses. Having said that, we should note some significant differences.

The dimensionality of the problem is only the number of samples in the wavelength domain, which is usually about $N = 31$, but is always less than 471, for 1 nm sampling from 360 nm to 830 nm. This means that the estimate can be computed with direct use of the algebraic equations.

The estimation methods that are based on the mean square error criterion require the use of the correlation of the response, $\mathbf{R_{mm}}$. This presents a problem, since there is a limited "ensemble" from which the response is drawn. Nevertheless, common constraints on smoothness can be used to give results that are useful in practice.

The POCS method has several advantages for this problem. It does not require the estimation of the correlation. The residual set of Eq. (14.15) can be easily modified for this case. The nonnegative set of Eq. (14.14) is very powerful, since most responses will have large portions that are zero or near zero. This is owing to their design to select portions of the spectrum and reject others. The smoothness set of Eq. (14.17) is useful since most response curves are smooth, owing to the physical properties of the materials from which they are made. This method is discussed in detail in [238]. A different approach is discussed in [246].

## 14.1.11    Color issues

It was mentioned that all of the mathematical forms that have been derived in the previous sections can work for color or monochrome. The implementation is quite another matter. The results for monochrome images can be implemented in the frequency domain by using two-dimensional DFTs. If we assume that the color channels are independent of each other, then the restoration problem can be decomposed into the processing of the monochrome bands. However, it is obvious that the color channels are, in fact, correlated. Using this information, should result in improved restorations. This was explored in [268]. The basic results of this research showed that correct knowledge of the color correlations gave improved performance. Problems arose when the knowledge of the cross-correlations of color channels was not exact. The color restoration methods that assume cross-channel correlations, or equivalently, cross-spectral correlations, are very sensitive to errors in the estimation of the cross-correlations. With this information, it is usually better to process the color channels independently, using the common methods of estimating the power spectra required for the various MMSE filters, [268].

If the channels are to be processed independently, then the user has a choice of color spaces in which to work. The obvious approach is to transform the image to a space with uncorrelated channels [124]. In this case, the tristimulus values can be transformed using a Karhunen–Loeve transformation to obtain uncorrelated channels (see Section 7.2.4). The image would be transformed back to the original color space for display. In [235], the authors say that the transformation to YIQ, a television standard and linear transformation of RGB, [217], is nearly as effective at decorrelating the channels. There have been many other approaches to using the color correlation combined with various modeling and filter criteria, e.g., [84, 85, 100, 139, 184, 235]. A criticism of this work is that it uses the RGB color space, or a linear transformation of it, and does not pay sufficient attention to color fidelity, as measured in colorimetric terms, such as $\Delta E_{ab}^*$. An example of the unintended color distortions is shown in the comparisons of different methods in [184]. Exceptions are described in [6], which uses the CIE space metrics to evaluate the effect of the number of recorded channels on blur restoration quality and [44, 82], which evaluate restoration of color quantization in colorimetric spaces.

## 14.2    Color and spectral correction

The previous sections considered correcting for noise and spatial frequency degradations of the image. In the recording process, it is likely that the image is recorded with a nonideal spectral sensitivity. Here we consider correcting for these degradations. Most monochrome value variations can be corrected by a simple functional form. The compensation for spectral effects requires vector manipulation. Recall from Chapter 8 that the expression for the measured value of a radiometric source is

$$c = \mathbf{m}^T \mathbf{f} + \epsilon,$$

where **m** is the vector representing the sampled sensitivity of the sensor, $\epsilon$ represents the measurement noise and **f** represents the radiometric source. This is the same form as the spatial blurring model of Eq. (14.1) and the scanner response of Eq. (14.20). Thus, the same methods can be applied.

## 14.2.1    Spectral radiance estimation

If the vector **f** is to be estimated, it is clear that several measurements are required. In particular, if the dimension of **f** is $N$, then $N$ independent measurements are needed. This may be difficult for various reasons including cost, time or available instrumentation. The simplest conceptual way of estimating **f** is to use a set of $N$ sensors with sensitivity

$$\mathbf{m}_k = \mathbf{e}_k, \quad 1 \leq k \leq N,$$

where $\mathbf{e}_k$ has a one in the $k$th position and zeros elsewhere. Unfortunately, such sensors are difficult to realize in practice. Even obtaining $N$ independent sensitivities is usually impossible. Thus, it is often possible to obtain only an estimate that is restricted to a subspace determined by the sensors.

Consider $K$ sensors, $\{\mathbf{m}_k\}_{k=1}^{K}$, which are independent. Independence is easily obtained for $K \ll N$. An estimate is obtained by the least squares method by solving

$$\text{minimize } ||\mathbf{c} - \mathbf{M}^T \mathbf{f}||^2$$

with respect to **f**. The $k$th column of the matrix **M** is $\mathbf{m}_k$ and the $k$th element of **c** is the measurement made with the $k$th sensor. The solution to the least squares problem, from Chapter 2, is

$$\hat{\mathbf{f}} = \mathbf{M}^+ \mathbf{c} = \mathbf{M}(\mathbf{M}^T \mathbf{M})^{-1} \mathbf{c}.$$

Recall that if **M** is ill-conditioned, the solution may be a poor one.

## 14.2.2    Constrained estimation

One way to overcome ill-conditioning is to impose constraints on the solution, similar to those of spatial deblurring in Section 14.1.7. In many cases, the solution may be known to be smoothly varying. A measurement of smoothness is the magnitude squared of the derivative, which can be written

$$e_s = \mathbf{f}^T \mathbf{D}^T \mathbf{D} \mathbf{f},$$

where

$$
\mathbf{D} =
\begin{bmatrix}
1 & -1 & 0 & \dots & 0 & 0 & 0 \\
0 & 1 & -1 & \dots & 0 & 0 & 0 \\
\vdots & \vdots & \vdots & \vdots & \vdots & \vdots & \vdots \\
0 & 0 & 0 & \dots & 0 & 1 & -1 \\
0 & 0 & 0 & \dots & 0 & 0 & 1
\end{bmatrix}.
$$

The constrained problem can be stated

$$
\min_{\mathbf{f}} e_s = \mathbf{f}^T \mathbf{D}^T \mathbf{D} \mathbf{f},
$$

$$
\text{subject to } ||\mathbf{c} - \mathbf{M}^T \mathbf{f}||^2 = e,
$$

where $e$ is determined by the noise characteristics of $\epsilon$ and the length of the vectors, $N$.

The constrained problem can be solved using Lagrange multipliers [101], using the methods of Section 14.1.7. The problem can be formulated as

$$
\min_{\mathbf{f}, \lambda} \mathbf{f}^T \mathbf{D}^T \mathbf{D} \mathbf{f} + \lambda \left[ (\mathbf{c} - \mathbf{M}^T \mathbf{f})^T (\mathbf{c} - \mathbf{M}^T \mathbf{f}) - e \right].
$$

Differentiating with respect to $\mathbf{f}$ and setting the result equal to zero, we obtain

$$
2\mathbf{D}^T \mathbf{D} \mathbf{f} + \lambda[-2\mathbf{M}^T \mathbf{c} + 2\mathbf{M}^T \mathbf{M} \mathbf{f}] = 0,
$$

which yields

$$
\hat{\mathbf{f}} = (\mathbf{M}^T \mathbf{M} + \frac{1}{\lambda} \mathbf{D}^T \mathbf{D})^{-1} \mathbf{M}^T \mathbf{c}.
$$

Substituting the estimate for $\mathbf{f}$ into the constraint equation yields

$$
||\mathbf{c} - \mathbf{M}^T (\mathbf{M}^T \mathbf{M} + \frac{1}{\lambda} \mathbf{D}^T \mathbf{D})^{-1} \mathbf{M}^T \mathbf{c}||^2 = e,
$$

where $\lambda$ can be found by numerical methods.

## 14.2.3 Minimum mean square error estimation

The constrained method used the a priori knowledge of smoothness to produce a well-conditioned problem. If statistical information about the spectra is available, the minimum mean square error estimate is usually a well conditioned solution. Recall that the problem is formulated

$$
\min_{\mathbf{W}} E\{||\mathbf{f} - \mathbf{W}\mathbf{c}||^2\}.
$$

The solution to the problem is

$$\hat{\mathbf{f}} = \mathbf{R}_{ff}\mathbf{M}^T[\mathbf{MR}_{ff}\mathbf{M}^T + \mathbf{R}_{\epsilon\epsilon}]^{-1}\mathbf{c},$$

where $\mathbf{R}_{ff}$ and $\mathbf{R}_{\epsilon\epsilon}$ are the autocorrelation matrices of the spectrum and noise, respectively.

## 14.3    Tristimulus value (color) correction

The computation of the tristimulus values was discussed in Chapter 8. There are several practical problems in the actual measurement of the values. The filters that are required to be a linear transformation of the CIE color matching functions may be only an approximation to such filters. If reflective samples are under investigation, the tristimulus values depend upon the viewing illumination. Measurements can be made to determine the values under one illuminant and later it is desired to compute the values under a different illuminant. Another problem with any measurement is noise. When noise is considered, the coefficients of the linear transformation to map the measurement space onto the tristimulus space are very important.

The measurement of the image data can be represented by

$$\mathbf{c} = \mathbf{M}^T\mathbf{f} + \boldsymbol{\epsilon},$$

where $\mathbf{M}$ is an $N \times M$ matrix representing the $M$ sensor spectral sensitivities (or filters) and $\mathbf{c}$ is an $M \times 1$ vector representing the measured values. This is the same form as the spatial blurring model of Eq. (14.1) and the scanner response of Eq. (14.20). Again, the same methods can be applied.[1] For most color problems, $M = 3$, since we are dealing with tristimulus values. The estimates of the tristimulus values are obtained by

$$\hat{\mathbf{t}} = \mathbf{Bc}.$$

The correction matrix $\mathbf{B}$ can be found by solving the least squares problem for a known data set, i.e.,

$$\min_{\mathbf{B}} E\{||\mathbf{t} - \mathbf{BM}^T\mathbf{f}||^2\}.$$

The expected value may be replaced with the sum of the squares over a given data set:

$$\min_{\mathbf{B}} \sum_{k=1}^{K} ||\mathbf{t}_k - \mathbf{Bc}_k||^2,$$

---

[1] We have applied the same methods to many different problems in imaging. It brings to mind a classic saying, "The good thing about mathematics is that you don't have to know what you're talking about."

where the $c_k$ vectors are measured from the samples of the data set; that is, the spectra of the data need not be known, only the measured values are needed. The minimization of the summation can be written in algebraic form using partitioned matrices. Let

$$\mathbf{T} = [\mathbf{t}_1, \mathbf{t}_2, \ldots, \mathbf{t}_K],$$

and

$$\mathbf{C} = [\mathbf{c}_1, \mathbf{c}_2, \ldots, \mathbf{c}_K].$$

The problem can be written

$$\min_{\mathbf{B}} \text{Trace}[(\mathbf{T} - \mathbf{BC})(\mathbf{T} - \mathbf{BC})^T].$$

The matrix $\mathbf{B}$ obtained for the known data set is used to correct all subsequent measured data. Thus, it is important to choose the set $\{\mathbf{t}_k, \mathbf{c}_k\}$ to be representative of the ensemble of interest.

## 14.4    Illuminant color correction

Often, measurements are taken to obtain the tristimulus values of reflective objects under a particular illumination and, later, it is desired to estimate the values under a different illumination. It has been noted that a color measuring device must use some illuminant to obtain the signal from which to compute the tristimulus values under a particular set of lighting conditions. Ideally, the illuminant used for the measurement is the same as the one under which the object is to be viewed. If this is not the case, then color correction is necessary. Even if it is the case and the tristimulus values under different viewing conditions are desired, color correction is necessary.

Let us consider data taken under an illuminant represented by the diagonal matrix, $\mathbf{L}_0$. Using a reflectance data set instead of the radiance data set of the previous problem, the measurements are given by

$$\mathbf{c}_{0k} = \mathbf{M}^T \mathbf{L}_0 \mathbf{r}_k + \boldsymbol{\epsilon}, \tag{14.21}$$

where the radiant spectrum is obtained from the reflective spectrum by $\mathbf{f} = \mathbf{L}_0 \mathbf{r}$. In this case, the goal of illuminant correction is to estimate the values

$$\mathbf{c}_{vk} = \mathbf{M}^T \mathbf{L}_v \mathbf{r}_k,$$

where $\mathbf{L}_v$ is the viewing illuminant. The problem can be addressed with the least squares approach using a fixed data set and the minimum mean square error approach using the statistics of the spectra. In both cases, the object is to develop a transformation that converts measurements taken with the device using illuminant $\mathbf{L}_0$ to an estimate of the ideal tristimulus values that would be obtained under illuminant $\mathbf{L}_v$.

The least squares approach finds the best transformation over a representative data set; then uses that transformation for all subsequent measurements. The transformation, $\mathbf{B}$, is obtained by solving the problem

$$\min_{\mathbf{B}} \sum_{k=1}^{K} ||\mathbf{c}_{vk} - \mathbf{B}\mathbf{c}_{0k}||^2,$$

where the values of $\mathbf{c}_{vk}$ and $\mathbf{c}_{0k}$ are obtained from the known reflectances of the data set. While Eq. (14.21) has the same form as the spatial blurring model of Eq. (14.1) and other previous models, the goal in this case is slightly different. The mean square approach is the same, so the results below should look familiar.

The minimum mean square error approach uses knowledge of the statistical characterization of the ensemble of interest, in particular, the autocovariance matrices of the spectra and noise. It is the solution to the problem

$$\min_{\mathbf{B}} E\{||\mathbf{c}_{vk} - \mathbf{B}\mathbf{c}_{0k}||^2\}.$$

The solution to this problem has been shown to be

$$\mathbf{B} = \mathbf{R}_{v0}\mathbf{R}_{00}^{-1},$$

where $\mathbf{R}_{v0}$ is the cross-correlation of $\mathbf{c}_{vk}$ and $\mathbf{c}_{0k}$ and $\mathbf{R}_{00}$ is the autocorrelation of $\mathbf{c}_{0k}$. This can be written in terms of the autocorrelation of the reflections, $\mathbf{R}_{rr}$, and the autocorrelation of the noise, $\mathbf{R}_{\epsilon\epsilon}$,

$$\mathbf{B} = \mathbf{M}^T \mathbf{L}_v \mathbf{R}_{rr} \mathbf{L}_0 \mathbf{M} [\mathbf{M}^T \mathbf{L}_0 \mathbf{R}_{rr} \mathbf{L}_0 \mathbf{M} + \mathbf{R}_{\epsilon\epsilon}]^{-1}.$$

The MMSE approach has the advantage of producing a well-conditioned system. The least squares approach tends to produce ill-conditioned systems, since the noise is not explicitly considered. This approach can be modified to produce a well conditioned system by using the pseudoinverse solution of a system whose singular values below a specified threshold have been set to zero. This modification can also be interpreted as finding the best estimate of the reflectance spectrum that is within a subspace defined by the eigenvectors of the autocovariance matrix, $\mathbf{R}_{rr}$. This is described by

$$\hat{\mathbf{r}} = \sum_{j=1}^{P} \beta_j \mathbf{v}_j,$$

where $\{\mathbf{v}_j\}_{j=1}^{P}$ are the eigenvectors corresponding to the $P$ largest eigenvalues. The coefficients, $\{\beta_j\}$, are found by solving the problem

$$\min_{\{\beta_j\}} ||\mathbf{c}_0 - \mathbf{M}^T \mathbf{L}_0 \sum_{j=1}^{P} \beta_j \mathbf{v}_j||^2.$$

The corrected tristimulus values are found from

$$\hat{\mathbf{c}}_v = \mathbf{M}^T \mathbf{L}_v \sum_{j=1}^{P} \beta_j \mathbf{v}_j.$$

## 14.4.1    White point mapping

A simple correction method that is in common use for illuminant correction is called *white point mapping*. The basic idea is that the illuminant defines the white point of the image; that is, if there is a perfect reflector in the image, it will appear the same as the illuminant. The defining point changes with the illuminant. White point mapping consists of computing a transformation such that the white point of the image under the scanning illuminant maps to the white point of the image under the viewing illuminant. If we assume that the reflective spectrum of the white point is uniform, the defining equation for the transformation is

$$\mathbf{A}^T \mathbf{L}_v \mathbf{u} = \mathbf{W} \mathbf{A}^T \mathbf{L}_0 \mathbf{u},$$

where $\mathbf{A}$ is the matrix of CIE color matching functions, $\mathbf{L}_0$ and $\mathbf{L}_v$ are the measurement and viewing illuminants respectively, $\mathbf{u}$ is the uniform reflector, $\mathbf{u} = [1, 1, \ldots, 1]^T$ and $\mathbf{W}$ is a diagonal matrix. Since there are three unknown parameters (on the diagonal of $\mathbf{W}$) and three equations, the problem is easily solved.

This approach is used in video camera adjustments where the gains of the three color guns are adjusted to produce equal output values. It is also used in color printing to determine the appropriate filters with which to print a negative. It is the basis for the normalization in the transformations to the $L^*a^*b^*$ and $L^*u^*v^*$ uniform color spaces and is related to the perceptual mapping discussed in Section 12.3.9.

## 14.5    Color photographic film exposure

The estimation of the exposure of color film requires the analysis of a two-step process. After the film is exposed, the resulting densities at the various wavelengths are a function of the D–log$E$ curve of each of the color sensitive layers (see Fig. 11.10). The density of the layers must be measured. As it is impossible to measure a single color layer, the density of the layers must be computed from measurements through all of them. After the densities are estimated, the exposure can be estimated. The densities of layers of film are given by the model

$$\mathbf{d} = \Gamma \log_{10}(\mathbf{S}^T \mathbf{f}),$$

where $\mathbf{f}$ is the radiant spectrum that exposes the film (product of intensity and time), $\mathbf{S}$ is the matrix of sensitivities of each layer, $\Gamma$ is diagonal matrix defined by the slopes of the D–log$E$ curves (assumed exposure in the linear region) and $\mathbf{d}$ is the density of the dye produced in the layers [217, 272]. The $\log_{10}(\cdot)$ operation is performed on each element of the vector independently. The offset constant used in the film characterization in Section 11.3.1 has been omitted. It would add only a constant to the density of each layer. The measurement of the density of the exposed and developed film is represented by

$$\mathbf{c} = \mathbf{M}^T \mathbf{L}_0 10^{-\mathbf{Pd}},$$

where $\mathbf{P}$ is the dye transmission of the three layers for unit density dyes. From the measurement of $\mathbf{c}$, it is desired to estimate $\mathbf{f}$. Of course, the best that can be done if $\mathbf{c}$ is a three-dimensional vector is estimate the product, $\mathbf{S}^T \mathbf{f}$.

Since the goal of measuring the film is to determine the amount of dye present in each layer, the filters used for the measurement are usually narrowband with transmission peaks that correspond to the dye absorption peaks, similar to the CMY status A density filters shown in Figure 8.25a. If the contribution of any two dyes is negligible at the dye peak of the third, the measurement of $\mathbf{c}$ can be directly related to $\mathbf{d}$. This may be a slightly weaker condition than the block dye assumption discussed in Section 8.4.2. On the other hand, the actual filters that are used may have significant width. For example, consider the density filters shown in Fig. 8.25. The status T filters are noticeably wider than the status A filters. In this case, the block dye assumption may be necessary for simplification. Once $\mathbf{d}$ is obtained, the product $\mathbf{S}^T \mathbf{f}$ can be computed.

If the dyes overlap significantly, the resulting equations are nonlinear and require nonlinear system solvers.

## 14.6        Problems

**14.1**    To evaluate the restoration methods, it is easiest to use one-dimensional signals first. A 1-D signal is given in the image folder of the text website (www.cambridge.org/9780521868532) called *lineofimage.asc*. The line is taken from a picture of a boy wearing a striped shirt.

(a) Using $\mathbf{h} = [1/5, 1/5, 1/5, 1/5, 1/5]$, blur the signal and add zero mean, Gaussian noise with standard deviation, $\sigma = 8$. Plot this signal.
(b) Estimate the original signal using the inverse filter. Compare the result with the original signal graphically. Compute the mean square error.
(c) Estimate the original signal using the MSE (Wiener) filter. Use the original signal to estimate the power spectrum that is required. Compare the result to the original signal graphically. Compute the mean square error.
(d) Estimate the original signal using a third method of your choice. Use the original signal to estimate any parameters than are required. Compare the result to the original signal graphically. Compute the mean square error.

**14.2**    Repeat the restorations of Problem 14.1 with different noise levels. Compare the results to see the effect of noise on the restorations.

**14.3**  Repeat the restorations of Problem 14.1 with blurs of different lengths. Compare the results to see the effect of the blur.

**14.4**  Using the definitions in Appendix B show that the inverse solution of Eq. (14.3) is the pseudoinverse solution.

**14.5**  The Wiener filter of Section 14.1.2 was derived assuming a zero mean process. Derive the Wiener filter assuming a nonzero mean $E\{\mathbf{f}\} = \bar{\mathbf{f}}$.

**14.6**  The forms of the filters in the frequency domain look very similar for the Wiener filter of Eq. (14.9) and the constrained least squares of Eq. (14.13).

(a) What is the relation of $P_{\epsilon\epsilon}(k,l)/P_{ff}(k,l)$ in Eq. (14.9) to $\tilde{c}(k,l)$ in Eq. (14.13)?
(b) Assume that $\mathbf{C}$ is given by Eq. (14.21), and we assume that the noise is white, i.e., $P_{\epsilon\epsilon}(k,l) = \sigma_\epsilon^2$, a constant. What would be the qualitative charcteristics of the equivalent image power spectrum, $P_{ff}(k,l)$ in the frequency domain of Eq. (14.9), to make the two filters equivalent, i.e., $P_{\epsilon\epsilon}(k,l)/P_{ff}(k,l) = \tilde{c}(k,l)$?

**14.7**  Using a uniform motion blur of five pixels, as in Problem 14.1, blur the image in the text website (www.cambridge.org/9780521868532) called *cameraman.tif* and add zero mean, Gaussian noise with standard deviation, $\sigma = 8$. Display this image.

(a) Estimate the original signal using the inverse filter. Compare the result with the original image using correct image display methods. Compute the mean square error.
(b) Estimate the original image using the MSE (Wiener) filter. Use the original image to estimate the power spectrum that is required. Compare the result with the original image using correct image display methods. Compute the mean square error.
(c) Estimate the original image using a third method of your choice. Use the original image to estimate any parameters that are required. Compare the result with the original image using correct image display methods. Compute the mean square error.

**14.8**  Repeat the restorations of Problem 14.7 with different noise levels. Compare the results to see the effect of noise on the restorations.

**14.9**  Repeat the restorations of Problem 14.7 with blurs of different lengths. Compare the results to see the effect of the blur.

**14.10**  Repeat the restorations of Problem 14.7 with blurs of different types. For example, use an out-of-focus lens blur of diameters 3, 5 and 9 pixels. Compare the results to see the effect of the blur.

**14.11**  Compute the Wiener restoration of the images of Problem 13.9e, both *blur_a* and *blur_b*. Use the frequency domain (FFT) implementation. Compare the results obtained from the two blurs. This shows the effects of the circular assumption that is not the case for an actual image.

**14.12**   Use the 64 spectral color patches found in the text website (www.cambridge.org/9780521868532) named *munsell.spectra.10*, and the spectral sensitivities in *scanning_set_1_10nm* for the scanning filters of a recording device (scanner) to create scanner data.

(a) From these data, use two methods from the chapter to estimate the scanner sensitivities and compare the results.

(b) Add noise to the data at a level of 30 dB and repeat the estimation of (a).

**14.13**   Using the 64 spectral color patches found in the text website (www.cambridge.org/9780521868532) named *munsell.spectra.10*, compute the tristimulus values (CIEXYZ) under illuminant D65. Use the spectral sensitivities in *scanning_set_1_10nm* for the scanning filters of a recording device (scanner).

(a) Compute the optimal $3 \times 3$ color correction matrix **B** to estimate the tristimulus values under illuminant D65 from the recorded values.

(b) Compute the average $\Delta E_{ab}^*$ error of the estimation for this estimation. Use the illuminant, D65, for the white point of the CIELAB transformation.

**14.14**   Using the 64 spectral color patches found in the text website (www.cambridge.org/9780521868532) named *munsell.spectra.10*, compute the tristimulus values (CIEXYZ) under illuminant D65. Repeat the computation for illuminant A.

(a) Compute the optimal $3 \times 3$ color correction matrix **B** to estimate the tristimulus values under illuminant A from the tristimulus values under D65.

(b) Compute the average $\Delta E_{ab}^*$ error of the estimation for this estimation. Use the target illuminant, A, for the white point of the CIELAB transformation.

# A  Generalized functions and sampling representation

The impulse signal is used extensively in this text, particularly in Chapters 5 and 6. The impulse signal is represented by the Dirac delta function, $\delta(t)$, [201, 107]. It has two major applications in signal and image processing. It is the basis for describing the transformation of signals by a linear, time-invariant system, and it is used to describe sampling of analog signals to create discrete signals. Mathematically, the Dirac delta function is a *generalized function*, since it does not have a finite value at every point. For this reason, the function must be treated in special ways. See [165,140] for a more mathematically detailed treatment.

## A.1  Basic definition

The function is defined as zero for $t \neq 0$ with an area of unity. The unit area property can be written

$$\int_{-\epsilon}^{\epsilon} \delta(u)\mathrm{d}u = 1, \tag{A.1}$$

for any $\epsilon > 0$. The restriction, $\epsilon > 0$, is assumed to avoid possible negating of the integral if the direction of integration is from positive to negative. The most useful property of the delta function is that of sifting, e.g., extracting single values of a continuous function. This is defined by the integral

$$s(t_0) = \int_{-\infty}^{\infty} s(t)\delta(t - t_0)\mathrm{d}t = \int_{-\infty}^{\infty} s(t_0)\delta(t - t_0)\mathrm{d}t. \tag{A.2}$$

This shows the production of a single sample. We would represent the sampled signal as a signal that is zero everywhere except at the sampling time, $s_0(t) = s(t_0)\delta(t - t_0)$. The sampled signal can be represented graphically by using an arrow, as shown in Fig. 2.2.

To describe mathematically the time scaling properties of the Fourier transform of delta functions, it is necessary to introduce a definition of the function that uses limits. One of the problems of using delta functions is that there are several possible definitions that can be used. The differences in the results are minor to most engineers but cause mathematicians great consternation. Since we, the authors, are engineers, we will ignore these difficulties and proceed. Two common definitions of the delta function are[1]

$$\delta(t) = \lim_{a \to 0} \frac{1}{\sqrt{2\pi a}} e^{-t^2/2a^2},$$

and

$$\delta(t) = \lim_{a \to 0} \frac{1}{a} \text{rect}(t/a),$$

where

$$\text{rect}(t) = \begin{cases} 1 & \text{if } -1/2 \leq t \leq 1/2 \\ 0 & \text{else} \end{cases}.$$

The use of the delta function makes the description of sampling easy to represent. However, the interpretation of the delta function is not straightforward. The function $\delta(t - t_0)$ does not have a finite value at the argument $t = t_0$. It does have a finite area at that point and the area is unity. This is in contrast to the usual case for functions with finite values. For a function with finite values, e.g., $s(t) = \cos(2\pi t) + t^2$, the area under a specific value of $t$ is zero. Mathematically, we would use the limit to represent this

$$\lim_{\epsilon \to 0} \int_{t_0-\epsilon}^{t_0+\epsilon} s(t)dt = 0,$$

for $\epsilon > 0$. For the delta function, we have

$$\lim_{\epsilon \to 0} \int_{t_0-\epsilon}^{t_0+\epsilon} \delta(t - t_0)dt = 1,$$

for $\epsilon > 0$. Multiplying by the constant $s(t_0)$ gives the result of Eq. (A.2).

A somewhat surprising property is the scaling of the delta function when the time scale is changed, as in

$$\delta(bt) = \frac{1}{|b|}\delta(t). \tag{A.3}$$

This is important when working with the time scaling of Fourier transforms. To see this property, consider the definition of the delta function as a limit,

$$\delta(bt) = \lim_{a \to 0} \frac{1}{a} \text{rect}(bt/a).$$

---

[1] For the really curious, one of the problems comes about when the definition of the rect function is changed to defining a pulse that is unity on [0, 1] or [−1, 0] instead of [−1/2, 1/2]. These variations will cause differences when working with discontinuous functions, which occur frequently as edges in images. The differences are minor in that the value of the shifting integral may change at the edge point. Since the edges form a set of zero measure, they have no significant effect on our computations.

The time scaling operation does not change the value of the function, but does change the region over which the function is nonzero. Thus, the area under the function is no longer unity but $1/|b|$. The absolute value is required since the area is positive, even if the function is time reversed by a negative $b$.

## A.2     Sampling, 1-D

The entire sampling sequence can be represented using the comb function,

$$\text{comb}(t) = \sum_{n=-\infty}^{\infty} \delta(t-n), \tag{A.4}$$

where the sampling interval is unity. The sampled signal is obtained by multiplication, as written,

$$s_d(t) = s(t)\text{comb}(t) = s(t)\sum_{n=-\infty}^{\infty}\delta(t-n) = \sum_{n=-\infty}^{\infty}s(t)\delta(t-n). \tag{A.5}$$

The sampling is represented graphically in Fig. 6.1. It is common to use the notation of $\{s(n)\}$ or $s(n)$ to represent the collection of samples in discrete space. The arguments $n$ and $t$ will serve to distinguish the discrete or continuous spaces, respectively.

A sampling interval of $T$ can be included by writing

$$\text{comb}_T(t) = \sum_{n=-\infty}^{\infty}\delta(t-nT) = T\sum_{n=-\infty}^{\infty}\delta(t/T-n) = T\text{comb}(t/T), \tag{A.6}$$

where the sampling interval is denoted by the subscript on the comb$(\cdot)$ function. The scale factor of $T$ in the second form is a result of the scaling property of Eq. (A.3).

## A.3     Frequency effects of sampling, 1-D

The 1-D effects of sampling in the frequency domain are discussed in most undergraduate signals and systems texts. To discuss the frequency domain effects, it is necessary to present the basic Fourier transform of a delta function and a comb function. The Fourier transform of a delta function is a constant. This is seen directly from the definition,

$$\mathcal{F}[\delta(t)] = \int_{-\infty}^{\infty}\delta(t)e^{-\omega t}\,dt = e^{-\omega t}|_{t=0}\int_{-\infty}^{\infty}\delta(t)\,dt = 1.$$

The extraction of the value of the complex exponential at $t = 0$ is a result of the sifting property illustrated earlier in Eq. (A.2).

The Fourier transform of a comb function in the time domain is a comb function in the frequency domain. This requires a more detailed explanation than the transform of the delta function. The comb function of Eq. (A.4) is a periodic function. As such, its Fourier transform is actually a Fourier series. The Fourier series of a periodic function, $s_p(t)$, with period $T$, is defined by a sequence of coefficients,

$$S_p(n) = \frac{1}{T} \int_{-T/2}^{T/2} s_p(t) e^{-\omega_0 n t} dt, \tag{A.7}$$

where $\omega_0 = \frac{2\pi}{T}$. The usual synthesis equation (inverse transform) gives the original function

$$s_p(t) = \sum_{n=-\infty}^{\infty} S_p(n) e^{\omega_0 n t}. \tag{A.8}$$

If we represent the Fourier transform of the periodic function by

$$S_p(\omega) = \sum_{n=-\infty}^{\infty} S_p(n) \delta(\omega - n\omega_0),$$

we can see the direct correspondence between the Fourier series and the Fourier transform. Using the sifting property of the delta function, we can take the inverse Fourier transform of $S_p(\omega)$ and obtain the summation form of $s_p(t)$ in Eq. (A.8).

Now, to obtain the Fourier transform of the comb function, we take the Fourier series representation of Eq. (A.7) of the $\text{comb}_T(\cdot)$ function,

$$\text{comb}_T(t) = \sum_{n=-\infty}^{\infty} \text{Comb}_T(n) e^{\omega_0 n t},$$

where the difference between the time and frequency functions is denoted by the upper case C in the transform. The series coefficients are computed as

$$\text{Comb}_T(n) = \frac{1}{T} \int_{-T/2}^{T/2} \delta(t) e^{-\omega_0 n t} dt = 1. \tag{A.9}$$

Using the notation change from Fourier series to Fourier transform, we get

$$\text{Comb}_T(\omega) = \sum_{n=-\infty}^{\infty} \text{Comb}_T(n) \delta\left(\omega - \frac{n2\pi}{T}\right) = \sum_{n=-\infty}^{\infty} \delta\left(\omega - \frac{n2\pi}{T}\right).$$

Substituting $\omega = 2\pi F$ gives the result in Table 5.2.

## A.4    Sampling, 2-D

The two-dimensional Dirac delta function can be defined in several ways. The easiest for most image processing purposes is as the separable product of one-dimensional delta functions, $\delta(x, y) = \delta(x)\delta(y)$. The 2-D delta function can also be defined using the limits of nonseparable functions, for example:

$$\delta(x, y) = \lim_{a \to 0} \frac{1}{\pi a^2} \text{disk}(x/a, y/a),$$

where

$$\text{disk}(x, y) = \begin{cases} 1 & \text{if } \sqrt{x^2 + y^2} \le 1 \\ 0 & \text{else} \end{cases}.$$

The extension of the comb function to two dimensions should probably be called a brush, but we will continue to use the term comb and define it by

$$\text{comb}(x, y) = \sum_{m=-\infty}^{\infty} \sum_{n=-\infty}^{\infty} \delta(x - m, y - n).$$

The equation for 2-D sampling is

$$s(m, n) = s_d(x, y) = s(x, y)\text{comb}(x, y), \tag{A.10}$$

where a normalized sampling interval of unity is assumed. This is shown in Fig. 6.6.

A change in the sampling interval is represented by $f(m, n) = f_a(m\Delta x, n\Delta y)$. It is possible to represent the change of sampling interval by scaling the argument of the comb function in Eq. (A.10) as

$$s(m, n) = s_d(x, y) = |\Delta x \Delta y| s(x, y) \text{comb}\left(\frac{x}{\Delta x}, \frac{y}{\Delta y}\right). \tag{A.11}$$

The scale factor of $|\Delta x \Delta y|$ is a result of the scaling property of Eq. (A.3).

The sifting property of the 2-D delta function is analogous to the 1-D function

$$f(m, n) = \iint f_a(x, y)\delta(x - m\Delta x, y - n\Delta y)dxdy.$$

Note that there is a difference in this and the similar function

$$\frac{1}{|\Delta x \Delta y|} f(m, n) = \iint f_a(x, y)\delta\left(\frac{x}{\Delta x} - m, \frac{y}{\Delta y} - n\right)dxdy.$$

The scaling property for 2-D functions yields the result

$$\int_{-\epsilon}^{\epsilon} \int_{-\epsilon}^{\epsilon} \delta(ax, by)dxdy = \frac{1}{|ab|}.$$

As in the case of the 1-D functions, we need only the value at the point where the delta function is nonzero:

$$f(m, n) = \iint f_a(m\Delta x, n\Delta y)\delta(m\Delta x - x, n\Delta y - y)dxdy.$$

## A.5      Frequency effects of sampling, 2-D

The two-dimensional sampling function can be transformed analogously to Eq. (A.9) to obtain

$$\text{Comb}_p(m, n) = \frac{1}{T^2} \int_{-T/2}^{T/2} \int_{-T/2}^{T/2} \delta(s, t) e^{-\omega_0(ms+nt)} dt = 1. \tag{A.12}$$

Using the notation change from Fourier series to Fourier transform, we get

$$\text{Comb}(\omega_m, \omega_n) = \sum_{m=-\infty}^{\infty} \sum_{n=-\infty}^{\infty} \delta(\omega_m - m2\pi, \omega_n - n2\pi).$$

## A.6      Generalized sampling

Shannon's sampling theorem is a cornerstone of digital signal processing. However, direct application of the theorem in real world problems can be difficult because:

- Real world signals and images are not bandlimited.
- The ideal low pass filter cannot be implemented.
- The sinc function has a very slow decay.
- Sampling systems do not use Dirac delta functions. For example, the sampling of reflectance or radiant spectra that is done by filters or color matching functions is not well represented by delta function sampling.

Many of these difficulties can be addressed by generalizing Shannon's sampling theorem. The details of this approach are discussed in [280] where the input signal is assumed to be a finite energy signal, i.e.,

$$\int_{-\infty}^{\infty} |f(x)|^2 dx < \infty.$$

Note that this is less restrictive than requiring that the input signal be bandlimited.[2] The goal is to design the sampling and interpolation system to obtain the "best" approximation of the input signal. This requires the designation of an approximation space in which the interpolation signal will reside. This general space is defined by a basis (see Section 7.1.3) that consists of shifted versions of a single function, $\phi(x)$. The space will be denoted by

$$V_\phi = \{ f(x) = \sum_{k=-\infty}^{\infty} c(k)\phi(x - k), \quad c(k) \in l_2 \}, \tag{A.13}$$

---

[2] Mathematically, the signal is required to be contained in the Hilbert space $L_2$, which is the space of square integrable functions.

where $l_2$ is the set of square summable sequences. Note that if $\phi(x) = \text{sinc}(x)$, then $V_\phi$ is the space of bandlimited signals. To provide a valid approximation space, the function $\phi(x)$ must satisfy certain requirements. A key requirement is the partition of unity, which is stated as

$$\sum_{k=-\infty}^{\infty} \phi(x - k) = 1. \tag{A.14}$$

This states that the summation of the shifted functions is a constant equal to unity. Given that $\phi(x)$ satisfies the above requirement,[3] we now want to design the sampling and interpolation system. It can be shown that the least squares approximation of a signal $f(x)$ by a signal in $V_\phi$ is given by

$$\hat{f}(x) = \sum_{k=-\infty}^{\infty} \left[ \int_{-\infty}^{\infty} f(y) \overset{\circ}{\phi}(y - k) dy \right] \phi(x - k), \tag{A.15}$$

where we have introduced a function $\overset{\circ}{\phi}(y)$, which is defined as the dual of $\phi(x)$. The dual of $\phi(x)$ is the unique function in $V_\phi$ that satisfies the property

$$\int_{-\infty}^{\infty} \phi(y - k) \overset{\circ}{\phi}(y - l) dy = \delta(k - l). \tag{A.16}$$

It is easy to show that the sinc function is its own dual. This is done by using the Fourier transform and the fact that convolution in time (or space), as in Eq. (A.16), is equivalent to multiplication in the frequency domain. For the sinc function, the Fourier transform is a rectangular function, which, multiplied by itself, is unchanged.

The computation in Eq. (A.15) can be broken into two components. The first component is a continuous convolution with the kernel $\overset{\circ}{\phi}(-x)$ followed by sampling, which is expressed as

$$c(k) = \int_{-\infty}^{\infty} f(y) \overset{\circ}{\phi}(y - k) dy. \tag{A.17}$$

The second component is a mixed convolution of the discrete sequence $c(k)$ with the continuous function $\phi(x)$, which is expressed as

$$\hat{f}(x) = \sum_{k=-\infty}^{\infty} c(k)\phi(x - k). \tag{A.18}$$

The complete system consists of a prefilter, followed by sampling, followed by a reconstruction filter, and is shown in Figure A.1. Note that in this formulation, the reconstruction will be exact, that is $\hat{f}(x) = f(x)$, provided the input is already in $V_\phi$. This is true even if $f(x)$ is not bandlimited.

---

[3] The functions $\{\phi(x - k)\}_{k=-\infty}^{\infty}$ must also form a Riesz basis of $V_\phi$.

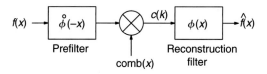

**Figure A.1.** Generalized sampling system.

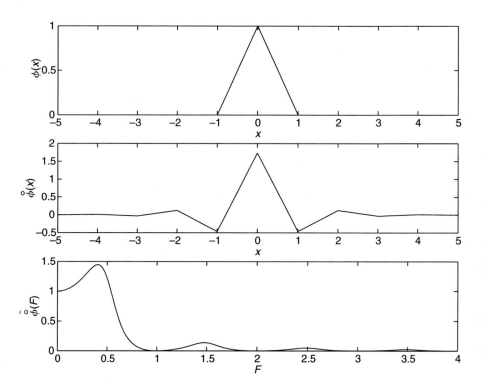

**Figure A.2.** Linear interpolation kernel with its dual and the frequency response of the dual for a sampling rate of $T = 1$.

Shannon's sampling theorem fits nicely in this generalization where the prefilter is an ideal low pass filter, which performs anti-aliasing, and the reconstruction filter is the sinc interpolator. As another example, consider the case where the interpolation function is given by the commonly used linear interpolation function $\phi(x) = \text{tri}_1(x)$, defined in Eq. (6.35). It is easy to show that this function satisfies the partition of unity requirement. The dual of this function is given by the mixed convolution

$$\overset{\circ}{\phi}(x) = \sum_{k=-\infty}^{\infty} p^{-1}(k)\phi(x - k), \tag{A.19}$$

where $p^{-1}(k)$ is the convolutional inverse of the finite sequence,

$$p(k) = \int_{-\infty}^{\infty} \phi(x)\phi(x - k) \, dx.$$

Figure A.2 displays $\phi(x)$, $\overset{\circ}{\phi}(x)$, and the frequency response of $\overset{\circ}{\phi}(x)$. Owing to its more gradual drop off, this frequency response is easier to implement than the ideal lowpass prefilter required when performing sinc interpolation. In addition, the linear interpolation is much simpler than a sinc interpolation.

# B  Digital image manipulation and matrix representation

In Chapter 2, we note that a digital image is represented by the function of discrete variables, $f(m, n)$. This discrete function can be represented by a matrix, which can be transformed to a vector using stacked notation. This transformation leads to the representation of images by vectors; and optical blurring functions, discrete Fourier transforms and various other image operations as matrices. By representing many image processing operations as matrix-vector operations, we can use the powerful methods of linear algebra to address our problems and formulate concise solutions. Here we review the properties of matrix theory that we need for this text. This is a brief summary and does not attempt to derive results. For a more complete presentation, a text on matrix algebra is suggested, such as [174, 181, 236].

## B.1  Basic matrix definitions and properties

To begin, let us summarize the important properties of matrix-vectors and their operations in Table B.1. We will then give more details of the less familiar definitions and operations and introduce the pseudoinverse and elementary matrix calculus.

## B.2  Kronecker product

The Kronecker product is useful for representing 2-D transformations, such as the Fourier transform and other transforms, on images using stacked notation. The definition of the product is

$$
\mathbf{A}_{K \times L} \otimes \mathbf{B}_{M \times N} =
\begin{bmatrix}
a_{11}\mathbf{B} & a_{12}\mathbf{B} & \cdots & a_{1L}\mathbf{B} \\
a_{21}\mathbf{B} & a_{22}\mathbf{B} & \cdots & a_{2L}\mathbf{B} \\
\vdots & \vdots & \vdots & \vdots \\
a_{K1}\mathbf{B} & a_{K2}\mathbf{B} & \cdots & a_{KL}\mathbf{B}
\end{bmatrix}_{KM \times LN}.
$$

The 2-D DFT is represented by

$$
\mathbf{W}_{N^2 \times N^2} = \mathbf{W}_{N \times N} \otimes \mathbf{W}_{N \times N}.
$$

**Table B.1.** Table of matrix definitions

| Item | Definition | Comments |
|---|---|---|
| Matrix | $\mathbf{H} = [h_{m,n}] = [H]_{m,n}$ | $\{m, n\} = \{$row,column$\}$ |
| Transpose | $\mathbf{H}^T = [h_{n,m}]$ | Rows and columns are interchanged |
| Complex conjugate | $\mathbf{H}^* = [h^*_{m,n}]$ | Conjugate of each element |
| Conjugate transpose | $\mathbf{H}^{*T} = [h^*_{n,m}]$ | Used often with the DFT |
| Symmetric matrix | $\mathbf{H}^T = \mathbf{H}$ | All eigenvalues are real |
| Hermitian matrix | $\mathbf{H}^{*T} = \mathbf{H}$ | Real symmetric is Hermitian |
| Identity matrix | $\mathbf{I} = [\delta(m - n)]$ | Ones on the diagonal; $\mathbf{I}$ is square. |
| Null matrix | $\mathbf{0} = [0]$ | Zero in each element |
| Matrix addition | $\mathbf{H} + \mathbf{G} = [h_{m,n} + g_{m,n}]$ | Add elements |
| Scalar multiplication | $\alpha\mathbf{H} = [\alpha h_{m,n}]$ | Multiply each element |
| Matrix multiplication | $\mathbf{HG} = \mathbf{F} = [f_{m,n}]$ $= \left[\sum_{k=0}^{N-1} h_{m,k} g_{k,n}\right]$ | Note dimensionality |
| Commutation | $\mathbf{HG} = \mathbf{GH}$ | Not generally true, be careful |
| Vector inner product | $\mathbf{h}^T \mathbf{g} = \sum_{k=0}^{N-1} h_k g_k$ | Scalar |
| Vector outer product | $\mathbf{h}\mathbf{g}^T = [h_m g_n]$ | Rank one matrix |
| Matrix outer product | $\mathbf{H} \otimes \mathbf{G} = [g_{m,n}\mathbf{H}]$ | If $\mathbf{H}$ is $K \times L$ and $\mathbf{G}$ is $M \times N$ then the outer product is $(KM) \times (LN)$ |
| Determinant | $|\mathbf{H}|$ | $\mathbf{H}$ must be square |
| Rank($\mathbf{H}$) | Number of linearly independent rows or columns | |
| Inverse | $\mathbf{H}^{-1}$ | $\mathbf{HH}^{-1} = \mathbf{H}^{-1}\mathbf{H} = \mathbf{I}$ |
| Singular | $\mathbf{H}^{-1}$ does not exist | |
| Trace | $Tr[\mathbf{H}] = \sum_{k=0}^{N-1} h_{k,k}$ | $\mathbf{H}$ is N×N |
| Eigenvalues, $\lambda_k$ | Roots of $|\mathbf{H} - \lambda_k \mathbf{I}| = 0$ | Note multiplicity |
| Eigenvectors, $\mathbf{v}_k$ | Solutions to $\mathbf{Hv} = \lambda_k \mathbf{v}$ | $\mathbf{H} \neq 0$ |
| ABCD lemma | $(\mathbf{ABCD})^{-1} = \mathbf{A}^{-1} + \mathbf{A}^{-1}\mathbf{B}$ $(\mathbf{C}^{-1} - \mathbf{DA}^{-1}\mathbf{B})^{-1}\mathbf{DA}^{-1}$ | $\mathbf{A}, \mathbf{C}$ are nonsingular |

## B.2.1    Properties of the Kronecker product

The Kronecker product has some very easily demonstrated properties that can be used in many of the operations that arise from the stacked notation. An example of the use of this is given in [274] for the application of demosaicking color images. The properties of interest here are

$$\mathbf{A} \otimes \mathbf{B} \neq \mathbf{B} \otimes \mathbf{A} \quad \text{in general,}$$

$$\mathbf{A} \otimes \mathbf{B} + \mathbf{C} \otimes \mathbf{D} \neq (\mathbf{A} + \mathbf{B}) \otimes (\mathbf{C} + \mathbf{D}) \quad \text{in general,}$$

$$(\mathbf{A} \otimes \mathbf{B})(\mathbf{C} \otimes \mathbf{D}) = \mathbf{AC} \otimes \mathbf{BD},$$

$$(\mathbf{A} \otimes \mathbf{B})^{-1} = \mathbf{A}^{-1} \otimes \mathbf{B}^{-1} \quad \text{if the inverses exist.}$$

## B.3     Properties of the trace of matrices

The trace is defined for square matrices by

$$\text{Trace}(\mathbf{A}_{N \times N}) = \sum_{k=1}^{N} a(k,k).$$

For nonsquare matrices $\mathbf{A}_{M \times N}$ and $\mathbf{B}_{N \times M}$, it can be shown that

$$\text{Trace}(\mathbf{AB}) = \text{Trace}(\mathbf{BA}).$$

This is particularly useful if $\mathbf{A}$ and $\mathbf{B}$ are vectors of compatible sizes. This relation says that the dot product is the trace of the outer product.

If dimensionality permits the re-ordering of the product, we have

$$\text{Trace}(\mathbf{ABC}) = \text{Trace}(\mathbf{CAB}).$$

This leads to the result that if $\mathbf{U}$ is an orthogonal matrix, then

$$\text{Trace}(\mathbf{UAU}^T) = \text{Trace}(\mathbf{A}).$$

This can be interpreted as Parseval's theorem when $\mathbf{U} = \mathbf{W}$ and $\mathbf{A} = \mathbf{HH}^T$, where $\mathbf{H}$ is circulant. Another special case for vectors is

$$\mathbf{f}^T \mathbf{g} = \text{Trace}(\mathbf{fg}^T).$$

For the Kronecker product, we also have

$$\text{Trace}(\mathbf{A} \otimes \mathbf{B}) = \text{Trace}(\mathbf{A})\text{Trace}(\mathbf{B}).$$

## B.4     Matrix derivatives

For scalar functions of the $N$-vector, denoted $\Psi(\mathbf{a})$ where $\mathbf{a} = [a_1, \ldots, a_N]^T$, or the $N \times N$ matrix, denoted $\Psi(\mathbf{A})$ where

$$\mathbf{A} = \begin{bmatrix} a_{11} & a_{12} & \cdots & a_{1N} \\ a_{21} & a_{22} & \cdots & a_{2N} \\ \vdots & \vdots & \vdots & \vdots \\ a_{M1} & a_{M2} & \cdots & a_{MN} \end{bmatrix},$$

the derivatives are defined by [174, 236]

$$\frac{\partial \Psi(\mathbf{a})}{\partial \mathbf{a}} = \left[ \frac{\partial \Psi(\mathbf{a})}{\partial a_1}, \frac{\partial \Psi(\mathbf{a})}{\partial a_2}, \ldots, \frac{\partial \Psi(\mathbf{a})}{\partial a_N} \right]^T,$$

$$\frac{\partial \Psi(\mathbf{A})}{\partial \mathbf{A}} = \begin{bmatrix} \frac{\partial \Psi(\mathbf{A})}{\partial a_{11}}, & \frac{\partial \Psi(\mathbf{A})}{\partial a_{12}}, & \cdots, & \frac{\partial \Psi(\mathbf{A})}{\partial a_{1N}} \\ \frac{\partial \Psi(\mathbf{A})}{\partial a_{21}}, & \frac{\partial \Psi(\mathbf{A})}{\partial a_{22}}, & \cdots, & \frac{\partial \Psi(\mathbf{A})}{\partial a_{2N}} \\ \vdots & \vdots & \vdots & \vdots \\ \frac{\partial \Psi(\mathbf{A})}{\partial a_{M1}}, & \frac{\partial \Psi(\mathbf{A})}{\partial a_{M2}}, & \cdots, & \frac{\partial \Psi(\mathbf{A})}{\partial a_{MN}} \end{bmatrix}.$$

There are several common functions whose derivatives are useful to know:

$$\frac{\partial \mathbf{b}^T \mathbf{a}}{\partial \mathbf{a}} = \mathbf{b},$$

$$\frac{\partial \mathbf{a}^T \mathbf{b}}{\partial \mathbf{a}} = \mathbf{b},$$

$$\frac{\partial \mathbf{a}^T \mathbf{B} \mathbf{a}}{\partial \mathbf{a}} = (\mathbf{B} + \mathbf{B}^T)\mathbf{a},$$

$$\frac{\partial \mathbf{b}^T \mathbf{A} \mathbf{c}}{\partial \mathbf{A}} = \mathbf{b} \mathbf{c}^T,$$

$$\frac{\partial \mathbf{b}^T \mathbf{A}^T \mathbf{A} \mathbf{c}}{\partial \mathbf{A}} = \mathbf{A} \mathbf{c} \mathbf{b}^T + \mathbf{A} \mathbf{b} \mathbf{c}^T,$$

$$\frac{\partial \text{ Trace}(\mathbf{B}\mathbf{A})}{\partial \mathbf{A}} = \mathbf{B}^T,$$

$$\frac{\partial \text{ Trace}(\mathbf{A}^T \mathbf{B}\mathbf{A})}{\partial \mathbf{A}} = (\mathbf{B} + \mathbf{B}^T)\mathbf{A},$$

$$\frac{\partial \text{ Trace}(\mathbf{B}\mathbf{A}^{-1})}{\partial \mathbf{A}} = -(\mathbf{A}^{-1} \mathbf{B} \mathbf{A}^{-1})^T.$$

It is a good exercise to verify these relations using the above definitions.

## B.5    Generalized inverse (pseudoinverse)

Frequently, we wish to solve a system of equations with the goal to find a vector $\mathbf{x}$ where

$$\mathbf{b}_{N \times 1} = \mathbf{A}_{N \times M} \mathbf{x}_{M \times 1}. \tag{B.1}$$

If $M > N$ there will exist many solutions to the problem. If $M = N$ and the equations are linearly independent, there is a unique solution. If $M < N$ then the problem becomes one of least squares minimization.

In color recording models, the case $M > N$ is frequently encountered, which is the source of spectral color aliasing (see Section 9.2). When modeling the effect of PSFs, the case of interest is $M < N$ where the equations are inconsistent. The inconsistencies are caused by

- Noise,
- Modeling errors,
- Nonlinearities,
- Estimation errors of $\mathbf{A}$ (impulse response or PSF).

An image formation model frequently encountered is

$$\mathbf{g} = \mathbf{Hf} + \epsilon \Rightarrow \mathbf{g} - \epsilon = \mathbf{Hf}$$

where $\epsilon$ is noise. We wish to find a solution to the problem of the form

$$\min_{\mathbf{x}} \quad ||\mathbf{b} - \mathbf{Ax}||^2, \tag{B.2}$$

or, in imaging, using $||\mathbf{g} - \mathbf{Hf}||^2$, as in Section 14.1.1. The solution to this problem that has the minimum norm is

$$\hat{\mathbf{x}} = (\mathbf{A}^T\mathbf{A})^{-1}\mathbf{A}^T\mathbf{b},$$

if the inverse exists. But since it may not, we need to generalize the definition of "inverse" to that of *pseudoinverse*. In cases where $(\mathbf{A}^T\mathbf{A})^{-1}$ exists, the matrix $(\mathbf{A}^T\mathbf{A})^{-1}\mathbf{A}^T$ can be thought of as an "inverse" of the matrix $\mathbf{A}$ that has no standard inverse.

The Moore–Penrose pseudoinverse of a matrix $\mathbf{A}$ is written $\mathbf{A}^+$ and is defined by the properties

1. $(\mathbf{A}^+\mathbf{A})^T = \mathbf{A}^+\mathbf{A}$,
2. $(\mathbf{AA}^+)^T = \mathbf{AA}^+$,
3. $\mathbf{AA}^+\mathbf{A} = \mathbf{A}$,
4. $\mathbf{A}^+\mathbf{AA}^+ = \mathbf{A}^+$.

The following are properties that can be derived from the above defining properties.

### Derived properties
1. $(\mathbf{A}^+)^T = (\mathbf{A}^T)^+$,
2. $(\mathbf{A}^+)^+ = \mathbf{A}$,
3. $(\mathbf{AB})^+ = \mathbf{B}^+\mathbf{A}^+$ if $\mathbf{A}_{m \times r}$ and $\mathbf{B}_{r \times n}$ are rank $r$,
4. Rank $\mathbf{A} = $ Rank $\mathbf{A}^+$.

The solution to Eq. (B.2) that is given by $\hat{\mathbf{x}} = \mathbf{A}^+\mathbf{b}$ is the *minimum norm* solution, since of all possible solution to Eq. (B.2), it has the smallest norm. We will justify this claim shortly.

## B.5.1    Computing $A^+$

From elementary matrix theory, we know that any real square matrix, $\mathbf{A}$, can be diagonalized by row and column operations,

$$
\mathbf{U}_R \mathbf{A} \mathbf{U}_C^T = \Lambda =
\begin{bmatrix}
\lambda_1 & 0 & 0 & \ldots & 0 & 0 & \ldots & 0 \\
0 & \lambda_2 & 0 & \ldots & 0 & 0 & \ldots & 0 \\
0 & 0 & \lambda_3 & \ldots & 0 & 0 & \ldots & 0 \\
\vdots & \vdots & \vdots & \vdots & \vdots & \vdots & \vdots & \vdots \\
0 & 0 & 0 & \ldots & \lambda_r & 0 & \ldots & 0 \\
0 & 0 & 0 & \ldots & 0 & 0 & \ldots & 0 \\
\vdots & \vdots & \vdots & \vdots & \vdots & \vdots & \vdots & \vdots \\
0 & 0 & 0 & \ldots & 0 & 0 & \ldots & 0
\end{bmatrix}.
$$

If $\mathbf{A}$ is symmetric then $\mathbf{U}_R = \mathbf{U}_C$.

Note that for an arbitrary matrix, $\mathbf{A}$, which may be nonsquare, $\mathbf{A}\mathbf{A}^T$ and $\mathbf{A}^T\mathbf{A}$ are symmetric, thus

$$
\mathbf{U}^T \mathbf{A}\mathbf{A}^T \mathbf{U} = \Lambda_u, \tag{B.3}
$$

$$
\mathbf{V}^T \mathbf{A}^T \mathbf{A} \mathbf{V} = \Lambda_v. \tag{B.4}
$$

If $\mathbf{A}$ is not square, $\Lambda_u$ and $\Lambda_v$ have identical nonzero elements on the diagonal but a different number of zero elements. This number of nonzero elements is the rank of the matrix $\mathbf{A}$.

The above equations define eigenvalues and eigenvectors for $\mathbf{A}\mathbf{A}^T$ and $\mathbf{A}^T\mathbf{A}$. The matrix $\mathbf{U} = [\mathbf{u}_1, \mathbf{u}_2, \ldots, \mathbf{u}_N]$ contains eigenvectors of $\mathbf{A}\mathbf{A}^T$ and the matrix $\mathbf{V} = [\mathbf{v}_1, \mathbf{v}_2, \ldots, \mathbf{v}_M]$ contains eigenvectors of $\mathbf{A}^T\mathbf{A}$.

Recall that the eigenvectors of a symmetric matrix are orthogonal. By normalizing the eigenvectors, we note the fact that $\mathbf{U}$ and $\mathbf{V}$ are unitary.

Finally, it can be shown that for any matrix, $\mathbf{A}$, we have [236]

$$
\mathbf{U}^T \mathbf{A} \mathbf{V} = \Lambda^{1/2} =
\begin{bmatrix}
\lambda_1^{1/2} & 0 & 0 & \ldots & 0 & 0 & \ldots & 0 \\
0 & \lambda_2^{1/2} & 0 & \ldots & 0 & 0 & \ldots & 0 \\
0 & 0 & \lambda_3^{1/2} & \ldots & 0 & 0 & \ldots & 0 \\
\vdots & \vdots & \vdots & \vdots & \vdots & \vdots & \vdots & \vdots \\
0 & 0 & 0 & \ldots & \lambda_r^{1/2} & 0 & \ldots & 0 \\
0 & 0 & 0 & \ldots & 0 & 0 & \ldots & 0 \\
\vdots & \vdots & \vdots & \vdots & \vdots & \vdots & \vdots & \vdots \\
0 & 0 & 0 & \ldots & 0 & 0 & \ldots & 0
\end{bmatrix}, \tag{B.5}
$$

where the $\lambda_i$ correspond to those of Eqs. (B.3) and (B.4). This implies that

$$\mathbf{A} = \mathbf{U}\Lambda^{1/2}\mathbf{V}^T.$$

The matrix $\mathbf{A}$ can be written as

$$\mathbf{A} = \sum_{k=1}^{r} \lambda_k \mathbf{u}_k \mathbf{v}_k^T, \tag{B.6}$$

which is the weighted sum of rank one matrices. Note that since the sum depends on only the $r$ nonzero singular values, the decomposition of Eq. (B.6) can be written using an $r$ by $r$ nonsingular diagonal matrix and eigenvectors associated only with the nonzero singular values.

The pseudoinverse of $\mathbf{A}$ is given by

$$\mathbf{A}^+ = \mathbf{V}\Lambda^{-1/2}\mathbf{U}^T = \mathbf{V} \begin{bmatrix} \lambda_1^{-1/2} & 0 & 0 & \cdots & 0 & 0 & \cdots & 0 \\ 0 & \lambda_2^{-1/2} & 0 & \cdots & 0 & 0 & \cdots & 0 \\ 0 & 0 & \lambda_3^{-1/2} & \cdots & 0 & 0 & \cdots & 0 \\ \vdots & \vdots & \vdots & \vdots & \vdots & \vdots & \vdots & \vdots \\ 0 & 0 & 0 & \cdots & \lambda_r^{-1/2} & 0 & \cdots & 0 \\ 0 & 0 & 0 & \cdots & 0 & 0 & \cdots & 0 \\ \vdots & \vdots & \vdots & \vdots & \vdots & \vdots & \vdots & \vdots \\ 0 & 0 & 0 & \cdots & 0 & 0 & \cdots & 0 \end{bmatrix} \mathbf{U}^T. \tag{B.7}$$

In general, the solution set for the least squares problem is

$$\hat{\mathbf{x}} = \mathbf{A}^+\mathbf{b} + (\mathbf{I} - \mathbf{A}^+\mathbf{A})\mathbf{g},$$

where $\mathbf{g}$ is an arbitrary vector. From this, it is easy to see that $\mathbf{A}^+\mathbf{b}$ has minimum norm.

## B.5.2    Relation to signal recovery

It can be shown that

$$\hat{\mathbf{f}} = \mathbf{H}^+\mathbf{g}$$

is the solution to the image deconvolution problem that minimizes the expected fitting error for the common linear model presented earlier,

$$\min_{\hat{\mathbf{f}}} \quad E\{||\mathbf{g} - \mathbf{H}\hat{\mathbf{f}}||^2\}.$$

Consider the DFT relation for circular convolution. Suppose that we approximate the optical image formation by

$$\mathbf{g} = \mathbf{H}_c \mathbf{f},$$

then a solution to the deconvolution problem is

$$\hat{\mathbf{f}} = \mathbf{H}_c^+ \mathbf{g}.$$

Using the DFT to find the pseudoinverse, we obtain a simple form for the solution, $\hat{\mathbf{f}}$. See Problem 14.4 for the exercise that obtains the explicit form.

## B.6     Ill-conditioned matrices (systems)

A system is *ill-conditioned* if a small change in the output of the system implies a large change in the input to the system. In the case of the system given by Eq. (B.1), this means that a small perturbation, such as noise, to the output vector, $\mathbf{b}$, results in a large change to the input vector, $\mathbf{x}$.

Consider the perturbed system,

$$\mathbf{b} + \epsilon = \mathbf{A}\mathbf{x}.$$

From the definition of the pseudoinverse matrix and basic linearity, a solution is

$$\hat{\mathbf{x}} = \mathbf{A}^+ \mathbf{b} + \mathbf{A}^+ \epsilon,$$

which is the original solution, $\mathbf{A}^+ \mathbf{b}$, plus a perturbation, $\mathbf{A}^+ \epsilon$. The relative magnitude of the perturbation depends on the relative magnitudes of the singular values. By examination of the form of the pseudoinverse of Eq. (B.7), we see that the relative magnitude of the perturbation is large if the dynamic range of the nonzero singular values is large. A rule of thumb is that a matrix or system is ill-conditioned if

$$\frac{\lambda_{max}}{\lambda_{min}} > 10^4,$$

where $\lambda_{max}$ and $\lambda_{min}$ are the maximum and minimum singular values respectively. An obvious question is whether a small nonzero singular value is really nonzero or just an artifact of noise or numerical computational rounding off errors. This is a justification for the thresholding of small nonzero terms in Eq. (14.3), which was discussed in Section 14.1.1.

## B.7      Properties of DFT matrices

The one-dimensional DFT matrix, $\mathbf{W}$, is constructed as an $N \times N$ matrix with the coefficients defined in terms of, $w_N = \exp(-j2\pi/N)$, as

$$
\mathbf{W} = \begin{bmatrix}
w_N^0 & w_N^0 & w_N^0 & \cdots & w_N^0 \\
w_N^0 & w_N^1 & w_N^2 & \cdots & w_N^{N-1} \\
w_N^0 & w_N^2 & w_N^4 & \cdots & w_N^{2N-2} \\
\vdots & \vdots & \vdots & \vdots & \vdots \\
w_N^0 & w_N^{N-1} & w_N^{N-2} & \cdots & w_N^1
\end{bmatrix},
\tag{B.8}
$$

where the term $w_N^k$ is $w_N$ raised to the $k$th power. In Chapter 5, we noted two properties of importance:

1. The inverse of $\mathbf{W}$ is the inverse DFT and is given by $\mathbf{W}^{-1} = \frac{1}{2}[w_N^{-mn}]_{mn}$.
2. The term $\mathbf{W}\mathbf{H}_c\mathbf{W}^{-1} = \boldsymbol{\Lambda}_H$ is a diagonal matrix that contains the terms of the DFT of $h(n)$ on the diagonal, where $\mathbf{H}_c$ is a circulant matrix with the first row equal to the vector $\mathbf{h} = [h(0), h(1), \ldots, h(N-1)]^T$.

We prove these properties here.

To prove the fact that $\mathbf{W}^{-1} = \frac{1}{2}[w_N^{-mn}]_{mn}$, it is sufficient to compute the elements of $\mathbf{A} = \mathbf{W}\mathbf{W}^{-1}$ and show that $\mathbf{A} = \mathbf{I}$. The $(m, n)$ element of $\mathbf{A}$ is given by

$$
[\mathbf{A}]_{m,n} = \sum_{k=0}^{N-1} w_N^{mk} \frac{1}{N} w_N^{-kn} = \frac{1}{N} \sum_{k=0}^{N-1} w_N^{(m-n)k}.
\tag{B.9}
$$

Using the formula for a geometric series,

$$
\sum_{k=0}^{N-1} \alpha_k = \frac{1 - \alpha^N}{1 - \alpha},
\tag{B.10}
$$

and noting that $w_N^N = e^{-j2\pi} = 1$, we have

$$
[\mathbf{A}]_{m,n} = \begin{cases} 1 & \text{if } m = n \\ 0 & \text{if } m \neq n \end{cases},
\tag{B.11}
$$

thus, $\mathbf{A} = \mathbf{I}$.

The second property requires more manipulation but relies on the same idea. Let $\mathbf{B} = \mathbf{W}\mathbf{H}_c\mathbf{W}^{-1}$ and compute the $(m, n)$ element of $\mathbf{B}$. This is

$$
[\mathbf{B}]_{m,n} = \sum_{k=0}^{N-1} w_N^{mk} \frac{1}{N} \sum_{l=0}^{N-1} h(k - l) w_N^{-ln},
\tag{B.12}
$$

where we use the fact that the $(k, l)$ element of the circulant $\mathbf{H}_c$ is $h(k - l)$. We will use a periodic extension of $N$ element vector $\mathbf{h}$ for the computation. We need to consider two cases, as before, $m = n$ and $m \neq n$. For the case where $m = n$, we have

$$
\begin{aligned}
[\mathbf{B}]_{m,m} &= \sum_{k=0}^{N-1} w_N^{mk} \frac{1}{N} \sum_{l=0}^{N-1} h(k - l) w_N^{-lm} \\
&= \frac{1}{N} \sum_{l=0}^{N-1} w_N^{-lm} \sum_{k=0}^{N-1} h(k - l) w_N^{km}.
\end{aligned}
\tag{B.13}
$$

We use the shifting property of the DFT to obtain

$$
[\mathbf{B}]_{m,m} = \frac{1}{N} \sum_{l=0}^{N-1} w_N^{-lm} w_N^{lm} \tilde{h}(m) = \tilde{h}(m).
\tag{B.14}
$$

For the off-diagonal terms, we consider the $N$ terms in the summation of Eq. (B.12) that contain a fixed $h(p)$. We will show that each of these summations of $N$ terms is zero. We make the substitution, $p = k - l$ and write the coefficient of this term as

$$
\frac{1}{N} \sum_{k=0}^{N-1} w_N^{-mk} w_N^{-n(k-p)} = \frac{1}{N} w_N^{np} \sum_{k=0}^{N-1} w_N^{k(m-n)}.
\tag{B.15}
$$

Since for this case $m \neq n$, the results of the summations of the geometric series are zero for all $p$, and the matrix $\mathbf{B}$ is diagonal with the diagonal elements equal to the DFT of $\mathbf{h}$.

# C  Stochastic images

Images can be considered representative of random processes. Given the values of pixels in a well defined region, it is not possible to predict exactly the values of pixels outside of that region. For most images, it is likely that there is some relation between the pixel values inside and outside the known region, but the relationship is statistical. The fact that most images are the result of the measurement of radiation means that there is always some uncertainty about the exact value of a pixel, even within any known region. In fact, deterministic images are usually of little interest. From an information theoretic viewpoint, it is the uncertainty of the values of pixels that makes the information conveyed by the pixels important. This appendix will review the fundamentals that are assumed as a prerequisite for treating the various aspects of noise and stochastic models that are used in this text.

This appendix gives only brief definitions of the terms that we will use repeatedly in the text. It will only briefly discuss the elementary properties and concepts of stochastic processes that are necessary for the description of many of the imaging modeling processes discussed in the main text. Thus, this should be seen as a refresher of material that the reader has seen previously, or perhaps it indicates the material that the reader will need to learn from some more appropriate text in order to understand certain parts of this text. Suggested probability and random processes texts for image processing workers include [95, 109, 115, 205, 252].

## C.1  Basic probability definitions

The *probability* that an event A will occur, denoted $P(A)$, is a measure of the frequency of occurrence of the event A. It is more usual to deal with *random variables*, which are quantitative, but closely linked to the random event. Without getting too deeply into the mathematical definitions, an example of an event is the side of a die showing four dots on the top face. The associated random variable is $X$, which can take the quantitative values $\{1, 2, 3, 4, 5, 6\}$, and the event that $X = 4$, is the event of interest. A more practical imaging example is an event that the radiation sensed at a pixel location measures between 3.1 and 3.3 candela. The associated random variable might be the pixel denoted $Y$, and the event could be $147 \leq Y \leq 149$, where the image has been quantized to 8 bits, according to some appropriate scale.

Random variables can be discrete, continuous or mixed. For discrete random variables, the probability for a random variable being equal to a particular value is well defined, e.g., for the example of a fair die toss, $P(X = 4) = 1/6$. We know that a probability is a nonnegative value and the sum of the probabilities of all possible values is unity,

$$\sum_{k=0}^{\infty} P(X = x_k) = 1,$$

where $x_k$ are the possible values of the random variable. For continuous random variables, it is possible to define a probability only for some range of values of the random variable. This probability is defined by using a *probability density function*, $p(x)$, which is defined by the following properties:

1. $p(x) \geq 0$,
2. $\int_{-\infty}^{\infty} p(x)\, dx = 1$.

where we omit the mathematical details, such as requiring the function to be integrable.

## C.1.1 Common discrete probability distributions and densities

The most common discrete probability distributions are:

- *Uniform*: over the range of integers $X \in \{a, a + 1, \cdots, b\}$, $P(X = n) = \frac{1}{b-a+1}$ for $a \leq n \leq b$ and zero otherwise.
- *Poisson*: $P(X = n) = \frac{\mu^n e^{-\mu}}{n!}$, for $n \geq 0$, where $\mu$ is the mean and variance of the distribution.
- *Binominal*: for a system with $N$ possible events, $P(X = n) = \frac{N!}{n!(N-n)!} p^n (1-p)^{(N-n)}$, for $1 \leq n \leq N$.

## C.1.2 Common continuous probability densities

The most common continuous probability densities are:

- *Uniform*: over the range $a \leq x \leq b$, $p(x) = \frac{1}{b-a}$ for $a \leq x \leq b$ and zero otherwise.
- *Gaussian* or *normal*:

$$p(x) = \frac{1}{\sqrt{2\pi}\sigma} e^{-\frac{(x-\mu)^2}{2\sigma^2}}, \text{ for } -\infty \leq x \leq \infty,$$

where $\mu$ is the mean and $\sigma$ is the standard deviation of the distribution.
- *Exponential*: $p(x) = ae^{-ax}$, for $0 \leq x \leq \infty$, where $a > 0$.
- *Laplacian*: $p(x) = \frac{a}{2} e^{-a|x|}$, for $-\infty \leq x \leq \infty$, where $a > 0$.

## C.1.3 Central limit theorem

Gaussian distributions are very useful because of their theoretical properties, and because they can be used to approximate a large number of practical distributions. For example, the central limit theorem is often invoked when dealing with functions of a large number of random variables.

**Central limit theorem**: let $X_1, X_2, \ldots, X_N$ be $N$ mutually independent random variables with probability density functions $P(x_1), P(x_2), \ldots, P(x_N)$, respectively, such that $E\{X_i\} = 0$ and $\mathrm{Var}[X_i] = \sigma_i^2$. Let

$$s_N^2 = \sum_{i=1}^{N} \sigma_i^2.$$

If for a given $\epsilon > 0$ and N sufficiently large, $\sigma_i$ satisfy

$$\sigma_i < \epsilon s_N, \quad i = 1, 2, \ldots, N,$$

then the normalized sum $Z = \frac{X_1 + X_2 + \ldots + X_N}{s_N^2}$ converges to the standard normal PDF, $N(0, 1)$ [252].

### C.1.4        Moments: mean, variance

The *mean* or *expected value* of a random variable $X$, denoted by $E\{X\}$, is defined by

$$E\{X\} = \sum_{k=0}^{\infty} x_k P(X = x_k),$$

for a discrete random variable, and

$$E\{X\} = \int_{-\infty}^{\infty} x p(x) \, dx,$$

for a continuous random variable.

The *variance* of a random variable $X$ is defined by

$$\mathrm{Var}\{X\} = \sum_{k=0}^{\infty} (x_k - E\{X\})^2 P(X = x_k),$$

for a discrete random variable, and

$$\mathrm{Var}\{X\} = \int_{-\infty}^{\infty} (x - E\{X\})^2 p(x) \, dx,$$

for a continuous random variable.

## C.2        Histograms

The histogram of a signal is an array that records the frequency of occurrence of the values of the signal. If the signal is scalar valued, the histogram can be defined as a vector and plotted as a graph or bar chart. For a signal, $s(n)$, for $1 \leq n \leq N$, each element of the occurrence histogram, $h_o(k)$, is the number of times the value of $s(n)$ lies in the interval $d_k \leq s(n) < d_{k+1}$, for $k = 0, \ldots, M$. The probability histogram is obtained by dividing the occurrence histogram by the total number of samples, $h(k) = h_o(k)/N$. This gives an approximation to the probability distribution of the signal values, that is, if the signal, $s(n)$, is a sample of a random variable, $X$, then

$$h(k) \approx P\{d_k \leq X < d_{k+1}\},$$

the probability that $X$ lies in the interval $[d_k, d_{k+1}]$.

Histograms are simple to compute, but care should be taken when interpreting them. The validity of the approximation of the histogram to the probability distribution depends on the number of samples, $N$, and bin boundaries, $\{d_k\}$. If there are only a small number of samples available, the bin widths must be selected to allow a reasonable number of values to fall in each bin. As the number of samples increases, the widths of the bins can be decreased and the resolution improved.

The bin widths should be chosen to span the useful range of values and show sufficient detail, as allowed by the number of samples. For example, if a signal has several isolated values that occur frequently, the bin widths should be chosen so that these values fall into different bins. The peaks and valleys of the distribution should be apparent in the histogram. The histogram of Fig. 10.10a shows six distinct peaks. Choosing a larger bin width might reduce some of the "noise," but might also obscure the two peaks between 25 and 50 or between 100 and 140. For this same image histogram, it would be imprudent to choose a range larger than 0 to 255.

The bin width should be consistent with the quantization of the signal values. For most images, the values are often integers between 0 and 255. Thus, bin boundaries should reflect this fact. Choosing a bin width of 0.25 would not result in increased resolution, but would produce three empty bins between every one that contained valid values. Using simple algorithms such as setting the bin width to the range of the signal divided by a fixed number of bins can yield this type of error. For example, for the distribution of Fig. 10.10a, setting the bin width

$$w = \frac{\text{max} - \text{min}}{256}$$

would yield $w = 0.92$, which would result in several bins (roughly every 12th one) that would be guaranteed to be empty. The appearance of nearly periodic zeros in a histogram is an indication that the original signal is quantized and the bin width chosen is not matched well with that quantization.

## C.3   Basic joint probability definitions

We are usually interested in the relation of multiple random variables. The basis for this is the joint probability and joint probability density functions. These have the same types of property as the functions for a single random variable. The probabilities are non-negative and must sum or integrate to unity. For discrete random variables, $X$ and $Y$, we have

$$\sum_{k=1}^{\infty}\sum_{l=1}^{\infty} P(X = x_k \text{ and } Y = y_l) = 1,$$

and for continuous random variables, we have

$$\int_{-\infty}^{\infty}\int_{-\infty}^{\infty} p(x, y)\mathrm{d}x\mathrm{d}y = 1.$$

### C.3.1    Marginal distributions and densities

The marginal probability of the random variable $X$ relative to the joint probability is simply

$$P(X = x \text{ and } Y = \text{anything}) = \sum_{l=1}^{\infty} P(X = x \text{ and } Y = y_l) = P(X = x).$$

For the continuous random variables, the marginal density of $X$ is

$$p(x) = \int_{-\infty}^{\infty} p(x, y)\mathrm{d}y.$$

### C.3.2    Correlation and covariance

The correlation between two random variables is defined as

$$\mathrm{Cor}(X, Y) = E\{XY\},$$

where the expected value operation is computed analogously to the mean in Section C.1.4, that is, for continuous variables

$$E\{XY\} = \int_{-\infty}^{\infty}\int_{-\infty}^{\infty} xyp(x, y)\mathrm{d}x\mathrm{d}y.$$

The covariance is defined for continuous variables by

$$\mathrm{Cov}(X, Y) = E\{(X - E\{X\})(Y - E\{Y\})\}$$

$$= \int_{-\infty}^{\infty}\int_{-\infty}^{\infty} (x - E\{X\})$$

$$(y - E\{Y\})p(x, y)\mathrm{d}x\mathrm{d}y.$$

The covariance of $X$ with itself is the variance.

Of particular interest is the multidimensional Gaussian distribution. A multidimensional Gaussian distribution for the $N$-vector $\mathbf{s}$ is defined by

$$P(\mathbf{s}) = \frac{1}{(2\pi)^{N/2}|\mathbf{K}_{ss}|^{1/2}} \exp\left[-\frac{1}{2}(\mathbf{s} - \mu_s)^T \mathbf{K}_{ss}^{-1}(\mathbf{s} - \mu_s)\right],$$

where $\mu_s$ is the mean and $\mathbf{K}_{ss}$ is the covariance matrix.

## C.3.3 Independence

Two random variables are *independent* if their joint probability (or density) is the product of their marginal probabilities (or marginal densities),

$$P(X, Y) = P(X)P(Y) \text{ or } p(x, y) = p(x)p(y).$$

Variables are *dependent* if they are not independent.

## C.3.4 Conditional probability distributions and densities; Bayes' theorem

The probability of a random variable may be conditioned upon knowledge of some constraint or auxiliary information. For discrete random variables, the *conditional probability* is written $P(X|Y)$ and referred to as the probability of $X$ given $Y$. For continuous probability densities, we have $p(x|y)$. The mathematical definition, in terms of joint and marginal probabilities is given by

$$P(X|Y) = \frac{P(X, Y)}{P(Y)} \text{ or } p(x|y) = \frac{p(x, y)}{p(y)}.$$

By interchanging the roles of $X$ and $Y$, we have

$$P(X, Y) = P(X|Y)P(Y) = P(Y|X)P(X).$$

Rewriting the last equation, we get *Bayes' theorem*

$$P(X|Y) = \frac{P(Y|X)P(X)}{P(Y)}.$$

This is extremely important, for it is the basis for many image restoration, pattern recognition, and classification algorithms. We can also see that if $X$ and $Y$ are independent, then $P(X|Y) = P(X)$.

## C.4 Stochastic processes

A *stochastic process* is an indexed set of random variables. The index set can be continuous or discrete. An example of a discrete stochastic process is the sequential values stored on a music CD, $X(n)$; or the pixel values of a digital camera, $S(m, n)$. In the music case, for each $n$, $X(n)$ is a random variable. In the image example, each pair $(m, n)$ identifies a random variable. The stochastic process can be indexed by a continuous variable as in the case of temperature as a function of time, or a radiation field as a function of spatial location. For this section, we will restrict ourselves to the discrete case.

The usual definitions of mean and variance can be used for stochastic processes. However, it is important to realize that those statistics are defined for each index, that is, the mean at index $n_1$ is not necessarily the same as the mean at index $n_2$. The mean of a stochastic process, $E\{X(n)\}$, is a deterministic function of $n$. Likewise, the variance is a deterministic function of $n$.

Since we have a sequence of random variables, the relation between the elements of the sequence is of interest. The correlation between elements of a random process is called the *autocorrelation* and defined as $\mathrm{Cor}_{XX}(m, n) = E\{[X(m), X(n)]\}$. When dealing with two random processes, we have the *cross-correlation* defined as $\mathrm{Cor}_{XY}(m, n) = E\{[X(m), Y(n)]\}$. *Autocovariance* and *cross-covariance* are defined by subtracting the means of the processes, i.e., $\mathrm{Cov}_{XX}(m, n) = E\{[(X(m) - \mu_x), (X(n) - \mu_x)]\}$ and $\mathrm{Cov}_{XY}(m, n) = E\{[(X(m) - \mu_x), (Y(n) - \mu_y)]\}$.

### Stochastic images

For a monochrome image denoted by $s(x, y)$, the value at each location $(x, y)$ is a random variable. The spatial location $(x, y)$ can be considered an index to an ensemble of random variables. The location indices can be continuous $(x, y)$ or discrete $(m, n)$.

The stochastic image is completely described by its joint probability distribution function (PDF). However, this is almost never known in practice. For most applications, it is sufficient to characterize the random signal by its mean, variance and covariance.

We will denote the mean of $s(x, y)$ by

$$\mu_s(x, y) = E\{s(x, y)\}.$$

The variance of $s(x, y)$ is defined by

$$\mathrm{Var}[s(x, y)] = E\{[s(x, y) - \mu_s(x, y)]^2\}.$$

The autocorrelation of $s(x, y)$ is defined by

$$R_{ss}(x, y, x', y') = E\{s(x, y)s(x', y')\}.$$

The autocovariance of $s(x, y)$ is defined by

$$K_{ss}(x, y, x', y') = E\{[s(x, y) - \mu_s(x, y)][s(x', y') - \mu_s(x', y')]\}.$$

The cross-correlation of $s(x, y)$ and $g(x, y)$ is defined by

$$R_{sg}(x, y, x', y') = E\{s(x, y)g(x', y')\}.$$

Two random variables are *uncorrelated* if

$$E\{s(x,y)g(x',y')\} = E\{s(x,y)\}E\{g(x',y')\},$$

for all indices $(x,y)$ and $(x',y')$.

Independent random variables are uncorrelated, but it is possible for random variables to be uncorrelated without being independent.

The cross-covariance of $f(x,y)$ and $g(x,y)$ is defined by

$$K_{sg}(x,y,x',y') = E\{[s(x,y) - \mu_s(x,y)][g(x',y') - \mu_g(x',y')]\}.$$

Note that the arguments $(x,y)$ can be continuous or discrete.

### Stochastic vectors

Images are usually defined as vectors, thus it is appropriate to consider the special case of random vectors. In many cases, the collection represents points on a rectangular sampling lattice. The process of vectorizing an image was described in Section 2.7. The stochastic image characterization can be easily expressed in terms of elementary probability. Let $s$ be a vector of $N$ random variables

$$\mathbf{s} = [s_1, s_2, \ldots s_N]^T.$$

Note that vectors of signals are usually written as column vectors. The mean of $\mathbf{s}$ is defined by

$$\mu_s = [E\{s_1\}, E\{s_2\}, \ldots E\{s_N\}]^T,$$

where the expected value is taken for each element in the vector. The autocovariance of $\mathbf{s}$ is defined by

$$\mathbf{K}_{ss} = E\{[\mathbf{s} - \mu_\mathbf{s}][\mathbf{s} - \mu_\mathbf{s}]^T\}.$$

The cross-correlation of $\mathbf{s}$ and $\mathbf{g}$ is defined by

$$\mathbf{R}_{sg} = E\{\mathbf{s}\mathbf{g}^T\}.$$

The autocovariance and cross-covariance are defined with the appropriate modifications.

### C.4.1    Stationary processes

A random process is said to be *stationary* if all of its joint distributions depend only on the difference in indices and not the specific indices. Heuristically, stationarity implies that one region of a signal is statistically like any other region of the signal. Mathematically, for any times, $\{n_1, n_2, \ldots, n_M\}$, we have

$$P[X(n_1), X(n_2), \ldots, X(n_M)] = P[X(n_1 - n_0), X(n_2 - n_0), \ldots, X(n_M - n_0)].$$

This definition is easily, if tediously, extended to two dimensions [252]. This is a very difficult condition to meet or verify. While many image processing algorithms require knowledge of image statistics, there may be a large problem in obtaining estimates of those statistics. For example, estimating the autocorrelation of a signal ensemble should be done by averaging many samples of signals from the ensemble, e.g.,

$$\hat{\mathbf{R}}_{ss} = 1/N \sum_{k=1}^{N} \mathbf{s}_k \mathbf{s}_k^T,$$

where the vector $\mathbf{s}_k$ is the $k$th sample of the signal. It may not be possible to find or use a large number of independent signals or images to estimate such an autocorrelation. If a process is *stationary*, then the computational burden can be significantly reduced, since the averaging can be done over different parts of a single realization of a signal. There is also a condition of ergodicity, which is mentioned later in Section C.7.2.

For practical processing algorithms, we use only first and second order moments, i.e., mean, variance, correlation and covariance. We say that a random process is *wide-sense stationary* if the first and second order moments are time-invariant, that is, for any times $m$ and $n$ and any time shift $n_0$,

$$E\{X(n)\} = E\{X(n - n_0)\} = \mu;$$
$$E\{X(n)X(m)\} = E\{X(n - n_0)X(m - n_0)\} = R_{xx}(m - n).$$

The autocovariance is defined similarly. A result of the wide-sense stationary assumption is that the autocorrelation matrix has a Toeplitz form in addition to being symmetric. This means that for a random signal (random process) of length $N$,

$$\mathbf{R}_{ss} = E\{\mathbf{ss}_k^T\},$$

the elements of $\mathbf{R}_{ss} = [r_{i,j}]$ are related by

$$r_{i,j} = R_{xx}(i - j).$$

The power spectrum of a stationary random process is defined as the Fourier transform of the autocovariance function,

$$P_{xx}(\omega) = \mathcal{F}[R_{xx}(n)],$$

where we use the appropriate Fourier transform depending on the continuity or discreteness of the domains. Since the assumption of stationarity yields a Toeplitz form for the autocorrelation, we can use the property of the discrete Fourier transform to diagonalize Toeplitz matrices to greatly simplify computation (see Section 2.7).

The assumption of stationarity is very important for most processing algorithms. However, as is shown in Chapter 7, images are not truly stationary. It is important to understand the limitations of this common assumption. We gain computation simplicity and efficiency, but lose optimality in our algorithms.

## C.5 Transformations of stochastic signals

The most common transformation of a stochastic signal, $\mathbf{x}$, is represented by the algebraic equation

$$\mathbf{y} = \mathbf{A}\mathbf{x}.$$

The properties of the new stochastic process, $\mathbf{y}$, are easily related to those of $\mathbf{x}$. The mean and correlation are given by

$$E\{\mathbf{y}\} = \mathbf{A}E\{\mathbf{x}\}$$

and

$$R_{yy} = E\{\mathbf{A}\mathbf{x}\mathbf{x}^T\mathbf{A}^T\} = \mathbf{A}E\{\mathbf{x}\mathbf{x}^T\}\mathbf{A}^T = \mathbf{A}R_{xx}\mathbf{A}^T.$$

Since we know that the correlation and covariance are related by the inclusion of the mean in the correlation, we can treat them simultaneously, by assuming a zero mean process. Of particular interest is the transformation that produces a new stochastic process that is *uncorrelated*, that is, the covariance matrix of the process is diagonal.

To obtain this transformation, we decompose the covariance matrix of the input process, $\mathbf{R}_{xx}$, using its eigenvectors, as

$$\mathbf{R}_{xx} = \Phi \Lambda \Phi^T,$$

where $\Lambda$ is a diagonal matrix that contains the eigenvalues of $\mathbf{R}_{xx}$ on the diagonal, and $\Phi$ is a matrix that contains the eigenvectors of $\mathbf{R}_{xx}$ in the columns. Since the matrix $\mathbf{R}_{xx}$ represents a covariance, it is positive and semi-definite, which implies that the diagonal elements of $\Lambda$ are nonnegative. The transformation on the vector $\mathbf{x}$ that produces an uncorrelated vector $\mathbf{y}$ is given by

$$\mathbf{y} = \Phi^T \mathbf{x}.$$

This is an application of the unitary transformation discussed in Section B.5 and [236]. This transformation is also known as the Karhunen–Loeve (K–L) transformation.

For two-dimensional stochastic processes, we use the stacked notation to keep the same matrix-vector format. Here the image vector, $\mathbf{x}$, is obtained from the stacking procedure. However, as was mentioned in Section 2.7, this notation is not useful for computation. The computation of the eigenvectors of the huge correlation matrix is extremely expensive and obtaining accurate values is a problem. If we make the assumption that the stochastic process is stationary and the correlation of the image is separable, then we can write the 2-D correlation matrix as a Kronecker product,

$$\mathbf{R}_{xx} = \mathbf{R}_c \otimes \mathbf{R}_r,$$

where $\mathbf{R}_r$ is the correlation matrix associated with the rows and $\mathbf{R}_c$ is that associated with the columns. The Kronecker product is defined in Section B.2. The K–L transform on images is discussed in more detail in [217].

The K–L transform for this limited case of a stationary, separable process is obtained by multiplying each column of the image by the eigenvector matrix associated with the columns, $\Phi_c$, followed by multiplying each row of the resulting image by the eigenvector matrix associated with the rows, $\Phi_r$. For an image represented as an $N \times N$ matrix, $\mathbf{X}$, this is written

$$\mathbf{Y} = \Phi_c \mathbf{X} \Phi_r^T.$$

This operation is computable in practical applications.

## C.6        Effects of shift-invariant linear systems on stochastic signals

If the input to a linear system is a stochastic image, then the output is also stochastic. For matrix transformations, the mean and covariance of the output were presented in the previous section. The relationships between the input and output stochastic images for convolutional systems are given below. The shift-invariant linear system is defined by its impulse response or point spread function (PSF), $h(x, y)$,

$$g(x, y) = h(x, y) * s(x, y),$$

where $s(x, y)$ is the input signal and $g(x, y)$ is the output.

The cross-correlation and autocorrelation matrices are given by

$$r_{sg}(x, y) = h(x, y) * r_{ss}(x, y),$$
$$r_{gg}(x, y) = h(-x, -y) * h(x, y) * r_{ss}(x, y) = r_{hh}(x, y) * r_{ss}(x, y),$$

where $h(-x, -y) * h(x, y) = r_{hh}(x, y)$.

The effect of a linear system on a stochastic image is characterized by the power spectrum, denoted

$$r_{sg}(x, y) \longleftrightarrow H^*(u, v) P_{ss}(u, v), \tag{C.1}$$

$$r_{gg}(x, y) \longleftrightarrow |H(u, v)|^2 P_{ss}(u, v). \tag{C.2}$$

An example of this property is shown in Section 7.4.3.

## C.7        Stochastic image models

A stochastic model permits the user to characterize a class or ensemble of random signals or images. The basis of a stochastic model is a set of instructions that define how the class of signals or images can be generated. For example, a common model is that of generating signals by putting stationary white noise through a linear, shift-invariant system. If the input to a linear, shift-invariant system is stationary, then the output is also stationary. In this case, the ensemble is completely characterized by the definition of the system. The system is usually defined by a mathematical model and characterized by the values of parameters used in its formulation. The characterization is done by selection of a mathematical model and the estimation of parameters that define the model.

Most image processing methods require the use of first and second order statistics, thus, wide-sense stationarity is assumed. The mean and autocorrelation function must be determined. The power spectrum, as the Fourier transform of the autocorrelation, is included in these second order statistics. The estimates of the mean, variance and power spectrum of an image are used in describing image characteristics in Chapter 7.

## C.7.1    Estimation of stochastic parameters

The mean and variance of stationary signals are usually estimated by simple averages. Given a set of samples, $\{s(n)\}_{n=1}^{N}$, the mean is estimated by

$$\hat{\mu} = \frac{1}{N} \sum_{n=1}^{N} s(n),$$

and the variance is estimated by

$$\hat{\sigma}^2 = \frac{1}{N-1} \sum_{n=1}^{N} [s(n) - \hat{\mu}]^2.$$

These estimates are *unbiased* since their expected values are equal to the statistic that is being estimated, i.e.,

$$E\{\hat{\mu}\} = E\left\{\frac{1}{N} \sum_{n=1}^{N} s(n)\right\} = E\{s(n)\}$$

and

$$E\{\hat{\sigma}^2\} = E\{[s(n) - E\{s(n)\}]^2\} = \text{Var}(s(n)).$$

Furthermore, the estimates are *consistent*, since they become more accurate as the number of samples increases. Mathematically, an estimator, $g(n)$, based on $N$ samples, is consistent if

$$\lim_{N \to \infty} \text{Var}[g(n)] = 0.$$

## C.7.2    Power spectrum computation

The power spectrum of an image ensemble is often estimated from a single image by the periodogram defined as the magnitude squared of the Fourier transform of the sample image. To make this estimate, it is necessary to invoke not only stationarity but also ergodicity. A random process is *ergodic* if every sample of the process is representative of the process. The problems of the periodogram as a spectral estimator are well known [200, 218]. The fact that it is neither a consistent nor unbiased estimator is problematic.

The consistency problem can be overcome by windowing and averaging periodograms as noted in the texts on 1-D signal processing [200, 218]. The windowing has the additional value of eliminating any discontinuities at the edges of the image, which eliminates the misleading horizontal and vertical lines in the spectral estimate.

Stochastic signals are most often modeled by passing a white noise random process, $w(n)$, through a linear filter, as

$$s(n) = h(n) * w(n) = \sum_{k=-\infty}^{\infty} h(k)w(n-k).$$

Since the white noise has a spectrum that is constant, the filter gives the output random process its characteristic shape. By taking Fourier transforms of the signals, we have

$$P_{ss}(\omega) = |H(\omega)|^2 P_{ww}(\omega) = \sigma^2 |H(\omega)|^2,$$

where $P_{ww}(\omega)$ is the power spectrum of the white noise with variance $\sigma^2$, $P_{ss}(\omega)$ is the power spectrum of the output image and $H(\omega)$ is the Fourier transform of the impulse response. Since the power spectrum is the Fourier transform of the autocorrelation function, the above relation defines the autocorrelation function as well.

Given a desired autocorrelation function, the process of finding a filter $H(\omega)$ that realizes a stochastic process with those characteristics is called *spectral factorization*. Determining this filter is usually an approximation process. If a rational polynomial is assumed for the functional form of $H(\omega)$, then the estimation problem is one of determining the coefficients of the polynomials of the numerator and denominator. In two dimensions, the PSF may be assumed to be separable in order to further simplify the problem.

If two stochastic signals, $f(n)$ and $g(n)$, are statistically independent, then the power spectrum of the sum is the sum of the power spectra,

$$s(n) = f(n) + g(n),$$
$$P_{ss}(\omega) = P_{ff}(\omega) + P_{gg}(\omega).$$

## C.7.3    One-dimensional models

We will use one-dimensional models to introduce the basic mathematical models for signals. Later, we will discuss the extension to two dimensions.

### Finite impulse response models

For digital systems, the simplest filter representation is a *finite impulse response* (FIR) or *moving average* (MA) system. The model of order $p$ is

$$x(n) = h(n) * w(n) = \sum_{k=0}^{p-1} h(k)w(n-k).$$

An advantage of this model is that the autocorrelation function can be matched exactly for the first $p$ values. The problem with this model is that the autocorrelation function is necessarily an estimated quantity and subject to error. There is a severe SNR problem when trying to estimate a large number of filter coefficients from a relatively small number of data samples. The length of the FIR filter required to match a common autocorrelation function, e.g., an exponential, is very large.

### Infinite impulse response models

The most common signal model is an autoregressive (AR) model. This is the standard all-pole filter:

$$y(n) = \sum_{k=1}^{p} a(k)y(n-k) + x(n).$$

For most stochastic signal models, the input, $x(n)$, is assumed to be white noise with variance $\sigma_n^2$. For 1-D signals, it is usually assumed to be zero mean as well. This means that the estimate of the output,

$$\hat{y}(n) = \sum_{k=1}^{p} a(k)y(n-k),$$

differs from the actual $y(n)$ by a noise term. The quantity $\hat{y}(n)$ is a predictor of the actual signal based on the last $p$ values of the signal. This model is appropriate for $p$th order *Markov processes*. It is frequently used because of its ease of computation and analysis.

The AR model can be written in the $z$-domain as

$$Y(z) = \frac{X(z)}{1 - \sum_{k=1}^{p} a(k)z^{-k}} = \frac{X(z)}{A_p(z)}. \tag{C.3}$$

The filter, $A_p(z)$ is known as a *whitening filter*, since when applied to the signal $y(n)$ the result is white noise, $x(n)$, that is, the result is an FIR filter,

$$X(z) = Y(z)A_p(z) \longleftrightarrow x(n) = \sum_{k=0}^{p} a(k)y(n-k),$$

where $a(0) = 1$.

The power spectrum of the signal is given by

$$P_{yy}(\omega) = \left. \frac{\sigma_n^2}{A_p(z)A_p(z^{-1})} \right|_{z=e^{j\omega}}. \tag{C.4}$$

This is easily computed by using the discrete Fourier transform. This is useful in the estimation of the power spectra for restoration methods of Section 14.1.

## C.7.4        Identification of AR models

The identification of the AR model coefficients reduces to solving a least squares problem

$$\min_{a(k)} \quad E\left\{ \left[ y(n) - \sum_{k=1}^{p} a(k)y(n-k) \right]^2 \right\}.$$

Taking the derivatives with respect to $a(l)$ and setting the result equal to zero yields the system of equations for $l = 1, \dots, p$,

$$-2E\{y(n)y(n-l)\} + 2\sum_{k=1}^{p} a(k)E\{y(n-l)y(n-k)\} = 0.$$

Since $y(n)$ is a stationary random process, we have

$$\sum_{k=1}^{p} a(k)r_{yy}(l-k) = r_{yy}(l).$$

This can be written using matrices as

$$\mathbf{Ra} = \mathbf{r},$$

where $\mathbf{R}$ is a $p \times p$ Toeplitz matrix. Note that since $\mathbf{R}$ is an autocorrelation matrix, it is also *positive definite*.

## C.7.5        Maximum entropy extension of $r_{yy}(m)$

Using the model

$$y(n) = \sum_{k=1}^{p} a(k)y(n-k) + x(n),$$

multiplying by $y(n-m)$ on both sides, and taking the expected value, we obtain

$$E\{y(n)y(n-m)\} = \sum_{k=1}^{p} a(k)E\{y(n-k)y(n-m)\} + E\{x(n)y(n-m)\}.$$

This can be written

$$r_{yy}(m) = \sum_{k=1}^{p} a(k) r_{yy}(m-k),$$

if $m > 0$, since the noise is uncorrelated with previous output and input. This relation gives the extension of the autocorrelation for all indices. This is sometimes used to extrapolate the autocorrelation function when it has been estimated from a finite number of samples. It can be shown (obviously not here) that this extension is the estimate of the autocorrelation that maximizes the entropy,

$$H = \frac{1}{2\pi} \int_{-\pi}^{\pi} \log[P_{yy}(\omega)] d\omega,$$

where $P_{yy}(\omega)$ is the Fourier transform of $r_{yy}(m)$. A heuristic interpretation is that the estimate is the "most random" process that is consistent with the $p$ estimated values of the autocorrelation.

## C.7.6 Problems with AR, MA and ARMA model identification

Note that adding noise to an AR system produces an ARMA system,

$$s(n) = y(n) + w(n),$$

which can be written in the $z$-domain as

$$S(z) = \frac{X(z)}{A_p(z)} + W(z) = \frac{X(z) + A_p(z)W(z)}{A_p(z)}.$$

The recursive relation for an ARMA(p,q) system defined by

$$y(n) = \sum_{k=1}^{p} a(k) y(n-k) + \sum_{k=0}^{q} b(k) x(n-k)$$

is given by

$$r_{yy}(m) = \begin{cases} \sum_{k=1}^{p} a(k) r_{yy}(m-k) & \text{if } m > q, \\ \sum_{k=1}^{p} a(k) r_{yy}(m-k) - \sum_{k=0}^{q} b(k) r_{xy}(m-k) & \text{if } 0 \le m \le q, \\ r_{yy}(-m) & \text{if } m < 0. \end{cases}$$

The obvious solution is to estimate $r_{yy}(m)$ for indices greater than $q$ and solve the first system for the AR coefficients, then substitute those values into the second system and solve for the MA coefficients.

The problem is one of signal-to-noise ratio (SNR). The magnitude of $r_{yy}(m)$ usually decreases rapidly, and so estimates for longer lags are much poorer than those for shorter lags. The resulting estimates for the AR coefficients are in error and this error results in poor estimates for the MA terms.

The computed error for any AR or MA process is monotonic decreasing with increasing order. Since the model can never predict the current sample exactly, the error is controlled by the white noise input. The common methods of estimating the model order depend on the variance of the error approaching the variance of the noise. When the error power stops decreasing rapidly as the order increases and starts to level off, the model order is thought to be reached. Determining exactly when this happens is the subject of many papers. A method that works for most practical problems is still awaited.

## C.8 Two-dimensional stochastic image models

The major difference in the 1-D and 2-D models is that the concept of *causality* cannot be naturally extended from one to two dimensions. The mathematical methods are virtually identical. It is also more difficult to keep track of indices.

The general form of the 2-D linear predictor is

$$y(m,n) = \sum_{(k,l) \in S_x} a(k,l)y(m-k,n-l) + \varepsilon(m,n), \tag{C.5}$$

where $a(k,l)$ are the prediction coefficients, $S_x$ is a subset of indices in the 2-D lattice that defines the *prediction region* and $\varepsilon(m,n)$ is the prediction error. The graphical representation of the prediction regions is shown in Fig. 7.18.

### C.8.1 Causal prediction

The region for causal prediction is obtained from an analogy to a scanning sequence. We define the set of indices used to predict the pixel at location $(m,n)$ in Eq. (C.5) by

$$S_1 = \{l \geq 1, \forall k\} \cup \{l = 0, k \geq 1\}.$$

This is also known as the *nonsymmetric half plane*. A subset of this region would be the quarter plane, which results in a *strongly causal* predictor. Note that, in practice, only a finite subset of the prediction region is used, e.g.,

$$W_1 = \{1 \leq l \leq q, \ -p \leq k \leq p\} \cup \{l = 0, \ 1 \leq k \leq p\}.$$

### C.8.2 Semicausal prediction

The *semicausal predictor* is causal in one index and noncausal in the other. A typical prediction region is given by

$$S_2 = \{l \geq 1, \forall k\} \cup \{l = 0, k \neq 0\}.$$

### C.8.3 Noncausal prediction

The noncausal predictor can be a function of all indices except the index that is predicted.

$$S_3 = \{\forall (k,l) \neq (0,0)\}.$$

## C.9 Determining prediction coefficients

### C.9.1 Minimum variance prediction

Estimating the coefficients for an AR model can be written as a typical least squares minimization problem,

$$\min_{a(k,l)} \epsilon^2(m,n) = E\left\{\left[y(m,n) - \sum_{(k,l)\in S_x} a(k,l)y(m-k,n-l)\right]^2\right\}.$$

The region of support, $S_x$, will be assumed to be limited to a finite number of terms. The solution is obtained by differentiating $\epsilon^2(m,n)$ with respect to $a(k,l)$, and setting the result equal to zero or by using the orthogonality principle directly. Since $(k,l)$ is used for the index of the summation, we will denote the differentiation with respect to $a(p,q)$ as

$$\frac{\partial \epsilon^2(m,n)}{\partial a(p,q)} = 2E\left\{\left[y(m,n) - \sum_{(k,l)\in S_x} a(k,l)y(m-k,n-l)\right]y(m-p,n-q)\right\}$$

$$\text{for } (p,q) \in S_x.$$

Setting this result to zero, we have

$$E\left\{\left[y(m,n) - \sum_{(k,l)\in S_x} a(k,l)y(m-k,n-l)\right]y(m-p,n-q)\right\} = 0,$$

$$\text{for } (p,q) \in S_x, \qquad \text{(C.6)}$$

which is a realization of the *orthogonality principle*, that is, the prediction error is orthogonal to the data on which the prediction is based. The result looks like Eq. (7.36), except for the $\beta\delta(p,q)$ term and the range of $(p,q)$. Gathering terms, we have

$$\sum_{(k,l)\in S_x} a(k,l)E\{y(m-k,n-l)y(m-p,n-q)\} = E\{y(m,n)y(m-p,n-q)\},$$

$$\text{for } (p,q) \in S_x.$$

Using the definition of autocorrelation for a stationary process,

$$r_{yy}(p,q) = E\{y(m,n)y(m-p,n-q)\},$$

we obtain the equation

$$\sum_{(k,l)\in S_x} a(k,l)r_{yy}(p-k,q-l) = r_{yy}(p,q).$$

It is common to write the prediction as

$$y(m,n) = -\sum_{(k,l)\in S_x} a(k,l)y(m-k,n-l),$$

or the prediction error as

$$\epsilon(m,n) = \sum_{(k,l)\in W_x} a(k,l)y(m-k,n-l),$$

where $(k,l) \in W_x = S_x \cup (0,0)$ and $a(0,0) = 1$. This allows us to add the $(p,q) = (0,0)$ term to $S_x$ in Eq. (C.6).

The autocorrelation of the error is defined by

$$r_{\epsilon\epsilon}(p,q) = E\{\epsilon(m,n)\epsilon(p-m,q-n)\},$$

which can be rewritten

$$r_{\epsilon\epsilon}(p,q) = E\left\{\left[y(m,n) - \sum_{(k,l)\in S_x} a(k,l)y(m-k,n-l)\right]\right.$$
$$\left.\left[y(p-m,q-n) - \sum_{(k,l)\in S_x} a(k,l)y(p-m-k,q-n-l)\right]\right\}. \quad \text{(C.7)}$$

This can be decomposed into parts to which the orthogonality principle can be applied, since we are dealing with the solution to that problem. We have

$$r_{\epsilon\epsilon}(p,q) = E\left\{\left[y(m,n) - \sum_{(k,l)\in S_x} a(k,l)y(m-k,n-l)\right]y(p-m,q-n)\right\}$$
$$- \sum_{(k,l)\in S_x} a(k,l)E\left\{\left[y(m,n) - \sum_{(k,l)\in S_x} a(k,l)y(m-k,n-l)\right]\right.$$
$$\left.y(p-m-k,q-n-l)\right\}, \quad \text{(C.8)}$$

which can be rewritten making the error terms explicit,

$$r_{\epsilon\epsilon}(p,q) = E\{\epsilon(m,n)y(p-m,q-n)\}$$
$$- \sum_{(k,l)\in S_x} a(k,l)E\{\epsilon(m,n)y(p-m-k,q-n-l)\}. \quad \text{(C.9)}$$

At this point, all terms except $(p, q) = (0, 0)$ are zero because of the orthogonality principle, and we have

$$r_{\epsilon\epsilon}(p, q) = \beta\delta(p, q). \tag{C.10}$$

The AR image generation model can be written as in Eq. (7.35),

$$y(m, n) = \sum_{(k,l)\in S_x} a(k, l)y(m - k, n - l) + w(m, n), \tag{C.11}$$

where $w(m, n)$ is white noise input with variance $\beta^2$. We can also represent the output as the convolution of the impulse response, $h(m, n)$, and the input noise,

$$y(m, n) = \sum_{(k,l)\in Q_x} h(k, l)w(m - k, n - l), \tag{C.12}$$

where $Q_x$ is the infinite set of causal indices for the equivalent system. Writing this in the $z$-transform domain, we have from Eq. (C.12),

$$Y(z_1, z_2) = H(z_1, z_2)W(z_1, z_2),$$

and from Eq. (C.11),

$$Y(z_1, z_2) = \frac{W(z_1, z_2)}{A(z_1, z_2)},$$

which is the 2-D equivalent of Eq. (C.3). Using the relations between autocorrelations and power spectra of shift-invariant systems of Section C.6, we can obtain the $z$-transform representation of the spectrum of the output,

$$S_{yy}(z_1, z_2) = \frac{\beta^2}{A(z_1, z_2)A(z_1^{-1}, z_2^{-1})}, \tag{C.13}$$

where the 2-D filter of the input noise is represented by

$$H(z_1, z_2) = \frac{1}{A(z_1, z_2)} = \left[1 - \sum_{(m,n)\in S_x} a(m, n)z_1^{-m}z_2^{-n}\right]^{-1}.$$

The equation for the power spectrum yields the useful AR estimation in the discrete frequency domain by substituting $z = e^{j\omega}$, as is done for the 1-D model of Eq. (C.4). This continuous spectrum may be easily sampled by use of the DFT. This was done for the examples of Fig. 7.19.

## C.9.2     Stability

For most image processing purposes, stability of the image model is not critical, since we are processing a limited number of pixels for any image. A 1-D time signal can continue for long intervals, and stability is an important property of such models. The common requirement of absolute convergence of the impulse response (point spread function) is sufficient to guarantee stability

$$\sum_{m=-\infty}^{\infty} \sum_{n=-\infty}^{\infty} |h(m,n)| < \infty.$$

For a causal system, the system represented in the nonsymmetric half plane by

$$A(z_1, z_2) = 1 - \sum_{m=1}^{p} a(m,0)z_1^{-m} - \sum_{m=-p}^{p} \sum_{n=1}^{q} a(m,n)z_1^{-m}z_2^{-n}$$

is stable iff

$$A(z_1, z_2) \neq 0, \quad |z_1| \geq 1 \quad and \quad z_2 = \infty,$$
$$A(z_1, z_2) \neq 0, \quad |z_1| = 1 \quad and \quad z_2 \geq 1.$$

Remember that 2-D polynomials are not necessarily factorable. Thus, there is no 2-D equivalent to the 1-D criterion that all poles lie inside the unit circle.

## C.10     Spectral factorization of 2-D models

Unlike 1-D polynomials, which always have real or complex factors, 2-D polynomials cannot usually be factored to yield real or complex roots. We require additional assumptions. One of the most common is separability of the autocorrelation or equivalently, the spectrum. If

$$r(m,n) = r_x(m)r_y(n),$$

then

$$P(u,v) = P_x(u)P_y(v),$$

and 1-D models can be used that are guaranteed to be factorable. Using the causal models in one dimension results in a strictly causal model in two dimensions.

### C.10.1     Solving for finite $a(m,n)$

The basic equation for a finite prediction region, $S_x$ is

$$r_{yy}(m,n) - \sum_{(k,l) \in S_x} a(k,l)r_{yy}(m-k,n-l) = 0.$$

It is noted that the set of indices needed for the correlation function is usually larger than that of the AR coefficients. For example, if

$$W_x = \{(1,0),(0,1),(1,1),(-1,1)\},$$

then the set of autocorrelation values that are needed for the above equation is

$$\{r(0,0), r(1,-1), r(0,-1), r(2,-1), r(-1,1), r(-1,0), r(1,0),$$
$$r(0,1), r(2,0), r(-2,1), r(-2,0)\}.$$

The symmetry of the autocorrelation can be used to reduce the number of distinct values. In any case, there are more distinct indices than in the prediction region. Thus, the correlations generated by the model may not match the correlations used to generate the model. This also means that the same MVR predictors can be generated by different correlation functions. This model is used to compute the power spectral estimates for the example in Section 7.4.2.

## C.10.2 High resolution spectral estimation

The AR model has the same advantage in 2-D as it does in 1-D, in that it is possible to obtain improved separation of frequency components over the Fourier transform based methods. Heuristically, this is the result of fitting a few parameters with a large number of samples (see [134] Example 6.13 pp. 218–19).

# D    Multidimensional look-up tables

## D.1    Introduction

A look-up table (LUT) is basically a function from one space to another that is defined in terms of a few samples, their corresponding function values, and a method to calculate any particular mapping from those samples. Mathematically, the LUT is defined as $\mathcal{L}[\{(\mathbf{x}_k, f(\mathbf{x}_k))\}, \mathcal{I}(\mathbf{x})]$, where $\{\mathbf{x}_k\}$ are the samples in the domain space, $\{f(\mathbf{x}_k)\}$ are the corresponding function values in the range space, and $\mathcal{I}(\mathbf{x})$ is the function, or algorithm, that is used to compute the value in the range space for an arbitrary point in the domain space, $\mathbf{x}$. The function $\mathcal{I}(\mathbf{x})$ interpolates the output if the point $x$ is within the convex hull of the sample set $\{\mathbf{x}_k\}$, and extrapolates the output if it is not.

Look-up tables are a simple and computationally efficient way to generate nonlinear and nonparametric functions. Because of their efficiency and ease of implementation, look-up tables are often used to compute standard functions, such as sinusoids and exponentials. The accuracy of the tabularized function depends upon the resolution of the table. The key to the efficiency is that the interpolation between elements in the table is simple and fast. This means that accuracy depends on the resolution of the table, rather than the approximation of the interpolation to an ideal functional form.

Multidimensional look-up tables (MLUTs) have been used for color space transformations for several years [11, 121, 138, 220, 234, 257]. MLUTs have been used in embedded systems of printers, copiers, multifunction peripherals (MFPs), cameras and scanners. In addition, they are used in ICC profiles and postscript color rendering dictionaries. Because of their commonality, we will review the mathematics of their use, as well as the major issues in their design.

In this appendix, we will first review the notation that we will need to describe the tables and the interpolation methods. Next, we will give the details of one simple interpolation method that can be used with any MLUT. Finally, we will describe how to create MLUTs for characterizing (see Chapter 12) input and output devices.

## D.2    Mathematics of MLUTs

Here we will focus on look-up tables that correspond to a uniform grid in the color space. The points on the grid can be considered samples. Tables with nonuniform sampling along each axis are discussed in [3, 45]. While a nonuniformly sampled table can provide a better approximation with fewer samples, they are rarely used in embedded systems owing to the complexity of the interpolation computations, and are not currently allowed in the ICC format.

## D.2.1 Sample points

Let the true mapping between the $M$-dimensional color space $C$ and the $N$-dimensional color space $D$ be given by $\mathcal{F}(\cdot)$, where, as in Chapter 12, we write $\mathcal{F}: C \to D$, which denotes

$$\mathcal{F}(\mathbf{c}) = \mathbf{d} \in D, \tag{D.1}$$

for $\mathbf{c} \in C$. Our goal is to approximate this mapping with an MLUT, $\mathcal{L}: C \to D$.

For simplicity, and to consider only cases of interest, let us assume that the elements of the vectors in $C$ range from 0 to $P$, that is, the vector $\mathbf{c} = [c_1, c_2, \ldots, c_M]$ has the property that $0 \leq c_i \leq P$. The input dimension $M$ would be three for RGB or CMY devices and four for CMYK printers. If we let $R$ be the number of samples in each dimension, then for each sample input vector, there is a corresponding $N$-dimensional output vector. Thus, there are $N$ entries in the MLUT for each of the $R^M$ possible input combinations. This yields a total of $NR^M$ entries. For ease of notation, let us assume that $M = 3$. In this case, the entries for a uniformly sampled MLUT, which approximates the mapping $\mathcal{F}$ are the values

$$\mathcal{F}(\mathbf{c}_{i,j,k}) = \mathbf{d}_{i,j,k}, \quad i,j,k \in \{0, \ldots, R-1\}, \tag{D.2}$$

where

$$\mathbf{c}_{i,j,k} = P \left[ \frac{i}{R-1}, \frac{j}{R-1}, \frac{k}{R-1} \right]. \tag{D.3}$$

The approximation of a value $\mathcal{F}(\mathbf{c})$, where $\mathbf{c}$ is not on a sample point, is calculated by an interpolation method. Two common MLUT interpolation methods are trilinear interpolation and tetrahedral interpolation. For ease of discussion later, let us define a function $\mathcal{H}$, which takes table indices as input and provides the table value at that location as output. The function $\mathcal{H}(\cdot)$ is represented by

$$\mathcal{H}([i,j,k]) = \mathbf{d}_{i,j,k} \quad i,j,k \in \{0, \ldots, R-1\}. \tag{D.4}$$

As an example, consider an MLUT where $P = 255$ and $R = 17$. For this sampling step size, the sample values at the grid points are given by

$$\{0, \ 15.9375, \ 31.875, \ 47.8125, \ 63.75, \ 79.6875, \ 95.625$$
$$111.5625, \ 127.5, \ 143.4375, \ 159.375, \ 175.3125$$
$$191.25, \ 207.1875, \ 223.125, \ 239.0625, \ 255\}.$$

In this case, the value of the table at location $[i, j, k] = [14, 6, 5]$ is denoted by

$$\mathcal{H}([14, 6, 5]) = \mathcal{F}([223.125, 95.625, 79.6875]), \tag{D.5}$$

which is the device output for an input of $[223.125, 95.625, 79.6875]$. Note that having float sample points is the defined method for MLUTs in the ICC profile format [129, pp. 51, 55]. In practice, the actual table is often created using rounded values, which in the above example are given by

{0, 16, 32, 48, 64, 80, 96, 112, 128, 143, 159, 175, 191, 207, 223, 239, 255}.

This rounding introduces a nonuniformly sampled table by one count in the middle of the table. In the above example, all the sample values are 16 steps apart except when going from 128 to 143.

## D.3      Interpolation

Given an arbitrary value $\mathbf{c} \in C$, the problem is to use the MLUT to approximate the value $\mathcal{F}(\mathbf{c})$. The first step is to determine which samples in the MLUT to use for the interpolation. Since the trilinear method uses all eight points of the cube around the point to be computed, it is easy to determine the appropriate samples using simple indexing. Other, more complex methods, like tetrahedral interpolation, use fewer samples, but require more computation to locate the best ones. The approximation using trilinear interpolation consists of three steps:

- Determining the cube that contains the point $\mathbf{c}$, which we will refer to as the cube index. The index $[I, J, K]$ defines the cube with vertices

$$C_{[I,J,K]} = \{[I, J, K], [I + 1, J, K], [I, J + 1, K], [I, J, K + 1], [I + 1, J + 1, K],$$
$$[I + 1, J, K + 1], [I, J + 1, K + 1], [I + 1, J + 1, K + 1]\}; \tag{D.6}$$

- Determining the subindexing or weight values within the cube;
- Computing the interpolation.

### D.3.1      Finding the cube index

Since $M = 3$, the MLUT consists of $(R - 1)^3$ cubes. Mathematically, the root index, $\mathbf{d} = [d_1, d_2, d_3] = [I, J, K]$, of the cube containing the value $\mathbf{c} = [c_1, c_2, c_3]$ can be determined using

$$d_i = \text{FLOOR}\left\{\frac{c_i(R - 1)}{P},\right\} \quad \text{for} \quad c_i < P, \quad i = 1, 2, 3, \tag{D.7}$$

$$= R - 2 \quad\quad\quad\quad\quad\quad \text{for} \quad c_i = P.$$

Note that the elements of $[I, J, K]$ are in the range 0 to $R - 2$.

Given this root index, it is possible to determine the table values that will be used in the trilinear interpolation. If the root index is given by the values $[I, J, K] < R - 1$, then the set of eight table values that are used in the calculation is given by

$$\mathcal{H}_{[I,J,K]} = \{\mathcal{H}([I, J, K]), \mathcal{H}([I + 1, J, K), \mathcal{H}([I, J + 1, K]),$$
$$\mathcal{H}([I, J, K + 1]), \mathcal{H}([I + 1, J + 1, K]), \mathcal{H}([I + 1, J, K + 1]),$$
$$\mathcal{H}([I, J + 1, K + 1]), \mathcal{H}([I + 1, J + 1, K + 1])\}. \tag{D.8}$$

### D.3.2    Finding subindices and weights

In addition to the above table values, the trilinear interpolation computation requires subindices into the cube along each of the three dimensions to determine how much weight to give each of the eight table values in a summation. Assuming that float values were used to create the table, the exact subindices are given by the elements of the vector,

$$\mathbf{s} = \mathbf{c} - \mathbf{c}_{I,J,K}, \tag{D.9}$$

and the weights are given by products of the elements of the vectors

$$\mathbf{w} = \frac{\mathbf{s}(R - 1)}{P}, \tag{D.10}$$

$$\mathbf{v} = 1 - \mathbf{w}. \tag{D.11}$$

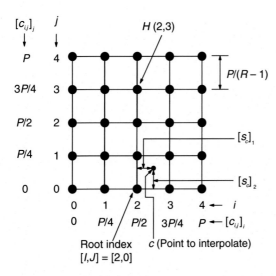

**Figure D.1.** Graphical illustration of 2-D MLUT indexing for interpolation; in this example, $R = 5$.

Note that the elements of **w** and **v** are in the range [0, 1]. Figure D.1 displays a graphic of these quantities when indexing in a 2-D MLUT.

In practice, the values **w** and **v** are not usually computed directly with floating point arithmetic. Instead, 1-D look-up tables are used, or bit AND and bit shift methods are used. These methods are discussed in [12, 297].

### D.3.3     Interpolation methods

In the case of trilinear interpolation, for $\mathbf{v} = [v_1, v_2, v_3]$ and $\mathbf{w} = [w_1, w_2, w_3]$, the interpolated value is computed as

$$
\begin{aligned}
\mathcal{I}(\mathbf{c}) = \mathbf{t} = \; & \mathcal{H}([I, J, K]) v_1 v_2 v_3 \\
& + \mathcal{H}([I + 1, J, K]) w_1 v_2 v_3 \\
& + \mathcal{H}([I, J + 1, K]) v_1 w_2 v_3 \\
& + \mathcal{H}([I, J, K + 1]) v_1 v_2 w_3 \\
& + \mathcal{H}([I + 1, J + 1, K]) w_1 w_2 v_3 \\
& + \mathcal{H}([I + 1, J, K + 1]) w_1 v_2 w_3 \\
& + \mathcal{H}([I, J + 1, K + 1]) v_1 w_2 w_3 \\
& + \mathcal{H}([I + 1, J + 1, K + 1]) w_1 w_2 w_3.
\end{aligned}
\tag{D.12}
$$

Tetrahedral interpolation and other methods, such as prism and pyramid interpolation, reduce the number of points used in the interpolation calculation, i.e., Eq. (D.12), by dividing the cube containing the vector **c** into subsections. In the case of tetrahedral interpolation, an additional test consisting of three comparisons is required to determine what subsection contains the vector **c**. Each subsection uses only four points to compute an interpolation as opposed to the eight points used in the trilinear interpolation. See [138] for additional details. The weights for these methods are computed based on the relative distances of the interpolated point to the vertices.

For all of these interpolation methods, the indexing into the table is performed identically to that of the trilinear interpolation example described in the above section. The difference occurs after this indexing process with the introduction of a sequence of subindex comparisons and a computationally simpler replacement for Eq. (D.12).

There are several acceleration methods for MLUT interpolation discussed in [12, Section 11.4]. These methods are designed to reduce the computational cost of indexing, as well as the interpolation in Eq. (D.12). One approach is to make use of a cache or hash coding method to avoid recomputing recently computed values. For an embedded system, it would be necessary to consider the trade-off of the cost of increased memory required by these methods versus the reduction in computational cost. The size of the cache, the statistics of the image data and the hash coding function will greatly affect the efficiency of these methods.

Another class of acceleration methods discussed in [12] takes advantage of the spatial frequency sensitivity properties of the human visual system (HVS) (see Appendix E).

Since the human visual system is less sensitive to high frequency chrominance errors than to luminance errors, methods that save computations at the cost of introducing high frequency chrominance errors are of interest. To work efficiently, these methods require the input color space to be a luminance or chrominance type such as YCrCb, Kodak YCC, or CIELAB. Embedded systems that process images for Color FAX (CIELAB) or JPEG images (YCC) may use MLUTs that have such a property. Color copy operation in multifunction peripherals (MFPs) will typically transform the scanner RGB data to the printer CMY(K) space. In this case, it is not a straightforward process to take advantage of these acceleration techniques.

---

**Example D.1.** Let us return to our earlier example where $P = 255$ and $R = 17$. Now consider a particular RGB input point given by $\mathbf{c} = [230,\ 100,\ 95]$. The root cube index is computed using Eq. (D.7) giving

$$[I, J, K] = [14,\ 6,\ 5],$$

which, using Eq. (D.3), is the table sample value $\mathbf{c}_{14,\,6,\,5} = [223.1250,\ 95.6250,\ 79.6875]$. The subindexes are given by Eq. (D.9), which gives

$$\mathbf{s} = [6.8750,\ 4.3750,\ 15.3125],$$

and from Eqs. (D.10) and (D.11), the weights for the interpolation are computed from various products of the values

$$\mathbf{w} = [0.4314,\ 0.2745,\ 0.9608]$$

$$\mathbf{v} = [0.5686,\ 0.7255,\ 0.0392].$$

These values would be substituted into Eq. (D.12) to obtain the output $\mathcal{I}(\mathbf{c})$.

---

# D.4 Creation of input device MLUTs

To create an MLUT for a 3-band input device, our goal is first to create pairs $\{(\mathbf{c}_r, \mathcal{H}(\mathbf{c}_r))\}$ for $r = 1, \ldots, R^3$, where $\mathbf{c}_r$ is a sample point in the $R \times R \times R$ grid in the device space, and $\mathcal{H}(\mathbf{c}_r)$ is its corresponding vector in the output color space. Once the grid is populated, the interpolation method, $\mathcal{I}$, can be selected. We begin with a target that has known values in a device-independent (DI) color space. Care should be taken in generating or choosing the target. The target should adequately span the range of the input device and provide good coverage of the gamut. Figure D.2 displays the Kodak Q60 scanner characterization target, which was adopted as a standard for the printing industry [8]. Figure D.3a displays the distribution of the Q60 colors in a device-dependent scanner color space. In this case, the target was scanned with a CIS scanner (see Section 10.1), and

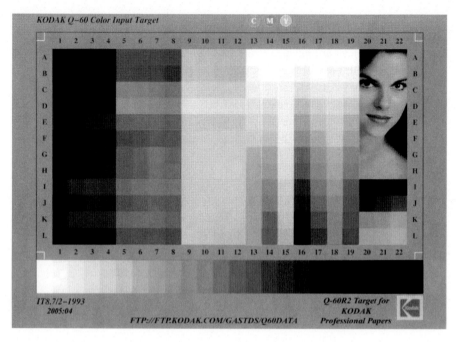

**Figure D.2.** Kodak Q60 color target; (for color version, please see Plate 30).

the pixels in each color square in the target were averaged to compute one of the points in the figure. To simplify visualization, let us reduce the problem to two dimensions by considering only the red and green components. In this case, the distribution of scanned values is shown in Fig. D.3b. Overlayed upon this distribution is a 2-D MLUT that represents the grid points, $\{c_r\}$, needed to create our MLUT. In the case of the scanner, we wish to have the table uniformly sampled in RGB color space on the $R \times R \times R$ grid with a CIELAB vector, or other device-independent color space vector, $\mathcal{H}(c_r)$, at each table entry.

There are basically two cases for grid points that we must consider: grid points that are within a convex hull of scanned values and those that are not. Determination of grid points that are outside the convex hull requires extrapolation, rather than interpolation. Figure D.4 indicates examples of such grid points on our 2-D illustration. There are a number of methods that can be used to perform the extrapolation. These include artificial neural nets, polynomial fits and locally linear mappings that use a linear extrapolation of nearby scanned values. These same methods or tetrahedral interpolation can be used for the grid points that are within a convex hull of scanned values. The interpolation method used to create the MLUT does not need to be the same as the method, $\mathcal{I}$, used to implement the MLUT. As shown in Fig. D.4, when using interpolation methods, it is necessary to determine what local scanned values should be used, since there may exist many choices. The decision is usually based upon a combination of the distance of the scanned values from the grid point, as well as the volume of the enclosing convex

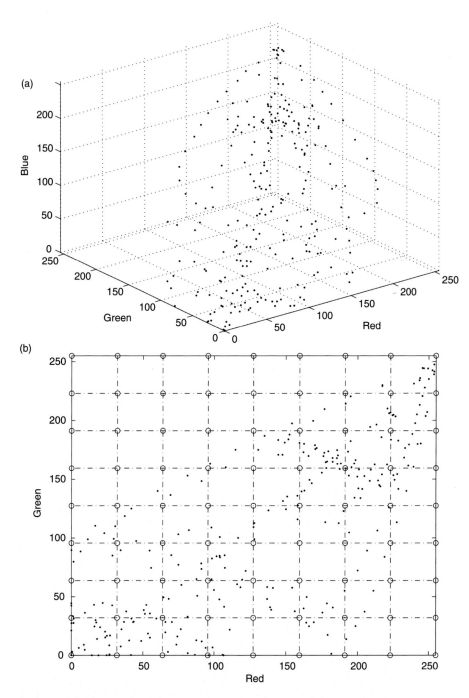

**Figure D.3.** (a) Distribution of Q60 colors in the RGB scanner color space; (b) projection of distribution of Q60 colors in RGB scanner color space onto the red–green color plane; each Q60 scanned value is denoted by a dot in the plot; the sample points of the grid for the MLUT are shown as circles on the uniform grid.

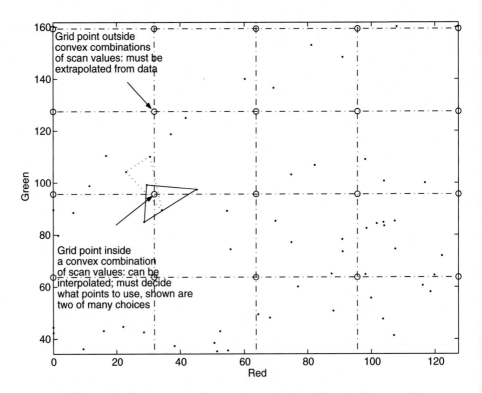

**Figure D.4.** Figure showing a grid point that must be extrapolated from the data, as well as one that can be interpolated: note that the interpolated point can be interpolated using a number of possible different scan values; alternatively, a large number of samples can be used and an estimation problem posed to compute the grid point.

region. The volume of the region is a necessary consideration, since it is important to avoid nearly co-planar samples that cause instability in the interpolation.

Note in Fig. D.3b that large regions within the convex hull of the scanner RGB color space have no measurement values from the target. The values that are interpolated in such regions may have greater error because of the sample spacing. Regions outside the convex hull must be extrapolated.

## D.5     Creation of output device MLUTs

In the case of output devices, the control values that are sent to the device are easily generated to create a uniform grid. To simplify notation, let us assume that the output device is a 3-band system, e.g., RGB or CMY. We produce the output by varying the control values, $\{\mathbf{c} = [i, j, k]\}$, over an $N \times N \times N$ grid to produce corresponding output vectors, $\{\mathcal{H}([i, j, k])\}$. This automatically provides an MLUT that can be used for a mapping from control values to a device-independent color space, usually CIELAB. This mapping is often referred to as the *forward mapping*, $\mathcal{F}: \Omega_{\text{device}} \rightarrow \Omega_{\text{CIE}}$. The

Gamut of device

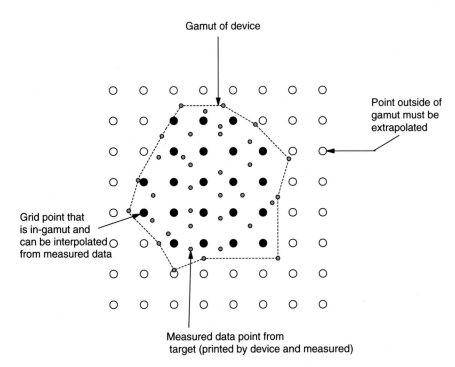

Point outside of
gamut must be
extrapolated

Grid point that
is in-gamut and
can be interpolated
from measured data

Measured data point from
target (printed by device and measured)

**Figure D.5.** The large circles represent the grid points; the small circles represent the measured data produced by the output device; the black grid points are in-gamut of the device and possible to interpolate from the measured data; the white grid points are outside the gamut of the device and must be extrapolated from the measured data; this extrapolation amounts to defining a gamut mapping since it describes what to print when a color outside the gamut is desired.

problem for the output device is creating the inverse of this mapping, that is, given a CIELAB value, $\mathbf{d}$, finding the control value, $\mathbf{c}$, that will cause the device to produce that CIELAB value at the output. This mapping is often referred to as the *inverse mapping*, $\mathcal{F}^{-1}: \Omega_{\mathrm{CIE}} \rightarrow \Omega_{\mathrm{device}}$. In this case, the inverse mapping MLUT is uniformly sampled in CIELAB color space, and each grid point contains a RGB or CMY control value.

It is possible to approach the problem in the same fashion used in the input device problem. That is, look at the distribution of CIELAB values created by the printer, and interpolate the grid points. The extrapolation of grid points that are outside the distribution of colors defines a gamut mapping for the device. This is shown in Fig. D.5, where it is clear that points outside the gamut must be extrapolated from the data. When a color that is outside the gamut is specified to be produced by the output device, these grid points that have been extrapolated will be used along with an interpolation method to compute the color that will be printed. Hence, these points define the gamut mapping.

Depending upon the shape of the gamut in the space in which the table is indexed and the selection of colors that are printed and measured, it is possible that some in-gamut grid points may need to be extrapolated from the data. To illustrate the problem, an example is shown in Fig. D.6 where the gamut that arises from the measured data

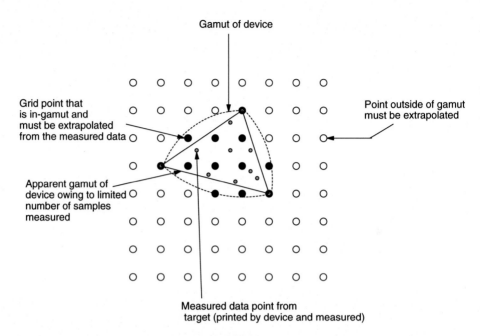

**Figure D.6.** The large circles represent the grid points; the small circles represent the measured data produced by the output device; the black grid points are in-gamut of the device, but in this case not every one can be interpolated from the measured data; the solid line represents the gamut as it appears from the measured data; points outside this boundary will need to be extrapolated.

is shown with the actual gamut of the device. As additional samples are measured, the size of this "measured gamut" will increase and eventually match the true gamut of the device.

Recall that the goal of building an output device MLUT is to find, for every vector, **d**, on an $R \times R \times R$ grid in the output color space, the corresponding control vector, **c**, in the device input space. To do this, we will need to find control values in our measured $N \times N \times N$ grid that produce vectors close to the sample **d**. Since the forward mapping is known from the measurements, we need to find the cube in the input space that contains the control vector that will produce **d**. Using the concept of root index introduced previously, $C_{[i,j,k]}$ of Eq. (D.6) defines the vertices of the cube indexed by $[i, j, k]$ and $\mathcal{H}_{[i,j,k]}$ of Eq. (D.8) defines the corresponding output vectors.

The forward mapping is defined by a collection of samples and an interpolation method, $\mathcal{I}(\cdot)$. Given a cubic collection of table indices $C_{[i,j,k]}$ and a control value **z** that is within that cube, the MLUT interpolated CIELAB value will be determined by the function

$$\mathcal{I}(\mathbf{z}, C_{[i,j,k]}, \mathcal{H}_{[i,j,k]}, \text{RANGE}(\mathbf{z})), \tag{D.13}$$

where RANGE(**z**) returns the minimum and maximum values possible for **z**, and the interpolation function $\mathcal{I}(\cdot)$ can be any desired multidimension interpolation function, e.g., trilinear, tetrahedral, pyramid, etc. [138].

Using the above notation, the construction of the inverse MLUT table $\mathcal{F}^{-1}$ is performed as follows:

- Select an arbitrary grid point **d** (a CIELAB value) of the $R^3$ points that we wish to fill. The goal is to determine what control value should be associated with that CIELAB grid point.
- Of the $N^3$ CIELAB values that were measured, find the closest one to **d** in terms of Euclidean distance ($\Delta E_{ab}^*$ distance), i.e., find

$$[I,J,K] = \arg(\min_{i,j,k} ||\mathcal{H}([i,j,k]) - \mathbf{d}||^2), \tag{D.14}$$

where $i,j,k \in [0,1,...,(N-1)]$.
- For the indices $[I,J,K]$ determine the eight (or fewer if an edge point) cubes that surround the point in the $N \times N \times N$ notation of the data. Assuming that $1 < I,J,K < N-2$, these eight cubes would consist of the cubes $C_{[I-1,J-1,K-1]}$, $C_{[I-1,J-1,K]}$, $C_{[I-1,J,K-1]}$, $C_{[I,J-1,K-1]}$, $C_{[I,J,K-1]}$, $C_{[I,J-1,K]}$, $C_{[I-1,J,K]}$, $C_{[I,J,K]}$. For ease of notation, denote these eight cubes simply as $C_l$, $l = 1,...,8$.
- For each cube, solve the following optimization problem:

$$\mathbf{z}_{\text{optim},l} = \arg(\min_{\mathbf{z}} ||\mathbf{d} - \mathcal{I}(\mathbf{z}, C_l, \mathcal{H}_l, \text{RANGE}(\mathbf{z}))||^2), \tag{D.15}$$

using a nonlinear optimization method.
- If the RGB vector $\mathbf{z}_{\text{optim},l}$ is within the cube $C_l$, then stop the optimizations and fill the grid point **d** that we are trying to fill with the RGB value $\mathbf{z}_{\text{optim},l}$. The test to determine if the point is within the cube is easily done by comparing $\mathbf{z}_{\text{optim},l}$ with the RGB grid points in $C_l$.
- If the RGB vectors $\mathbf{z}_{\text{optim},l}$ are all outside of their respective cubes, then the CIELAB value **d** is outside of the printer gamut; in other words, the printer cannot create that color. In this case, the following optimization problems are solved:

$$\delta e(l) = (\min_{\mathbf{z}} ||\mathbf{d} - \mathcal{I}(\mathbf{z}, C_l, \mathcal{H}_l, \text{RANGE}(\mathbf{z}))||^2),$$

for $l = 1,...,8$ with the constraint that the RGB vector **z** must remain in the cube $C_l$. The optimal constrained arguments $\mathbf{z}_{\text{outgamut},l}$ are saved with each computation. Once the $\delta e(l)$ values are determined and the minimum error

$$L = \arg(\min_l \delta e(l))$$

is found, the gamut mapped RGB vector $\mathbf{z}_{\text{outgamut},L}$ is placed in the grid point **d**.

Note that many different approaches to gamut mapping could be used in the above algorithm. The choice of the color space in which the table is indexed will affect the simplicity of the calculation for computing the actual grid point value that is out of gamut. For example, if CIELAB is the grid space, then as discussed in Section 12.3.10, a common gamut mapping is to map along lines of constant hue and lightness. This calculation is rather straightforward once the in-gamut grid points are determined. If the indexing color space is sRGB or a device-dependent color space, the computation of the out-of-gamut grid points is not as simple. One approach in this case is to create a gamut mapping in CIELAB and use this mapping for the creation of the table that is indexed in sRGB.

For example, consider the problem of creating a table that is indexed in scanner RGB space and provides printer CMY values as output. The best approach to creating such a table would be to create a mapping from scanner RGB to CIELAB and a mapping from CIELAB to CMY. These two mappings are then combined to create one mapping from scanner RGB to CMY. In this approach, the approximate uniformity of the CIELAB color space can be used to advantage when dealing with colors that are outside the gamut of the printer, and outside the range of colors that are in the scanner target.

# E     Psychovisual properties

In many cases, the human observer is the final judge of the quality of a recorded and reproduced image. The perceived quality is dependent upon the expectations and needs of the viewer, as well as the properties of the human visual system (HVS). Algorithms and devices should be designed using knowledge of the limitations of the human visual system. Such algorithms and devices typically run faster, use less bandwidth and cost less than a device designed with little thought regarding the human observer. In this appendix, we will review many of the characteristics of the human visual system that are useful when designing algorithms and devices for image recording and reproduction. For an in-depth look at this topic see [300].

The human visual system is a highly nonlinear, adaptive system making it very difficult to model completely. As with most systems, linear models can offer a level of approximation that is sufficiently close and significantly more tractable. One approach to model the human visual system is to divide it into a number of subsystems. One such division is given by:

- Optical elements, including lens and pupil aperture,
- Sensing elements, consisting of cones and rods,
- Processing elements, consisting of interconnected neurons in the eye and the visual cortex.

Let us look at each system individually.

## E.1     Optical system

The optical elements of the human visual system are shown in Fig. E.1. The image is focused onto the retina by the lens. The lens shape is altered by the attached ciliary muscle and zonule ligaments, which change the shape of the lens and hence bring objects at various distances into focus. As we age, the range of focus decreases, which results in the need for bifocals. Since the visual system consists of a single lens, only one wavelength of light can be in exact focus. This can cause interesting visual effects such as a red object being in focus, but near a blurry blue object, making the blue object appear to be farther away. Plate 31 (see figure E.2) displays an example of an image that can be used to demonstrate this effect. View the image as close as is comfortable. To the observer, it should appear that the red letters are closer than the blue letters.

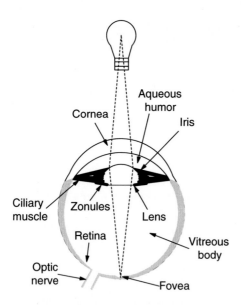

**Figure E.1.** Optical elements of human eye.

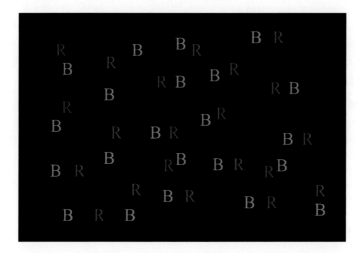

**Figure E.2.** The colored version of this image can be used to demonstrate an effect caused by the fact that the human visual system is a single lense system and can only focus one wavelength exactly: when viewed closely, it should appear that the red letters are closer than the blue letters even though they are in the same spatial plane (for color version, please see Plate 31).

As with any optical system, the optical system of the HVS has spatial resolution limitations. These limitations are caused by two factors. One is imperfections in the lens itself, the other is diffraction due to the size of the aperture. The pupil or aperture size is controlled by the iris. The size of the pupil can vary from about 1 mm in a bright environment to about 7 mm in a dark environment. At 7 mm, the primary source of blur

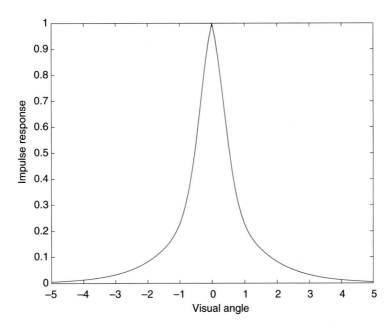

**Figure E.3.** Cross section of HVS point spread function for 3 mm wide pupil: note that the abscissa is in degrees and the maximum value of the point spread function is normalized to one.

is due to imperfections in the lens and cornea. At 1mm, diffraction is a significant source of blur in the optical system [300]. Figure E.3 displays the typical optical point spread function for the human visual system with a 3 mm pupil, where we assume circular symmetry. The modulation transfer function is shown in Fig. 8.1.

## E.2 Sensing elements

The light that passes through the pupil is focused onto the retina, which contains the sensing elements. The rods are the sensors that give rise to our low-light vision. Since all the rods have the same spectral sensitivity, they cannot provide any color information about the sensed radiation. The rods are distributed over a large area of the retina and extremely sensitive. Multiple rods are tied to a single neuron, which greatly limits the spatial resolution of low-light vision, but improves sensitivity.

In bright light, the rods are saturated and the cones are the primary sensing elements. There are three types of cones, each with its own spectral sensitivity. This variation gives rise to the phenomenon of color. The relative spectral sensitivity of the three types of cones, referred to as L, M, and S for long, medium and short wavelengths are shown in Fig. 8.8. The cones are unevenly distributed in the retina, with a large number in a small region defined as the fovea, where we can focus most acutely. Unlike the rods, each cone is connected to multiple neurons, implying that significant processing is performed early in the visual system.

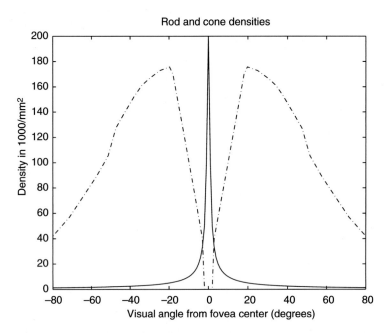

**Figure E.4.** Density of rods (dashed) and cones (solid) on surface of retina: figure is roughly based upon Figure 3.1 of [300] and Figure 12.5 of [160].

Figure E.4 displays the spatial density of the cones and rods on the retina. The distribution of the different cone types is of significance. In particular, there are no S type cones in the fovea. In other areas of the retina, there are far fewer S cone types than there are L and M cone types. Figure E.5 displays an example distribution of cones outside the fovea. A hypothesis for insensitivity to blue-yellow variations is that the optical system has already introduced a blur in the short wavelengths owing to chromatic aberration, and hence a lower spatial sampling rate is optimal for the short wavelengths compared with the spatial sampling rate for the longer wavelengths. In any event, this variation in spatial sampling rate as a function of wavelength greatly affects the ability of the human visual system to detect certain color stimuli and is used to advantage in the design of digital imaging systems and methods. The variation in the distribution of cones is one of the reasons for needing both the 2° and 10° color matching functions (see Section 8.3.2).

## E.3    Processing elements

While a discussion of neural processing is beyond the planned scope of this book, this is a significant contributor to what we "see." The property that each cone feeds multiple neurons leads to significant initial processing of the visual signal to extract edge information, perform motion detection, extract color and luminance information.

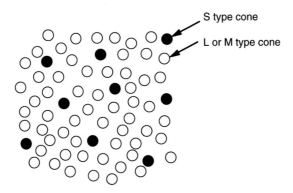

S type cone

L or M type cone

**Figure E.5.** Example of sampling distribution of cones outside fovea.

So significant is the neural processing that it led Edwin H. Land[1] to question the usefulness of the color matching functions in defining color as well as the trichromatic nature of the human visual system [300, p 287].

Many optical illusion images are designed to exploit such neural processing and adaptation. For example, the apparent brightness of a gray tone or color patch depends on the gray tone or color surrounding the patch. The visual system adapts to the average of the area in the field of view. In addition, the responses of the rods and cones can be changed by fatigue. *After images* are an effect of this fatigue.

Plate 32 (see Fig. E.6) can be used to demonstrate neural fatigue. The observer should stare at the yellow cross for 10 to 15 seconds and then look at the white square. An after image appears, which is the inverse of the original image. In this case, the observer will see a blue cross on a yellow square.

Plate 33 (see Fig. E.7) can be used to demonstrate *simultaneous contrast*. In this case, the red squares are spectrally the same, but appear significantly different owing to the surrounding color. The source of the phenomena is termed lateral inhibition and occurs from one area inducing an inhibitory response on an adjacent area.

Finally, Fig. E.8 displays an image that induces an interesting visual effect that is neural processing. This effect is still not completely understood. As the observer views the image, black dots fill in the white circles in regions that are not focused upon the fovea. As the observer's eyes scan the picture, the black spots disappear in regions imaged upon the fovea, giving a flickering effect. This type of image is called a Hermann grid [160]. The effect was studied at least as early as 1870 [110].

Studies have shown that the neural processing in the human visual system encodes the color image in an *opponent-color* format. Roughly, the opponent-color signals can be considered as a luminance or gray scale component (L), a red/green component (R-G), and a blue/yellow component (B-Y). The (R-G) and (B-Y) channels are referred to as the

---

[1] Edwin H. Land was the inventor of instant developing film and founder of the Polaroid Corporation. He also conceived and produced the first modern filters to polarize light.

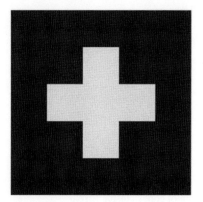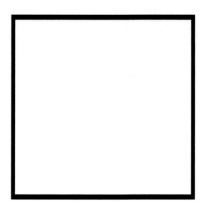

**Figure E.6.** Figure that can be used to demonstrate the effects of neural fatigue: stare at the yellow cross for 10 to 15 seconds and then stare at the white square; an "after image" of a blue cross in a yellow square will appear (for color version, please see Plate 32).

**Figure E.7.** Example of the effects of simultaneous contrast: spectrally the red areas are the same, but the areas on the right appear to be more yellow (for color version, please see Plate 33).

chrominance channels. This encoding becomes important in experiments to characterize the color spatial frequency characteristics of the human visual system.

## E.4    Mathematical modeling

There are a number of models that have been proposed for modeling both monochromatic and color visual effects. Closely related to creating a model for the human visual system

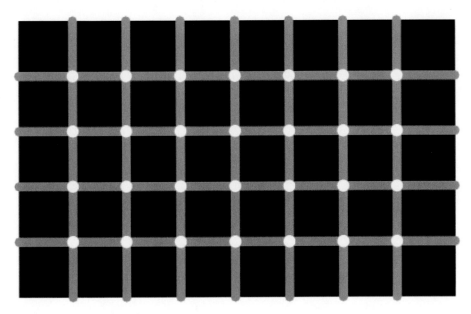

**Figure E.8.** The scintillating grid: as the observer's eyes scan the picture, the black spots disappear in regions imaged upon the fovea, giving a flickering effect.

is the problem of quantifying the visual difference between two images. Such a measure can be used to develop algorithms that display minimal processing distortions.

### E.4.1      Weber's law

Weber's law is a general statement of "just noticeable differences." If the intensity value of $I_0$ is just noticeably (perceptually) different from $I$, Weber's law states that

$$\frac{|I - I_0|}{I} = \frac{dI}{I} = \text{constant.} \tag{E.1}$$

This holds for colors, luminances, sounds, weights, etc. For luminances, the constant is about 0.02, which indicates that a minimum of 50 discrete gray levels are required for good representation of black and white images. Note that because of the adaptive properties of the eye, more gray levels are required for the display of large, high quality images.

A log-like function is often used to represent perceived luminance. In other words, perceived luminance for an intensity of $I$ is of the form

$$c(I) = \log(I). \tag{E.2}$$

Differentiating $c(I)$ with respect to $I$ results in

$$\frac{dc(I)}{dI} = \frac{1}{I}, \tag{E.3}$$

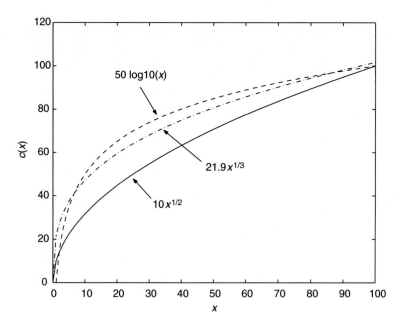

**Figure E.9.** Comparison of eye sensitivity models.

which implies that the change in perceived luminance is given by

$$dc(I) = \frac{dI}{I}, \tag{E.4}$$

which, from Weber's law, is a constant.

While the log function is often used for normal light conditions, it is not a popular model for low light level conditions owing to the singularity at zero. In many cases, the root law model is used,

$$c(I) = \alpha_1 I^p, \tag{E.5}$$

where $p = 1/2$ and $p = 1/3$ are popular models. These functions approximate the log function and eliminate the singularity problem, as shown in Fig. E.9. The $1/3$ nonlinearity in the mapping from CIEXYZ to CIELAB arises from Weber's law.

### E.4.2    Spatial-color properties and opponent color spaces

As mentioned earlier, the finite aperture of the optical system of the eye limits the bandwidth of the signal that is passed to the brain. This optical effect will result in a low pass filtering of visual images. Chapter 8 covered the basics of the frequency response or resolution of the human visual system for the case of monochrome imaging.

Color image models are significantly more complex. There have been a number of experiments to determine the spatial frequency response of the human visual system as a

**Figure E.10.** An example of a frequency pattern in the blue–yellow direction at a constant luminance (for color version, please see Plate 34).

function of color [214, 219]. These experiments often have the viewer adjust the contrast at which a frequency pattern becomes visible or invisible. The frequency patterns are commonly displayed on a monitor at various orientations for various color patterns. An example of one such pattern is shown in Fig. E.10. In this figure, the luminance is constant and there is a frequency pattern in a blue-yellow direction.[2] With this process, it is possible to develop a color/spatial frequency model of the human visual system. Obviously, viewing conditions are critical in an experiment such as this. A special viewing environment is required to assure that the modulated color presented is all that reaches the eye. As with the monochrome case, images can be created that display the MTF of the human visual system. Figure E.11 displays one such image in the blue color region, modulating towards yellow. In this case, the image is a constant luminance, but the magnitude of variation in the blue-yellow direction increases along the vertical axis.[3] The frequency of the variation increases along the horizontal axis.

As mentioned, studies have shown that the neural processing in the human visual system encodes the color image in an opponent-color type of format. Almost every model of the human visual system performs some encoding of the colorimetric signals in this fashion. The blue-yellow (B-Y) channel relies heavily on the S cone. As such, it

[2] While every attempt was made to maintain constant luminance, the process of printing the image for the text and the viewing illumination will introduce some color distortions. The constant luminance sRGB image for viewing on a monitor is available at the text's website (www.cambridge.org/9780521868532). To ensure visibility in the printed version, we have modulated in the blue-yellow direction well beyond the point of being just noticeable.

[3] Again, due to printing limitations, the image on the text's website may be better suited for viewing.

**Figure E.11.** Demonstration of MTF of eye in blue region modulating towards yellow: spatial frequency varies on horizontal axis, magnitude of variation in a blue–yellow direction varies along the vertical axis, and the image is constant luminance (for color version, please see Plate 35).

can be sampled at a much lower sampling rate than for the other channels. Visual studies have shown that the red-green (R-G) channel can also be spatially sampled at a lower rate than for the luminance channel. This property of the HVS is heavily exploited by a variety of algorithms and devices. Example devices include color television, which uses less bandwidth for the chrominance channels than for the luminance channel, and digital cameras, which use Bayer color filter arrays (see Fig. 10.13) to sample the green wavelengths at a higher rate than the red and blue wavelengths. Processing methods that exploit this property include [167] for temporal noise reduction, [15] for computational improvements on color correction, [78] for color halftoning and, of course, color image and video compression methods, like JPEG and MPEG [182, 212].

Essentially, the algorithms can take advantage of this property of the human visual system by either reducing the amount of data that is handled through subsampling the chrominance channels or by using simpler computations, which may introduce errors in spatial-color areas that are difficult to see. Essentially, the goal is to spend the computational resources to reproduce image data that will be observable. The most common method for determining if an algorithm has introduced artifacts is to perform a qualitative visual comparison. To complement this approach, there have been studies on developing image difference metrics to quantify the difference between color images. Work on image quality began early in the history of digital image processing and primarily concentrated on blur and noise effects. More recent work considered coding and halftoning artifacts. Reviews of this work contain most of the references of interest [10, 208, 245, 303]. More recent work that includes color fidelity includes [21, 73, 321, 322].

### E.4.3    sCIELAB

Most color difference metrics, such as CIE $\Delta E_{ab}^*$ and $\Delta E_{94}^*$, were developed for solid patches. These measures fail to take into account the frequency response of the HVS. Zhang and Wandell [321] introduced a color image metric that incorporated the opponent color and spatial filtering characteristics of the human visual system. The measure takes two color images and performs the following operations:

- Transforms each to an opponent color space.
- Spatially filters each channel with filters derived from visual experiments. The support (size) of the spatial filters depends upon the viewing distance and the display resolution.
- Recombines the filtered channels into a color image in CIELAB color space. This color space is approximately uniform, which implies that mean square error is a good indicator of color difference.
- Computes the standard $\Delta E_{ab}^*$ or $\Delta E_{94}^*$ color difference metric between the filtered images.

The new color space, called sCIELAB can provide some quantification of the effectiveness of an algorithm to distribute errors where they are less visible. The details to transform from sRGB to sCIELAB [321] are as follows:

First transform from sRGB to CIEXYZ using Eqs. (8.61) and (8.62). The CIEXYZ values are then transformed to an opponent-type color space via

$$\begin{bmatrix} O_1 \\ O_2 \\ O_3 \end{bmatrix} = \begin{bmatrix} 0.279 & 0.72 & -0.107 \\ -0.449 & 0.29 & -0.077 \\ 0.086 & -0.59 & 0.501 \end{bmatrix} \begin{bmatrix} X \\ Y \\ Z \end{bmatrix}. \tag{E.6}$$

At this point, the opponent color planes are spatially filtered by dimensionally separable filters where

$$Of_i(x, y) = O_i(x, y) * v_i(x) * v_i(y) \quad i = 1, 2, 3, \tag{E.7}$$

where $*$ represents convolution. The $Of_i$ image planes are transformed back to XYZ using the equation

$$\begin{bmatrix} X \\ Y \\ Z \end{bmatrix} = \begin{bmatrix} 0.6266 & -1.8672 & -0.1532 \\ 1.3699 & 0.9348 & 0.4362 \\ 1.5057 & 1.4213 & 2.5360 \end{bmatrix} \begin{bmatrix} Of_1 \\ Of_2 \\ Of_3 \end{bmatrix}, \tag{E.8}$$

and then transformed to CIELAB using the standard CIEXYZ to CIELAB transformation (see Eq. (8.42)) with the appropriate white point. Note that if the image is an sRGB image, the white point is D65. The error metric between two images is computed using the standard CIELAB $\Delta E_{ab}^*$ calculation, i.e., Euclidean distance, and the sCIELAB error is denoted as $\Delta E_s^*$.

The impulse response of the circularly symmetric spatial filters, $v_i(x)$, $\quad i = 1, 2, 3$, depend upon the pixel width of the displayed image, as well as the viewing distance. Typically, display resolution is given in dots/inch (dpi). Assuming an image with $d$ dpi and a viewing distance of $v$ inches, the separable continuous filters are given by[4]

$$v_1(x) = \frac{1}{\beta\sqrt{\pi}} \left( 35.451\, e^{-\left(\frac{x}{0.0283*\beta}\right)^2} + 0.8603\, e^{-\left(\frac{x}{0.133*\beta}\right)^2} \right.$$

$$\left. -0.0271\, e^{-\left(\frac{x}{4.336*\beta}\right)^2} \right),
\tag{E.9}$$

$$v_2(x) = \frac{1}{\beta\sqrt{\pi}} \left( 15.733\, e^{-\left(\frac{x}{0.0392*\beta}\right)^2} + 7.7586\, e^{-\left(\frac{x}{0.0494*\beta}\right)^2} \right),
\tag{E.10}$$

$$v_3(x) = \frac{1}{\beta*\sqrt{\pi}} \left( 10.595\, e^{-\left(\frac{x}{0.0536*\beta}\right)^2} + 11.195\, e^{-\left(\frac{x}{0.0386*\beta}\right)^2} \right),
\tag{E.11}$$

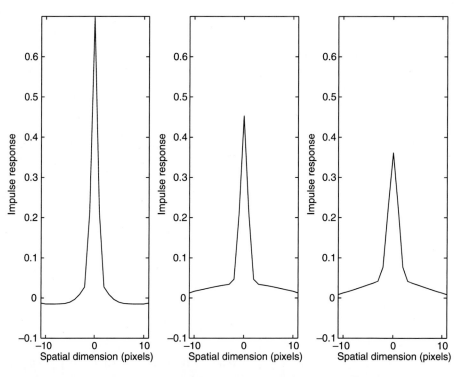

**Figure E.12.** Impulse response of spatial filters used in transformation to sCIELAB space. The resolution is 72 dpi with a viewing distance of 18 inches. The luminance filter $v_1$ will pass more high frequency information compared to the chrominance filters.

---

[4] Note that this formulation is equivalent to that given in [321].

where $\beta$, the ratio samples/degree of the display, is given by

$$\beta = 2vd \tan(\pi/360). \tag{E.12}$$

For digital filtering, the support of the above filters are given by a visual angle of one degree. They are also forced to have an odd number of sample points, denoted by $[-M, ..., 0, ..., M]$, where

$$M = \text{ceil}(\beta/2) - 1. \tag{E.13}$$

Note that if $\beta$ is less than 224, then care must be taken to avoid aliasing. One approach is to oversample the continuous filters, low pass filter these samples, and then subsample to the desired rate. The impulse response of each digital filter should be normalized to unity area. The impulse responses are plotted in Fig. E.12 for a resolution of 72 dpi and a viewing distance of 18 inches, which is typical for monitor viewing conditions.

# References

[1] J. E. Adams, "Interactions between color plane interpolation and other image processing functions in electronic photography," in *Proc. SPIE*, vol. 2416, pp. 144–151, Mar. 1995.

[2] J. E. Adams, "Design of practical color filter array interpolation algorithms for digital cameras," in *Proc. SPIE*, vol. 3028, pp. 117–125, Mar. 1997.

[3] A. U. Agar and J. P. Allebach, "A minimax method for function interpolation using an SLI structure," *Proc. IEEE International Conference on Image Processing*, vol. 1, pp. 671–674, 1997.

[4] F. Aghdasi and R. K. Ward, "Reduction of boundary artifacts in image restoration," *IEEE Transactions on Image Processing*, vol. 5, no. 4, pp. 611–618, Apr. 1996.

[5] R. L. Alfvin and M. D. Fairchild, "Observer variability in metameric color matches using color reproduction media," *Color Research and Application*, vol. 22, no. 3, pp. 174–188, Jun. 1997.

[6] H. Altunbasak and H. J. Trussell, "Colorimetric restoration of digital images," *IEEE Transactions on Image Processing*, vol. 10, no. 3, pp. 393–402, Mar. 2001.

[7] M. Anderson, R. Motta, S. Chandrasekar and M. Stokes, "Proposal for a standard default color space for the internet – sRGB," *Proc. IS&T/SID Fourth Color Imaging Conference*, pp. 238–246, Nov. 1996.

[8] ANSI IT8.7/2-1993, *"Graphic Technology – Color Reflection Target for Input Scanner Calibration,"* 1993.

[9] S. Ardalan and J. Paulos, "An analysis of nonlinear behavior in delta-sigma modulators," *IEEE Transactions on Circuits and Systems*, vol. 34, no. 6, pp. 593–603, Jun. 1987.

[10] I. Avcibas, B. Sankur and K. Sayood, "Statistical evaluation of image quality measures," *Journal of Electronic Imaging*, vol. 11, no. 2, pp. 206–223, Apr. 2002.

[11] R. Bala, "Chapter 5: device characterization," *Digital Color Imaging Handbook*, Boca Raton, CRC Press, 2003.

[12] R. Bala, "Chapter 11: efficient color transformation implementation," *Digital Color Imaging Handbook*, Boca Raton, CRC Press, 2003.

[13] R. Balasubramanian, "A printer model for dot-on-dot halftone screens," in *Proc. SPIE*, vol. 2413, pp. 356–364, Apr. 1995.

[14] R. Balasubramanian, "Colorimetric modeling of binary color printers," *Proc. IEEE International Conference on Image Processing*, vol. 2, pp. 327–330, Nov. 1995.

[15] R. Balasubramanian, "Reducing the cost of lookup table based color transformations," *Proc. IS&T/SID Seventh Color Imaging Conference,* pp. 65–68, Nov. 1999.

[16] F. A. Baqai and J. P. Allebach, "Computer-aided design of clustered-dot color screens based on a human visual system model," *Proceedings of the IEEE*, vol. 90, no. 1, pp. 104–122, Jan. 2002.

[17] H. B. Barlow and J. D. Mollon, *The Senses*, Cambridge, U.K., Cambridge University Press, 1982.

[18] E. Barnes, "Integrated solutions for CCD signal processing," *Analog Dialogue*, Published by Analog Devices, vol. 32, no. 1, pp. 6–8, 1998. www.analog.com/library/analogDialogue/archives/32-1/contents.html.

[19] C. J. Bartleson and F. Grum, *Optical Radiation Measurements*, vol. 3, *Radiometric Measurements*, New York, Academic Press, 1984.

[20] C. J. Bartleson and F. Grum, *Optical Radiation Measurements*, vol. 5, *Visual Measurements*, New York, Academic Press, 1984.

[21] K. H. Bauml, X. Zhang and B. Wandell, "Color spaces and metrics," in *Vision Models and Applications to Image and Video Processing*, C. J. van den Branden Lambrecht, ed., Kluwer Academic Pub., 2001.

[22] B. E. Bayer, "Color imaging array," U.S. Patent 3,971,065, 1976.

[23] C. S. Bell, "Contrast-based autofocus mechanism," U.S. Patent 5,170,202, 1992.

[24] A. R. Robertson and J. F. Fisher, "Color vision, representation and reproduction," in *Television Engineering Handbook*, K. B. Benson and J. Whitaker, eds., McGraw-Hill, 1992, (see page 2.32).

[25] R. S. Berns, R. J. Motta and M. E. Gorzynski, "CRT colorimetry. part I: theory and practice," *Color Research and Application*, vol. 18, no. 5, pp. 299–314, Oct. 1993.

[26] R. S. Berns, M. E. Gorzynski and R. J. Motta, "CRT colorimetry. part II: metrology," *Color Research and Application*, vol. 18, no. 5, pp. 315–325, Oct. 1993.

[27] R. S. Berns, "Spectral modeling of a dye diffusion thermal transfer printer," *Journal of Electronic Imaging*, vol. 2, no. 4, pp 359–370, Oct. 1993.

[28] F. W. Billmeyer, "Survey of color order systems," *Color Research and Application*, vol. 12, no. 4, pp. 173–186, Aug. 1987.

[29] T. Blu, P. Thevenaz and M. Unser, "How a simple shift can significantly improve the performance of linear interpolation," *Proc. IEEE International Conference on Image Processing*, vol. 3, pp. 377–380, 2002.

[30] B. P. Bogert, M. J. R. Healy and J. W. Tukey, "The quefrency alanysis of time series for echoes: cepstrum, psuedo-autocovariance, cross-cepstrum and saphe cracking," *Proceedings of the Symposium on Time Series Analysis*, M. Rosenblat, ed., NY, Wiley, pp. 209–243, 1963.

[31] C. F. Borges, "Trichromatic approximation method for surface illumination," *Journal of the Optical Society of America*, A, vol. 8, no. 8, pp. 1319–1323, 1991.

[32] A. C. Bovik (ed.), *Handbook of Image and Video Processing*, 2nd edn., Academic Press, 2005.

[33] R. N. Bracewell, *Two-Dimensional Imaging*, Englewood Cliffs, NJ, Prentice-Hall, 1995.

[34] D. H. Brainard, "Calibration of a computer controlled color monitor," *Color Research and Application*, vol. 14, no. 1, pp. 23–34, Feb. 1989.

[35] K. M. Braun, R. Balasubramanian and R. Eschbach, "Development and evaluation of six gamut-mapping algorithms for pictorial images," *Proc. IS&T/SID Seventh Color Imaging Conference*, pp. 144–148, Nov. 1999.

[36] K. M. Braun, R. Balasubramanian and S. J. Harrington, "Gamut-mapping techniques for business graphics," *Proc. IS&T/SID Seventh Color Imaging Conference*, pp. 149–154, Nov. 1999.

[37] L. M. Bregman, "The method of successive projection for finding a common point of convex sets," *Doklady Akademiia Nauk SSSR*, vol. 162, pp. 487–490, 1965. (English translation in *Soviet Mathematics – Doklady*, vol. 6, no. 3, pp. 688–692, 1965.)

[38] E. O. Brigham, *The Fast Fourier Transform*, Prentice-Hall, 1974.

[39] K. Buckley, "Selecting an analog front end for imaging applications," *Analog Dialogue*, Published by Analog Devices, vol. 34, no. 6, pp. 40–44, 2000. www.analog.com/library/analogDialogue/archives/34-06/imaging/index.html.

[40] D. E. Bugner, "A review of electrographic printing," *Journal of Imaging Science*, vol. 35, no. 6, pp. 377–387, Dec. 1991.

[41] S. A. Burns, J. B. Cohen and E. N. Kuznetsov, "Multiple metamers: preserving color matches under diverse illuminants," *Color Research and Application*, vol. 14, no. 1, pp. 16–22, Feb. 1989.

[42] W. G. Carrara, R. M. Majewski and R. S. Goodman, *Spotlight Synthetic Aperture Radar: Signal Processing Algorithms,* Artech House Publishers, 1995.

[43] M. A. Cayless and A. M. Marsden (eds.), *Lamps and Lighting*, 3rd edn., London, Edward Arnold, 1983.

[44] Y. H. Chan and Y. H. Fung, "A regularized constrained iterative restoration algorithm for restoring color-quantized images," *Signal Processing*, vol. 85, no. 7, pp. 1375–1387, Jul. 2005.

[45] J. Z. Chang, J. P. Allebach and C. A. Bouman, "Sequential linear interpolation of multidimensional functions," *IEEE Transactions on Image Processing*, vol. 6, no. 9, pp. 1231–1245, Sep. 1997.

[46] E. Chang, S. Cheung and D. Pan, "Color filter array recovery using a threshold-based variable number of gradients," in *Proc. SPIE*, vol. 3650, pp. 36–43, 1999.

[47] CIE Publication 63, *Spectroradiometric Measurement of Light Sources*, CIE Central Bureau, 1984.

[48] CIE Publication 15.2, *Colorimetry*, CIE Central Bureau, 1986.

[49] CIE, "Industrial colour difference evaluation," Technical Report 116–1995, 1995.

[50] CIE, "Improvement to industrial colour-difference evaluation," CIE Publication no. 142–2001, Central Bureau of the CIE, Vienna, 2001.

[51] J. B. Cohen, "Dependency of the spectral reflectance curves of the Munsell color chips," *Psychonometric Science*, vol. 1, pp. 369–370, 1964.

[52] J. B. Cohen and W. E. Kappauf, "Metameric color stimuli, fundamental metamers, and Wyszecki's metameric blacks," *American Journal of Psychology*, vol. 95, no. 4, pp. 537–564, Winter 1982.

[53] J. B. Cohen and W. E. Kappauf, "Color mixture and fundamental metamers: theory, algebra, geometry, application," *American Journal of Psychology*, vol. 98, no. 2, pp. 171–259, Summer 1985.

[54] J. B. Cohen, "Color and color mixture: scalar and vector fundamentals," *Color Research and Application*, vol. 13, no. 1, pp. 5–39, Feb. 1988.

[55] P. L. Combettes and H. J. Trussell, "Set theoretic estimation by random search," *IEEE Transactions on Signal Processing*, vol. 39, no. 7, pp. 1669–1671, Jul. 1991.

[56] P. L. Combettes, "The foundations of set theoretic estimation," *Proceedings of the IEEE*, vol. 81, no. 2, pp. 182–208, Feb. 1993.

[57] P. L. Combettes, "Convex set theoretic image recovery by extrapolated iterations of parallel subgradient projections," *IEEE Transactions on Image Processing*, vol. 6, no. 4, pp. 493–506, Apr. 1997.

[58] J. N. Cook, P. A. Sample and R. N. Weinreb, "Solution to spatial inhomogeneity on video monitors," *Color Research and Application*, vol. 18, no. 5, pp. 334–340, Oct. 1993.

[59] P. C. Cosman, K. L. Oehler, E. A. Riskin and R. M. Gray, "Using vector quantization for image processing," *Proceedings of the IEEE*, vol. 81, no. 9, pp. 1326–1341, Sep. 1993.

[60] W. B. Cowan, "An inexpensive scheme for calibration of a color monitor in terms of standard CIE coordinates," *ACM SIGGRAPH Computer Graphics*, vol. 17, no. 3, pp. 315–321, Jul. 1983.

[61] W. B. Cowan and N. Rowell, "On the gun independency and phosphor constancy of colour video monitors," *Color Research and Application*, vol. 11, S34–S38, Supplement, 1986.

[62] G. P. Crawford, "A bright new page in portable displays," *IEEE Spectrum*, vol. 37, no. 10, pp. 40–46, Oct. 2000.

[63] J. C. Curlander and R. N. McDonough, *Synthetic Aperture Radar*, John Wiley and Sons, 1991.

[64] N. Dantera-Venkata, B. L. Evans and V. Monga, "Color error-diffusion halftoning," *IEEE Signal Processing Magazine*, vol. 20, no. 4, pp. 51–58, Jul. 2003.

[65] W. E. R. Davies and G. Wyszecki, "Physical approximation of color-mixture functions," *Journal of the Optical Society of America*, vol. 52, no. 6, pp. 679–685, Jun. 1962.

[66] S. G. deGroot and J. W. Gebhard, "Pupil size as determined by adapting luminance," *Journal of the Optical Society of America*, vol. 42, no. 7, pp. 492–495, 1952.

[67] *Digital Visual Interface DVI*, Digital Display Working Group, Revision 1.0, Apr. 1999, www.ddwg.org/.

[68] D. E. Dudgeon and R. M. Mersereau, *Multidimensional Digital Signal Processing*, Prentice-Hall, 1984.

[69] F. Ebner and M. D. Fairchild, "Gamut mapping from below: finding minimum perceptual distances for colors outside the gamut volume," *Color Research and Application*, vol. 22, no. 6, pp. 402–413, Dec. 1997.

[70] P. G. Engeldrum, "Almost color mixture function," *Journal of Imaging Technology*, vol. 14, no. 4, pp. 108–110, Aug. 1988.

[71] R. Eschbach, "Reduction of artifacts in error diffusion by means of input-dependent weights," *Journal of Electronic Imaging*, vol. 2, no. 4, pp. 352–358, Oct. 1993.

[72] M. D. Fairchild, "Refinement of the RLAB color space," *Color Research and Application*, vol. 21, pp. 338–346, Oct. 1996.

[73] M. D. Fairchild and G. M. Johnson, "iCAM framework for image appearance, differences and quality," *Journal of Electronic Imaging*, vol. 13, no. 1, pp. 126–138, Jan. 2004.

[74] M. D. Fairchild, *Color Appearance Models*, 2nd edn., Chichester, UK, Wiley, 2005.

[75] V. Falletti, A. Premoli and M. L. Rastello, "Optical glass filters: an algorithm for optimal design," *Applied Optics*, vol. 21, no. 23, pp. 4345–4350, Dec. 1982.

[76] Z. Fan and S. Harrington, "Improved quantization methods in color error diffusion," *Journal of Electronic Imaging*, vol. 8, no. 4, pp. 430–438, Oct. 1999.

[77] J. E. Farrell and J. M. Booth, *Design Handbook for Imagery*, Seattle, WA, Boeing Aerospace Company, 1975 (see pp. 3.2–56).

[78] T. J. Flohr, B. W. Kolpatzik, R. Balasubramanian *et al.*, "Model-based color image quantization," in *Proc. SPIE*, vol. 1913, pp. 270–281, Sep. 1993.

[79] R. W. Floyd and L. Steinberg, "An adaptive algorithm for spatial gray scale," *Digest of SID International Symposium*, Los Angeles, pp. 36–37, 1975.

[80] S. Forrest, P. Burrows and M. Thompson, "The dawn of organic electronics," *IEEE Spectrum*, vol. 37, no. 8, pp. 29–34, Aug. 2000.

[81] See Foveon website for information on latest technology. www.foveon.com.

[82] Y. H. Fung and Y. H. Chan, "POCS-based algorithm for restoring colour-quantised images," *IEE Proceedings – Vision, Image and Signal Processing*, vol. 151, no. 2, pp. 119–127, Apr. 2004.

[83] B. Furht, S. W. Smoliar and Z. H. Zhang, *Video and Image Processing in Multimedia Systems,* Kluwer Academic Publishers, 1995.

[84] N. P. Galatsanos and R. T. Chin, "Digital restoration of multichannel images," *IEEE Transactions on Acoustics, Speech and Signal Processing*, vol. 37, no. 3, pp. 415–421, Mar. 1989.

[85] N. P. Galatsanos, A. K. Katsaggelos, R. T. Chin and A. D. Hillery, "Least squares restoration of multichannel images," *IEEE Transactions on Signal Processing*, vol. 39, no. 10, pp. 2222–2236, Oct. 1991.

[86] R. S. Gentile, E. Walowit and J. P. Allebach, "A comparison of techniques for color gamut mismatch compensation," *Journal of Imaging Techology*, vol. 16, pp. 176–181, 1990.

[87] E. J. Giorgianni and T. E. Madden, *Digital Color Management*, Reading, Mass., Addison-Wesley, 1998.

[88] J. W. Glotzbach, R. W. Schafer and K. Illgner, "A method of color filter array interpolation with alias cancellation properties," *Proc. IEEE International Conference on Image Processing*, vol. 1, pp. 141–144, 2001.

[89] K. R. L. Godfrey and Y. Attikiouzel, "Polar backpropagation – determining the chromaticity of a light source," *International Neural Network Conference*, Paris, INNS and IEEE, Jul. 9–13, 1990.

[90] J. R. Goldschneider, E. A. Riskin and P. W. Wong, "Embedded multilevel error diffusion," *IEEE Transactions on Image Processing*, vol. 6, no. 7, pp. 956–964, Jul. 1997.

[91] G. H. Golub and C. F. Van Loan, "An analysis of the total least squares problem," *SIAM Journal on Numerical Analysis*, vol. 17, no. 6, pp. 883–893, 1980.

[92] J. W. Goodman, *Introduction to Fourier Optics*, 3rd edn., Roberts and Company, 2005.

[93] H. G. Graßmann, "Zur Theorie der Farbenmischung," *Poggendorffs Annalen der Physik und Chemie*, vol. 89, pp. 69–84, 1853.

[94] H. Grassmann, "On the theory of compound colours," *Philosophical Magazine*, vol. 7, no. 4, pp. 254–264, 1854.

[95] R. M. Gray and L. D. Davisson, *Random Processes: a Mathematical Approach for Engineers,* Prentice-Hall, 1986.

[96] B. Grob and C. Herndon, *Basic Television and Video Systems*, New York, NY, McGraw-Hill, 1999.

[97] L. G. Gubin, B. T. Polyak and E. V. Raik, "The method of projections for finding the common point of convex sets," *Zhurnal Vychislitel'noi Matematiki i Matematicheskoi Fiziki*, vol. 7, no. 6, pp. 1211–1228, 1967. (English translation in *USSR Computational Mathematics and Mathematical Physics*, vol. 7, no. 6, pp. 1–24, 1967).

[98] B. K. Gunturk, Y. Altunbasak and R. M. Mersereau, "Color plane interpolation using alternating projections," *IEEE Transactions on Image Processing*, vol. 11, no. 9, pp. 997–1013, Sep. 2002.

[99] B. K. Guntruk, J. Glotzbach, Y. Altunbasak, R. W. Schafer and R. M. Mesereau, "Demosaicking: color plane interpolation in digital cameras," *IEEE Signal Processing Magazine*, vol. 22, no. 1, pp. 44–54, Jan. 2005.

[100] Y. P. Guo, H. P. Lee and C. L. Teo, "Multichannel image restoration using an iterative algorithm in space domain," *Image and Vision Computing*, vol. 14, no. 6, pp. 389–400, 1996.

[101] R. W. Hamming, *Numerical Methods for Scientists and Engineers*, McGraw-Hill, 1973.

[102] H. Haneishi, T. Hirao, A. Shimazu and Y. Mikaye, "Colorimetric precision in scanner calibration using matrices," in *Proc. Third IS&T/SID Color Imaging Conference*, pp. 106–108, Nov. 1995.

[103] R. A. Hann and N. C. Beck, "Dye diffusion thermal transfer (D2C2) color printing," *Journal of Imaging Technology*, vol. 16, no. 12, pp. 238–241, Dec. 1990.

[104] J. Y. Hardeberg and F. Schmitt, "Color printer characterization using a computational geometry approach," *Proc. IS&T/SID Fifth Color Imaging Conference*, pp. 96–99, Nov. 1997.

[105] J. Y. Hardeberg, "Acquisition and reproduction of colour images: colorimetric and multispectral approaches," Ph.D. thesis, Ecole Nationale Supérieure des Télécommunications, Jan. 1999.

[106] S. Haykin, *Adaptive Filter Theory*, 4th edn., 2002, Englewood Cliffs, NJ, Prentice Hall.

[107] S. Haykin and B. Van Veen, *Signals and Systems,* Wiley, 2003.

[108] D. A. Hays, "The evolution of color xerographic development systems," *Journal of Imaging Science*, vol. 17, no. 6, pp. 252–258, Dec. 1991.

[109] C. W. Helstrom, *Probability and Stochastic Processes for Engineers,* Macmillan, 1984.

[110] L. Hermann, "Eine Erscheinung simultanen Contrastes," *Pflügers archiv fur die gasamte Physiologie*, vol. 3, pp. 13–15, 1870.

[111] R. H. Hibbard, "Apparatus and method for adaptively interpolating a full color image utilizing luminance gradients," U.S. Patent 5,382,976, 1995.

[112] S. M. Highnote and G. W. Flint, "Extending the gamut: microlaser-based display technology," *Proc. IS&T/SID Fifth Color Imaging Conference*, pp. 41–43, Nov. 1997.

[113] K. Hirakawa and T. W. Parks, "Adaptive homogeneity-directed demosaicing algorithm," *IEEE Transactions on Image Processing*, vol. 14, no. 3, pp. 360–369, Mar. 2005.

[114] J. Ho, B. Funt and M. S. Drew, "Separating a color signal into illumination and surface reflectance components: theory and applications," *IEEE Transactions on Pattern Analysis and Machine Intelligence*, vol. 12, no. 10, pp. 966–977, Oct. 1990.

[115] P. G. Hoel, S. C. Port and C. J. Stone, *Introduction to Probability Theory*, Boston, Houghton Miffin Company, 1971.

[116] R. Holub, W. Kearsley and C. Pearson, "Color systems calibration for graphic arts: II. output devices," *Journal of Imaging Technology*, vol. 14, no. 2, pp. 53–60, Apr. 1988.

[117] R. Holub, C. Pearson and W. Kearsley, "The black printer," *Journal of Imaging Technology*, vol. 15, no. 4, pp. 149–158, Aug. 1989.

[118] B. K. P. Horn, "Exact reproduction of colored images," *Computer Vision, Graphics and Image Processing*, vol. 26, no. 2, pp 135–167, 1984.

[119] T. Hoshino and R. S. Berns, "Color gamut mapping techniques for color hard copy images," in *Proc. SPIE,* vol. 1909, pp. 152–165, Aug. 1993.

[120] R. E. Hufnagel and N. R. Stanley, "Modulation transfer function associated with image transmission through turbulent media," *Journal of the Optical Society of America*, vol. 54, no. 1, pp. 52–61, Jan. 1964.

[121] P. C. Hung, "Colorimetric calibration in electronic imaging devices using a look-up table model and interpolations," *Journal of Electronic Imaging*, vol. 2, no. 1, pp. 53–61, Jan. 1993.

[122] P. Hung and R. S. Berns, "Determination of constant hue loci for a CRT gamut and their predictions using color appearance spaces," *Color Research and Application*, vol. 20, no. 5, pp. 285–295, Oct. 1995.

[123] B. R. Hunt and J. R. Breedlove, "Scan and display considerations in processing images by digital computer," *IEEE Transactions on Computers*, vol. 24, no. 8, pp. 848–853, Aug. 1975.

[124] B. R. Hunt and O. Kubler, "Karhunen-Loeve multispectral image restoration. Part 1: theory," *IEEE Transactions on Acoustics, Speech and Signal Processing*, vol. 32, no. 3, pp. 592–600, Jun. 1984.

[125] R. W. G. Hunt, *The Reproduction of Colour*, Tolworth, Fountain Press, 1987.

[126] R. W. G. Hunt, *Measuring Colour*, 2nd edn., New York, NY, E. Horwood, 1991.

[127] R. W. G. Hunt, "Revised color-appearance model for related and unrelated colors," *Color Research and Application*, vol. 16, no. 3, pp. 146–165, Jun. 1991.

[128] R. Hunter and R. W. Harold, *The Measurement of Appearance*, 2nd edn., Wiley, 1987.

[129] International Color Consortium, *ICC Profile Format*, Version 4.2.0.0, available at www.color.org/.

[130] K. Iino and R. S. Berns, "The effect of black printer separation algorithms on perceived spatial image quality," *Proc. IS&T/SID Fifth Color Imaging Conference*, pp. 163–168, Nov. 1997.

[131] Y. Inoue, "Dominant in mobilecom, LCDs adopt futuristic refinements," *Display Devices*, no. 24, pp. 17–21, Summer 2001.

[132] ISO 5-3:1995 *Photography – Density measurements – Part 3: Spectral conditions*, Nov. 1995.

[133] S. Itoh and M. Tanaka, "Current status of field-emission displays," *Proceedings of the IEEE*, vol. 90, no. 4, pp. 514–520, Apr. 2002.

[134] A. K. Jain, *Fundamentals of Digital Image Processing*, Englewood Cliffs, N.J., Prentice-Hall, 1989.

[135] J. F. Jarvis, C. N. Judice and W. H. Ninke, "A survey of techniques for the display of continuous tone pictures on bilevel display," *Computer Graphics and Image Processing*, vol. 5, pp. 13–40, 1976.

[136] H. R. Kang and P. G. Anderson, "Neural network applications to the color scanner and printer calibrations," *Journal of Electronic Imaging*, vol. 1, no. 2, pp. 125–134, Apr. 1992.

[137] H. R. Kang, "Color scanner calibration," *Journal of Imaging Science and Technology*, vol. 36, no. 2, pp. 162–170, Mar./Apr. 1992.

[138] H. R. Kang, *Color Technology for Electronic Devices*," Bellingham WA, SPIE Press, 1997.

[139] M. G. Kang and A. K. Katsaggelos, "Simultaneous multichannel image restoration and estimation of the regularization parameters," *IEEE Transactions on Image Processing*, vol. 6, no. 5, pp. 774–778, May 1997.

[140] R. P. Kanwal, *Generalized Functions Theory and Applications*, 3rd edn., Birkhauser, 2004.

[141] J. M. Kasson and W. Plouffe, "An analysis of selected computer interchange color spaces," *ACM Transactions on Graphics*, vol. 11, no. 4, pp. 373–405, Oct. 1992.

[142] N. Katoh and M. Ito, "Gamut mappings for computer generated images (II)," *Proc. IS&T/SID Fourth Color Imaging Conference*, pp. 126–129, Nov. 1996.

[143] H. Kawamoto, "The history of liquid-crystal displays," *Proceedings of the IEEE*, vol. 90, no. 4, pp. 460–500, Apr. 2002.

[144] S. M. Kay, *Modern Spectral Estimation: Theory and Application,* Prentice-Hall, 1988.

[145] K. L. Kelly, "Lines of constant correlated color temperature based on MacAdam's (u, v) uniform chromaticity transformation of the CIE diagram," *Journal of the Optical Society of America*, vol. 53, pp. 999–1002, 1963.

[146] C. H. Kim, S. M. Seong, J. A. Lee and L. S. Kim, "Winscale: an image-scaling algorithm using an area pixel model," *IEEE Transactions on Circuits and Systems for Video Technology*, vol. 13, no. 6, pp. 549–553, Jun. 2003.

[147] C. Y. Kim, I. S. Kweon and Y. S. Seo, "Color and printer models for color halftoning," *Journal of Electronic Imaging*, vol. 6, no. 2, pp. 166–180, Apr. 1997.

[148] S. H. Kim and J. P. Allebach, "Impact of HVS models on model-based halftoning," *IEEE Transactions on Image Processing*, vol. 11, no. 3, pp. 258–269, Mar. 2002.

[149] J. Kimmel, J. Hautanen and T. Levola, "Display technologies for portable communications devices," *Proceedings of the IEEE*, vol. 90, no. 4, pp. 581–590, Apr. 2002.

[150] R. Kimmel, "Demosaicing: image reconstruction from CCD samples," *IEEE Transactions on Image Processing*, vol. 8, no. 9, pp. 1221–1228, Sep. 1999.

[151] M. A. Klompenhouwer, "The temporal MTF of displays and related video signal processing," *Proc. IEEE International Conference on Image Processing*, vol. 2, pp. 13–16, Sep. 2005.

[152] K. T. Knox and R. Eschbach, "Threshold modulation in error diffusion," *Journal of Electronic Imaging*, vol. 2, no. 3, pp. 185–192, Jul. 1993.

[153] B. W. Kolpatzik and C. A. Bouman, "Optimized error diffusion for image display," *Journal of Electronic Imaging*, vol. 1, no. 3, pp. 277–292, Jul. 1992.

[154] F. Kretz, "Subjectively optimal quantization of pictures," *IEEE Transactions on Communications*, vol. 23, no. 11, pp. 1288–1292, Nov. 1975.

[155] M. S. Kulkarni, "Fundamentals of digital signal processing of color signals," M.S. thesis, North Carolina State University, 1994.

[156] T. Kurita, A. Saito and I. Yuyama, "Consideration of perceived MTF of hold type display for moving images," *Proc. International Display Workshops '98*, pp. 823–826, Dec. 1998.

[157] K. M. Lam, "Metamerism and colour constancy," Ph.D. thesis, University of Bradford, 1985.

[158] C. Lee, M. Eden and M. Unser, "High-quality image resizing using oblique projection operators," *IEEE Transactions on Image Processing*, vol. 7, no. 5, pp. 679–692, May 1998.

[159] H.-C. Lee, "Method for computing the scene-illuminant chromaticity from specular highlights," *Journal of the Optical Society of America*, A, vol. 3, no. 10, pp. 1694–1699, Oct. 1986.

[160] H.-C. Lee, *Introduction to Color Imaging Science*, Cambridge University Press, 2005.

[161] J. H. Lee and J. P. Allebach, "Colorant-based direct binary search halftoning," *Journal of Electronic Imaging*, vol. 11, no. 4, pp. 517–527, Oct. 2002.

[162] J. H. Lee and J. P. Allebach, "Inkjet printer model-based halftoning," *IEEE Transactions on Image Processing*, vol. 14, no. 5, pp. 674–689, May 2005.

[163] P. Li and J. P. Allebach, "Tone dependent error diffusion," *IEEE Transactions on Image Processing*, vol. 13, no. 2, pp. 201–215, Feb. 2004.

[164] D. J. Lieberman and J. P. Allebach, "A dual interpretation for direct binary search and its implications for tone reproduction and texture quality," *IEEE Transactions on Image Processing*, vol. 9, no. 11, pp. 1950–1969, Nov. 2000.

[165] M. J. Lighthill, *Introduction to Fourier Analysis and Generalized Functions,* Cambridge University Press, 1958.

[166] Y. Linde, A. Buzo and R. M. Gray, "An algorithm for vector quantizer design," *IEEE Transactions on Communications*, vol. 28, no. 1, pp. 84–95, Jan. 1980.

[167] L. Lucchese and S. K. Mitra, "A new method for denoising color images," *Proc. IEEE International Conference on Image Processing*, vol. 2, pp. 373–376, Sep. 2002.

[168] M. R. Luo, "Color science," Chapter 3 in *Colour Image Processing Handbook*, S. J. Sanguine and R. E. N. Horne, eds., Chapman and Hall, 1998.

[169] M. R. Luo, G. Cui and B. Rigg, "The development of the CIE2000 colour-difference formula: CIEDE2000," *Color Research and Application*, vol. 26, pp. 240–350, Oct. 2001.

[170] R. Lyon and P. Hubel, "Eyeing the camera: into the next century," *Proc. IS&T/TSID 10th Color Imaging Conference*, pp. 349–355, Nov. 2002.

[171] D. L. MacAdam, "Visual sensitivities to color differences in daylight," *Journal of the Optical Society of America*, vol. 32, no. 5, pp. 247–274, May 1942.

[172] L. W. MacDonald, "Gamut mapping in perceptual color space," in *Proc. IS&T/SID's 3rd Color Imaging Conference,* pp. 193–196, Nov. 1993.

[173] A. Macovski, *Medical Imaging Systems,* Prentice-Hall, 1983.

[174] J. R. Magnus and H. Neudecker, *Matrix Differential Calculus,* New York, John Wiley and Sons, 1988.

[175] V. Mani, "Calibration of color monitors," Master's thesis, Raleigh, North Carolina State Univ., 1991.

[176] S. L. Marple, *Digital Spectral Analysis with Applications*, Prentice-Hall, 1987.

[177] J. Max, "Quantizing for minimum distortion," *IEEE Transactions on Information Theory*, vol. 6, no. 1, pp. 7–12, Jan. 1960.

[178] E. Meijering, "A chronology of interpolation: from ancient astronomy to modern signal and image processing," *Proc. of the IEEE*, vol. 90, no. 3, pp. 319–342, Mar. 2002.

[179] D. E. Mentley, "State of flat-panel display technology and future trends,"*Proceedings of the IEEE*, vol. 90, no. 4, pp. 453–459, Apr. 2002.

[180] R. B. Merrill, "Color separation in an active pixel cell imaging array using a triple-well structure," U.S. Patent 5,965,875, 1999.

[181] C. D. Meyer, *Matrix Analysis and Applied Linear Algebra,* Society for Industrial and Applied Mathematics, 2000.

[182] J. L. Mitchell, D. J. Legall and C. Fogg, *MPEG Video Compression Standard*, NY, Chapman-Hall, 1997.

[183] MATLAB is a software package produced and supported by The MathWorks, Inc., Natick, MA (www.mathworks.com).

[184] R. Molina, J. Mateos, A. K. Katsaggelos and M. Vega, "Bayesian multichannel image restoration using compound Gauss-Markov random fields," *IEEE Transactions on Image Processing*, vol. 12, no. 12, pp. 1642–1654, Dec. 2003.

[185] E. D. Montag and M. D. Fairchild, "Psychophysical evaluation of gamut mapping techniques using simple rendered images and artificial gamut boundaries," *IEEE Transactions on Image Processing*, vol. 6, no. 7, pp. 977–989, Jul. 1997.

[186] J. Morovic and M. R. Luo, "Gamut mapping algorithms based on psychophysical experiment," *Proc. IS&T/SID Fifth Color Imaging Conference*, pp. 44–49, 1997.

[187] J. Morovic and M. R. Luo, "Cross-media psychophysical evaluation of gamut mapping algorithms," *Proc. AIC Color 97*, 1997.

[188] J. Mukherjee, R. Parthasarathi and S. Goyal, "Markov random field processing for color demosaicing," *Pattern Recognition Letters*, vol. 22, no. 3, pp. 339–351, Mar. 2001.

[189] D. C. Munson, "A note on Lena," *IEEE Transactions on Image Processing*, vol. 5, no. 1, p. 3, Jan. 1996.

[190] A. C. Naiman and W. Makous, "Spatial nonlinearities of gray-scale CRT pixels," in *Proc. SPIE*, vol. 1666, pp. 41–56, 1992.

[191] Y. Nayatani, T. Mori, K. Hashimoto, H. Sobagaki and K. Takahama, "Comparison of color-appearance models," *Color Research and Application*, vol. 15, pp. 272–284, Oct. 1990.

[192] A. N. Netravali and B. G. Haskell, *Digital Pictures: Representation, Compression and Standards*, 2nd edn., Plenum Publishing, 1994.

[193] H. E. J. Neugebauer, "Die theoretischen Grundlagen des Mehrfarbenbuchdrucks," *Zeitschrift fur wissenschaftliche Photographie Photophysik und Photochemie.*, vol. 36, no. 4, pp. 73–89, Apr. 1937, reprinted in [231].

[194] H. E. J. Neugebauer, "Quality factor for filters whose spectral transmittances are different from color mixture curves, and its application to color photography," *Journal of the Optical Society of America*, vol. 46, no. 10, pp. 821–824, Oct. 1956.

[195] K. N. Ngan and H. C. Koh, "Predictive classified vector quantization," *IEEE Transactions on Image Processing*, vol. 1, no. 3, pp. 269–280, Jul. 1992.

[196] M. Nielsen and M. Stokes, "The creation of the sRGB ICC profile," *Proc. IS&T/SID Sixth Color Imaging Conference*, pp. 253–257, Nov. 1998.

[197] S. I. Nin, J. M. Kasson and W. Plouffe, "Printing CIELAB images on a CMYK printer using tri-linear interpolation," in *Proc. SPIE*, vol. 1670, pp. 316–324, May 1992.

[198] Y. X. Noyes, J. Y. Hardeberg and A. Moskalev, "Linearization curve generation for CcMmYK printing," *Proc. IS&T/SID 8th Color Imaging Conference*, Scottsdale, Arizona, pp. 247–251, Nov. 2000.

[199] N. Ohta, A. R. Robertson, *Colorimetry: Fundamentals and Applications,* Wiley, 2005.

[200] A. V. Oppenheim and R. W. Schafer, *Discrete-Time Signal Processing*, Prentice-Hall, 1989.

[201] A. V. Oppenheim and A. S. Willsky, *Signals and Systems*, 2nd edn., Prentice-Hall, 1996.

[202] M. T. Orchard and C. A. Bouman, "Color quantization of images," *IEEE Transactions on Signal Processing*, vol. 39, no. 12, pp. 2677–2690, Dec. 1991.

[203] H. Pan, X.-F. Feng and S. Daly, "LCD motion blur modeling and analysis," *Proc. IEEE International Conference on Image Processing*, vol. 2, pp. 11–14, Sep. 2005.

[204] H. Pan, X. F. Feng and S. Daly, "LCD motion blur analysis and modeling based on temporal PSF," *SID2006*, pp. 1704–1707, May 2006.

[205] A. Papoulis and S. U. Pillai, *Probability, Random Variables, and Stochastic Processes*. 4th edn., McGraw-Hill, 2002.

[206] T. N. Pappas and D. L. Neuhoff, "Printer models and error diffusion," *IEEE Transactions on Image Processing*, vol. 4, no. 1, pp. 66–80, Jan. 1995.

[207] T. N. Pappas and D. L. Neuhoff, "Least-squares model-based halftoning," *IEEE Transactions on Image Processing*, vol. 8, no. 8, pp. 1102–1116, Aug. 1999.

[208] T. N. Pappas, R. J. Safranek and J. Chen, "Perceptual criteria for image quality evaluation," Chapter 8.2 in *Handbook of Image and Video Processing*, 2nd edn., A. C. Bovik, ed., Academic Press, 2005.

[209] K. Parulski and K. Spaulding, "Chapter 12: color image processing for digital cameras," in *Digital Color Imaging Handbook*, G. Sharma, ed., CRC Press, 2003.

[210] G. B. Pawle, "Inside the ICC color device profile," in *Proc. IS&T/SID Third Color Imaging Conf.*, pp. 160–163, Nov. 1995.

[211] S. C. Pei and C. M. Cheng, "Color image processing by using binary quaternion-moment-preserving thresholding technique," *IEEE Transactions on Image Processing*, vol. 8, no. 5, pp. 614–628, May 1999.

[212] W. B. Pennebacker and J. L. Mitchell, *JPEG Still Image Data Compression Standard*, NY, Van Nostrand-Reinhold, 1993.

[213] I. Pobboravsky and M. Pearson, "Computation of dot areas required to match a colorimetrically specified color using the modified Neugebauer equations," *Proc. Technical Association of the Graphic Arts*, vol. 24, pp. 65–77, 1972.

[214] A. B. Poirson and B. A. Wandell, "Pattern-color separable pathways predict sensitivity to simple colored patterns," *Vision Research*, vol. 36, no. 4, pp. 515–526, Feb. 1996.

[215] D. L. Post and C. S. Calhoun, "Further evaluation of methods for producing desired colors on CRT monitors," *Color Research and Application*, vol. 25, no. 2, pp. 90–104, Apr. 2000.

[216] W. Praefcke, "Color separation for four color printing," *Proc. IS&T/SID Sixth Color Imaging Conference*, pp. 189–192, Nov. 1998.

[217] W. K. Pratt, *Digital Image Processing*, 3rd edn., John Wiley and Sons, 2001.

[218] J. G. Proakis and D. G. Manolakis, *Digital Signal Processing*, 2nd edn., MacMillan, 1992.

[219] S. A. Rajala, H. J. Trussell and B. Krishnakumar, "Visual sensitivity to color-varying stimuli,", in *Proc. SPIE*, vol. 1666, pp. 375–386, 1992.

[220] S. A. Rajala and A. P. Kakodkar, "Interpolation of color data," *Proc. IS&T/SID Color Imaging Conference*, pp. 180–183, Nov. 1993.

[221] S. A. Rajala, H. J. Trussell and A. P. Kakodkar, "The use of extrapolation in computing color look-up tables," in *Proc. SPIE*, vol. 2170, pp. 53–62, 1994.

[222] R. Ramanath, W. E. Snyder, Y. Yoo and M. S. Drew, "Color image processing pipeline in digital still cameras," *IEEE Signal Processing Magazine*, vol. 22, no. 1, pp. 34–43, Jan. 2005.

[223] B. D. Rao, "Unified treatment of LS, TLS, and truncated SVD methods using a weighted TLS framework," in *Recent Advances in Total Least Squares Techniques and Errors-in-Variables*, S. van Huffel, ed., Philadelphia, SIAM, pp. 11–20, 1997.

[224] M. S. Rea, ed., *IESNS Lighting Handbook: References and Applications*, Illuminating Engineering Society of North America, 2000.

[225] S. J. Reeves, "Fast image restoration without boundary artifacts," *IEEE Transactions on Image Processing*, vol. 14, no. 10, pp. 1448–1453, Oct. 2005.

[226] W. Rhodes, "Fifty years of the Neugebauer equations," in *Proc. SPIE*, vol. 1184, Neugebauer Memorial Seminar on Color Reproduction, pp. 7–18, Dec. 1989.

[227] A. Rosenfeld and A. C. Kak, *Digital Picture Processing*, 2nd edn., vol. 1, Academic Press, 1982.

[228] A. E. Savakis and H. J. Trussell, "On the accuracy of PSF representation in image restoration," *IEEE Transactions on Image Processing*, vol. 2, no. 2, pp. 252–259, Apr. 1993.

[229] A. A. Sawchuk, "Space-variant system analysis of image motion," *Journal of the Optical Society of America*, vol. 63, no. 9, pp. 1052–1063, Sep. 1973.

[230] A. A. Sawchuk, "Space-variant image restoration by coordinate transformations," *Journal of the Optical Society of America*, vol. 64, no. 2, pp. 138–144, Feb. 1974.

[231] K. Sayangi, ed., *Proc. SPIE: Neugebauer Memorial Seminar on Color Reproduction,* vol. 1184, Dec. 1989.

[232] A. Schaum, "Theory and design of local interpolators," *CVGIP: Graphical Models and Image Processing*, vol. 55, no. 6, pp. 464–481, Nov. 1993.

[233] R. Scheps and J. S. Schoonmaker, "Acousto-optic tunable filter hyperspectral imaging system," U.S. Patent 6,490,075, 2002.

[234] W. F. Schreiber, "A color pre-press system using appearance variables," *Journal of Imaging Technology*, vol. 17, no. 4, pp. 200–211, Aug. 1986.

[235] R. R. Schultz and R. L. Stevenson, "Stochastic modeling and estimation of multispectral image data," *IEEE Transactions on Image Processing*, vol. 4, no. 8, pp. 1109–1119, Aug. 1995.

[236] S. R. Searle, *Matrix Algebra Useful for Statistics,* New York, NY, John Wiley & Sons, 1982.

[237] H. Seetzen and L. A. Whitehead, "A high dynamic range display using low and high resolution modulators," in *Society for Information Display International Symposium Digest of Technical Papers*, pp. 1450–1453, 2003.

[238] G. Sharma and H. J. Trussell, "Set theoretic estimation in color scanner characterization," *Journal of Electronic Imaging*, vol. 5, no. 4, pp. 479–489, Oct. 1996.

[239] G. Sharma and H. J. Trussell, "Digital color imaging," *IEEE Transactions on Image Processing*, vol. 6, no. 7, pp. 901–932, Jul. 1997.

[240] G. Sharma and H. J. Trussell, "Figures of merit for color scanners," *IEEE Transactions on Image Processing*, vol. 6, no. 7, pp. 990–1001, Jul. 1997.

[241] G. Sharma, H. J. Trussell and M. J. Vrhel, "Optimal nonnegative color scanning filters," *IEEE Transactions on Image Processing*, vol. 7, no. 1, pp. 129–133, Jan. 1998.

[242] G. Sharma, "Set theoretic estimation for problems in subtractive color," *Color Research and Application*, vol. 25, no. 5, pp. 333–348, Aug. 2000.

[243] G. Sharma, "LCDs versus CRTs – Color calibration and gamut consideration," *Proceedings of the IEEE*, vol. 90, no. 4, pp. 605–622, Apr. 2002.

[244] G. Sharma, W. Wu and E. N. Dalal, "The CIEDE2000 color-difference formula: implementation notes, supplementary test data, and mathematical observations," *Color Research and Application*, vol. 30, no. 1, Feb. 2005.

[245] H. R. Sheikh and A. C. Bovik, "Information theoretic approaches to image quality assessment," Chapter 8.4 in *Handbook of Image and Video Processing*, 2nd edn., A. C. Bovik, ed., Academic Press, 2005.

[246] H. L. Shen and J. H. Xin, "Spectral characterization of a color scanner by adaptive estimation," *Journal of the Optical Society of America*, A, vol. 21, no. 7, pp. 1125–1130, 2004.

[247] L. D. Silverstein, "Color display technology: from pixels to perception," *Proc. IS&T/SID Thirteenth Color Imaging Conference*, pp. 136–140, Nov. 2005.

[248] M. Soumekh, *Fourier Array Imaging,* Prentice Hall, 1994.

[249] M. Soumekh, *Synthetic Aperture Radar Signal Processing with* MATLAB *Algorithms,* John Wiley and Sons, 1999.

[250] K. E. Spaulding, R. N. Ellson and J. R. Sullivan, "UltraColor: a new gamut mapping strategy," *Proc. SPIE*, vol. 2414, pp. 61–68, Feb. 1995.

[251] K. E. Spaulding, R. L. Miller and J. Schildkraut, "Methods for generating blue-noise dither matrices for digital halftoning," *Journal of Electronic Imaging*, vol. 6, no. 2, pp. 208–230, Apr. 1997.

[252] H. Stark and J. W. Woods, *Probability, Random Processes and Estimation Theory for Engineers*, 3rd edn., Prentice-Hall, 2001.

[253] E. Steinberg, R. Rolleston and R. L. Easton, "Analysis of random dithering patterns using second-order statistics," *Journal of Electronic Imaging*, vol. 1, no. 4, pp. 396–404, Oct. 1992.

[254] P. Stoica and R. Moses, *Introduction to Spectral Analysis,* Prentice-Hall, 1997.

[255] M. Stokes, M. D. Fairchild and R. S. Berns, "Precision requirements for digital color reproduction," *ACM Transactions on Graphics*, vol. 11, no. 4, pp. 406–422, Oct. 1992.

[256] M. Stokes, M. Anderson, S. Chandrasekar and R. Motta, "A standard default color space for the Internet – sRGB," www.color.org/srgb.html.

[257] M. C. Stone, W. B. Cowan and J. C. Beatty, "Color gamut mapping and the printing of digital color images," *ACM Transactions on Graphics*, vol. 7, no. 4, Oct. 1988.

[258] S. Süsstrunk, R. Buckley and S. Swen, "Standard RGB color spaces," *Proc. IS&T/SID Seventh Color Imaging Conference*, pp. 127–134, Nov. 1999.

[259] K. Tang, J. Astola and Y. Neuvo, "Nonlinear multivariate image filtering techniques," *IEEE Transactions on Image Processing*, vol. 4, no. 6, pp. 788–798, Jun. 1995.

[260] K. Tarumi, M. Heckmeier and M. Klasen-Memmer, "Advanced liquid-crystal materials for TFT monitor and TV applications," *Journal of the Society for Information Display*, vol. 10, no. 2, pp. 127–132, Jun. 2002.

[261] A. M. Tekalp and H. J. Trussell, "Comparative study of some statistical and set-theoretic methods for image restoration," *Computer Vision, Graphics and Image Processing: Graphical Models and Image Processing*, vol. 53, no. 2, pp. 108–120, Mar. 1991.

[262] A. M. Tekalp, *Digital video processing*, Prentice-Hall, 1995.

[263] P. Thevenaz, T. Blu and M. Unser, "Image interpolation and resampling," *Handbook of Medical Imaging, Processing and Analysis*, I. N. Bankman, ed., Orlando FL, USA, Academic Press, pp. 393–420, 2000.

[264] P. Thevenaz, T. Blu and M. Unser, "Interpolation revisited," *IEEE Transactions on Medical Imaging*, vol. 19, no. 7, pp. 739–758, Jul. 2000.

[265] H. J. Trussell and B. R. Hunt, "Improved methods of maximum a posteriori image restoration," *IEEE Transactions on Computers*, vol. 28, no. 1, pp. 57–62, Jan. 1979.

[266] H. J. Trussell and M. R. Civanlar, "The initial estimate in constrained iterative restoration," *Proc. International Conf. Acous., Speech and Sig. Proc.*, pp. 643–646, Apr. 1983.

[267] H. J. Trussell and M. R. Civanlar, "The feasible solution in signal restoration," *IEEE Transactions on Acoustics, Speech and Signal Processing*, vol. 32, no. 2, pp. 201–212, Apr. 1984.

[268] H. J. Trussell, M. I. Sezan and D. Tran, "Sensitivity of color LMMSE restoration of images to the spectral estimate," *IEEE Transactions on Acoustics, Speech and Signal Processing*, vol. 39, no. 1, pp. 248–252, Jan. 1991.

[269] H. J. Trussell, "Application of set theoretic methods to color systems," *Color Research and Application*, vol. 16, no. 1, pp. 31–41, Feb. 1991.

[270] H. J. Trussell and M. J. Vrhel, "Estimation of illumination for color correction," *Proc. IEEE International Conference on Acoustics, Speech and Signal Processing*, vol. 4, pp. 2513–2516, Apr. 1991.

[271] H. J. Trussell and S. Fogel, "Identification and restoration of spatially variant motion blurs in sequential images," *IEEE Transaction on Image Processing*, vol. 1, no. 1, pp. 123–126, Jan. 1992.

[272] H. J. Trussell, "DSP solutions run the gamut for color systems," *IEEE Signal Processing Magazine*, vol. 10, no. 2, pp. 8–23, Apr. 1993.

[273] H. J. Trussell and M. S. Kulkarni, "Sampling and processing of color signals," *IEEE Transactions on Image Processing*, vol. 5, no. 4, pp. 677–681, Apr. 1996.

[274] H. J. Trussell and R. E. Hartwig, "Mathematics of demosaicking," *IEEE Transactions on Image Processing*, vol. 11, no. 4, pp. 485–492, Apr. 2002.

[275] H. Uchiike and T. Hirakawa, "Color plasma displays,"*Proceedings of the IEEE*, vol. 90, no. 4, pp. 533–539, Apr. 2002.

[276] R. Ulichney, *Digital Halftoning*, Cambridge, Massachusetts, MIT Press, 1987.

[277] R. Ulichney, "The void-and-cluster method for dither array generation," in *Proc. SPIE*, vol. 1913, pp. 332–343, Sep. 1993.

[278] M. Unser, A. Aldroubi and M. Eden, "Enlargement or reduction of digital images with minimum loss of information," *IEEE Transactions on Image Processing*, vol. 4, no. 3, pp. 247–258, Mar. 1995.

[279] M. Unser, "Splines: a perfect fit for signal and image processing," *IEEE Signal Processing Magazine*, vol. 16, no. 6, pp. 22–38, Nov. 1999.

[280] M. Unser, "Sampling 50 years after Shannon," *Proceedings of the IEEE*, vol. 88, no. 4, pp. 569–587, Apr. 2000.

[281] S. van Huffel and J. Vandewalle, *The Total Least Squares Problem*, Philadelphia, SIAM, 1991.

[282] N. D. Venkata and B. L. Evans, "Design and analysis of vector color error diffusion halftoning systems," *IEEE Transactions on Image Processing*, vol. 10, no. 10, pp. 1552–1565, Oct. 2001.

[283] M. Vetterli and J. Kovacevic, *Wavelets and Subband Coding,* Prentice-Hall, 1995.

[284] J. A. S. Viggiano, "Modeling the color of multi-colored halftones," *Proc. Technical Association of the Graphic Arts*, pp. 44–62, 1990.

[285] P. L. Vora and H. J. Trussell, "Measure of goodness of a set of colour scanning filters," *Journal of the Optical Society of America*, A, vol. 10, no. 7, pp. 1499–1508, Jul. 1993.

[286] P. L. Vora and H. J. Trussell, "A mathematical method for designing a set of colour scanning filters," *IEEE Transactions on Image Processing*, vol. 6, no. 2, pp. 312–320, Feb. 1997.

[287] P. Vora and H. J. Trussell, "Mathematical methods for the analysis of color scanning filters," *IEEE Transactions on Image Processing*, vol. 6, no. 2, pp. 321–327, Feb. 1997.

[288] P. L. Vora, J. E. Farrell, J. D. Tietz and D. H. Brainard, "Image capture: simulation of sensor responses from hyperspectral images," *IEEE Transactions on Image Processing*, vol. 10, no. 2, pp. 307–316, Feb. 2001.

[289] M. J. Vrhel and H. J. Trussell, "Color correction using principal components," *Color Research and Application*, vol. 17, no. 5, pp. 328–338, Oct. 1992.

[290] M. J. Vrhel and H. J. Trussell, "Physical device illumination color correction," *Proc SPIE*, vol. 1909, pp. 84–91, Aug. 1993.

[291] M. J. Vrhel, R. Gershon and L. S. Iwan, "Measurement and analysis of object reflectance spectra," *Color Research and Application*, vol. 19, pp. 4–9, Feb. 1994.

[292] M. J. Vrhel and H. J. Trussell, "Filter considerations in color correction," *IEEE Transactions on Image Processing*, vol. 3, no. 2, pp. 147–161, Mar. 1994.

[293] M. J. Vrhel, H. J. Trussell and J. Bosch, "Design and realization of optimal color filters for multi-illuminant color correction," *Journal of Electronic Imaging,* vol. 4, no. 1, pp. 6–14, Jan. 1995.

[294] M. J. Vrhel and H. J. Trussell, "Optimal color filters in the presence of noise," *IEEE Transactions on Image Processing*, vol. 4, no. 6, pp. 814–823, Jun. 1995.

[295] M. J. Vrhel and H. J. Trussell, "Color scanner calibration via a neural network," *Proc. IEEE International Conference on Acoustics, Speech and Signal Processing*, vol. 6, pp. 3465–3468, Mar. 1999.

[296] M. J. Vrhel and H. J. Trussell, "Color device calibration: a mathematical formulation," *IEEE Transactions on Image Processing*, vol. 8, no. 12, pp. 1796–1806, Dec. 1999.

[297] M. J. Vrhel, "Indexing of multidimensional lookup tables in embedded systems," *IEEE Transactions on Image Processing*, vol. 13, no. 10, pp. 1319–1326, Oct. 2004.

[298] M. J. Vrhel, E. Saber and H. J. Trussell, "Color image generation and display technologies," *IEEE Signal Processing Magazine*, vol. 22, no. 1, pp. 23–33, Jan. 2005.

[299] B. A. Wandell, "The synthesis and analysis of color images," *IEEE Transactions on Pattern Analysis and Machine Intelligence*, vol. 9, no. 1, pp. 2–13, Jan. 1987.

[300] B. A. Wandell, *Foundations of Vision,* Sunderland, MA, Sinauer Assoc., Inc., 1995.

[301] X. Wang, E. Chan, M. K. Mandal and S. Panchanathan, "Wavelet-based image coding using nonlinear interpolative vector quantization," *IEEE Transactions on Image Processing*, vol. 5, no. 3, pp. 518–522, Mar. 1996.

[302] Y. Wang, J. Ostermann and Y.-Q. Zhang, *Video Processing and Communications*, Prentice Hall, 2002.

[303] Z. Wang, A. C. Bovik and E. P. Simoncelli, "Structural approaches to image quality assessment," Chapter 8.3 in *Handbook of Image and Video Processing*, 2nd edn., A. C. Bovik. ed., Academic Press, 2005.

[304] K. I. Werner, "The flat panel's future," *IEEE Spectrum*, vol. 30, no. 11, pp. 18–26, Nov. 1993.

[305] K. I. Werner, "The flowering of displays," *IEEE Spectrum*, vol. 34, no. 5, pp. 40–49, May 1997.

[306] R. L. Wisnieff and J. J. Ritsko, "Electronic displays for information technology," *IBM Journal of Research and Development*, vol. 44, no. 3, pp. 409–422, May 2000.

[307] I. H. Witten and R. M. Neal, "Using peano curves for bilevel display of continuous-tone images," *IEEE Computer Graphics and Applications*, vol. 2, no. 3, pp. 47–52, 1982.

[308] M. Wolski, J. P. Allebach and C. A. Bouman, "Gamut mapping: squeezing the most out of your color system," *Proc. IS&T/SID Second Color Imaging Conference*, pp. 89–92, Nov. 1994.

[309] M. Wolski, C. A. Bouman, J. P. Allebach and E. Walowit, "Optimization of sensor response functions for colorimetry of reflective and emissive objects," *IEEE Transactions on Image Processing*, vol. 5, no. 3, pp. 507–517, Mar. 1996.

[310] P. W. Wong, "Error diffusion with dynamically adjusted kernel," *Proc. IEEE International Conference on Acoustics, Speech and Signal Processing*, vol. 5, pp. 113–116, Apr. 1994.

[311] H. Wright, C. L. Saunders and D. Gignac, "Design of glass filter combinations for photometers," *Applied Optics*, vol. 8, no. 12, pp. 2449–2455, Dec. 1969.

[312] G. Wyszecki and G. H. Fielder, "New color matching ellipses," *Journal of the Optical Society of America*, vol. 62, no. 9, pp. 1135–1152, Sep. 1971.

[313] G. Wyszecki and W. S. Stiles, *Color Science: Concepts and Methods, Quantitative Data and Formulae,* 2nd edn., New York, NY, John Wiley and Sons, 1982.

[314] M. Xia, E. Saber, G. Sharma and A. M. Tekalp, "End-to-end color printer calibration by total least squares regression," *IEEE Transactions on Image Processing*, vol. 8, no. 5, pp. 700–716, May 1999.

[315] L. A. Yoder, "The TI digital light processing micromirror tech: putting it to work now," *Advanced Imaging Magazine*, vol. 11, no. 6, pp. 43–46, Jun. 1996.

[316] J. M. Younse, "Mirrors on a chip," *IEEE Spectrum*, vol. 30, no. 11, pp. 27–31, Nov. 1993.

[317] J. A. C. Yule and W. J. Nielsen, "The penetration of light into paper and its effect on halftone reproduction," *Proc. Technical Association of the Graphic Arts*, vol. 4, pp. 65–75, 1951.

[318] J. A. C. Yule, *Principles of Color Reproduction*, New York, John Wiley & Sons, 1967.

[319] A. Zakhor, S. Lin and F. Eskafi, "A new class of B/W and color halftoning algorithms," *IEEE Transactions on Image Processing*, vol. 2, no. 4, pp. 499–509, Oct. 1993.

[320] H. Zeng and P. G. Anderson, "An expanded Neugebauer model for printer color formation," *Proc. SPIE*, vol. 3648, pp. 27–36, Jan. 1999.

[321] X. Zhang and B. A. Wandell, "A spatial extension of CIELAB for digital color image reproduction," *Journal SID*, vol. 5, no. 1, pp. 61–63, Mar. 1997. http://white.stanford.edu/~brian/scielab/scielab.html.

[322] X. Zhang and B. A. Wandell, "Color image fidelity metrics evaluated using image distortion maps," *Signal Processing*, vol. 70, no. 3, pp. 201–214, 1998.

# Index

Printed in the United States
by Baker & Taylor Publisher Services